Teaching and Learning in Middle and Secondary Schools

Student Empowerment Through Learning Communities

Clifford H. Edwards

Brigham Young University

PEARSON

Merrill
Prentice Hall

Upper Saddle River, New Jersey
Columbus, Ohio

Library of Congress Cataloging-in-Publication Data

Edwards, Clifford H.
   Teaching and learning in middle and secondary schools: student empowerment through
learning communities / Clifford H. Edwards.
     p. cm.
   Includes bibliographical references and index.
   ISBN 0-13-098547-3
     1. School improvement programs—United States. 2. Middle school teaching —United States. 3. High school
teaching—United States. 4. Teacher-student relationships—United States. I. Title.

LB2822.82.E394 2005
373.12—dc22   2003066609

Vice President and Executive Publisher: Jeffery W. Johnston	**Cover Designer:** Robin Chukes
Executive Editor: Debra A. Stollenwerk	**Cover image:** Index Stock
Associate Editor: Ben M. Stephen	**Photo Coordinator:** Cynthia Cassidy
Editorial Assistant: Mary Morrill	**Production Manager:** Susan Hannahs
Production Editor: Kris Robinson-Roach	**Director of Marketing:** Ann Castel Davis
Production Coordination: Carlisle Publishers Services	**Marketing Manager:** Darcy Betts Prybella
Design Coordinator: Diane C. Lorenzo	**Marketing Coordinator:** Tyra Poole

This book was set in Minion by Carlisle Communications, Ltd. It was printed and bound by R. R. Donnelley & Sons Company. The cover was printed by The Lehigh Press, Inc.

Photo Credits: Barbara Schwartz/Merrill, p. 3; Anthony Magnacca/Merrill, pp. 28, 36, 90, 127, 172, 230, 278, 310, 331, 339, 415; Scott Cunningham/Merrill, pp. 47, 71, 247, 263, 297, 317, 348, 428; Photo by Tim McCabe, USDA Natural Resources Conservation Service, p. 99; Photo courtesy of USDA Natural Resources Conservation Service, p. 117; Ken Karp/Prentice Hall School Division, pp. 141, 275; Anne Vega/Merrill, pp. 155, 193, 204, 374; Larry Hamill/Merrill, p. 386.

Pearson Education Ltd.
Pearson Education Singapore Pte. Ltd.
Pearson Education Canada, Ltd.
Pearson Education—Japan

Pearson Education Australia Pty. Limited
Pearson Education North Asia Ltd.
Pearson Educación de Mexico, S.A. de C.V.
Pearson Education Malaysia Pte. Ltd.

10 9 8 7 6 5 4 3 2 1
ISBN: 0-13-098547-3

Preface

A society's greatest treasure is its children. Through children, important cultural phenomena are perpetuated and basic social institutions are transmitted from one generation to the next. It is also through children that needed modifications are created and infused into values, lifestyles, and social living. Despite the value of maintaining culture and society, changes inevitably occur that transform it. One of the important purposes of schools is to help students achieve a balance between continuing the social good while at the same time helping them prepare for the changed society in which they will live. At the present time, an unprecedented movement of society exists in less-knowable directions with less-predictable consequences coming from various influential forces. Problems have become more global in nature with no explicit solutions. Even small communities have become complicated because of the influx of different cultures.

In addition to concerns regarding children's ability to live successfully in a changing society, there is also an ethic of caring for children that should greatly influence school operations. Children's personal welfare and well-being are prime concerns. Children need to be protected from potential harm and be provided the best possible circumstances for living full and happy lives, in addition to being prepared for the work world. They also need to learn social values and norms so they can become appropriately integrated into their communities. In the present world, with its changing conditions and a whole new set of problems to be faced, children are best served in schools where they receive preparation to live successfully in modern communities and learn how to effectively solve current, complex problems. In the past, life preparation consisted of knowing a set of facts regarding the various areas of knowledge generated from human experience and research. While this knowledge is important, putting it to use in solving a plethora of ever-changing problems is a far more critical kind of life preparation. Children not only need to become expert problem solvers, but they also need to achieve the level of sensitivity required to successfully work with others in solving these community problems consisting of divergent cultures and social orientations. This is a substantial change from earlier times when each community had a more stable set of cultural expectations and values.

Teachers must be trained so that they can help students solve problems and adjust to changing circumstances in complex communities. They should know how to formulate authentic learning communities capable of helping students effectively deal with life as it currently exists. They should also know how to promote better relationships among students and create greater solidarity and less divisiveness. They must learn to help their students become advocates for one another and help defuse problems that threaten group members. To do this, teachers have to learn to function more autonomously and responsibly. Few problems exist that can be prescriptively solved; they require personal ingenuity and insight. Teachers should provide their particular group of students with the kind of experiences that realistically prepare them for living in a modern world perpetually fraught with unanticipated difficulties and expectations. In particular, teachers must become skilled in how to help transform schools into institutions that can effectively accomplish these purposes. Teachers should understand current school operations, along with ways to modify education to accommodate the needed changes mentioned.

CONCEPTUAL FRAMEWORK

The purpose of this text is to promote teaching excellence and prepare teachers to become involved in school improvement. The learning communities model for school improvement is designed to promote a better education for students in several important dimensions. Learning communities support better student-teacher relationships, promote more effective learning, help eliminate student alienation and violence, provide students with a format for functioning responsibly in real communities, effectively satisfy student needs, encourage better self-esteem, and help develop student decision-making skills.

Schools are often criticized for their failure to accomplish these important goals. These criticisms have spawned a plethora of changes and suggestions for change over the years, many of which have been employed and later abandoned. Unfortunately, many of the suggested changes fail to address the fundamental ailments that affect schools and instead attend to peripheral considerations. For example, many of the recommended changes do not attend to the way children naturally learn or how to effectively satisfy student needs within a school context. In addition, many of the proposed changes do not provide students with meaningful experiences that they can value and apply in solving current problems. Rarely are their school experiences a valid representation of the roles they will occupy in community life later on.

This text suggests that many of the fundamental education problems can be solved by employing learning communities as the basic learning configuration in the schools. In recent years, learning communities have increasingly been recommended as the most valid approach to school improvement. They supply an ordered, consistent way for students to satisfy their needs and achieve excellence in meaningful and useful learning, as well as develop the moral attributes that will equip them to successfully relate to others in their communities. In learning communities, students acquire a sense of being cared for and accepted, along with opportunities for leadership growth and academic excellence. Learning communities provide a means for greater personal and interpersonal growth and direction for life within a democracy.

While the focus of the text is on putting learning communities into operation in the schools, instruction is also given regarding traditional approaches to teaching so that prospective teachers can not only employ the methods of learning communities, but also learn to teach effectively in traditional schools. Teachers can learn how to plan curricula and provide effective instruction, as well as become skilled in other teacher responsibilities.

School improvement is a basic theme of the text. Those aspects of schooling most in need of change are identified, such as the application of invalid learning processes, use of inappropriate motivational strategies, and failure to satisfy student needs. Explanations are given regarding how these failures occur, along with the fundamental changes necessary to remedy these problems.

TEXT ORGANIZATION

A comprehensive description of the learning communities approach to education is given in Chapter 1, along with a rationale for its value and usefulness in improving schools. Chapter 2 provides a description of student needs, along with supporting research, and the kind of school experiences that help students best satisfy their interpersonal and academic needs. Chapter 3 focuses on autonomy, with a description of how students can be empowered by having more self-directed school opportunities. A model is provided that shows how students can be helped to become more responsible decision makers and take a more substantial role in curriculum determination. The most critical aspect of schooling is learning. Chapter 4 presents constructivist theory as the appropriate learning model, along with the way in which this theory can be put into operation in schools, particularly where the emphasis is on learning communities. In Chapter 5, discussions of multicultural education and exceptionality are combined in an effort to help teachers learn how to provide all students more effective school experiences. The learning idiosyncrasies and problems of various student populations are delineated, along with suggested ways to help them effectively learn.

Teachers can greatly improve their practice if they carefully reflect on their experiences and apply available research to their teaching, as shown in Chapter 6. The reader is taught the appropriate function of theory and the strategic place of personal decision making for improving teaching and learning. Chapter 7 helps teachers become more expert in curriculum construction and in formulating instruction plans that take into account all aspects of learning and related considerations. Teachers learn how to formulate objectives from each of the three domains of knowledge and create plans for instruction with varying purposes. They learn how to formulate a course of study, create units of instruction, and organize daily lesson plans.

In Chapter 8, the reader learns the special nature of thinking and how to foster thinking and problem solving in learning communities. Cooperative learning models are described as ways to promote both cognitive and affective growth. Chapter 9 provides a detailed description of motivation research. Intrinsic versus extrinsic motivation, along with motivation to learn, are discussed. Other topics include ways to motivate students who suffer from learned helplessness or who have a preoccupation with self-worth, as well as the strategic connection that exists between motivation and human needs. Discipline has long been identified as one of the most critical problems that limit teacher effectiveness in the classroom. In Chapter 10, the reader is shown not only how to effectively deal with discipline problems, but also how to prevent them. The nature of school violence is presented, as are recommendations for violence prevention.

Chapter 11 provides instruction on the measurement of achievement. Issues regarding student assessment are outlined, along with various means for evaluating student work. Alternative assessment and portfolios are given as ways to validly determine the quality of student work in learning communities. Teaching improvement is the focus of Chapter 12. The obstacles to improvement are presented, along with ways to improve teaching practice individually and in groups. The value of action research and personal empowerment are also delineated. Methods of improving teaching in learning communities are described. Chapter 13 details a plan for involving parents in the education of their children, including ways that parents can support learning communities. This chapter also includes a rationale for including the entire community at large in the school's operation.

PEDAGOGICAL FEATURES

Each chapter begins with a list of learning objectives that the reader is encouraged to use as a study guide. The objectives focus on the most important potential outcomes.

Vignettes are placed in a variety of locations in the text to stimulate interest and create a framework for study, as well as promote practical conceptualizations of key concepts, ideas, and issues. They allow the reader to connect theories and practices with real life problems.

To help the reader carefully consider various points presented in the text and make practical applications regarding what has been learned, questions for reflection, decision points, and reflections about self are placed in strategic locations in the various chapters.

- *Questions for Reflection* allow the reader to consider various points about the information presented and think about implications and associated issues. The individual has an opportunity to compare theories and ideas and make judgments about educational policies and practices. Opportunities are given to analyze practical situations, policies, and educational methods and to make comparisons and solve problems.

- *Decision Points* give the reader an opportunity to apply what he or she has learned by completing practical exercises. To successfully complete decision points the reader must use theoretical knowledge as the basis for creating instructional materials, formulating sequences of activities which appropriately articulate with student needs and skill, and determining personal approaches to problem solving.

- *Reflections About Self* provide an opportunity to introspectively examine one's personal philosophy in light of contrasting educational practices and to justify points of view and proposed teaching methods. The reader is asked to contrast personal views of the nature of learning along with human nature and needs with the various theoretical considerations presented.

- Each chapter closes with a list of *Central Ideas*. This list provides the reader with a convenient way to review and summarize the contents of the chapter. Each central idea is a conceptual statement about the most significant content of the chapter.

- Each chapter contains *National Board for Professional Teaching Standards* placed strategically within the text to help the reader gain familiarity with the standards as they relate to teacher performance and to help focus attention on achieving teaching excellence. The standards provide specific expectations for readers as they prepare for teaching careers.

This book has been primarily designed for undergraduate courses in general methods, but may also be suitably used for graduate methods courses, introduction to education courses, and curriculum courses.

The following is the reference for the National Teaching Standards that appear throughout the text: National Board for Professional Teaching Standards. (1990). *Toward high and rigorous standards for the teaching profession: Initial policies and perspectives of the National Board for Professional Teaching Standards.* (2nd ed). Washington, DC: Author.

ACKNOWLEDGMENTS

I would like to thank the reviewers who provided thoughtful insight in reviewing this manuscript: Sally Armstrong, Northeastern State University; David Boger, North Carolina A&T State University; Frank Brathwaite, D'Youville College; Sandy Buczynski, University of San Diego; Mary C. Markowitz, Ohio University; Eunice M. Merideth, Drake University; Laura C. Stokes, University of North Alabama; and Barbara N. Young, Middle Tennessee State University.

I would also like to thank Sharon Black, Brigham Young University, for her skillful editing of the text.

Educator Learning Center:
An Invaluable Online Resource

Merrill Education and the Association for Supervision and Curriculum Development (ASCD) invite you to take advantage of a new online resource, one that provides access to the top research and proven strategies associated with ASCD and Merrill—the Educator Learning Center. At www. EducatorLearningCenter.com you will find resources that will enhance your students' understanding of course topics and of current educational issues, in addition to being invaluable for further research.

How the Educator Learning Center will help your students become better teachers

With the combined resources of Merrill Education and ASCD, you and your students will find a wealth of tools and materials to better prepare them for the classroom.

RESEARCH

- More than 600 articles from the ASCD journal *Educational Leadership* discuss everyday issues faced by practicing teachers.
- A direct link on the site to Research Navigator™ gives students access to many of the leading education journals, as well as extensive content detailing the research process.
- Excerpts from Merrill Education texts give your students insights on important topics of instructional methods, diverse populations, assessment, classroom management, technology, and refining classroom practice.

CLASSROOM PRACTICE

- Hundreds of lesson plans and teaching strategies are categorized by content area and age range.
- Case studies and classroom video footage provide virtual field experience for student reflection.
- Computer simulations and other electronic tools keep your students abreast of today's classrooms and current technologies.

Look into the value of Educator Learning Center yourself

A four-month subscription to Educator Learning Center is $25 but is FREE when used in conjunction with this text. To obtain free passcodes for your students, simply contact your local Merrill/Prentice Hall sales representative, and your representative will give you a special ISBN to give your bookstore when ordering your textbooks. To preview the value of this website to you and your students, please go to www.EducatorLearningCenter.com and click on "Demo."

Brief Contents

Contents

Note: Every effort has been made to provide accurate and current Internet information in this book. However, the Internet and information posted on it are constantly changing, so it is inevitable that some of the Internet addresses listed in this textbook will change.

The Basis

For teachers to be successful in the classroom it is important that they understand their students in terms of their basic needs and motivations, along with how they learn. The instructional program must take into account student attributes and a complex combination of critical considerations regarding how to satisfy a balance of student needs and goals, how to ensure that learning activities appropriately map onto natural learning proclivities, and how to be certain that student differences are thoughtfully considered. In addition, because students are part of ongoing communities, it is essential that the dynamics of school and classroom operations be patterned after life in democratic communities. Furthermore, students need to learn problem-solving strategies by becoming involved in solving personal as well as significant community problems in which they have vested interests.

Schools commonly have difficulty meeting the needs and interests of students. They tend to emphasize policies and procedures that keep students from satisfying their basic needs and limit the level of academic excellence of which students are capable. Learning communities can alleviate many of these deficiencies and help students acquire the educational experiences they need to become successful citizens in an increasingly complex society.

Traditional schools are ordinarily oriented toward competition, which tends to disenfranchise many students and reduce their learning effectiveness. Schools need to be restructured to incorporate learning communities as the basic organization for instruction. Learning communities can effectively satisfy all student needs, along with alleviating problems which lead to social and academic disenchantment, learning and discipline problems, and school violence.

Student autonomy within learning communities is the primary means for empowering students to achieve excellence as well as helping them to make appropriate social and intellectual progress. Autonomy helps students become enthusiastic, committed participants in the learning process who take personal responsibility for becoming self-directed learners. Autonomy is essential in encouraging students to become responsible participants in learning communities. A balance between personal autonomy and community involvement produces conditions for learning excellence and personal growth.

An understanding of the learning process is essential to classroom instruction. Without an accurate conception of how students learn, teachers are unable to provide experiences which are powerfully educative and growth promoting. It is generally accepted that learning is a generative process with the learner idiosyncratically constructing knowledge. Because many of the traditional methods of instruction emphasize the presentation and assimilation of information, they are out of sync with how children naturally learn. Learning communities provide an instructional format articulated through natural learning and encourage students to become more naturally and enthusiastically involved.

Many of the learning problems students encounter go unrecognized when ethnic, class, and gender issues are not properly considered. The situation is complicated further with the inclusion of students with various learning disabilities in regular classrooms. It is quite difficult for teachers to provide the right kind of learning experiences for such a broad spectrum of children. Teachers must become skilled in providing the kind of learning experiences that help all children make optimum progress in school.

Learning Communities

CHAPTER OBJECTIVES

This chapter is designed to help you

1. Defend the need for moral teachers and explain the role of moral teaching in children's personal development.
2. Explain the need for and nature of moral learning communities.
3. Explain how moral learning communities can help children satisfy their basic needs.
4. Explain the fundamental changes needed in schooling before genuine learning communities can be successfully created.
5. Describe the nature of relationships in moral learning communities and explain how these relationships can be developed.
6. Describe the critical attributes of moral learning communities.

Learning communities promote learning excellence and positive relationships.

7. Explain the actions needed to promote a properly functioning learning community.

8. Discuss ways in which teachers can be successfully involved in professional learning communities.

9. Discuss the value of school-community relationships and activities, and describe the kind of activities in which students might become involved in the community at large.

10. Explain how learning communities can promote more positive, personal teacher behavior and how this contributes to student learning.

11. Identify those characteristics of schools which may alienate students and indicate how learning communities can help schools avoid these problems.

INTRODUCTION

Schools seem to be perpetually under attack for their shortcomings. Historically, various innovations designed for improvement have been tried, but many fail because they don't adequately address the real problems. Instead, they focus on peripheral matters or merely symptoms. For example, many innovations address administrative concerns rather than teaching and learning, so their impact is minimal; continuous progress schools and flexible schedules are examples of these efforts. Many reform efforts are incremental and aimed at improving existing school structures to make them run more efficiently. They assume that basic institutional structures are sound and need only limited tinkering to help schools effectively function. However, it is becoming increasingly evident that the organization and practices of schools are irremediably flawed and that more fundamental changes are needed (Newman, 1998). The superficial changes commonly made have had little or no impact in dealing with school ills.

Sometimes new procedures designed to solve problems become part of the problem. In the case of competency testing, testing does not examine school practices nor provide valid suggestions for improvement. In addition, it is assumed that these tests validly measure desired school outcomes. Given how standardized tests are created, this is impossible, as is any hope of using test scores either to judge the quality of education or create means for improvement (Meier, 2002). It does, however, result in teachers abandoning the intended curriculum and scrambling to help students get passing scores on the test (Clinchy, 2001; Merrow, 2001).

There is no question that schools, manifested in a plethora of problems such as violence, high dropout rates, low achievement, and poor motivation, need fundamental changes. However, appropriate changes cannot be made until the problems are properly characterized. Chief among these problems is an improper conceptualization of learning as well as a failure to satisfy basic student needs (Darling-Hammond, 1997). Authentic learning, in addition to a full array of need-satisfying conditions, can be provided in an appropriately operated learning community. The following vignette illustrates how the dynamics of common school practices contribute to student alienation and violence.

Mark had been an outcast most of his school years. In elementary school he was often excluded from play activities, or else was chosen last when teams were being organized on the playground. In the classroom the other students considered him a "nerd." Upon reaching high school, he felt even more distanced from his peers. Never coordinated enough to excel at sports, he always felt like he was on the "outside looking in" while other boys were accepted and admired for their athletic abilities. As a result, he became more withdrawn over the years. He lacked social skills, due in part to having been withdrawn in school, and spent most of his time at home by himself studying science books and listening to rap music in his room.

Mark's mother would occasionally ask about his school work while looking in on him, and he routinely told her he completed it at school. She knew that wasn't true, since she occasionally received calls from his teachers, but felt helpless to change the situation. In the past she had nagged him, but soon found this to be fruitless. In addition, after working all day in an insurance agency, she didn't have the energy to do much more than fix dinner and do a little cleaning. Mark's father drove a truck transporting office furniture to various locations across the country and was frequently gone for periods as long as two weeks. When he was at home, he frequently criticized the government or any other group he viewed as infringing on his rights and privileges. His interactions with Mark consisted essentially of complaints about Mark's poor performance at school. His father frequently reminded him that he would have no chance for a college education if he continued to fail in high school. Mark's father also expected him to "take up some of the slack" at home in his absence. But it was rare for him to be satisfied with Mark's efforts to help out, and he generally ignored him. Soon Mark deliberately refused to do what his father assigned him, and he learned to suffer through the rebukes. Mark's mother often came to his defense, putting her relationship with her husband at risk. Despite her husband's long absences, she succeeded in maintaining a minimum of family goodwill. She was usually able to convince Mark that his father loved him but was overwhelmed by problems with his work that intruded on their family life. She told him he needed to be grateful for a father who never failed to bring home a paycheck.

Mark seemed cordial enough to his mother, but he rarely accepted her invitations to spend time with her. Instead he spent his evenings sequestered in his room. Mark rarely applied himself to his school work, hiding his intelligence from his teachers. He felt that what they were teaching was so "simple-minded" that he refused to get involved in class. He deliberately wrote the wrong answers to test questions lest the appearance of an attempt to succeed might seem to validate their "trivial curriculum." At first his teachers pleaded with him to at least turn in his assignments so he could get credit toward graduation, but they eventually gave up and left him alone. That was how he preferred it. They usually let him sit in the back row and read. At least then he wasn't disturbing the class.

Mark had a particularly strong dislike for the school athletes. As a group they made his life miserable, singling him out to torment and getting their "kicks" out of teasing him, often circling him in the hall to poke fun at him. This made it necessary to find various alternative routes to and from classes. He often ducked under one of the stairwells to wait for the bell to ring before going to class. He had so many tardies that teachers were continually threatening him, but this was of no consequence to Mark. They couldn't dock his grades when they were all "F"s, anyway.

Mark had recently taken an interest in girls, particularly Maria Rosales, a girl in his U.S. history class. He admired the way she often took exception to the platitudinous, vapid remarks of the teacher, Mr. Hartley, whose opinions about history always seemed to support Eurocentric acculturation and a view of America as the great "melting pot." Mark had read enough, and Maria had experienced enough, to consider his views just a lot of propaganda. Her family had lived in the United States for four generations, but she still felt disenfranchised. Yet the other students in class seemed content with Mr. Hartley's views. Mark secretly laughed at their gullibility, but he thought that in Maria he might have found an ally. His fascination with her led to fantasies about the two of them attending school dances and concerts together. He imagined dancing with her and talking to her about various topics of mutual interest. He fantasized about meeting her family and about introducing her to his mother. Sometimes he even formed mental pictures of their wedding.

Finally Mark became bold enough to approach Maria and ask if he could walk her home from school. He knew exactly where she lived, as he had followed her home many times, carefully keeping himself out of sight. He had carefully outlined in his mind what he would talk with her about, knowing what subjects were of great interest to her. Maria's reply to his invitation really stunned Mark. First she looked at him in complete surprise, like he was a stranger—and an undesirable one at that. Then she laughed at him incredulously and told him he must have taken leave of his senses. Her look communicated unquestioningly that she looked on him as scum. Because he had given himself to her completely in his mind, it was easy to hate her in an instant. She was the one person he had come to care about, maybe even to love. Her dislike for him was the final rejection. He didn't go to school for a week; instead, he locked himself in his room, coming out only to eat an occasional meal.

However, Mark's life significantly changed the day Reuben came to town and enrolled at Lincoln High School. He had transferred from a large school in the Midwest when his father had taken a position managing the local department store in this small Mountain West community. In Reuben, Mark found a sympathizer. Reuben had also been consistently rejected in school, partly because of his Jewish parentage and partly because he lacked athletic and social skills. Like Mark, he was ignored at home. His parents had not discovered his gun collection or found out that he had learned how to make timing devices for explosives on the Internet. He had stolen all the guns, as well as a respectable cache of ammunition, and pilfered dynamite from his uncle's construction site. No one suspected Reuben of the theft, and his Uncle Silas never officially disclosed that the explosives had been taken, since he had his reputation to protect.

Mark met Reuben in his physics class. They were seated across the aisle from one another. Reuben quickly discerned that Mark was rejected by his peers and was full of the same kind of hate that boiled inside him. They naturally turned to one another to fulfill their need for acceptance and recognition, sharing the venomous feelings they both had for their peers, their teachers, and the school. Mark and Reuben started spending a great deal of time together in the evenings. At school they both wore black pants and shirts, along with dark trench coats which they left open down the front. As they made themselves conspicuous, they received an additional dose of criticism and teasing.

Seven weeks into their friendship, Reuben showed Mark his collection of guns and explosives, and they began planning how they would use these weapons for revenge. They meticulously planned a particular day to plant the dynamite. All the explosives had to be placed strategically where and when they would not arouse suspicion or be detected. Exact timing was planned so that the explosions could distract, as well as maim, school officials and students while the pair carried out their operation. Members of the football team were specifically targeted; Reuben and Mark had determined the exact time when most of them would be in the dressing room. Other students' schedules and habits were also checked, as Mark wanted revenge on two of his teachers and a couple of boys from his physical education class who had tormented him over the years. Most notably, he wanted to confront Maria Rosales, point a gun at her, and ask if he could walk her home now.

QUESTIONS FOR REFLECTION

1. What kind of experiences tend to precipitate violence after it has been building for a period of time?
2. What are some of the subtle things teachers need to watch for in anticipating potential violence problems in school? What teacher interventions may help avoid violence problems regarding these factors?
3. What could have been done by teachers to help prevent the violence in Mark's case?

The Need for Change

Attending school can be very difficult for students. Some students, like Mark and Reuben, are tormented by their peers; others suffer from poor student-teacher relations or are bored by what they consider to be irrelevant curricula. When students do not do well academically or fail socially, they may withdraw or perhaps turn violent. Violence, along with gang activity, drug dealing, and drug consumption, tend to proliferate under conditions of student neglect and alienation (Hyman & Perone, 1998). There is an apparent need for changes in school to address these problems and to support the kind of education that more students find valid in modern society. Paramount among the changes needed is for teachers to become more explicit, moral examples for students and to provide a caring environment in which students can become caring, moral people themselves, equipped to actively participate in democratic living (Fenstermacher, 1990; Meier, 2002; Noddings, 2002). Moral people are tolerant and open-minded. They exhibit such virtues as honesty, fairness, justice, and even-handedness. They are very unlikely to engage in violent activities like those of Mark and Reuben or to reject and torment fellow students.

NATIONAL TEACHING STANDARDS

Proficient teachers are models of educated persons. They should exemplify character and competence as well as curiosity and a love of learning. They should also exhibit tolerance and open-mindedness; fairness and justice; appreciation of cultural and intellectual heritages; respect for human diversity and dignity; and such intellectual capacities as the ability to carefully reason, to take multiple perspectives, to question and receive wisdom, to be creative, to take risks, and to adopt an experimental and problem-solving orientation. These are attributes of moral teachers.

The Need for Moral Teachers

Educational theorists point out that changes in American society may be responsible for much of the conflict and desolation manifest in today's schools (Goodlad, 1994). Beginning with the industrial age and continuing through the information age, social and geographical mobility have increased. The sense of community tends to dry up and close associations with friends diminish. Because humans are inherently social, the lack of a solid community erodes the individual's sense of well-being and connectedness, along with the level of commitment usually associated with community membership. In addition, the moral imperatives, like those described as needed by teachers in the national teaching standards, and which are usually associated with community living, become less important. In a study of 13 of the world's major civilizations, Meyers (1968) discovered that, in their later stages of development, teaching became less morally focused, with more emphasis given to forms, rituals, and technical knowledge. The result was the spread of decadence throughout these societies. At the beginning, each of these societies stressed intimate tutor/learner relationships, as opposed to those found in formal institutions such as schools. Person-to-person contacts were promoted, and the primary goal of education was for teachers to transmit moral knowledge and to practice morality in dealing with their students. "Poor teaching" was recognized to have grave moral ramifications for the proper development of students in particular and society in general.

In appropriately defined moral education, such themes as moral conduct, character formation, diligence, respect for elders, community responsibility, personal integrity, and other important virtues are stressed. According to Meyers (1968), today the role of teachers in **moral education** has been tempered in deference to the prevailing secular—and even antireligious—intellectual climate. Rather than moral educators, teachers are seen as highly skilled technicians who deliver technical information to clients. However, the moral role of teachers is critical in a harmonious, properly functioning society. Children, because of their immaturity and lack of experience, are often incapable of defending themselves from negligent or selfish teachers. They are in a process of growth and development that requires moral nurturing. Irresponsible or careless teaching can have profound negative effects on their life opportunities (Wynne, 1995).

Teaching is a moral endeavor, specifically because it is a human action undertaken with regard to other human beings. Consequently, moral matters regarding what is fair, right, just, and virtuous are always present. Because students are young and immature, it makes it all the more necessary that teachers be morally oriented (Fenstermacher, 1990). Unfortunately, at the present time, though considerable emphasis is being placed on restructuring education, little attention is given to the enlightenment of youth, the freeing of their minds and souls for effective thinking, or their development of essential human virtues. The focus is on the status and prestige of teachers, on testing for teacher competence and student achievement, and on career advancement (Fenstermacher, 1990).

The moral aspects of learning communities currently being emphasized by educators should not be confused with earlier efforts at moral education. These earlier curricula focused on values education and character education as ends in themselves rather than as a mechanism to enhance interpersonal relationships, community responsibility, and authentic learning. Moral education as a focus in learning communities helps define the nature of relationships between students and between students and their teachers as they engage in personally meaningful learning that benefits not only individuals but groups as well.

The induction of students into moral living requires teachers who are themselves examples of moral living. In their teaching and personal lives they need to model moral attributes (McHenry, 2000; Noddings, 2002). One of the most critical of the moral attributes for teachers is that of teaching and learning **reciprocity**—of shared accountability for student learning. In current practice, teachers are usually held accountable when students fail to learn. It is assumed that teachers can ensure that even the most recalcitrant youth learn effectively, regardless of their attitudes or negative influences in their lives. Making the teacher totally responsible denies the learner a role in making decisions about life at school. Without shared involvement, students cannot be counted on to do their part in the learning process. Unfortunately, in far too many schools neither parents nor students, or even teachers, seem to know who makes decisions or how they are made. More often than not, no one in the school itself is deciding anything of importance; these decisions are being made in places far removed from the schools, such as state departments and central offices, yet teachers are increasingly being held accountable for results when they have little input in curriculum decisions (Darling-Hammond, 1997; Meier, 2002).

Perhaps the most critical ingredient for reciprocity in student learning is an appropriate balance of agency for both teachers and students. Teachers need sufficient autonomy to make important decisions regarding their classes and students, which generally requires less interference from the administration and fewer state restrictions regarding curricula. This is particularly true when teaching students with special needs. Research indicates that instead of rescuing young people from risk, some regular school practices put them at further risk, intensifying the problems of children and youth who are already in desperate circumstances. Many of these difficulties are within the power of educators to solve, such as problems associated with grouping and tracking practices, inappropriate expectations and language of teachers, and poor curricular and instructional decisions (Goodlad, 1994).

A requisite degree of autonomy must also be offered to students. When teachers have sufficient personal control over the curriculum, they are at liberty to share decision making with their students, *but only to the extent students demonstrate they are able to make reasonable choices.* This not only empowers students and promotes greater interest and effort on their part, but it also provides a way to achieve a balanced reciprocity for learning. Empowering students can be effectively accomplished in moral learning communities, which provide for each participant to be a valued member, for caring relationships to be formed, and for shared expectations to result in meaningful learning. In providing students greater autonomy, teachers should carefully monitor the extent to which students make responsible decisions and provide instruction on how to make better choices. Greater decision-making opportunities should be given as students gradually develop a greater capacity for wise judgment. Ordinarily this involves incorporating important relevant problems that students are currently experiencing as central curricular elements and allowing students to formulate personal and group strategies for solving these problems.

 ## QUESTIONS FOR REFLECTION

1. Think about your personal experiences in school. Make a list of teaching practices and learning activities from your experience which have moral implications. From your experience, what changes would have made your schooling more of a moral endeavor?

2. How do your personal beliefs about education compare with the kind of education involved in moral learning communities? What modifications to your personal beliefs would be necessary to be compatible with learning communities?

The Need for Moral Learning Communities

There are a number of important reasons for employing moral learning communities in the schools. Moral learning communities:

- promote better student-teacher relationships
- promote more effective learning
- help eliminate alienation and violence
- help students adjust better to the community at large
- help students better satisfy their basic needs
- help students learn better self-esteem
- help students assume more responsibility for their conduct and their learning
- promote community decision making
- help students learn to function in the real world

In American society, societal advancement has been claimed to be a function of "rugged individualism," referencing the solitary frontiersman who used his personal ingenuity to conquer the frontier and prepare the way for those who followed. In reality, it was the groups who settled the frontier by "putting down roots" and establishing lasting communities who really created conditions for social advancement. Amitai Etzioni, a noted sociologist, is among those who challenge the idea of the individual as central in human motivation and decision making. He believes too much emphasis has been placed on rational choice and individual decision making (Etzioni, 1988). In reality, decisions are influenced by norms: People commonly take into account what others believe and how they are likely to react to the decisions. Emotions, preferences, values, and beliefs in connection with social bonds and obligations are paramount in decision making. Various communities within which the individual holds membership shape thinking and constrain the ways in which one's needs get satisfied. Thus, group norms influence choice. Self-interest is moderated and selfless behavior is undertaken. It is common to respond selflessly to duties and obligations that come from valued group causes or social connections.

It is sometimes declared that "what is rewarded gets done." A more community-oriented interpretation is "what is rewarding gets done," or "what one values and believes to be good gets done." The first view is based on extrinsic gain, while the second emphasizes intrinsic worth. There is no doubt that individuals may respond to the possibility of receiving a reward. However, intrinsic motivation can also be a powerful influence. Extrinsic value promotes calculated involvement: Students respond because of what others can supply as a reward. Intrinsic motivation, in contrast, comes from within: The individual does something that is enjoyed and perceived as meaningful. In addition, intrinsic involvement has a way of being sustained independent of external factors. A third motivating factor, called a moral tie, emerges from the acceptance of duties and obligations toward others and toward work that comes from commitments regarding shared values and beliefs. Like intrinsic motivation, moral ties come from within. Because moral ties are grounded more in cultural norms and expectations than in personal gratification, they are usually much stronger than either extrinsic or intrinsic motivation (Sergiovanni, 1994). For example, students are likely to be more highly motivated when they undertake group projects like limiting drug abuse or cleaning up pollution in a local river.

Perhaps the most potent source of moral guidance is found in religious values. One's family background and personal values also contribute to decisions made regarding value questions. In interviews with school administrators, Marshall (1992) found that they consistently relied on religious values and on family and personal values, as well as their commitment to the ethic of caring and their respect for the value of the communities in which they live and work, to make choices. These sources were consistently referred to in discussions regarding conflict situations. The administrators who were studied consistently articulated the value of justice, equity, and fairness. They also included openness, honesty, and evenhandedness as dominant themes in their values and administrative actions.

Learning communities depend on teachers who have internalized principles like those previously listed to provide the moral guidance needed to moderate classroom interactions appropriately (Noddings, 2002). Johnson (1990) found that teachers commonly enter the profession with purposes consistent with these principles, which provide an appropriate social orientation toward the development of learning communities. Teachers who are employed in the private school sector tend to maintain these values and attitudes, while their public school counterparts move in the direction less conducive to building community. Private school teachers maintain a "we" identity, while public school teachers assume an "I" or "me" identity. With a "we" identity there is an emphasis on bonding with others and sharing a common habitat, thereby developing a sense of neighborliness or kinship. Teaching and learning are characterized by collegiality between teachers and students, as well as between students. Relationships are based on understandings about what is shared and the obligations associated with them. Public school teachers tend to develop a contractual value orientation. Their connections are contrived instead of being authentic, and result in disconnectedness, isolation, and loneliness.

Johnson (1990) found that private school teachers were more likely than public school teachers to have cultural bonds with others in the school. They expressed clearer descriptions of their school's goals and purposes, articulating with precision the values they share with others in their schools. They were able to explain how these values were grounded in the school's history and were reinforced and expressed in its traditions. In contrast, public school teachers seldom mentioned the defining nature of cultural bonds. They represented their schools as having mixed purposes, vague histories, artificial traditions, and a neutral stance toward values. It appears that schools as organizations influence teachers toward either community or isolationist orientations to teaching. Of course, the issue here is not whether or not teachers may or may not respond to cultural connections. Early on they are equipped to do so. The question is whether or not schools are willing to modify their operations in ways which promote these connections.

In understanding the human need for community, various theories provide insight. Durkheim (1964) proposed that humans have a basic need to belong, to be connected to each other, and to identify with a set of norms that give direction and meaning to life. He indicates that without mores, values, goals, and norms, people become alienated from themselves, from others, and ultimately from society. Negative consequences are the result both socially and personally. The antidote for such possibilities, according to Durkheim, is community. This kind of involvement provides for the development of a collective conscience, with moral awareness as well as the emergence of mutual obligation. Community involvement includes three elements:

1. duty
2. attachment
3. self-determination

Duty implies a level of self-constraint achieved through a sense of obligation to the community. Attachment involves a sense of membership, commitment to the group, and development of community identity. Self-determination is achieved when personal agency becomes integrated within a rational sense of awareness regarding the reasons for duty and attachment to the community (Durkheim, 1964).

To have successful relationships with others and to experience fruitful community life, individuals must moderate need satisfaction to a level where everyone's needs can be appropriately fulfilled. All needs require some degree of fulfillment and this can only occur when members of a community help one another satisfy their needs. Community members who fail to reciprocate fulfillment of needs can expect less fulfillment of their own needs than they desire. To create a successful learning community, all members must have an appropriate level of satisfaction and realize that achieving their desires requires a degree of sacrifice for others in the community. They must also realize that their needs cannot be satisfied outside a social context. Part of the community's work is to help all members understand that the fulfillment of their needs requires the simultaneous satisfaction of the needs of all community members. All have a reciprocal responsibility to look after one another's interests, for that is the only way personal needs can be consistently met. The quality of relationships necessary for community maintenance involves choosing not to coerce, force, compel, punish, reward, manipulate, boss, motivate, criticize, blame, complain, nag, badger, rank, rate, or withdraw. Instead, community members must choose to care, listen, support, negotiate, encourage, love, befriend, trust, accept, welcome, and esteem (Glasser, 1984).

Decision Points

Assume you are a high school teacher. In your class there are several students who routinely dominate others and monopolize class time. It is obvious that other class members despise them and deliberately avoid working with them.

Questions:
1. What needs to happen so everyone's needs are fulfilled?
2. What seems to be the most potent need students have?
3. What could you do as the teacher to promote a greater sense of moral commitment between students?

Task:
1. Design a list of learning activities you believe will help students balance their needs so all students can achieve a greater sense of complete fulfillment. Include activities you believe will be particularly effective in creating greater interpersonal cohesiveness between students.

NATIONAL TEACHING STANDARDS

To fulfill their responsibilities, teachers must create, enrich, and alter the organizational structures in which they work with young people.

School Changes Needed

To establish moral learning communities, fundamental modifications are needed in basic school operations and teaching practices. However, school practices have a long tradition, and much about their daily operation has become generally accepted routine. Many educators find it difficult to imagine changes beyond minor adjustments. Some popular current recommendations for change are of this variety. Unfortunately, they rarely examine what is really ailing the schools, focusing instead on superficial modifications, like a physician dealing with symptoms instead of addressing the causes of disease (Newman, 1998). Commonly the cry is to return to "the basics" as the most appropriate format for improving education. Interestingly, no one has bothered to ask whether the traditional education that proponents so highly treasure was ever the best education for anyone (Noddings, 2002). The return to basics emphasizes the need for schools to meet prescribed standards, enforced through high-stakes standardized testing, as is the case in the "no child left behind" imperative issued by the federal government. However, even if all concerned agree about the standards, and even if they manage to create valid tests, there is still very little evidence that what schools teach matters in the real world (Merrow, 2001).

One of the problems commonly identified for modern schools is the fact their operations are based on an agricultural or manufacturing economy even though society has entered the information age. The increase in complexity associated with this technological society requires citizens who can understand and evaluate difficult problems and alternatives and who can manage complicated social systems. However, school curricula, with their orientation to fact recall, have changed little in the past 100 years and consequently are out of sync with these changing conditions. These traditional fact-based, rote-dominated structures do not develop necessary decision-making skills or social sensitivities. Schools do not promote long-term teacher-student relationships or in-depth study, both of which are needed to help students achieve the kind of skills needed in modern society. Schools are still administered, essentially, by hierarchical decision making. Policies are formulated at the top and filter down through the system where they are translated into rigid rules and procedures. Little or no credence is given to the decision-making role of teachers in their individual classrooms, nor do students have a role in deciding how and what they learn (Darling-Hammond, 1997).

Various recommendations have been proposed to alleviate the current distress of schools and to promote the change necessary to adjust to current economic, social, and cultural realities (McHenry, 2000). These recommendations are substantially different from those routinely made in earlier times (Smith, 2001). Instead of recommending flexible schedules, site-based management, teacher-proof materials, and the like, it is suggested that schools be substantially restructured from their traditional functions. For example, Darling-Hammond (1997) recommends that the curriculum change to focus on higher-order cognitive functioning, taking students beyond recall, recognition, and reproduction of information to evaluation, analysis, syntheses, and production of arguments, ideas, and performances. Students should engage in extensive, in-depth inquiry experiences that have current meaning in their lives, rather than being limited to the superficial memorization of massive amounts of factual information (McHenry, 2000; Smith, 2001). This obviously will require that the current evaluation system, which relies heavily on recall, be revised to emphasize such methods as self-evaluation and portfolios. More sophisticated means will be required to determine depth of understanding, and students will need to apply their skills and ideas in personally meaningful contexts and engage in activities they have personal reasons to undertake (Glickman, 1993). Educational experiences should build upon students' prior learning, but press them toward more disciplined understandings. Such an approach will not require careful diagnoses and prescription, but rather sensitive creation of experiences which take into account considerable student input and choice. Students and teachers must be provided extended blocks of time to work together around meaningful, authentic problems (Darling-Hammond, 1997).

It is also recommended that schools foster truly democratic experiences for students, employing structures of caring to promote a greater sense of community among students, teachers, and administrators. In far too many schools, relationships between students and teachers are characterized by mistrust, manifested in authoritarian treatment, demeaning statements, and petty rules that most students will break sooner or later (Darling-Hammond, 1997; Noddings, 2002). Schools must include families and communities at large in meaningful school experiences before truly authentic democratic understanding and participation can be faithfully applied to school activities (Meier, 2002). These experiences must extend far beyond bake sales and visits to nursing homes, although such activities have value. Students need to be involved in solving community problems such as drug dealing, gang activity, and public violence. The roles they play should allow for bona fide decision-making with real community problems (Glickman, 1993).

The quality of education depends more on teachers than on any other component of the education process. Neither textbooks nor state or district curricula have the power to effect learning the way teachers do. Consequently some recommended school improvement schemes focus on the nature of teacher training and the characteristics of teaching as a craft. For teachers to effectively employ their skills, they must be empowered with far more decision-making opportunities than most currently enjoy (Bohn & Sleeter, 2000). It is generally conceded that current teacher training programs are deficient in preparing teachers for this much-enhanced role. Currently most teachers see themselves as information transmitters with little moral responsibility. The common view of teaching is one of employing technically defined practice in routine ways, with teachers engaging their students in carefully guided learning activities which incorporate specific methods. The methods are both means of instruction and ends as well, and the ends of instruction are justified in terms of employing "appropriate" methodological means. The important task of teachers carefully scrutinizing the ends of instruction receives little support. One place where this means-ends problem has been particularly noticeable is in the formulation of educational objectives. Greater emphasis has been placed on framing objectives in a proper format than in ensuring that they constitute a well-articulated and justifiable end for instruction (Smith, 1972).

Perhaps morality should be the central feature in the development of teachers if they are to develop students' capacities to choose and hold visions of the good and thus prepare them to participate in and benefit from the general autonomy and opportunities of adult society. Teachers must enable their students to exercise their basic freedoms responsibly (Bull, 1990). There can be no moral behavior without the requisite level of autonomy, a rule that holds for teachers as well as their students. Teachers must be morally developed in order to help their students become moral people. They must be honest themselves if they expect honesty from their students, generous if they expect generosity, and diligent if they hope to see diligence. Students must observe their teachers thinking critically in their presence as a template for their own development of critical thinking. Teachers must exemplify moral principles and virtues in order to elicit them from their students (Fenstermacher, 1990). In addition, for moral instruction to succeed it must be intentional and properly conceptualized. Moral development must be the central purpose of instruction rather than a hoped-for incidental outcome. When memorizing large quantities of information takes precedence over more substantive moral outcomes, moral development can be seriously thwarted (Noddings, 2002). One very important component of moral teaching is an appropriate context. Because the purpose of moral instruction in school is to prepare students for life in their families and communities, life in school should be a fair representation of those conditions, and moral development should be an integrated component of the curriculum. School learning communities provide an excellent format for this kind of education if in fact the community environment created is authentic and appropriately connected to real community life (Meier, 2002).

 ## QUESTIONS FOR REFLECTION

1. What kinds of community problems can students legitimately deal with? Identify any exceptions and explain why some of these problems would be inappropriate for students to deal with.

2. What obstacles are likely to be encountered in creating school experiences for students that authentically prepare them for life in their communities? How can these obstacles be overcome?

3. What kind of experiences would encourage the development of a high degree of personal morality in students? What would your role as the teacher be?

Reflections About Self

1. Ascertain the degree of commitment you need to have to promote the moral development of students.
2. Create a list of moral principles you feel strongly about. What experiences have you had that have bolstered your commitment to these principles? Create a list of experiences you believe would help solidify these principles as a significant part of your value system.

The Need for a New Theory of Schooling

Not only must teachers provide examples of moral living for students, but teaching and learning practices must help students acquire the skills, attitudes, and understandings that allow them to become meaningfully integrated into social and cultural realities. This requires experiences which are authentic, satisfy student needs, and articulate appropriately with their learning proclivities. Learning approaches must be encouraged which recognize the complexity of human learning and development. Unfortunately, most policies aimed at monitoring and regulating teaching and learning in the public schools presume that learning is simple and predictable, a development due to a long tradition of applying behavioristic learning theories to schooling. B. F. Skinner and other advocates believed that even complex learning could be produced by presenting reinforcing stimuli immediately following a demonstration of desired behavior. From this perspective, instructional sequences have traditionally provided small, discrete pieces of information to be mastered in a predetermined sequence, short responses to be learned by rote memorization, immediate reinforcement for correct answers, many opportunities for correct performance, a gradual progression of individual discrete skills intended to cumulate in a more complex performance, and use of reinforcement for maintaining student attention and participation. Standardized curricula based on these behavioristic principles are currently prescribed in all states but Iowa (Bohn & Sleeter, 2000). School systems search for teacher-proof curricula and dictate the use of standardized testing, a clear indication of mistrust for teachers' capabilities to make sound decisions about how and what students should be taught (Meier, 2002). Such curricula mandate specific textbooks and provide teachers with hundreds of state- or district-generated objectives with associated lessons and tests. Evidence suggests that highly prescriptive curricular mandates do not improve learning, especially if they effectively control teaching (Darling-Hammond, 1997).

Behavioristic learning theories have been ineffective for less-than-obvious reasons. No doubt many educators believed that incentives provided for defined learning sequences should stimulate more and better learning, assuming that learning would eventually become self-rewarding if students could be induced to begin the process through various reinforcers. However, experience has shown that when students become conditioned to the reward, learning fails to become naturally rewarding and students eventually refuse to engage in learning activities without rewards. Thus, learning that was intrinsically rewarding in the past would not be undertaken without an extrinsic reinforcer. It was clearly demonstrated that extrinsic rewards can undermine the intrinsic, self-rewarding power of learning (Kohn, 1993).

TABLE 1.1   *Comparison Between Behaviorism and Constructivism.*

Educational Activity	Behaviorism	Constructivism
Assumptions About Learning	Information is absorbed.	Students actively construct their own meaning.
	New information automatically replaces old erroneous information.	New concepts that are taught must be compared to existing conceptions and then integrated or rejected.
	Students regularly acknowledge and change conceptions that are wrong.	Students resist changing their conceptions.
Teaching	Information has to be broken down into small pieces and sequenced.	Students are provided with opportunities to explore and create their own investigations.
	Teaching is by rote.	Teaching is by inquiry.
Curriculum	Programmed instruction, computer-assisted instruction, and teacher-proof materials are provided.	Bodies of information to explore are recommended.
Administration	Top-down administration.	Learning communities.

Behaviorism has had a potent influence on education for a couple of reasons. First, it presumes predictability, viewing children as passive raw material that can be readily manipulated. It reduces learning tasks to their simplest form and sequences them in a uniform manner which is simple to manage and can be stimulated by appropriately dispensed rewards. Second, simplistic schemes for teaching were devised to respond to inherent weaknesses in the teaching profession as well as the under education of teachers. This condition prevented any organized move to oppose these practices (Darling-Hammond, 1997). Currently, behavioristic principles have been challenged by constructivist learning theory. (See the comparisons between behaviorism and constructivism in Table 1.1.) The constructivist position is that children do not simply absorb information that has been carefully organized and sequenced by teachers; students create their own meaning. They organize their own conceptions of the world and compare current learning with previous conceptions, accepting new material as meaningful if it can be successfully organized to fit with what is already stored in memory. Behaviorism sees the human brain as a sponge that simply sops up what is presented; constructivism describes the brain as an agent that actively and selectively examines information and constructs personal meaning. Information judged to be incongruous with what is already stored may not be seriously considered (Trowbridge, Bybee, & Powell, 2000).

From the behavioristic viewpoint, children's school behavior must be managed and controlled by teachers and other adults; they are unable to assume any responsibility for their own learning. As this view has been accepted for a very long time, change in this perspective challenges practices that have previously appeared sensible, but which now appear to be seriously flawed. The constructivist conception of learning requires fundamental changes in the way schools are viewed as well as in the activities they provide, administratively and pedagogically.

Schools need to abandon top-down forms of administration that emphasize control in favour of procedures that focus more on trust and caring relationships (Darling-Hammond, 1993; Newman, 1998; Noddings, 2002). In addition, the number of students per teacher needs to be reduced to accommodate a broader professional role for teachers. Compensatory reductions would occur in the number of administrative and support personnel needed. Teacher training should be more comprehensive, allowing teachers to become familiar with administrative and support requirements and to teach a broader range of subjects to the same students. Such changes would contribute to the context needed to employ learning communities as the primary learning configuration. With this approach teachers are able to spend more time with the same group of students and to provide a more integrated curriculum (Noddings, 2002; Sizer, 1984). In addition, fewer subjects would be taught, with more in-depth study of these subjects, thus avoiding the superficial nature of learning so prevalent in American schools (Darling-Hammond, 1997). Thus, students would have a format to become deeply involved in meaningful topics of their own choosing. Noddings (2002) suggests that schooling might consist of new subjects such as *People: Their Growth, Customs, and Relationships.* These new subjects should have the same status as all current school subjects and be studied over a three- or four-year period in the same way math and English currently are. A course about *people* might contain practical components in which students do part of their work outside the classroom in such places as kindergarten classrooms and nursing homes. Learning communities could be used to implement these suggested curricular changes.

Learning Communities

Learning communities provide an excellent format for exploring personally meaningful study, while emphasizing student preparation to function in a democratic society. Children involved in learning communities gain experiences with a template for current and future roles in authentic community life. Much of human experience involves life in communities. Unfortunately, traditional schools and curricula impose different kinds of goals and experiences on students. In school, students are generally encouraged to do their own work so that educators can verify that their level of competency is exclusively their own. Most school learning involves students sitting quietly doing their own work, which is then evaluated through testing (Goodlad, 1984). There are few opportunities for independent inquiry or involvement with other students. Rarely do students engage in extended learning which produces extensive, high-quality products and reports. Their work does not authentically represent the kind of human activity common in all walks of life and in all kinds of employment. When children graduate from high school, they frequently lack preparation for life in the workforce or involvement in their neighborhoods.

Transforming traditional schools into caring learning communities will require deep changes. Past efforts at school restructuring have never produced substantial changes in the process of teaching and learning due to the stabilizing effect of the dominant culture of schools. Most proposed changes have been accommodated within the existing structure without substantial adjustments or significant differences (Newman, 1998; Sergiovanni,

2000). In the end, schooling remains much the same, despite the fact that little or no research data support schools as they are (Merrow, 2001; Noddings, 2002). Schools have evolved into bureaucratic institutions that are organized more for administrative convenience than for maximum student learning.

Faced with the usual criticism of schools, policy makers have ordinarily dictated changes based on strategies which have little or no effect on learning. Commonly standard outcomes have been mandated along with management systems that emphasize supervision, evaluation, and penalties for noncompliance. Such mandates often rely on corporate images of vision and leadership to motivate, inspire, or otherwise persuade schools to change. Market theories are applied which have never been evaluated for school application. Inappropriate models of competition are often employed, along with backup rewards that administrators hope will produce desired changes. They rarely do. Schools seem impervious to these initiatives. Market forces seem able to change school structure, but have little effect on the essential school purposes of teaching and learning (Sergiovanni, 2000). To produce deep changes, the power of localism is recommended by which democratic actions through learning communities formulate action plans and all members of the community are substantially involved (Hiatt & Diana, 2001). This involves input by students and their teachers, as well as parents and administrators. But the most significant determiners of school curricula must be students and their teachers (Keefe & Jenkins, 2002). Outsiders have limited knowledge regarding the kinds of learning experiences students find meaningful and are not able to detect the changes in teaching strategies necessary to engender responsible self-direction and high-quality student learning.

 ## QUESTIONS FOR REFLECTION

1. If possible, spend some time in a school observing what is happening there and the kind of student behavior that tends to be promoted in these circumstances. What specific connections do you make regarding schools and student behavior?

2. From your experience, what evidence is there that schools need to make fundamental changes in their operations? Explain what could be done to make these changes and what obstacles might be met in trying to make changes.

3. Why do you believe schools remain much the same despite efforts to restructure them? Explain your reasoning.

4. What changes do you believe are essential for schools to make in order to prepare students for a productive life in democratic communities? What do you believe the teacher's role should be in making these changes?

5. What challenges are present when schools try to change? What kind of participation by community members might help meet these challenges?

NATIONAL TEACHING STANDARDS

Teachers must like all students and become dedicated to and skilled at making knowledge accessible to all students.

TABLE 1.2   *Comparisons Between Traditional Schools and Learning Communities.*

Traditional Schools	**Learning Communities**
Curriculum is common.	Curriculum is unique.
Curriculum is prescribed.	Community creates the curriculum.
Needs and interests of the students are assumed to be the same.	Community members' unique desires are taken into account.
Purposes are prescribed from outside the classroom; commitment to purposes varies.	Commitment to community purposes are created within the community.
Agreements are contractual.	Agreements evolve out of interpersonal understandings and shared obligations.
Teacher control is essential.	Autonomy and responsibility are promoted.
Teacher-administrator relations depend on power and authority.	Teacher-administrator relations are based on mutual respect.
Motivation depends on rewards provided by superiors.	Motivation depends on a combination of personal interest and collective significance.
Decisions depend on dictated, universal rules.	Decisions are made in connection with the community rendering collective judgment about specific situations.
Individuals are valued for their achievements.	Individuals are valued unconditionally.
Expectations are narrowly defined.	Roles are loosely defined for members.
Focus is on self-interest.	Community interests and associations are considered valuable in and of themselves.
Each person has to look after his or her own interests.	There is a covenant regarding the vision of the community and its purposes.

Relationships in Communities

The coercive methods often used in schools to teach the prescribed curriculum are diametrically opposed to how learning communities operate (see Table 1.2). Learning communities cannot be run with recipes. There are no workshops or training packages that will provide the necessary kind of preparation. This is because each learning community is unique: Participants must invent their own practice. Certain guidelines can be followed, but many of the essential elements of any community are created by the community members themselves. This is what gives each community uniqueness and also delineates the difficulties they encounter in the community building process (Sergiovanni, 1994). Because each community depends on its members for definition and function, each has to engage in a process of community building that accommodates the needs and desires of its members and provides for collaboration and sharing of the results of community labors and learning, as well as the growth of group identity. Group identity must include strong commitment to community purposes, along with acceptance and caring by all community members.

Relationships in a community are not based on contracts as they are in some formal organizations (Wickett, 2000). Interpersonal agreements about what is shared gradually develop into a set of obligations concerning what group members hold in common.

Relationships in a community are mutually reinforcing, as the needs of each group member are the *primary agenda* of the community. The community is healthy and strong when group members help one another satisfy personal needs and desires.

In a learning community, student-teacher relationships reflect kinship and love along with duty and acceptance. Teachers treat their students with the same sense of care they would give their own children. On the highest level of this kinship, teachers extend the greatest level of personal autonomy, which students are capable of responsibly using. Student autonomy will vary over time as students gain experience working in the community and assuming increased control over their own learning. Teacher-administrator relationships should reflect mutual respect, teacher autonomy, and genuine caring.

Members of a learning community share common interests. Any learning activity should be examined for its collective significance according to community values that constitute a public moral code; however, learning can be constrained by personal interests as well. The *common good* of a learning community is the *collective good* of all of its members: Personal interests can and should be pursued in connection with the community achieving its purposes, as determined through active interaction and collaboration (Glickman, 1993).

Problems that arise in a learning community should be dealt with without reference to universal rules. Decisions should be made in connection with the specifics of the situation itself, with the unique circumstances in the problem situation requiring a unique resolution. Thus, the same problem may be handled differently on different occasions.

In learning communities, members value one another more than their separate achievements. When acceptance is contingent on one's achievements, love and acceptance are conditional, and children will not feel a steady flow of acceptance and appreciation. Having to satisfy conditions for acceptance undermines each individual's sense of worth and approbation.

The roles of learning community members should not be too strictly defined. A good deal of latitude allows individuals to determine their own roles within the community. Stereotyping one another creates narrow expectations which interfere with personal flexibility and relegate roles to preset requirements. Learning communities function best when both teachers and students experience a spirit of inquiry and when personal satisfaction can be enhanced by determining one's own role in the community.

In a learning community, means and ends have equal importance. Thus, interest in learning itself as a process is intrinsically valued and not considered as merely a means for high achievement and good grades. Rules are valued as a means for enhancing learning, not as a way to manage student behavior. Improving the quality of the teachers' workplace should be valued because it is the right thing to do, not because it can manipulate teacher improvement.

Altruism characterizes learning communities. Relationships are close and informal as well as cooperative. Individual needs and circumstances are taken into consideration, and individual concerns are considered legitimate. Acceptance is unconditional. Sacrificing self-interest in deference to the needs of other community members should be common. Members associate with one another for the intrinsic value of association, not because of the personal use to which such associations may be put. Knowledge is valued and obtained for its own sake. The acceptance and love of children is the business of the community. These community characteristics emerge through the ties engendered by this kind of kinship. A sense of community identity is created by sharing common experiences in the school, and a compact of mutual obligations and commitments is created out of common purposes (Sergiovanni, 1994). Building community seems to require the development of a common mind, consisting of shared values, conceptions, and ideas about schooling and about human nature. There can be no dialogue or communication unless beliefs, values, commitments, and even emotions are shared in common. These conditions are not easily achieved in a diverse population, but can be developed through the process of community building. It is possible to build communities that cherish individual freedom. However, there can be enormous problems. Participants may find it difficult to care for others who are radically different and to respect ideological diversity (Noddings, 2002).

In building learning communities, common purposes must be achieved. Leaders both in the school and in each classroom represent these purposes as their actions suggest clarity for group actions, promoting consensus among group members and stimulating commitment to community purposes. Under these conditions a value framework evolves, allowing daily routine activities to take on special meaning and significance. Norms thereby created guide specific actions, and an identity emerges for the school that differentiates it from other schools. As a result the school is transformed from a common workplace to a sacred enterprise—sacred in the sense that the work done there has special meaning and importance to those involved. What makes these schools different from many others is their clarity of purpose and their grasp of the broader values and principles central to real school achievement (Sergiovanni, 1990).

In a properly developed learning community, purposes involve the vision of leaders in and out of the classroom, as well as a covenant shared by the group. The covenant provides the value dimension needed for extraordinary performance by students, and the vision of the school reflects the hopes, dreams, needs, and interests of students, as well as the values and beliefs of everyone who has a stake in the school. Ultimately, the vision provides the conception of what the school stands and lives for. In the hearts of the members, this vision drives their daily behavior toward community purposes (Brandt, 1992). The term **covenant** emphasizes that agreements entered into are binding and solemn commitments for which trust is an essential element. Covenants define what the learning community is as well as the commitments members make to one another. The process of building consensus about purposes and beliefs binds people together around common themes, with a sense of mission and group ownership (Sergiovanni, 1990). Unfortunately, research into present-day schooling reveals a near vacuum with respect to mission (Goodlad, 2000).

 ## QUESTIONS FOR REFLECTION

1. What kind of projects would provide an appropriate kind of learning activity for a learning community?

2. How would you determine the degree of autonomy to provide students in a learning community? How would you define the level of students' maturity as a means of determining when students are prepared for having more freedom and responsibility in the classroom?

Decision Points

1. Create a list of purposes you believe should undergird a learning community.
2. Formulate a list of learning activities in the subject you teach that would provide students a means of achieving the purposes you have defined.

Attributes of Learning Communities

As learning communities become stronger, more and more of the actions taken by individuals and groups are compelled from within, while fewer are centered outside the group. These actions tend to be self-sustaining. Students become eager, empowered participants in group learning activities as well as more responsible self-managing partners, bound to one another and to their teachers by reciprocal webs of moral obligation. Personal rights, discretion, and freedom connect with commitments, obligations, and duties that they feel toward others and toward the school (Sergiovanni, 1999). Schools develop into productive learning communities as they become

- *Reflective communities*—in which students and teachers develop insights into their own strengths and weaknesses as learners and use these insights to improve learning strategies.
- *Developmental communities*—in which students and teachers learn to acknowledge and accept the fact that community members develop at different rates and are more or less ready to learn particular ideas at particular times.
- *Diverse communities*—in which the various talents and interests of students and teachers are acknowledged and allowed to provide direction to curriculum construction, teaching, and evaluation.
- *Conversational communities*—in which high priority is given to promoting active discourse among members, with in-depth exploration of values and interests.
- *Caring communities*—in which students and teachers learn to be kind to one another and to respect one another's differences, with emphasis on helping one another develop as learners and persons.
- *Responsible communities*—in which students and teachers develop a sense of responsibility toward one another, and a moral obligation evolves including not only present behavior, but also future behavior as citizens (Sergiovanni, 1999).

Perhaps the strongest force in moving schools toward becoming these types of communities is establishing a covenant (Sergiovanni, 1999), which represents the establishment of principles of operation from which the school will not be moved. The mission, goals, and plans that emanate from community deliberations are considered too important to abandon for other purposes (Glickman, 1993).

A covenant community in the school consists of students, teachers, administrators, and parents who share certain purposes, values, and beliefs, and who feel a strong sense of belonging. This doesn't mean that all members are the same or expected to be alike in many ways. In fact, learning communities are strengthened by diversity. Yet individuals in diverse groups can come to think the welfare of the group is paramount so long as the desires and welfare of *each member* define group purposes and operations. Membership in the community inspires deep loyalty, compelling individuals to work together for the common good. In a covenant community, leaders not only work toward a consensus of ideas and commitments, but they model these ideas and commitments and help others apply them in their daily lives. Successful groups do not force members to comply with expectations. Rather, they foster common commitments which grow out of the ability of members to accomplish together what they could not do alone. Group goals become the ultimate fulfillment both of the collective and of the individual (Glickman, 1993).

The covenant is created by all people who participate in the educational process and is used as the basis for decision making, as well as establishing school priorities with respect to staff, schedules, materials, assessment, the curriculum, staff development, and resource allocation (Allen, Rogers, Hensley, Glanton, & Livingston, 1999; Glickman, 1993).

Covenants should perhaps be differentiated from contracts. Contracts ordinarily contain agreements, with associated punishments for noncompliance, and specify acceptable minimums. Covenants, however, employ the concept of maximums along with promoting societal thinking and policy making (Qvortrup, 1997). In a covenant one goes beyond what is required and initiates multiple actions designed to nourish and sustain the community (Wickett, 2000). A covenant is fulfilled for what Sergiovanni (1996) calls "sacred reasons," full of collegiality, unity, and care. Individuals are interdependent based on affection and reciprocal devotion. These dependencies are not debilitating, as are those based on extrinsic rewards, but are enlarging because they are reciprocal. Thus, a covenant contains a promise or pledge for each member to help further the welfare of *each* group member and consequently that of the community as a whole.

Creating a covenant raises questions regarding how the school can become a purposeful, caring, inquiring, and respectful community:

How do students learn?

What kind of learning activities accentuate the learning process?

What kind of learning activities engage students in personally satisfying, meaningful learning?

What kind of experiences will help students become persons of character in a democratic society?

What will help students think deeply about themselves, about others, and about what they learn?

What is it that students should come to know?

What processes should students become skilled in using?

How can students learn to work with adults?

How can parents and the community at large become involved in the learning community?

How can students be helped to truly care about one another and about the school and to focus on common purposes?

How can obligations and commitments be promoted in a learning community?

What should accountability mean to community members?

How will leadership evolve, and how can the burdens of leadership be shared? (Sergiovanni, 1996)

Each school must find its own answers to these and other questions. There will of course be commonalities, but no effort should be made to duplicate particular aspects of any other learning community. Communities achieve differing insights in some of these areas, but to ensure its ownership, each community should forge its own questions as well as answers, giving sufficient effort to ensure good answers. Difficulties and disagreements can be expected, but eventually consensus must develop concerning those things which are central to the purposes and operations of the community in supporting community building and sustenance. For example, as learning in a community involves considerable student interaction, conceptions of learning that isolate students or learning practices that sort children on their relative achievements are unacceptable. Children must be considered as inherently capable of high achievement, and effort must be a basic determinant of academic success; students must understand that one can learn from mistakes and that good students solicit help from one another. These views of children's learning and capacities are consistent with community.

Teachers will have to decide whether or not to treat children as though they were family members, and whether to treat their students as individuals or in terms of uniform standards, rules, and regulations. They will have to address questions like the following:

Will role relationships and job descriptions narrowly define the topics taught and discussed with students, or will relationships be unbounded by roles?
Will students have to earn high regard through their achievements, or will they be inherently valued?
How closely can teachers and students associate?
Is there a magic line between students and teachers that must be maintained to avoid role conflicts?
Will good relationships with students be sought in order to motivate them to learn, or will good student relationships be valued in and of themselves?

Relationships in learning communities should be ethical. Ethics deal with which acts are morally right or wrong, the conditions under which individuals are morally responsible for what they do, and what moral rules or principles are justified. They also deal with what traits or dispositions are morally good or bad, and with what things are desirable from a moral point of view. Within the teaching profession, pre-eminent values relating to ethical standards may reflect a particular, powerful enclave or group which is at odds with the values of some community members. During attempts to clarify group values, these enclaves can be expected to coerce acceptance of their views. However, moral considerations and ethical standards should be drawn from the entire community, not coercively or arbitrarily imposed. Once these standards are formed, they should not be mechanistically restrictive, but should be considered as guidelines with sufficient flexibility to provide for autonomy in decision making by all community members. These expectations of group processes and development must be accepted up front by members in order for a true learning community to evolve (Coombe, 1999).

Members of learning communities need to understand that knowledge is always partial and somewhat fallible and that growth can be enriched through sharing meanings and interpretations of the learning of all members of the community (Howard & England-Kennedy, 2001). Thus, what is learned should be considered tentative during investigations. The learning agenda should always be related to something that is intrinsically human, with inquiry directed to questions important to humans as individuals and as social beings. It is also wise for the school curricula to consist of comprehensive projects related to strategic questions involving not only the current era but also the influence of the past. All disciplines of learning should be experienced by students in terms of their history so that they appreciate the nature of human development. Finally, school meanings should be continuously related to students' everyday experiences in order to infuse learning with personal interest, to provide students a way to make sense of current experiences relative to the past, and to enable valid, insightful decisions regarding matters especially important to them (Glickman, 1993; Meier, 2002; Starratt, 1996).

Strong school communities have their own culture. They have acquired a sense of mission and share a covenant which enables them to achieve personal and group purposes with a high degree of community commitment. However, school communities also share a set of attributes which include the following (Raywid, 1993):

- respect
- caring
- inclusiveness
- trust
- empowerment
- commitment

Respect involves students and teachers having true regard for one another as unique persons. There is no room in a community for stereotyping human attributes and capabilities. Communities are made up of a wide variety of individuals with various personal idiosyncracies. These differences are to be celebrated, not discriminated against. Many find differences to be threatening, particularly when the focus is on a misguided effort to achieve higher self-esteem. Respect requires that all community members render authentic courtesy to one another.

Caring is more particularistic and proactive than respect. It involves reaching out to initiate positive interaction with others. While respect involves passive acceptance, caring individuals actively look out for one another. A caring person will anticipate acts of kindness to relieve discomfort or provide additional comfort for others. Such an individual will acquire a sense of satisfaction through helping others achieve a higher state of learning, often sacrificing personal desires to ensure that comrades receive help and assistance. Students' sense of caring should be so heightened that to do deliberate harm to another human being is nearly unthinkable (Noddings, 2002).

Inclusiveness requires group members to do all they can to ensure that all community members are drawn into the whole range of interactions available throughout the school, so that no one is left out. There are *no* physical or psychological divisions; no cliques exist. Bias is unacceptable according to religion, race, culture, economic level, or any other characteristic. Deliberate efforts are made to integrate all individuals in order to provide the greatest possible diversity, thus presenting a fuller array of possibilities from which to understand meanings. No discriminatory practices exist between students and their teachers. There is no separate lunchroom for teachers; the place of teachers during lunch as well as during all school activities is with their students. Students should be included in teacher meetings, where they can begin to understand some of the problems teachers confront and can have an opportunity to provide their insights regarding problem situations. Most importantly, students and teachers should share a common culture, with its attendant values and assumptions about conduct and expectations; thus, they will have unity rather than being pitted against one another, as is often the case in traditional schools.

Trust is essential to the workings of a community. Without trust there is no significant interaction between community members. Genuine trust in a community provides an atmosphere in which participants are prepared to make authentic disclosures, working energetically with colleagues to promote more meaningful relationships and more useful learning. They are assured that no one will ever use the disclosed information inappropriately. In society children have been cut adrift without the necessary support or nurturance of grown-ups, without the surrounding of a community in which they might feel it is safe to try out various roles, or even ally themselves with the world of adults that they might some day want to join as full members. Children best learn the complex skills and dispositions of adulthood through keeping real company with the knowledgeable adults. If they are part of trusting relationships, they won't be afraid to take risks, make mistakes, or do something dumb. "Learning works best, in fact, when the very idea that it's risky hasn't even occurred to kids" (Meier, 2002).

Both students and teachers can acquire a sense of *empowerment* in an authentic community because they know they are listened to carefully and taken seriously when they communicate. They know that community members will not intentionally hurt their feelings. In traditional schools, students rarely have decision-making power, and they are not ordinarily consulted for their opinions regarding many of the matters which concern them. Because of their age and inexperience, their opinions are not respected. Empowering students can significantly impact teaching and learning. It allows student interests to be taken into account, as well as stimulates vigor and commitment along with a greater sense of ownership.

Commitment in a community promotes strong interpersonal attachments and energizes the work in which community members engage. Unless a sense of family evolves, members have little reason to attach themselves to the goals and values of the school. However, when all community members are committed, they are motivated to achieve the best results both for themselves and for all others concerned. When there is commitment, the quality of teaching and learning can be expected to substantially increase.

To some degree all of the previously listed attributes of a community are interrelated. Commitment could not materialize without empowerment, and empowerment would be impossible without trust. Until community members are respected, valued unconditionally, and are cared for, trust will never occur. All of these factors must be integrated for an authentic community to develop. For this to take place, schools must decentralize operations. Bureaucratic schools keep learning communities from becoming sufficiently empowered (Hiatt & Diana, 2001).

QUESTIONS FOR REFLECTION

1. How would you promote the development of a covenant among the members of a learning community in your classroom? How would you handle points of conflict between students and encourage cooperation?
2. In what way is inquiry an essential activity in learning communities?
3. How can lack of any one of the following attributes of a learning community promote its demise: respect, caring, inclusiveness, trust, empowerment, or commitment?

Professional Learning Communities

Teachers participate in learning communities with their students, and they also need to become involved in professional learning communities composed of other teachers and administrative personnel. Forming communities of professionals is an approach which is radically different from the top-down administration common in schools. With the community approach, schools are governed democratically. Administrators do not have special status, and they do not have a responsibility to ensure that particular things get accomplished. In fact, they are not required to ensure anything regarding the work of the group. They are members of a group of professionals engaged in a common struggle to educate themselves so that they can better educate their students. In the community, numerous opportunities for leadership emerge from the membership. New, informal

Professional learning communities increase excellence in teaching and learning.

categories tend to develop. For example, teacher scholars, teacher researchers, conference coordinators, or area experts might emerge in connection with the work being accomplished. Leadership opportunities arise regardless of status or rank. Those who lead should have a greater sense of vision about the possibilities for change in a particular subject or activity and have greater commitment to and understanding of group functions and membership. Leadership is a matter of facilitating, brokering, and linking rather than pointing directions (Lieberman, 1996).

Professional groups must find ways to transform the school culture from a traditional organization governed by externally imposed rules, regulations, and policies to a responsible, democratic, inquiring learning community. Emphasis needs to be placed on how to guide teaching and learning toward authentic understanding; how to provide for freedom of inquiry; how to maximize growth in knowledge, understanding, and social responsibility; and how to put principles of democracy into operation in a climate of reflection and continuous adaptation, despite cynicism and frequent deliberate attempts at obstruction by others (Hackney & Henderson, 1999).

One important rationale for organizing teachers into learning communities is that students learn best from teachers who have insatiable appetites for learning. The role of teachers includes learning new ways to teach, trying them out, sharing their experiences, making refinements, and then trying them again. Learning communities are built on the premises that learning to teach successfully is a lifelong process and that outstanding teachers learn and grow while investigating their craft and communicating their discoveries to colleagues. For this process to be successful, learning communities must choose their own topics for investigation. It is the process of learning that is important, not the topics chosen or the outcomes achieved (Dodd & Rosenbaum, 1986).

Successful professional learning communities depend on the development of collegiality, a professional virtue that involves the fulfillment of membership obligations. Being a member of the teaching profession and of a specific school faculty should engender a strong sense of responsibility. Membership in a professional community provides teachers with certain rights and privileges and exacts certain obligations and duties. Teachers have the right to expect support from other members of the profession and the school community, and they have the obligation to give similar support to other group members. The basic conditions which make people colleagues are sharing a common membership in a community, having unwavering commitment to the common cause of educating the young, and sharing professional values and a common professional heritage. Without this shared base, there can be no meaningful collegiality. True colleagues share a congeniality through their shared goals and purposes. They develop mutual respect and confidence in both the abilities and intentions of the individuals with whom they work as the source of growth in a professional education community (Sergiovanni, 1992). In the development of professional learning communities, collegiality must be deliberately encouraged. Members must agree that it is essential to group success. Group development and maintenance will require members to periodically assess the components of collegiality. This kind of activity should not be delayed until interpersonal difficulties emerge. Dysfunctions in interpersonal relationships should be anticipated and prevented from materializing or from escalating.

QUESTIONS FOR REFLECTION

1. As a member of a professional learning community, choose three topics of particular importance for schooling that you would favor addressing as a community member.

2. What do you consider to be the greatest impediment to the formation and operation of professional learning communities? Explain why.

Decision Points

Assume you are a public school teacher who is interested in a leadership role in changing from curricula based on traditional learning to those based on constructivist learning.

1. Explain how you would approach the learning community with your proposal for leadership.
2. Explain how you would create conditions in the learning community that would bring about positive work conditions regarding an understanding of constructivist learning.
3. Assuming that the professional learning community decides to implement constructivist learning practices, explain how you would provide leadership for implementing these practices.

Schools and Outside Communities

Some of the most valuable learning can occur in the community surrounding the school. Too often school work is viewed as unrelated to ongoing community concerns, or as preparation for future community involvement. Often students believe their school work is irrelevant, possibly due, in part, to the fact that little is ordinarily done to help students make real-life connections between school and the neighborhoods they live in. Life outside school consists of a series of problems to be solved to improve living conditions or to understand various phenomena that may impact individuals in both positive and negative ways. For many children, survival is more important than getting into the most prestigious universities; the problems in their neighborhoods may have little to do with achieving a college education. However, an important purpose of an education is to provide students with the means for economically and socially advancing themselves. Consequently, schooling must be viewed as a many-faceted endeavor, and children should learn to appreciate the many possibilities it can provide. Teachers who encourage a broader perspective on the purposes of schooling and help their students articulate learning with real community problems will provide a more useful education for them. They can also anticipate far fewer objections regarding the relevance of the curriculum.

One of the problems of traditional schooling is that concepts are dealt with as though they abstract, self-contained entities, although most mental activities outside the school require children to use concepts and skills as tools in a variety of activities unique to their culture. School involves manipulation of symbols to deal with information that is detached from the real world of students. In school, children commonly fail to learn because they have no context within which to make proper associations, nor can they apply what they learn to the problems they regularly face each day. In addition, school emphasizes symbolic thinking, while mental activity outside the school engages children directly with real objects, situations, and problems. School attempts to equip students with general skills and knowledge that they may be able to apply to needs later in life. Learning in a real-life context, however, requires students to acquire specific competencies which they can use to solve specific problems in current situations and relationships (Resnick, 1987). Learning without a proper context not only handicaps students when they enter the job market and find themselves unable to apply what they have learned in school to the real world of work, but it also makes it difficult for them to understand conceptual knowledge and realize its significance. **Conceptualizing** requires the ability to engage in abstract thought with the aid of concrete referents. Meaningful referents are difficult to supply in a school context. For learning to be useful, it must be actively pursued using the appropriate tools within a real-world context (Brown, Collins, & Duguid, 1989). These conditions can be more effectively supplied when students are helping to solve significant problems in their communities.

Not long ago, young people learned occupational skills by working and developed their role in the community by participating directly in the community. In the industrial age, production was mechanized and the workplace was reorganized into large factory units, destroying a pattern of life in which living, working, and learning were effectively interconnected. As the industrial age was being transformed into the information age, living/working/learning patterns did not seem any more amenable to traditional schooling. In pre-industrial days, young people experienced meaningful involvement in society. They learned from their elders skills that were part theoretical, part practical, and part intuitive. Modern science has learned that brains are more efficient when all the senses are stimulated and when they are confronting new ideas and being challenged. Humans tolerate ambiguity and delight in searching for new and novel solutions to problems. Seeking new solutions seems to have been a survival skill. Those who could not constructively reflect on their practice and improve went out of business (Abbott, 1996). Modern society needs individuals who can offer both a high level of technical skill and basic collaborative, social, and problem-solving skills. Students must be equipped to formulate unique solutions to modern-day problems; to deal with ambiguity and uncertainty; and to be especially creative and enterprising. Unfortunately, these capabilities have been largely ignored in schools designed primarily for a manufacturing economy. These important educational goals are more achievable in community settings where the context is authentic and the problems are real. In natural settings, inherent learning processes can proceed unadulterated. Learning can then be based on personal construction of meaning and less on transfer of irrelevant knowledge.

It is often very useful for schools to form long-term school-community partnerships. Through these partnerships, students can become involved with projects that have continuity and have been underway long enough to have limited management problems. Projects with a service component provide students with important affective consequences to go along with their intellectual and group processing experiences. School-community experiences should thus have the following components:

- The experience should engage students in activities which allow them to be of service in the community.
- Students should work with adult mentors or advisors who serve as masters of skill development.

- The experience should be directly connected to the ongoing affairs of the community—an authentic experience for a particular community—and not just a category of general activities.
- Students should make genuine contributions to the community. Their service should be needed and valued.
- Projects should be individualized as much as possible, satisfying students' personal as well as social needs.

Decision Points

Describe three projects you believe would be particularly appropriate for participation by a learning community in a community you are familiar with.

CENTRAL IDEAS

1. Historically, education has focused primarily on moral and character issues. When this focus has been lost in various civilizations, decadence has spread throughout these societies. Currently more emphasis is given to forms, rituals, and technical knowledge than to the moral aspect of education.
2. Teaching is primarily a moral enterprise. Thus, the curriculum must emphasize learning about one's role in a democratic society and the teacher must model as well as teach moral principles.
3. Students need sufficient autonomy, with the requisite emphasis on personal responsibility, to share accountability for their own learning.
4. Moral learning communities not only provide for better student-teacher relationships and increased learning, but they also reduce alienation and violence in the school, promote self-esteem, and develop students' ability to make valid decisions about meaningful problems in the school and in society.
5. Community involvement helps create moral ties which bind community members in highly motivated community actions.
6. The needs of individuals are connected to the needs and actions of communities. Each person can only fulfill his or her needs in concert with other community members satisfying their needs.
7. The school curriculum needs to be changed so that students gain more in-depth understandings by applying higher-order cognitive learning activities. Such activities often involve an inquiry process which emphasizes group projects involving democratic structures of caring and community.
8. Learning occurs when students create their own meaning rather than memorize information that has been carefully structured and reinforced.
9. Each learning community depends on its members to define roles and functions. The process of community building accommodates the needs and desires of the members and stimulates collaboration.

10. Learning communities engender kinship and love, and members share common interests. Community members must value one another and emphasize group accomplishments more than separate achievements.
11. Learning communities share a common vision and establish a covenant, a sacred enterprise devoted to the well-being of the community. Strong communities develop their own culture. Their sense of mission enables them to achieve both personal and group purposes with a high degree of commitment.
12. Community empowers students and teachers because both are seriously listened to and respected.
13. Learning communities cannot come into existence by edict, nor can they be forced to change. They exist, develop, and adapt to serve the members of the group.
14. Learning communities function better when all members value the thoughts and feelings of others, listen nonjudgmentally, and achieve a state of empathy.
15. Professional learning communities provide a way for teachers to become involved with other educators in seeking to improve teaching and learning in the schools.
16. Learning in the community outside the school provides students with authentic, meaningful experiences which better articulate their natural way of learning than most classroom sequences.

REFERENCES

Abbott, J. (1996). Children need communities. *Educational Leadership, 53* (8), 6–10.

Allen, L., Rogers, D., Hensley, F., Glanton, M., & Livingston, M. (1999). *A guide to renewing your school: Lessons from the league of professional schools.* San Francisco: Jossey-Bass.

Bohn, A. P., & Sleeter, C. E. (2000). Multicultural education and the standards movement: A report from the field. *Phi Delta Kappan, 82* (2), 156–159.

Brandt, R. (1992). On building learning communities: A conversation with Hank Levin. *Educational Leadership, 50* (1), 19–23.

Brown, J. S., Collins, A., & Duguid, P. (1989). Situated cognition and the culture of learning. *Educational Researcher, 18,* 32–42.

Bull, B. L. (1990). The limits of teacher professionalism. In J. I. Goodlad, R. Soder, & K. A. Sirotnik (Eds.), *The moral dimensions of teaching.* San Francisco: Jossey-Bass.

Clinchy, E. (2001). Needed: A new educational civil rights movement. *Phi Delta Kappan, 83* (7), 493–498.

Coombe, K. (1999). Ethics and the learning community. In J. Retallick, B. Cocklin, & K. Coombe (Eds.), *Learning communities in education: Issues, strategies and contexts.* New York: Routledge.

Darling-Hammond, L. (1993). Reframing the school reform agenda: Developing capacity for school transformation. *Phi Delta Kappan, 74* (10), 753–761.

Darling-Hammond, L. (1997). *The right to learn: A blueprint for creating schools that work.* San Francisco: Jossey-Bass.

Dodd, A. W., & Rosenbaum, E. (1986). Learning communities for curriculum and staff development. *Phi Delta Kappan, 67* (5), 380–384.

Durkheim, E. (1964). *The division of labor in society* (G. Simpson, trans.). New York: Free Press (originally published in 1893).

Etzioni, E. (1988). *The moral dimensions.* New York: Free Press.

Fenstermacher, G. D. (1990). Some moral considerations on teaching as a profession. In J. I. Goodlad, R. Soder, & K. A. Sirotnik (Eds.), *The moral dimensions of teaching* (pp. 130–151). San Francisco: Jossey-Bass.

Glasser, W. (1984). *Control theory.* New York: Harper & Row.

Glickman, C. D. (1993). *Renewing America's schools: A guide for school-based action.* San Francisco: Jossey-Bass.

Goodlad, J. I. (1984). *A place called school: Prospects for the future.* New York: McGraw-Hill.

Goodlad, J. I. (1994). Retrospect and prospect. In J. I. Goodlad & P. Keating (Eds.), *Access to knowledge: The continuing agenda for our nation's schools* (pp. 329–344). New York: College Entrance Examination Board.

Goodlad, J. I. (2000). Education and democracy. *Phi Delta Kappan, 82* (1), 86–89.

Hackney, C. E., & Henderson, J. G. (1999). Educating school leaders for inquiry-based democratic learning communities. *Educational Horizons, Winter,* 67–73.

Hiatt, M., & Diana, B. (2001). School learning communities: A vision for organic school reform. *School Community Journal, 11* (2), 93–112.

Howard, A., & England-Kennedy, E. S. (2001). Transgressing boundaries through learning communities. *Journal of Cooperative Education, 36* (1), 76–82.

Hyman, I. A., & Perone, D. C. (1998). The other side of school violence: Educator politics that may contribute to student misbehavior. *Journal of Student Psychology, 36* (1), 7–27.

Johnson, S. M. (1990). *Teachers at work: Achieving success in our schools.* New York: Basic Books.

Keefe, J. W., & Jenkins, J. M. (2002). Personalized instruction. *Phi Delta Kappan, 83* (6), 440–448.

Kohn, A. (1993). *Punished by rewards.* Boston: Houghton Mifflin.

Lieberman, A. (1996). Creating intentional learning communities. *Educational Leadership, 54* (3), 51–55.

Marshall, C. (1992). School administrators' values: A focus on atypicals. *Educational Administration Quarterly, 28* (3), 368–386.

McHenry, I. (2000). Conflict in schools: Fertile ground for moral growth. *Phi Delta Kappan, 82* (3), 223–227.

Meier, D. (2002). *In schools we trust: Creating communities of learning in an era of testing and standardization.* Boston: Beacon Press.

Merrow, J. (2001). Undermining standards. *Phi Delta Kappan, 83* (9), 653–659.

Meyers, E. A. (1968). *Education in the perspective of history.* New York: Harper Brothers.

Newman, J. M. (1998). We can't get there from here: Critical issues in school reform. *Phi Delta Kappan, 80* (4), 228–294.

Noddings, N. (2002). *Educating moral people: A caring alternative to character education.* New York: Teacher's College Press.

Qvortrup, J. (1997). Children, individualism, and community review of "the missing child" in liberal theory: Towards a covenant theory of family, community, welfare, and the civic state by John O'Neill. *Childhood: A Global Journal of Child Research, 4* (3), 359–368.

Raywid, M. A. (1993). Community: An alternative school accomplishment. In G. A. Smith (Ed.), *Public schools that work: Creating community.* New York: Routledge.

Resnick, L. B. (1987). Learning in school and out. *Educational Researcher, 16,* 13–20.

Sergiovanni, T. J. (1990). *Value-added leadership: How to get extraordinary performance in schools.* San Diego: Harcourt Brace Jovanovich.

Sergiovanni, T. J. (1992). *Moral leadership: Getting to the heart of school improvement.* San Francisco: Jossey-Bass.

Sergiovanni, T. J. (1994). *Building community in school.* San Francisco: Jossey-Bass.

Sergiovanni, T. J. (1996). *Leadership for the schoolhouse.* San Francisco: Jossey-Bass.

Sergiovanni, T. J. (1999). The story of community. In J. Retallick, B. Cocklin, & K. Coombe (Eds.), *Learning communities in education: Issues, strategies and contexts* (pp. 9–25). New York: Routledge.

Sergiovanni, T. J. (2000). *The life world of leadership: Creating culture, community and personal meaning in our schools.* San Francisco: Jossey-Bass.

Sizer, T. R. (1984). *Horace's compromise: The dilemma of the American school.* Boston: Houghton Mifflin.

Smith, F. (2001). Just a matter of time. *Phi Delta Kappan, 82* (8), 573–576.

Smith, P. G. (1972). On the logic of behavioral objectives. *Phi Delta Kappan, 53,* 429–431.

Starratt, R. J. (1996). *Transforming educational administration: Meaning, community, and excellence.* New York: McGraw-Hill.

Trowbridge, L. W., Bybee, R. W., & Powell, J. C. (2000). *Teaching secondary school science; Strategies for developing scientific literacy* (7th ed.). Upper Saddle River, NJ: Prentice Hall.

Wickett, R. E. Y. (2000). The learning covenant. *New Directions for Adult and Continuing Education, 35,* 39–47.

Wynne, E. A. (1995). The moral dimensions of teaching. In A. C. Ornstein (Ed.), *Teaching: Theory into practice* (pp. 189–202). Boston: Allyn & Bacon.

CHAPTER 2

Student Differences and Needs

CHAPTER OBJECTIVES

This chapter is designed to help you

1. Understand the intellectual, physical, social, and moral growth of adolescents; be able to create a classroom environment; and formulate instructional experiences which are consistent with these growth patterns.

2. Explain the specific differences between various theories regarding adolescent needs.

3. Formulate a list of needs from various theories regarding adolescent needs and provide descriptions of educational experiences which help to satisfy all these needs.

4. Explain how teachers can support the self-concept of their students without putting them at risk for depression.

Learning communities help to counter the rejection and isolation often encountered in the schools.

5. Describe how students view authority in the school and how teachers and administrators can provide a viable form of authority.

6. Describe a comprehensive program for supplanting students' misbehavior with socially acceptable behaviors.

7. Explain the nature of resilience and ways that resilience can help protect students from possible deleterious effects in school, and discuss how resilience can be promoted in schools.

INTRODUCTION

Significant differences exist between students in terms of their learning styles, needs, and interests. Although a good deal of educational writing identifies ways to differentiate instruction to cater to these differences, much instruction ignores this critical educational imperative. Taking student differences and needs into account provides a means of enhancing learning and making classrooms more manageable for teachers. However, many believe that taking all students' interests and needs into account requires a forfeiture of standards, not to mention an increase in complexity. The complexity created by negative student reactions to a system that ignores their needs and interests can be quite complicated and difficult to manage.

Luis Gonzales, upon entering high school, was given an IQ and an achievement test. He quickly discovered that there were very few words on these tests, including the directions, that he understood. Even though he pointed this out to the test administrator, he was told to do the best he could.

Spanish was almost exclusively spoken in Luis's home, and he had few associations outside school where English was used. The same situation applied to many of his friends, who also had a difficult time deciphering the exam. As a result, educators found it hard to get an accurate assessment of their abilities.

Luis and many of his Hispanic friends found themselves tracked through many of the same courses. Frequently, the curriculum was repetitiously focused on elementary information designed for a group of educable mentally retarded students. Often various physical activities and games were substituted for normal school work. Anyone interested in pursuing more intellectual work was categorically discouraged.

Eventually Luis and many of his friends dropped out of school and wound up on the streets, as they had very few of the skills necessary to find jobs. Most got into trouble of one kind or another. Drugs and theft were common problems, some individuals were involved in armed robbery, and a few engaged in gang fights and killings. Luis spent time in reform school, after which he enlisted in the air force. He scored well on the admission tests, and was assigned to attend a special school to prepare him to operate complex radar equipment, a career path he requested. This was the first time Luis realized that his abilities were far greater than his high school experience led him to believe. He was not only amazed that he did well on the tests, but that the air force would allow him to pursue a course of study consistent with his interests, one which promised to involve considerable intellectual ability.

After his discharge from the air force, Luis enrolled in one of California's state colleges and immediately distinguished himself academically. He earned mostly "A"s in his courses and eventually went on to achieve a doctorate. He then took a job teaching and doing research in a prominent Colorado university.

QUESTIONS FOR REFLECTION

1. What kinds of categorizations may put students into settings for which they are ill prepared or which allow them to be given learning experiences far below their ability?

2. How might IQ and achievement tests fail to adequately measure students' intellectual ability besides the case of insufficient language development?

3. What adjustments are necessary in the school to ensure that what happened to Luis and his friends does not routinely occur?

Adolescent Growth and Development

Understanding the nature of adolescent growth and development, along with adolescents' needs and differences, offers teachers important information needed to determine the kind of educational environment and learning activities most appropriate for their students. Learning communities require teachers to have a deep understanding of students' needs and interests. The very essence of learning communities is to provide learning experiences that focus on student interests and satisfy the needs of all students.

A knowledge of intellectual development must be applied in order to ensure that students are provided the educational experiences that articulate with the ways they think and are consistent with the capacity to engage in different levels of thinking as students grow and develop. Physical, moral, and social development must be added to an understanding of needs, culture, language, and customs to define the total educational program. Ignoring these important considerations is the same as denying the existence of the critical and strategic factors needed for successful teaching and learning. These factors impact all youth in one way or another as they try to satisfy their needs and achieve their ambitions within an authoritarian, compulsory education system. Depending on the educational philosophy accepted, the various growth concepts can either be used to encourage youth to behave as directed and acquire the skills and information deemed appropriate, or they can be used to gain the necessary educational modifications to provide a better fit between development patterns and human inclinations on the one hand and learning arrangements on the other.

What is adolescence? This question has stirred considerable interest for a good many years among philosophers, scientists, and educators. At times the behavior patterns of youth have defied explanation and led parents, as well as teachers, to explore various options to help young people learn better, adhere to family and social values, and generally fulfill adult expectations, hopes, and desires. Adults, of course, see themselves as guides and mentors, well equipped to lead youth through various perils and into more satisfying life conditions. In many cases youth appear to lack the knowledge and judgment to make critical decisions about important questions and issues. Their behavior is commonly inconsistent with the available knowledge and necessary judgment to capitalize on opportunities in a timely way and to avoid circumstances that might sabotage a happy, healthy life. In the face of these efforts to guide youth are their inclinations and personal aspirations. Many times adult actions directly conflict with the needs of youth and interfere with growth and adjustment patterns. A correct understanding of growth and development, along with students' needs, can prepare educators to teach more effectively and help students to acquire those skills and abilities that will best prepare them to live successfully in democratic communities.

NATIONAL TEACHING STANDARDS

Teachers should use their knowledge about adolescent growth and development to form decisions about how they teach.

Intellectual Development

Piaget's work has had an enormous impact on the way educators view the nature and growth of human intellect. Psychologists and educators currently give less credence to the previously popular behavioristic view of learning and development, a view that accepts humans as being born without any inclinations or will. Behaviorists believe that we routinely respond in particular ways as a result of exposure to reinforcing stimuli. Their view is that information is learned by arranging it in carefully sequenced packages and then providing appropriate feedback and reinforcement (Good & Brophy, 2003). The learning goal from this viewpoint is to somehow accurately symbolize the content of the external world within the mind. This is done through language, with less attention being given to concrete referents. Thus, it is not considered essential to provide students with opportunities to manipulate real objects or conduct experiments regarding personal questions and issues (Resnick, 1987).

Piaget (1954, 1955) believed, however, that all individuals actually have to act upon the external world, and must personally reconstruct the world to truly know it. In this process new conceptions of reality can be created, and more accurate perspectives on phenomena and ideas can be achieved. The mind, according to Piaget, does not absorb information by sopping it up like a sponge. Instead, students act upon their environment and reconstruct reality by forming **schemata,** previously held conceptions that are personally modified to reflect new insights achieved by examining new information or engaging in new searches for meaning and understanding. Humans appear to be internally driven to achieve competence for successful living. Thus, schemata comes about not by passive experiences, but by force of logic and interaction with the external world. Thus, education must consist of experiences that promote thinking while helping the student achieve a personally relevant and meaningful understanding of personally interesting phenomena.

According to Piaget, we interact with the world in two basic ways: (1) *assimilation* and (2) *accommodation.* **Assimilation** is the process of taking in new sensory experiences that fit into the existing structure or schemata of the individual. Thus, the external world is modified to fit into already formed conceptual constructs. The modification must be minimal for this process to work successfully; otherwise, serious misconceptions may result.

Accommodation refers to the process of changing existing schemata or constructing new cognitive structures to be more compatible with new sensory data or experiences. This involves such acts as questioning, manipulating, or reconceptualizing actions. As students try to solve problems and encounter inconsistencies through these activities, new schemata are created for more correctly acting upon the world.

These processes provide a way for the individual to fit into the real world. In any novel situation, experiences are either assimilated into existing structures or accommodated by changing existing structures. This interplay is called **adaption.** If assimilation is not accurately accomplished, such as when salient aspects of a situation are disregarded, a state called **egocentrism** occurs. Intellectual growth requires that the individual change his or her egocentric view of the world and develop more mature accommodations of other perspectives (Inhelder & Piaget, 1958; Piaget & Inhelder, 1969).

Piaget (1970) believed age to be an important factor in learning ability. In his view, children pass through a set of well-ordered stages to finally achieve full thinking capacity. (See a summary of these stages in Table 2.1.) During the first year of life, infants gradually acquire

TABLE 2.1   *Piaget's Stages of Intellectual Development.*

Name of Stage	Age of Development	Description
Sensorimotor	Birth to 18 months	Hidden objects are located through random physical searching. Objects exist only when in the perceptual field of the child.
Preoperational	18 months to 6–7 years	Children cannot conserve area, volume, etc.; beginning of organized language and symbolic function; have difficulty realizing an object may have several properties.
Concrete operations	6–7 years to 11–12 years	Child thinks concretely rather than abstractly; can group and classify; has developed the ability to conserve number, substance, length, area, weight, and volume; thinks in a step-to-step progression without relating each link to all others.
Formal operations	11–12 years to 14–15 years	Child can engage in hypothetical deductive reasoning based upon the logic of all possible combinations; can conduct controlled experiments; can hypothesize and think in terms of chance operations.

the ability to mentally represent the external world. At 18 months they are generally still unable to accept the existence of objects outside their perceptual field. Hidden objects are located through random physical searching. By the end of their second year, they can visualize events and to some degree mentally follow them through. Children in this stage can discover solutions to problems without trial and error. They anticipate the location of an object that is being moved without seeing its actual trajectory. This is called the *sensorimotor stage*.

This stage is followed by the *preoperational stage*, during which children can manipulate symbols that represent the environment. They are only able to evaluate and understand what they perceive. Thus, they can imitate the speech of another individual but are unable to comprehend another person's point of view, since a point of view cannot be perceived. This stage lasts until about age 6 or 7.

When children pass to the *concrete operations stage*, they become capable of elementary logical thought. This can occur only after children have had sufficient experience with their environment, have accumulated a store of relevant concepts, and have mentally organized these thoughts. They still think in concrete terms. Actual objects need to be observed and manipulated for children to process information about them. They are able to make elementary logical operations, make groupings and classifications, and perceive relationships. In this stage the ability to conserve gradually develops. Conservation involves the ability to retain a consistent view of volume, length, area, weight, substance, or number while these are being manipulated and altered. For example, a child who is unable to conserve substance will think a piece of clay rolled between the palms of the hands and elongated has been increased in amount, even though this manipulation is done as the child watches. A child who thinks the volume of a liquid has changed when it is poured from one container into one of a different shape cannot conserve volume. A child who is unable to see that changing the outside dimensions of a rectangle does not necessarily change the area cannot conserve area. The stage of concrete operations lasts until children are about 11 or 12 years of age.

Formal operations is Piaget's final stage of intellectual development. In this stage, children can engage in four basic mental operations. First, they can make hypotheses and use deductive thinking, like that used in the scientific method or in problem-solving. They are able to conduct controlled experiments, discerning potentially confounding variables and arranging strategies for setting all factors equal but the one in question. Second, they have the ability to engage in inductive thinking. They can form conclusions based on data or information. These two abilities are commonly engaged in simultaneously. Third, children engage in reflective thinking, the ability to think about their own thoughts as well as consider the thoughts of another person. This skill is useful for analyzing and criticizing logical arguments and debates and for understanding another person's point of view. At this stage, children are able to address questions like "Should there be metal detectors and surveillance cameras in American high schools?" The fourth ability is called *interpropositional logic*. Children with this skill are able to discern whether conclusions drawn from two or more propositions are indeed logical. For example, examine the two following propositions and the conclusion:

Proposition 1: All teenage drivers drive recklessly.
Proposition 2: Reckless drivers should have their driver's license revoked.
Conclusion: All teenage drivers should have their driver's license revoked.

At this level, students should be able to ascertain the inappropriateness of the conclusion and determine what in the propositions is not valid (Jensen, 1985).

One question that often arises is whether or not teachers, by using particular strategies, can speed up the child's progression through the stages of development. Educators are often encouraged to get their students to accomplish more in less time; thus, efficiency may be emphasized more than effectiveness. However, it is generally felt among proponents of Piaget's ideas that little or nothing is gained by trying to accelerate the natural development pattern. Instead, sufficient time should be given so that the changes that occur are in concert with the natural processes. Of course, there are many experiences which children should encounter as a part of the natural processes of growth.

Sometimes it is concluded that all youth will eventually achieve formal operations abilities. Actually, research shows this assumption is false. For example, Higgens-Trenk and Gaite (1971, p. 202) indicate that many adolescents may not attain the formal operations stage until their late teens or early twenties. Even within the oldest group in their study, with a mean age of 17.7 years, over 50 percent were not at the formal operations level. Shayer (1979, p. 272) points out that there is no definitive proof that Piaget's original assumption that all adolescents achieve formal operations abilities in their early teens is true. Piaget eventually conceded this point and suggested that some may attain formal operations as late as 20 years of age (Manaster, 1989). Most studies have found that only about 50 percent of adult subjects perform at the formal operations level (Jensen, 1985). The nagging, unanswered question is whether some individuals are inherently unable to achieve this higher level of thinking or whether they would have attained it with more appropriate educational experiences.

Researchers have indicated that an additional stage might be included with the four identified by Piaget. Arlin (1975) suggested that the formal operations stage be renamed the *problem-solving stage* to differentiate it from this fifth stage, the *problem-finding stage*. Adding this stage acknowledges the difference between solving problems and accurately determining problems to solve. Certainly students find more difficulty ascertaining viable problems to solve than they do organizing research to solve problems presented to them by others.

From Piaget's (1970) point of view, the basic purpose of education is to teach children to think and develop their minds, not to transmit knowledge. For maximum learning to occur, children must be able to use their dominant mode of thinking and stage of development in much of what they do. They should also have some experiences that challenge their thinking or promote accommodation. The purpose of this is not to accelerate abilities, but rather to provide experiences that are compatible with growth. Teachers should not just provide learning opportunities that are narrowly consistent with specifically identified ability levels, but rather provide freedom of experience so that students can progress in terms of personal readiness. These experiences should not have external rewards attached. Motivation is a natural part of human growth and does not need to be compelled. Dilemmas and problems help promote development in learning, because they often create disequilibrium that stimulates the growth of new structures and schemata for appropriate accommodation.

In school, the intellect of students should not be too narrowly defined. This was partially illustrated in the chapter-opening vignette describing Luis Gonzales and his friends. Although the misidentification primarily occurred because of language deficits, there are other important aspects of human intelligence that are not measured by IQ and achievement tests. IQ tests are supposed to measure general intelligence, but they actually measure only a small part of the more than 100 separate intellectual abilities identified by J. P. Guilford (1972). Any particular individual has different combinations of these abilities, with each having different levels of strength. IQ and achievement tests correlate well with one another, and to a great extent with success in traditional schooling. However, many of the abilities identified by Guilford, which tend to be ignored in traditional schooling, are needed for success in various occupations. Students who have these important strengths have few opportunities to develop them and experience success in school. Their potential for occupational success, consequently, is also limited.

QUESTIONS FOR REFLECTION

1. What can be anticipated regarding the intellectual development of a typical group of twelfth-grade students?
2. Compare common school practices with those necessary to promote thinking.

Decision Points

Create a sequence of instruction in your teaching field you believe would be appropriate for twelfth-grade students, given the most likely state of their intellectual development.

Moral Reasoning and Development

While Piaget addressed some specifics regarding the development of moral reasoning, Lawrence Kohlberg considered his conclusions regarding the stages of intellectual growth inadequate to explain how moral reasoning develops (Kohlberg, 1969). He, therefore, undertook the arduous task of creating a series of 10 moral dilemmas that he used in interviews to place students in one of six moral reasoning categories (see Table 2.2). These categories, arranged in a developmental sequence carefully researched across a number of cultures, are represented as stages in an invariant progression. Each individual moves sequentially through the stages without skipping any, but does not necessarily reach the highest stage (Kohlberg, 1973).

One important distinction to make regarding stages of moral reasoning is that they do not represent an individual's values or choices, but rather reflect the frame of reference through which the individual thinks and builds his or her thoughts. It is also important to distinguish stages from motives and behavior (Boyce & Jensen, 1978). A child, a youth, and an adult may all refrain from some behavior like lying, but their reasons for doing so may be substantially different and their ways of explaining their behavior may also vary. A child may choose not to lie to avoid punishment, while a youth may do so to gain acceptance. An adult may do the same thing because he or she considers lying to be a violation of principles. In addition, it is fairly common for any individual's reasoning to be inconsistent with the level of his or her behavior. There is also evidence that males and females are different in their patterns of moral reasoning, with females predominating in a caring orientation and males focusing on justice (Gilligan & Attanucci, 1988). Kohlberg has generally failed to make this distinction (Gilligan, 1977).

Kohlberg acknowledged a relationship between Piaget's cognitive states and these stages of moral development (Kohlberg & Gilligan, 1971). He believed that, although growth to a new, higher cognitive stage is not sufficient to acquire a new, higher moral stage, cognitive maturation is necessary before moral maturation can occur.

The first of Kohlberg's moral reasoning levels is called *pre-conventional.* Kohlberg (1969, 1976) believed that children in the concrete operations stage are able to reason at this

TABLE 2.2   *Kohlberg's Levels of Moral Reasoning.*

Level 1 Pre-Conventional

	Stage 1–Obedience and punishment orientation	Child acts to avoid punishment.
	Stage 2–Naivety egoistic orientation	Child seeks personal pleasure regardless of whether or not actions conflict with the rights of others.

Level 2 Conventional

	Stage 3–Good-boy or good-girl orientation	Child seeks approval and avoids disapproval; believes no one has the right to do evil.
	Stage 4–Authority and social order maintaining orientation	Child tries to escape feelings of guilt if behavior might be disapproved by authorities. A right is an earned privilege given by others.

Level 3 Post-Conventional

	Stage 5–Contractual legalistic orientation	Child acts upon moral principles in terms of approval or disapproval of the greater community.
	Stage 6–Conscience or principle orientation	Morality is based upon universal principles. Life and human dignity is respected. Feeling good personally is the motivation moral for action.

level, which is divided into two stages. In *Stage 1, obedience and punishment orientation,* children act to avoid punishment. A student may, for example, tell peers that they should get back to class immediately when the bell rings or they will be punished. In *Stage 2,* the *naivety egoistic orientation,* behavior is motivated by the hope to achieve personal pleasure regardless of whether or not these actions conflict with the rights of others. In this case, a child may believe he or she should be allowed to choose a team ahead of others because some of the child's friends are on that team, instead of realizing that others have similar rights to choose.

The second level is the *conventional level,* which includes adolescents and adults who are at the early formal operations stage. There are also two stages in this level. The first, *Stage 3,* is the *good-boy* or *good-girl orientation* in which behavior is motivated by the desire to obtain social approval and good relationships with others. As a result, actions are taken to avoid the disapproval of others. The concept of what is right is expanded to include the idea that no one has the right to do evil. At this point, students may be worried more about what others think than about the inherent appropriateness of their actions. They will, however, express strong disapproval of the actions of others they consider bad. In *Stage 4,* the *authority and social order maintaining orientation,* the individual is motivated to escape feelings of guilt or blame by actions that might be disapproved of by recognized authorities. A right is an earned privilege or payment from others. At this point, youth see authorized authority as the appropriate index of right and wrong. They conscientiously try to avoid feelings of guilt associated with disobeying constituted authority. Their compliance can be bought if compensation is offered by those in authority positions.

The final level is the *post-conventional level,* which is ordinarily achieved by adolescents and adults who have developed true formal operations capabilities. *Stage 5* within this level, called *contractual legalistic orientation,* identifies moral principles as the controlling element in one's actions. Motivation is sparked by the approval or disapproval of particular actions by the greater community. In this stage, individuals are particularly cognizant about the law. To them, the laws of the land, instituted by constitutional authority, form the basis for all actions. Thus, laws of conscription to fight in a war where lives of people will be sacrificed is considered appropriate even though the war may be judged by some to be immoral. When *Stage 6, conscience or principle orientation,* is achieved, the individual's behavior is based upon universal moral principles regarding the dignity of man. Feeling good about one's self and one's involvement become the motivation for moral action. Rights take on the broad meaning of genuine concern for individual life and respect for human dignity. Reasoning in this stage can transcend the law and some principles are considered more fundamentally appropriate than the constituted law. For example, blocking the doorway of a draft board office to protest what is judged to be an immoral war is considered a higher order of thinking than submitting to the law as a conscript, manifesting allegiance to laws instituted by constituted authority.

Piaget's stages appear to relate directly to specific moral stages through Level 2. However, teaching the formal operations stage is considered to be a necessary but insufficient condition for Stages 5 and 6. After this level has been reached, it is not the cognitive stage achieved that determines whether a person makes moral judgments from a perspective of social contract and higher law (Stage 5) or from a perspective of universal ethical principles (Stage 6). Rather, the perspective is determined by the differences in motivation, background, and experience that allow individuals at the formal operations level to reach Stage 5 or Stage 6. Interestingly, Kohlberg considered it rare for a person to achieve Stage 6 (Manaster, 1989).

Kohlberg (1973) believed that moral development continues on into adulthood. Adolescents may develop an awareness of principled moral reasoning, but an actual commitment to employing ethical principles does not develop until adulthood.

From Kohlberg's perspective, cognitive methods should be employed to develop moral reasoning abilities. This competence is a capacity to exercise reason in moral judgment and can be developed to some degree by confronting moral dilemmas. Dilemmas can be used not only to determine the moral reasoning ability of students but also as a method of instruction to promote the advancement from one stage to the next.

Moral Development and the Ethic of Care

Whereas Kohlberg advocates the direct teaching of virtues in a cognitive format, care theorists rely more heavily on establishing conditions, experiences, and expectations likely to encourage goodness in individuals. Students would not initially be taught basic principles relating to morality, as these do not motivate. In fact, there is some evidence that students exposed to cognitive approaches often come to believe that almost any decision can be justified, and that the strength of their arguments is what really counts (Katz, Noddings, & Strike, 1999). Care theorists prefer students to be involved in caring activities modeled by teachers in institutions like kindergarten classrooms and nursing homes so that the virtues needed are taught within real-life contexts. For students to develop virtues, they have to be shown by adults how to care, regularly engage in dialogue with adults about caring, and have many opportunities for practice in caring. Such virtues as congeniality, amiability, good humor, emotional sensitivity, and good manners are emphasized. As caring individuals, students need to learn to act according to the real needs of others, not on contrived conditions (Noddings, 2002).

The development of care is promoted through self-understanding and a critical appreciation of groups to which the individual belongs. However, not only should there be a strong group ethic supported, but also the acceptance of others outside the group. Otherwise, the danger exists for community members to become self-righteous and draw strong lines between themselves and others whose values and ways of life are different and who may be judged inferior.

Stories are an essential starting place for moral instruction. Not only do stories provide a means for initiating moral sentiment, but they can provide students a broader base for considering the basis of human behavior (Noddings, 1992, 1993). Students need to understand that people who are usually good sometimes give way to temptation or even evil. They must realize that whole tribes or nations can go wrong, that individuals can be led to betray friendships out of fear, that when we try to be good we sometimes become confused over what "good" means, and that we are dependent on one another for moral goodness. Children must realize that each person is in part responsible for the moral development of others encountered. The way we treat others can be the means of bringing out either the best or worst in them. It is empowering for students to learn that they can provide a model for associates to follow to grow and become better (Noddings, 2002). It is hoped that, through stories, students will develop a sense of sympathy that is intelligently guided by moral understanding (Thayer-Bacon, 2000).

Children need continuity. For this reason, learning communities need to remain together for long periods of time. For example, groups may stay together all during their high school years, involving students in a curriculum including feminist perspectives, human issues, and social concerns. Students might study the topic of love, for example, as well as address related ideas regarding feuds, violence, hatred, despair, suicide, regret, adultery, compassion, fidelity, community, prejudice, ambition, jealousy, passion, gratitude, and loneliness. Friendship might also be studied. Students might examine such questions as, "What does it mean to be a friend?"

Teachers can have real, in-depth conversations with their students about topics students feel are important. However, students must receive an assurance from their teachers that they are taken seriously and that they are accepted and liked. Students must be listened to and their ideas respected; the interaction between teachers and students should bring enjoyment to both.

Schools must make substantial changes to fully implement a curriculum focused on caring. Schools and teachers must eliminate many of the practices designed to control students, like grading and testing, and implement student self-evaluation and student self-government. Uniform requirements for all students must be abandoned, particularly college entrance requirements. The curriculum must incorporate caring in its conceptualizations and applications. Students must have numerous opportunities to experience caring relationships and to learn that caring broadens and strengthens them (Noddings, 2002).

QUESTIONS FOR REFLECTION

1. Compare Kohlberg's stages and Noddings' description of moral development through caring. How could these approaches be used in conjunction with one another in the schools?
2. Why is it that the actions of people may be inconsistent with their level of moral thinking?
3. What kind of caring experiences might be created for students in public schools?

Decision Points

What level of moral reasoning is reflected in the following questions and statements?

1. How are we going to make sure we don't get caught?
2. I know we shouldn't cheat, but I've got to get an "A" on this exam.
3. I need to turn this paper in today because I told Mr. Krump I would.
4. Don't you guys know that the rule about food fights in the cafeteria is to protect us students?
5. I realize little white lies are usually wrong, but sometimes they are necessary to protect someone from getting hurt.

Differences in physical maturity promote adjustment problems among adolescents.

Physical Development

The timing of physical development has important implications for learning communities in the public schools. Learning communities depend on evolving social interactions and interdependencies. The physical development and attractiveness of youth greatly influence social actions and levels of acceptance by peers, as well as self-concept and general behavior. Teachers need to be cognizant of the relationships between the physical growth of adolescents in their classes and various adjustment problems their students may confront, along with intervention strategies they might employ to help students become more readily accepted as group members so they can take an active and responsible role in group learning activities.

In general, research shows early maturing girls to be at a disadvantage compared to their later maturing peers. They experience more crises, loss of control, and unrest (Peskin, 1973). Girls tend to be particularly dissatisfied with their weight. Early maturing boys, however, are generally satisfied with their appearance (Crockett & Peterson, 1887). Peterson (1987) found that early or late maturing adolescents were less satisfied with their appearance and their body image than those whose maturation could be considered average. She found early maturing girls in the higher grades were generally less satisfied with their weight and appearance than their less mature classmates. In other research, a disproportionate number of late maturing females experienced difficulty which led to crises in connection with the development of womanhood. Early maturing boys, however, make great social and personal gains from their maturation and do not stand out from the total group the way early maturing girls do. Though they may be ahead of slow maturing boys, their development coincides well with later maturing girls (Manaster, 1989). In addition, early maturing boys usually have physical attributes like strength and coordination that give them an advantage over smaller boys, attributes that are prized by boys but not by girls.

Although physical maturation, particularly puberty, is primarily a function of genetics and age, diet and exercise also play an important role. Girls who restrict food intake or who engage in high levels of intensive exercise have a delay in the onset of puberty (Brooks-Gunn, 1987). These students may need to receive counseling about the potential causes, particularly if they are seriously restricting their diet. Female students may be particularly vulnerable to social expectations regarding their weight and develop conditions like anorexia nervosa and bulimia, which have serious health consequences and may require professional assistance.

Body shape is another factor that differentiates youth from one another and makes them more or less acceptable to their peers. Adolescents with a mesomorphic body type (triangular shape) are dominant, assertive, confident, aggressive, enterprising, talkative, active, reckless, energetic, and outgoing. This makes them more attractive not only to their peers, but to adults as well. Both endomorphs (heavier or fatty appearance) and ectomorphs (thin and tall) are less well accepted. Endomorphs tend to be dependent, relaxed, calm, kind, self-satisfied, complacent, amiable, and generous, while ectomorphs are detached, tense, anxious, introverted, self-centered, reflective, inhibited, and suspicious (Jensen, 1985). Mesomorphic individuals have attributes that allow them to more easily assimilate into learning communities and take an active role. The other two body types are more likely to experience some difficulty and may need special assistance from teachers to make needed adjustments to achieve acceptance and become productive group learners.

Physical attractiveness has a powerful influence upon adolescent popularity, peer acceptance, and self-evaluation. Attractive individuals seem to be better adjusted socially, have better self-concepts, develop more healthy personality attributes, and display more positive social behavior. They are also more able to resist peer pressure (Adams, 1977a, 1977b; Adams & Crossman, 1978). If these consequences are allowed to take course without teacher intervention, less attractive youth may fail to achieve their potential in attitude and skill development. Members of learning communities must pay attention to this issue so that they understand the consequences of various forms of favoritism based on relative attractiveness. Researchers have concluded that when others see us as attractive, they do various subtle things that encourage the development of confidence and skills. However, if an individual is considered unattractive, he or she is treated in ways that cause deterioration of social behavior and adjustment (Jensen, 1985).

Decision Points

Describe a conversation you might have with a group of eighth-grade students about problems they may experience regarding physical growth, and discuss ways a learning community might properly deal with these problems.

Reflections About Self

1. How would you compare your own moral, intellectual, physical, and social development with the theories presented here?

Schooling and Student Needs

Jeremy had long felt that he had no control over his life, as his parents had already laid out a plan for him to attend medical school. His father was a doctor. His grandfather, who had just recently retired from practice, remained active in the medical community by serving on the local hospital board. Jeremy felt his parents had already cast his lot in school for him. His teachers from elementary school on seemed to acknowledge in various ways that he was destined to be a doctor and, therefore, he was expected to perform academically a step above his peers. Whenever his grandfather used the term family pride to describe his aspirations for him, something seemed to get stuck in Jeremy's throat. He could already tell he didn't have what it took to succeed in medical school. He thought high school should be easy, but he had to work hard to get good grades. Some of his friends didn't spend a fourth as much time as he did studying, and they got the same grades he did. He approached each school year with terror, anticipating another rise in expectations just like there had been each year since second grade. Now, as he sat outside the school counselor's office, he silently rehearsed what he was going to say to the counselor in the hopes of somehow getting out from under the conditions that threatened to smother the life out of him. He could hardly breathe as Ms. Selby opened her door and beckoned for him to enter.

As Jeremy sat down and started to unburden himself, it was difficult to hold back the tears. He told Ms. Selby the whole story from beginning to end, and then finished by asking what he could possibly do that wouldn't alienate his family but would remove the burden he suffered.

"Ms. Selby, I don't even like medicine. I don't like the smells in the hospital; the sight of blood nearly makes me pass out. And I can't imagine spending my life tied to a pager, a cell phone, and a long line of patients who all need me desperately. And I know I'm not smart enough. I don't even like to learn about things related to medicine. What am I going to do?"

"Well," Ms. Selby said. "You say you have never told your parents what you have just said to me?"

"No. I never dared. They are counting on me too much. I'm supposed to be just one more in the long line of doctors in the family."

"That's the first thing you need to do. You may be anticipating more of a reaction than you will actually get. What will you tell them you want to do with your life?"

"That's the hard part. I want to be a biology teacher. I volunteered last summer to teach science lessons at a youth camp, and then both last year and this I am Mr. Herod's teaching assistant in biology. I love it. But I can just imagine what my parents will say about that."

"You've not told them about your interests I take it."

"Not really. I've told them how much I enjoy teaching experiences, but I don't think they have any conception of me as a teacher. When they look at me, they only see a doctor."

"This is what I'm going to recommend," said Ms. Selby. "Meet together with your parents. I suggest that your grandfather not be involved. Tell your parents exactly what you have just told me. It may shock them, but maybe they are not as committed to your being a doctor as you have imagined."

Jeremy spent two days going over the speech he planned to make to his parents before he could muster the courage to actually approach them. When he finally got them to sit down and listen to him, his desires had filled him with courage. He was determined to tell them exactly how he felt and stick to his plan of becoming a teacher. After he finished speaking, and even before his parents responded, he felt as though a huge load was lifted from his shoulders. He studied both of their faces as he spoke and first saw disbelief, horror, and even disgust. But as he continued on they took on looks of sympathy, acknowledgment, and even acceptance. After it was over, to his surprise, his parents told him that his happiness was far more important than their aspirations that he enter the medical field. They had always been certain that Jeremy wanted to be a doctor, and never imagined anything else for him. They explained that it would take some adjusting for them, but that they would support him in his desires.

This case study illustrates some of the needs children have, as well as the way these needs may be unknowingly frustrated. Students will live happier, more productive lives in school when their needs are routinely met and when these needs are expressly connected to their learning experiences. Jeremy found that his need for personal control was being frustrated. He felt as though his whole life was being stifled because of the priority his parents gave to their desires and the limited opportunity they apparently offered for him to be more self-directed. They were wise to acknowledge his need to plot his own course in life, recognizing that his happiness depended on it. Sometimes parents and teachers assume students are unable to make their own decisions and, therefore, require considerable guidance. However, youth have an inherent need for personal control over their lives.

Researchers have identified a number of basic human needs with interesting consensus (Brendtro, Brokenleg, & Van Brockern, 1990; Coopersmith, 1967; Glasser, 1998; Kohn, 1993) (see Table 2.3). All agree that satisfying needs is essential to living effectively in the school environment. They also agree that students require positive relationships with classmates and teachers to reach their potential (significance, belonging, collaboration, love, and acceptance). Three of the theorists specifically indicate that academic success is essential (competence, mastery, content). Significantly, all four indicate that students should have valid choices and the ability to influence the environment in which they live (power, independence, choice, freedom). The final category of needs has to do with the desire to share in significant undertakings and to impart something to others. This, of course, involves making a difference in the lives of others and establishing meaningful relationships with them, as is the case in learning communities. These designated categories of needs correspond well with expressions from students. For example, Topper, Williams, Leo, Hamilton, and Fox (1994) interviewed students and, in correlating their data with a review of research, made a list of student needs:

- to have reciprocal, caring relationships with close friends
- to be challenged to do one's best within a context of enjoyment
- to be provided with a full range of choices and receive instruction on how to make useful and valid choices
- to have opportunities to achieve the necessary competence to pursue one's dreams, to become an effective self-advocate, and to achieve meaningful cultural interdependence
- to achieve a sense of physical well-being
- to acquire acceptable status and be looked upon by peers as "cool"
- to receive unconditional love and know there is someone who will always be there to give support
- to have opportunities to make a difference in someone's life

Children can be expected to have significantly different experiences and have acquired various patterns of behavior in their quest to satisfy their needs. In addition, though their needs may be somewhat common, they will have different intensities of desire, as well as different

TABLE 2.3 *Basic Human Needs.*

Brendtro (1990)	Coopersmith (1967)	Kohn (1993)	Glasser (1998)
Belonging	Significance	Collaboration	Love & acceptance
Mastery	Competence	Content	Fun
Interdependence	Power	Choice	Power/freedom
Generosity	Virtue		Survival

levels of success in achieving what they desire. Some children may be extremely suspicious of others and reluctant to enter into meaningful relationships with them. Others may be overly defensive or extremely coercive, given their experiences with authority figures. Still others may be so starved for affection and validation that they perpetually seek it and sense rejection when they do not receive it in the way they wish (Glasser, 1984). In learning communities, many of these problems can be successfully dealt with, providing students a greater sense of need satisfaction. For example, strong caring relationships can be more readily achieved in which students can be challenged to do their best without being threatened. In learning communities, students are provided choices and given instruction in how to make more valid decisions. They are encouraged to pursue their personal desires with vigor and to receive help from classmates in these endeavors. Unconditional support and acceptance by classmates add to the reasonable and responsible views they have of themselves.

Student Needs and School Adjustment

The failure of schools to adequately satisfy students' needs is likely the most potent deterrent to school achievement. There are at least two basic reasons for this. First, needs cry out to be fulfilled, and all else may become subordinate. Most human behavior involves an effort to achieve personal needs (Glasser, 1998). Some students may give up their search for gratification when it becomes evident they cannot achieve it within the school context. However others will engage in various aberrant, disruptive actions that teachers find difficult to interpret. Why would a child, for example, be uncooperative or attack a teacher from whom the child wants acceptance and approval? Why risk the hope of establishing a positive relationship with the teacher? Such behavior can hardly inspire acceptance, even from the most conscientious teachers. When youth behave aberrantly in an effort to satisfy their needs, teachers are unlikely to be supportive (Glasser, 1990).

The second reason unfulfilled needs have a negative impact on achievement is that failure to satisfy them can lead students to think disparagingly of themselves. Unfulfilled needs can cause students to react negatively, or in some cases to withdraw (Glasser, 1998). Students who withdraw fail to satisfy their needs because they tend to be ignored by their teachers, since teachers usually pay little attention to students who do not cause trouble. They are more likely to devote their time and energy working with more outgoing students or spending an inordinate amount of time trying to achieve order in the classroom. Positive behavior, thus, is ignored, while most teacher attention is focused on the negative actions of a few students. These teacher actions fail to help either the disrupting students or their more reticent counterparts. Needs go unfulfilled, and the development of positive self-concepts is unsupported.

The greatest need in schools is for educators to make a conscientious effort to validly and consistently satisfy student needs. Unfortunately, schools often engage in practices that are an affront to students and their desires. Instead of ensuring that students are satisfied with what happens in school, many routine school procedures result in the opposite (Glasser, 1998). These procedures may be based on assumptions about students that are untrue. For example, when students are not allowed to make decisions about what and how they learn, this policy is based on the assumptions that they are unable to validly do so. This kind of policy also assumes that students have little need for self-determination and that this need can be set aside with few ill consequences. Another false assumption is that school learning should rarely be fun; supposedly, it is just hard work. However, learning can be fun if it is meaningful, provides a sense of accomplishment, and is judged by the student to be useful. Otherwise, it is drudgery. Other school routines that keep students from satisfying their needs include testing and grading, inflexible assignments and deadlines, emphasis on the memorization of facts, and excessive rules accompanied by punitive rule enforcement (Glasser, 1990).

The discipline effort of schools is largely required to manage students whose needs are not being adequately met. Aberrant behavior is usually a manifestation of frustrated need fulfillment. Students are not inherently disruptive. Acting out, even when it appears to have no purpose, is designed to fulfill needs. This is a point educators often have difficulty grasping. It is wise to look at all student behavior as purposeful in terms of inherent needs. If all needs were routinely satisfied, as they tend to be in learning communities, teachers would not have the arduous task of managing students' disruptive behavior.

Theoretical Constructs Regarding Needs

Human needs receive considerable attention from researchers, and this attention provides a solid basis upon which to make decisions about teaching strategies as well as student-teacher relationships and school operations. This work can be characterized as hierarchical in its orientation, or it can be viewed as interactive or based on social needs.

Hierarchical Needs Theories

Abraham Maslow. A particularly useful conception of human needs is provided by Abraham Maslow (1954). He assumed that the purpose of all human behavior is to satisfy some need and that these needs are arranged in a hierarchy. The hierarchical arrangement is in terms of pre-potency: Needs lower in the hierarchy have to be satisfied before higher-level needs assert themselves. The list of needs includes the following, starting from the most pre-potent need to higher, more life-fulfilling needs:

- physiological needs
- safety and security
- belongingness and affection
- self-respect
- self-actualization

As long as lower-level needs go unmet, the individual will continue to seek their fulfillment, ignoring higher-level needs. Thus, if there are unmet physiological needs such as hunger, the individual will submit himself or herself to danger in order to get something to eat. A starving soldier, for example, may put himself in harms' way to get food. Once his hunger has abated, safety becomes the primary concern. For years, schools have sponsored breakfast programs for students who habitually arrive without having eaten. This has obviously been done because students cannot focus on their school work when their stomachs are empty. Also, a chronically insecure boy is more concerned about feeling safe than achieving satisfactory social experiences or satisfying academic demands.

As needs are satisfied, they don't just disappear; they simply assume a position of less importance as far as motivation is concerned. Thus, an individual who is working to achieve higher needs can revert to lower levels as these needs assert themselves. Obviously, the goal is for students to have lower needs sufficiently satisfied so that these needs don't occupy their attention and dominate their behavior. Thus, they can eventually satisfy higher-order needs consistently. Maslow held the view that all people are basically good, and they have an innate need to be competent and accepted. He believed that being unproductive, therefore, is not an indication that a student is bad, but rather an indication of frustrated need fulfillment. He also suggested that basic needs cannot be met without assistance from other people. Thus, not only individuals like teachers, but anyone associated with the student, can be a source of need fulfillment. Finally, only when basic needs are met can the individual become motivated to become self-actualized and attain his or her fullest potential (Jones & Jones, 2001).

Maslow (1962) describes human growth and development in terms of what he calls "holistic-dynamic" psychology. His basic propositions about this process provide some guidance for teachers as they interact with their students and provide learning opportunities for them. All of these assumptions about the growth process articulate well with practices and procedures of learning communities:

1. Humans have an essential inner nature that is intrinsic, given, natural, and very resistant to change.
2. Each person's inner nature has some characteristics that all others have, and some that are unique to the individual.
3. Even when repressed by abuse or similar trauma, the inner nature persists toward self-actualization.
4. In addition to the self-actualization that occurs through discovery and acceptance of inherent aspects of one's nature, each person also creates much of what he or she is through a series of choices made as the individual interacts with others and the environment.
5. No psychological health is possible unless the essential core of an individual is fundamentally accepted, loved, and respected by others as well as by himself or herself.
6. The main source of illness comes from the frustration of needs, of personal potential, of the expression of self, and of the tendency of each individual to grow in his or her own style.
7. Even though the inner core is inherent in all humans, it is easily overcome and suppressed.
8. Generally speaking, children will, given the choice, select what is good for their personal growth.
9. The complete absence of frustration is dangerous. To be strong, a person must acquire frustration tolerance, including the ability to acknowledge the difference between physical reality and personal wishes. Each individual must be able to satisfy many of his or her own needs without exclusive dependence on others.
10. Humans have an innate need to use their capacities, to test their limits, and to grow to the fullest extent possible.

11. Humans need a validated, usable system of values that they strongly believe in and are devoted to, which can be used consistently as a guide in life.

12. The highest maturity includes a childlike quality. Work seems to be the same as play. Duty becomes pleasant, and it is pleasant to do one's duty.

13. In self-actualized persons, impulses are more expressed and less controlled. Controls are less rigid, inflexible, and anxiety-determined.

14. What self-actualized persons want and enjoy is apt to be just what is good for them. Their spontaneous reactions are as capable, efficient, and right as if they had been taught to them in advance.

15. Self-actualized behavior is not driven by fear, but rather by a desire to be good and to live successfully with others.

Eric Erickson.   Although Erickson's approach is primarily developmental, it is also essentially hierarchical. Thus, failure to reach satisfactory resolution of an early stage, such as trust, would negatively affect an individual's ability to work through later developmental stages. Erickson defined eight stages of psychosocial development characterized by a conflict in which the individual either attains an important psychosocial understanding or develops an emotional liability.

The first stage is infancy, during which a child develops either a sense of trust and hope or a sense of mistrust and despair. Though children go through this stage early in life, it is not unusual for children's interpersonal relationships to suffer because they have never achieved a sense of trust for adults. Consequently, they may be withdrawn or, in some cases, overdependent on adults. In these cases, they constantly seek reassurance and support.

The second stage, which occurs early in childhood, is the period in which children achieve a sense of autonomy. For this stage to be effectively achieved, children need opportunities to test themselves within a context of support. Otherwise destructive behavior can be expected, along with the development of a sense of doubt and shame.

In the third stage, support for children's autonomy is also essential. In this stage, children learn to take initiative and avoid guilt. They need considerable practice in developing independence and in learning to successfully interact with others. To take initiative, children learn to plan and organize activities and carry them through (Erickson, 1963).

Moving away from playing make-believe to producing real things characterizes the fourth stage. In this stage, children must learn to do something well and develop a sense of their own competence, which depends on meaningful contact with others, particularly adults, so that achievements can be appropriately acknowledged, verified, and expanded (Erickson, 1968).

The next two stages occur in adolescence, assuming children have successfully negotiated the first four stages. In the first of these stages, children are in search of a personal identity. In the beginning there is a dramatic increase in self-consciousness and a decrease in self-esteem. Children seem to feel "on stage" with an imaginary audience. They also feel alone, as if no one understands them and their problems. Teachers need to create classroom conditions for these youth that help them to be comfortable with others and to feel secure that they are not going to be singled out for some reason (Elkind, 1967).

In the last two stages, youth begin challenging previously accepted beliefs and values. They begin to view the world in more subjective and critical terms. At this time students are less inclined to accept things by examining them personally. They start to question why they are supposed to do various things that they earlier accepted without question. They are likely to question rules or adult behavior they consider illogical or indefensible. In these stages, teachers need to provide an environment that allows for the examination of curriculum, rules, and procedures along with values.

In the secondary schools, teachers must not only help students develop positive resolution of the stages characteristic of this age, but also provide help for students struggling with unsatisfactory resolution of earlier stages. Much of this work has to do with helping students develop confidence and independence, and realistically visualizing personal competence while others acknowledge and accept their work as valid. Students with unresolved difficulties will not be able to successfully make their way through successive stages as they encounter them. In learning communities, students are much more able to develop positive attitudes about their abilities and achievements, as well as acquire meaningful feedback that others accept and value their contributions to the group.

Rudolph Dreikurs. The behavior of children is best understood as an attempt to achieve particular needs, according to Dreikurs. At first, behavior is driven by the need for success and recognition or *attention.* This can ordinarily be achieved by making contributions that are approved of by others, through which the individual achieves a sense of acceptance for what he or she does. If this need is not satisfied, the individual may be disruptive to get attention. If these actions are not successful, a hierarchy of misguided goals emerges. The first of these is a power motive. Only when the need for attention is not satisfied does the *power* motive become active. If the individual does not achieve the power he or she sought, he or she will become deeply discouraged and seek *revenge.* Then, if the revenge motive is sufficiently thwarted, the individual will manifest a *display of inadequacy.* This final goal is defined as just giving up. When a child tries various levels of attention-getting in order to achieve a sense of belonging and fails, he or she may become discouraged, lose all hope of being a significant person, and eventually expect only failure and defeat (Dreikurs & Cassel, 1972; Dreikurs, Grunwald, & Pepper, 1971).

Interactive Need Theories

Interactive need theories are not hierarchical; in other words, needs are not dependent on other needs in a hierarchy to become active. With interactive theories, all needs are present all the time. They are related in the sense that fulfilling one's needs depends on the relative strength of each need and the willingness of the person to forgo complete satisfaction of one need in order to satisfy others. Needs are satisfied within a social context, making need satisfaction a reciprocal process. A person can only adequately satisfy his or her needs to the extent that the individual is willing to help others satisfy their needs as well.

William Glasser. Each individual seeks to fulfill his or her desires to the greatest extent possible. It is part of the genetic code. Behavior is understood as the strongest attempt the person can make at the time to satisfy his or her needs or motives. These needs include the following:

- to survive and reproduce
- to belong, love, and be accepted
- to gain power
- to experience freedom
- to have fun (Glasser, 1986)

Glasser believes that students require sufficent control over their environment in order to feel a sense of self-determination and to fulfill their other needs. He says that schools should do away with the boss-management style of administration and teaching and adopt one of lead-management in which students are empowered to be more self-regulating (Glasser, 1990). Students should be taught how their desires may have to be modified in social situations so that all needs are minimally met as they strive to help others satisfy their needs as well. The motive for fun, for example, may conflict with that of power. Teachers may be unwilling to forfeit all the control required by students to achieve the need they have for fun. The necessary adjustment is for teachers to allow the students more control and for students to seek a little less fun. However, both have to modify their position in order for both to achieve fulfillment. Children often wish for more fun in school, which may mean that teachers have to relinquish some control since fun often requires a greater measure of freedom than traditional classrooms allow.

Because all individuals strive to satisfy their needs and because doing so may interfere with others satisfying their needs, balance must be struck. There is a necessary balance that must be created between satisfying others' needs and fulfilling our own. For example, a person's need for power may interfere with satisfying his or her need to belong and be loved. Thus, a person from whom affection is desired may be turned off by power overtures. Neither person may be willing to relinquish power, and thus they both must suffer the consequence of affection being withdrawn.

A balance of needs is also necessary within any one person. Because not all needs can be satisfied to the extent the individual may desire, personal desires must usually be modified so that all needs can be met at a level that doesn't deprive associates of an opportunity to satisfy their needs as well. For example, perhaps one person's desire for control over others exceeds what those others are willing to allow, or perhaps certain individuals are unwilling to extend the degree of affection someone desires to satisfy his or her needs. Under these conditions, the individual cannot justifiably manipulate those he or she wishes to control or to receive affection from. The way in which this might play out is illustrated in the following vignette.

Blaine loved Willow for as long as he could remember. They were now seniors in high school, and he began hoping that they might start to think more seriously about their future plans together. They had been next-door neighbors most of their lives, first as playmates, and later as good friends. Their families routinely shared activities together, and through their high school years the two of them studied together two or three nights a week. They had also been on quite a few dates. Nearly all of these experiences were very pleasant, and the couple seemed drawn to one another by common beliefs and values. Blaine came to think of Willow romantically as his girl, and was interested in no one else. Willow, however, had very tender feelings toward Blaine but was also starting to develop an interest in dating other boys. During the past year a couple of boys had shown an interest in her and had asked her for dates on occasions when she had already promised to go out with Blaine. Then, about mid-year, Randy Montague asked her to go to the Junior Prom with him, and she accepted. She initially had second thoughts because of her close association with Blaine, but she wanted to see what it would be like to be with someone else. When Blaine found out, he was angry.

"I thought you would be going to the Junior Prom with me. It's the most important dance of the year."

"Well, Randy asked me first, and I decided I needed to start dating other boys. We shouldn't just date each other. We need to see what it's like to have dates with others. You can get a date with someone else, too. That doesn't mean we won't date any more."

"I thought we . . . well, you know, I thought we were kind of steady."

"We've never really talked about that. I never really considered us that way."

"I guess we had different ideas about that. I don't have anyone else I want to go with. I guess you'll just have to do what you want."

Later Blaine asked Willow to go to a basketball game with him. She refused, indicating that she had a test the next day and needed to study. Blaine volunteered to study with her, but she declined.

"I'm going to study with Ryan tonight," she said. "We have chemistry together, and he can help me with the parts I don't understand."

Blaine sulked away, visibly disturbed and angry. He started asking Willow to activities he knew she either could not or would not likely want to attend, as a test of how much she cared for him. She turned him down most of the time. Sometimes Blaine got a little "pushy" with his invitations. Willow was completely turned off by his attempts at control, and they occasionally argued. As Blaine got more controlling, Willow felt less and less affection for him. Soon she decided she didn't like him much at all and requested he not ask her out any more. With this rejection, Blaine sulked all the more. He devoted his life to stalking Willow and mentally objected to most of her activities. When Willow became aware she was being stalked, she was so angry she confronted Blaine and made him promise to stop. Her anger made Blaine dislike her in a way he had never believed he could. Now Willow and Blaine actually disliked one another.

To have successful relationships with others and to experience fruitful community life, individuals must moderate need satisfaction to a level where everyone's needs can be appropriately fulfilled. In the case of Blaine and Willow, excessive control destroyed a relationship that had formerly been full of affection and acceptance. All needs require some degree of fulfillment, and this can only occur when members of a community help one another satisfy their needs. Blaine might have retained his relationship with Willow if he had relinquished his need to control her and permitted her more freedom. Community members who fail to help others fulfill their needs can expect less fulfillment of their own needs. To create a successful learning community, all members must have an appropriate level of satisfaction and realize that achieving their desires requires a degree of sacrifice for others in the community. The quality of relationships necessary for community maintenance involves choosing not to coerce, manipulate, boss, criticize, complain, or withdraw. Instead, community members must choose to care, listen, support, negotiate, encourage, love, befriend, trust, accept, welcome, and esteem (Glasser, 1984).

One reason students do poorly in school is because their desire for self-direction goes unfulfilled. However, if they complain about what they are forced to do in school and rebel, they are punished. Schooling is best defined in terms of two destructive practices, both of which are unsuccessfully enforced by low grades and failure. The first is making students memorize facts that have no value for anyone, including students, in the real world. The second practice is to force students to acquire knowledge that may have some value in the real world, but nowhere near enough to justify having every student learn it. Schools have never been successful in forcing students to learn information that students do not see as relevant either in their present or future lives (Glasser, 1998). These conditions can be changed through the application of constructivist learning theory in the classroom (see Chapter 4). Constructivist theory assumes students naturally learn by investigating personally meaningful problems and that knowledge retention depends on the importance students give to what they learn.

Stanley Coopersmith.   The views of Coopersmith (1967) are likewise related to other theories. In his research, Coopersmith found that high self-esteem is essential to achieving needs of significance, competence, and power. *Significance* is best defined as being valued by others due to positive two-way relationships in which each individual sincerely cares about the other. *Competence* is evidenced by being able to perform tasks that are valued by others. Performances must occur at the right age. *Power* is indicated by the ability to control one's environment and to achieve desires and expectations. Needs can only be met when students experience a sense of trust and personal involvement as they acquire competence. In school these needs can be met when students are allowed to choose what they study and are included in determining classroom rules and regulations. It is best if they are provided opportunities consistent with their personal learning styles.

Developmental Theories

Developmental theory often focuses on the stages of growth and on the effects of having inappropriate levels of support during the growth process. The kind of support ordinarily needed includes giving trust, love, and acceptance and providing children an environment in which they can hone their skills and achieve a sense of competence as judged by their peers. Without this support, various aberrant reactions can be expected, including poor social and school adjustment and even violence.

Stanley Greenspan.   The needs of an individual can be very personal, and making sense of them may only be possible in light of the person's experience (Greenspan, 1997; Greenspan & Wieder, 1998). Greenspan's research indicates that it is essential to understand each youth's individual profile of developmental strengths and weaknesses and to use this profile to develop interventions that can help the individual reach his or her potential. Each individual has natural intentions and feelings that are personal ways to approach situations in life, including school learning. Emotions are a central mediating factor in intelligence and academic performance, as they are used to organize experience and behavior, help the individual make valid connections with the world, and achieve a sense of competence. Teachers are responsible for helping youth make the necessary connections between learning and their emotions and desires. Otherwise the youth, particularly those who have trouble connecting their experiences to the world, will have difficulty learning and achieving their potential.

James Garbarino.   Garbarino (1999), who worked extensively with youth who have committed violent crimes, found that nearly all these youth had histories of neglect and abuse and hid their true selves in an effort to protect themselves from further hurt. He found that these youngsters responded well to unconditional love. They craved love and acceptance, and though their pasts indicated to them that love could not be reliably anticipated, they could learn to change their views. Garbarino also found that these children were capable of developing new attachments and that they desperately needed to do so, as others could take the place of a primary caregiver in providing needed affection and acceptance. In Garbarino's studies, these new connections proved to be potent in reducing the level of depression experienced by many youth. This was significant, as Garbarino found that depression and rejection were significant precursors to violent crimes. Connections with surrogate caregivers were found to be essential to the recovery process of these youth, as well as positive peer relationships characterized by acceptance and support; both significantly curtailed violent behaviors. With a greater incidence of violent behavior in the schools, it is important to modify whatever alienates these youngsters and makes them feel unaccepted. Often children who are abused at home only find more rejection in school.

Social Needs Theories

Though social needs theories have similarities to other categories of theory, they are best characterized as being centered around the need of youth and children to share relationships with one another and with adults in order to gain a sense of well-being and life adjustment. It is thus through social interactions that needs can best be satisfied and the individual can make appropriate social and school adjustments.

David Elkind.   Elkind (1981) describes three basic contracts between adults and children that, if violated, can create stress for children. The first of these is *responsibility–freedom.* This contract requires adults to monitor youth's intellectual, social, and emotional development in order to provide the requisite level of freedom, along with sufficient opportunities to exercise their freedom responsibly. The responsibility–freedom contract is violated when adults fail to reward responsible behavior with greater freedom. For example, if students are denied more opportunities for self-direction when they have demonstrated their ability to be responsibly self-governing, it is an affront to their growth and development.

Achievement–support, Elkind's second category, refers to the necessity of adults providing personal and material support to help children effectively achieve their age-related goals. Support is lacking when teachers provide inadequate instruction, insufficient materials, and limited opportunities for optimum growth and development. Teachers may fail to provide timely feedback or clear explanations in answer to student questions. They may also support their own agenda for learning and ignore or refuse to support students' learning wishes.

Loyalty–commitment, Elkind's third category, is defined as an adult expectation that students respond with loyalty to, and acceptance of, their teachers because of the time, effort, and energy teachers give to teaching. This contract can be violated when teachers give up on students and criticize them rather than trying to understand their problems by thoughtfully and openly discussing them. This ordinarily happens with low-achieving students, who seem less able to provide payback for what teachers feel is the inordinate amount of time and effort they give them.

From a social standpoint, all individuals have needs that are fulfilled by others. Each in turn supplies what is necessary according to inherent human contracts. Failure on the part of any participant, teacher or student, violates the contract. Specific social patterns and expectations are continually changing, even though the implicit nature of the contract does not. As aspects of children's needs change, teachers must make appropriate adjustments to expedite the tacit agreement without violating it. This means teachers must monitor students to ascertain their current capabilities and then supply them opportunities that incorporate a learning environment that maximizes growth and development.

Joan Lipsitz.   The work of Lipsitz (1984) focuses on the inability of adults to understand youth well enough to adequately satisfy their needs. According to Lipsitz, the failure of teachers to understand youth is the major reason for so much unproductive student behavior in school. Excessive frustration is experienced by teachers as they try to manage student behavior after making incorrect assumptions about student needs and growth patterns. In the list of needs identified by Lipsitz, there are similarities to the lists of other therapists:

- The need for *diversity*. Students require considerable variety and a full range of options in their lives.
- The need for *self-exploration* and *self-definition* opportunities. Youth require extensive experiences which focus on personal identity and values.
- The need for *meaningful participation* in school and community. Whenever students are members of a group that provides goals, experiences, and expectations, they become involved in deciding what these are and how they can individually incorporate them into their lives.
- The need for *positive social interactions* with peers and adults. Many needs can only be satisfied during interpersonal associations. In addition, youth inherently seek affiliation with others. Some of these associations can be disruptive unless teachers make deliberate plans to incorporate meaningful social interactions during instruction.
- The need for *physical activity*. Students of all ages require movement. When movement is strategically planned for and carried out in an orderly way, this need can be satisfied without undue interruption of the instructional program.

- The need for *competence* and *achievement.* Because so much is made of school achievement in modern society, children's sense of well-being is explicitly tied to it. Otherwise, more emphasis may be put on other kinds of competence and achievement. Because of the school emphasis, teachers have an enormous responsibility to help all their students achieve genuine competence. Grading practices make this very difficult.
- The need for *structure* and *clear limits.* This need is often improperly defined. The need for order or structure is essential to ensure that students' rights are not violated and that students do not feel a need for others to control them because they feel unable to control themselves. To conclude that students want to be directed by others ignores the overwhelming need for personal control that many theorists have identified. Instead, structure is a manifestation of the need to know what can be expected of others in social interactions, and to ensure that personal rights are not abridged.

Attribution Theory

Research on attribution theory indicates that when students have an internal locus of control, they learn to attribute their success to ability and effort. However, if they have an external locus of control they believe their success is because of luck or fate while failures are the result of low ability. When students view their success or failure as being within their control, they routinely assume that they can be successful, even though they have initially failed at something, if they practice more or modify their approach in some way. When failure is attributed to ability, luck, or the difficulty of the task, however, students assume they have less control over outcomes and believe that making greater effort or organizing themselves more carefully will have little effect on what they can accomplish (Smith & Price, 1996). Modifying an external locus of control is difficult, particularly in a school setting where in all likelihood this frame of reference developed in the first place. This perspective comes primarily from the school practice of only providing teachers to assess the work of students. If students have little or no role in assessment, no amount of praising them for their efforts or providing success experiences is likely to alter their view. Rather, students with an external locus of control must learn to make valid assessments of their own work. This is best accomplished when students are given tasks for which it is evident that greater effort and time were given to performances of better quality. This way students can gradually appreciate the fact that effort does count toward quality performance and that their performance can be improved when effort is increased. These conditions can be greatly enhanced in learning communities.

Martin Seligman.   One of the most important contributions teachers can make in their teaching is to help their students develop an optimistic view of life. When optimism fails to develop, pessimism takes its place and depression often results. An optimistic life orientation does not come from being told positive things or from having images of victory, but rather from thinking about causes in particular ways. According to Seligman (1995), there are three crucial dimensions youth always use to explain why any particular good or bad event happens to them: *permanence, pervasiveness,* and *personalization.*

Young people who are most at risk for depression ordinarily believe that the bad things that happen to them are permanent, or that there is nothing they can do to change what has happened. With this viewpoint they reason that bad will happen perpetually; there is no way to escape it. They commonly use terms like *never, always,* and *no matter what* to describe negative events in their lives. Optimistic people, however, see bad events as temporary. They resist depression by realizing that they will eventually recover from setbacks and that problems can be overcome. They not only believe that problems are only temporary and can be altered with effort on their part, but also that there are high points in life as well as low points, and that the highs can be maximized and the lows minimized. Optimistic adolescents explain good events in terms of being permanent. They are able to see their positive traits, like being a hard worker or being likeable, as being under their control and as permanent characteristics.

Pervasiveness allows the individual to project causes and effects across many situations. Thus, optimistic individuals see their success as predictable from one kind of activity to another, while pessimistic persons tend to use global explanations for their failure and give up, for they anticipate failing on most endeavors. A pessimistic youth may conclude from a poor golf score that she is bad at all sports, while an optimistic one may say she doesn't do well at golf, yet not include other sports in this declaration. The optimistic individual thinks globally about good events. If he receives a high grade in math, he concludes that he is smart rather than restricting the victory to "good at math," as a pessimistic person might do.

Personalization is the third way young people might explain how good or bad events happen to them. In personalization, the individual tries to decide who is at fault for what happens. When bad things occur, children can blame either themselves, other people, or circumstances. Youth who blame themselves when they fail usually suffer low self-esteem. Those who blame other people or circumstances feel better about themselves when confronted with bad events. This doesn't mean that children should be taught to blame others for their failure. Self-esteem is not the only concern. Children should not be encouraged to blame others when things go wrong, but instead hold themselves accountable to rectify the situation so it isn't repeated. Youth need to see themselves realistically so that they can take responsibility for problems that are their fault. They also need to realize that they can anticipate and alter circumstances in which problems commonly occur and that they can solve problems effectively if they give time and effort.

Seligman believes that the effort traditionally given to protect the self-concepts of children is responsible for the rising tide of depression manifest in society over the last five or six decades. Society's fear of damaging the self-concepts of children has led to shielding them from experiences and consequences that would have strengthened them and helped them avoid these debilitating illnesses. He indicates that this damage is caused by accepting mediocre student performances and approving of students' work when they are much more capable than their efforts show.

Educators and parents have feared dire consequences unless students' feelings of anger, sadness, and anxiety were cushioned. However, these feelings serve an important purpose. They motivate individuals to make the adaptations necessary in order to achieve their goals. In making these adaptations, negative emotions can be controlled. In reality, depression occurs when people fail to achieve their goals; it can be countered when they actually accomplish what they desire. When youth encounter obstacles, if parents or teachers jump in to bolster self-esteem, soften the difficulties, and distract them with distortions of what real success requires, it is harder for the young people to actually test their limits and achieve the best of which they are capable. If they are deprived of mastery, their self-esteem is weakened just as certainly as if they had been belittled, humiliated, and physically thwarted at every turn (Seligman, 1995). Teachers do not help adolescents develop positive self-concepts by providing artificially contrived success experiences, or by praising students' performances that are mediocre, in an effort to provide encouragement. Instead, they need to help children understand the nature of excellence and show them how to achieve it. Young people must be helped to realize that doing well takes time, patience, and considerable effort and that everyone has the capacity to be good at something. It is necessary to broaden the range of acceptable achievements to which children can aspire. When this is done, students are more likely to develop a quality called **resiliency.** Individuals who develop resiliency are able to handle frustrating conditions with considerable equanimity. They are unlikely to get so upset that they resort to violence. According to Benard (1993), resiliency is promoted when children experience caring relationships, high expectations, and opportunities for participation within communities. It is critical to note that the high expectations needed must come from students themselves so they experience personal relevance and ownership of what they learn.

 ## QUESTIONS FOR REFLECTION

1. What is significant about hierarchical theories as compared to other theories about needs?
2. Which theory do you believe provides the most insightful and useful view of students' needs? Why?

 ## *Decision Points*

1. Make a comparison between various theories regarding needs, showing commonalities and differences. Indicate school practices, both academic and extracurricular, that are consistent with these theories.
2. Examine each of the theories presented in this chapter and make comparisons to the description of learning communities as presented in Chapter 1. Note consistencies and inconsistencies between learning community practices and the assumptions about human needs associated with each theory. Formulate a description of needs that best fits learning communities.

 ## *Reflections About Self*

1. Think about your own needs and the way in which they have either been fulfilled or thwarted in your life. To what degree do you believe theorists have identified an appropriate list of student needs to feel fulfilled in school? What would you either add or subtract from what is suggested?

How to Ensure Student Needs Are Met

Satisfying student needs is not limited to diagnosing individuals or groups of students to see what their needs are, as there appears to be considerable agreement among theorists regarding human needs. The task for teachers is to help students alter their misguided efforts to fulfill their needs, adapt by using more socially acceptable strategies, and conduct school in a way so that all students satisfy their needs at an acceptable level. Most student misbehavior encountered by teachers consists of misguided efforts to fulfill needs. Much of this behavior has been conditioned over a period of time and is well-ingrained in students' behavioral repertoire. Because these behaviors have been fulfilling needs to some degree, they are in a sense validated and probably defended as necessary by the youth. Students probably see efforts to terminate their aberrant behavior as a threat to need gratification, and thus to their well-being. It is, therefore, a daunting task in many cases to encourage students to trade their behaviors for more acceptable ones, especially when the socially acceptable behaviors are promoted by the very people who in the past have denied them legitimate need satisfaction. If changes are to be made, the best hope is found in learning communities, where if students will take an active part, their needs will be well met through doing personally satisfying and socially satisfactory things that are an integral part of learning community operations.

What actions can teachers take to alter old patterns of misbehavior and supplant them with viable alternative behaviors? The following listed activities will be helpful:

- Make a careful analysis of the needs theories. Make a full list of the needs you believe motivate human behavior. Determine whether or not you think there are some hierarchical connections between various needs, and apply this concept as seems appropriate.
- Examine the behavior of students in your classes. Satisfy yourself that even various categories of aberrant behavior can be interpreted as need satisfying. You may wish to connect these behaviors to particular needs to get a comprehensive view of behavior and motives so you have a better grasp of how student behavior is related to needs.
- Conduct a group discussion with the purpose of having students examine various behaviors and the needs they satisfy. Have them make an appraisal of their own behavior to determine what needs they are trying to fulfill.
- Have students identify various appropriate behaviors that satisfy their basic needs and consider group and personal implications for changing behavior so that personal needs can be more fully satisfied within the social context.
- A teacher might at this point interview students individually to help them realize the consequences of their misbehavior and replace their behaviors with those having consequences they prefer. Have them create a list of activities which they believe will satisfy their needs more fully and which help other members of the learning community likewise satisfy their needs.
- Teach group members the necessity of balancing their need gratification. Help them understand that they are dependent on the group to have their needs met and that they have a responsibility to group members to help them satisfy their needs. A balance must be struck between each individual's needs and those of other members of the community so that all can satisfy all their needs as fully as possible in a group setting. Students must also realize that need satisfaction must take place not only in a school community but also the community at large. There may be ethical, legal, or moral considerations which must be acknowledged in striking an appropriate balance. For example, students may need to take a more active role in the community to limit crime, promote positive recreational activities, or encourage youth employment possibilities.

- Operate the class as a learning community. Do this in a way that ensures that all class members' needs are satisfied. Teachers must keep in mind that they may have as many as 120 students in five or six classes. Each of these classes constitutes a separate learning community and must have sufficient autonomy to create their own learning and management procedures. Each class must have its own context in which needs are satisfied.

 ## Decision Points

1. a. Make an analysis of the needs presented by various theorists and decide upon a list of the needs you feel are most characteristic of youth.
   b. Make a list of misbehaviors which can be expected from youth in school.
   c. List the needs students are most likely trying to satisfy with such misbehavior.
   d. Make a list of socially acceptable behaviors which could be traded for the unacceptable ones.
2. With a group of peers, role-play a discussion that might be expected from high school students regarding their needs and behavior. Include a comparison between acceptable and unacceptable behavior for satisfying needs.
3. With a peer, role-play a situation in which a student has habitually failed to follow classroom procedures which he or she has been involved in creating. Help the misbehaving student to identify the consequences of his or her actions and formulate a plan for changing the inappropriate behavior.
4. Conduct a discussion in which the group is trying to decide how to best balance their needs in a learning community.
5. Visit a school and observe student behavior. Try to make connections between student needs and behavior.

CENTRAL IDEAS

1. During the concrete operations stage of intellectual development, students require concrete representation of what they are learning.
2. Many older students, and even adults, do not achieve the formal operations stage of intellectual development. Teachers, therefore, must continue to provide concrete referents, and encourage students to engage in formal thought.
3. Students' behavior may not be consistent with the level of moral reasoning they have acquired.
4. Moral thinking develops in an invariant sequence; thus, each individual moves sequentially through the stages, but does not necessarily achieve the highest stage.
5. Variations in physical development can result in considerable trauma for youth. Teacher intervention can often rescue them from dire consequences.
6. Researchers generally agree that students need to feel accepted and appreciated, to have positive social relationships, to achieve a sense of autonomy in directing their own affairs, to achieve a satisfactory level of competence, and to experience fun in school.

7. Maslow's theory indicates that needs are related hierarchically, with lower-order needs having to be satisfied before attention is directed toward satisfying higher-order needs.

8. According to Erickson, to achieve the highest level of development youth must first satisfactorily negotiate earlier stages. They go from developing a sense of autonomy to becoming intellectually capable.

9. In Dreikur's theory, attention is the predominating need. When it is not satisfied, the levels of power, revenge, or display of inadequacy may appear in a hierarchical order as each of the succeeding needs is thwarted.

10. Glasser believes all behavior is purposeful to achieve the needs of survival, love and acceptance, power, freedom, and fun. Satisfying these needs has to be balanced between oneself and others in social situations.

11. Seligman believes that optimism is best attained through achieving competence and that depression can be the result of supplanting a focus on genuine achievement with an emphasis on promoting self-esteem without encouraging excellence.

12. Rejection and depression preludes to violence, but can be avoided by caring association with surrogate caregivers.

13. If students are denied opportunities for self-direction when they have demonstrated an ability to be responsibly self-governing, it is an affront to their growth and development.

14. Specific aspects of children's needs are constantly changing, and teachers must make appropriate adjustments in order to adequately fulfill these needs.

15. Students can learn that their efforts result in quality when they are given opportunities to assess their own work.

16. The vast increase in depression over the past several decades may be due to society's emphasis on self-concept and the fear of damaging self-concept by high expectations.

17. Optimism acquired through high achievement can protect children from depression.

18. Optimistic children believe that negative happenings are temporary and that their success in one setting can predict success in many others.

19. School purposes are best met within a context of students satisfying their needs.

20. When students' needs are met through learning communities, they develop resiliency, which tends to protect them from various debilitating challenges that face them.

21. Children often respond to the exercise of authority with disruptive or violent behavior. A caring environment, devoid of excessive control, can reduce these problems.

22. When authority is abused in schools, trust never evolves, feelings of being cared for are never achieved, and a sense of empowerment is never realized.

23. The role of the teacher is to help students achieve their needs in socially acceptable ways and avoid behavior which is disruptive and which fails to satisfy social needs.

REFERENCES

Adams, G. R. (1977a). Physical attractiveness: Personality and social reactions to peer pressure. *Journal of Psychology, 896,* 287–296.

Adams, G. R. (1977b). Physical attractiveness: Towards a developmental social psychology of beauty. *Human Development, 20,* 217–239.

Adams, G. R., & Crossman, S. M. (1978). *Physical attractiveness: A cultural imperative.* Rosen Heights, NY: Libra.

Arlin, P. K. (1975). Cognitive development in adulthood: A fifth stage? *Developmental Psychology, 11* (5), 602–606.

Benard, B. (1993). Fostering resiliency in kids. *Educational Leadership, 51* (3), 44–48.

Boyce, D., & Jensen, L. (1978). *Moral reasoning.* Lincoln: University of Nebraska Press.

Brendtro, L., Brokenleg, M., & Van Brockern, S. (1990). *Reclaiming youth at risk: Our hope for the future.* Bloomington, IN: National Educational Service.

Brooks-Gunn, J. (1987). Pubertal process and girls' psychological adaption. In R. M. Lerner & T. T. Foch (Eds.), *Biological-psychosocial interactions in early adolescence* (pp. 123–153). Hillsdale, NJ: Lawrence Erlbaum Associates.

Coopersmith, S. (1967). *The antecedents of self-esteem.* San Francisco: W. H. Freeman.

Crockett, L. J., & Peterson, A. C. (1987). Pubertal status and psychosocial development: Findings from the early adolescence study. In R. M. Lerner & T. T. Foch (Eds.), *Biological-psychosocial interactions in early adolescence* (pp. 173–188). Hillsdale, NJ: Lawrence Erlbaum Associates.

Dreikurs, R., & Cassel, P. (1972). *Discipline without tears: What to do with children who misbehave.* New York: Hawthorne.

Dreikurs, R., Grunwald, B., & Pepper, F. (1971). *Maintaining sanity in the classroom: Illustrated teaching techniques.* New York: Harper & Row.

Elkind, D. (1967). Egocentrism in adolescence. *Child Development, 38,* 1025–1034.

Elkind, D. (1981). *The hurried child: Growing up too fast too soon.* Reading, MA: Addison-Wesley.

Erickson, E. (1963). *Childhood and society* (2nd ed.). New York: Norton.

Erickson, E. (1968). *Identity, youth, and crisis.* New York: Norton.

Garbarino, J. (1999). *Lost boys: Why our sons turn violent and how we can save them.* New York: The Free Press.

Gilligan, C. (1977). In a different voice: Women's conception of self and morality. *Harvard Educational Review, 47* (4), 481–517.

Gilligan, C., & Attanucci, J. (1988). Two moral orientations: Gender differences and similarities. *Merrill Palmer Quarterly, 34* (3), 223–237.

Glasser, W. (1986). *Control theory in the classroom.* New York: Harper & Row.

Glasser, W. (1984). *Control theory: A new explanation of how we control our lives.* New York: Harper & Row.

Glasser, W. (1990). *The quality school: Managing students without coercion.* New York: Harper & Row.

Glasser, W. (1998). *Choice theory: A new psychology of personal freedom.* New York: Harper Collins.

Good, T. L., & Brophy, J. E. (2003). *Looking in classrooms* (9th ed.). Boston: Allyn & Bacon.

Greenspan, S. (1997). *The growth of the mind.* Reading, MA: Perseus Books.

Greenspan, S. (1998). *The child with special needs.* Reading, MA: Perseus Books.

Greenspan, S. L., & Wieder, S. (1997). Learning to interact. *Scholastic Early Childhood Today, 12*(3), 23–24.

Guilford, J. P. (1972). Thurstone's primary mental abilities and structure of intellect abilities. *Psychological Bulletin, 77,* 129–143.

Higgens-Trenk, A., & Gaite, A. (1971). Elusiveness of formal operational thought in adolescents. *Proceedings of the 79th Annual Convention of the American Psychological Association.*

Inhelder, B., & Piaget, J. (1958). *The growth of logical thinking from childhood to adolescence.* New York: Basic Books.

Jensen, L. C. (1985). *Adolescence: Theories, research, applications.* St. Paul, MN: West.

Jones, V. F., & Jones, L. S. (2001). *Comprehensive classroom management: Creating communities of support and solving problems* (6th ed.). Boston: Allyn & Bacon.

Katz, M., Noddings, N., & Strike, K. (1999). *Justice and caring.* New York: Teachers College Press.

Kohlberg, L. (1969). The cognitive development approach to socialization. In D. A. Goslin (Ed.), *Handbook of socialization theory and practice* (p. 375). Chicago: Rand McNally.

Kohlberg, L. (1973). Continuities in childhood and adult moral development revisited. In P. Baltes & K. W. Shaie (Eds.), *Lifespan developmental psychology: Personality and socialization.* New York: Academic Press.

Kohlberg, L. (1976). Moral stages and moralization: The cognitive-developmental approach. In T. Lickona (Ed.), *Moral development and behavior.* New York: Holt, Rinehart & Winston.

Kohlberg, L., & Gilligan, C. (1971). The adolescent as philosopher: The discovery of the self in a postconventional world. *Daedalus (Fall),* 1051–1086.

Kohn, A. (1993). *Punishment by rewards: The trouble with gold stars, incentive plans, A's, praise, and other bribes.* Boston: Houghton Mifflin.

Lipsitz, J. (1984). *Successful schools for your adolescents.* New Brunswick, NJ: Transaction Books.

Manaster, G. J. (1989). *Adolescent development: A psychological interpretation.* Itasca, IL: F. E. Peacock Publishers.

Maslow, A. H. (1954). *Motivation and personality.* New York: Harper.

Maslow, A. H. (1962). Some basic propositions of a growth and self-actualization psychology. In A. W. Combs (Ed.), *Perceiving, behaving, becoming: A new focus on education* (1962 Yearbook). Washington, D.C.: Association for Supervision and Curriculum Development.

Noddings, N. (1992). *The challenge to care in schools.* New York: Teachers College Press.

Noddings, N. (1993). *Educating for intelligent belief or unbelief.* New York: Teachers College Press.

Noddings, N. (2002). *Educating moral people: A caring alternative to character education.* New York: Teachers College Press.

Peskin, H. (1973). Pubertal onset and ego functioning. *Journal of Abnormal Psychology, 72,* 1–15.

Peterson, A. C. (1987). Those gangly years. *Psychology Today* (September), 28–34.

Piaget, J. (1954). *The construction of reality in the child.* New York: Basic Books.

Piaget, J. (1955). *The language and thought of the child.* New York: Meridan Books.

Piaget, J. (1970). *Science of education and the psychology of the child.* New York: Orion Press.

Piaget, J., & Inhelder, B. (1958). *The growth of logical thinking*. New York: Basic Books.

Resnick, L. B. (1987). Learning in school and out. *Educational Researcher, 16*, 13–20.

Seligman, M. E. P. (1995). *The optimistic child*. New York: Harper Collins.

Shayer, M. (1979). Has Piaget's construct of formal operational thinking any utility? *British Journal of Educational Psychology, 49*, 265–276.

Smith, J. O., & Price, R. A. (1996). Attribution theory and developmental students as passive learners. *Journal of Developmental Education, 19* (3), 2–4.

Thayer-Bacon, B. (2000). *Transforming critical thinking*. New York: Teachers College Press.

Topper, K., Williams, M., Leo, A., Hamilton, H., & Fox, R. (1994) A positive approach to understanding and addressing challenging behaviors: Supporting educators and families to include students with emotional and behavioral difficulties in regular education. Montpelier, Vermont: Vermont University, Center for Developmental Disabilities.

Autonomy and Student Empowerment

CHAPTER OBJECTIVES

This chapter is designed to help you

1. Explain the central place of personal autonomy in human activity and its strategic worth to student learning.
2. Explain the need for autonomy in learning communities.
3. Explain the relationships between autonomy, maturity, and responsibility in the moral development of youth.
4. Explain the relationship between autonomy and achievement, problem solving, creativity, motivation, and inquiry.
5. Explain the teacher's role in promoting autonomy and problem solving.

In learning communities students aquire independence and responsible self-direction.

INTRODUCTION

The quest for personal freedom is a central feature of the human endeavor (Glasser, 1998). The desire for agency appears early in life, as evidenced by the independent searching and learning engaged in by toddlers, as well as their insistence to do many things on their own like feed themselves, tie their own shoes, or sweep the floor long before they have the requisite ability to do these things well without assistance. The desire for freedom continues to predominate in each individual's needs through childhood, adolescence, and into adulthood.

Challenges to freedom or autonomy are often met with stern resistance or outright rebellion. This is particularly noticeable during adolescence, when youth feel they can accomplish many things without adult direction and interference, but are commonly restricted until adults believe they have the proper education, skills, and sense of responsibility. Although young individuals may already have the necessary skills or proper attitudes, adults, because of their inherent need to direct the activity of others, are reluctant to relinquish control. In defending the adult coercive role, the controlling person often claims that adolescent children who are given freedom will act irresponsibly, when in fact their rebellious behavior is a reaction to excessive control. Not uncommonly, the youth who rebel as a result of being under too much control are then exposed to increased control in an effort to keep them within bounds. The adult thus tries to solve the problem of rebellion with its cause. The result is usually more recalcitrant resistance, along with increased resentment and rebellion.

Even when students comply with teacher demands, there is no assurance they are sincerely submitting themselves to what teachers consider to be more expert knowledge and rational judgment. Many youth probably see no alternative but to give in under the circumstances. After all, adults are the gatekeepers to rewards and attractive vocations. They get to decide when youth are ready for more autonomy, thereby reserving the privilege to those individuals who comply with demands. However, responsible autonomy requires an environment of freedom in order to develop and thus cannot logically serve as a prerequisite for its own achievement. In other words, responsible autonomy is learned only within a context of freedom, and therefore youth cannot be expected to first show that they are responsible before being given the right of self-direction. There is also little reason to believe that students who have limited autonomy will adequately learn decision-making skills and establish themselves as well-adjusted, contributing members of society.

One reason commonly given for controlling adolescent behavior is that students will later find similar conditions in the workplace to which they must learn to adjust. What society actually needs are individuals who strive for meaningful relationships in their employment and sense a high degree of personal autonomy in their community role, rather than begrudgingly comply with others' expectations.

It is often difficult to understand how autonomy can be an integral part of learning communities and, in fact, be essential to their functions and operations. On the surface, autonomy and community appear to be contradictory elements. Autonomy is ordinarily viewed as independence from others and their influence. However, though autonomy is an authentic constituent of independence, it is also an essential component of community. Both are necessary because most individuals desire sufficient autonomy along with community membership. Thus, we desire social interactions, but only so long as these associations do not subvert our need for autonomy. Communities that function smoothly depend on a good deal of cooperation, but also require that community actions be laced with an appropriate level of freedom. When community actions and interactions are restricted and personal agency is thwarted, community life stagnates and cooperation falters. The personal fulfillment sought in social interactions is diminished, and the afflicted individuals either seek to alter these unacceptable conditions or overtly rebel against those who they consider perpetrators of coercion.

Autonomy in learning communities is a matter of self-generated contributions that the individual believes are helpful to the group. These contributions do not come by assignment, but rather develop from personal interests and desires. Thus, they are personally invigorating and meaningful. They also carry the strength of personal commitment and are thus likely to be of higher quality. In such a community, each member provides a unique contribution based upon his or her individual interests and qualifications. Thus, each member's role is idiosyncratically determined with an expectation that what is done will be sufficiently useful to the whole community. Each individual has the personal task of specifically determining how he or she might best serve the learning community, while at the same time satisfying personal needs for growth and development. This process is illustrated in the following vignette.

Huia enthusiastically volunteered to participate in Mr. Keck's experimental class in her school. She learned that the class was organized as a learning community and that community-based learning projects would be emphasized along with efforts to strengthen group membership. As a Pacific Islander, specifically a Maori, she had not been successfully integrated into the predominantly European-American culture of the school. Not only did she feel like an outsider, but she was commonly singled out for various forms of abuse by her peers. In addition, she had difficulty applying herself to her studies, which generally consisted of memorizing factual material that she found irrelevant. She anticipated that the experimental class might help her feel more accepted, and also make her a more successful learner. She discovered that students would have an opportunity to formulate their own learning plans and activities according to their personal interests, and that each class member would be part of a larger learning community, with the specific purpose of cooperating in the learning experience so all could mutually benefit.

In the initial meeting, Mr. Keck further explained that the class would be broken up into smaller learning groups formed according to learning interests. He also explained the necessity for collegiality and outlined a series of team-building activities in which all would eventually participate.

Huia's initial learning adventure was to explore the First Amendment of the United States Constitution with her group. Other groups in the class took other amendments to learn about. Huia, along with two other students, became interested in the freedom of speech and press components of the First Amendment. At that time, a controversy had arisen in school about some material concerning a local pollution problem that students desired to publish in the school newspaper. Students felt that their freedom of speech rights were inappropriately prohibited when the faculty advisor censored it. They wanted to expose a local company for polluting a nearby river, and felt that the information they had was true because its source was a local engineer, although it was a rumor at that point. In the controversy with their advisor, the student editor and reporters became greatly incensed and were outspoken about how they were restricted. They achieved considerable support from other students. In their studies, Huia and her group learned enough about free speech to realize that the students had a serious misunderstanding about their rights under the First Amendment. The study group arranged to make a presentation to the student newspaper staff, and Huia took the lead in explaining the nature of student rights with regard to free speech.

"Students have many of the rights of adults in America," she began. "But there are also some restrictions. Teachers in the school also are restricted in some ways. For example, as students we could publish and distribute materials regarding our own religious beliefs. Teachers, however, would be unable to do the same, because students are considered vulnerable to being inappropriately persuaded by teachers to accept particular religious beliefs. Student maturity is also an issue when it comes to what can be written in a school newspaper. Because we are underage, we are protected from being sued for libel by someone for what we print in the school newspaper. But if the school allows us to publish libelous material, they are in a position to be sued. The school can, therefore, legitimately protect itself from such legal action by regulating what is published at school. As students we have a lot of rights that are protected that we need to learn about. One of them is in regards to what we can wear. The school cannot restrict what we wear unless it can be shown to interfere with the learning process. For example, someone may come with such outlandish clothing or hair styles that it attracts undue attention and disrupts class. In this case it could be restricted. The same is true of items of clothing that are worn by gang members.

As students we also have some protection regarding the right of the school administration to search our lockers. There are some schools where students have signed a statement allowing the school to search their lockers for any reason. It is done as a condition for getting a locker. In effect, they have signed away their right of protection from unwarranted searching. In our school this has not been done. Therefore, if the administration wishes to search the lockers there must been a good reason, like when it is reported that guns or other weapons have been brought into the school. They can also search lockers to retrieve school property or to remove any item that is a suspected health hazard, like spoiling food. Usually the principal would tell us in advance that a search was being made unless it became a matter of student safety, like if there was a bomb threat. So you can see that our rights are protected unless there is what is called a 'compelling state interest' that can take precedence. These compelling state interests are designed to protect the whole society and have to be given more importance than the rights of any individual."

As Huia talked, the other students showed respect and appreciation for the high level of understanding she had of the subject and the helpful way she explained it. She completely defused the situation. Later the principal, along with the faculty advisor, were liberal in their praise, the student newspaper staff thanked her for helping them see the situation better, and her group members heartedly congratulated her for how well she represented them. After this presentation there was a noticeable increase in Huia's acceptance in the school. The growth in collegiality was especially noticeable within her group. Huia's confidence in her ability to learn meaningful things and apply them successfully to life's problems grew considerably. She also realized that she could successfully take a leadership role with her peers.

 QUESTIONS FOR REFLECTION

1. In what way was agency central to the success Huia experienced in her learning?

2. What is the relationship between learning communities and an environment of freedom?

3. Why was Huia successful in defusing the conflict whereas teachers and administrators had been unsuccessful?

Decision Points

1. Make a list of the obstacles that might be encountered by increasing student autonomy and using learning communities as an instructional format for secondary schools. How might the effects of each of these obstacles be minimized?
2. Make a statement of your position regarding student autonomy and learning communities in secondary schools. Defend your position.

Children's Response to Authority

There is little question that classrooms need order to promote optimum learning, but a question does exist regarding how it is established. This may be the most important factor influencing student behavior in the schools. Discipline problems in school can more often be traced to dysfunctions in the interpersonal climate and organizational patterns of the school than to student malfunctions (Wayson & Pinnell, 1982). Obviously, a safe, quiet environment is necessary for optimum learning to occur. However, students often engage in noisy disruptions and unsafe actions. The confrontations that occur can be explosive and sometimes lead to catastrophic violence. From what has been learned about student needs and behavior, it is clear that students require an accepting, caring environment, one in which they have considerable control over what happens to them as well as conditions that promote a true sense of competence. The lack of these conditions is the primary reason there may be a lack of order in the classroom.

Perhaps control is the most potent need of youth. Young people may be particularly concerned with personal control if they have previously been excessively regulated, and if they see such regulation as depriving them of a means of satisfying their needs. Unfortunately, schools routinely prevent students from fulfilling their needs, and in particular their needs for autonomy and self-government (Glasser, 1990). Youth who have been subject to excessive control in their homes or in school have the most difficult time adapting to authority.

All humans, including students, abhor the arbitrary use of power, which, as defined by students includes, but is not limited to, (1) power exercised without the backing of constituents, (2) power exercised without requisite knowledge, (3) power exercised without prior consultation, (4) power exercised for personal gain, (5) power exercised which alters or cancels agreements made regarding events and activities, (6) power exercised to prove who is boss, (7) power exercised because of being an authorized agent, (8) power exercised even though someone else in the system is more qualified to make judgments and decisions, (9) power exercised without seeking all necessary information, (10) power exercised when it is assumed that students are not mature enough to render judgments and make decisions on their own, (11) power exercised to escape responsibility, (12) power exercised to defeat popular undertakings of students or faculty, (13) power exercised to impose unnecessary or illogical rules and procedures, (14) power exercised when it is unnecessary, (15) power exercised to create visibility, (16) power exercised in the face of disagreements regarding what the nature of curriculum should be, (17) power exercised to limit the options available to students, (18) power exercised to undermine the power of others, and (19) power exercised without due consideration of already established rules and procedures.

Abuses of authority are commonly seen in all aspects of society, and particularly in the schools where students ordinarily feel unable to declare their grievances with any hope that appropriate actions will be taken to remedy them. As they see it, they are left with no recourse but to rebel and make life miserable for those in authority (Glasser, 1998). Because the means to deal appropriately with authority appears unavailable to them, they react in negative, irrational ways even though these actions have no hope of achieving what they desire. They may never have been included in deliberations about school concerns, nor have their contributions seriously considered. Under these conditions, trust never evolves, feelings of being cared for are never achieved, and a sense of empowerment is never realized. Thus, in students' contact with authority in the schools, they may learn to view authority figures antagonistically and to generalize this attitude to other individuals in authority (Glasser, 1984).

The establishment of order in schools will fail so long as there is an improper exercise of authority. Youth can be expected to react negatively to an abuse of control. In contrast, if authority is used to empower students, to help them acquire the competency they value, and to help them become involved in meaningful interactions with their peers and others in bonafide learning communities, they will come to understand the appropriate use of power and to accept and foster appropriately exercised authority.

Autonomy and Learning: A Model

Many teachers have found that, when they provide students an increase in autonomy, anarchy prevails. Students are commonly provided freedom only with the provision that they act responsibly. It usually takes only a short time before students are openly disruptive, convincing the teacher that they are not ready for the freedom they have been offered. This often happens with neophyte teachers' first fledgling attempts at teaching. They may explain that the students are trusted and expected to behave like adults, but these declarations usually fail to produce the desired results.

Students who have previously been exposed to the usual school rules and restraints will be unlikely to use their newfound freedom responsibly at first. Instead, they will probably assume the freedom is simply a sign of teacher weakness or bad judgment and take advantage of it by being more disruptive. The usual teacher reaction is to assume students are not ready for increased freedom because they are immature. Thus, the teacher increases control and imposes punishments for unacceptable behavior. It is inappropriate to assume that students' readiness to assume personal responsibility in the classroom is simply a matter of age maturity or teacher edict.

If students were trusted and allowed more freedom, most believe they would responsibly use it. Actually, responsible autonomy is not a matter of age but rather a consequence of experience and training. Therefore, students cannot be expected to engage autonomously and responsibly in their classroom affairs just by receiving more freedom and a declaration of trust. Instead, the amount of freedom they receive must correspond to the level of personal and social responsibility they have currently achieved. When the amount of freedom students receive is commensurate with their current degree of maturity, and is combined with experiences designed to promote the development of responsible autonomy, they are able to gradually grow toward a higher level of social responsibility. The development of responsible autonomy cannot be acquired in the absence of freedom; sufficient freedom is a necessary component.

The relationship between autonomy, maturity, and responsibility is illustrated in Figure 3.1 (Edwards, 1995). This model shows that responsible autonomy is a function of growing maturity and that this relationship is enhanced through teaching and learning. The nature of the learning process is a critical matter. Students must not be expected to prove themselves before they are allowed freedom of action. In addition, they should

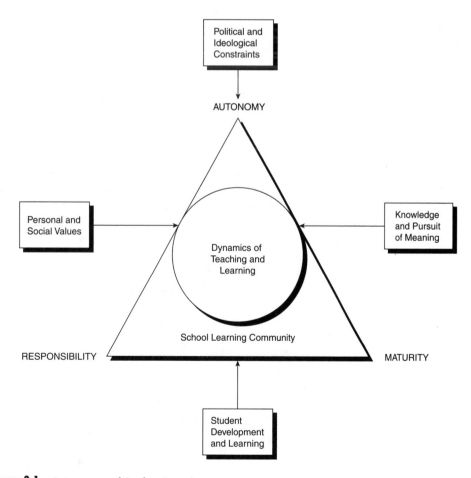

Figure 3.1 Autonomy and Student Learning

TABLE 3.1   *Attributes of Maturity.*

Increasingly aware of shared human experience	Increasingly willing to accept responsible share of common human experience
Increasingly behaves in terms of consequences	Increasingly articulates expressions of belief
Increasingly empathetic	More comprehensive and philosophical in developing meanings

not be granted more freedom than they can responsibly apply. This requires an instructional format designed to help students solve real-life problems and allow them to direct much of their own learning and other classroom affairs. Too often school tends to be divorced from the real world with textbook mastery replacing natural learning experiences. This involves memorizing textbook content rather than using textbooks as resources (Darling-Hammond, 1997). Textbooks can be a valuable resource to use while completing self-directed learning projects and solving personal and community problems. However, as far as possible, learning should be placed within a community context. This provides more meaningful experiences for students and helps them learn that most of life's activities to some degree have community connections; therefore, school experiences should reflect that fact (Sergiovanni, 2000).

Maturity is a growing experience. Jelinek (1979) indicates that maturity has the following attributes (see Table 3.1). First, the individual becomes increasingly willing to accept a responsible share of the common human enterprise and becomes increasingly aware that human experiences are shared. Second, the individual becomes increasingly adept at behaving appropriately in terms of consequences. Thus, consequences are used to guide experiences and make adjustments to life's problems. Third, the individual becomes increasingly articulate in expressing his or her beliefs and opinions and more persuasive in presenting arguments. Fourth, the individual becomes increasingly more empathetic. Without empathy, others' perspectives cannot be truly appreciated nor can the individual show genuine interest in others. An individual who lacks empathy is unlikely to accept group objectives or to participate enthusiastically in group activities. Fifth, the individual becomes more comprehensive and philosophical in developing meanings. Group cohesiveness and productivity depend on the members becoming more meaningfully involved in community affairs, and having this involvement become more deeply significant to each individual. Only when community affairs become a reflection of its members' important beliefs does commitment evolve. Commitment is what drives communities toward more active and fulfilling participation (Sergiovanni, 1992).

Learning for responsibility should incorporate personal and social values (see Figure 3.1). Values are essential elements of any community. Not only do they provide the basis upon which community members can relate and work together successfully, but they stimulate the level of activity that can be expected. Whatever is valued gives focus to community action. When there are shared values, the entire community can become powerfully involved. All individuals in a community not only must value things in common but must know that they value them and why. This allows for discussion and conceptualization. When values are conceptualized, their critical importance to the community can be appreciated and communicated. Communicating values among community members helps solidify allegiance, promote support, acknowledge involvement in the learning community, learn roles in responsible community membership, and indicate ways that their autonomy can be appropriately integrated within this responsibility. It provides a format within which their need for personal freedom can be connected to community action (Sergiovanni, 1994). For example, children might discuss their views regarding the indigent population in their community and discuss things they might do to render aid. Their values regarding the poor might be examined and their views about the welfare system explored. They might examine how they feel about those who have the ability to work and those who do not, living instead off the dole, in contrast to those who are temporarily out of work due to situations beyond their control. Students might identify different populations who are destitute for varying reasons. The needs of unwed mothers who lack the necessary training to finds jobs with sufficient pay to support themselves might be explored. Students might also examine ways in which school dropouts might become members of the unemployed, and possibly homeless, population. After reaching consensus, a service-learning activity may be initiated by combining efforts of the learning community toward solutions for the indigent population. As part of this effort, individuals or small groups of students might be encouraged to become involved in ways that are personally meaningful, but also represent the overall position of the group.

The nature of learning, human development, and student needs are also essential elements of this model: the way in which children naturally learn, the needs they try to satisfy, and the ways of providing appropriate learning experiences for them. Increasingly, the nature of learning is thought to be constructivist: children generate their own meanings and construct their own knowledge. They often fail to assimilate information in the form it is given, as new information may be discarded in favor of already existing knowledge structures (Osborn & Wittrock, 1983; Phillips, 2000; Trowbridge, Bybee, & Powell, 2000). The constructivist approach dictates substantial changes in many educational experiences that affect children. Instead of simply transmitting information for students to absorb, teachers need to give children opportunities to initiate their own learning and regulate their own personal growth. Learning communities provide direction without coercion, and thereby promote personal autonomy within the context of community responsibility. Thus, students help create and achieve personally meaningful learning tasks that contribute to community agreements (Coombe, 1999).

Student needs are also part of this component. Students' energy is often directed at satisfying their needs, and their educational experiences should supply them with the necessary knowledge and skills. One need that tends to dominate, the need for autonomy, often provides a vehicle for individuals to satisfy their other needs.

Meaningful knowledge and its acquisition are central to achieving greater maturity and becoming more responsibly autonomous. The search for meaning is a growing experience in and of itself. When done in the social context of a learning community, there are even more opportunities for growth. Yet, when school experiences are too tightly structured or when the information students are asked to learn is judged to be irrelevant, little growth is possible (Darling-Hammond, 1997). Students can feel empowered by what they learn, particularly when they perceive the knowledge or skill to be an instrument for achieving their needs and goals (Glasser, 1998). Unless children make learning goals their own, the goals will only be grudgingly pursued.

There are political and ideological constraints that influence the development of responsible independence. Some of these constraints are culturally imposed while others are the product of an individual's desires and aspirations. For example, in some cultures students are expected to acquire large amounts of information that they will retain and use in the future even though data, available for years, indicates a very steep curve of forgetfulness from this kind of learning (Cronbach, 1963). The nonessential nature of these facts was graphically illustrated in research conducted by Shaw and Buhler (1984), who interviewed 250 successful people from different educational backgrounds: high school dropouts, high school graduates, college graduates (non-teaching), and teachers. Participants were asked simple factual questions in the subjects of social studies, English, and math. In social studies, subjects were asked questions regarding names of states, capitals, presidents, continents, oceans, important dates and people, and specific terms like *peninsula*. In English, questions included definitions of such terms as *participle, preposition, direct object, adjective, metaphor,* and *simile.* In math, participants were asked to define such terms as *quotient, common denominator, exponent, divisor,* and *integer.* High school dropouts achieved 23 percent in social studies, 8 percent in English, and 0 percent in math. High school graduates scored 33 percent in social studies, 35 percent in English, and 20 percent in math. College graduates faired better, with scores of 48 percent in social studies, 47 percent in English, and 27 percent in math. The highest, and yet interestingly low, scores were achieved by teachers. They scored 63 percent in social studies, 58 percent in English, and 36 percent in math. It appears from this study that memorized facts are not well retained, nor do they have significant influence on success in adulthood.

Decision Points

Create a detailed description of how you would organize a class in your major where an appropriate balance between autonomy, maturity, and responsibility is sought. In doing this, create a sequence of instruction and describe what you might do to deal with discipline problems.

The Influence of Autonomy on Achievement

Parents and educators often voice concerns over whether or not student achievement will be adversely affected if learning is significantly self-regulated. Students are generally considered to be too immature to appropriately judge what and how they learn or to follow through on learning commitments. However, these opinions result from the observation of children who are usually conditioned to learn under strict control. It is inappropriate to assume that children are inherently unable to learn to behave responsibly. Instead, irresponsible, disruptive behavior is more likely a reaction to excessive control (Kohn, 1993). Once these barriers are lowered, former excessive constraint can encourage more acting out.

In reality, most students who are allowed to regulate their own learning tend to have better achievement results. This is true at various levels through secondary school

(Williams, 1996), and into the university level (Linder & Harris, 1993). The same results have been obtained in research regarding gifted students (DelBello, 1988) and students with learning disabilities (Rooney & Hallahan, 1988), as well as corrections education students (Linder, 1994). In her study, DelBello (1988) found that moderately gifted students outdistanced highly gifted peers when their parents had high expectations of them, encouraged a "can do" attitude, created a balance between structure and freedom, provided a sounding board for children's ideas, questioned rather than dictated to children, and encouraged their children to make lists, sketch diagrams of proposed projects, and follow self-imposed deadlines. Thus, with some instruction on decision making along with encouragement and an atmosphere of freedom, children seem able to regulate their own learning and achieve at higher levels than more capable but highly controlled peers.

The degree of students' autonomy to support increased achievement depends on conditions in the school. McNeil (1988a) found that educational quality is reduced through teacher control, which in turn is promoted through greater administrator control of teachers. This is commonly done in an effort to make schools smooth running organizations and to meet minimum standards. When teachers believe administrators' greatest concern is that minimum standards be met, they start to elicit minimal compliance from their students. They also tend to maintain tight control over the course content rather than allowing students to become actively involved in gathering and interpreting information. Instead, they lecture and reduce their teaching to having students memorize lists of terms and unelaborated facts.

In order to avoid student failure and appear to be teaching information of some substance, teachers tend to gradually eliminate extensive reading assignments, all writing assignments, and most class discussions. They parcel out course content in the form of manageable facts contained on simple worksheets and handouts (McNeil, 1988b). Students find such school experiences lack credibility; thus, these students fall into patterns of minimal compliance that administrators condemn as boring, disinterested teaching, as well as the result of student apathy. They see their schools as "out of control" and move to institute still more behavioral and administrative controls. Thus, a vicious cycle of lowering expectations is set into motion and the school begins to lose its legitimacy as a place for serious learning. Both teachers and students report feeling "herded." These conditions cause administrators to make disproportionate attempts to control behavior that come across as acts of desperation, thereby making students rebel in such petty ways as littering the halls and cafeteria (McNeil, 1988a).

However, when teachers do not have to teach in conflict with administrative policies, they are more likely to demand the best of their students and to learn along with them. Such teachers place few barriers between their professional knowledge and their classroom learning. Instead of students misreading the dullness of lectures as a lack of teacher knowledge, and teachers mistaking student disappointment with this diluted content for apathy and lack of curiosity, greater teacher and student autonomy can lead to more invigorating school experiences for students and more advanced achievement (McNeil, 1988c). Thus, what happens in schools is shaped by the tension between the conflicting goals of educating students and controlling or processing them. Many times the controlling atmosphere in schools may be the result of pressures imposed on school administrators from state education departments, boards of education, and various special interest groups. They are also governed by school codes and regulations imposed by state legislatures as well as national imperatives designed to manipulate schools through funding inducements. These influences may be contradictory, coercive, and sometimes counter-productive. School administrators may find themselves unable to encourage sufficient teacher and student autonomy if they feel unable to resist such pressures.

One way to manage students is through high-stakes tests that must be passed at specified levels. The purpose of these tests is to stimulate greater adherence to national standards, but in reality these tests may actually be a threat to standards (Merrow, 2001). The use of high-stakes tests have produced extensive "teaching to the test," along with greatly undermining curriculum quality and discriminating against various groups of students (Clinchy, 2001; McNeil, 2000). Some teachers actually teach subjects included on the test rather than the ordinary components of the courses for which they have been trained. In some cases, teachers and school administrators have blatantly cheated in an effort to increase student scores. This is an especially potent problem when retaining one's job is contingent on test results (Merrow, 2001).

High-stakes testing not only stimulates undesirable excesses from teachers and administrators, but it limits student learning opportunities. First, the focus on tests greatly diminishes the breadth and fullness of the curriculum. Second, the mandates of testing limit the decision-making opportunities for students. Third, test administration conditions students to follow instruction and respond in prescribed ways instead of promoting attitudes of investigation and inquiry. Fourth, students lose the potential for excellence. Fifth, there is little assurance that high-stakes tests, with their focus on acquiring information, are valid assessments of life preparation. Sixth, high-stakes testing covers a narrow range of measures that do not include many of the valid interests and abilities of students.

In preparing for high-stakes tests, an inordinate amount of time is devoted to test preparation that could more profitably be used to provide students with a wide range of critical learning opportunities (Meier, 2002). Achievements regarding many of these experiences cannot be validly measured by multiple-choice test items, the preferred testing format for high-stakes tests. Thus, school experiences tend to focus exclusively on what can be simply measured rather than on what teachers have traditionally felt students ought to learn.

Problem-solving and decision-making skills are particularly useful, not only for adult life, but also for current use. Many of the problems youth face require greater decision-making prowess than they possess, as shown by the poor decisions students make both in school and outside its walls. For example, far too many young people are involved in gang activity, sexual promiscuity, and poor academic application, along with drug trafficking and use. Many of these activities may be simple rebellion, but it is also clear that many youth do not understand the implications and consequences of such behavior. Little effort is apparently devoted to planning life experiences toward defensible and desirable ends. The hallmark of good decision-making skill is a plan of life that has been consistently organized around long-term goals that have personal meaning for the individual and that provide for a lifetime of satisfying, carefully thought out experiences and consequences.

Prescriptive living robs life of its zest. School experiences that require a narrow range of prescribed learning in which students see little personal, practical use tends to dull learning as an important life experience. Learning is inherent in humans and central to life experience. However, its continued importance is a function of how free the individual feels to direct his or her own learning. Because preparation for high-stakes tests is prescriptive in the extreme, students can become conditioned to a way of learning that has little motivation aside from passing a test they judge to have limited usefulness. Humans naturally engage in investigation and inquiry in approaching life's problems. This learning orientation is personally satisfying as well as instructive and useful. Often problems are unpredictable and complex, as well as varying from time to time. Limiting preparation to prescriptive approaches is far less valid than providing experiences that promote more creativity and self-judgment.

Excellence, rather than minimum achievement levels, should be the goal of education. However, high-stakes testing is devoted to helping all students achieve minimum standards. Unfortunately, for many students achieving minimums is far below their ability. However, when minimums are emphasized, particularly in a system that allows little freedom and limits personal incentives, capable students are likely to achieve at levels far below their potential (Glasser, 1990). Minimums thus become maximums, as there is little reason to do more. Students are robbed of opportunities to achieve a true sense of accomplishment. They may go away either feeling cheated or deceived into thinking they are more capable than they really are. Students should have an opportunity to do their very best and to recognize that academic achievement as significant.

Life is not a matter of test taking. Tests are often criticized for not representing a valid assessment of life preparation. High-stakes testing makes this criticism all the more potent. In the desire to construct tests that are easy to score, instruments have been created that are devoted less to life skills and more to memorized facts (Meier, 2002). Life preparation should primarily focus on skill development and the acquisition of information used to solve personally relevant problems. In addition, they would be learned within a real context by helping students use what was learned in valid life experiences (Glasser, 1986).

The range of students' interests is much broader than those included in high-stakes tests. However, the legitimacy of any particular interest or skill is inherently determined by whether or not it is included on the tests. Not only does this limit what is considered valid, but it can possibly reduce the extent of a student's success in taking the exam, particularly if the individual has devoted any substantial time to his or her interests away from test subjects. Thus, students are penalized for following after their inherent interests and forced to pursue goals with less meaning, thereby emphasizing test-taking purposes rather than enlarging personal capacity. Such forced restrictions have obvious detriments for life in a democratic society.

QUESTIONS FOR REFLECTION

1. What can be expected from high-stakes testing and test-driven curricula as compared with what might be anticipated when schools use teacher-made tests to assess student achievement and when teachers have sufficient autonomy to make their own decisions regarding curricula and instruction?

2. What is the role a school administrator might take to empower teachers given the effect of excessive control on teachers and students and the pressures often imposed on school administrators by state education departments, state legislators, special interest groups, and the federal government?

NATIONAL TEACHING STANDARDS

Teachers believe in the dignity and worth of all their students and the potential that exists with each one of them.

Autonomy as the Basis for Motivation

When Nathaniel Shaler went to study with Professor Louis Agassiz, he learned important lessons regarding the motivation to learn as well as the meaning of excellence, which apply not only to university students but to secondary level students as well. In their first meeting, Professor Agassiz sat Nathaniel Shaler down in front of a rusty tin pan containing a small fish. Shaler was instructed to study it, but on no occasion talk to anyone concerning it, nor read anything relating to fishes until he had permission to do so. When Shaler inquired as to what was expected, he was told to find out what he could without damaging the specimen. He was further told that, when he had finished, Professor Agassiz would question him. Shaler worked on the specimen for most of an hour, thinking he had completely compassed the fish and learned what there was to know. He consequently appeared before Professor Agassiz with the intention of providing a summary report and getting on with things. But the professor, who was always within call, concerned himself no further with Shaler for that day, nor the next, nor for a week.

Shaler was left with a distressing set of circumstances that he suspected involved a game being played out for specific purposes. He eventually realized that he was being covertly watched, so he set his wits to work upon the fish endlessly and in the course of a hundred hours or so thought he had done an excessive amount of study—at least a hundred times as much as seemed possible at the start. He got interested in finding out how the scales went in series, then examined their shape, studied their form and the placement of teeth, and so on. Eventually he felt full of the subject, and he probably expressed the same in his bearing. Yet Agassiz said nothing, and simply expressed a cheery good morning each day. At length, on the seventh day, the question came—"Well?"—to which Shaler proceeded for an hour to express all he knew about the fish. At the end of an hour's recital, Agassiz walked away saying, "That is not right."

It was clear to Shaler at that point that the game was to find out whether or not he was capable of doing hard work and seeking excellence continuously without the support of a teacher. The result was to induce Shaler to work harder. He went at the task anew. He discarded his first notes, and in another week of 10-hour days achieved results that astonished him and seemed to satisfy his mentor. However, there was no trace of praise in Agassiz's words or manner. He signified acceptance by placing before Shaler a half of a peck of bones, telling him to see what he could make of them, with no further directions as a guide. He soon found that the bones were from about half a dozen fishes of different species. He spent two months or more fitting the separate bones together in their proper order, with no more help than an occasional remark coming from Agassiz that something was not right. When he finished with the bones, Shaler set upon a study of a large number of fish specimens preserved in alcohol, which represented about 20 species of side-swimmers.

Through this new form of study Shaler reached a sense of power in his learning that he had never before achieved and that he never forgot. The experience forged greater thoroughness in his work and provided a new standard of excellence. After he had thus prepared himself, Shaler was permitted to read and interact with others. After this substantial investment in self-directed learning, his mind was prepared to interact with the views of others without being easily turned from his own. In this process Shaler found what he thought was a discrepancy in the knowledge of his mentor. One of the species he had studied had cycloid scales on one side and ctenoid on the other. He planned to take malicious pleasure in exhibiting his find to Agassiz, expecting to repay in part the humiliation the professor had inflicted on Shaler's conceit. To his question as to how to classify the nondescript species, Agassiz replied as though to validate the excellence of his student's independent work, "My boy, there are now two of us who know that." That exchange inducted Shaler into a collegial relationship with his mentor that Agassiz built upon in the coming months by encouraging an even greater level of learning independence (Cooper, 1917).

QUESTIONS FOR REFLECTION

1. Compare traditional teaching, characterized by knowledge transmission, to Nathaniel Shaler's experience with Professor Louis Agassiz. What are the most likely outcomes of these two different approaches to teaching in terms of excellence?

2. To what extent can the model of teaching used by Professor Agassiz be used with high school students? What modifications might be necessary?

Professor Agassiz's story reveals the strategic prominence of the drive for competence as a motivating factor in learning. This experience illustrates a common misconception of the nature of excellence and the work required to achieve it. School experiences are usually provided to students without much input from them. With learning parameters being defined by teachers, students often not only resist teacher expectations, but fail to realize anything near the level of competence possible (Glasser, 1998). The longer children are in school, the more recalcitrant they become in clinging to low levels of accomplishment. They can become content with mediocrity. In addition, they no doubt would be as surprised as Nathaniel Shaler was at the thoroughness and effort required to achieve excellence. Such experiences show the connection between accomplishment and motivation, particularly when what is achieved is self-directed. They also show teachers that their students' complacent acceptance of reinforced mediocrity is resistant to change so that, if efforts are made to modify these conditions, sufficient time and patience must be allowed, along with responsibility-oriented teaching. Teachers who undertake the difficult task of deprogramming students who have adopted minimal expectations of themselves will find considerable resistance. Not only will students be reluctant, but school practices and policies will not be supportive.

It is not possible to substantially alter the false perceptions of students by simply pointing out that their views are unfounded, wrong, misguided, or inconsistent. The basis for these false definitions and consequent self-fulfilling prophesies are deeply rooted in individual and group norms and are difficult for students to recognize and change (Banks, 2000). Instead, the situation in which students operate must be substantially changed. As with Nathaniel Shaler, the conditions that led to the misconception about quality have to be eliminated. It must become impossible for mediocre performances to be acceptable; otherwise, the self-fulfilling prophesy cycle cannot be broken (Wilkins, 1976). As William Glasser

(1990) has explained, students believe they are capable of doing work of much higher quality in class than they ever actually accomplish. All but a few admit that they have never done it and have no plans to do it in the future. They have become comfortable with low quality because nothing else has been expected of them. Most behavior stems from efforts to satisfy our needs. Students must find that low performance interferes with satisfying their need for competence. This can be accomplished only when the acceptable level of accomplishment is the best of which each student is capable.

Motivation depends not only on meeting challenges and demonstrating excellence, but on choice and collaboration as well (Turner & Meyer, 1995). Choice is particularly important to adolescents. Adolescence is characterized by a sudden drive for independence as opposed to a gradual one, and its impact is immense, particularly in the area of self-discovery. When these inclinations are suppressed, the individual commonly manifests excessive aggressiveness and intolerance (Norton, 1970). There is nothing new about the idea that students should be permitted to participate, individually and collectively, in making decisions about curricula and classroom management. It has long been advocated and carried out in progressive, democratic, open, free, experimental, or alternative schools. In these schools, and sometimes in regular public schools, such practices as constructivist learning, holistic learning, learner-centered curricula, discovery-based science, or authentic assessment are carried out in an effort to more fully empower children by providing them extensive decision-making opportunities. Yet, despite the fact that self-directed learning is not a particularly novel idea, it has not been extensively employed, despite having received considerable support from research (Eccles et al., 1991).

Why is it so important for youth to decide what and how they learn and determine the conditions under which they do it? How might opportunities to be more self-directed be provided? What are the common barriers to student self-determination? What can be done to eliminate the irrational limits commonly placed on student decision making? These questions require answers, as they are too important to be ignored. They have critical and strategic implications for students' attitudes toward school as well as their achievements.

Although Americans live in a democratic society, little is done to represent democracy in the schools (Smith, 2001). Yet, students are expected to assume lives of democratic involvement once they leave school, even though they haven't had sufficient opportunities to learn the nature and virtue of democratic living in practical terms. This learning experience might be accomplished if youth become active participants in their own education. At this period in their lives they not only desire greater independence, but they also crave interpersonal experiences. Also during this period they spend time with their age mates and with teachers who can provide appropriate conditions for learning.

Nothing deprives youth of motivation to learn more than being powerless to regulate themselves. The inherent desire for free choice helps students through difficult and challenging situations. When teachers provide all the direction, students who face challenging circumstances are more inclined to shift responsibility to their teachers and assume a role of resistance. However, according to Kohn (1993), self-determination provides at least the five following benefits that contribute to greater motivation and an elevated sense of well-being.

First, there are psychological as well as general health benefits. For example, individuals who rarely become physically ill despite having to deal with considerable stress tend to be those who feel more personal control over what happens to them. Adequate emotional adjustment depends on achieving a strong sense of self-determination. However, in contrast, few conditions lead more reliably to depression and other forms of psychological distress than feelings of helplessness (Seligman, 1995).

Second, providing children more opportunities for self-regulation promotes greater levels of responsibility. It is ironic that adults commonly insist that youth refuse to take responsibility for their own behavior, yet provide few if any opportunities for this kind of growth. To learn responsibility, children must be given experiences that provide them the necessary freedom and decision-making opportunities to develop responsibility. Not only is lack of free choice in decision making a deterrent to learning responsibility, but it foments rebellion and stimulates irresponsibility. If we truly value democracy we need to prepare youth to productively participate in a democratic culture. The most obvious way to do this is to teach them decision-making skills and help them acquire an inclination to use these skills. The important values associated with democratic living cannot be successfully promoted in the absence of choice (Kohn, 1993). Autonomy thus provides the necessary motivation to thrive in democratic communities.

Third, motivation toward academic achievement depends upon students having sufficient decision-making power. One's enthusiasm quickly evaporates when one is controlled. Waning enthusiasm robs students of potential achievements, as their motivation is cut short by the stifling effects of coercion. Concerns about the effects of coercive school management and the potential for greater motivation under conditions of increased self-determination led researchers to conduct the Eight-Year Study, where 30 high schools were encouraged to develop innovative programs that incorporated democratic principles. The students in these programs, who were studied during their four years of high school, as well as four years into their university careers, showed significantly more motivation and success than their traditionally trained counterparts (Aiken, 1942). Other research has shown that student choice motivates students to work more efficiently and effectively on their school work, be more creative, miss less school, score better on national tests of basic skills, have increased reasoning skills, and be more persistent in their school work (Kohn, 1993). All these provide evidence that students are indeed motivated by being self-directed.

Fourth, sharing decision-making power with students provides benefits for teachers as well. Teachers report that their jobs become a good deal more interesting when they collaborate with students about what happens in the classroom. In addition, with students making more decisions for themselves, teachers experience less need to monitor and supervise them. There is less need to motivate students when their motivation comes from within.

Fifth, allowing youth to make decisions is more respectful and consistent with the basic values to which most of us claim to subscribe. It is also more in tune with the way students are expected to eventually interact with others in their communities. Thus, it provides a way to authentically relate to youth and does not necessitate the compromise of basic democratic values with its inherent hypocrisy. Teachers can feel a greater sense of motivation as they experience youth growing toward increased responsibility. This in turn can increase student motivation.

QUESTIONS FOR REFLECTION

1. Why in the schools of our democratic society, where schools are supposed to prepare children and youth for democratic living, are there so many restrictions and so much control with a clear lack of modeling for democracy?

2. What do you believe could be done to provide students more clear and consistent models of democratic living that they could readily practice as part of their life in the schools?

 ## *Decision Points*

Design and administer a survey for teachers and students in a secondary school to use in determining their perceptions regarding the degree of control versus autonomy they believe exists in their school. Make a list of changes in school operations which the data indicate might increase teacher and student autonomy.

Promoting Autonomous Learning

To what extent is responsible autonomy valued in a community? Can it be fostered? Is the school a logical place to promote its development? These questions are central in considering whether or not to organize school experiences that promote autonomy. It seems self-evident that in a democratic society autonomy should be highly valued. In fact, the development of responsible autonomy should be the primary goal of such a society, because its perpetuation depends on the extent to which citizens have both the skill and inclination to live autonomously as responsible community members. A person accepts this role by engaging in activities of the mind, such as choosing, deciding, deliberating, reflecting, planning, and judging, and has a complex understanding of these processes while engaging in them. Autonomous individuals must have both independence from external authority and at the same time mastery of themselves and their own intellectual powers (DeVries, Hildebrandt, & Zan, 2000). Not only must there be freedom from the dictates and interferences of others, but there must also be freedom from disabling conflicts or lack of coordination between various elements of personality that might fail to bring sufficient logic and judgment to decision making (Gibbs, 1979).

The following qualities define an autonomous person.

- The individual wonders about things and asks about them with a sense of his or her right to ask, think about, and justify various events and happenings that could quite naturally be taken for granted.
- The individual refuses to agree or comply with what others suggest when these suggestions seem critically unacceptable.
- The individual defines what is wanted or in his or her personal best interest as distinct from what may be conventionally accepted.
- The individual conceives of goals, policies, and plans independent of others and of pressure that might be imposed to obtain compliance.
- The individual chooses among alternative proposals and ideas, making deliberate choices consistent with personal purposes.

- The individual forms personal opinions on various topics of interest.
- The individual governs behavior and attitudes through a process of deliberate decision making, based on careful consideration of personally accepted principles and ideals (Dearden, 1975).

Thus, an autonomous person must not only be free from others' coercive influence, but he or she must also be free from personal compulsions and rigidities. Autonomy implies a responsiveness to the environment and an ability to make creative and unique responses to situations as they arise rather than being burdened by patterns and stereotypical responses that are established through one's past experiences. Mature autonomy requires both **emotional independence**—a condition of freedom from continual and pressing needs of reassurance and approval from others—and **instrumental independence**—the ability to carry on activities and skillfully deal with problems without needing help from others. Simultaneously, the individual relishes interdependence, recognizing that one receives benefits from society by contributing to it and that personal rights have a corollary social responsibility (Chickering, 1969).

Teachers need to develop specific plans and strategies to help students become more responsibly autonomous and self-directing. They must then give a high priority to these plans. Otherwise students are unlikely to achieve this important goal. It is possible for students to get this kind of training in various aspects of their schooling. They can, for example, help make decisions about course content and learning activities, as well as about discipline and management procedures. They can also be actively involved in deliberations regarding the school's extracurricular program.

Student autonomy does not mean that students should work alone, isolated from others. Rather, it implies that students need experiences coordinating their views with those of others and must learn how to achieve a higher level of personal satisfaction in their learning by becoming involved with other students. In addition, training in responsibility should not be postponed until students are old enough to be expected to act autonomously. Postponing the opportunity to exercise responsibility discourages the development of this capacity (Boud, 1981). Autonomous learning can take place at any level or any age; however, it will not have the same appearance in all situations. Because of its responsibility component and because children become more able decision makers as they develop intellectually, self-guided learning will achieve greater levels of sophistication over time. Children and youth will also acquire better skills for interacting with one another as they are provided opportunities for social growth and development. Intellectual and social growth are key elements in the development of responsible autonomy. The following vignette describing the instruction of middle school children in diagramming sentences illustrates how children can be empowered with greater autonomy.

Ms. Halinski's seventh-grade class was divided into six groups of four or five students each. When they arrived after lunch, she wrote a rather tricky sentence on the chalkboard and gave the groups the task of diagramming it. After this was done, a representative of each group put their group's diagram on the chalkboard. Two of the six diagrams were immediately erased, because they were duplications. Each group then offered arguments either favoring or opposing one or another of the remaining four diagrams. The authors of the various

Ms. Halinski empowers her students by helping them think critically and independently.

diagrams vigorously defended their diagrams in an intense debate that lasted well into the next period. After careful consideration, the class agreed that two of the diagrams were inadequate and had to be erased.

Ms. Halinski then asked if the class wanted her to provide the answer. Some answered "Yes," but others said, "No, because you'll give us the wrong answer just to see if you can trick us!" Ms. Halinski admitted that she planned to do just that. Therefore, the arguments and counter-arguments continued, and the class finally agreed on the superiority of one diagram. They spent another period on that one sentence until they were convinced of the superiority of the final diagram. Many students offered wrong ideas along the way, but Ms. Halinski encouraged them to defend their opinions until they themselves were convinced that their opinions were wrong (Kammi, 1984).

 ## QUESTION FOR REFLECTION

1. What are the potential advantages and disadvantages of employing a teaching method where students are permitted to offer wrong ideas and draw their own conclusions regarding problems and issues?

A debate about the superiority of one idea or another is good because it provides children an opportunity to think critically and assess ideas in relationship to one another. It also encourages students to modify their ideas and conclusions when they are convinced new ones are better. In the previous vignette, the teacher simultaneously tried to foster the development of intellectual and moral autonomy. Youth can develop intellectual and moral autonomy only when all ideas, including wrong ones, are respected and given serious consideration (Noddings, 2002). These kinds of exchanges also help students better comprehend various concepts being considered.

In teaching greater autonomy, it is essential to help students validly assess their own thinking without incrimination. This involves providing students many problems that do not have only one right answer. Even if only a single right answer applies, students should present their current thinking with the knowledge that expressions of their thinking are tentative. All contributions are subject to change at any time without any negative connotation being allowed. Thus, mistaken ideas are subject to change at any time with little or no finality being attached to student contributions. Discussions are to be considered as a time to exchange ideas and build understanding, with modifications in thinking being the norm.

Learning Strategies for Encouraging Autonomy

Students can achieve better self-regulation in their school experiences through a number of strategies. For example, students should learn self-monitoring skills and problem solving to acquire greater self-regulation skill. Self-monitoring involves youth carefully assessing their work to see that it meets the appropriate standards. If students cannot assess their own behavior, they will not be able to responsibly control it. An increase in appropriate behavior can therefore be expected as a consequence of students' self-evaluation. However, youth do not inherently know appropriate standards nor how to apply them in assessing their work. The teacher has a critical role in helping students address the issue of standards, as well as applying them. This involves showing students both poor and excellent examples and discussing the features that distinguish them from one another. Students need to learn how to formulate and employ criteria to make valid judgments and to provide acceptable rationales for their choices.

Specific student learning questions and teacher objectives are essential components of the Self-Determined Learning Model of Instruction (Wehmeyer, Palmer, Agran, Mithang, & Martin, 2000), a comprehensive set of recommendations regarding specific actions teachers may take to encourage students to direct their own learning toward preferred goals. This model is an excellent format for promoting a greater sense of personal responsibility. The first phase is goal setting, designed to have students address issues regarding their learning goals and to have teachers help them answer relevant questions regarding their goals, thereby providing conditions for them to act comprehensively, thoughtfully, and responsibly.

Student Question 1: What do I want to learn?
- Encourage students to identify specific strengths and instructional needs.
- Encourage students to communicate preferences, interests, beliefs, and values.
- Show students how to prioritize their needs and interests.

Student Question 2: What do I know about the particular subject now?
- Have students identify their current knowledge and skills relative to needs.
- Have students identify opportunities for and barriers to learning.

Student Question 3: What must I change to learn what I need to know?
  • Have students determine how to modify constraints on their learning.
  • Have students choose a specific need to address from the prioritized list.
Student Question 4: What can I do to ensure my goal is met?
  • Instruct students how to state their goals and associated criteria for achievement.

As part of Phase 1, teachers teach students how to assess their interests, abilities, and instructional needs. Because this task is likely unfamiliar to students, teachers will need to help them make valid assessments and differentiate between their simple desires and the needs that can be related to fuller, more complex living. Students will also have to learn the basic skills of making choices and solving problems. This involves determining what assumptions may be associated with various proposed courses of action and validating them. Validation involves determining the truthfulness of assumptions and relating this determination to the problem being solved. For example, memorizing the orders of insects in a biology class may be viewed as excellent preparation for college when, in fact, conducting a research project on insects may be more valid. Memorized information will be easily forgotten, but a well-organized project will provide skills essential to conducting a research project at the university.

Phase 2 of the Self-Determined Learning Model of Instruction involves taking action to implement learning goals. Generally students are not only told what to learn but directed by their teachers in the learning process. Students are unlikely, therefore, to know what experiences will provide the most effective means to achieve what they desire. The following strategies are designed to help them take the proper actions to achieve their goals.

Student Question 5: What can I do to find out what I don't know?
  • Help students assess their current knowledge and how it compares with goals.
Student Question 6: What are the obstacles to timely action?
  • Help students determine how to bridge the gap between current status and goals.
Student Question 7: What can I do to remove barriers to learning?
  • Help students identify strategies of instruction which overcome barriers.
  • Help students learn to employ student-directed learning strategies.
  • Provide sufficient support to help students apply their learning strategies.
  • Provide teacher instruction as appropriate and desired by students.
Student Question 8: When is an appropriate time to take action?
  • Encourage students to determine a schedule for their plan of action.
  • Provide resources and time for students to implement plans.
  • Encourage students to consistently monitor their own progress.

In Phase 2, teachers help students learn how to schedule and follow through on plans. As with the action phase, students most likely had adults impose deadlines regarding various learning assignments and projects. Without these directions, youth are prone to flounder and miscalculate appropriate timing for coordinating and sequencing their work.

Phase 3 of the Self-Determined Learning Model of Instruction focuses on the adjustments that have been made to facilitate learning and the students' assessment of these activities. It encourages students to look at what they have learned and how effective their strategies are in removing barriers and supporting effective learning.

> *Student Question 9: What actions have been taken to specifically apply learning strategies?*
> - Encourage students to evaluate their progress toward goal achievement.
>
> *Student Question 10: What barriers have been removed and what has the impact been?*
> - Help students assess the effectiveness of removing barriers and promoting success.
>
> *Student Question 11: What has been the personal impact on me regarding what was learned?*
> - Help students examine progress in terms of their goals.
> - Encourage students to determine if their goals need modification.
> - Have students assess their action plans for effectiveness.
> - Collaborate with students regarding necessary changes in their action plans.
>
> *Student Question 12: Have I found out what I really wanted to know?*
> - Have students assess the usefulness of goals achieved.

Assessment and modification are the key features of Phase 3. In addition, it is important for students to determine the true value of what they have learned and to assess its usefulness to them in achieving their overall goals in life. This implies that a careful evaluation be made not only of what was achieved and how effectively it was done, but also of how these results relate to overall goals. In the process of learning, new understandings often occur that bring new insights to learning and its purposes.

As they implement strategies for increased student autonomy, teachers need to be aware of the potential for misunderstanding. Even when the purpose of educational experiences is to encourage greater agency for students, the message is sometimes communicated that the teacher is still in charge and that very little opportunity exists for students to really become self-governing. Apparently, even when teachers claim to value autonomy and employ strategies to encourage its development, students report that it does not exist in the classroom (Edwards & Allred, 1990).

QUESTIONS FOR REFLECTION

1. What are the likely difficulties you might encounter as a teacher implementing the Self-Determined Learning Model of Instruction? What would you do to avoid these problems?

2. What do teachers do that might communicate to their students that the teacher is still in charge, even though students have been told they are to experience autonomy in their learning?

NATIONAL TEACHING STANDARDS

Teachers recognize that learning and behavior are connected to particular settings or contexts. They strive to provide multiple contexts in which to promote student abilities.

Autonomy and Moral Learning Communities

Perhaps the best hope for achieving a comfortable relationship between authority and responsibility in the schools is through learning communities. No doubt authority will always be vested in educators who carry the important responsibility of providing instructional leadership. However, one critical mistake often made in such a system is to assume that the person in authority is responsible for ensuring that learning takes place. This shifts responsibility away from students, who ultimately must assume this role. The purpose of authority in learning communities is not to control participants and insist on predetermined goals or force students to achieve them. Instead, that person is to take on a role of participant and use his or her skills to help others undertake better leadership and decision making within a democratic atmosphere.

Students appear to jealously guard their freedom and resist their teachers when personal freedom is at risk. It is, therefore, essential that teachers attempt to promote better group cohesiveness, helpfulness, and social responsibility so that students do not feel pressured to respond as directed. Human beings apparently have a built-in resistance to control by others along with a strong desire to be self-directed. Yet, there is no question that teachers must be the ultimate authority in the classroom. They cannot simply pass authority on to students and ignore questionable activities initiated by students. At the same time they cannot treat youth in a "heavy handed" way, depriving them of the freedom necessary for growth and development in a democratic society. A balance must be struck with teachers *gradually empowering* students to the greatest extent possible, given their growth in judgment and responsible decision making.

Not only must students have an appropriate environment in which to develop personal autonomy and accompanying social responsibility, but they must also have achieved a sufficient level of independence from authority and adequate mastery of themselves as well as their power of thinking and decision making. Students must have the skills of choosing, deciding, deliberating, reflecting, and judging if they are to take full advantage of the freedom necessary to develop greater independent judgment along with social responsibility.

The truly autonomous person operates comfortably with independence as well as providing a strong personal flavor to group interactions and appropriate interdependence. He or she must work out a well-orchestrated viewpoint and course of action that incorporates the necessity for personal rights to have a related social responsibility. To promote these behaviors, students must not only acquire appropriate attitudes, but also decisive actions. This involves instruction in which they are coached to feature their point of view without backing down prematurely and to formulate their own views and goals, which they are taught how to defend and expertly implement. Sensitivity is required of teachers to help students gain genuine insight into how personal autonomy is inextricably connected to social discourse and action. Teachers need to ensure that students stay focused on thoughtful independent actions that enhance group growth and development, as well as achieve these personal needs that can only be supplied through responsible group participation. In connection with these recommendations, it is important to note that people work with greater commitment toward collective goals than individual ones (Csikszentmihalyi, 1990). Thus, communities provide a powerful learning configuration in which to increase both need satisfaction and commitment.

QUESTION FOR REFLECTION

1. How can teachers help students to understand and apply themselves to the task of increased personal autonomy within a responsible social context?

 ## *Decision Points*

1. With a group of four other students, role-play a problem-solving session in which participants attempt to determine whether or not school uniforms should be implemented as the only appropriate attire in school.
2. In a group, formulate a strategy to teach a group-determined topic that you believe would help students satisfy their needs and promote greater commitment.
3. With a group of four other students, role-play the following situations and attempt to come to a conclusion as you think secondary school students might:
   a. A close friend admits to you that he or she has stolen something from a store and wants you to remain quiet about it. Revealing the theft would put your friendship in jeopardy.
   b. You are told that you can become a member of an elite group of students in school if you will relinquish your friendship with another student. This friendship started just a month earlier as an assignment from a teacher in school.
   c. You are asked to discuss the value of considering honesty as having gray areas in some situations rather than being black or white.
   d. A friend asks you to make an assessment of the clothes she is wearing, and you realize she is simply seeking a compliment. Determine how the values of honesty and courtesy would enter into the response you would make to her request.

 ## *Reflections About Self*

1. Think about your own experiences in school. To what extent do you believe you have received sufficient freedom to maximize your personal growth and development?
2. What experiences have you had in school that were more restrictive than needed?
3. What do you believe is the appropriate level of autonomy that should be provided to students in the school?

CENTRAL IDEAS

1. The desire for personal autonomy is inherent, and abridging it may cause student rebellion.
2. Although autonomy appears to be a divisive element in a community setting, it is in fact essential to individual growth and action in smooth functioning communities.
3. Responsible autonomy depends on the development of maturity, which can come about only as youth experience sufficient freedom while learning to make wise choices.
4. Autonomy is positively related to achievement, effective problem solving, and motivation to learn.

5. Responsible autonomy can be enhanced through solving personal problems and being involved in making decisions regarding the curriculum and learning activities.
6. Autonomous individuals engage in distinctive thought processes which distinguish them as independent, responsible group members.
7. Autonomy is essential for moral development.

REFERENCES

Aiken, W. M. (1942). *The story of the eight-year study.* New York: Harper.

Banks, J. A. (2000). The social construction of differences and the quest for educational equality. In R. Brandt (Ed.), *Education in a new era* (pp. 21–45). Arlington, VA: Association for Supervision and Curriculum Development.

Boud, D. (1981). Toward student responsibility for learning. In D. Boud (Ed.), *Developing student autonomy in learning* (pp. 21–37). New York: Nichols.

Chickering, A. W. (1969). *Education and identity.* San Francisco: Jossey-Bass.

Clinchy, E. (2001). Needed: A new educational civil rights movement. *Phi Delta Kappan, 82* (7), 493–498.

Coombe, K. (1999). Ethics and the learning community. In R. Retallick, B. Cocklin, & K. Coombe (Eds.), *Learning communities in education: Issues, strategies and contexts.* New York: Routledge.

Cooper, L. (1917). *Louis Agassiz as a teacher.* Ithaca, NY: The Comestock Publishing Co.

Cronbach, L. (1963). *Educational psychology.* New York: Harcourt, Brace and World.

Csikszentmihalyi, M. (1990). *Flow: The psychology of optimal experience.* New York: Harper & Row.

Darling-Hammond, L. (1997). *The right to learn: A blueprint for creating schools that work.* San Francisco: Jossey-Bass.

Dearden, R. F. (1975). Autonomy as an educational ideal. In S. C. Brown (Ed.), *Philosophers discuss education* (pp. 3–18). London: Macmillan.

DelBello, M. S. (1988). Fostering independent workers: A parent's view. *Gifted Child Today, 11* (May-June), 45–46.

DeVries, R., Hildebrandt, C., & Zan, B. (2000). Constructivist early education for moral development. *Early Education & Development, 11* (1), 9–24.

Eccles, J. S., Bachanan, C. M., Flanagan, C., Fuligni, A., Midgley, C., & Yee, D. (1991). Control versus autonomy during early adolescence. *Journal of Social Issues, 47* (4), 53–68.

Edwards, C. H. (1995). *A systematic approach to instructional design* (2nd ed.). Champaign, IL: Stipes Publishing L.L.C.

Edwards, C. H., & Allred, W. E. (1990). Autonomy in the classroom: The contrast between teachers' beliefs and students' perceptions. *Illinois School Research and Development, 26* (3), 186–196.

Gibbs, B. (1979). Autonomy and authority in education. *Journal of Philosophy of Education, 13,* 119–132.

Glasser, W. (1984). *Control theory: A new explanation of how we control our lives.* New York: Harper & Row.

Glasser, W. (1990). *The quality school: Managing students without coercion.* New York: Harper & Row.

Glasser, W. (1998). *Choice theory.* New York: Harper Collins.

Jelinek, J. J. (1979). *A curriculum proposal for the development of maturity in students.* Arizona State University, Educational Research Information Center #ED 176286.

Kamii, C. (1984). Autonomy: The aim of education envisioned by Piaget. *Phi Delta Kappan, 65* (6), 410–415.

Kohn, A. (1993). Choices for children: Why and how to let students decide. *Phi Delta Kappan, 75* (1), 8–20.

Linder, R. W. (1994). Self-regulated learning in correctional education students and its implications for instruction. *Journal of Correctional Education, 45* (3), 122–126.

Linder, R. W., & Harris, B. (1993). Self-regulated learning: Its assessment and instructional implications. *Educational Research Quarterly, 16* (2), 29–37.

McNeil, L. M. (1988a). Contradictions of control, part 1: Administrators and teachers. *Phi Delta Kappan, 69* (5), 333–339.

McNeil, L. M. (1988b). Contradictions of control, part 2: Teachers, students, and curriculum. *Phi Delta Kappan, 69* (6), 433–438.

McNeil, L. M. (1988c). Contradictions of control, part 3: Contradictions of reform. *Phi Delta Kappan, 69* (7), 478–485.

McNeil, L. M. (2000). Creating new inequalities: Contradictions of reform. *Phi Delta Kappan, 81* (10), 729–734.

Meier, D. (2002). *In schools we trust: Creating communities of learning in an era of testing and standardization.* Boston: Beacon Press.

Merrow, J. (2001). Undermining standards. *Phi Delta Kappan, 82* (9), 653–659.

Noddings, N. (2002). *Educating moral people: A caring alternative to character education.* New York: Teachers College Press.

Norton, D. L. (1970). The rites of passage from dependence to autonomy. *School Review, 79* (November), 19–41.

Osborn, R. J., & Wittrock, M. C. (1983). Learning science: A generative process. *Science Education, 67,* 489–508.

Phillips, D. C. (2000). An opinionated account of constructivist landscape. In D. C. Phillips (Ed.), *Constructivism in education; Opinions and second opinions on controversial issues.* Ninety-ninth yearbook of the National Society for the Study of Education (pp. 1–16). Chicago: The University of Chicago Press.

Rooney, K. J., & Hallahan, D. P. (1988). The effects of self-monitoring on adult behavior and student independence. *Learning Disabilities Research, 3* (2), 88–93.

Seligman, M. E. P. (1995). *The optimistic child.* New York: Harper Collins.

Sergiovanni, T. J. (1992). *Moral leadership: Getting to the heart of school improvement.* San Francisco: Jossey-Bass.

Sergiovanni, T. J. (1994). *Building community in school.* San Francisco: Jossey-Bass.

Sergiovanni, T. J. (2000). *The life world of leadership: Creating culture, community and personal meaning in our schools.* San Francisco: Jossey-Bass.

Shaw, D. G., & Buhler, J. H. (1984). What's the capital of North Dakota? *Educational Leadership, 41* (5), 90.

Smith, F. (2001). Just a matter of time. *Phi Delta Kappan, 82* (8), 573–576.

Trowbridge, L. W., Bybee, R. W., & Powell, J. C. (2000). *Teaching secondary school science: Strategies for developing scientific literacy.* Upper Saddle River, NJ: Merrill/Prentice Hall.

Turner, J. C., & Meyer, D. K. (1995). Motivating students to learn: Lessons from fifth grade math class. *Middle School Journal, 27,* 18–25.

Wayson, W., & Pinnell, G. (1982). Creating a living curriculum for teaching self-discipline. In D. Duke (Ed.), *Helping teachers manage classrooms.* Alexandria, VA: Association for Supervision and Curriculum Development.

Wehmeyer, M. L., Palmer, S. B., Agran, M., Mithang, D. E., & Martin, J. E. (2000). Promoting casual agency: The self-determined learning model of instruction. *Exceptional Children, 66* (4), 439–453.

Wilkins, W. E. (1976). The concept of self-fulfilling prophesy. *Sociology of Education, 49,* 175–183.

Williams, J. E. (1996). The relation between efficacy for self-regarded learning and domain specific academic performance. *Journal of Research and Development in Education, 29* (2), 77–80.

How Students Learn

CHAPTER OBJECTIVES

This chapter is designed to help you

1. Describe common school practices that limit learning.
2. Apply various models of learning to teaching.
3. Understand the differences between behavioristic and constructivist learning theories and indicate the kinds of learning activities that are consistent with each.
4. Explain the nature of true inquiry learning and the role of teachers in promoting this kind of learning.
5. Explain how constructivism is consistent with learning in communities.
6. Describe how the purposes of education are determined and how standardized achievement tests affect this process.

Students learn naturally through self-guided inquiry.

7. Explain how individuals construct knowledge and make sense of their world and how teachers can help students acquire an accurate picture of reality.

8. Describe the nature of student learning styles and create learning activities for students that cater to their particular learning style, as well as being consistent to their particular blend of multiple intelligences.

INTRODUCTION

Effective learning is a continuing problem in schools. Ordinarily the question is asked, "How can a teacher get children to learn?" The way this question is commonly worded contains a substantial part of the problem: It implies that students won't learn on their own volition, and that they have to be made to learn in one way or another by their teachers.

When teachers try to motivate their classes, they assume that students are not inherently interested in learning, or at least they are not interested in learning what is provided in school. It is also assumed that what students may choose to learn would not be legitimate in a school setting, or that teachers, curriculum committees, or other authoritative groups are the only justifiable source of school curricula. There are various levels of input regarding school curricula, ranging from state curriculum committees who provide approved textbook lists and lesson objectives to school curriculum committees and individual teachers. Even on the national level, school learning experiences are guided by national standards and benchmarks (National Research Council, 1996). The various standards and curriculum guides, along with so-called "teacher proof" instructional materials, often deny teachers opportunities to make curricula decisions. It is also rare for students to have a role in determining the curriculum, despite the fact that they are the ones who do the learning. However, they are motivated by helping to choose what they do in school. Regarding student interest and motivation, many educators make two fatal errors. First, they do not capitalize on the intrinsic interests of students. Second, they assume students will abandon personal desires and interests in favor of those provided by the teacher. Perhaps in some cases students may abandon their own motives in favor of those supplied by teachers, if they find these motives sufficiently meaningful or useful (e.g., they enhance the chances of getting into college). However, examining the interests of students and then empowering them to make decisions about their own learning simplifies this process, while at the same time supplying more powerful motivation for learning. Students often resist even the most logical and useful school experiences because they have had little or no role in making decisions about what they learn. School learning will be impeded less if students are allowed to supply input and if their input is taken seriously in making decisions regarding learning.

Some additional practices that impede learning include excessively structured curricula and classroom procedures. In addition, poor learning conditions are created when students' needs are not met. This is particularly true when rules are enforced through punishment and when opportunities for students to receive acceptance and credibility are denied them. Focusing on competition instead of community learning often sets students up for failure and keeps them from becoming competent learners who are valued by their teachers and classmates.

Another school procedure that limits authentic learning is content memorization. Memorizing facts and concepts assumes that information is simply absorbed in the form given. This, of course, is not true. However, the practice of students memorizing facts and then being tested continues. It is also assumed that students will remember and apply the memorized facts as needed months and years later. It has long been known that memorized facts and principles are not retained long unless they are associated with some useful purpose for which students desire to apply them (Cronbach, 1963). Not only must the information learned be purposeful, but it must also be learned in a manner that articulates with students' constructivist learning processes (Osborne & Wittrock, 1983).

Mr. Davenport determined that his students couldn't learn. He believed he had tried everything possible to encourage learning, and still his students found it difficult to understand complex concepts. They openly resisted his teaching, even when he carefully explained how they would need to know the concepts he taught later in their lives. He was particularly outspoken about how college-bound students could make use of the information from his class. In addition to telling students how useful his class was, he also tried to motivate them by using various rewards, including an emphasis on grades. It appeared many of his students did not care about grades; at least, they made no attempt to learn when he threatened them with lower grades for not performing. There were only a few who seemed to be motivated by grades; they were the ones who routinely earned "A"s. Mr. Davenport found himself interacting more with high-achieving students and ignoring the less-able members of the class. He told himself it wouldn't do any good to spend more time with the underperformers anyway; they didn't seem to have either the necessary ability or the interest.

Mr. Davenport tried various kinds of punishment to get low-achieving students to perform. He assigned them extra work when they wasted time in class, kept them after class, and had them come in after school. He also wrote letters home to their parents and made quite a few phone calls to the parents of the more disruptive students. He occasionally yelled at students and routinely belittled them publicly, hoping to embarrass them into studying. The rewards he offered seemed to do the most good, particularly when he provided some tangible reinforcement like candy. He also offered rewards such as leaving for lunch early or playing games in class if students finished their work early. Eventually he gave up this program because it was costing him too much to buy candy and because a parent of one of his students requested that Mr. Davenport not bribe his son any longer. He also noticed that after a while, students seemed more interested in receiving the reinforcers than in doing the work required to get them. He occasionally heard students joke about his reward program when they thought he could not hear them. As time passed, some students lost all interest in rewards; a few hard-to-manage students never were significantly influenced by them. Eventually students seemed much more interested in talking to one another or disrupting class in other ways than earning rewards. Observing this, Mr. Davenport allowed them to talk to friends on specified occasions if they conformed to his rules and were productive in class. This didn't work well because students talked with their friends whenever they wanted anyway.

QUESTIONS FOR REFLECTION

1. Identify mistakes you believe Mr. Davenport made in managing his classes. What is there about these practices you believe created classroom problems?

2. Compare student interests with forms of motivation typically supplied by teachers to promote learning. How well do these map on to each other?

3. What can teachers do to create school activities which correspond to students' interests?

 Decision Points

Create a list of 15 teacher objectives in your teaching field. Rate them as you think students might in terms of their importance to students personally. Use the following scale: (1) very important, (2) somewhat important, (3) limited importance, and (4) unimportant. Then have a group of high school students rate the same set of objectives; compare your ratings with theirs.

NATIONAL TEACHING STANDARDS

Teachers use their knowledge of individual and social learning theory to form their decisions about how they teach. In doing so, they integrate this with their own personal theories of learning that they have acquired from their own practice.

Learning Purposes

Learning purposes are in part defined by the nature of learning itself. Although the learning process is not usually the way learning purposes are determined, it cannot be ignored because of its strategic importance. Ordinarily the objectives held for schooling consist of outcomes defined by various philosophical positions. One of these, **essentialism,** attempts to transmit cultural heritage to the next generation. A second philosophical tradition, **pragmatism,** rejects the usefulness of transmitting the cultural heritage because the future cannot be known; therefore, adherents maintain there is little certainty that the current canon of knowledge will be viable. It advocates training students to use their capacities and to prepare themselves with the skills needed for a broad range of possible adjustments and adaptations. **Reconstructionism,** a third philosophical tradition, points to the need for education to prepare students to reconstruct society and suit it to the ends they desire in the future. Thus, students are not expected to apply old knowledge to the future or simply prepare for conditions that may come; rather, they are expected to become architects of the kind of society they desire. All of these philosophies focus on a desired end result of education, indicating only in a minimum way the virtue of the learning process itself. To be sure, each philosophy dictates a kind of learning approach that articulates with desired ends, but the process of learning is not considered as critical as the final outcomes.

To focus on the "means" rather than the "ends" of education seems antithetical to the need for justifiable purposes. Historically, the means have been of little importance in defining what is educationally valuable. It didn't matter so much how a result was achieved if the end product was acceptable. This kind of thinking allowed the acceptance of educational practices that were highly questionable because, though they held promise for achieving specified outcomes, they also produced unacceptable "side effects." For example, it is hoped that rewarding students for scoring well on examinations may increase future test scores, but rewards can also lead students to dislike the thing for which they receive the reward, namely the content being learned (Kohn, 1993).

Many times the means of instruction are equal to or more important than the ends. This is particularly true with group activities in learning communities. The processes of group development and inquiry learning are examples of the critically important means featured in learning communities. The intention here is not to undermine the importance of conceptual knowledge, but to assert the importance of the learning processes. There is sufficient viable content that can be included when the focus is on the learning processes, meaning the fear that instruction contains insufficient substantive information is not an issue.

When the learning process becomes the central feature of classroom activities, students can be encouraged toward responsible autonomy. They can learn much about the society in which they live by investigating various issues and problems and trying to function as a responsible agent in various deliberations and decisions. If real problems are examined and students acquire a sense of commitment for life in the community, their autonomous learning efforts will help them become skilled problem solvers, expert in assuming various roles in the community. These activities all focus on process, and the skills developed are process skills.

In recent years, schooling has been defined by standardized achievement tests: The purpose of schooling is to pass these tests. This purpose is currently challenging all other previously important goals and objectives. Yet, society appears to continue valuing the more traditional educational purposes and assumes that these objectives are still central to school operations. Unfortunately, they may not be. This illustrates how easy it is to lose sight of purposes and confuse more important outcomes with less important ones. The excessive emphasis on content objectives and the diminution of process goals is an example of this.

 ## QUESTIONS FOR REFLECTION

1. What do you think the purposes of education are? Compare your view with those of some of your peers.

2. In your experience, how carefully do schools follow the purposes you have outlined?

Learning Theory and Teaching Models

Schools have historically emphasized a behavioristic basis for learning. Behaviorism emphasizes the orderly accumulation of facts that have been conceptually organized and presented. Carefully organized information would seem to be easier for students to learn and retain than less well-organized material. Therefore, it is assumed that students can make more meaningful interpretations of facts and concepts if they can visualize them consistently in terms of their relationships. Later, when asked to recall what they have learned, students should simply reconstruct the information as presented.

Behaviorism was challenged by the research of Piaget, which essentially indicated that learning needs to be orchestrated by each individual and that the level of learning depends on a predictable sequence of intellectual development. As defined by Piaget, development depends on growth that is stimulated by efforts to learn. Thus, trying to solve problems using higher mental operations stimulates the growth in capacity to subsequently deal with these problems successfully. Piaget believed humans are internally motivated to make sense of the world in order to suit their own purposes (Piaget, 1950). Thus, teaching becomes a matter of creating conditions that provide students more opportunities for self-direction. Behaviorists, however, conclude that learning must be carefully orchestrated by teachers and that proper understanding requires teachers to present appropriate information and arrange contingencies of reinforcement (Skinner, 1948). In this case, teachers conceptually organize information and present it to students using a variety of strategies.

A number of teaching models apply different levels of student self-direction and have various orientations regarding the learning process. Joyce and Weil (1996) have placed learning models into families including, (1) information processing, (2) personal, (3) behavioral systems, and (4) social. These model families provide a convenient way to visualize different approaches to teaching and provide teachers a way to characterize the purposes and processes of different teaching approaches. In addition, they help teachers achieve considerable flexibility in their teaching.

The Information Processing Family

Information processing focuses on cognition and concept formation. Students are taught to seek and master information, organize it, build and test hypotheses, and apply what they are learning in class to their independent reading and writing, as well as their exploration of themselves and the world around them. Some of the models encourage students to collect information and build their own concepts while others teach them how to profit from direct instruction through assigned readings, lectures, and instructional systems. These models include inductive thinking, concept attainment, inquiry training, and advance organizers.

Inductive Thinking

Strategies for teaching **inductive thinking** come from the work of Taba (1967). She identifies three inductive thinking skills that are strategically arranged to advance the level of students' thinking. They are first taught to conceptualize by, (1) identifying and enumerating the data relevant to a topic or problem, (2) grouping these items into categories whose members have common attributes, and (3) developing labels for the categories. For example, students may be asked to describe the actions taken by the Coalition Forces in connection with the 2003 invasion of Iraq. Second, they may be asked to categorize these activities in terms of attributes like prewar activities, diplomatic activities, United Nations activities, activities of noncoalition countries opposed to the war, activities and attitudes of Arab countries regarding the war, war strategy and operations, attitudes of Iraqi citizens regarding the fall of the Saddam Hussein Government, effects of the war on the Iraqi infrastructure, and the change of attitudes of various countries before, during, and after the war. Third, students may be asked to categorize this data in terms of the nature and background of countries who oppose the war or the nature of change in attitudes in terms of the various countries' religious or economic relationships with Iraq.

The second teaching strategy involves interpreting, inferring, and generalizing. At this level students may be asked to explain how economic and religious interests interact in producing attitudes regarding the war with Iraq. They might also be asked to interpret the actions taken by various U.N. member nations in terms of U.N. resolutions relating to weapons of mass destruction and the war effort, including the various efforts at inspections, sanctions, and the illegal activities of Iraq and other countries that violated United Nations sanctions.

The third strategy is the application of principles. In this case, students may be asked to do one or more of the following: (1) project what might be expected from Coalition Forces occupying Iraq for different periods of time, (2) indicate what might have been expected if the United Nations had given its full approval for the invasion, (3) explain what might have been the result had there been unanimous backing and involvement by other Arab countries, (4) hypothesize the course of action that may be expected by the United States and Great Britain in the event no weapons of mass destruction could be found in Iraq or neighboring Syria, (5) project how the whole scenario of the Iraqi Freedom Invasion may have played out differently in terms of Arab support if the United States took a stronger position against Israel and for the Palestinian Movement, or (6) show how ethnic differences and economic considerations, as well as biased news reports, can be expected to frame the attitudes and actions of various countries of the world regarding the Iraqi War.

Concept Attainment

Whereas the inductive model promotes concept formation based on how students build categories, **concept attainment** requires students to figure out the *attributes* of preformed categories by comparing and contrasting examples that contain the characteristics or attributes of the concept with examples that do not contain those attributes. For example, students may be asked to differentiate between countries and cities. Both have boundaries, but countries are different in that they can deal independently with other countries while cities cannot.

Concepts can also be differentiated in terms of the *value* of their attributes, which refers to the degree an attribute is present in any particular example. For instance, honesty is sometimes characterized in terms of telling "black" or "white" lies. White lies are sometimes told to protect an individual for some reason or to more appropriately characterize a situation that the complete truth may inappropriately color. When things are characterized, we acknowledge that some attributes are present to various degrees. Students must decide whether any amount of the presence of an attribute is sufficient to place something in a particular category and what the range of density is that qualifies something to belong to a category. For example, consider the category *poisonous*. Chlorine is put into culinary water because it is poisonous; just enough is added to the water supply to kill bacteria, but not harm humans. Consequently, tap water is not an exemplar of the category of *poisonous* because it contains insufficient chlorine to harm us. Similar value considerations apply to such concepts as short and tall, cold and hot, and friendly and hostile, as well as rich and poor (Joyce & Weil, 1996).

Once a category is established, it is symbolically named. Desks, fruit, dogs, and parents are examples of categorical names. Keep in mind, however, that although individual items are commonly grouped together into a single category, they may differ from one another in certain respects. For example, there are many kinds of fruit. In teaching concepts, it is important to provide negative examples so students can make contrasts against them and thereby identify the boundaries of the concept. Part of knowing a concept is recognizing positive instances of it and also distinguishing closely related but negative examples (Bruner, Goodnow, & Austin, 1967). For example, significant differences exist in the operations of different forms of democracy. Democracries involving town meetings differ from representative forms of government, much like the parliamentary government of Great Britain differs from the government of the United States.

Scientific Inquiry and Inquiry Training

In **scientific inquiry,** designed by Schwab (1965), students are first presented with an area for investigation, including the methodologies used in the investigation. Next, the problem is structured so that the student can identify a particular problem or difficulty to solve. The difficulty may be one of data interpretation, data generation, the control of experiments, or the making of inferences. Third, students are asked to speculate about the problem, so that they can identify the difficulty involved in the proposed inquiry. Fourth, students are asked to determine ways of clearing up the difficulty by redesigning the experiment, organizing data in different ways, generating data, and developing constructs. For example, students may be supplied with information regarding the salinity of the soil in a particular area and consequent plant distribution, as well as the interaction of other factors like soil pH, moisture, and soil nutrients, to provide a more accurate interpretation of what is observed. They would need to design properly controlled experiments that took into account the possible role of these factors and their interactions.

Inquiry training, a teaching strategy developed by Richard Suchman (1962), suggests students work through the process of scientific investigation through questioning the teacher. They are first presented with a discrepant event to engage their interest, ordinarily consisting of a puzzling situation designed to encourage students to ask questions. This represents a significant departure from the usual process of teachers originating questions in the classroom. In this process, the teacher is only allowed to answer "Yes" or "No" to student questions. For example, students may be taken to a quaking aspen forest that appears to have grown up in the middle of a douglas fir tree community. They would be asked to think of questions regarding what they observe. However, the teacher may have to direct students' attention to specific items until they become used to this kind of teaching strategy.

The second phase, data-gathering, prompts students to ask questions that help verify the nature of objects and conditions associated with the problem situation. It may be necessary to direct their attention to the location and apparent association of various plants and have them think up questions to help clarify what they are observing. In the third phase, student questions are designed to indicate the kind of experiments that could validly be used to achieve a clear understanding of the problem; this involves isolating relevant variables and formulating hypotheses for testing. In this case, students may ask questions like whether or not testing the soil in terms of nutrients or pH would be in order. The teacher would eventually focus the students' attention as indirectly as possible on the connection between what they observe and the history of environmental events that may have taken place in the area. Students may appropriately conclude that they may need to examine other similar areas, make comparisons, and question the teacher about this possibility. They may propose that factors such as fire, insect infestation, and the like may be responsible for what they observe.

The fourth phase consists of creating explanations for the gathered data. In this phase, students are encouraged to exercise care to avoid drawing incorrect conclusions. Students may ask questions that simulate an examination of the vicinity for evidence of fire, insect damage, or other factors. The teacher would answer "Yes" or "No" to their inquiries. Finally, students would analyze their inquiry strategy and then try to develop more effective ones. This simulated inquiry process provides students an opportunity, with coaching from teachers, to practice inquiry skills in preparation for conducting their own formal experiments.

Advance Organizers

David Ausubel (1963), the chief spokesman for teaching with **advance organizers,** advocates the mastery of academic information through teacher presentation. His concern is to help teachers convey large amounts of information as meaningfully and efficiently as possible. To do this, teachers must first help students create a conceptual framework that provides a mental structure around which additional information can be meaningfully organized. Ausubel believes that a person's existing cognitive structure is the foremost factor governing whether new material will be meaningful and how well it can be acquired and retained. Each of the academic disciplines is composed of a structure of concepts that are hierarchically organized. Thus, each discipline has a number of very broad, abstract concepts that include more concrete concepts at lower stages of organization. After students understand this structure, they are more able to incorporate related meaningful information and remember it longer. For example, to understand art, students might be taught that changes in culture over time as well as the evolution in artistic techniques frame the kind of art that has been done. Thus, art created during the Renaissance is characteristically more expressive of the human body than that in earlier generations. In addition, artistic style has varied through time. Realism has given way to more abstract, expressionistic representations. Acquiring this conceptual information can help students place particular pieces of art in the proper time period.

The Personal Family

Teachers must lead students toward greater mental and emotional health by helping them develop self-confidence, a realistic sense of self, and empathetic reactions to others. Students also need to have opportunities to fulfill their own needs and aspirations as they define them. In doing this, each student needs to be taken on as a partner in determining what he or she will learn and how this will take place. Each needs opportunities for creativity and personal expression. Nondirective teaching provides a means to accomplish these goals.

Nondirective Teaching

Nondirective teaching focuses on facilitating learning rather than directing it. An environment is created in which students are able to attain greater personal effectiveness and realistic self-appraisal. The teacher's role involves stimulating student expression and personal analysis. Students are helped to examine their needs and values in light of projects they wish to accomplish. The goal is for students to recognize how to effectively direct their own educational decisions. Teachers employ the basic techniques of Carl Rogers (1971) in helping students realistically assess their educational efforts and direct their learning activities. When being nondirective, a teacher tries to understand the student's world empathetically and to simply state their interpretation of student communications. Student feelings are accepted, especially those that the student may be fearful of publicly disclosing. Thus, the teacher communicates to the student that all thoughts and feelings are acceptable. A student may come to the teacher, for example, hoping to find out the teacher's assessment of a social studies project. The teacher may help initiate a discussion by having the student describe accomplishments and what he or she felt about them. The student is encouraged to explore the various ramifications of the project and how it corresponds to his or her educational goals. Once the student indicates what has been done, the teacher interprets and reflects back to the student what is understood. This is done without making any judgments about the value of the project; rather, the student is led to draw his or her own conclusions and to make whatever changes are personally desired. The student makes decisions, with the teacher providing clarifying feedback along with encouragement and support for whatever direction is chosen. Along with developing greater problem-solving abilities, students acquire stronger concepts of themselves as capable, self-directed human beings. They eventually achieve confidence that, in their interactions with others and with the environment, they will be productive and successful. As a result, they become self-actualized (Maslow, 1962).

Behavioral Systems Family

Behavioral theory indicates that once a behavior has been learned, the probability that it will occur can be strengthened or weakened by stimuli from the environment. For the educator, this involves designing instructional materials and student-teacher interactions that encourage productive learning and avoiding environmental conditions that discourage it. All human behavior is assumed to be under the control of the external environment. Thus, by manipulating the environment, educators can reinforce whatever behaviors they wish to encourage. Ordinarily behaviorists arrange instruction with high success predictability. This is done by creating small sequenced steps with appropriately designed feedback to provide students immediate and frequent knowledge of their progress. Rewards of various kinds are often provided to encourage learning. Mastery learning and direct instruction are examples of behavioristic schooling.

Mastery Learning

Mastery learning involves strategies for increasing the likelihood that students will attain a satisfactory level of performance. This requires a modification of the traditional definition of human aptitude. Instead of viewing aptitude in terms of an individual's achievement capacity, it is taken as the amount of time needed to learn any given material (Bloom, 1971; Carroll, 1971). In this view, it is possible for nearly all students to master any given set of objectives if sufficient time is provided, along with appropriate instruction. From an instructional perspective, this involves considerable individualized, self-paced instruction with frequent evaluations of pupil progress. Objectives must be very specific and should be grouped in meaningful streams of content. The learning experiences should be sequenced so that they build on those that logically precede them. Thus, in mathematics instruction, learning experiences would be grouped into such areas as numeration, place value, addition, subtraction, and so on (Joyce & Weil, 1996).

Direct Instruction

The most prominent features of *direct instruction* are an academic focus, a high degree of teacher direction and control, high expectations for pupil progress, a system for managing time, and a positive learning atmosphere. An academic focus refers to the high priority placed on assignments and completion of academic tasks. Teachers explain new concepts to large groups of students and direct their controlled practice. The presenting of new material is preceded by giving students a lesson framework that clarifies instructional purposes and procedures and shows how these shape proposed learning activities. Students are provided sufficient time to learn and practice new skills and knowledge and are given clear explanations and demonstrations so that they have a high degree of understanding. Teacher presentations include, (1) giving material in small steps; (2) providing many, varied examples of the new skills or concepts; (3) modeling, or giving narrated demonstrations of the learning task; (4) avoiding digressions, staying on the topic; and (5) reexplaining difficult points (Rosenshine, 1985).

Following the teacher's explanation of concepts, the teacher checks student understanding through discussion. The teacher asks questions that require specific answers or seek explanations of how answers were found. It is critical that all students have an opportunity to answer questions, and teachers must provide each student feedback on his or her responses. Errors are not allowed to go uncorrected.

The Social Family

Teaching with a social orientation has the central role of enhancing the personal and social life of students and ensuring a productive democratic social order. Cooperative learning inherently enhances the quality of life, providing a sense of interpersonal connectedness and reducing alienation and unproductive social conflict. In addition, cooperative learning endeavors also stimulate intellectual growth. Social theorists take issue with the efficacy of schooling patterns that emphasize excessive cognitive structuring as well as patterns where students spend the bulk of their time learning on an individual basis. Jurisprudential inquiry is an example of this kind of learning.

Jurisprudential Inquiry

Donald Oliver and James P. Shaver (1966/1974) created the **jurisprudential inquiry** model to help students learn to think systematically about contemporary issues. This model basically trains students in citizenship and helps them confront legal, ethical, and social questions in the context of ongoing cultural and social changes. Students are given tools for analyzing and debating social issues, which helps them successfully participate in the redefinition of social values. Citizens in any community are assumed to differ in their views and priorities, resulting in potential conflicts over social values. To preserve the social order and increase interpersonal human productiveness, complex, controversial issues must be resolved.

With this model, students play the role of a competent judge requiring three types of competence. First is familiarity with the values of the American creed as embedded in the Constitution and the Declaration of Independence. These documents and associated principles establish a framework used to judge public issues and make legal decisions.

Second, students need competence in clarifying and resolving issues. Ordinarily, controversy arises due to value conflicts or because public policies do not adhere to the core values of society. Whenever a conflict regarding values arises, three kinds of problems are likely present: (1) value problems where there is uncertainty regarding which values or legal principles are in conflict, (2) factual problems involving what particular facts are associated with the conflict; and (3) definitional problems that center on the meaning of words used to describe the controversy. Clarifying and resolving issues involves clarifying definitions, establishing facts, and identifying the values important to the issues.

The third area of competence needed by students is knowledge of contemporary political and public issues. This requires students to be exposed to a full spectrum of political, social, and economic problems that face American society. In the jurisprudential inquiry model, students focus on the specific legal aspect of a situation rather than more general values.

This model's teaching strategy involves students taking a position regarding issues and having the teacher challenge them using a Socratic mode of questioning. Students are pushed to carefully consider their stance and learn the following:

- Does the student point of view hold up well against positions reflecting alternative values?
- Is the student position consistent across many situations?
- Are the reasons used for maintaining a particular position relevant to the situation?
- Are the assumptions supporting the position valid?
- What are the consequences for holding a particular position?
- Can the position be held in spite of its consequences?

The model is employed for students in six phases: (1) orienting to a particular case; (2) identifying the issues; (3) taking positions; (4) exploring the stances underlying the positions taken; (5) refining and qualifying positions; and (6) testing assumptions about facts, definitions, and consequences.

In the first phase, students are introduced to the case materials through stories or historical narratives. Events in the case are outlined and participants' behavior is analyzed. In Phase 2, students synthesize the facts into a public issue, characterize the values involved, and identify conflicts between values. Phase 3 involves students taking a position regarding the issue and stating a defense for their position.

Phase 4 explores the various student positions, with the teacher using a confrontational style in an effort to help students probe their positions. Students may be asked to identify the point at which a value is violated, clarify the value conflict through analogies, provide a description of desirable or undesirable consequences of their position, or establish value priorities by explaining precisely how values are in conflict with one another.

Phase 5 consists of refining and clarifying the various issues and showing their points of contrast. Student reasoning is focused on, and students are given an opportunity to indicate how their position differs from others being considered.

Finally, in Phase 6, a careful analysis is made in which assumptions associated with various positions are examined to determine if they are in fact true and relevant. Consequences are explored to determine their validity. Students try to assess whether or not the proposed consequences will actually occur.

Constructivism

The most conspicuous psychological influence on curriculum thinking during the past two decades has been the **constructivist** view of learning (Fensham, 1992). Generally considered an extension of Piaget's work, its strength is in its effort to connect with the reality of human cognitive processes and thus guide effective teaching and learning in the various school subjects. Constructivists believe that teaching, curriculum, and school organization should fit the way in which children learn (Matthews, 2000). The basic premises of constructivism are that each individual has a unique conceptual structure of reality in his or her brain and that the individual constructs a unique conception of the world through personal experiences. In simple terms, constructivism is a theory about the limits of human knowledge. It is a belief that all knowledge is necessarily a product of each individual's cognitive acts. A person can have no direct or unmediated knowledge of any external or objective reality, but must construct his or her own understanding through personal experiences; thus, the nature of one's learning is profoundly influenced by previous experiences and by the way each individual has learned to view and process information (Confrey, 1990). Clearly the conceptual organization of any one individual is unique to him or her and significantly different from that held by anyone else.

The brain is not a passive consumer of information. Instead, it actively constructs its own interpretations of information and draws inferences from them. The brain selectively ignores some information and attends to other information. To learn with understanding, the learner must actively construct meaning (Phillips, 2000). To comprehend anything, the individual must invent a model or explanation for it that organizes the information to fit logic, real-world experiences, or both. People retrieve information from long-term memory and use their information-processing strategies to generate meaning from the incoming information, or to organize it, code it, and store it in long-term memory (see Table 4.1).

To some theorists, the reality that individuals construct of the world is limited to sensory inputs, requiring that information be perceived and stored as pictures. This idea is deeply flawed. People do not build-up meanings from sensory inputs; rather, the varied

TABLE 4.1   *Comparisons Between Traditional Learning and Constructivism.*

	Traditional	**Constructivism**
Learning purposes	To acquire a standardized conception of the world	To create an idiosyncratic conception of the world
Learning processes	Passively absorbs information	Actively constructs meaning
Storage in the brain	Information stored in the form in which it is given	Stored information modified to be consistent with information already stored
Selectivity of storage	Accepts all information	Selectively accepts or rejects information

inputs received must be converted to ideas like pressure, elasticity, force, and stress. These ideas have to be defined in order to have meaning. Definitions are not ascertained by the learner from direct experience, but from having teachers explain their meaning. As a result, definitions are in the public domain of knowing and not exclusively personal. Consequently, learning cannot be conceived as 100 percent personal even though one's conceptualization of what is taught is personal.

Since knowledge is personally constructed rather than simply being imparted by teachers and learned by students, how can children come to the knowledge of complex conceptual schemes that have taken the best minds hundreds of years to build up? For example, when would children think to understand ideas regarding velocity, acceleration, force, gene, social structure, and democracy on their own, and what would their conceptions be, given their limited backgrounds? In addition, what hope is there for schools to provide opportunities for children to have direct experiences with phenomena that require sophisticated equipment to study? How can teachers teach a body of knowledge which is in large part abstract (that is, removed from students' experience) that has no connection to their prior conceptions, and that is alien to common sense and in conflict with everyday experience, expectations, and concepts (Matthews, 2000)? If students are given access to fundamental knowledge of the world, the process of knowledge construction must go beyond personal empirical inquiry. Learners not only need to be given access to knowledge through personal self-directed experiences, but also through models and conventional knowledge of the subjects (Solomon, 1994). The challenge is to provide instruction in such a way that students construct meaning for themselves that is essentially consistent with conceptual knowledge on the subject.

Theoretical ideas and conventions can be made available to students without explaining them, illustrating them, and showing the interconnections of knowledge; in brief, without explicitly teaching them. This, of course, is the dilemma of constructivist learning, and is related to another question: Are students unable to efficiently alter prior knowledge conceptions, or will they resist on the grounds of preferring self-direction in their learning? In either case, students may incorrectly construct meaning. However, if students resist altering their views, it creates an entirely different problem than if they simply have difficulty doing this.

Ordinarily, literacy in any subject consists not only of knowing basic information, but also of using the methods of the particular discipline to increase one's knowledge and understanding. Thus, the processes used to acquire knowledge are an essential part of an adequate education. Since forgetting conceptual information happens rapidly, familiarity with the methods of inquiry in a subject may be essential, particularly if students acquire accurate conceptions of knowledge as a byproduct of their inquiries. Constructivist learning fits an emphasis on methods of inquiry better than a focus on acquiring conceptual information, so it serves as a useful theory to guide learning. This does not mean that acquiring an understanding of a subject is not important; rather, it illustrates the necessity of having knowledge acquisition come from inquiry experiences rather than exclusively from teaching approaches that foster information transmission. Methods are needed that feature student-teacher interactions that draw attention to aspects of the learning experiences that will deepen understanding and provide a relevant avenue for study. Student-teacher interactions help students conceptualize by providing contrasting views, clarifications, and explanations and by suggesting similar or different avenues of research. Teachers can thus help students visualize more promising directions for their inquiries, directions that are more likely to lead to substantial information rather than to frivolous, less critical data. Teachers can also provide students with help in thinking through the inquiry process, determining proper controls, and drawing defensible conclusions. These activities will help students become more thorough in their research and more exacting in the inferences they make. This approach will also help students acquire a more accurate knowledge base, which they will buy into because they have had considerable involvement in formulating it.

Osborne and Wittrock (1984), while studying about children learning science, found that they exhibited a number of interesting characteristics that have enormous implications for teaching:

- Children understand the world from a child's point of view.
- Many of the views of the world and meanings held by older students are the same as those they had as young children even though they have had considerable additional exposure to instruction on the subjects.
- Children's ideas can be amazingly tenacious and resistant to change.
- If children's ideas and views of the world are changed through instruction, the changes are sometimes quite different from those the teacher intended.
- Students consider each lesson as an isolated event, while the teacher assumes that students appreciate the connecting links between lessons.
- Student purposes for a lesson are often subtly but significantly different from the purposes intended by the teacher.
- Pupils often show little interest in or concern about those features of learning that the teacher or the textbook writer consider to be critical.
- Pupils' knowledge structures frequently are not the structures teachers assumed they have.
- Pupils' understandings developed from the outcomes of experimental work are frequently not those the teacher assumes have developed.
- Children often unknowingly modify the information they are taught so that it is not in conflict with their earlier ideas.

These data indicate that teachers need to be alert to subtle learning problems during instruction, since information that is ordinarily taken for granted cannot be relied upon. Teachers need to examine the thinking of their students routinely so they can provide experiences that will help students confront inconsistencies in their observations and conclusions. It is obviously unwise to assume that information can simply be transmitted. More sophisticated interactions between teachers and their students are necessary if students are to have bonafide learning experiences.

Learning How to Construct Knowledge

Constructivism involves actively making connections between new information and existing networks or *schema* of prior knowledge. Before knowledge becomes useful in a generative sense—usable for interpreting new situations, solving problems, thinking and reasoning, and learning generally—students must learn how to frame and elaborate critical questions about what they are exposed to and how to examine the new information in relation to more familiar content, while in the process building new knowledge structures. Otherwise, what is learned remains inaccessible for understanding and solving problems in everyday life (Resnick & Klopfer, 1989).

Knowledge construction is much more efficient when learners can relate new information to their existing background knowledge (Adams, 1990). Nothing is understood initially as an abstraction; instead, it is understood within a concrete context supplied by previous experiences and existing knowledge (Anderson, 1984). For example, consider the following paragraph:

> When Roy arrived, the man acknowledged his entry into the room and put a mark in a book to indicate he was present. Roy then seated himself in his place and waited. While he was doing so, the person next to him engaged him in a conversation about events of the day. Soon the man stood up and chastised the group for failure to appropriately complete an assignment. He then got after them for not paying attention while he was talking to them and prescribed a punishment for these infractions of the rules.

You probably had little difficulty recognizing that this event took place in a school room. Though this was a very sketchy narrative, it is clear that the person taking attendance is the teacher, that discussion with peers about the day's activities is consistent with what might take place in a classroom, and that teachers often chastise their classes for not completing assignments and for failing to pay attention. Because of past experiences, most former students have a "classroom schema" and readily use this as the context by which to understand the paragraph.

Now let's change the context. Assume this is a description of a group of prisoners assembling for a work assignment: The man in charge is the guard, the conversation is between inmates, the failed assignment refers to the previous day's work, and chastisement occurs as often in a prison environment as in school. Most people would choose a school as the context of the paragraph, however, because more people have been in schools than in prisons. This difference in contexts illustrates the importance of using conceptual contexts to shape student views as they try to learn new information. It is necessary that relevant background knowledge be activated so the schema used are consistent with the concepts to be learned. Teachers can prepare students by drawing familiar analogies or providing examples that link the new content to familiar ideas or experiences. They can take an inventory of what students know or think about the topic before starting instruction. They can also ask students questions that require predictions about outcomes or solutions to related problems.

When existing schema are inaccurate or unsuitable for the concepts being learned, their activation will interfere with learning (Alvermann, Smith, & Readence, 1985). This interference can occur when schema are oversimplified or inaccurate. At times these inaccurate schema are part of the primitive view children have of the world based on their naive experiences. For example, a small child riding in a car sees the moon as moving relative to her. Children also commonly hold the view that the sun revolves around the earth rather than realizing that the rotating earth accounts for the rising and setting sun. This kind of perception was a common sense, but inaccurate view held in most societies prior to the advent of modern science.

Mere exposure to correct conceptions does not necessarily help create better understanding. On the contrary, as mentioned earlier, children's misconceptions are tenacious. Children will not readily alter their present schema to fit new data. It may be helpful to present children with the contradiction their views create or with the lack of utility of their ideas (Good & Brophy, 2000). The best way is probably to have students conduct experiments or make detailed observations that help provide clarification but are sufficiently self-directed that reconceptualization is not forced.

Meaning construction works well in social settings where several individuals engage in sustained discourse about a topic or undertake it in cooperative inquiry. This is known as **social constructivism.** Such discussions and investigations expose students to input from others and make them aware of previously unknown things, thereby leading to an expansion of their cognitive structures. Exposure to ideas that contradict their own may cause students to examine their beliefs more carefully and increase their willingness and ability to reconstruct them. In addition, when students engage in extensive communication with others, they are forced to more clearly articulate their views. These interactions should consist of sustained dialogues and discussions in which participants pursue topics in depth through exchanging views and negotiating meanings and implications as they explore ramifications (Pearson & Iran-Negate, 1998). This sharpens their own conceptions and may lead to appropriate alterations of their views. In connection with this, cognition and language development begin as two separate functions. As children move along in school, more and more of their learning is mediated through language. This is especially true of some cultural knowledge that is difficult, if not impossible, to acquire through direct experience (Vygotsky, 1962, 1978).

From a social constructivist viewpoint, instruction in school should be modeled as much as possible on how things are learned in natural settings. In these settings students don't merely acquire knowledge, but they learn viable life skills while being socialized within learning communities. To become involved in *authentic learning,* youth need an apprenticeship experience within the community during which they gradually acquire expertise and achieve enhanced social roles. Over time their roles can change from being peripheral to becoming more central to the community's purposes and activities. The knowledge and skills normally provided in schools have been abstracted and removed from the application settings where they originate. School learning separates *knowing* from *doing* and reduces not only the effectiveness of learning but also the application of learning to real-life situations (Lave & Wenger, 1991). However, cognition is situational; that is, it is adapted to the settings, purposes, and tasks to which it is best applied and for which it was constructed in the first place. Thus, if students are to retain the knowledge in a form that makes it usable for application, they need to develop the knowledge in its natural setting, using the methods and tasks suited to that setting.

Decision Points

1. Prepare a description of an event in which you believe students operating out of different contexts may have different interpretations of the event.
2. Describe a concept in your field of study that you believe may be confusing to students. Explain how you would go about helping students achieve a more accurate picture of the concept.

Inquiry Learning

Inquiry learning fits well with the constructivist views of how children achieve an understanding of their world. First, if properly done, it provides students a way to investigate questions they are curious about. Second, if the inquiry process is held to an adequate level of rigor, authentic information can be obtained that is both interesting and basic to the field of study. Third, if the teacher is skillfully involved, students can learn how to acquire information in a controlled format similar to that used by experts in the field. More valid information can consequently be anticipated from study. Fourth, because of the potential for student self-direction, a higher level of interest and commitment can be expected.

True inquiry is primarily a learning process by which student questions are investigated. However, unless there is significant teacher involvement, the questions asked are likely to be of low quality and limited importance. During interaction with students, teachers need to help them understand the difference between substantial questions and those of little consequence. For example, students may express an interest in finding out something about plant growth and decide to determine if plants need water and fertilizer to grow. If this is presented as the research question, the following dialogue might take place:

TEACHER: Do you really think that fertilizer and water may not promote better plant growth?

STUDENT: No. But I just wanted to try it out and see what happens.

TEACHER: Is there anything about fertilizer you could find out that might add to your knowledge on the subject?

STUDENT: Well, I could use different brands of fertilizer. Maybe some are better than others.

TEACHER: Do you have any reason to suspect that some brands may be better than others?

STUDENT: They tell you that in advertisements, don't they?

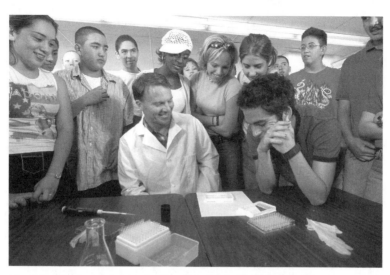

Teachers can promote inquiry through carefully selected questions.

TEACHER: Yes, I believe that's right, but have you made any observations that would lead you to think this would provide you with important information in science?

STUDENT: Not really. I just wanted to do something that would be easy to figure out.

TEACHER: Can you think of some other question about plant growth that interests you for which you don't already have an answer?

STUDENT: Well, I have wondered why roots grow down and stems up. I know it's gravity or something. At least that's what the book says.

TEACHER: What is there about this process that interests you?

STUDENT: I've just wondered if the roots have to grow down and the stems up. Maybe there is some way to change that. Maybe there is a stronger force than gravity that could reverse everything.

TEACHER: What kind of a force are you talking about?

STUDENT: You know, like when you swing a bucket around and over your head the water stays in the bucket even though it is upside down with gravity pulling on it.

TEACHER: That's centrifugal force. So you think centrifugal force may counteract the force of gravity in plant growth. What makes you think that?

STUDENT: You know, it's like I said, when you spin a bucket around, the centrifugal force seems stronger than gravity. Maybe it is the same in a plant. Maybe the roots won't go down. They could grow in the direction of the centrifugal force.

TEACHER: That sounds like an interesting question and a reasonable hypothesis. How would you set up an experiment to test your hypothesis?

STUDENT: I noticed you have one of those ceiling fans in your office that spins all the time. It has centrifugal force, doesn't it?

TEACHER: Yes, certainly. So you think that the force it creates could counteract gravity?

STUDENT: Yes, I think it would. I want to find out anyway.

TEACHER: You're welcome to use the fan. Let's see if it looks feasible. As you look at the fan, is there anything about it that might propose a problem for your research?

STUDENT: Well, I could plant some seeds in some containers and then tape them to the fan. I'd have to put a container of seeds on each fan blade to make sure it was balanced.

TEACHER: I think that is right. Do you see anything on the fan that might influence the results you might get?

STUDENT: There is the light. It's in the center of the fan so the stems might grow toward the center of the fan because of light rather than away because of centrifugal force like my hypothesis indicates. I can just take the light bulb out.

TEACHER: That would take care of that problem, I suspect. Are there any other things to consider to make sure your experiment is properly controlled?

STUDENT: Yes, I need to have some control plants that receive the same treatment as the experimental group, but are not put on the fan. I'd have to water them the same and have them in the same room. You know, there is another experiment I might try. Do stems grow away from gravity or do they grow toward the light? Once I know that, I could see which has the most power to influence plant growth: light or centrifugal force. I saw some plants once that were grown without light. They were white instead of green, and they were long and spindly. They just didn't grow right, but the stems did grow up and the roots went down.

TEACHER: It sounds like you might be able to devise an interesting study about that once you have some idea about centrifugal force. How might trying to find out more than one thing at a time confound the results you might get?

STUDENT: If I didn't do it right, I might confuse the results.

TEACHER: So what is the best course of action for you to take?

STUDENT: I should do the study of centrifugal force and make sure it is controlled properly.

In this dialogue the teacher helps nudge the student away from common knowledge and toward a more demanding and thought-provoking experience. It encourages the student to create a more sophisticated question to research and to exercise better control over possible confounding variables. It also provides an opportunity for the student to achieve a higher level of understanding about forces in the physical world. When the student formulates the question and designs research with appropriate help from the teacher, he or she benefits from a more sophisticated view of the phenomena being studied. A greater understanding of basic concepts is also possible once the research is completed.

Students are more likely to have difficulty with formulating viable questions than with other aspects of the inquiry process, due to the common school practice of teachers asking most of the questions, while the students answer those questions. These habits are hard to break. The other deterrent to creating valuable questions for study is grading students and having them regulate their academic life in terms of achieving minimums. Students often do just enough to get by when what is actually needed in inquiry teaching, and learning is for students to reach for higher and higher levels of sophistication in their research and search for projects that will help them achieve a deep understanding of fundamental concepts in a field. This objective will likely be unfulfilled if students don't feel personally compelled to achieve higher levels of competence. Being satisfied with minimums can significantly deter the quest for excellence.

How can teachers prepare themselves to promote appropriate levels of questioning by their students? Of course they do not want to just give the research questions to students, yet they want to be prepared to provide clues to guide students toward viable research questions. A prepared teacher will have already formulated a list of potential research questions that can be referred to but not given to students. This list provides a background out of which teachers can lead students toward asking their own questions. Teachers should also have a lot of materials for ready access in student research. In social studies this might include printed materials, access to Internet sites, videos, and addresses of various social and government agencies, along with descriptions of the kind of information these agencies may provide. In addition to these kinds of resources, science teachers should have ready access to laboratory facilities and materials for research, along with possible connections to universities and other places where more sophisticated equipment and expert assistance may be available. The school may have an arboretum available, as well as a greenhouse, garden plots, facilities, and materials that may support year-round biology research and learning. English teachers obviously need a lot of printed, video, and Internet resources. Students should have access to as broad a range of resources as the schools can provide or arrange. In physical education, some students could be provided with the means to study exercise physiology and other appropriate topics that are quite different from the usual physical activity encountered in traditional physical education teaching.

Conducting carefully controlled experiments is essential for valid inquiry experiences. Depending on the students level of intellectual development, different levels of sophistication can be expected as they design research to answer their questions. Students who are not at the formal operations level of intellectual development will experience difficulty understanding the possibility of multiple causation for various phenomena and events. Their limited thinking ability leaves them confined to events with single causes and unable to think in terms of probability. These limitations will handicap them to some degree, but should not be considered justifiable reasons for not having them engage in research. Their fledgling efforts to engage in bonafide research can be assumed to improve their subsequent ability to do it well.

The teacher's role in promoting student research excellence is coaching. A teacher may initially provide more help than he or she will later give by drawing attention to the need for proper control as well as an appropriate means for achieving it. In the end they will mostly just look on and ask students to explain their design. Eventually students should be able to design properly controlled research projects without much input from the teacher.

At first, students may be overzealous in drawing research conclusions. Though they might have tried to use randomly selected, representative samples or opinions and may have designed their research well, the conclusions drawn should reflect reasoned judgment. Extrapolations should be justified by the data collected as well as by the quality of the research design and the sampling. Students also need to understand that it can be just as important and useful for research hypotheses to fail as it is for them to be confirmed by the research data.

Inquiry learning should be a significant aspect of education because it provides a useful way for students to understand the social, historical, artistic, political, and physical worlds and to become acquainted with how important information has come into being. It also provides a format for students to satisfy their inherent desire to investigate their world, understand it, and use this knowledge for their own purposes. Inquiry learning within learning communities is an excellent format for implementing constructivist learning theory.

Decision Points

Create a scenario for teaching a lesson in your teaching field using true inquiry methods. Provide both a description of the scenario and examples of the conversations you might have with your students.

NATIONAL TEACHING STANDARD

Teachers recognize that learning and behavior are connected to particular settings or contexts. They strive to provide multiple contexts in which to promote student abilities.

Teachers understand that there are multiple intelligences which require different approaches to learning and can capitalize on this knowledge to provide students experiences consistent with their personal strengths and gifts.

Learning Styles and Multiple Intelligences

Historically, "learning styles" referred to an innate capacity of students to greatly benefit from visual, auditory, or tactile learning. Later there came an emphasis on learning preferences based on **brain hemisphericity,** the individual's inclination to process information in either the left or right hemisphere of the brain. Researchers found that learning preferences and processing skills could be measured to some degree with an encephalograph (EEG), which detects reductions in alpha readings during problem solving, thereby indicating that a particular hemisphere has become active (Springer & Deutsch, 1981). Research indicates that each hemisphere specializes in different kinds of learning. The left hemisphere is more adept at verbal functions, as it contains speech centers located in the parietal and broca regions. Left hemisphere learners tend to emphasize technical, scientific, rational, analytical, logical, factual, convergent, and quantitative skills. They learn well from lectures, particularly if these presentations are well organized. In addition, they read well and excel at test taking. In contrast, right hemisphere learners are more visual and holistic. They are more imaginative and divergent in their thinking, more adept at hands-on activities, and they readily engage in holistic conceptualization.

To cater to these different learning styles, educators recommend modifying traditional teaching, which is characterized by presentation, practice, and evaluation, and including more activities consistent with right hemisphere learning. Learners who are right hemisphere dominant have predictable difficulty with the traditional curriculum.

Jared spent most of the period trying to memorize the list of terms and definitions from his U.S. Government class, but it was hopeless. He was getting nowhere. The definitions just wouldn't get into his head; somehow he could not visualize their meaning. They were just words. He experienced the same problem in biology until Mr. Cirigliano recognized his difficulty and set him to work building models of cells and various organisms. By the time he was finished with each model, Jared knew more about what those models represented than any member of the class. Mr. Cirigliano used his models to show other class members the structures of various cells and organisms, and told members of the class that Jared had provided the models and explained how hard he worked both in school and at home to complete them. Jared's sense of self-worth grew considerably as class members expressed their approval for his work. He also learned more in his biology class than in any other class he had taken. He was starting to feel a real sense of accomplishment in school for the first time.

Howard Gardner's (1991) work on human intelligence has greatly expanded our understanding of student learning preferences. He explains that children, during the first years of life, become proficient in their native language, as well as throwing and catching balls, riding bikes, dancing, organizing their belongings, and dozens of other skills. They also develop theories about how the world works, as well as their own minds. All this is done with little formal instruction. Ironically, these very young children who readily master complex symbol systems like language, as well as art forms like music, and can develop theories about how the world operates along with intricate theories of the mind, often experience great difficulty learning what they are taught in school. Gardner believes students possess different minds and, therefore, learn, remember, perform, and understand in different ways. This is illustrated by Jared's story. He was a spatial learner who found difficulty learning linguistically; therefore, he required concrete representations of concepts in order to acquire meaning about them.

Gardner refers to the different ways of understanding and learning as **multiple intelligences.** He has identified eight distinct ways of knowing and representing the world; each is an intelligence with its own unique rules, codes, and symbols. Various learners operate out of different intelligences; consequently, they have different approaches to problems and learn in different ways. In addition, each person has a different mix of these intelligences, with varying tendencies for a predominant learning orientation. A listing of the eight intelligences follows, including descriptions of how they can be implemented in a classroom setting.

Bodily kinesthetic: Meaning is created through movement. Students can apply the bodily kinesthetic learning orientation with experiences including drama, role-playing, simulations, dancing, games, demonstrations, physical exercises and sports, and field trips. In some classes, like math and science, it is not easy to employ bodily kinesthetic learning. Yet, to the extent possible, teachers should provide learning opportunities that correspond to the preferred learning orientation of their students. This will include such adaptations as having students present a creative drama of how two scientists interact when they disagree about scientific research and concepts. Students who learn kinesthetically have body awareness, space awareness, tactile discriminating ability, grace and coordination, mastery of nonverbal communication, authentic acting ability, a flair for the creative and dramatic in various artistic expressions, the ability to make appropriate physical movements in a variety of games and sporting activities, and the ability to use various kinds of manipulatives.

Linguistic: Individuals with strong linguistic intelligence excel at creating and understanding meaning through language. Linguistic talents can be promoted by writing stories and poems, as modeled by the teacher. Stories can be used in introducing various learning units, especially concepts related to culture. Linguistic skills can be developed as students compare their ideas with those of their classmates and attempt to draw conclusions and formulate questions for inquiry investigations. Students can also examine what they hear routinely from others in terms of appropriateness, soundness, and relevance to their lives.

Logical-mathematical: A logical-mathematical individual excels at using highly organized, logical, and rule-based systems to create and understand meaning. This learner creates and demonstrates an understanding of number systems. To promote logical-mathematical thinking, teachers should (1) use diverse questioning strategies, (2) pose open-ended problems for students to solve, (3) have students construct models of key concepts, (4) have students predict and verify logical outcomes, (5) have students discern patterns and connections in diverse phenomena, (6) ask students to justify their statements or opinions, and (7) provide students opportunities for observation and investigation.

Inquiry learning is an excellent way to employ logical-mathematical thinking. The use of various questioning strategies designed to encourage higher-level thinking are useful. Students can be asked to detect patterns or break codes. Patterns are evident in nearly all traditional school subjects. In the life sciences, plant and animal interactions are commonly observed in various ecosystems. In art, patterns can be observed in studying art history. Structure and patterns can also be discerned in novels, poetry, and musical compositions. Students can be asked to discern patterns in mathematical models, architecture, clothing designs, and the characteristics of various elements and compounds in chemistry.

Visual-spatial: The visual-spatial intelligence involves creating and understanding meaning through visual and spatial symbols and conceptions. Most subjects present opportunities for promoting visual-spatial learning. Teachers need to supply students with a variety of tools and materials that can be used to create various kinds of objects and displays. Creations might include flow charts representing complex processes, concept maps that show relationships between ideas, models of various structures and processes, and visual representations of stories or poems students are writing.

In biology, students might be asked to construct a cell model with all its organelles arranged in their proper configuration. In language arts, students might create puppets or paint murals and backdrops, as well as illustrate literature by creating storyboards.

Musical: Musical intelligence enables the individual to create an understanding of meaning through musical symbols. Musical skills include composing and performing various kinds of music, as well as developing expertise in music criticism. Musical talent development requires early experiences. A critical period for developing sensitivity to sound and pitch is between ages 4 and 6. At this time a rich musical environment can provide a foundation for later development. Music is an aural language in which the three basic components of pitch, rhythm, and timbre can be arranged in countless combinations and give rise to a remarkable variety of musical sounds. There is also a strong connection between musical sounds and the emotions, providing a means for enhancing life in the classroom. Music can be used to heighten the suspense, sadness, tragedy, or joy of stories from literature and history. Humorous songs can add zest and warmth to almost any classroom.

Teachers can use music to create a variety of emotions and images in the classroom, and they can invite students to compose their own music. Students might create background music, music that is an integral part of a play, music to generate or enhance emotions, or music to help in memorizing important conceptual information.

Interpersonal: Interpersonal intelligence involves creating and obtaining meaning through the social world. This includes skill in understanding society and its problems and processes, and is often developed through the procedures that promote group work. All students need greater sensitivity and skill in working with others. In particular, such skills are very useful for learning to manage conflict, as well as ensuring that individual needs are met, that power is equitably distributed, that communication is effective, that values and priorities are considered and properly addressed in activities and deliberations, that perceptions of situations that vary from person to person are dealt with appropriately, and that members of learning communities know that learning approaches and personalities differ and can have enhancing or denigrating effects on group activities. Developing interpersonal intelligence involves learning about and appreciating diverse points of view and successfully working with a variety of individuals who represent these various positions and inclinations. Students can develop these skills by working on projects alongside members of various age groups, classes, and racial groups, and ultimately assuming leadership roles in conducting these activities.

Intrapersonal: Intrapersonal intelligence inclines a person toward creating and understanding meaning through intrapersonal symbols. Intrapersonal intelligence involves self-reflection philosophically, psychologically, and religiously. Higher-order thinking skills are essential to self-analyses, as is an understanding of one's emotions and feelings. Emotions need to be understood and expressed in ways that promote a sense of well-being. Sufficient intellectual capacity is necessary so values can be understood and consistent value systems can be created. Students should understand how their personal preferences and values must be consistent with social expectations and standards. The development of an integrated, well-adjusted personality depends on an adequate understanding of self and self-expression, and an ability to fit these in with important societal morals and ideals.

One way to enhance self-reflection is through journal writing. Students can be encouraged to write about their self-explorations, their own life philosophy and how it articulates with predominant social values, what they have learned from life experiences, and how these experiences have shaped their values and hopes. Writing about personal strengths and weaknesses, along with self-improvement changes, can help students achieve greater personal understanding, so they can make adjustments that will enhance their opportunities and achievements. Some students may wish to make their journal confidential, given the personal nature of some items recorded there. They may also wish to share other information and receive feedback. Students should be allowed to determine what should be shared and what should not.

Naturalist: The person with high naturalist intelligence uses the natural world as the means for creating and understanding meaning. This kind of learning focuses on making meaningful distinctions in the natural world in order to visualize patterns and relationships between living organisms (Carreiro, 1998; Gardner, 1994). Naturalist intelligence involves the capacities of observing, reflecting, making connections, classifying, integrating, and communicating perceptions of the natural and man-made worlds. To encourage the development of naturalist intelligence, teachers might have students make observations, conduct research, and formulate explanations of interpretations and conclusions. Themes for study might include change, adaptation, balance, biotic resources, diversity, competition, cycles, patterns, and populations.

Students need tools for observation, like microscopes, and sufficient reference and laboratory facilities to study a wide variety of plant and animal specimens. They also need opportunities to study plant and animal communities in natural settings so they can achieve more realistic perceptions. Student development can be supported with greenhouses, arboreta, and field trips into the various plant and animal communities.

It may not be readily apparent how each of these intelligences can be promoted in any one classroom. The fact remains, however, that students have different combinations of these intellectual abilities and that these combinations determine their areas of greatest inclination and skill. Thus, learning can be increased when there are better matches between student abilities and the work students do in the classroom. Teachers need to give some of their students experiences that are different from the ordinary. Otherwise, these youth may not find success. Traditional schooling focuses on far too few of the defined intelligences, making some appear more legitimate than others. The curriculum needs to include a much wider range of experiences so that some students are not unfairly discriminated against.

 ## *Decision Points*

Describe a project for a learning community in which there are planned activities for all the multiple intelligences.

CENTRAL IDEAS

1. Student enthusiasm for learning depends on the degree of students' involvement in deciding what is learned and how.
2. Learning practices that fail to satisfy student needs and that deny them opportunities to be appropriately self-governing significantly interfere with learning.
3. Behavioristic learning theory is currently less accepted than constructivism. Behaviorism makes assumptions about learning that cannot be confirmed. Constructivism, however, is accepted as a more valid view of natural learning.
4. There are various models designed to employ different theories of learning and to achieve different academic purposes.
5. Constructivism is a theory of learning which indicates that the brain is not a passive consumer of information. Instead, the brain actively pursues understanding, constructs its own interpretations of information, and draws inferences from them. Concept construction in each individual depends on how well new information corresponds to what is already stored in the brain.
6. Learners are particularly resistant to changing their cognitive structures. Changing conceptual structures can best be accomplished by providing experiences for students that allow them to see for themselves, in a practical way, how their current view must be modified to accommodate a more accurate picture of a particular understanding.
7. Despite the personalized way each individual constructs meaning for himself or herself by actively pursuing an understanding of the world, not all learning can focus on independent learner inquiries. Students also need to learn from the store of established information. This must be accomplished with skillful directing by teachers who are equipped to provide questions and give guidance that can lead to productive thinking and understanding.

8. Inquiry learning is an excellent approach to teaching and learning in learning communities.

9. Inquiry learning is most fundamentally a process of students asking and then answering their own questions. Teachers can improve the rigor of inquiry learning by directing students' attention toward substantive problems, by asking thoughtful questions, and by inviting questions from students that relate to the subject being considered.

10. The purposes of learning ordinarily center on student outcomes, with little emphasis on the value of processes. The processes of learning have value aside from outcomes.

11. Each individual constructs knowledge in terms of contextual information drawn from personal experiences. Accurate knowledge construction can be enhanced through social interaction, which provides various views that can sharpen personal conceptions and bring deeper meanings.

12. Youth have various learning styles and different blends of the multiple intelligences. Learning can be improved when students are given learning opportunities that correspond to their intelligences.

REFERENCES

Adams, M. (1990). *Beginning to read: Thinking and learning about print.* Cambridge: MIT Press.

Alvermann, D., Smith, L., & Readence, J. (1985). Effects of interactive discussion and text type on learning counterintuitive science concepts. *Journal of Educational Research, 88,* 420–435.

Anderson, R. (1984). Role of the reader's schema in comprehension, learning, and memory. In R. Anderson, J. Osborn, & R. Tierney (Eds.), *Learning to read in American schools: Basal readers and content texts.* Hillsdale, NJ: Lawrence Erlbaum Associates.

Ausubel, D. P. (1963). *The psychology of meaningful verbal learning.* New York: Grune & Stratton.

Bloom, B. (1971). Mastery learning. In J. H. Block (Ed.), *Mastery learning: Theory and practice* (pp. 47–63). New York: Holt, Rinehart & Winston.

Bruner, J., Goodnow, J. J., & Austin, G. A. (1967). *A study of thinking.* New York: Science Editions.

Carreiro, P. (1998). *Tales of thinking: Multiple intelligences in the classroom.* York, ME: Stenhouse Publishers.

Carroll, J. B. (1971). Problems of measurement related to the concept of learning for mastery. In J. H. Block (Ed.), *Mastery learning: Theory and practice* (pp. 37–41). New York: Holt, Rinehart & Winston.

Confrey, J. (1990). What constructivism implies for teaching. In R. Davis (Ed.), *Constructivist views on the teaching and learning of mathematics* (p. 109). Reston, VA: National Council of Teachers of Mathematics.

Cronbach, L. J. (1963). *Educational psychology.* New York: Harcourt Brace & World.

Fensham, P. (1992). Science and technology. In P. W. Jackson (Ed.), *Handbook of research on teaching* (p. 801). New York: Macmillan.

Gardner, H. (1991). *The unschooled mind: How children think and how schools should teach.* New York: Basic Books.

Gardner, H. (1994). Multiple intelligences: A theory in practice. *Teachers College Record, 95* (4), 576–583.

Good, T. L., & Brophy, J. E. (2000). *Looking in classrooms.* New York: Longman.

Joyce, B., & Weil, M. (1996). *Models of teaching.* Boston: Allyn & Bacon.

Kohn, A. (1993). *Punished by rewards: The trouble with gold stars, incentive plans, A's, praise, and other bribes.* Boston: Houghton Mifflin.

Lave, J., & Wenger, E. (1991). *Situated learning: Legitimate peripheral participation.* Cambridge: Cambridge University Press.

Maslow, A. (1962) *Toward a psychology of being.* New York: Van Nostrand.

Matthews, M. R. (2000). Appraising constructivism in science and mathematics education. In D. C. Phillips (Ed.), *Constructivism in education: Opinions and second opinions on controversial issues* (pp.161–192). Ninety-ninth yearbook of the National Society for the Study of Education, Part I. Chicago: The University of Chicago Press.

National Research Council. (1996). *National science education standards.* Washington, DC: National Academy Press.

Oliver, D., & Shaver, J. P. (1966/1974). *Teaching public issues in the high school.* Boston: Houghton Mifflin.

Osborne, R. J., & Wittrock, M. C. (1983). Learning science: A generative process. *Science Education, 67,* 489–508.

Pearson, P. D., & Iran-Negate, A. (Eds.) (1998). *Review of Research in Education* (Vol. 23). Washington, DC: American Educational Research Association.

Phillips, D. C. (2000). An opinionated account of the constructivist landscape. In D. C. Phillips (Ed.), *Constructivism in education: Opinions and second opinions on controversial issues.* Ninety-ninth yearbook of the National Society for the Study of Education, Part I. Chicago: The University of Chicago Press.

Piaget, J. (1950). *Psychology of intelligence.* New York: Harcourt Brace.

Resnick, L., & Klopfer, L. (Eds.). (1989). *Toward the thinking curriculum: Current cognitive research: 1989 yearbook of the association for supervision and curriculum development.* Alexandria, VA: Association for Supervision and Curriculum Development.

Rogers, C. (1971). *Client centered therapy.* Boston: Houghton Mifflin.

Rosenshine, B. (1985). Direct instruction. In T. Husen & T. N. Postlethwaite (Eds.), *International encyclopedia of education* (Vol. 3, pp. 1395–1400). Oxford: Pergamon Press.

Schwab, J. (1965). *Biological sciences curriculum study: Biology teachers' handbook.* New York: Wiley.

Skinner, B. F. (1948). *Walden two.* New York: Macmillan.

Solomon, J. (1994). The rise and fall of constructivism. *Studies in Science Education, 23,* 1–19.

Springer, S. P., & Deutsch, G. (1981). *Left brain, right brain.* San Francisco: W. H. Freeman and Company.

Suchman, R. J. (1962) *The elementary school training program in scientific inquiry, Report to the U.S. Office of Education, Project Title VII, Urbana: University of Illinois.*

Taba, H. (1967). *Teachers handbook for elementary school social studies.* Reading, MA: Addison-Wesley.

Vygotsky, L. (1962). *Thought and language.* Cambridge, MA: MIT Press.

Vygotsky, L. (1978). *Mind in society: The development of higher psychological processes.* (Edited by M. Cole, V. John-Steiner, S. Scribner, & E. Souberman). Cambridge: Harvard University Press.

Multicultural Education and Exceptionality in Learning Communities

CHAPTER OBJECTIVES

This chapter is designed to help you

1. Help multicultural students and students of exceptionality achieve success within learning communities.

2. Understand the nature of cultural assimilation in American society and express ways that these assimilation efforts have affected various cultures immigrating to the United States.

3. Explain the differences between various assimilation theories and show which is the most likely explanation of how assimilation actually takes place in society.

4. Explain the myths which surround multicultural education and discuss why these myths have no substance.

The special needs of a diverse student population must be addressed by teachers.

5. Explain the role of *voice* in helping multicultural students gain a fuller understanding of cultural disparities.

6. Explain the provisions of the Individuals with Disabilities Education Act.

7. Explain how to avoid class, ethnic, and gender problems in dealing with students.

8. Identify various behavioral disorders, along with various treatments that may be applied to help students who have these problems.

9. Characterize various learning disabilities and indicate some of the interventions possible for helping students with learning disabilities.

10. Explain how gifted, creative, and talented students can be helped to function appropriately in learning communities.

INTRODUCTION

The diversity of the student population creates one of the most difficult problems that teachers have to face: providing useful and appropriate instruction. Students come from many cultures and represent different races as well as different ethnic and class groups. Students with various learning challenges are often integrated into regular classrooms, although teachers may have very little experience or training in effectively teaching in such complex circumstances. The students themselves are often confronted with conditions that make both learning and social conditions difficult. The experience of Johanna and her classmates in the following vignette illustrates this problem.

Johanna, a 16-year-old, came to the United States from Puerto Rico six months ago. Although she has been exposed to English in school during this time, her parents still speak Spanish exclusively in their home. As a result, she has considerable difficulty understanding what is going on in school. There are 10 other Hispanic students there; four are Native Americans, while the other six are immigrants like herself. None of these students are in her other classes, although three of the immigrant youth eat lunch with her daily. They speak in Spanish as they talk of their aspirations and desires, as well as problems they encounter at school. None claim to have friends outside their little circle and all express some fear for their safety. There has been some taunting in the halls, and some of the boys in school look at them and laugh.

Johanna tries to make up for her language inadequacies by excelling in art. Her teacher often makes a point of showing her artwork, which is excellent, to the class. A few of her teachers try to take time to help her while the class is doing seat work, but most of the instruction comes from lectures and reading the text. She occasionally is assisted by a special education teacher who does not speak Spanish, but who is warm and loving. This teacher comes into the regular classroom, sits by Johanna, and gives her help when she is working on seat work. Johanna loves to interact with her, but some of her classmates laugh when she works with this special teacher. It makes her feel like she is dumb and not accepted. She wishes that there was some way to get the help she needs without drawing attention to herself.

Recently Johanna became aware of how different the meanings of English words are when compared to Spanish and how some words have multiple meanings that are difficult to keep straight. She was often laughed at for not understanding these differences or the small nuances in speech between the languages. One particularly troublesome issue was the cultural voice Johanna carried over from her native language. For example, she was trying to explain what it meant to respect your mother and father last Monday, and told the class that to respect her mother she would shut her mouth and go to her room when scolded. "If I don't," she explained, "my mother will smack me." The class laughed at this and had to be quieted by the teacher. Later, Jane, the girl who sat next to her, told Johanna that *respect* means having manners. Johanna has trouble keeping all these meanings straight.

Johanna's difficulties are common ones. Youth with special needs often feel like misunderstood outsiders. Their natural reaction is to withdraw or restrict interactions to a limited number of associates who have similar difficulties. Some youth have language problems, while others have to deal with racial or class prejudice. A few students have behavioral disorders and disabilities, or impairments to sight or hearing. When these children are included in regular classrooms, teachers have the difficult task of providing instructional strategies that ensure these special students, along with all of their peers, are provided the best educational opportunities possible. Having such a diverse student population greatly complicates the work of teachers, particularly when they assume that all their students should achieve the same educational objectives.

Giving all youth common educational experiences is not only difficult, but it is inappropriate. Just because students share the same classrooms doesn't mean that their goals, learning activities, and assessment should also be the same. Rather, it is because students have different learning proclivities, as well as interests, that learning opportunities should be differentiated. It is virtually impossible for all students to go through the same set of experiences common in traditional schooling and still achieve what is most appropriate for them. Nonetheless, providing each student exactly what he or she needs is daunting, a goal that is next to impossible for many teachers. To provide learning experiences that are suited to individual learners, teachers need to take into account students' constructivist learning inclinations, learning styles, interests, and needs, as well as special learning problems they may have. Each student will have individual life experiences as well as personal learning approaches. It can be mind boggling just to accommodate a few differences between students, let alone cater to the full spectrum of variations.

Actually, teachers have an impossible task if they try to direct all learning activities while catering to the various differences between students. For this reason, teachers ignore most differences and deal with the few students they can reach, given the time they have. To increase the amount of learning that specifically relates to each student, teachers need to take on a new role: empowering students to direct their own learning, which can be responsibly achieved in learning communities.

Exemplary teachers do not focus on youth with special needs as though they are in a separate category. Rather, it is more effective if all students are considered to have special needs. They do, in fact. Each person is sufficiently different from any other person that he or she can benefit greatly from classroom experiences that take these differences into account. If students are responsibly self-directed, the burden of deciding the most beneficial experiences for each student is partially taken out of the teacher's hands. This has the added benefit of promoting more student enthusiasm and commitment for learning. Learning communities may provide the best format for accommodating student differences and appropriately varying the learning environment. In learning communities, activities can be differentiated as needed, while students assume responsibility for directions and adjustments. It doesn't matter how broad the differences are between students. Each can be provided experiences that articulate with group learning, but also foster personal growth. For example, if Johanna had been in a learning community, the group's priority would be to ensure that her language difficulty did not interfere with her learning. They would find a way to provide her the needed help and to engage the group in personally meaningful learning activities. In addition, there would be no disparaging comments or actions directed toward Johanna, nor intimidating laughter. Such things would be unthinkable within the group. If mocking or teasing came from outside the group, her community "family" would immediately act to solve the problem; Johanna, as part of the family, would be protected and supported. Johanna's language difficulties would be openly addressed by the community, and her role adjusted to accommodate changes in her ability as she grew in her language facility. All in the community would revel in her growth and development.

Decision Points

Identify six fellow students from your own public school experience who you believe needed special help. List the things you believe were done by teachers that was helpful. Create another list of happenings you believe were detrimental to those individuals. What should have been done to be more helpful?

Multicultural and Diversity Concerns

Multicultural education was a response to the belief, fueled by societal unrest and racial discrimination, that children with different cultural backgrounds did not have their needs appropriately met. Conscientious efforts were taken to ensure these children received the best education possible, since existing educational practices generally did discriminate against children, not only because of class, gender, or race, but also because of various learning, behavior, or physical problems (Banks, 2003a).

Youth groups needing special attention have been steadily increasing. With regard to ethnicity, demographers predict that by the year 2020 one of every three people in the United States will belong to what we now refer to as a minority (Sobol, 1990). By 2050, African Americans, Latinos, and Asian Americans will make up 48 percent of the U.S. population (Martin & Midgley, 1999). Interestingly, in 1996 students of color constituted the majority population in 70 of the nation's 130 largest school districts (districts with 36,000 students or more). The range was from 50.7 percent in Toledo, Ohio, to 96.9 percent in Brownsville, Texas (Gay, 2003).

To effectively work with diverse populations, teachers must acknowledge that all people have similar needs, desires, and problems, but they have different ways of satisfying their needs and solving their problems. Teachers who realize that people who act differently are still essentially the same will attain greater respect for their students, thereby helping their students to more fully grow and develop (Grossman, 1995).

NATIONAL TEACHING STANDARDS

Teachers recognize that intelligence is culturally defined; that is, intelligent behavior is largely determined by the values and beliefs of the culture in which that behavior is judged.

Teachers recognize that, in a multicultural nation, students bring to the schools a plethora of abilities and aptitudes that are valued differently by the community, the school, and the family.

Understanding Cultural Differences

Culture defines the way we think, feel, and act, as well as the way we judge the world. Thus, culture restricts alternative ways of looking at the world, including the way we view others and assess their social value. This **ethnocentric** view sees one's own culture traits as natural, correct, and superior to those of other cultures, whose traits are considered odd, amusing, inferior, or immoral (Yetman, 1985).

In modern society, it is increasingly important that all citizens achieve an accurate picture of other cultures and learn to treat them fairly. This means not only understanding other cultures and appreciating them, but valuing them and viewing them as viable constituents of America's cultural plurality. It involves understanding other cultural systems from their perspective rather than from one's own. This is necessary in order to maintain positive relationships with the numerous cultural groups, not only in America but throughout the world. Failure to understand and accept other ways of life is largely responsible for poor relationships, hatred, and war.

One of the difficulties often encountered in understanding other races and cultures is the practice of stereotyping. This not only occurs in general society but also in school textbooks. For example, African Americans are often portrayed in service occupations, sports, and entertainment, rather than in professions like law, medicine, and teaching. Native Americans are often portrayed in historical settings, but rarely in contemporary circumstances. In addition, they are characterized from the perspective of the majority culture, rather than as they might view themselves. Hispanic groups are stereotyped as violent, and are often portrayed as living in segregated, poor neighborhoods (Hardman, Drew, & Egan, 1999). These stereotypes often obscure the positive features of various cultures that might make positive contributions to other groups.

Another impediment to understanding other cultures is the emphasis placed on assimilation in American society. **Assimilation** is a process where various cultural groups adopt the dominant culture. During assimilation, cultural patterns that distinguish different groups might disappear, the distinctive patterns of these groups might become part of the dominant culture, or a combination of the two might occur (Gollnick & Chinn, 1994). Assimilation develops through stages in which the new cultural group (1) adjusts its cultural patterns to be more consistent with the dominant group, (2) develops significant large-scale relationships with the dominant group, (3) intermarries fully with the dominant group, (4) loses its sense of identity as separate from the dominant group, (5) encounters no discrimination, (6) doesn't experience prejudiced attitudes, and (7) is not involved in power struggles and value incompatibilities with the dominant group.

The speed of assimilation varies, depending on how isolated and segregated a particular group is from the dominant society. Native Americans, for example, have been isolated on reservations, so their assimilation has been very slow. The same is true for any groups who are discriminated against (Gordon, 1964). A more advanced stage of assimilation is referred to as **structural assimilation,** which takes place when various groups share primary relationships such as membership in the same cliques and social clubs. In the United States, structural assimilation has mainly been seen with white Protestant immigrants from northern and western Europe. Other groups forfeit their cultures and languages and behave like the dominant culture, at least publicly, but still have not achieved full acceptance by the dominant culture (Gollnick & Chinn, 1994).

There are different ideas about assimilation methods. The Anglo-conformity theory holds that an individual can only be assimilated by renouncing his or her ancestral culture in favor of an Anglo-Saxon one. There is also the melting pot theory, which contends that disparate cultures from all over world can assemble in "America's divinely inspired crucible" and merge into a single, unique American culture, although it is generally conceded that this has never taken place. Instead, the specific cultural contributions of the various groups have been limited by the dominant culture (Gordon, 1964).

Actually, neither the melting pot theory nor the Anglo-conformity theory adequately explain what has taken place historically in America. A better picture comes from **cultural pluralism:** enough subsocietal separation is maintained to guarantee the continuance of various ethnic cultural traditions and the perpetuation of various subgroups without interfering with the operation of general American civic life. When minorities fail to be assimilated into the dominant culture, they tend to maintain their own ethnic identity and only participate peripherally in the larger cultural life (Gollnick & Chinn, 1994).

An even more telling explanation of assimilation in American society comes from a modified version of cultural pluralism. According to this view, assimilation and pluralism are ongoing processes. In practical terms, cultural diversity should be accommodated in public education, and interactions of individuals from different cultural groups should be supported. Thus, various groups continue to retain elements of their own culture, but take on certain aspects of the majority culture. When applied to the schools, modified cultural pluralism advocates different emphases depending on circumstances. If group maintenance and support are the primary concerns, schools tend to remain segregated. The emphasis is on community control, native language instruction, and a curriculum strong in ethnic studies. However, when the goal is to achieve a better balance between the dominant culture and ethnic attachments, similarities as well as differences are integrated and highlighted. The curriculum focuses on the national identity and interests while at the same time valuing cultural diversity and pluralistic perspectives. This approach usually emphasizes the integration of students and staff, equal educational opportunity, and a curriculum sensitive to group needs (Hernandez, 1989).

 ## QUESTIONS FOR REFLECTION

1. Why is it that the "melting pot theory" of assimilation could have apparent acceptance by Americans yet never have been truly achieved?

2. Why is the modified version of cultural pluralism a better explanation of how assimilation has taken place in the United States than the melting pot theory?

Myths and Realities About Multicultural Education

Some form of multicultural education has been practiced since the 1920s. During early times its purpose was to make the dominant majority populations more tolerant and accepting of immigrants in order to foster and maintain a greater sense of national unity and social control (Montalto, 1978). Later, during the 1960s, desegregation was enforced in the schools. At the same time, children of color were described as *culturally deprived* of the background required to optimally benefit from a curriculum essentially defined by the dominant society. Eventually these groups were described as *culturally different;* thus, value was attached to other cultures. Yet, schooling emphasized the need to help children develop the cultural patterns of the dominant society so they could fit into mainstream American life (Sleeter & Grant, 1988).

The civil rights movement of the 1960s and 1970s stimulated an interest in ethnic studies, discrimination, and intergroup relations. Racial and ethnic pride emerged, and people demanded African American or other ethnic studies programs. Participants in these programs were primarily members of the groups being studied; in some cases, students outside the group were deliberately excluded. These programs focused mainly on the various ethnic histories and cultures, with the main objectives being to provide students with insight and to instill pride in personal racial/ethnic backgrounds. Most of these programs featured only one ethnic group; the scope of a program was seldom multiethnic. There was, however, occasionally a limited focus on understanding the relationship and conflict between the particular ethnic group and the dominant population.

Programs were eventually developed that focused on human relations. The objectives were to promote interracial understanding and to eliminate stereotypes. There was an emphasis on students' attitudes and feelings about others and about themselves (Sleeter & Grant, 1988). Along with the development of these efforts came the realization that ethnic studies by themselves would provide no guarantee of support for cultural diversity. Students from the dominant culture also needed to learn about the history, culture, and contributions of subordinate groups. Thus, ethnic studies were expanded into multiethnic studies. The curriculum emphasized the contributions of various subordinate groups and indicated that America was indeed a multiethnic country.

Accompanying the ethnic and racial emphasis of the civil rights movement came a call to deal with inequities regarding the poor, women, the disabled, the bilingual, and the aged.

This broader concept centered on the various microcultures to which individuals belong, emphasizing the interactions involved in being members of those microcultures, especially race, class, and gender. Yet, after six decades of concern for civil and human rights, there have been few real improvements in the management of cultural diversity and equality in the schools. Classrooms may be desegregated and mainstreamed, but many gaps still exist between various groups of students. The following inequities continue to be maintained:

- Students of color still score below white students on national standardized tests.
- There is still a great gap in income between whites and people of color.
- Whites occupy most of the managerial/professional jobs.
- More African American and Hispanic families than white families are below the poverty level (Gollnick & Chinn, 1994).

These problems can, in part, be solved if all students receive better educational experiences and if students become proactively involved in social improvement. Longstanding prejudices tend to rigidly enforce these inequalities. To solve these problems, students must be prepared to occupy a more significant role in modifying the social conditions that perpetuate them.

Educational reform efforts in America have generally consisted of little more than bureaucratic shuffling with little learning improvement. More comprehensive approaches are needed so the myriad influences on student achievement can be properly taken into account. The changes needed require multicultural applications in which factors influencing the education of diverse student populations are properly applied. This can best be accomplished by promoting student decision making along with the development of social action skills (Nieto, 2003). Reforms in multicultural education must be broadly conceptualized to help increase the quality of learning experiences for all students. They need to move beyond viewing diversity as a passing fad and genuinely take the history of integration into account, as well as the inequality and exclusion characteristic of past educational practices, to continue to effect the quality of students' educational experiences. Educators must realize that multicultural education is appropriate for everyone regardless of ethnicity, race, language, social class, religion, gender, or ability (Nieto, 1996).

Many of the multicultural education approaches have characterized groups of students on the basis of culture or ethnicity. However, given the differences within these groups, this stereotyping simply adds to the problems. In addition, many of the multicultural approaches tend to be single faceted and focus simplistically on procedures like mentioning the accomplishments of various racial groups in textbooks as though this would solve ethnic and racial problems. However, this has just diverted attention from real problems like the institutional discrimination characteristic of many schools. It is primarily through institutional discrimination being applied by those who control schools and other institutions that oppressive policies and practices are reinforced and legitimized (Nieto, 1996).

Many efforts at multicultural education have a very low impact in actually solving problems and promoting better educational experiences for students. For example, efforts like a "taco day" focus primarily on attitudes rather than activities that really make a difference. In addition, multicultural education may fail because of the ordinary practice of lumping all the problems of diverse groups together, rather than addressing the unique problems of each (Kailin, 2002).

To really make a difference, multicultural education should involve resistance to social oppression, including opposition to white supremacy and also patriarchy (Sleeter, 1996). Unfortunately, multicultural teachers ordinarily limit instruction to helping students make adjustments in the world as it exists rather than encouraging them to take actions to improve society. What is needed is a **critical pedagogy** that stresses the need for students to challenge the existing social order and initiate change. This is difficult because schools, as they currently operate, do not relate to students' real-life problems. Therefore, students don't see school as a mechanism for improving their oppressive social conditions. Consequently, students may see their education as irrelevant and simply offer a minimum effort. Thus, they unwittingly restrict their academic empowerment by not actively resisting the school's low demand of them. Students therefore get little help in achieving their potential and realizing their dreams in the real world. They go through school with no clear view of what they must do and how well they must perform to be academically and socially successful (Sleeter, 1996).

Multicultural education must be a basic education for all, not just peripheral experiences for a few students. It cannot be an add-on to the European-based curriculum already in place. Instead, it must incorporate critical multicultural elements and must be pervasive enough to permeate everything in the school: school climate, physical environment, curriculum, and relationships between teachers, students, and the community. This emphasis must be apparent in all lesson materials, curriculum guides, and other instructional materials as well as other features of the school like extracurricular activities and communications with parents. Multicultural education must prepare students for active membership in a democratic society and involve both teachers and students in applying what is learned to initiate justifiable social action (Nieto, 2002). Students should be helped to view things from multiple perspectives and process information critically and reflectively in advance of taking appropriate social action (Banks, 1997). The curriculum should not be passive, but rather help empower students in taking active roles to seek social justice.

Cultural and linguistic diversity should be celebrated rather than suppressed. Students should spend time reflecting on multiple and contradictory perspectives in order to more fully understand reality and to respect viewpoints with which they disagree. Only in this way can they learn to work successfully with others in a diverse society (Gay, 1995).

Schools should mentor students in their native language and culture. Native languages are currently downplayed and their use encouraged as little as possible. Students usually are denied instruction in their native language until after they have mastered English. However, having minority students maintain their native languages and cultures and verify their validity is essential for them to support and sustain academic achievement (Gay, 1995).

Banks (2003a) suggests a comprehensive curriculum plan for multicultural education that includes: (1) a focus on heroes and holidays; (2) the creation of themes and perspectives about various cultures that are added to the school program in the form of special units; (3) a focus on themes, events, concepts, and issues from multiple ethnic and cultural perspectives (For example, the Revolutionary War might be examined from the perspective of the British, Native Americans, and African Americans. Another possibility would be to study how different groups have influenced the development of the English language or to study and compare the history and style of art forms from various cultures.); and (4) helping students learn how to make decisions on important issues and problems and then taking action to help solve them. The teacher's role is to help students acquire decision-making skills and political efficacy. They should encourage students to become reflective social critics and skilled directors of social change. This involves a substantial change from the current practice of socializing students to unquestioningly accept the existing ideologies about the social order (Hahn, 1998).

Multicultural education should be based on sound principles with appropriate philosophical underpinnings (Bennett, 2003). First, it is imperative for multicultural experiences to foster acceptance and appreciation for cultural diversity itself. This goes beyond simply tolerance to intensely valuing diversity. Diversity is celebrated for the various perspectives it provides and the enlarged views it promotes. It gives insights so students can understand complex issues and solve problems for which they might not otherwise be prepared.

Second, in multicultural education there should be respect for human dignity and universal human rights. Students are taught that essential harmony is impossible without safeguarding everyone's rights and protecting human dignity. Divisiveness hampers social progress when attacks are made against the personal integrity of group members. Serious repercussions can be expected if anyone in a diverse population has special privileges over others.

Third, all societies have a responsibility to the world community. Unfortunately, when the cultures and the intentions of others are unknown or vague, the result may be war and other atrocities. Cordiality and cooperation are critical for the continuation of peaceful relations and courteous interactions. These attitudes and skills should be a central focus of schools.

Fourth, students should be taught a cooperative reverence for the earth. In America, the environment has commonly been exploited for personal gain. Exploiters assume that the earth has unlimited resources and an unlimited capacity to absorb toxic substances. Forests have been cut down with little thought taken regarding regeneration. Pollutants have been dumped into the ocean and rivers and released into the atmosphere in dangerous quantities. Nuclear waste has been created with insufficient consideration for how it might be properly disposed. Plant and animal habitats have been encroached upon for the sake of development, causing the extinction of species at an alarming rate. These and other issues need to be seriously considered by students as part of the ecology agenda of the school and of the entire world community.

The philosophical principles previously outlined provide a framework for the construction of a comprehensive multicultural education composed of the following interactive dimensions (Banks, 1995, 1996, 2003b; Bennett, 2003; Sleeter, 1996):

Curriculum content: The content of the curriculum should be composed of examples and illustrations from a variety of cultures. Key concepts, principles, generalizations, and theories should be drawn from various cultural areas and provide multiethnic and global perspectives. Students should be engaged in active inquiry and development of new knowledge about cultural differences along with the history and contributions of many ethnic groups and nations. The goal is for students to acquire multiple historical perspectives about culture and ethnicity.

Multicultural competence and understanding: Students need multiple ways of perceiving, evaluating, believing, and doing. They must be able to investigate and determine implicit cultural assumptions, frames of reference, perspectives, and biases within the various disciplines and how these views influence the way in which knowledge is constructed. For example, students might analyze knowledge construction in science by examining how racism has been perpetuated in science by genetic theories of intelligence. Students also need to acquire a cultural consciousness and be able to accurately interpret the nuances of style of other cultures and appreciate their unique contributions and value.

Prejudice reduction: Students must understand the forms of racism and sexism and how these contribute to prejudice and discrimination. Students need to develop positive attitudes toward different racial, ethnic, and cultural groups. In addition, they must learn to actively combat racism and sexism and their negative effects.

Equity pedagogy: The school environment must accommodate instructional strategies, discipline practices, school-community relations, and classroom climates that support diversity. Teachers must also be able to successfully determine the extent to which their teaching properly reflects multicultural issues and concerns. Teachers should be skilled in facilitating the academic achievement of students from diverse cultures and social class groups along with providing gender-appropriate instruction. They should appreciate the differences in learning styles of different students and be able to provide appropriate learning activities for students with different learning styles.

Employing empowering, social justice oriented learning: Critical pedagogy should be employed that emphasizes students challenging the existing social order. Myths and racial stereotypes must be examined by students and processed. They must be able to address school issues from multiple perspectives and use these insights to restructure the schools. Some practices that may be examined include labeling, grouping, sports participation, disproportionate achievement, enrollment in gifted and special education programs, and the interaction of staff and teachers across racial, ethnic, and gender lines.

Reverence for the earth: Students should understand the global dynamics of the earth and actively participate in conservation. Students should raise awareness for planetary improvement and encourage the perpetuation of a vibrant healthy earth. They must see their role in preserving the earth for future generations as a sacred responsibility.

 ## QUESTIONS FOR REFLECTION

1. What problems do you see in connection with ethnic studies? How can these problems be avoided?

2. What would a viable program of multicultural studies contain in specific terms? List some examples of the kind of experiences students might have that would be consistent with how multicultural studies were defined in the previous section.

NATIONAL TEACHING STANDARDS

Teachers are attuned to the diversity found among students and develop an array of strategies for working with them. This involves providing educational experiences that capitalize on and enlarge the repertoires of learning and thinking that students bring to school.

Teachers are vigilant in ensuring that all students receive sufficient attention and that biases based on real or perceived ability differences, handicaps or disabilities, social or cultural background, language, race, religion, or gender do not distort relationships between themselves and their students.

Nondiscriminatory Assessment of Diverse Populations

Unfortunately, a disproportionate number of minority students find themselves in special education classes due to cultural and language differences between them and the dominant culture. Referrals and placements in special classes are ordinarily based on various standardized assessments of such factors as intellectual and social functioning. Such assessments may be biased against children from ethnically and culturally different backgrounds. Courts have determined that particular tests discriminate against Hispanic students (*Diana v. State Board of Education*, 1970, 1973) and African American students (*Larry P. v. Riles*, 1972, 1979). This litigation has successfully established precedents for placing students in special programs: (1) children tested for potential placement in special education programs must be assessed in their native or primary language, and (2) children cannot be placed in special classes on the basis of culturally biased tests.

Assessment errors have been at the heart of the controversy regarding minority over-representation in special and multicultural education. Sometimes the measurement error is due to cultural phenomena, while at other times it is a function of the breadth and depth of children's experiences. Those who construct tests can hardly escape their own cultural background as they prepare items; thus, their culture is reflected in the questions. The environment of children from advantaged families is far more diverse and stimulus-rich than the environment of less-affluent families. Children from advantaged families will have traveled more, had more conversations with their parents about the world around them, and had experiences involving a greater variety of items that can be purchased or viewed in different settings. Tests ordinarily don't account for these differences. For example, one item on a nationally recognized standardized achievement test asks elementary students the following question: A plant's fruit always contains seeds.

Which of the items below is not a fruit?

A. Orange
B. Pumpkin
C. Apple
D. Celery

What if certain children, because of their poverty and/or life experiences, have never encountered celery or seen inside a pumpkin (Popham, 1999)? The test maker may find it inconceivable that a third-grade child has never eaten celery or carved a pumpkin. Consequently, he or she may not correctly recognize the potential bias. Even when tests have been purged of biases, there are good reasons to reject their use. For example, the test may not serve its intended purpose. There may be more valid means of determining student placement, like personal interviews.

One major culprit interfering with valid assessments of culturally diverse students is language differences. Assessments of children who are linguistically different have generally been biased and are an inaccurate reflection of the child's abilities (Figueroa, 1989). A large number of children do not speak English, or if they do they are handicapped to a degree by retaining the *voice* of their culture, which they unsuccessfully try to apply to their understanding of English. These children may also suffer a delay in language development. Some have fluency in conversational English, but not an adequate proficiency to sustain academic work. The usual result for these students is less success than expected, due simply to the lack of language proficiency, not to the lack of ability. Though an assessment may be necessary for placement in the students' native language, it is likely impossible to provide instruction in the same way. Therefore, placement is only part of the problem these students face. If students are placed using tests administered in their native language, but they are put in situations incongruous with the assessment, little may be gained until their language skills are brought up to the necessary level. No matter what the placement, this should be the design for all students who lack the necessary language skills to benefit optimally from ongoing instruction.

 ## QUESTION FOR REFLECTION

1. What alternative assessments might be appropriate for multicultural education?

NATIONAL TEACHING STANDARDS

Teachers need to ensure that mainstreamed students are being educated in the least-restrictive environment and must work with special education teachers to achieve this. They must work at successfully coordinating English as a second language, bilingual, and English-immersion programs.

Teachers need to be able to appropriately identify students in need of special attention and work in tandem with specialists to help them.

Education in the Least-Restrictive Environment

Education in the least-restrictive environment usually means placement in the educational mainstream. The 1975 Individuals with Disabilities Education Act (IDEA) requires students with disabilities to be taught in settings with non-disabled peers as much as possible. The same is true for students who are culturally different. Depending on the degree of disability or the level of language proficiency, students may need to be placed in a separate classroom situation for a portion of the time where their particular problem can receive appropriate attention. This tactic is usually reserved for students in unique circumstances.

Even in the 1997 amendment to IDEA, the basic principles have remained unchanged. All special children are to be accepted into a program of instruction designed especially for them. Nondiscriminatory identification of children with special needs and the evaluation of their achievements should be consistently employed (Turnbull & Cilley, 1999). Children are to receive instruction as a **continuum of services.** This is a flexible arrangement where students' placement can be changed from one level to another over time. It is represented as a pyramid composed of seven levels (Heward & Cavanaugh, 2003):

- *Level 7— Specialized facilities in a nonpublic setting:*   Instruction is intensive and in a protected environment.
- *Level 6 — Special schools:*   A prescribed program is delivered from a specially trained staff.
- *Level 5 — Full-time special class:*   Pupils receive a prescribed program under the direction of a special class teacher.
- *Level 4 — Regular classroom and resource room:*   Pupils receive a prescribed program under the direction of a regular classroom teacher, with some time spent in a specially staffed and equipped resource room.
- *Level 3 — Regular classroom with supplementary instruction and services:*   Pupils receive a prescribed program under the direction of the regular teacher. In addition there is instruction from an itinerant or school-based specialist.
- *Level 2 — Regular classroom with consultation to the teacher:*   Pupils get a prescribed program under the direction of the regular classroom teacher who is supported by ongoing consultation from specialists.
- *Level 1 — Regular classroom:*   Pupils receive a prescribed program under the direction of the regular teacher.

Language instruction and disability remediation can take place in several ways. One approach is to give students instruction both in English and in their native language, decreasing the use of native language instruction over time. This is the *transition model.* A second approach provides for instruction to be in English for the regular curriculum, accompanied by instruction in the native language during the part of the day focused on the ethnic heritage. This is called the *restoration/maintenance model.* The third model, called the *maintenance model,* has the regular curriculum taught primarily in English, while various other curriculum areas are taught primarily in the native language. Each of these approaches has merit and their use is ordinarily determined by conditions in specific school districts (Hardman, Drew, & Egan, 1999).

IDEA also requires the development of an individualized educational program (IEP) for each student who is disabled. Each IEP must consider cultural factors, such as language proficiency, as well as learning and behavioral problems. A student with disabilities or a language deficiency may receive specialized instruction from various professionals for each appropriate facet of his or her education. To be maximally effective, IEP should address all phases of the student's life. For example, children who live in poverty come to school with a different set of experiences and problems than their peers from more affluent backgrounds. Care must be exercised to avoid stereotyping in the preparation of IEPs. For example, assumptions may be made regarding a particular ethnic group: the foods eaten, family leadership, child-rearing practices, or methods of confronting problems.

The following criteria must be adhered to in preparing IEPs:

- A team composed of parents, the child's teacher, a special education teacher, a school district representative, and the child, if this is determined to be appropriate.

- A statement indicating the child's present level of performance and how the disability affects learning and participation in school activities, goals, and objectives; services to be provided; and modifications needed to achieve the goals.
- An explanation of the extent to which the child will not participate with non-disabled children in the regular classroom.
- Statement of modifications in the administration of assessments needed, or the need for exclusion from assessments and tests.
- Date for starting services and modifications and the anticipated frequency, location, and duration of those services and modifications.
- Statement of how progress will be measured and how parents will be kept informed about the child's progress, and the extent to which the progress achieved is sufficient to enable the child to meet the goals by the end of the year.
- For students 14 and older, the IEP must also include information about how the child's transition from school to adult life will be supported (Turnbull & Turnbull, 1998).

NATIONAL TEACHING STANDARDS

Teachers should counter potential inequities and avoid favoritism.

Teachers do not treat all children alike, for similar treatment is not necessarily equivalent to equitable education.

Teachers employ what is known about ineffectual and effective practice with diverse groups of students, while striving to learn more about how best to accommodate those differences.

Diversity and Learning Communities

Learning communities are especially appropriate for helping students with disabilities or ethnic differences to have a fuller, more successful educational experience since learning

Teachers can help multicultural students advance themselves socially and academically.

communities assume a helping role; participants look after one another's needs and concerns. The community's basic agenda is to be an advocate for all members and to help them experience academic and social success. If strong ties are promoted between members, and roles are defined to ensure that each member of the community has his or her needs met and his or her problems addressed by the group, these important matters will not be left to chance and ignored as they often are in regular classrooms. Even in situations where IEPs have been written, and where specialists are employed to help students with special needs, the important matter of having students look after one another is usually not a high priority. The focus is ordinarily on achievement, not on caring relationships.

The teacher's role in a learning community that includes students with special needs is to ensure that critical issues regarding all of these students are addressed. This includes some considerations and activities that do not ordinarily occur in school. For example, the role of students with special needs in relation to their peers is substantially different than it would be in the regular classroom. In a normal classroom situation, students with special needs are simply recipients of the specified help. However, with learning communities the role of students with special needs includes looking after the interests of other students, not just receiving help. Everyone in the group, including students with special needs, has a part to play in the life of other members. This is a critical difference between these two different approaches. Exclusively receiving help limits the growth of these students and steers them toward an egocentric orientation to life.

Focusing on others' needs will likely be a new experience for all students, but students with special needs may find this particularly different and challenging. They have typically spent most of their lives having others help them, so being in a helper role will be a huge adjustment for them. Teachers will need to provide guidance and encouragement so there is a smooth transition from acting as a recipient of help to being a helper. This may not be a comfortable transition for some students because their life experiences have not given them sufficient opportunities for this kind of growth. They are looked upon as needing help, not as capable of rendering assistance to others. Some of the help ordinarily given to students with special needs not only is unwarranted, but it may be detrimental. Thus, many of these students may be victims of a "self-fulfilling prophesy" regarding some of their supposed inabilities, and consequently they may exhibit learned helplessness.

Specialists of various kinds should be involved in helping students with special needs in learning communities. Their expertise is essential to help students define their roles and coach as needed. Care will obviously be needed to avoid excessive dependence on specialized support. Much of the assistance for these students should be generated from the group, with professionals providing direction as needed. The professionals' role should be to give insights for group members about how to provide appropriate assistance.

In learning communities, many of the same principles still apply as in the traditional classroom, except that the context is different. Some of the tasks teachers or professionals ordinarily perform in a classroom should be turned over to group members. When and how this takes place will vary according to the circumstances and individuals involved. The judgment of professionals is critical in making this determination. Their recommendations should not only reflect knowledge about what is most helpful to students with special needs, but also demonstrate how these suggestions can be carried out within a learning community. All actions in a learning community should support the group agenda as well as the needs and well-being of each individual member.

Decision Points

1. Visit a public secondary school and make observations of the diverse student population. Make a record of instances where multicultural considerations are ignored or dealt with inappropriately and where teachers and students promote positive experiences for minority students.
2. Create a description of a specific learning project from your teaching subject and explain how specific arrangements could be made to appropriately involve all members of a diverse learning community.

Understanding Class, Ethnic, and Gender Problems in Schools

Teachers must understand the specific characteristics and sensitivities of different multicultural groups to help their students in relating personally to the groups and in preparing class members with the attitudes and skills needed to successfully interact with one another. In doing this, it is important not to overgeneralize. Asian and Hispanic cultures, for example, vary from one country to the next. There may also be regional differences. Teachers need to explore other cultures individually so they will be able to supply the guidance necessary to promote better student understanding as well as encourage helpful interactions and cohesiveness within the class and provide necessary support to individuals.

Social Class

There are two different views about social class structure in the United States, with two significantly different beliefs regarding the possibility of individuals achieving equity and advancing socially and economically. The first position supports the idea that it is possible to move to a higher class with sufficient effort. There is an inherent struggle between those who control most of the resources and those who are oppressed. The oppressed are usually believed to be inferior, and their hardships are blamed on their lack of effort. In this kind of society, individuals who are the ablest and most meritorious, ambitious, hard-working, and talented achieve the highest social levels. Affirmative action is discouraged, as it is believed to be alien to democratic principles and encourages mediocrity.

In the second view of social class, a few families and individuals own and control corporations, banks, and other means of gaining wealth; these comprise the privileged upper class. Those who sell their labor to make a living make up the other classes. Inequality is acknowledged, but it is not explained in terms of class differences and conflicts. Rather, various classes exist due to low motivation and inability. Thus, it is the individual's fault for not advancing socially. This is called "blaming the victim." From this perspective, most people are caught in the socioeconomic stratum they were born into, and the politicoeconomic system ensures that they remain there. Equity cannot be achieved in this view through providing oppressed individuals an equal chance; instead, equal results are sought. Affirmative action is considered necessary to help people achieve a more advanced social status. Equity comes when the same results are achieved by all in terms of such indicators as school dropout rates, college attendance and graduation, and access to high-paying jobs (Gollnick & Chinn, 1994).

Some people have considerable difficulty raising their class status; others advance themselves fairly naturally through their own ingenuity and efforts. This disparity often defies explanation. Yet, it is clear that those with wealth protect their advantage, both for themselves and their children, by occupying important positions on boards that determine state and local policies, on boards of colleges and universities, and on corporation boards. By controlling policies that can influence their investments, they are able to protect their interests (Parenti, 1988).

Economic inequality is most pronounced among African Americans, Hispanic Americans, and Native Americans. Many believe that education can be a powerful force for helping individuals advance socially and reduce poverty. In keeping with this belief, the federal government has initiated educational programs to raise the economic levels for impoverished people (e.g., Head Start, Upward Bound, Title I, Job Corps, and Neighborhood Youth Corps). Unfortunately, these programs have not realized the desired goals. As a result, some have come to believe that public education, rather than being an agent for social reform and improvement, has become a mechanism for inculcating the values and developing the skills necessary for maintaining the current socioeconomic and political systems (Gollnick & Chinn, 1994). Perhaps one reason for this failure could be the organized effort of affluent parents to derail educational reforms they believe are not in the best interest of their children. They believe their children deserve more consideration than those from the lower socioeconomic classes and that the programs initiated to help the underprivileged should be abolished (Kohn, 1998).

The current socioeconomic order is perpetuated in some ways that may seem benign, but have devastating consequences for lower-class children. For example, children get categorized into reading and mathematics groups as early as the eighth day of school, and these groupings are typically made according to nonacademic factors. Children who come to school in clean clothes, interact with teachers more readily, are more verbal, use standard English, and come from more advantaged families are generally placed in the more advanced groups (Rist, 1970).

A lower-quality education is given to lower-class children. They are given less-effective learning experiences than their more-advantaged counterparts. Because they are commonly provided remedial compensatory education, they miss out on learning that involves critical thinking. Educators assume these children do not learn easily and consequently cannot understand difficult concepts. Thus, these children have fewer opportunities to engage in creative thinking, and instead participate in recitation activities and structured writing experiences (Gamoran & Berends, 1987).

Tracking is one of the educational practices that adversely affects lower-class children. This system assigns children to specific classes according to test scores, socioeconomic status, and teacher grades and recommendations. Initial tracking tends to permanently lock children in to a particular level of expectation and, as a result, a set amount of academic success. The feedback lower-track children get from teachers and peers suggest that little can be expected from them because they are inferior (Banks & Banks, 1989).

What can be done to eliminate inequitable educational practices? Tracking, of course, should be eliminated. Students with disadvantages need the benefit of experiences that have here-to-fore been reserved for the more advantaged youth (Wheelock, 1992). They need to learn to think and make decisions as well as participate in democratically oriented classrooms where the emphasis on community undermines prejudice and class distinctions. They need to be empowered with all their classmates to fight against social practices that elevate one person above another; they must be allowed to achieve at the highest possible level. The diversity of cultures should be honored, and youth should be taught that they can improve their situation socially in concert with their classmates (Banks, 2000).

 ## QUESTIONS FOR REFLECTION

1. From an educational standpoint, what can be done to promote more economic equity?
2. To what extent does seeking economic equity support a democratic society?

Ethnic Diversity

The United States is reportedly composed of at least 276 separate ethnic groups, based on national origin, religion, and race, including 170 different Native American groups (Gollnick & Chinn, 1994). Ethnic groups are commonly broken down into several general categories: European Americans, Asian Americans, African Americans, Hispanic Americans, and Native Americans. However, this is a superficial view. The subgroups in any one of these general categories have their origins in different countries and consequently have distinctive cultures. People from different countries have been subject to different political and economic pressures and concerns, and they have developed a variety of customs and social interactions. There are also significant differences in language usage and local idioms. People from South and Central America, for example, share ancient cultural origins, but have had more than 200 years to develop their own cultural characteristics (Omi & Winant, 1986).

Socially and politically dominated groups have experienced the most severe academic disadvantage in American schools. For example, Koreans and members of the Buraka caste in Japan do poorly in Japanese schools, but perform well as immigrants in American schools. Finns do poorly in Sweden, but succeed as well as Sweds in Australia. The Maori do poorly when compared to other Pacific Island Immigrants in New Zealand Schools. In the United States, newly arrived immigrants do better and have higher self-esteem than their counterparts born in America. However, these students may not learn well due to preoccupations regarding political resistance to the dominant society (Jacob & Jordan, 1993).

The situation with African Americans is different from Hispanic cultures. African Americans are tied together by race and common heritage. Because their skin color ranges from light to very dark, it does not define them as a group; rather, their identification is based more on sharing a common national origin. Most importantly, they have become a single ethnic group because they share a common history, language, economic life, and culture, which has developed after more than four centuries of living in the United States. Race, however, remains an important part of their identity (Appiah, 1990). This is in contrast to people of color who have recently immigrated. These individuals identify themselves with other ethnic groups like Puerto Ricans, Nigerian Americans, or West Indians. Historically, race has been a dominant factor in singling out certain groups as inferior and thereby eligible for discriminatory treatment. The existence of many ethnic groups has not been important. However, from an educational standpoint, it is necessary to understand the uniqueness of each ethnic group so students from these groups can be treated appropriately by their teachers.

Students are commonly placed in an educational environment based on test scores. Through this tracking process, many African American and Hispanic students get placed in classes with slow learners because of their low test scores. In this case, the self-fulfilling prophesy takes over and students begin to act and think as though they are mentally challenged (Banks, 2000). Experts believe all forms of tracking should be abolished (Oakes & Guiton, 1995). The longer African American, Hispanic, and Native American youth stay in tracking configurations, the further they fall behind academically (Gay, 2003).

Ethnic groups other than the dominant Western European group are usually given minority status. These groups experience a wide range of discriminatory treatments, and consequently a lot of oppositional behavior is expressed. Some individuals who succeed in crossing the boundaries into the dominant group may experience both internal opposition or identity problems, as well as opposition and pressure from their original ethnic group (Ogbu, 1988, p. 176).

The members of some minority groups grow-up in ethnic enclaves such as Chinatown, Little Italy, Harlem, and Little Saigon. Youth from these environments often become culturally encapsulated. Nearly all of their primary relationships occur within their group, and they lack awareness of other cultures. When they are forced out of their ethnic encapsulation in their quest to achieve economic mobility, they often encounter considerable difficulty making the transition into a multicultural environment. These individuals usually form secondary relationships with members of other ethnic groups with whom they work, but rarely with members of the dominant culture (Gollnick & Chinn, 1994).

As a result of prejudice, members of oppressed groups are denied full access to the economic, political, and social spheres of the dominant group. Unfortunately, in an effort to become assimilated into the dominant group, these ethnic minorities may reject their own ethnic group and culture. If they are not fully accepted by the dominant group, they find themselves suspended between two cultures, resulting in self-identity problems. Educators must realize that youth are products of their own experiences; therefore, a specific individual may not fit a stereotypical definition of the ethnic group to which he or she belongs. This is exemplified by the migration of Vietnamese families in the 1970s. In the early 1970s, immigrants predominantly came from the wealthy and professional middle class. In the late 1970s, most Vietnamese immigrants came from peasant and rural backgrounds. Unfortunately, some educators have expected the same academic performance from all Asian Americans. Teachers need to be more familiar with the various microcultures to increase their effectiveness working with students from these backgrounds (Gollnick & Chinn, 1994).

Ethnicity has a significant impact on the school experiences of youth. Because the school environment may be incongruous with students' cultural experiences, teachers will have to provide necessary support. They need to create a hospitable classroom climate so that all students are comfortable. Students must be able to participate in the dominant society while maintaining distinct ethnic identities if they choose. Youth who belong to the dominant culture require instruction and experiences that acquaint them with the cultures and behavior of their minority classmates. Children need to feel that cultural diversity is not only normal, but desirable within the learning communities to which they belong (Gay, 2003).

Learning communities can provide the acceptance and caring needed to ensure that all ethnic groups feel needed and wanted, thereby avoiding patterns of resistance and opposition that commonly appear when minority students are subordinated in the school. Otherwise, these students may become discipline problems, denying the value of academic achievement and other important school purposes (Ogbu, 1988; Solomon, 1988).

Understanding very subtle differences between cultural patterns of expression can help immensely as teachers interact with their students (see Table 5.1). For example, African-American adults seldom ask their children questions when they already know the answer. However, teachers ordinarily ask questions just to ascertain what students know. Obviously, they know more about the subject than their students. This confuses African American students, particularly in the early grades. In addition, African American adults usually ask questions about children's experiences, while teachers ask about other things. Youth consequently may be unprepared to give intelligent answers. Finally, European American teachers tend to be more indirect, while African American parents issue direct orders to their children and give them specific instructions about what they want them to do. When their teachers ask them to do "such and such," African American students take these instructions as suggestions rather than expectations (Brice-Heath, 1982).

Native Americans also confront significant cultural disparities in school. For example, Native Americans are less concerned with the exactness of time than are European

TABLE 5.1   *Differences in Cultural Patterns of Expression.*

Minority Cultures	**Some Cultural Generalizations**	**European Americans' Cultural Generalizations**
African Americans	Don't ask questions to which adults know the answer	Ask questions to find out what students know
	Give direct orders	Give less-direct orders that students take as suggestions
	Avert eyes to show respect	Use eye contact to show respect
Native Americans	Do not be concerned with exactness of time	Value punctuality
	Do not prepare for unknown eventualities	Engage in future-oriented activities
	Value patience	Value quick action
	Value preserving resources	Value consumption
	Value personal freedom	Value group consensus
	Avoid saying what they believe another doesn't want to hear	Value absolute truthfulness
Asian Americans	Shun frankness	Make direct expressions
	Emphasize interpersonal harmony	Emphasize truthfulness
Hispanic Americans	Avert eyes to show submissiveness	Make eye contact
	Actively avoid admission of guilt	Be less passionate about admission of guilt
	Touch while communicating	Avoid touching, as it may be offensive

Americans, who consider punctuality a virtue, if not a necessity. In addition, Native Americans hold that because the future is uncertain, preparing for unknown eventualities is a waste of time and effort. Western Europeans, however, buy insurance, fret over savings and investments, and engage in many future-oriented activities that make little sense to Native Americans. Western Europeans admire quick action, while Native Americans value patience. Teachers may judge Native American children's slow reactions as evidence of their being dull. The seemingly obvious solution of encouraging these students to act more quickly may have negative consequences.

Another reason that Native Americans may have difficulty respecting European American culture is its emphasis on consumption, particularly the indiscriminate use of earth's resources. Native Americans believe in achieving balance with nature, thereby ensuring the preservation of the environment. They believe that the Great Spirit is in all things and, therefore, that all nature deserves respect.

Native American peoples greatly prize individual freedom. It is a little different view of freedom, however, than is found among Western Europeans. Even though the emphasis is on making choices that ensure group survival, no one in the group has the right to force the choice of another. Historically, this was true even in important matters like war. If someone wanted to organize a raiding party, only those who volunteered would go. Leadership among the Native Americans depended on ability. The best hunter led the hunting party, and the best warrior led the tribe into war. In European American society, leadership is often inherited or awarded rather than earned. Once the group votes, all members are expected to go along with the group. For example, those who do not want to go to war are conscripted. The same is true of our two-party political system. The losing party is still active in government, but those who win the elections govern. It is common for unsuccessful candidates for political office to concede their loss and voice support for the winner. Native American youth may find some difficulty accepting such expectations, and therefore, find themselves at odds with their teachers and peers (Bennett, 1986).

Though membership in an ethnic group endows individuals with common attributes, they also have significant differences due to socioeconomic class and gender. All of these factors provide a complex mix that makes it necessary for teachers to understand each student as an individual. Each student brings to the classroom a complex, dynamic, and unique blend resulting from the interaction of race, gender, and class, as well as personal characteristics (Hernandez, 1989).

Difficulties may result from mismatches between students' and teachers' communication styles. Teachers, for example, may not correctly interpret expressions of shyness, insecurity, or disrespect. Sometimes students may be unable to determine whether their teachers are serious or joking. The communication styles of Hispanic Americans and some Asian and Pacific American groups are more formal than those of either European Americans or African Americans. In addition, African Americans tend to be more passionate when they express their feelings, while European Americans value objectivity. European Americans are more likely to express themselves with directness, while Asian Americans may shun frankness, and even employ the help of a mediator for communicating rather than directly approach another person (Howells & Sarabia, 1978). Teachers should obviously avoid excessive directness with youth who are uncomfortable with it.

There are also differences in the extent to which various cultures value honest expressions. It may be more critical to avoid disagreements and conflicts than to be perfectly honest. For example, Cambodians, Laotians, or Vietnamese consider intentions to be more important than whether or not a statement is true or false. Does the statement facilitate interpersonal harmony? Does it indicate a wish to change the subject? These are far more important considerations (Nguyen, 1984). Out of respect, some Native Americans will tell others what they assume they want to hear, while never believing that their words are untruthful. They will avoid telling things they believe that person does not want to hear. Some Native Americans have a custom of giving their possessions to someone to honor him or her. However, they do not want to achieve honor in return; such honor would destroy the essence of sharing. Therefore, when members of this ethnic group give something out of kindness, it may be considered rude to thank them or publicly acknowledge the gift (Bennett, 1986).

Different cultures have various ways to express guilt or make accusations. European Americans tend to express guilt by lowering the eyes and avoiding eye contact. When falsely accused, they may make vigorous denials. African Americans, however, lower their eyes as a sign of respect, not as an admission of guilt. They proclaim their innocence by making emotional statements. Southern European cultures and some Latin American groups may be voraciously emotional when defending themselves (Grossman, 1995). Eye contact is also differentially used by various cultures to express defiance or submissiveness. European Americans ordinarily express defiance with a silent stare. African Americans roll their eyes, while many Asian and Pacific Americans form a smile (Johnson, 1971). Direct eye contact is expected by European Americans as a sign of respect, while African Americans, Asians, Pacific Americans, and Hispanic Americans typically avert their eyes to show submissiveness (Grossman, 1995).

Some cultures find it unnatural to ask for help, because of the imperative to be sensitive to others' needs and notice when assistance is required. Students from these groups are left in a quandary when rebuked for not asking for help as they need it.

Hispanic individuals are more active in avoiding the admission of errors and mistakes than are some other cultures. They may even experience difficulty finding an expression in English that allows them to sufficiently avoid blame and avoid feelings of guilt for mistakes (Jaramillo, 1973).

Various cultures differ regarding the nature of physical contact used to communicate. Hispanics, for example, show affection and acceptance through touching another person. Lack of touching communicates lack of acceptance (Grossman, 1995). Hawaiian children put their hands on adults while trying to communicate. Their teachers may find this uncomfortable, and they may misinterpret the student's intentions. If a teacher is repulsed by these physical actions, a child may feel rejected. Hawaiians have a taboo about touching the head; in contrast, Western Europeans commonly pat a child on the head or tousle the hair to show affection and acceptance. The reaction of the Hawaiian child may range from vague feelings of discomfort to resentment, anger, or feelings of physical violation (Grossman, 1995).

Teacher effectiveness in multicultural classrooms depends on how well teachers understand cultural differences while interacting with their students and integrating culture with the curriculum and instructional concerns. Learning in multicultural classrooms is greatly enhanced when teachers create (1) a learning atmosphere in which their students feel respected and connected to them, (2) a favorable disposition toward the learning experiences through encouraging personal relevance and choice, (3) learning experiences that are challenging and include student perspectives and values, and (4) an understanding that students are effective in learning something they value (Wlodkowski & Ginsberg, 1995). These demonstrably effective teaching methods are central to learning communities.

Decision Points

Assume you are a teacher in a classroom with a lot of ethnic diversity, including African Americans, Native Americans, European Americans, Asian Americans, and Pacific Americans. Describe a learning project designed to help these students learn about one another and gain skills for learning effectively as a group.

Reflections About Self

1. In your experience, how have racially, culturally, and socially different students been treated in school by both teachers and their peers?
2. How do you feel about students who are different than yourself?
3. What specific ways do you believe you, as their teacher, will likely interact with students of a different race, culture, or social class than yourself?

Eliminating Gender Bias

Role expectations traditionally associated with gender exist in all ethnic communities and class levels that have been defined and enforced through various subtle and explicit social actions. The role of women was historically based on assumed physical and intellectual inferiority. Women were denied opportunities to perform professional and administrative work, as well as jobs involving manual labor that required significant strength. These historical restrictions have given way, in recent years, to much more enlightened views. Women now are credited with an intellectual capacity equivalent to that of men, and they have shown that they can effectively operate most of the labor-saving equipment once reserved to men.

Despite sufficient capacity to perform most of the work men have traditionally done, women are still relegated to lower-paying jobs with less responsibility than men, although in recent years this situation has improved because of affirmative action laws and because women themselves have taken a more realistic view of their potential. Women have traditionally selected lower-paying, less-prestigious jobs due to cultural bias. From the time they were little children, they were provided with gender roles and encouraged to follow them. The messages of parents, teachers, and others have a virtually irreversible effect on the child's gender role identity (Strickland, 1995).

When women accept the roles society provides for them, they often also accept lower expectations for themselves. For example, it is common to think of math and science as the exclusive academic domain of males. Woman are taught both overtly and covertly that they are less capable in these subjects, which often leads them to devalue their own potential and assume that men's careers are more important than their own. On the other side of this issue, homemaking is devalued in today's society. Women may be caught in a double bind: They may try to escape homemaking because it is not valued, but they find little acceptance in certain male-dominated occupations they wish to enter.

Schools generally perpetuate gender bias. It used to be common for textbooks to depict boys as active and adventuresome, while girls were shown as passive. There were stereotypes of girls playing with dolls, giving tea parties, or working in the kitchen while boys engaged in important activities to prepare for careers. Much of this bias is a thing of the past, but there still exist subtle classroom biases that primarily occur during student-teacher interactions. For example, boys are spoken to more frequently than girls in most science classes and are asked more questions that invoke productive thinking skills (Becker, 1981). Boys are praised more for the quality of their work, whereas girls are praised for being neat. Teachers tend to give boys general instructions on how to complete their science projects while they are more likely to show girls exactly what to do on the project, or even do it for them. In addition, boys receive more attention in the classroom than girls do, in the form of praise, criticism, remediation, and expressions of acceptance (Sadker & Sadker, 1985).

One common problem is in how occupations are defined. With male dominance, occupations have come to be characterized in ways that fit male behavior and attitudes. It appears that for women to be successful they have to mimic these typically male dispositions and actions. These biased occupational definitions assume that the only acceptable approach is a strictly male one (Noddings, 2002). One area in which male dominance currently may be seen as less acceptable is medicine. When women combine compassion and understanding with their medical skills, they may more effectively relate to their patients. Many patients, particularly females, may have a strong preference for treatment by female doctors.

In schools, the kinds of learning activities girls prefer should be emphasized through all the grades. They will likely do better with a curriculum that emphasizes relationships, cooperation, and caring. These things are currently promoted in the early school years, but are later replaced by a greater emphasis on competition, justice, objectivity, and self-interest. What is needed is a pedagogy that encourages more interactions, feelings, and democratic dynamics (Scering, 1997). Here again, learning communities are the favored format to ensure that these important classroom dynamics characterize the education of young women and help eliminate the biases to which they are routinely exposed.

Too often teachers focus on young women as if they were problems that need to be corrected. For example, if there are fewer than a desirable number of girls who sign up for math and science courses, teachers try to encourage them to participate. When girls lack what is presumed to be a requisite level of aggressiveness and competitiveness to participate successfully with boys in class, teachers wonder how to make them more aggressive and competitive. However, rather than trying to change female students to be more like boys, so they more adequately fit a male-dominated stereotype of learning in science and math, efforts must be made to teach these and other subjects in the way in which young women actually learn best and that better fits a female disposition. A female pedagogy is needed (Banks, 2003b; Rasool & Curtis, 2000). In this respect, young women prefer personalized knowledge rather than abstract, objective information. They like to learn from firsthand observations rather than complex abstractions.

Women's noteworthiness cannot be elevated by identifying obscure contributions and giving them inflated status, or defining their accomplishments in a way common to men. In addition, acclaiming insignificant contributions of women as though they were key events does not help to raise the status of women. Rather, formal historical omissions must be candidly admitted, and actions should be taken to avoid future prejudice. In addition, women need to be recognized for their own brand of excellence. Accepting male imitations exclusively narrows the range of acceptable contributions women can make. Also, the issue is not whether women have been given sufficient credit for past accomplishments, but rather what is going to be done now to promote significant involvement for all women. They can and must be involved in doing those things for which they have an inclination and inherent skill. Women can provide a different perspective on social and other issues and a different brand of solutions to problems. Through their participation in community and government affairs, more enlightened social practices and governmental procedures might be determined. Their input might lead to a more vibrant and equitable society.

Though blatant bias and discrimination has become less frequent, there still exists subtle and pervasive gender bias in schools. It is interesting to note that even though teachers are generally unaware of their gender bias, 76 percent of their students are. However, evidence shows that biases can be reduced with training. Nonetheless, little is currently being done to effectively solve the problem. Regrettably, gender bias is responsible for 15 percent of the girls wishing they were the opposite sex (Sadker & Sadker, 1994; Sadker & Sadker, 2003; Sadker, Sadker, & Shakeshift, 1992).

Sadker and Sadker (2003) identify seven forms of bias that need to be dealt with by teachers:

- *Invisibility:* These are biases of omission. Often information about the activities and achievements of women is excluded from student learning materials.
- *Linguistic bias:* Terms like *cavemen, airman, city fathers, manpower, repairman, little old lady, forefathers, policeman, fireman, ladylike,* and *mankind* express bias, as do expressions like the following: "I'd like you to meet Dr. Jones and his wife, Susan." "This fabric is man-made." "All men are created equal." "What do you guys think?"
- *Stereotyping:* Women are shown as dependent, passive, fearful, and docile, while men are depicted as ingenious, creative, brave, athletic, achieving, and curious.
- *Imbalance:* Interpretation of situations from the perspective of only one gender. For example, an individual may declare that the trouble in a friend's marriage comes from a nagging wife, when nagging may be precipitated by a male partner who routinely leaves dirty dishes in the sink and clothing strewn all over the bedroom.
- *Unreality:* Pretending biasing conditions do not exist as a pretense of not wanting to offend people.
- *Fragmentation:* Putting women into an adjunct status. References to women's achievements are given as add-ons instead of being a substantial component of ongoing instruction.
- *Cosmetic bias:* Women's accomplishments may be depicted in a glitzy or showy way, because special attention must be provided in order to give them substance.

Student sexual orientation is another concern teachers must address. Research indicates that lesbian, gay, and bisexual youth have more suicidal thoughts and behaviors (D'Augelli, Hershberger, & Pilkington, 2001; Russell & Joyner, 2001). D'Augelli, Pilkington, and Hershberger (2002) indicate that half of the lesbian, gay, and bisexual youth in their study report experiencing verbal abuse and 11 percent indicate they have been physically assaulted.

Mental problems are more prevalent among these young people. However, external support can significantly reduce the risk of suicide among these youth (Rutter & Soucar, 2002).

Decision Points

Describe an activity that may be undertaken in school that would encourage girls to make reasoned choices about motherhood and a profession that shows no bias toward being a homemaker or a professional.

Reflections About Self

1. What have you observed in your personal experience regarding gender discrimination in the schools?

2. What specific things about your usual way of interacting with members of the opposite sex might interfere with providing gender-appropriate instruction in your teaching?

Thomas was the most difficult student Ms. Larsen ever encountered. The first day Thomas walked into her class, the sneer on his face almost made Ms. Larsen wince. The look reflected a lifetime of abuse, at home as well as in school. Ms. Larsen could also detect humor in Thomas's sneer, an "I'm going to get you" attitude. Thomas knew no teacher was a match for the trouble he could create. There were other students in the school who secretly admired Thomas for his outrageous actions, wishing they had the courage to do the same. They silently approved of his disruptive antics. Ms. Larsen just barely avoided a confrontation with Thomas that first day when Thomas took one of the goldfish out of the aquarium and flung it across the room into Janice's lap. Janice leaped up screaming and ran from the room. Ms. Larsen restrained herself, simply nodding for Thomas to take his seat and watching him as he sneered and audibly laughed. There was only a couple of minutes to wait until the bell rang, and Ms. Larsen sighed in relief as Thomas exited the classroom with three or four of the boys tagging along with him, visibly amused at what had happened. Ms. Larsen feared the next day more than any day she could remember in her teaching career. She knew of no way to deal with Thomas.

It was with a prayer of thanks when Ms. Larsen learned the very next day that Thomas had been kicked out of school. Thomas acted up in his history class after being given one last chance to change his behavior, and Mr. Henry saw to it that the principal got involved. The principal recommended that the school board take action, and so Thomas was expelled. Ms. Larsen could not believe her good fortune. She was enormously relieved.

A month or so later, Ms. Larsen learned that Thomas was shot while trying to steal drugs from a local medical clinic. Ms. Larsen was relieved that Thomas would be taken off the streets. She hoped it would be permanent, but later discovered that after Thomas recovered from his wounds he merely spent six months in a juvenile correction facility. Two or three months later, Ms. Larsen read in the paper that Thomas was arrested for driving down a canyon road at night with his lights off; he ran into a car driven by a local physician, killing him. At first Ms. Larsen believed Thomas should get what was coming to him. She then realized that Thomas was a victim of his life experiences. Things might have happened at Thomas's home of which Ms. Larsen was unaware, stimulating resentment and rebellion. She even thought about what might have happened in the schools to shape the boy's behavior. Finally, Ms. Larsen wondered what she might have done to help Thomas. "Surely I could have done something," she said over and over to herself as she thought about the tragedy, not only to Thomas, but to all those his aberrant behavior had touched.

Behavioral Disorders

Teachers need to be on the lookout for behaviors that indicate severe behavioral disorders. There are a variety of serious problems that may be encountered in the school that need to be recognized and dealt with, and many of these problems should not be addressed exclusively by teachers. Specialized training is required. However, teachers have a role to play in helping some youth modify their behavior so they can remain in school. In the case of Thomas, for example, an individual teacher may have little impact on changing his behavior. In contrast, earlier intervention or significant involvement in a learning community may have provided Thomas the help needed to eliminate his aberrant behavior and encourage him to become productively involved in learning.

Children with behavioral disorders may act depressed, aggressive, suicidal, anxious, delinquent, hyperactive, socially withdrawn, or extremely shy. The broad area of behavior disorders includes many different types of problems. Consequently, it is not surprising that many approaches have been used to classify them. Unfortunately, there is no consistent, standardized set of criteria for determining the nature and severity of behavior disorders (Forness, 1988). Nonetheless, the American Psychiatric Association (1994) has prepared a manual, *Diagnostic and Statistical Manual of Mental Disorders* (4th ed.), or *DSM-IV*, that identifies seven major groups of disorders: (1) pervasive developmental disorders, (2) attention deficit and disruptive behavior disorders, (3) anxiety disorders, (4) feeding and eating disorders, (5) tic disorders, (6) elimination disorders, and (7) other disorders of infancy, childhood, or adolescence.

Pervasive Developmental Disorders

Pervasive developmental disorders may include significant problems in relating to parents, siblings, and others; very poor communication skills; and unusual behaviors evidenced in gestures, postures, and facial expressions. These disorders are generally accompanied by chromosomal abnormalities, structural abnormalities in the nervous system, and congenital infections. These disorders are usually evident at birth or occur very early in a child's life, and include severe delays in the acquisition of cognitive, language, motor, and social skills. These may be evidenced as a general delay, as in autism or mental retardation, or as a failure to show normal growth in the acquisition of specific skills, such as receptive and expressive language.

Attention Deficit and Disruptive Behavior Disorders

Children with attention deficit disorder have difficulty responding well to typical academic and social tasks and controlling their physical activity. Their physical activity commonly ap-

Disabled students must be provided a way to become fully accepted by their peers.

pears random or purposeless. Children with disruptive behavior disorders frequently hurt other individuals or animals or destroy property belonging to others. They repeatedly participate in theft and deceitful activities and regularly violate rules and social conventions. Some children with this disorder are highly oppositional with a recurring pattern of negativism, opposition to authority, blaming others for problems and mistakes, and being spiteful. Children with this disorder have difficulty attending to and completing tasks, responding carefully and reflectively to academic and social demands, and controlling or restricting their level of physical activity. They engage in such activities as stealing, running away from home, lying, setting fires, being truant from school, breaking into others' homes, destroying others' property, torturing animals, forcing sexual activity, using weapons in a fight, and being cruel to others.

Anxiety Disorders

Youth with anxiety disorders have problems dealing with anxiety-provoking situations and with separating themselves from parents or other attachment figures (e.g., close friends, teachers, coaches). They characteristically worry about future events, are overconcerned about achievement, have an excessive need for reassurance, and frequently complain about how their body functions. They may also have difficulty acting independently.

Feeding and Eating Disorders

The eating disorder Pica involves eating nonnutritive materials, such as cloth, string, hair, plaster, or even paint. This category also includes anorexia nervosa and bulimia, disorders characterized by gross disturbances in eating behavior that are more prevalent among girls and women. Individuals with anorexia nervosa have a body weight that is 15 percent below that expected. Individuals with this condition are intensely afraid of weight gain and exhibit grossly distorted perceptions of the shapes and sizes of their bodies. Bulimics engage in repeated episodes of binging, followed by self-induced vomiting, in order to prevent weight gain. Both of these conditions may result in a depressed mood, social withdrawal, irritability, and serious medical conditions. Teachers need to be alert for evidence of these problems. Eating disorders have become much more prevalent in recent years.

Tic Disorders

Tic disorders involve stereotyped movements or vocalizations that are involuntary, rapid, and recurrent. They take the form of eye blinking, facial gestures, sniffing, snorting, repeating certain words or phrases, and grunting. Stress often stimulates an increased frequency of tic expression. The individual may, for example, incessantly tap her pencil on her desk.

Elimination Disorders

Youth with elimination disorders have problems with bowel and bladder control that are not a function of any physical disorder.

Other Disorders of Infancy, Childhood, or Adolescence

The remaining conditions include disorders that are not easily placed in the other categorical areas. They include separation anxiety disorder, characterized by an inordinate fear about leaving home or being separated from persons to which the individual is attached. The individual may refuse to go to school; be afraid to go to sleep; and exhibit repeated complaints about headaches, stomachaches, and nausea. Another condition, elective mutism, includes individuals who refuse to talk in typical social, school, and work situations.

Youth with behavior disorders ordinarily have average to below average intelligence and school achievement (Scruggs & Mastropieri, 1986) and have difficulty relating to others. In school they experience difficulty listening, asking for teacher assistance, bringing materials to class, following directions, completing assignments, and ignoring various distractions prevalent in school. They also have difficulty introducing themselves, beginning and ending conversations, sharing, playing typical age-appropriate games, and apologizing. They are unable to deal appropriately with situations that produce strong feelings, such as anger and frustration.

Once a teacher suspects that a student has a disorder, he or she should meet with the child's parents. Difficulties may be the product of family problems such as the illness of a parent, marital difficulties, or a difficult financial situation. If problems persist, the teacher may want to make a referral for testing and evaluation. Parents' permission is essential for testing as well as prescribing treatment. It may be necessary to employ the skills of specialists who can work with parents and teachers to help these youth overcome their problems and become more productive in school.

Treatment may include any of a number of possible therapies supplied by experts. Teachers need to coordinate their treatment of children who have behavior disorders with those being provided by these therapists. This might include the application of cognitive-behavioral training or token reinforcement systems. Token reinforcement involves supplying students with rewards for normal behavior. Cognitive-behavioral training includes the following steps:

1. *Motor cue/ impulse delay.* Stop and think before you act; cue yourself.
2. *Problem definition.* Say how you feel and exactly what the problem is.
3. *Generation of alternatives.* Think of as many solutions as you can.
4. *Consideration of consequences.* Think ahead to what might happen next.
5. *Implementation.* When you have a really good solution, try it (Etscheidt, 1991).

 ## QUESTION FOR REFLECTION

1. How could you enlist members of a learning community to help students who have various behavioral disorders?

Learning Disabilities

Specific learning disabilities are defined by delays, deviations, and performance discrepancies in basic academic subjects (e.g., arithmetic, reading, spelling, and writing) and speech and language problems that cannot be attributed to mental retardation, sensory deficits, or emotional disturbance (Frederickson & Reason, 1995). The Individuals with Disabilities Education Act (IDEA) of 1990 uses a definition for learning disabilities first developed by the National Advisory Committee on Handicapped Children (Roberts & Mather, 1995):

> *"Specific learning disability" means a disorder in one or more of the basic psychological processes involved in understanding or in using language, spoken or written, which may manifest itself in an imperfect ability to listen, think, speak, read, write, spell or to do mathematical calculations. The term includes such conditions as perceptual handicaps, brain injury, minimal brain dysfunction, dyslexia, and developmental aphasia. The term does not include children who have learning problems which are primarily the result of visual, hearing, or motor handicaps, of mental retardation, of emotional disturbance, or of environmental, cultural, or economic disadvantage."* (PL 101–476, Sec. 5[b][4])

The IDEA definition was exclusionary in some ways, in that it defined conditions that are not learning disabilities but failed to offer substantive explanations of what constitutes a learning disability. The definition was also ambiguous because it lacked a clear way to measure learning disabilities. A definition provided by the National Joint Committee for Learning Disabilities (1988) contains important elements not stated in the IDEA statement:

> *"Learning disabilities is a general term that refers to a heterogeneous group of disorders manifest by significant difficulties in the acquisition and use of listening, speaking, writing, reasoning, or mathematical abilities. These disorders are intrinsic to the individual, presumed to be due to central nervous system dysfunction, and may occur across the life span. Problems in self-regulatory behaviors, social perception, and social interactions may exist with learning disabilities but do not by themselves constitute a learning disability. Although learning disabilities may occur*

concomitantly with other handicapping conditions (for example, sensory impairment, mental retardation, serious emotional disturbance) or with extrinsic influences (such as cultural differences, insufficient or inappropriate instruction), they are not the result of those conditions or influences."

There are a variety of problems referred to as learning disabilities. They range from mild difficulties experienced by individuals who have near normal intelligence but "poor neurological wiring" to problems that are more debilitating. Technically, **learning disability** refers to a disorder in one or more of the basic psychological processes involved with understanding or using spoken or written, language. These can manifest themselves as a limited ability to listen, think, speak, write, spell, or do mathematical calculations. **Attention deficit/hyperactivity disorder** (**ADHD**) is also considered to be a learning disability by some, but is not listed as such by IDEA. However, the essential features of ADHD have long been recognized in many children with learning disabilities. The distinctions between learning disabilities and ADHD are not at all clear specifically because they have historically overlapped and been applied to very heterogeneous groups of people (Goodyear & Hynd, 1993).

There is considerable disagreement about the cause of ADHD. Both biological and environmental influences have been proposed (Denckla, 1996). It has been speculated that causes may include such influences as genetic inheritance, neurological injury during birth, vitamin deficiencies, and food additives. As many as 5 percent of all children may have the disorder (APA, 1994; Parker, 1990). In the past, more boys than girls have been diagnosed with ADHD by a ratio of 9 to 1. Recent research indicates that the actual occurrence of learning disabilities may be more nearly equal between the sexes because females tend to remain unidentified (Lyon, 1995; Shaywitz, Fletcher, & Shaywitz, 1995). Identification problems occur because young males' behavior may be more disruptive, thus making them more readily recognizable to teachers (Clements, Clare, & Ezelle, 1995; Lyon, 1996). Children with ADHD experience considerable difficulty concentrating and exhibit various impulsive actions. However, they may not show the other behaviors characteristic of students within the usual categories of learning disabilities. Hyperactivity is a behavior characteristic commonly associated with children with learning disabilities, but they ordinarily have other debilitating conditions.

Some students with learning disabilities have perception problems that may come from deficiencies in a constellation of abnormalities: visual, auditory, and hapatic sensory (touch, body movement, and position sensation) systems. Students with visual problems may see a visual stimulus as unrelated parts rather than as an integrated pattern. They may not be able to identify a letter in the alphabet because it is perceived as unrelated lines rather than as lines comprising a meaningful whole. Students may also be unable to adequately make figure-ground discriminations to distinguish an object from its background. For example, students may be unable to focus on a word or sentence on the page of a textbook. They may also have difficulties distinguishing one visual stimulus from another; for example, determining the difference between the words *sit* and *sat*, or between such letters as *V* and *W*. They commonly reverse such letters as *b* and *d* (Hardman, Drew, & Egan, 1999).

Some children have deficiencies in auditory perception, such as poor auditory discrimination and the inability to tell the sound of one word or syllable from another. They also may be unable to discriminate a sound such as a ringing telephone from other sounds. Problem students may experience difficulty with auditory blending, auditory memory, and auditory association. Blending problems involve the inability to blend word parts into an integrated whole as children pronounce them. Auditory memory problems occur when the individual is unable to recall verbal information. Those with auditory association difficulties may be unable to put related ideas together to form an interrelated whole. These conditions naturally create school performance problems (Hardman, Drew, & Egan, 1999).

Another disabling condition is the failure of haptic perception (touch, body movement, and position sensation), which may result in poor handwriting. Almost any body movement may be adversely affected where this problem exists. Children with this disability may experience difficulty spacing letters and staying on the lines of the paper. However, problems may also be due to visual perception abnormalities; therefore precisely attributing some behaviors to a single factor is difficult (Hardman, Drew, & Egan, 1999).

Some children are disabled in terms of cognitive processing. This involves the way a person acquires, retains, and manipulates information (Hamachek, 1995; Lefrancios, 1995). In many cases material learned one day cannot be recalled the next. Yet, the research is confusing, with some results indicating that children with learning disabilities have poor memory (Agawal & Kaushal, 1987), while other evidence suggests that children with learning disabilities do not perform as well as children without them on some memory tasks but show no differences on other tasks (Denckla, 1996; Male, 1996; Perrig & Perrig, 1995; Swanson, 1988; Swanson & Berninger, 1995). Research also suggests that children with learning disabilities have different, rather than uniformly deficient, cognitive abilities (Denckla, 1996). These findings suggest that instruction should be specific and highly focused for individuals with learning disabilities rather than generic, and that children should engage in classroom activities in which they have been given an opportunity to give input.

A short attention span may interfere with some children's learning. Research shows that some children may be generally characterized as having a short attention span while others attend selectively (Richards, Samuels, Tumure, & Ysseldyke, 1990; Zentall & Ferkis, 1993). Students with selective attention problems experience difficulty focusing on centrally important tasks and pay attention more to peripheral or less relevant information. Teachers need to determine which students have selective attention problems and provide them experiences that fit their specific selectivity.

Students with learning disabilities routinely have difficulty reading, writing, spelling, and performing elementary mathematical skills. They may not only have a limited knowledge of words, but also may be unable to effectively recognize them. This second skill involves recognizing novel words, applying rules, generalizing letter patterns, and drawing sufficiently flexible analogies. In addition, children with learning disabilities may be unskilled in using context to determine meaning. Good readers routinely infer the general meaning of unknown words from contextual information while poor readers do not (Smith, 1994; Sorrell, 1990). Reading improvement can be achieved by helping students with learning disabilities enhance their word recognition skills (Billingsley & Ferro-Alemeida, 1993; Englert & Palincsar, 1988; Lerner, 1997) and apply context in their reading (Wong & Sawatsky, 1984). Students with learning disabilities often have letter-order confusion in their spelling, as well as a tendency to omit letters or add unnecessary ones. However, teaching these students learning strategies such as skills in organizing and summarizing, the use of mnemonics, problem solving, and relational thinking can offset these difficulties and enhance reading performance (Lauterbach & Bender, 1995; Vauras, Lehtinen, Olkinuora, & Salonen, 1993; Wong, 1993).

Mathematically, children with learning disabilities may have trouble counting, writing numbers, and mastering simple math concepts (Parmar, Cawley, & Frazita, 1996; Zentall & Ferkis, 1993). They may have problems with place value and be unable to understand that a particular digit has a different value depending on number position. According to Grinnell (1988), there are four problems students with learning disabilities have in math: (1) understanding the grouping process, (2) understanding that each position to the left represents another multiple of 10, (3) understanding the placement of one digit per position, and (4) understanding the relationship between the order of the digits and the value of the numeral.

These basic mathematics difficulties constitute major obstacles for students with learning disabilities as they move through schools. Mastery of fundamental quantitative concepts is vital to understanding more abstract and complex math concepts. These topics have traditionally received minimal or no attention in curricula designed for students with learning disabilities. Instead, students are exposed primarily to a mathematics curriculum that emphasizes computational skills (Lerner, 1997; Wong, 1993).

Various programs have been created to help students with learning disabilities have meaningful educational experiences; these include medical and academic, as well as behavioral, interventions. Medically, psychostimulants have been administered, although some professionals have seriously questioned their use (Pelham, 1986; Rosenburg, 1987). On the positive side, psychostimulants appear to promote improvement with as many as 75 percent of children with ADHD (Barkley, 1995). However, some researchers have expressed caution about using drugs like methylphenidate (Ritalin). Carlson and Bunner (1993) reviewed a number of investigations on the use of drugs to control hyperactivity and concluded that it improves classroom behavior, but doesn't necessarily improve academic performance. Other research indicates hyperactive students do not have an unusual response to the medication and exhibit no significant improvement in long-term academic or social adjustment when taking it (DuPaul, Barkely, & McMurray, 1991; Swanson et al., 1993). A lot of research is needed in this area for a number of reasons. First, exactly which drug will be effective is seldom known until after treatment has begun. Second, there is often confusion regarding dosage level, which some studies have shown to be from 50 to 400 percent higher than the dosage recommended as the maximum to improve cognitive abilities (Pelham, 1983). Third, there are physical side effects from using these medications that include insomnia, irritability, depressed appetite, and headaches. However, though these side effects appear to be relatively minor and mostly temporary, they vary greatly among individuals (Swanson et al., 1993). There may be clear benefits to the use of medications, but they may be overprescribed, and expectations that they will produce generalized improvement simply are not supported by research evidence (Hardman, Drew, & Egan, 1999).

Academic interventions include a variety of programs that deal with perceptual, cognitive, attention, spoken language, reading, writing, and mathematics treatments. Within each of these areas there is an array of instructional procedures aimed at pinpointing specific problems. These strategies are devised to address specific problems with a particular population. The needs of individual students should be assessed before prescribing any particular program. As required, expert opinion should be sought in solving a specific problem. Academic intervention should be applied within the learning community so support can be sought from group members. The community should receive instruction regarding the best ways to help any group member with learning problems so that all can take an active and appropriate role in helping one another.

Decision Points

Take a position and defend it regarding the use of psychostimulants to moderate the behavior of students with attention deficit/hyperactivity disorder (ADHD).

Reflections About Self

1. When you were in school, how did you feel about students who experienced difficulty learning or who disrupted class because of some developmental problem they had?
2. What do you remember about efforts you made as a student in the public schools to relate to students who had learning or behavioral problems?

Gifted, Creative, and Talented

A common misconception is that gifted students do not require special attention in order to be successful in school. However, they need help in pacing and in deciding what to do when they outrun the class (Subotnik & LeBlanc, 2003). In addition, because of an emphasis on the common curriculum, along with reliance on standardized achievement tests for placement, these students have generally been ignored. There has been more emphasis on getting low-performing children to do better than on preparing a way for unusually able students to excel. In fact, with standards set by traditional grading practices, many of these students are not expected to perform at the levels of which they are capable. Standardized achievement tests are not designed to measure the ability of gifted students. Because of the restricted range of the test items, **ceiling effects** are created that keep gifted students from demonstrating their true level of achievement. How many such children are there? This of course depends on how giftedness is defined. As more categories of giftedness have been added over the years, the percentage has gone from 2 to 3 percent prior to 1950 to 15 to 20 percent of the general school population after that time (Conant, 1959). Currently, 3 to 15 percent of the students in the school population may be identified as gifted depending on the regulations of a particular state (Hardman, Drew, & Egan, 1999).

Though there is no federally mandated definition of giftedness, Tannenbaum (1997) has proposed a definition consisting of the potential of children to eventually develop talent that exists only in adults. They can either become critically acclaimed performers or exemplary producers of ideas in spheres of activity that enhance the moral, physical, emotional, social, intellectual, or aesthetic life of humanity. Performers provide "staged artistry" or highly skilled "human services." Producers generate remarkable "thoughts" and "tangibles."

Subotnik and LeBlanc (2003) provide the following characteristics of gifted students:

- They learn at an accelerated pace.
- They have a capacity for seeing relationships and patterns at an exceptional level.
- They are intensely motivated, curious, and need in-depth learning experiences.
- They have high expectations of themselves and others.
- They are impatient with slow physical development, agility, or vocabulary to carry out solutions to problems they can easily visualize.
- They notice inconsistencies between ideal and real behavior as evidence of hypocrisy.

Definitions of giftedness are useful because they help differentiate the many different categories of giftedness and the forms in which each is expressed. It is a formidable undertaking to create measures to determine the presence and magnitude of these special capacities. IQ tests were once used as the only measure of giftedness and at present are used as a major source of information for screening and identifying general ability or intellectual giftedness (Assouline, 1997). However, intelligence tests have been found to do a poor job of predicting future creative and productive achievements of gifted students (Wallach, 1976).

There are currently various means for determining giftedness. Sometimes parents can provide helpful information in making a determination. Teachers can also provide some data. However, teachers tend to favor students who are well-dressed, cooperative, and task oriented. Many of the gifted do not fit this mold and are judged by their teachers as academically unable, when in fact they may be rebelling against unwarranted constraints on their creative inclinations. The dilemma of identifying the presence of creative ability can, in part, be resolved by administering one or more of a number of available creativity tests. It is probably wise to use multiple measures of creativity in order to ensure that the particular prowess of students doesn't go unrecognized (Callahan, 1991).

There are a number of recommended classroom configurations designed to provide gifted and talented students with differentiated learning opportunities (Clark, 1997). One of these is to leave the gifted students in the regular classroom and provide them special experiences there. A second is to arrange pullout activities where gifted students are taken from the regular classroom and provided specialized learning opportunities in the form of independent studies, seminars, mentorships, and cooperative studies. Pullout activities have the advantage of providing more appropriate learning opportunities, but they may be a disadvantage if after returning to the regular classroom these students are required to make up missed assignments. In addition, there may be significant gaps in their learning after they return to class.

Gifted students may also be put into special classes with their peers. In these cases, they may have a common curriculum, or they may have an individualized curricula. Sometimes special classes will be created just for students with a particular talent. Thus, those gifted in art may be in one setting, while those who emphasize science may be in another. There may also be a common special class for the gifted with pullout opportunities for special projects. There have also been special schools created for the gifted, creative, and talented; for example, there are special "schools for the arts."

Gifted students have sometimes been allowed to *accelerate* by skipping grades, thus allowing early matriculation at a university. Research on acceleration suggests that certain students benefit greatly from such experiences (Brody & Benbow, 1987). These benefits include improved motivation and confidence, as well as early completion of advanced training. Acceleration also helps prevent the mental laziness sometimes prevalent in gifted students who are forced to remain in regular classrooms (Van Tassel-Baska, 1989). Unfortunately, acceleration does not provide gifted students with opportunities to receive a differentiated curriculum suited to their specific needs (Schiever & Maker, 1997)

Accelerating gifted students, however, may have negative social implications. As a result, *enrichment* programs have been provided for these students. They remain in regular classrooms while their teachers cater to their learning proclivities. Enrichment can be either horizontal or vertical. Horizontal enrichment refers to the practice of adding courses of study to gifted children's schedules, like music appreciation, foreign languages, and mythology. Vertical enrichment involves increasing the depth of student experiences. They are given opportunities to engage in projects that deepen their understanding and develop sophisticated thinking patterns. Quality enrichment programs are characterized by carefully selected activities; challenging, but not overwhelming, assignments; and evaluations that are rigorous, yet fair. In addition, good enrichment programs focus on learning activities that stress higher-order thinking and application skills (Schiever & Maker, 1997).

Many of the needs of gifted, creative, and talented students can be appropriately met in learning communities, where they can be involved in specifically tailored learning projects. They can also be provided opportunities to mentor others as well as learn how to use their skills appropriately in real-life settings. Isolating the gifted and talented from the diverse population, as often happens in public schools, creates an artificial environment and limits growth. Most will eventually find themselves in situations involving diversity, and their success depends on their ability to successfully relate to a broad spectrum of work associates. Various programs initiated in the public schools have the potential for producing exclusivity. In addition, students may focus on their particular talent, but without having the necessary connections made to real-life problems and situations. Both of these potential problems can be successfully avoided in learning communities, where gifted students can provide leadership in learning projects related to their area of interest. They can teach their peers so all can benefit from their expertise. It is also appropriate to have gifted students work with experts outside the learning community, thereby allowing them to sharpen their skills and appreciate higher expectation levels. In addition, gifted students can also work on projects individually or in small groups. In a learning community, there are opportunities for individuals to share the results of their learning with the whole group. When there is an appropriate mix of independent and group activity, students can experience more authentic democratic learning along with opportunities to personally grow.

 ## QUESTIONS FOR REFLECTION

1. List a set of learning activities that provide appropriate learning opportunities for exceptional students in various categories. How are the different kinds of activities appropriate for different students?

2. What is the better approach to working with gifted and talented students, acceleration or enrichment? Explain why.

CENTRAL IDEAS

1. To provide an optimum environment for learning, teachers must take into account constructivism, learning styles, and the interests and needs of students, as well as various learning problems experienced by students.

2. Each and every student has specific needs and is different in significant ways from peers. All students' learning can be enhanced when these differences are appropriately considered.

3. Culture defines the way we think, feel, and act. In a diverse society, it is necessary for all to understand and appreciate other cultures and to learn how to respond appropriately to them.

4. Stereotyping other cultures should be avoided. Stereotyping can often lead to inaccurate conclusions and poor relationships.

5. In American society, there has been poor structural assimilation of various minorities into the dominant Western European culture.

6. The melting pot theory regarding the emergence of a single unique American culture has never been fulfilled.

7. The most accurate explanation of assimilation of minorities into American society is a modified version of cultural pluralism. This involves limited assimilation of minorities into the dominant culture with some retention of each minority culture.

8. Despite considerable efforts through multicultural education to reduce inequities in America, many problems still exist that limit full participation of minorities in American society. Schools need to help students become active in making improvements in the social conditions of all ethnic groups.

9. There are a number of false assumptions that promote resistance to multicultural education. They (a) promote divisiveness, (b) destroy the cultural melting pot, (c) fail to build societal harmony, (d) distract from educational basics, and (e) promote exclusiveness.

10. Many youth of ethnic minorities are improperly placed in school due to biases in the assessment instruments used.

11. Learning communities provide opportunities for diverse learners not only to receive help, but to grow through giving assistance to others.

12. Various professionals who provide help for special needs students must modify the application of their expertise so it can be effectively applied in learning communities.

13. The learning of students who are socially disadvantaged can be enhanced by their participation in democratically oriented classrooms.

14. There are significant differences between various ethnic groups that have important implications regarding how teachers interact with their students, as well as how they teach students to successfully relate to one another.

15. Schools perpetuate gender bias in subtle ways. These must be identified and eliminated, paving the way for both boys and girls to take on various roles in society that are credible and acceptable.

16. Students with behavioral disorders often require the help of experts in a coordinated classroom therapy program.

17. There are various programs available to help the learning disabled. Medical intervention with psychostimulants may be a poor choice for some students. Appropriate dosage is a serious issue, as are potential side effects.

18. Gifted, creative, and talented students have important growth-promoting opportunities in learning communities. They can take leadership roles as well as teach their peers. Their skills can be enhanced through independent and group projects, and through contacts with outside experts.

REFERENCES

Agawal, R., & Kaushal, K. (1987). Attention and short-term memory in normal children, aggressive children, and nonaggressive children with attention deficit disorder. *Journal of General Psychology, 14,* 335–344.

American Psychiatric Association. (1994). *Diagnostic and statistical manual of mental disorders* (4th ed.). Washington, DC: Author.

Appiah, A. (1990). *Early African American classics.* New York: Bantam.

Assouline, S. G. (1997). Assessment of gifted children. In N. Colangelo & A. D. Davis (Eds.), *Handbook of gifted education* (2nd ed., pp. 89–108). Boston: Allyn & Bacon.

Banks, J. A. (1995). Multicultural education: Historical development, dimensions, and practice. In J. A. Banks & C. A. M. Banks (Eds.), *Handbook of research on multicultural education* (pp. 3–24). New York: Macmillan.

Banks, J. A. (1996). *Multicultural education, transformitive knowledge, and action.* New York: Teachers College Press.

Banks, J. A. (1997). *Teaching strategies for ethnic studies* (6th ed.). Boston: Allyn & Bacon.

Banks, J. A. (2000). The social construction of differences and the quest for educational equality. In R. Brandt (Ed.), *Education in a new era* (pp. 21–45). Arlington, VA: Association for Supervision and Curriculum Development.

Banks, J. A. (2003a). Approaches to multicultural curriculum reform. In J. A. Banks & C. A. M. Banks (Eds.), *Multicultural education: Issues and perspectives* (4th ed., pp. 225–246). New York: John Wiley & Sons.

Banks, J. A. (2003b). Multicultural education: Characteristics and goals. In J. A. Banks & C. A. M. Banks (Eds.), *Multicultural education: Issues and perspectives* (4th ed., pp. 3–30). New York: John Wiley & Sons.

Banks, J. A., & Banks, C. A. M. (1989). *Multicultural education: Issues and perspectives.* Boston: Allyn & Bacon.

Barkley, R. (1995). *Taking charge of ADHD: The complete authoritative guide for parents.* New York: Guilford.

Becker, J. R. (1981). Differential treatment of females and males in mathematical classes. *Journal of Research in Mathematical Education, 12,* 40–53.

Bennett, C. I. (1986). *Comprehensive multicultural education: Theory and practice.* (2nd ed.). Boston: Allyn & Bacon.

Bennett, C. I. (2003). *Comprehensive multicultural education: Theory and practice* (3rd ed.). Boston: Allyn & Bacon.

Billingsley, B. S., & Ferro-Alemeida, S. C. (1993). Strategies to facilitate reading comprehension in students with learning disabilities. *Reading and Writing Quarterly: Overcoming Learning Difficulties, 9* (3), 263–278.

Brice-Heath, S. (1982). Questioning at home and at school: A comparative study. In G. Spindler (Ed.), *Doing ethnography: Educational anthropology in action* (p. 173). New York: Holt, Rinehart & Winston.

Brody, L. E., & Benbow, C. P. (1987). Accelerative strategies: How effective are they for the gifted? *Gifted Child Quarterly, 31* (3), 105–110.

Callahan, C. M. (1991). The assessment of creativity. In N. Colangelo & G. A. Davis (Eds.), *Handbook of gifted education* (pp. 219–235). Boston: Allyn & Bacon.

Carlson, C. L., & Bunner, M. R. (1993). Effects of methyl-phenidate on the academic performance of children with attention-deficit hyperactivity disorder and learning disabilities. *School Psychology Review, 22,* 184–198.

Clark, B. (1997). *Growing up gifted* (5th ed.). Columbus, OH: Merrill.

Clements, J., Clare, I., & Ezelle, L. A. (1995). Real men, real women, real lives: Gender issues in learning disabilities and challenging behavior. *Disability and Society, 10,* 425–435.

Conant, J. B. (1959). *The American high school today.* New York: McGraw-Hill.

D'Augelli, A. R., Hershberger, S. L., & Pilkington, N.W. (2001). Suicidality patterns and sexual orientation: Related factors among lesbian, gay and bisexual youth. *Suicide and life threatening behavior, 31* (3), 250–264.

D'Augelli, A. R., Pilkington, N. W., & Hershberger, S. L. (2002). Incidence and mental health impact of sexual orientation victimization of lesbian, gay, and bisexual youth in high school. *School Psychology Quarterly, 17* (2), 148–167.

Denckla, M. B. (1996). Biological correlates of learning and attention: What is relevant to learning disability and attention-deficit hyperactivity disorder. *Journal of Developmental and Behavioral Pediatrics, 17* (2), 114–119.

Diana v. State Board of Education. (1970, 1973). C–70, 37 RFP (N.D. Cal, 1970, 1973).

DuPaul, G., Barkely, R., & McMurray, M. (1991). Therapeutic effects of medication on ADHD: Implications for school psychologists. *School Psychology Review, 20,* 203–219.

Englert, C. A., & Palincsar, A. S. (1988). The reading process. In D. K. Reid (Ed.), *Teaching the learning disabled: A cognitive developmental approach* (pp. 162–189). Boston: Allyn & Bacon.

Etscheidt, S. E. (1991). Reducing aggressive behavior and improving self-control: A cognitive-behavioral treatment program for behaviorally disordered adolescents. *Behavior Disorders, 16* (2), 107–115.

Figueroa, R. A. (1989). Psychological testing of linguistic-minority students: Knowledge gaps and regulations. *Exceptional Children, 56,* 145–152.

Forness, S. R. (1988). Planning for the needs of children with serious emotional disturbance: The National Special Education and Mental Health Coalition. *Behavior Disorders, 13* (2), 127–133.

Frederickson, N., & Reason, R. (1995). Discrepancy definitions of specific learning difficulties. *Educational Psychology in Practice, 10* (4), 195–205.

Gamoran, A., & Berends, M. (1987). The effects of stratification in secondary schools: Synthesis of survey and ethnographic research. *Review of Educational Research, 57* (4), 415–435.

Gay, G. (1995). Mirror images on common issues: Parallels between multicultural education and critical pedagogy. In C. E. Sleeter & P. L. McLaren (Eds.), *Multicultural education, critical pedagogy, and politics of difference.* Albany, NY: State University of New York Press.

Gay, G. (2003). Educational equality for students of color. In J. A. Banks & C. A. M. Banks (Eds.), *Multicultural education: Issues and perspectives* (4th ed., pp. 197–224). New York: John Wiley & Sons.

Gollnick, D. M., & Chinn, P. C. (1994). *Multicultural education in a pluralistic society* (4th ed.). Upper Saddle River, NJ: Merrill/Prentice Hall.

Goodyear, P., & Hynd, G. W. (1993). Attention-deficit disorder with (ADD/H) and without (ADD/WO) hyperactivity: Behavioral and neuropsychological differentiation. *Journal of Clinical Child Psychology, 24,* 273–305.

Gordon, M. M. (1964). *Assimilation in American life: The role of race, religion, and national origins.* New York: Oxford University Press.

Grinnell, P. C. (1988). Teaching handwriting and spelling. In D. K. Reid (Ed.), *Teaching the learning disabled: A cognitive developmental approach* (pp. 245–278). Boston: Allyn & Bacon.

Grossman, H. (1995). *Teaching in a diverse society.* Boston: Allyn & Bacon.

Hahn, C. L. (1998). *Becoming political: Comparative perspectives on citizenship education.* Albany, NY: State University of New York Press.

Hamachek, D. (1995). *Psychology in teaching, learning, and growth* (5th ed.). Boston: Allyn & Bacon.

Hardman, M. L., Drew, C. J., & Egan, M. W. (1999). *Human exceptionality: Society, school, and family* (5th ed.). Boston: Allyn & Bacon.

Hernandez, H. (1989). *Multicultural education: A teacher's guide to contents and process.* Upper Saddle River, NJ: Merrill/Prentice Hall.

Heward, W. L., & Cavanaugh, R. A. (2003). Educational equality for students with disabilities. In J. A. Banks & C. A. M. Banks (Eds.), *Multicultural education: Issues and perspectives* (4th ed., pp. 295–326). New York: John Wiley & Sons.

Howells, G. N., & Sarabia, I. B. (1978). Education and the Filipino child. *Integrated Education, 16* (2), 17–20.

Jacob, E., & Jordan, C. (1993). *Minority education: Anthropological perspectives.* Norwood, NJ: Ablex.

Jaramillo, M. L. (1973, November). *Cautions when working with the culturally different child.* Paper presented at the Teacher Corps Associates Conference, Madison, WI.

Johnson, K. R. (1971). Black kinetics: Some nonverbal communication patterns in the Black culture. *Florida Reporter, 57,* 17–20.

Kailin, J. (2002). *Antiracist education: From theory to practice.* Lanham, MD: Rowman and Littlefield.

Kohn, A. (1998). Only for my kid: How privileged parents undermine school reform. *Phi Delta Kappan, 79,* 568–577.

Larry P. v. Riles. (1972, 1979). 343 F. Supp. 1306, 502 F. 2d 963 (N.D. Cal. 1979).

Lauterbach, S. L., & Bender, W. N. (1995). Cognitive strategy instruction for reading comprehension: A success for high school freshmen. *High School Journal, 79,* 58–64.

Lefrancios, G. R. (1995). *Of children: An introduction to child development* (8th ed.). Belmont, CA: Wadsworth.

Lerner, J. (1997). *Learning disabilities: Theories, diagnosis, and teaching strategies* (7th ed.). Boston: Houghton Mifflin.

Lyon, G. R. (1995). Toward a definition of dyslexia. *Annals of Dyslexia, 45,* 13–30.

Lyon, G. R. (1996). Learning disabilities. *The Future of Children, 6* (1), 54–76.

Male, D. B. (1996). Metamemorial functioning of children with moderate learning difficulties. *British Journal of Educational Psychology, 66,* 145–157.

Martin, P., & Midgley, E. (1999). Immigration to the United States. *Population Bulletin, 54* (2), 1–44. Washington, DC: Population Reference Bureau.

Montalto, N. V. (1978). The forgotten dream: A history of the intercultural education movement, 1924–1941. *Dissertation Abstracts International, 39*A, 1061. (University Microfilms No. 78–13436).

National Joint Committee on Learning Disabilities. (1988). [Letter to NJCLD member organizations.]

Nguyen, L. D. (1984, March). *Indochinese cross-cultural adjustments and communication.* Paper presented to the annual meeting of the Teachers of English to Speakers of Other Languages, Houston, TX.

Nieto, S. (1996). *Affirming diversity: The sociopolitical context of multicultural education* (2nd ed.). New York: Longman.

Nieto, S. (2002). *Language, culture and teaching: Critical perspectives for a new century.* Mahwah, NJ: Lawrence Erlbaum Associates.

Nieto, S. (2003). School reform and student learning: A multicultural perspective. In J. A. Banks & C. A. M. Banks (Eds.), *Multicultural education: Issues and perspectives* (4th ed., pp. 381–401). New York: John Wiley & Sons.

Noddings, N. (2002). *Educating moral people: A caring alternative to character education.* New York: Teachers College Press.

Oakes, J., & Guiton, G. (1995). Matchmaking: The dynamics of high school tracking decisions. *American Educational Research Journal, 32* (1), 3–33.

Ogbu, J. (1988). Class stratification, racial stratification, and schooling. In L. Weis (Ed.), *Class, race, and gender in American education* (pp. 176–177). Albany, NY: State University of New York Press.

Omi, M., & Winant, H. (1986). *Racial formation in the United States: From the 1960s to the 1980s.* New York: Routledge & Kegan Paul.

Parenti, M. (1988). *Democracy for the few* (5th ed.). New York: St. Martin's Press.

Parker, H. C. (1990). *C.H.A.D.D.: Children with attention deficit disorder: Parents supporting parents.* Education position paper, Plantation, FL.

Parmer, R. S., Cawley, J. F., & Frazita, R. R. (1996). Word problem-solving by students with and without mild disabilities. *Exceptional Children, 62,* 415–429.

Pelham, W. E. (1983). The effects of psychostimulants on academic achievement in hyperactive and learning-disabled children. *Thalmus, 3* (1), 2–48 (Newsletter of the International Academy of Research in Learning Disabilities).

Pelham, W. E. (1986). What do we know about the use and effects of CNS stimulants in the treatment of ADD? *Journal of Children in Contemporary Society, 19,* 99–110.

Perrig, P., & Perrig, W. J. (1995). Implicit and explicit memory in mentally retarded, learning disabled and normal children. *Swiss Journal of Psychology, 54* (2), 77–86.

Popham, W. J. (1999). Why standardized tests don't measure educational quality. *Educational Leadership, 56* (6), 8–15.

Rasool, J. A., & Curtis, A. C. (2000). *Multicultural education in middle and secondary classrooms: Meeting the challenge of diversity and change.* Belmont, CA: Wadsworth.

Richards, G. P., Samuels, S. J., Tumure, J. E., & Ysseldyke, J. E. (1990). Sustained and selective attention in children with learning disabilities. *Journal of Learning Disabilities, 23,* 129–136.

Rist, R. C. (1970). Student social class and teacher expectations: The self-fulfilling prophesy in ghetto education. *Harvard Educational Review, 40* (3). 70–110.

Roberts, R., & Mather, N. (1995). Legal protections for individuals with learning disabilities: The IDEA, Section 504, and the ADA. *Learning Disabilities Research and Practice, 10* (3).

Rosenburg, M. S. (1987). Psychopharmocological interventions with young hyperactive children. *Topics in Early Childhood Special Education, 6* (4), 62–74.

Russell, S. T., & Joyner, K. (2001). Adolescent sexual orientation and suicide risk: Evidence from a national study. *American Journal of Public Health, 91* (8), 1276–1281.

Rutter, P. A., & Soucar, E. (2002). Youth suicide risk and sexual orientation. *Adolescence, 37* (146), 289–299.

Sadker, D., & Sadker, M. (1985). Is the O.K. classroom O.K.? *Phi Delta Kappan, 55,* 358–361.

Sadker, D., & Sadker, M. (1994). *Failing at fairness.* New York: Charles Scribner's Sons.

Sadker, D., & Sadker, M. (2003). Gender bias: From colonial America to today's classrooms. In J. A. Banks & C. A. M. Banks (Eds.), *Multicultural education: Issues and perspectives* (4th ed., pp. 125–151). New York: John Wiley & Sons.

Sadker, D., Sadker, M., & Shakeshift, C. (1992). Sexuality and sexism in schools: How should educators be prepared? In S. S. Klein (Ed.), *Sex equity and sexuality in education* (pp. 363–375). Albany, NY: State University of New York Press.

Scering, G. E. S. (1997). Themes of a critical/feminist pedagogy: Teacher education for democracy. *Journal of Teacher Education, 48* (1), 62–67.

Schiever, S. W., & Maker, C. J. (1997). Enrichment and acceleration: An overview and new directions. In N. Colangelo & A. D. Davis (Eds.), *Handbook of gifted education* (2nd ed, pp. 113–125). Boston: Allyn & Bacon.

Scruggs, T. E., & Mastropieri, M. A. (1986). Academic characteristics of behavioral disordered and learning disabled students. *Behavior Disorders, 11* (3), 184–190.

Shaywitz, B., Fletcher, J., & Shaywitz, S. (1995). Defining and classifying learning disabilities and attention deficit hyperactivity disorder. *Journal of Child Neurology, 10* (Suppl. 1), S50-S57.

Sleeter, C. E. (1996). *Multicultural education as social activism.* Albany, NY: State University of New York Press.

Sleeter, C. E., & Grant, C. A. (1988). *Making choices for multicultural education: Five approaches to race, class, and gender.* Columbus, OH: Merrill.

Smith, C. R. (1994). *Learning disabilities: The interaction of learner, task, and setting* (3rd ed.). Boston: Allyn & Bacon.

Sobol, T. (1990). Understanding diversity. *Educational Leadership, 48* (3), 27–30.

Solomon, R. P. (1988). Black cultural forms in schools: A cross national comparison. In L. Weis (Ed.), *Class, race, and gender in American Education* (pp. 249–265). Albany, NY: State University of New York Press.

Sorrell, A. L. (1990). Three reading comprehension strategies. TELLS, story mapping and QARs. *Academic Therapy, 25,* 359–368.

Strickland, B. R. (1995, January). Research on sexual orientation and human development: A commentary. *Developmental Psychology, 31,* 137–140.

Subotnik, R. F., & LeBlanc, G. (2003). Teaching gifted students in a multicultural society. In J. A. Banks & C. A. M. Banks (Eds.), *Multicultural education: Issues and perspectives* (4th ed., pp. 353–376). New York: John Wiley & Sons.

Swanson, H. L., (1988). Toward a metatheory of learning disabilities. *Journal of Learning Disabilities, 21,* 196–209.

Swanson, H. L., & Berninger, V. (1995). The role of working memory in skilled and less skilled readers' comprehension. *Intelligence, 21,* 83–108.

Swanson, J. M., McBurnett, K., Wigal, T., Pfiffner, L. J., Lerner, M. A., Williams, L., Christian, D. L., Tamm, L., Wilcutt, E., Crowley, K., Clevenger, W., Khouzam, N., Woo, C., Crinella, F. M., & Fisher, T. D. (1993). Effect of stimulant medication on children with attention deficit disorder: A "review of reviews." *Exceptional Children, 60,* 154–162.

Tannenbaum, A. J. (1997). The meaning and making of giftedness. In N. Colangelo & A. D. Davis (Eds.), *Handbook of gifted education* (2nd ed., pp. 27–42). Boston: Allyn & Bacon.

Turnbull, H. R., & Turnbull, A. P. (1998). *Free appropriate public education: The law and children with disabilities* (5th ed.). Denver: Love.

Turnbull, R., & Cilley, M. (1999). *Explanations and implications of the 1997 amendments to IDEA.* Upper Saddle River, NJ: Merrill/Prentice Hall.

Van Tassel-Baska, J. (1989). Acceleration. In C. J. Maker (Ed.), *Critical issues in gifted education: Defensible programs for the gifted.* Rockville, MD: Aspen.

Vauras, M., Lehtinen, E., Olkinuora, E., & Salonen, P. (1993). Devices and desires: Integrative strategy instruction from a motivational perspective. *Journal of Learning Disabilities, 26,* 384–391.

Wallach, M. A. (1976). Tests tell us little about talent. *American Scientist, 64,* 57.

Wheelock, A. (1992). The case for untracking. *Educational Leadership, 50* (2), 6–10.

Wlodkowski, R. J., & Ginsberg, M. B. (1995). A framework for culturally responsive teaching. *Educational Leadership, 53* (1), 17–21.

Wong, B. Y. (1993). Pursuing an elusive goal: Molding strategic teachers and learners. *Journal of Learning Disabilities, 26,* 354–357.

Wong, B. Y. L., & Sawatsky, D. (1984). Sentence elaboration and retention of good, average, and poor readers. *Learning Disability Quarterly, 7,* 229–236.

Yetman, N. R. (Ed.) (1985). *Majority and minority: The dynamics of race and ethnicity in American life* (4th ed.). Boston: Allyn & Bacon.

Zentall, S. S., & Ferkis, M. A. (1993). Mathematical problem-solving for youth with ADHD, with and without learning disabilities. *Learning Disabilities Quarterly, 16,* 6–18.

Planning for Instruction

Skillful teaching depends on careful planning, so teachers need to make the best possible decisions. Instructional planning requires a good deal of reflection about the individual teacher and the students, as well as about societal expectations and the dynamics of teaching and learning. Reflection about teaching involves a careful consideration of hoped-for results as well as the processes for achieving them. Teachers must engage in a good deal of introspection in an effort to better understand themselves and their capabilities. They must also attempt to ascertain how their particular capabilities can best be used to accomplish important educational objectives.

It is not easy to determine what should take place in the classroom, as there are many considerations that must be addressed. Some of these factors are very complex, with various interested parties having quite different ideas about them. Teachers are often left with the unenviable task of making choices regarding issues with disparate expectations from their constituency. Teachers make an enormous number of decisions each day, with some regarding trivial matters and others involving considerations that are critically important to the well-being of students. Many times these decisions have to be made quickly with little time to adequately consider consequences. Consequently, teachers must be armed with appropriate knowledge and excellent decision-making skills.

After examining the curricular expectations of the state core curriculum for the subjects they teach, along with student needs and interests and the dynamics of teaching and learning, teachers must formulate instructional plans that achieve the goals defined by state curriculum committees and that incorporate learning experiences that satisfy student needs and learning styles. They must be able to anticipate what might be expected when they teach lessons to their students and plan for possible modifications that might be necessary. The complexity of this process is daunting, but successful teachers take more factors into account and more judiciously include them in their decision making. Teachers who fail to plan, plan to fail.

CHAPTER 6

Teaching as Reflection and Decision Making

CHAPTER OBJECTIVES

This chapter is designed to help you

1. State the kind of decisions that must be made before, during, and after teaching in the classroom.

2. Explain the function of theory in decision making and teaching, and how theory can be used to simplify teaching and make it more predictable.

3. Incorporate theory and experience with a personal philosophy of education that can be carefully articulated and applied.

4. Apply personal constructivist thinking inclinations to decision making about teaching, taking into account the possibility of making errors in interpreting student behavior and attitudes.

5. Identify personal potential teaching problems and employ techniques and practices that avoid these problems.

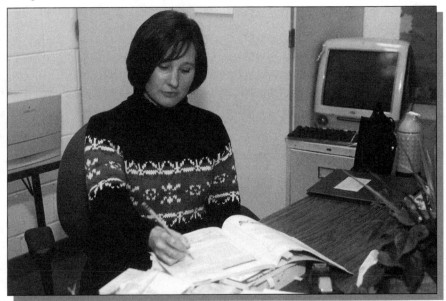

Excellence in teaching requires teachers to reflect on their practice.

6. Analyze the culture of schools and determine how school practices can be arranged to coincide with and enhance the culture.

7. Understand what constitutes good teaching and become committed to improving teaching through reflective practice.

8. Apply a personal philosophy to educational decision making.

9. Determine the validity of assumptions in decision making and use this information to make wise, informed decisions.

10. Apply appropriately prioritized criteria to curriculum decision making.

11. Successfully participate in reflective practices as individuals, in groups, and on a schoolwide basis.

12. Become an expert listener and apply this skill to make more successful interactions with others.

INTRODUCTION

Each teacher is uniquely qualified for decision making in his or her classroom. Each group of students is different from any other, and teachers know these differences more intimately than any other individual. In knowing the situation in their classrooms, teachers can make decisions that are more appropriate for the student population. Student interests are therefore more likely to be met and their needs satisfied. In addition, teachers who are given sufficient autonomy to make decisions in their own classrooms are more likely to be committed to teaching excellence and tend to work harder to ensure student success.

Mr. Cutler had a very diverse group of students in his biology class, including six Hispanic students whose ancestry included six different Central or South American countries; three African Americans; one Native American; and two Asian Americans. The Asian Americans were both from Vietnam, with one coming from the peasant class and the other from the upper level of society. The socioeconomic configuration of Mr. Cutler's class varied from lower working class to upper middle class. There was an even split between boys and girls. Mr. Cutler made a conscientious effort to ascertain learning styles and found all the multiple intelligences about evenly represented. He also tried to find out the hobbies of his students and was amazed at the diversity of interests.

With all these facts in mind, Mr. Cutler sat down to plan a biology unit on the causes of, and transmission of, human diseases. This unit was a departure from the traditional biology curriculum, but he could not imagine any of his classes being interested in studying traditional biology with its emphasis on the classification of various plants and animals. He found it difficult to think of many of his students wanting to study different tissues, organs, and organ systems, or to learn the characteristics of plants and animals, nearly all of which his students had never seen and were not likely to see. He decided to do this unit anyway because the subject was so applicable to all his students. They all had contact with diseases of many kinds, and in some cases these contacts had devastating implications either for themselves or for acquaintances. Since the topic of diseases would be very comprehensive, many subjects in biology could be studied in connection with it. It would be easy, he thought, to get students to talk about their experiences with various diseases. Once they were interested in the topic, he could help the class see that diseases have different origins. Some have genetic origins, while others are caused by bacteria, viruses, protozoans, and prions. There were also vitamin deficiency diseases and various-cause diseases like cancer. Studying diseases with possible genetic origins would require in-depth investigations about cells and cell division; infected tissues, organs, and organ systems; blood; and immune responses. Disease transmission required detailed study of various vectors like insects. Environmental factors, along with prevention, were also important areas for study. Mr. Cutler felt the evolution of disease would be interesting to many students, and decided to focus on these different topics once students reached the point where they considered them important to their study of disease.

Mr. Cutler talked to the whole class about his proposal to make sure the students were interested and there was sufficient commitment to engage in this kind of long-term study. The enthusiasm for the unit was excellent. Students immediately saw the topic as relevant and important. They all had firsthand experiences with diseases, and they realized how necessary it was not only to understand diseases but to know how to prevent them.

Mr. Cutler decided to start the unit right after Christmas break. During the first class, he showed the importance of the cell and how it divides. He put up diagrams of the cell and talked about all the organelles and their functions. He immediately sensed that students were not interested, and he realized he had made a mistake. After school that day he sat down to critically evaluate what had happened. His mistake had been of trying to teach the basics before promoting student interest. Without stimulating student interest and making sure students were enthusiastic about a particular topic before embarking on studying it, his efforts were in vain. Clearly his students were not inherently interested in studying cells and cell division, even though they expressed interest in various diseases. Once they became involved in studying diseases, the students would simply realize the importance of the related basic knowledge. This was particularly important regarding hereditary diseases, where understanding required a good knowledge of genetics, which likewise required a proper understanding of cells. He decided that his approach was essentially backwards. The next day he told the class they would drop the study of cell structures and functions as well as cell division for the time being. Instead, each student was to look up information on a chosen disease to bring to class. They would then have an opportunity to explain what they had learned and survey the interest others might have in the topic. Once this was done, Mr. Cutler arranged a schedule for students to do their research, report it to their peers, and make decisions about additional research. As time went by, students could readily see that their knowledge base needed to be improved. Most notably, students came to Mr. Cutler and asked for help in understanding specific questions about genetics.

A week after Mr. Cutler implemented his plan, he noticed that some of his students were growing dissatisfied. Several students with language difficulties didn't know what was going on. It was also apparent that some of the assigned learning tasks didn't fit the students' learning styles very well. Mr. Cutler decided to visit with each learning group and find out what adjustments needed to be made. He had the groups carefully discuss their projects, indicating anything they thought failed to help them learn well. During each of these discussions, Mr. Cutler asked each group to make any necessary modifications, and establish a regular time each week to make follow-up assessments. He also arranged for resource people to help increase the language skills of students with limited language facilities. He asked the groups to ensure that these students were receiving the full benefit of the learning projects.

Decision Points

Describe all the decisions Mr. Cutler had to make and explain what these decisions were based on.

NATIONAL TEACHING STANDARDS

Teachers make decisions ranging from what aspects of the subject matter to emphasize, to how to pace instruction. In making these decisions, teachers bring to bear their knowledge of students and learning as well as their experience with the teaching and understanding of the subject matter.

The Countenance of Teacher Decision Making

Teachers make many decisions each day; hence, they must be excellent decision makers in order to be successful (Pietig, 1998). These decisions involve a wide variety of items related to their teaching responsibilities, including decisions made before, during, and after teaching. *Before teaching,* teachers consider issues regarding the learning process, learning styles, ethnic differences, gender, nature of the subject matter, student interests, learning objectives, appropriate learning activities, organization and sequence of instruction, classroom organization, resources needed, forms of evaluation, personal beliefs and educational philosophy, anticipated problems, and so on. All these are included in the development of an instructional plan. They all tend to relate to one another, and decisions about any of them depend on related issues.

As complex as decision making before teaching is, decisions made *during teaching* are usually more difficult because they are done on the spot, during active teaching. This complexity results from the dynamics of a group of students who have brought their own agendas to class, along with their current problems. The dynamics of the class will vary on any particular day, depending on the personal, family, and social lives of students, as well as school activities, time of day, and events of all kinds in the community, state, nation, and the world. In addition, the teacher may discover, as Mr. Cutler did, that the best laid plans can go awry. Sometimes anticipated student interest does not materialize, or some students may have difficulty learning a particular concept or idea. Students may not find what is taught to be meaningful and useful. Discipline problems may also erupt. These and other unanticipated happenings make it necessary for teachers to make decisions quickly but effectively. Successful teachers consistently make these decisions, yet keep a critical eye on the particulars of each situation to determine if there are specific considerations that should in-fluence the decision.

Decisions are also made *after teaching* by reflective teachers. They must initially assess the success of the class and then try to formulate necessary modifications for subsequent instruction. Questions like the following might be asked: (1) Did students seem interested and apply themselves to the learning? (2) Were all students, including special needs students, involved in a meaningful way? (3) What modifications in the teaching approach would help the lesson be more successful? (4) Were on-the-spot decisions consistent and effective? (5) Was a proper context created for learning? (6) Was instruction sequenced so that concepts were accurately built upon one another? (7) Did the lesson promote group as well as independent learning? (8) Were the personal objectives of students achieved? (9) Was my role as the teacher helpful and productive? (10) Did I, as the teacher, promote better relationships between myself and my students as well as among students?

Decision Making: An Essential for Teachers

Good teaching depends on effective decision making by teachers. Teaching is anything but routine. Teachers who assume that teaching is routine and treat all students the same or who, in contrast, prescribe all learning activities individually for each student are doomed to failure. Because of its complexity, teaching cannot be reduced to a particular set of operations applied in the same way during each class period. However, because of its complexity teachers need to simplify teaching to reduce the number of required decisions down to a manageable level. This involves building and applying theory. The purpose of theory is threefold: description, explanation, and prediction. *Description's* function is to supply an organized system of classifying and interrelating knowledge to give a coherent definition of related facts and concepts. *Explanation's* purpose is to provide a meaningful account of how the associated facts and concepts that make up a theory relate to selected phenomena. Finally, theories feature of *predictability*. Since they are ordinarily backed by considerable research, theories consistently predict the outcome of particular interactions and events in specific circumstances. Description and explanation allow teachers to properly conceptualize the theory and create appropriate applications. Prediction, however, indicates what can be expected when the theory is properly applied. Thus, teachers can anticipate a particular outcome if they correctly apply a theory. For example, a theory predicts that increased student autonomy along with greater acceptance and attention are related to decreased student disruptiveness in class. If this theory predicts well, teachers should experience less disruptiveness if the theory is properly administered.

A theory simplifies because it shows how circumstances, actions, and outcomes are predictably related. Otherwise, teachers would be left with the arduous task of trying out various approaches depending on circumstances, with little hope that a predictable outcome can be expected. Without theory, teachers are left to employ tactics on a trial and error basis. With the trial and error approach, it is common to think that each student is different and, therefore, has to be taught differently than his or her peers. Imagine a teacher taking 30 students, whose behavior and learning preferences vary depending on personal idiosyncrasies as well as on many possible conditions and circumstances, and providing an effective, coherent instructional program without the proper application of theory. Many teachers claim to teach in this manner, but the results are questionable. For example, a teacher may severely punish a particularly recalcitrant student, assuming it is necessary, only to experience greater disruptiveness. A few students may be given a lot of responsibility, while others are deprived of this opportunity because the teacher considers them unprepared for it. Students who are less involved may become disengaged learners. Some disruptive students may have their names written on the board, primarily as a threat with no consequences, resulting in an increase in misbehavior. The teacher, no doubt, believed his or her efforts would produce better behavior when, in fact, they did not. Because of inconsistency and a poor understanding of theory, some students commonly find intended punishments to be rewarding.

Decision making by teachers in reality involves applying both theory and experience in connection with a personal philosophy of education. These decisions don't involve an effort to determine which theory or practice should be applied to a particular student at a particular time and in particular circumstances. Rather, decision-making concerns the application of one's personal educational philosophy and associated theory (i.e., theory that is consistent with personal philosophy) in practical situations. If the theories used have sufficient predictability, the assumption is that the desired ends of instruction will be achieved consistently for most students, most of the time. Sometimes minor modifications in applications may be required, but using different theories depending on circumstances should be avoided. Because different theories commonly are based on different assumptions and their applications are often contradictory and confusing to students, it is wise to avoid changing to different theories for different students or different circumstances. Not only is this inconsistency confusing, but there is no research that supports doing this, or which describes how and when this can most appropriately be done. Teachers would be simply guessing at when any particular approach would be best.

Decision Points

Make a list of as many kinds of teacher decisions as you can. Identify those decisions that allow time for thinking and those that have to be made on the spot. Estimate how many of each kind of decision a teacher may make in a typical class period.

Research on Teacher Decision Making

Decision making may be *the* basic teaching skill (Shavelson, 1973), as teachers may make as many as 4,000 decisions each day (Danielson, 1996; Jackson, 1968). Many times these decisions occur in rapid succession, making it necessary for the teacher to decide issues and problems with very limited time. Yet, these decisions must be made. It is generally desirable that these decisions are a consistent reflection of theory. However, with the ambiguous, complex nature of classroom life there is enormous potential for teachers' personal traits and viewpoints to shape their perceptions and behavior, rather than an astute application of theory (Lazarus & Folkman, 1984).

Cognitive theories of information processing are primarily *constructivist*. This implies that incoming information takes on decision-making meaning for the teacher only to the extent it can be related to knowledge that already exists in the teacher's mind. In addition, the mind is only able to consciously process a limited amount of information at any given time. The result is a highly personal process that is partially outside conscious awareness (Shepard, 1995). In addition to inherent biases with constructivist processing, people are also reluctant to alter their viewpoints or accept things from a different perspective because of their emotional attachments to their beliefs. Because each person is defined by his or her beliefs, evidence that may contradict or challenge those beliefs is often regarded as a threat to the self and consequently resisted or simply ignored (Head & Sutton, 1985). Thus, beliefs teachers have about their students and about learning substantially influence their goals and decisions (Kagan, 1992). Interestingly, teachers' beliefs are similar to the experiences they had as students (Richardson, 1990). Teacher decision making may consequently be more of an extension of individual identity than a rational evaluation of applicable information. Further, given the unconscious, value-laden nature of cognitive processes, it is unlikely that teachers will accurately perceive their own biases and even less likely that they will make changes in attitudes and beliefs.

For teachers to reduce the complexity of the classroom environment and teach effectively, it is necessary to separate significant events from the more incidental ones, and to apply teaching strategies that reflect bonafide research (Corno, 1981). However, even competent teachers may be unaware of important happenings in the classroom that may be critical to making appropriate decisions. For example, many teachers tend to focus on negative actions by students and give more credence to negative than positive input in decision making (Fiske & Taylor, 1984). Teachers also make **attribution errors** by interpreting students' actions in terms of personal attributes rather than in terms of the context in which the behavior takes place. Thus, teachers may react to stereotypical interpretations of a student's personality or other personal features and ignore more salient data embodied in ongoing classroom activities. Teachers may also interpret various events in the classroom in a general way. Thus, similar actions born of disparate causes may appear to have the same cause and require the same reaction (Holland, Holyoack, Nisbett, & Thagard, 1986). These decisions and consequent reactions may be processed automatically and be outside the teacher's conscious awareness (Uleman, 1987). Given the multidimensional, simultaneous, and immediate nature of classroom events, automatizing some elements involved in the act of teaching may be necessary so that sufficient conscious processing may be devoted to monitoring student behavior (Doyle, 1977). However, by allowing automatic reactions to occur, teachers run the risk of responding in set ways when conscientious decision making is called for. Inflexibility may be the result. Teachers, for the most part, do not consider various alternative options, but rather employ a single approach in a number of situations even when different reactions are indicated (Clarke & Peterson, 1986).

The difficulties encountered in getting teachers to make use of instructional theories and educational concepts have been well-documented (Kagan, 1992; Richardson 1990). These difficulties may be explained by teachers' inclination to maintain the status quo. Resistance to change may occur because of automatic mental processing routines, the constructivist nature of human learning, or the strong personal attachments people have toward their personal beliefs. To simply recommend, without qualification, that teachers be more reflective ignores the reality of how the human mind works. Teachers who are encouraged to analyze their beliefs and practices may simply reinforce previously established, unexamined concepts and automatic patterns of thinking.

One way to deal with this problem is to avoid simple reflection and capitalize on the constructivist nature of learning in a more formal way. Obviously, teachers cannot be indoctrinated. Instead, teachers need to appreciate the underlying processes that constrain objective reasoning, and thus achieve a heightened sensitivity to their unconscious biases as well as commit to continuous learning. Thus, teachers may be asked to examine the roots of their own beliefs and then be confronted with the histories of others' belief systems. By this means, a generalized constructivist approach is more likely to emerge than would occur through simple self-reflection alone. If teachers were exposed to the relative nature of various beliefs, they would be less likely to feel threatened than they would by a single approach. Teachers can be trained to recognize their own automatic biases by learning to examine how others spontaneously interpret and respond to situations in contrast to the ways that they do (Shepard, 1995).

QUESTIONS FOR REFLECTION

1. What can you do as a teacher to minimize bias in your decision making?
2. From your experience, what are the mistakes most common among teachers? Why are these mistakes made?

Decision Points

Make a list of examples from your experience of teachers misinterpreting the actions of their students. Prepare a list of safeguards to prevent you from making the same mistakes yourself.

NATIONAL TEACHING STANDARDS

Teachers can validly evaluate the usefulness of curricular material based on their understanding of curriculum theory, of students, of subject matter, and of the school's and their own educational aims.

Necessary Classroom Decisions

Student needs and interests, as well as social expectations, factor into deciding what should take place in classrooms. All schools establish policies detailing specific goals and objectives for education along with accepted textbooks and other instructional materials. Most states have specific outcomes defined for schooling. State codes commonly include such topics as drug abuse and various goals such as good citizenship. In addition, state departments of education ordinarily provide a core curriculum that details the goals for all approved courses of study. Teachers have the task of translating these expectations into student learning experiences that allow students some degree of autonomy and that satisfy their other needs. Student interests must be taken into account, and the means provided for students to pursue their interests within the prescribed curriculum. The teacher must decide how to adequately satisfy both state expectations and student needs and interests without substantially violating either. In doing this, teachers need to capitalize on intrinsic student interests. This involves strategies that use student interests to initiate instruction, but that eventually incorporate social needs and expectations. Students will need less teacher motivation to engage in learning for which they already have an interest.

Teachers have to make decisions regarding the relative importance of various possible curriculum components. Though not necessarily explicitly defined in the state core curriculum, the more important concepts and ideas should receive greater emphasis. However, unless they are identified as being of particular importance they will likely receive insufficient attention.

Teachers must make decisions about various possible approaches to the curriculum, although care should be taken to involve students so that intrinsic motivation can provide a focus for the decision. Various approaches can ordinarily be taken that involve student input but do not violate the prescribed curriculum. For example, in the chapter-opening case of Mr. Cutler, a biology course could conceivably take a medical approach focusing on the nature of disease, specifically its transmission and prevention, and still include all the appropriate topics outlined in the state core objectives for the course. The study of disease can include biochemistry, genetics, cells, tissues, organs, various vectors like insects, and so on.

QUESTION FOR REFLECTION

1. How can students be involved in curriculum construction?

Decision Points

How should you deal with conflicts between state curriculum requirements and personal educational philosophy? Show this with a specific example.

NATIONAL TEACHING STANDARDS

Teachers use their experience to acquire a deep understanding of their students, and the communities from which they come, that shape students' outlooks, values, and orientation toward schooling.

Reflection on Teaching

Excellent teachers constantly examine their own practice and look for ways to make improvements, which involves a thorough understanding of the culture of the classroom along with a valid view of teaching excellence. The nature of students, their interests, and their learning proclivities also need attention. Finally, the special problems presented by the classroom and the school need to be examined for ways they may or may not contribute to student learning. Continuous analysis is essential, not only because things change but because the dynamics brought on by change have important implications for classroom instruction. For example, a teacher may find that various student populations have different inclinations for interacting with one another. In addition the absence of certain class members may precipitate very different learning conditions, making it necessary to make adjustments if the necessary level of student interaction is to take place.

The Culture of Schools

The school's culture has an enormous impact on teaching and learning. Each school must be examined because each is different in significant ways (Orlich et al., 1990). Teachers must understand school culture as clearly as possible, not only to adjust to conditions appropriately, but also to initiate changes for improvement. However, cultural features and possible improvements are not ordinarily very explicit. School culture is characterized by considerable uncertainty. Values are often obscure, and there may be little agreement about them (Lieberman & Miller, 1984). The interactions possible between the school and society may also vary depending on the nature of the influences imposed on schools. In addition, within the school itself there are subsystems that may interact differently as circumstances and personnel change. Unique school cultures tend to develop over time, as initiatives and reactions occur both inside and outside the school.

One important contributor to school culture is the community in which the school is located. Within each community there are many entities that have viable input for schools. The ethnicity and social class of the parents, along with churches and various social organizations, provide a backdrop of influence. Different communities expect different things from their schools. Some may view the school as a way to move children out of poverty conditions into more affluent living and therefore will focus on college entrance preparations. Others believe school should provide a basic education for entry into a working class society. In multicultural communities, schools may be considered the appropriate means for minority groups to enter mainstream society.

Schools are also greatly influenced by student purposes, which are naturally impacted by parental expectations. If parents expect schools to ensure that their children enter a college or university of their choice, the focus is likely to be on grades as opposed to learning and achievement. Under these conditions, grades are likely to be inflated, with students being more concerned about what is being tested than what is meaningful. Consequently, pressure may be imposed on teachers to lower standards.

While this is going on, there may be pressure from outside the school to raise standards. During the past two decades, various educational task forces have been initiated with the expressed purpose of making recommendations for school improvement. Chance (1988) reported that more that 275 such task forces were organized in the United States, with each of them publishing a list of recommendations. As a result of these recommendations, states have increased high school graduation standards and college admission standards. They have also created additional student assessment tests to determine if expectations are being met. Teachers are given the arduous task of preparing their students for these year-end tests while at the same time adhering to state-prescribed curricula. This creates enormous pressure for teachers, particularly when the standardized tests are not a valid measure of school achievement (Popham, 1999).

Students are greatly influenced by past school experiences, which may be why proposed reforms often do not meet expectations. Students may resist, for example, the expectation to act more responsibly when given more autonomy. If they are used to considerable control, more freedom won't initially produce more responsible students. Similarly, raising standards won't necessarily improve student achievement. These efforts often fail to have the intended effect because they do not deal with fundamental flaws in the schools, or they may not be properly implemented. Giving students more autonomy may fulfill an important student need, but it requires skilled applications by carefully trained teachers who have sufficient commitment to face potential opposition.

The training and values of teachers are important aspects of school culture. Interestingly, teachers tend to operate within a system of values acquired in their own schooling experiences. Teacher training has a limited impact on how they teach (Nagel & Driscoll, 1992; Shulman, 1987). In addition, if new teachers enter the school with different ideas about teaching than those generally practiced, subtle pressure is often applied to get them to conform to the norms. They may be told that the real world of the school is much different from the classrooms portrayed in their university training. They are expected to set aside their research-based university training in favor of a style consisting primarily of lecturing and directing seat work (Goodlad, 1984), the kind of teaching practices often criticized in reform efforts (Orlich et al., 1990). In traditional schooling, teachers do the bulk of the talking, there are few hands-on activities, and teachers spend most of their time managing routines and employing whole-group instruction. Teachers tend to work alone, controlling the content of instruction, and providing very little praise or student feedback. Students tend to be passive, showing little or no initiative regarding what they learn. Instruction in the schools is described as "flat." Since a good deal of interaction and inquiry is recommended for classroom instruction (National Research Council, 1996), an obvious disparity exists between traditional schooling and teachers' instructional inclinations when compared to university training and recommendations by professional education groups.

State legislatures and state departments of education also impact school culture by establishing guidelines and rules regarding many aspects of education. Accepted courses of study, along with specific goals of instruction and textbooks, are commonly prescribed. State departments are also involved in teacher certification and consequently set standards for teacher preparation. During the past two or three decades, state legislatures have been particularly active in reforming the schools. During the 1980s alone, virtually every state legislature passed laws that impacted schools, teachers, teacher education, teacher licensing, school financing, and curriculum. By some estimations, over a thousand pieces of legislation were enacted in an effort to reform schools and their operations (Darling-Hammond & Berry, 1988). These state-mandated reforms focused first on efficiency, then on teacher-proof curricula, and finally on "a return to basics."

Decision Points

For a school with which you are familiar, list as many cultural components as you can. Explain their impact on the school in general and on the instructional program. Explain how you, as a classroom teacher in that school, would use the culture of the school and community to create a viable curriculum.

NATIONAL TEACHING STANDARDS

Teachers learn to "read" their students to determine potential learning problems for students and alter plans as necessary. They can then work with individual students.

Teachers learn from their students, from watching them interact with their peers, and from reading what they write.

Characteristics of Good Teaching

With all the efforts to improve education, little has been done to employ theories and ideas that actually change what happens in schools. Schooling tends to remain essentially the same regardless of the changes that take place. Teaching methods remain the same, assessment processes are unchanged, and test scores are not improved. Even students are aware that they are not progressing academically as they move through school; the meaningful experiences students report involve friends, sports, and other activities. Classes and teachers are at the bottom of the list (Goodlad, 1984). Students apparently do not find the curriculum and their experiences with their teachers as meaningful as their contact with peers and their participation in extracurricular programs.

What kind of teaching-learning experiences would make a difference? This question has to be qualified before it can be intelligently answered. It must first be decided whether or not high scores on standardized achievement tests can be considered a valid outcome for schooling. Politically, the answer may be "Yes." From an educational standpoint, however, the relative standing of students in the world is less important than achieving goals like the ability to function adequately in a democratic community and be gainfully employed in a satisfying job. It is also important to understand social systems and learn how to provide an excellent home environment in which to raise well-adjusted children. It is important that children learn how to solve problems of all kinds and apply their intellectual skills toward making a better world in which to live. Preparing for standardized achievement tests is unlikely to achieve these goals.

Once the goals of education are clear, it becomes a matter of determining the kind of educational experiences that can best achieve them, and the kind of teaching that can help children acquire the knowledge and skills desired (see Table 6.1). Good teaching consists of caring relationships in which students feel accepted, appreciated, and enabled to engage in learning activities that empower them to expertly solve relevant problems and become integrated into a variety of communities where they can function well. These include societal, family, spiritual, and occupational communities.

Excellent teaching is based on principles and purposes, not on techniques or methods. Various techniques or methods may be employed in connection with applying appropriate teaching principles, but unlike in traditional teaching, they are not an end in themselves. For example, a good PowerPoint presentation is frequently used as a criterion to judge the quality of a teacher's performance. If the PowerPoint presentation is well-organized and interesting, with humorous anecdotes and colorful illustrations, it may be

TABLE 6.1   *Characteristics of Good Teaching.*

Mediocre Teaching	Good Teaching
Experiences with teachers are not meaningful.	Caring relationships are formed with acceptance and appreciation.
Students memorize information.	Students experience empowering problem-solving learning activities.
Teaching is based on techniques and methods.	Teaching is based on theory and principles.
Students work on structured, prescribed curriculum.	Students work on meaningful projects.
Teachers do all the assessments.	Teachers help learners to make personal assessments of their work.

assumed to represent excellent teaching. However, the presentation of information is inconsistent with children's inherent constructivist learning inclinations. In addition, students would be much better off learning how to solve relevant problems rather than trying to assimilate a body of facts. Therefore, teaching excellence depends on the relevance of what is learned as well as the learning process, not the way in which information is presented. Excellent teaching is more likely to involve interaction skills and the ability to create active learning situations than it is to focus on knowledge and on creating well-organized presentations.

Because student-teacher interaction skills are critical, teachers need to master these skills in a way that promotes good relationships, helps students focus on significant problems, and allows students to approach these problems with the highest intellectual capacity of which they are capable. Teachers must get students involved in projects that are meaningful to them and will help them become skilled members of learning communities. In addition, teachers must know how to help learners make valid assessments of their work and initiate desired improvements.

The principles and purposes that support this kind of teaching activity include the following:

1. School learning should satisfy students' needs for attention and affection, autonomy, enjoyment, and personal control.
2. In learning, students should acquire those intellectual skills that help them effectively solve relevant problems. They should have many opportunities to apply their skills in problem solving.
3. What students learn should be personally meaningful to them and help them accomplish their goals.
4. In the learning environment, students should acquire a sense of well-being and personal satisfaction, and they should achieve an ability to successfully regulate their own lives.
5. In classroom situations, students should learn how to participate effectively in learning communities that adequately represent the nature of communities in which they will be involved throughout their lives.
6. Students should acquire skills for interacting with others, both as leaders and as followers.

7. Students should participate in activities that promote the development of their intellectual capacity.
8. Students should develop sufficient sensitivity to others to productively work with others in a variety of ways.
9. Students should develop an inclination to ask critical life questions and acquire the research skills to find answers to their questions.

Decision Points

Think about the teachers you have had in your own schooling. What teaching characteristics do excellent teachers have? Compare your observations with your peers and with information presented in this chapter about good teaching and attempt to reconcile any discrepancies.

NATIONAL TEACHING STANDARDS

Teachers' decisions should be grounded in established theory and reasoned judgment.

Decision Making and Educational Theory

Rather than simply applying various methods and judging their effectiveness with simplistic criteria like a quiet classroom or high test scores, teachers can make use of educational theories that have been researched and validated. These can be combined with personal experiences to supply a more comprehensive, useful approach to teaching. Without the use of theory, teaching strategies may be applicable in a limited number of circumstances, or they may promote unacceptable effects in addition to those sought. For example, some teachers use the "don't smile until Christmas" approach. In practical terms, this means that the teacher treats children roughly for the first part of the school year and then starts to treat them more kindly later on. Generally, there is a single objective: to keep students quiet. However, even though students might be quiet, they also may learn to dislike the teacher and become disenchanted with school overall because of the rough treatment they have experienced. Consequently, they may be unenthusiastic learners and low achievers.

Theories have the benefit of being comprehensive: they take a broad spectrum of important considerations into account, and they are generally applicable over a wide range of situations. Ordinarily, their use is carefully defined and the results of their application are predictable. In being comprehensive, they address issues in a cohesive way. Thus, a theory may provide, in addition to detailed explanations about the source and nature of educational goals, such information as how they can best be implemented, what should be done in the classroom to keep students motivated and interested, how to avoid problems, and how to properly manage the classroom and create a stimulating atmosphere for learning. In addition, theories provide principles for their application rather than prescriptive practices. In using theories, teachers apply principles to various classroom situations and make adjustments to practices that accommodate classroom differences without violating the applicable principles.

Educators may choose from different theories that vary in fundamental ways. Ordinarily, they are based on different assumptions about how children learn and develop, to what extent humans are self-regulating and can become self-governing, what the purposes of education should be, how students should be treated, and how instruction should be arranged. Perhaps the major difference between theories lies in the assumptions they make about human nature and learning. Behavioristic theories, for example, indicate that humans are only motivated externally, that there is limited uniqueness between individuals at birth, that humans have no will, and that each individual is shaped exclusively by the environment. This theory, results in carefully organized perspective school curricula, and shapes student behavior through reinforcement contingencies, with a lot of feedback given to inform students when they are following the approved procedures and practices. Humanistic theories, however, focus on the uniqueness of students and their behavior; they encourage student learning activities that correspond to student uniqueness.

Teachers can either function as technicians or theoreticians. As technicians, they routinely apply various techniques and prescriptively engage their students in activities. Thus, a technically oriented teacher might employ a well-organized PowerPoint presentation because it is assumed that students can come to a better understanding when a concept is appropriately represented and illustrated. If the teacher finds such an approach to be ineffective, a different approach, such as a discussion, might subsequently be used. Theoreticians are more likely to study a group of students and make adaptations appropriate to the theory on which they base their teaching. If additional adjustments are needed, these are made, but the theory continues to guide practice in order to maintain consistency and predictability. In making adaptations, the theoretician uses a broad base of inputs like student learning and development, human nature, and learning styles, along with the nature of the subject itself. These are orchestrated so that the learning approach used is sufficiently comprehensive to take all these sources of information into account. Theories ordinarily provide explanations about various features of teaching and learning, and guidelines for applying them appropriately in the classroom. All of the applications recommended are based on a common set of principles. With a technical approach to teaching, various methodologies may be used that are composed of disparate principles and applications. Thus, technicians use various methods that aren't necessarily based on a common set of principles but rather on folklore and traditions, while theoreticians faithfully base their practice on a defined set of principles that ordinarily are part of a consistent educational philosophy. Sometimes educational theories are criticized for lacking practicality, but in reality theories are much more practical and useful than technically oriented tradition and folklore (Johnson, 1998). Teachers are more effective when their teaching is based on theory, judgment, and wisdom than on various traditions (Hunter, 1988).

A Model for Decision Making in Teaching

A decision making model is particularly useful because it can provide consistency in dealing with problems that may be extremely complex and thus have many features that make adequate solutions difficult to achieve. A model provides a structure for ensuring comprehensive decision making, with all possible inputs to problem-solving considered and the relative importance of each input carefully evaluated and appropriately applied. Problem solving is often restricted by personal biases and by the failure to consider all contributing data. Sometimes assumptions are not taken into account and properly validated. In addition, evaluation criteria may not be broadly enough based or appropriately prioritized. These biasing features, along with applications of personal biased standards that may not have been properly delineated, can lead to inappropriate conclusions and poor decisions.

Decision Making and a Personal Philosophy of Education

There are many classroom decisions to make each day, and there is often little time to consider the strength of various possibilities before rendering a judgment or deciding on a course of action. Without a formalized decision process and a philosophy of education to guide decision making, the sheer volume of variations requiring teacher decisions and actions can be overwhelming. Decisions can be more efficiently and effectively made when a well-articulated approach is used and when decisions have the benefit of consistency that a philosophy of education can provide.

A philosophy of education's purpose is to bring together all the various aspects of teaching and learning into a single set of consistent principles that can be explicitly articulated and applied in the classroom. Being able to explain a theory in detail provides a way to fine-tune its conception and applications, as well as create a means for assessing effectiveness and guiding modifications while planning instruction and teaching. Education philosophies are composed of principles that have been examined and tested. These principles are consistent not only with education research, but also with personal beliefs. A teacher might, for example, have a strong belief that education should articulate with democratic principles and consequently establish learning communities in the classroom. The task then is to validate the usefulness of learning communities along with their characteristics and applications. Examining research and conducting trial-runs, along with making formal and informal assessments, are essential. In the process, the teacher can examine his or her original ideas regarding the appropriateness of democratic principles in the classroom, as well as assessing the ease of implementing them and the results. Over a succession of applications and analyses, the teacher can make an appraisal of the basic ideas as well as the problems of putting them into practice. A decision can then be made about the appropriateness of applying democratic principles in the classroom. This approach allows teachers not only to examine their philosophy of education more closely, but also to take a careful look at problems associated with implementation. It may even cause teachers to reconsider the principles they have accepted as strategic components of their educational philosophy.

In developing a personal philosophy of education, it is essential to examine personal beliefs as well as educational theory and research. The essential components of an educational philosophy include the following:

- a conception of human nature and needs in connection with how needs shape behavior and why
- a conception of the nature of human development and learning
- a conception of the nature of individual differences regarding learning styles and inclinations

- a conception of teaching given the nature of human development and learning
- a conception of curricular organization that articulates with learning and teaching

Teachers should realize that different views of education can be reflected in educational philosophy. A variety of theories with extensive research bases are currently incorporated into philosophy and applied in schools. Philosophy is not exclusively a result of research; in fact, research technically is an extension of philosophy that consists of one of a number of ways of knowing, namely the empirical mode. Although schools should theoretically be run as research indicates, research and its results are actually framed by philosophical considerations and associated assumptions. For example, research designed to determine which of a number of teaching approaches is the best may use achievement test scores as criterion measures, assuming that higher test scores correlate with a good education. The first question to address is whether or not the measures of achievement are sufficiently valid. Often they are not. The next step may be to challenge the assumption that high achievement test scores validly indicate a good education. This, of course, depends on how a good education is defined. One might define excellence in education as a student's ability to think clearly at high levels, to make excellent decisions, and to work and learn effectively in learning communities. These outcomes for schooling are not validly reflected in achievement test scores. Another question may be whether or not achievement test scores measure a sufficiently broad range of skills and abilities to reflect the full spectrum of multiple intelligences. Clearly they do not.

Different philosophies also may dictate what schools desire to achieve in terms of student discipline. One philosophy may require students to be compliant, while another may prefer that they learn self-regulation. There are various theories that strive to achieve both these ends. Research may indicate that all of them are effective for their intended purpose but never indicate which is the best outcome; in other words, the outcome is a matter of choice, not a matter of research results. If greater student autonomy and self-regulation are desired, various procedures designed to achieve these results can be tested to determine which are superior. If educators desire students to become excellent in achieving prescribed school purposes, then theories designed with this end in mind can be tested. However, determining if one or the other of these educational quests is superior is a matter of opinion.

Decision Points

Create a written statement of your philosophy of education that you believe is not only based on research but is also consistent with your personal experiences.

Assumptions and Their Validity

At all levels, decision making requires skill in determining and validating assumptions. **Assumptions** are often ignored, even when very crucial decisions are made, and the results can be catastrophic. An assumption is something presumed to be true or false. For example, it might be assumed that students attend school because they are interested in school learning. In fact, their attendance may be due to a desire to prepare for college entrance, satisfy their parents, or just avoid trouble. These goals have little to do with the desire to learn per se. If learning experiences are planned assuming that of students have an inherent desire to learn what school has to offer, teachers may be operating on a false assumption. All theories in the field of education are based on assumptions. They assume humans have particular needs, grow and develop in a certain way, have specified social behaviors, and learn in defined ways. From theory to theory these attributes are defined in different, often contradictory ways. It is wise, consequently, to carefully determine the assumptions associated with various theories and then validate them.

Validating assumptions means determining whether or not they are true, which is done by assessing appropriate empirical studies, as well as making careful analyses of one's own and others' experiences. This is not a simple process, for contradictory evidence may be supplied by research, and differences of opinion may result from individual experiences. Therefore, it is necessary to examine whatever evidence is available and make a judgment about its validity. Failure to do this is unconscionable. Engaging in educational processes that are based upon false, unexamined assumptions is likewise unacceptable.

Decision making also depends on the use of prioritized criteria. When **criteria** are used as standards for judgment, they allow for more consistent, analytical decision making. They also communicate to others the basis upon which decisions are made. When decision-making criteria are public, others are able to immediately determine how various choices are made. When criteria are prioritized, an even clearer picture is possible. Prioritized criteria tell explicitly what is being emphasized and why; they indicate the values of the decision maker and show the relative strength of criteria. To prioritize criteria, the decision maker must explain the relative importance given each criterion and why.

QUESTIONS FOR REFLECTION

1. What are some of the assumptions made in common school practice that you think are not valid? What evidence is there for this assertion?

2. What criteria do you think are appropriate to use to determine the kind of experiences students should receive? Make a list of these and prioritize them.

Reflective Practice and School Improvement

Excellent decision making is an essential component of reflective practice for school improvement. What is reflective practice? **Reflective practice,** a learning process that underlies all forms of high professional competence (Bright, 1996), ensures that disparate inputs in conversations about educational improvement are fully considered and that, through higher-level thinking processes, all potential educational considerations are carefully examined. Teachers who engage in this process examine one another's beliefs, goals, and practices to acquire new and deeper understandings that lead to positive actions for school improvement. These actions may involve changes in behavior, skills, attitudes, or perspectives within an individual, partner, small group, or the entire school. Reflective processes may take place within student learning communities, by individual teachers, with teacher partners, within small teacher groups, or within the entire school. These levels are components of a reflective practice model presented by York-Barr, Sommers, Ghere, and Montie (2001).

In this reflection model, beliefs are carefully examined, including values, visions, biases, and paradigms. Beliefs, which result primarily from experiences, influence how we think and behave. They form the lens through which we view the world and acquire an understanding of it. Goals are also analyzed. In this effort, aims, outcomes, and intentions are compared. Thoughtfully considered differences are used to clarify and refocus educational efforts. Reflecting on practice refers to an analysis of dispositions, behaviors, and skills related to teaching performance. This process involves designing instruction and assessment strategies, interacting with and influencing students, developing family relationships, collaborating with colleagues, and initiating schoolwide reforms.

Students' learning is linked to the learning of their teachers (Richardson, 1997, 1998). When teachers reflect on their practice, conditions are created to improve teaching because reflection accomplishes the following:

- It creates opportunities for continuous learning.
- It provides a variety of perspectives to draw on in addressing the many challenging and complex components of teaching.
- It provides new knowledge and understandings that have immediate applications because they are created within the context of teaching.
- It provides a sense of efficacy for teachers, helping them believe they can make a real difference for their students because of the context-generated solutions they create.
- It provides teachers a sense of personal responsibility for learning and improvement.
- It provides an avenue for strengthening relationships with other teachers and developing shared goals and developmental activities.
- It helps teachers build bridges between theory and practice.
- It reduces the likelihood that external mandates will be imposed because schools based on reflective practice already show improvements (York-Barr et al., 2001).

What does it mean to be a reflective educator? First, reflective educators must have a high level of commitment to their own professional development (Zeichner & Liston, 1996). They also must have a self-sustained interest in learning, which drives them to devote time and energy to inquiry, questioning, and discovery regarding ways to improve their practice (Bright, 1996). Their quest for improvement addresses instructional effectiveness, and they also focus on the underlying assumptions, biases, and values they possess. They consider the paramount issues of justice, equity, and morality as they seek to reflect on their practice and design their instruction. Instead of blindly accepting new ideas, they carefully analyze suggestions for change to ensure that they are appropriate in terms of previous experiences, various contexts, and desired educational goals (Clarke, 1995; Zeichner & Liston, 1996). Reflective teachers are able to synthesize data gleaned from the research (*content knowledge*) with their own personal teaching experiences (*contextual knowledge*). A blend of both types of knowledge are essential to achieve excellence in practice (Brookfield, 1992).

What personal capacities and skills promote effective reflection? Among the skills and dispositions that enhance the effectiveness of reflective practice, the ability to promote *trusting relationships* assures participants that information they share will not be used against them (Osterman & Kottkamp, 1993). Trust and respect contribute powerfully to supportive collaboration, reflective dialogue, and the growth of the professional community (Bryk, Camburn, & Louis, 1999). Reflection promotes change, and change involves risk. Teachers will be reluctant to talk about problems associated with potential change unless they feel secure in risk taking (Osterman & Kottkamp, 1993).

Reflective teachers also have to learn to be *present* to themselves and others. This attribute requires teachers to broaden their attention to include more than the usual immediate experience. They have to realize what is happening in a broader context while filtering out competing priorities. This allows individuals to bring themselves more fully to the task at hand and to fully and productively interact with others (Kahn, 1992).

An individual with an *open* mind will consider multiple perspectives. Reflective teachers need open-mindedness in order to listen to all sides of an issue and avoid viewing situations exclusively from personal perspectives. Without openness, the individual merely perpetuates his or her own current views, while an open person senses that there are alternative ways to think and act. This state of mind is critical in fostering inquiry (Hatton & Smith, 1995).

During reflection, teachers need to be able to *listen without judgment and with empathy*. Learning depends on one's ability to effectively listen. Individuals tend to use their own personal experiences to filter what is heard. (Carlson & Bailey, 1997; Isaacs, 1999). Thus, a speaker's intended meaning may be misinterpreted. Listening requires a suspension of personal thoughts in order to focus on what is being said. Listeners ordinarily calculate their next statement rather than listening intently to what others say. Listeners also commonly engage in appositional thinking while half-listening to a speaker. They have staked out their own position and resist being changed or influenced by another point of view (Isaacs, 1999). Empathetic listening occurs at a deeper level as the listener tries to make a genuine connection to another person and understand him or her completely. Temporarily setting aside personal concerns and ideas prepares a person to empathetically listen.

Understanding occurs with thoughtful listening. One doesn't have to agree in order to achieve a valid understanding of what is communicated. When genuine understanding is sought, communicants achieve a higher level of trust, and participants become more willing to modify their views to accommodate a broader range of input by others. Mutual understanding is the foundation of reflective practice (York-Barr et al., 2001).

Participant mutuality is essential if all individuals involved are to enthusiastically participate. There are ordinarily hierarchical structures in schools that tend to separate individuals by age, years of experience, degrees held, or positions occupied. Often younger, less-experienced teachers or students are viewed as lesser contributors and consequently of less value to the school community. This, of course, undermines their enthusiasm and diminishes their participation. Even when there are substantial differences between individuals, there should be an earnest valuing of what can be contributed by everyone. There should not be a pretext of experts that relegates lesser participants to less-valued roles. In learning communities, all participants can be enriched by everyone else, and through this mutual enrichment all can grow and make more important contributions to the whole group.

In an effective learning community, participants need to have *confidence in the process* of reflection. Because reflection is a time-consuming endeavor, those involved need to trust that the process will eventually lead to positive outcomes to which they have given significant input. Unless participants believe positive outcomes will occur, they will be unwilling to devote the necessary time to the process. Group development and trust take time. Once community members are informed of these time requirements, they need opportunities to assess the progress being made on improving student learning and must judge the development of the group.

The heart of reflective practice is inquiry, involving an active search to find answers to carefully constructed questions. Statements tend to stimulate analytic thinking and judgment, while questions spark creative thinking and promote either a search for answers, a negotiation of meaning, or a continuation of dialogue (York-Barr et al., 2001).

Successful reflection depends to a great extent on how participants respond to one another. Costa and Kallick (2000) provide appropriate response strategies. First, individuals need to *listen silently*. For thoughtful reflection, time must be given for adequate contemplation. Deeper meanings can then be expected. Second, listeners can improve reception by *paraphrasing* what they hear and sincerely stating their understanding of what was said. Third, listeners should accept what was said *nonjudgmentally*. Judgments tend to shut down thinking and interrupt the flow of the thinking process while the speaker deals with the apparent disagreement. Fourth, listeners sometimes need *clarification* of an idea or process. Questions of a non-interrogating nature can be asked to increase understanding and improve reflection. Fifth, speakers should *extend* by saying more about the topic. This allows individuals to broaden the information and bring better understanding.

As participants interact with one another, thinking can hopefully be expanded so that more possibilities are considered when solving problems. In thinking together, participants should no longer take a position as final. With less certainty, each individual can listen to various options, enlarge the scope of considerations, and bring to bear more useful input (Isaacs, 1999). It is essential that dialogue continue until enough appropriate input has been given to derive useful, mutually acceptable decisions. Hasty decision making should be avoided.

Teachers who are capable of reflecting on their practice have a greater potential to influence colleagues. Associates are drawn to and respect colleagues who are thoughtful, strive for continuous improvement, and are flexible and approachable. Teachers whose attention is focused primarily on the improvement of student learning can have a profound influence on guiding the thinking and decision making of other educators (Butler, 1996).

To engage in personal reflection, teachers can benefit from a written dialogue with themselves, asking strategic questions about their teaching such as:

What are the basic components of competent teaching?
How do children learn?
What should the goals of education be?
What should the role of students be in making decisions about their school experiences?

What conflicts can be discovered between beliefs and values about teaching and learning and the actual behavior of students?
How do students relate to me?
What differences between students may dictate different teaching approaches?

One way to expand thinking in self-reflection is to write down as many perspectives as possible about an event or experience: What did I see happen? What happened from the viewpoint of others? How can I interpret a situation positively without placing blame on others for their actions? How can I achieve an attitude of empathy about others' thoughts and actions? How can I come to understand that there are legitimate differences between the views of various people? It is valuable to understand one's own pattern of thinking; in other words, to think about thinking. Accepting the necessity of working with others is also essential. This interdependence requires empathetic understanding of various points of view, along with an ability to accept them without undue bias.

To be effective, reflective practice should occur not only with individual teachers, but in various group configurations. These learning communities provide a basis to improve the practice of individual teachers and also to revitalize and improve the entire school. A teacher may choose to interact with one other teacher as a partner or with small groups or teams of teachers. They can also become involved in schoolwide reflective practice.

Decision Points

Think about your personal attributes as a teacher, both positive and negative. In addition, think about the kind of classroom you believe is most appropriate in your subject matter

Teachers who interact with teaching partners can greatly enhance their classroom performance.

area. Prepare a narrative explanation of your hopes and aspirations about teaching, along with your strengths and weaknesses. Describe how you might determine whether or not your views and aspirations are the best way to promote student learning. Explain what actions you might take to improve your proposed practice.

Reflection with Partners

Teachers are commonly isolated from other teachers for most of the day and do not have any formal structure to promote interaction on critical school matters. Because of this isolation, and because each individual tends to filter experiences and thinking exclusively through his or her personal biases, reflecting without interacting with others can result in self-validation and justification (Bright, 1996; Butler, 1996; Levin, 1995). Involving others in reflection is a safeguard against perpetuating personal thoughts and values without examining them. Colleagues can be very helpful in detecting unsupported assumptions and biases (Bright, 1996).

Partnering should be done with a trusted colleague, as the level of trust will determine the productiveness of the association. It is also wise, initially, to have a partner who has common interests, along with similar experiences and values. Partnering with individuals holding excessively different views can be taxing if undertaken before the skills for positive interaction have been mastered.

Early in the reflection process, partners should indicate to one another what their learning desires and needs are. Productive associations are enhanced when there is a common, desirable agenda to follow. In the beginning, partners might clarify what they want from the interaction. Once the interaction process and agenda are solidified, the partners should move toward altering their usual frame of reference. This is ordinarily difficult and time-consuming, as well as uncomfortable (Butler, 1996). To alter the frame of reference, the following elements given by Ross (1990) can be useful:

*   Identify a number of educational dilemmas.
*   Analyze the dilemmas and determine both the similarities to other familiar situations and the unique qualities of each particular situation.
*   Frame the dilemmas in familiar perspectives, and then in new perspectives.
*   Experiment with different perspectives on each dilemma to discover the implications of applying various solutions to problems.
*   Evaluate both intended and unintended consequences of a solution after it has been implemented, and determine whether the consequences are desirable.

In addition to face-to-face interactions, partner teachers may also want to create dialogue journals that can be exchanged and then read outside of formal meetings. This approach allows teachers to interact without having to schedule meetings and provides an excellent format for careful thinking, which face-to-face meetings often cannot do. Some individuals do not do as well in face-to-face meetings and require more time, not only to consider what to say to their colleagues but also to think about the input and responses from associates.

Some reflective experiences should involve an analysis of teaching performances, which can be done as an observation scheme or as formal action research. Observations can be made and analyzed in terms of previous interactions, where intentions are defined and outcomes are measured against these intentions. When action research is indicated, teachers should first select a focus and clarify what theories are being tested. Next, research questions can be identified and a design created for controlling the experiment. The design is then implemented, and data is collected and analyzed. Finally, a report is made for further analysis.

Effective listening is critical in reflective practice. Most people do not listen well, but rather attend to their own views and opinions, and only wait during the remarks by others to insert their own agenda into the conversation. The following practice sequence can be helpful in reducing the inclination to focus on personal agendas while ignoring what others say in a conversation:

Step 1.
In a dyad, one person is designated as the listener and the other as the speaker.
Step 2.
The person designated as the speaker talks about a particular topic for three minutes. During this time, the listener just listens and does not talk.
Step 3.
At the end of the three minutes, both the speaker and listener reflect on how their roles felt.
Step 4.
The participants switch roles and go through another sequence of speaking, listening, and analyzing.

During these episodes, the speaker doesn't have to worry about having his or her train of thought interrupted. Likewise, the listener does not have to think about whether he or she agrees or disagrees with the speaker or how to respond. This kind of practice helps promote better listening for understanding and develops greater sensitivity to what others say.

Decision Points

With a partner, reflect on the kind of classroom each of you envisions as the best. Try to indicate areas in each description that you might give more attention to improving. Create as many different approaches as you can that are different from your own. Identify the strengths and weaknesses of both your approach and the various alternatives.

NATIONAL TEACHING STANDARDS

Teachers face stiff challenges that do not lend themselves to simple solutions. They must become proficient in fashioning compromises that satisfy multiple parties.

Reflection in Small Groups

Through experience, teachers have learned that working in groups is often risky, frustrating, and unproductive. They need to learn that risk can be minimized and that productive work can be accomplished if participants are committed and willing to devote the necessary time. Educators are more likely to engage in reflective group work if the agenda has meaning for their immediate practice and is likely to improve learning conditions for students (York-Barr et al., 2001).

What considerations must be addressed in promoting group cohesiveness and productivity? One critical factor is group size. According to Johnson and Johnson (1999), four to six people is optimal for a group. This size provides for varied perspectives and skills while still allowing adequate participation by all members. This does not negate the value of larger groups at times when they are necessary, so long as relationships are carefully developed and processes are well-designed and implemented (Thousand & Villa, 2000).

Group composition is also an important consideration. It is imperative that all *voices from the school* are represented and heard. Workable plans are possible only after all points of view have been expressed and considered. Heterogeneity has the potential to enhance learning, given the enlarged pool of information, perspectives, and skills it makes available. This arrangement also provides connections among teachers who rarely see one another. Valuable associations can emerge, providing important insights for potentially improving student learning.

As much as possible, teachers should be involved in determining reflective group composition as well as setting the agenda. With self-direction there will be a greater motivation for learning, along with increased ownership and commitment. Mandated assignments and task determination not only strip groups of their enthusiasm, but also remind teachers of the hierarchical organization of the school and the power relationships that subvert personal goals and directions, depriving teachers of personal drive and initiative.

There are a number of roles that may be occupied by group members: facilitator, recorder, researcher, observer, and so on. These can be rotated as determined by the group. Some group members may be assigned particular tasks because of their expertise in an area. One person may be particularly adept at research or knowledgeable about some aspect of the topic being studied, while another individual may be an excellent facilitator. The facilitator must be able to focus the development of group skills and processes and thus promote task accomplishment. He or she must be able to help create and sustain an environment in which participants feel comfortable enough to participate extensively without fear. Effective facilitators must also be skilled at promoting thinking through the questions they help create and at guiding the groups through constructive dialogue, as they consider issues and events from different perspectives in implementing action plans and solving problems.

It cannot be assumed that individuals know how to interact effectively in groups (Will, 1997). Leadership is necessary to appropriately interpret contexts and expand the repertoire of skills and processes needed for success. Each group will require different approaches. Because group development is an interactive process, it cannot be specifically defined in advance. Well-managed group development is required. Personal considerations regarding group members must be attended to while focus is maintained on the essential task of improving student learning. Group meetings should begin with participants receiving an assurance of safety and respect along with an understanding of the importance of the meeting and the way in which time will be effectively used.

In the initial meeting, the group should help identify purposes and objectives. They should specifically define what members want to learn and be able to do as a result of the activity. Next, the needed resources should be selected. An agenda can then be prepared that fits the time available, formatted as follows: (1) Engage in an activity to activate thinking; (2) include brief input from various resources; (3) participate in interaction so all have an opportunity to reflect on the topic and respond to one another; and (4) summarize the activity and bring attention to important aspects of what was learned as well as personal commitments that have been made that require follow-up (Magestro & Stanford-Blair, 2000).

One way to establish an agenda for study is to have each member write a question on an index card that he or she feels requires the most attention regarding student learning. These cards can then be sorted and the agenda laid out in terms of which questions the whole group believes are most critical. A similar approach can be taken in summarizing the work of the group and making action plans. Members can again be asked to write on an index card what they believe is the best answer to the designated questions, along with actions they feel should be taken. These can then be sorted, and actions can be planned that reflect group consensus.

Six Hats is another reflective strategy used to assist groups in moving forward after interacting about various study questions (de Bono, 1970). The purpose of this approach is to help the group look at potential actions and interventions from six different perspectives:

1. A white hat refers to data input. This symbolizes a focus on what the research indicates about the topic being studied. How effective have various practices been? What are the problems of implementation? What is the cost?

2. A yellow hat shifts discussion to how the potential plan will benefit students and staff. Will staff morale be lifted? How will students benefit? How will problem-solving skills be increased?

3. A black hat indicates caution. What problems may be expected that may adversely affect staff or students? What are the budgetary constraints? How difficult will the changes be to implement? Who might oppose changes and why? Will there be an unusual investment in time and resources to implement what is proposed?

4. A red hat symbolizes emotion. Will some teachers panic? Will some individuals consider the proposed changes in a negative light? Will people feel more connected and committed to one another? Will there be excitement on the part of students for the proposed changes?

5. A green hat focuses attention on growth. Will a lot be learned by all? Will teachers become more skilled and satisfied? Will teachers find new, more meaningful ways to teach? Will there be an increase in the number and quality of instructional strategies?

6. A blue hat symbolizes process. What will have to be done to communicate information to all concerned parties about decisions and proposed changes? How can the process of change be organized and executed? Who will provide leadership to ensure the success of what is planned?

When participants engage in conversations from these different perspectives, needs and constraints can be anticipated and potential problems can be avoided. Reflection for action is just as important as deliberations for creating a plan for improvement. In this process, insight can be gained that not only helps improve implementation, but may also help to identify new and better perspectives on the original problems and questions.

 ## QUESTIONS FOR REFLECTION

1. What do you believe would be the most difficult problem found in a group trying to improve teaching and learning? What strategies would you propose to help eliminate the problem?

NATIONAL TEACHING STANDARDS

Teachers face choices that force them to sacrifice one goal for another. They have to make hard choices even in the face of criticism and alienation.

Reflection in Schoolwide Learning Communities

Schools should continuously reflect on purposes and practices involving everyone in the organization, including students, teachers, administrators, and the community outside the school (Costa & Kallick, 2000). The best hope for school improvement lies with the collective thinking, inquiry, understanding, and action of all members of the school community. This, of course, is a complex process that requires considerable leadership, as well as organizational and interpersonal skills by members of the learning community.

What would schoolwide reflective practice look like? How might it be organized? Who would occupy the various roles? For some problems and questions, the entire school staff may be involved with a common topic. There might also be interdisciplinary groups established to provide their expertise in solving problems that require broad-based input. For example, teachers from different subjects or grade levels might meet. Sometimes problems have administrative as well as instructional implications. Appropriate personnel need to be assigned to groups dealing with such problems so that all necessary perspectives are considered. It is not wise to have excessively large groups for problem solving, yet necessary sources of input should be included so that diverse members of the school community are represented. This provides a broader, more appropriate knowledge base, as well as giving greater credence to decisions made. It also helps in achieving support from all members of the school community.

Researchers have found that successful schools have an active professional learning community that focuses on learning and on continuous improvement of instructional practice (Newmann & Wehlage, 1995). The result is lower rates of student absenteeism, lower dropout rates, and less class cutting. There is also an increase in the quality of teaching and learning as indicated by student achievement. There are many identifiable improvements in various aspects of the instructional program (Hord, 1997). In addition, there is a substantial increase in teacher efficacy and empowerment, increased satisfaction in professional accomplishment, and increased assumption of collective responsibility for student learning. Five characteristics emerge in the presence of a school-based professional community: (1) shared norms and values, (2) reflective dialogue, (3) deprivation of practice (i.e., more sharing of teaching practices), (4) a focus on student learning, and (5) responsible collaboration (Kruse, Louis, & Bryk, 1995).

NATIONAL TEACHING STANDARDS

Teachers must employ their professional knowledge of what makes for sound practice, with the interest of their students being given paramount consideration.

In schoolwide decision making and change, individuals are first concerned about how change will personally affect them. Next comes concerns about managing the new tasks that must be accomplished. Finally, the concern shifts to the impact of change on school learning and subsequent improvement strategies (Horsley & Loucks-Horsley, 1998). This shift in concerns must be recognized and managed for effective change to occur.

Successful school improvement initiatives involve shared leadership (Bryk, Camburn, & Louis, 1999). Improvement will falter as long as it depends on a single person, a few people, or outside directions and forces (Lambert, 1998). It is especially helpful if teachers assume roles as leaders rather than always having that role fall to administrators. When teachers function as leaders, there is an increased likelihood that curriculum and teaching improvements will be integrated into the school and sustained (Feiler, Heritage, & Gallimore, 2000). Principals have a pivotal role in making sure that teachers occupy positions of leadership. Effective principals ensure teacher involvement and provide an atmosphere for innovation and risk-taking (Bryk et al., 1999). They foster among teachers both reflection and collegial interaction about teaching and learning (Blase & Blase, 1999). Successful strategies by principals to promote school improvement include inspiring a shared vision, creating a positive culture of high expectations for staff and students, challenging existing practices, and promoting relationships with and among staff members. They intentionally foster reflection and learning, with dialogue as the primary learning format. The most powerful influence school leaders can have on their colleagues is to model ongoing reflection and learning about their practice and about student learning (Schwahn & Spady, 1998).

To put schoolwide reflection into operation, the school might first ask all community members to engage in independent reflection regarding specified school practices. Individuals are asked to record their thoughts in their journals and participate in small dialogue groups. Next, group members are organized into educational planning groups that make sense of the information generated in the dialogue groups and then determine what the next steps should be. They then make recommendations for implementation in the areas of agreement, disagreement, and confusion. Finally, inquiry and advisory teams comprised of all interested staff members are created. Their task is to determine priorities and give clear directions for implementation (Kronberg & Lunders, 1997).

QUESTION FOR REFLECTION

1. What do you believe the role of students and the community should be in helping to improve teaching and learning?

CENTRAL IDEAS

1. Teachers make hundreds of decisions each day regarding teaching and learning: before, during, and after the teaching occurs.
2. The purpose of theory is threefold: description, explanation, and prediction.
3. Decision making by teachers involves the use of educational theory and experience, along with a personal philosophy of education.
4. Teachers make decisions from a constructivist perspective, which means that their decisions are based on what they find meaningful.
5. Teachers not only make attribution errors by interpreting students' actions in terms of their own attitudes, but they experience difficulty applying instructional theories and educational concepts, relying primarily on personal experiences in the schools to frame their teaching.
6. Because of their constructivist tendencies in thinking and decision making, teachers should be encouraged to avoid previously established, unexamined concepts and automatic patterns of thinking.
7. Teachers often fail to consider student needs, understand students' learning and thinking processes, or maintain good student-teacher relationships. This is because they may not examine, research, or reflect carefully on their practice.
8. The culture of the schools greatly influences teaching and learning. Teachers must examine the culture from a full perspective to include school purposes, student goals and aspirations, and the desires and hopes of parents and other members of the community at large.
9. Students find little meaning in traditional schools. They are more interested in one another and in the activity program than in learning what is provided in the school curriculum.
10. Excellent teaching is based on principles and purposes, not techniques and methods.
11. Teachers are more successful if they operate as theoreticians than as technicians in their teaching.
12. The purpose of a personal philosophy of education is to bring together all the various aspects of teaching and learning into a single set of consistent principles that can be explicitly articulated and applied in the classroom.
13. Examining assumptions is an essential aspect of educational decision making, which helps teachers avoid acting on false information in their teaching.
14. Reflective practice in teaching requires a trusting relationship with others, a desire to engage in dialogue with colleagues to improve practice, a willingness to view educational issues from alternative perspectives, and a commitment to implement school improvement.

15. Reflective teachers focus primarily on the means to improve student learning, and they conform their practice to satisfying all student needs.
16. Being an effective communicator in learning communities requires excellent listening skills. Most teachers will require training in listening to become sufficiently proficient.
17. Successful schools have active professional learning communities that focus on learning and on the continuous improvement of instructional practice. They are broad-based in membership and share leadership.

REFERENCES

Blase, J., & Blase, J. (1999). Principals' instructional leadership and teacher development: Teacher's perspectives. *Educational Administration Quarterly, 35*(3), 349–378.

Bright, B. (1996). Reflecting on "reflective practice." *Studies in the Education of Adults, 28* (2), 162–184.

Brookfield, S. (1992). Why can't I get this right? Myths and realities in facilitating adult learning. *Adult Learning, 3* (6), 12–15.

Bryk, A., Camburn, E., & Louis, K. S. (1999). Professional community in Chicago elementary schools: Facilitating factors and organizational consequences. *Educational Administration Quarterly, 35* (Suppl), 751–781.

Butler, J. (1996). Professional development: Practice as text, reflection as process, and self as locus. *Australian Journal of Education, 40,* 265–283.

Carlson, R., & Bailey, J. (1997). *Slowing down to the speed of life: How to create a more peaceful, simpler life from the inside out.* San Francisco: Harper Collins.

Chance, W. (1988). *The best of education.* Chicago: The John D. and Catherine T. MacArthur Foundation.

Clarke, A. (1995). Professional development in practicum settings: Reflective practice under scrutiny. *Teaching and Teacher Education, 11* (3), 243–261.

Clarke, C. M., & Peterson, P. L. (1986). Teacher's thought processes. In M. Wittrock (Ed.), *Third handbook of research on teaching* (pp. 255–296). New York: Macmillan.

Corno, L. (1981). Cognitive organizing in the classroom. *Curriculum Inquiry, 11,* 359–377.

Costa, A. L., & Kallick, B. (2000). *Activating and engaging habits of mind.* Alexandria, VA: Association for Supervision and Curriculum Development.

Danielson, C. (1996). *Enhancing professional practice: A framework for teaching.* Alexandria, VA: Association for Supervision and Curriculum Development.

Darling-Hammond, L., & Berry, B. (1988). *The evolution of teacher policy.* Santa Monica, CA: RAND Corporation.

de Bono, E. (1970). *Lateral thinking.* New York: Harper & Row.

Doyle, W. (1977). Learning in the classroom environment: Ecological analysis. *Journal of Teacher Education, 28,* 51–55.

Feiler, R., Heritage, M., & Gallimore, R. (2000). Teachers leading teachers. *Educational Leadership, 57* (8), 66–69.

Fiske, S. T., & Taylor, S. E. (1984). *Social cognition.* Reading, MA: Addison-Wesley.

Goodlad, J. I. (1984). *A place called school: Prospects for the future.* New York: McGraw-Hill.

Hatton, N., & Smith, D. (1995). Reflection in teacher education: Towards definition and implementation. *Teaching and Teacher Education, 11* (1), 33–49.

Head, J. O., & Sutton, C. R. (1985). Language, understanding, and commitment. In L. H. T. West & A. L. Pines (Eds.), *Cognitive structure and conceptual change* (pp. 91–100). Orlando, FL: Academic Press.

Holland, J. H., Holyoack, K. J., Nisbett, R. G., & Thagard, P. R. (1986). *Induction.* Cambridge, MA: MIT Press.

Hord, S. (1997). *Professional learning communities: Communities of continuous inquiry and improvement.* Austin, TX: Southwest Educational Development Laboratory.

Horsley, D. L., & Loucks-Horsley, S. (1998). CBAM brings order to the tornado of change. *Journal of Staff Development, 19* (4). 17–20.

Hunter, M. (1988). Response to Slavin: Improving teacher decisions. *Educational Leadership, 46* (2), 29.

Isaacs, W. (1999). *Dialogue and the art of thinking together.* New York: Currency.

Jackson, P. W. (1968). *Life in classrooms.* New York: Holt, Rinehart & Winston.

Johnson, D. W., & Johnson, R. T. (1999). *Learning together and alone: Cooperative, competitive, and individualistic learning* (5th ed.). Needham Heights, MA: Allyn & Bacon.

Johnson, E. C. (1998). The importance of theory. *Teacher Education Quarterly, 25* (4), 37–38.

Kagan, D. M. (1992). Implications of research on teacher belief. *Educational Psychologist, 27* (1), 65–90.

Kahn, W. A. (1992). To be fully there: Psychological presence at work. *Human Relations, 45* (4), 321–349.

Kronberg, R., & Lunders, C. (1997). A school-wide reflection and dialogue process at Mountain View School. In J. Montie, J. York-Barr, & R. Kronberg (Eds.), *Reflective practice: Creating capacities for school improvement* (pp. 27–45). Minneapolis, MN: University of Minnesota, Institute on Community Integration.

Kruse, S. D., Louis, K. S., & Bryk, A. (1995). An emerging framework for analyzing school-based professional community. In K. S. Louis & S. D. Kruse (Eds.), *Professionalism and community: Perspectives on reforming urban schools* (pp. 23–42). Thousand Oaks: Corwin.

Lambert, L. (1998). *Building leadership capacity in schools.* Alexandria, VA: Association for Supervision and Curriculum Development.

Lazarus, R. S., & Folkman, S. (1984). *Stress, appraisal, and coping.* New York: Springer.

Levin, B. B. (1995). Using the case method in teacher education: The role of discussion and experience in teachers' thinking about cases. *Teaching and Teacher Education, 11* (1), 63–79.

Lieberman, A., & Miller, L. (1984). *Teachers, their world and their work.* Alexandria, VA: Association for Supervision and Curriculum Development.

Magestro, P. V., & Stanford-Blair, N. (2000). A tool for meaningful staff development. *Educational Leadership, 57* (8), 34–35.

Nagel, N., & Driscoll, A. (1992). Dilemmas caused by discrepancies between what they learn and what they see: Thinking and decision-making of preservice teachers. Paper presented at the annual meeting of the American Educational Research Association, San Francisco.

National Research Council. (1996). *National science education standards.* Washington, DC.: National Academy Press.

Newmann, F., & Wehlage, G. (1995). *Successful school restructuring.* Madison: University of Wisconsin, Center on Organization and Restructuring of Schools.

Orlich, D. C., Harder, R. J., Callahan, R. C., Kauchak, D. P., Pendergrass, R. A., Keogh, A. J., & Gibson, H. (1990). *Teaching strategies: A guide to better instruction.* Lexington, MA: D. C. Heath and Company.

Osterman, K. F., & Kottkamp, R. B. (1993). *Reflective practice for educators: Improving schooling through professional development.* Newbury Park, CA: Corwin.

Pietig, J. (1998). How educational foundations can empower tomorrow's teachers: Dewey revisited. *Teacher Education Quarterly, 25* (4), 102–106.

Popham, W. J. (1999). Why standardized tests don't measure educational quality. *Educational Leadership, 56* (6), 8–15.

Richardson, J. (1997). Putting student learning first put these schools ahead. *Journal of Staff Development, 18* (2), 42–47.

Richardson, J. (1998). We're all here to learn. *Journal of Staff Development, 19* (4), 49–55.

Richardson, V. (1990). Significant and worthwhile change in teaching practice. *Educational Researcher, 19* (1), 10–18.

Ross, D. D. (1990). Programmatic structures for the preparation of reflective teachers. In R. T. Clift, W. R. Houston, & M. C. Pugach (Eds.), *Encouraging reflective practice in education: An analysis of issues and programs* (pp. 97–118). New York: Teachers College Press.

Schwahn, C. J., & Spady, W. G. (1998). *Total leaders.* Arlington, VA: American Association for School Administrators.

Shavelson, R. J. (1973). What is the basic teaching skill? *Journal of Teacher Education, 24,* 144–151.

Shepard, R. (1995). Teaching: Decision making, cognitive inference. *Education, 115* (4), 509–515.

Shulman, L. S. (1987). Knowledge and teaching: Foundations of reform. *Harvard Educational Review, 57* (1), 1–22.

Thousand, J. S., & Villa, R. (2000). Collaborative teams: Powerful tools for school restructuring. In R. Villa & J. S. Thousand (Eds.), *Restructuring for caring and effective education* (2nd ed., pp. 254–291). Baltimore: Paul H. Brookes.

Uleman, J. S. (1987). Consciousness and control: The case of spontaneous trail inferences. *Personality and Social Psychology Bulletin, 13,* 337–354.

Will, A. M. (1997, Winter). Group learning in workshops. *New Directions for Adult and Continuing Education, 76,* 33–40.

York-Barr, J., Sommers, W. A., Ghere, G. S., & Montie, J. (2001). *Reflective practice to improve schools: An action guide for educators.* Thousand Oaks, CA: Corwin Press.

Zeichner, K. M., & Liston, D. P. (1996). *Reflective teaching: An introduction.* Mahwah, NJ: Lawrence Erlbaum Associates.

CHAPTER 7

Instructional Planning in Learning Communities

CHAPTER OBJECTIVES

This chapter is designed to help you

1. Describe what constitutes a good classroom climate for learning.

2. Explain what the foundations of curriculum are and describe the roles these elements play in curriculum construction.

3. Formulate properly constructed instructional objectives for the various levels of the cognitive, affective, and psychomotor domains.

4. Determine conditions that call for measurable objectives and those that require the use of experiential objectives.

5. Write objectives that include appropriately constructed parameters and evaluative adjuncts.

In learning communities, students are involved in planning their own learning experiences.

6. Create strategies for instruction in diverse student populations that promote higher-level thinking as well as affective growth and development.

7. Formulate instructional strategies for structured and unstructured classroom situations including learning communities.

8. Create instructional plans for a course, for units, and for individual lessons.

INTRODUCTION

Some teachers claim that, for the sake of flexibility, it is unwise to create instructional plans. There is no doubt that teachers need to be flexible, as they cannot always anticipate what will take place in their classrooms from day to day. However, flexibility requires more preparation, not less. Well-prepared teachers can quickly implement plans that include various options as needs arise. This allows viable changes in plans that provide the back-up preparations needed to ensure effectiveness. A biology teacher, for example, without ready access to biological materials that can be quickly assembled and distributed as appropriate is not sufficiently prepared. Of course, teachers cannot plan for every contingency, but preparing for some possible, viable options aids in quality teaching. Without such a plan, teachers are not likely to make flexible changes that meet student needs and interests. Thus, teachers without instructional plans that include contingencies are really much less flexible than those who are so prepared. The lack of a plan does not provide greater flexibility; instead, it reduces that possibility.

Teachers also need to carefully think through their goals and objectives and make instructional plans that are defensible from multiple perspectives. State education departments and the school district curricular expectations must be considered along with the teacher's own training and experience. Various philosophical considerations must be included in any schooling decision, as well as the students' role in helping to plan their educational experiences. Instructional planning requires a careful consideration of many factors and a thoughtful construction of lessons that appropriately satisfy these various inputs.

Ms. Ramirez was planning for some time to employ a new teaching and learning format in her classroom. Through the years she felt that some of her students were uncooperative while others appeared to be bored and disinterested. Using the core curriculum provided by the state, she created a series of lessons that she believed represented the state expectations, as well as lessons that would help her students meet modern challenges. She knew a few of her students would attend college and wanted them to be well-prepared. She anticipated others would attend technical schools in the area, while some would likely fill jobs in construction, clerking, housekeeping, and the like. The challenge was to figure out how to accommodate such a diverse student population in her U.S. Government classes.

She finally concluded that the only reasonable solution was to stop assuming students were just information repositories. She also had to stop assuming her students would take an interest in learning information simply because it would be helpful later in life. She routinely explained to her students that U.S. Government would be helpful as they later married, had families, and became involved in their communities.

Recently, however, she realized that her students were preoccupied with pressing concerns. They had very little inclination to devote their time and energy to something that would only be useful some time in the future. She also concluded that, although she wanted to prepare all students for the future, she really only provided experiences geared toward the college bound students. The state core curriculum, as well as her own experiences and inclinations, were focused toward scoring well on the year-end achievement test. She always considered knowledge about the Constitution and its amendments, along with a background in government operations, would be essential for effective living, and it was her sacred responsibility to help students see this as she did. During a conversation with one of her students, Raul Martinez, she finally concluded she was mistaken. Raul came in after school to get help with some missed assignments, and confronted Ms. Ramirez with a commonly asked question, "Why do we have to know this stuff, Ms. Ramirez? Where will I ever use it?"

Ms. Ramirez thought long and hard, even seeking help from other faculty members, and decided her reasons to justify the students' education could not be defended. She was especially uneasy about stating they would need the content of her course in college; she'd felt for a long time that this justification was pithy. Although she sincerely believed that studying U.S. Government was essential, it was easy to see that her expectations would not prepare students for responsible citizenship. She had to determine what students actually needed to learn, and felt they needed to be involved in the process. Raul's implied accusation indicated that much. Students might be naive, but their involvement was imperative. Maybe that was sufficient to start the process without predetermined goals and expectations, aside from those dictated in the state core. After examining the state core, she found it less prescriptive than she had assumed. There was room to accommodate a number of alternative approaches; the one she decided on was to organize a learning community in her classroom.

Decision Points

1. Make an analysis of Ms. Ramirez's reasons for organizing a learning community in her classroom. Decide whether or not you believe this decision was a good one and explain why.
2. If you have access to the state core in your state for the subject you teach, decide what components of it would allow for a learning community approach and which would not.

Traditional Curriculum Development

Ms. Ramirez faced a difficult task: Deciding what the curriculum should be, given the various needs and interests of her students. She needed to take into account multicultural concerns, learning theory, and the expectations of society, and organize a plan for instruction combining all these elements. She also needed to organize instruction based on a defensible curriculum plan and implement it in a classroom atmosphere allowing each student to develop intellectually and emotionally to the greatest extent possible.

The curriculum depends more on values and philosophy than empirical research. Different educational philosophies dictate different learning outcomes as well as educational procedures, and thus conceptualize the learning process. The role of empirical research is to ascertain whether the intended outcomes have been achieved, not to decide the value of what is intended. It is, therefore, critical to first determine from a philosophical point of view what kind of outcomes are preferred, and to seek the most useful procedures for achieving them. Even the assessment procedures must be philosophically determined. To be valid, student achievement assessment must accurately ascertain intended outcomes rather than measure information retrieval, as often happens in testing. When the curriculum and instructional program are evaluated, the chief concern is whether or not the intentions dictated by the philosophy have been properly met. Assessment considerations will be addressed in Chapter 11.

The Foundations of Curriculum—A Model

Traditional curriculum development is a complex, comprehensive process of examining various contributing areas of knowledge and formulating instructional plans that are consistent with these interrelated, foundational components. These components usually consist of various psychological, social, and educational theories. Theoretical knowledge provides information about the educational process from different carefully researched perspectives. Much of the research is limited, as it is based on a set of inconclusive assumptions. In fact, most assumptions about education are inconclusive. Consequently, assumptions are identified as such to differentiate them from truth. This distinction is helpful so that teachers will not erroneously conclude that their practices are based on true principles. In the social realm, very little absolute truth is available, and even if there were true principles available, differences of opinion would still exist. It is better to say a principle is consistent with a particular philosophical perspective rather than rank it as absolutely "true" or "untrue." A teacher usually accepts a particular philosophical position on faith or because it embodies personally meaningful and acceptable values.

Curriculum development involves the systematic examination of basic foundation areas of knowledge related to teaching and learning. These foundation areas include, (1) educational philosophy, (2) social and cultural implications, (3) learning and development, (4) values and value analysis, (5) interpersonal interaction and influence, and (6) the nature and structure of knowledge and meaning (see Figure 7.1). Each of these areas of knowledge should be consulted and their potential inputs considered during the curriculum construction process. These instructional objectives and the learning activities designed to accomplish them can be more rationally formulated when these foundation areas of knowledge are systematically taken into account during curriculum construction.

Educational Philosophy

Educational philosophies are systems of thought organized around a set of consistent principles. They ordinarily carry a particular orientation and development plan toward the kind of person schools should produce. They embody particular theories of human nature, development, and learning, and they serve the purpose of conceptualizing, explaining, and

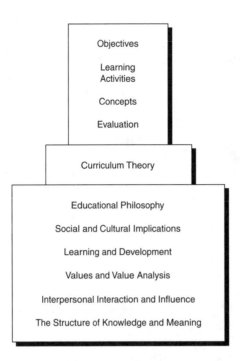

Figure 7.1   Curriculum Theory

predicting the behavioral consequences of activities and student and teacher interactions. They provide the benefit of consistency in the educational enterprise, forming a framework for discourse about teaching applications. Essentially, an educational philosophy describes the nature of educational experiences and the purposes toward which they are directed, providing clarity and vivid descriptions about curriculum and instruction.

Philosophy provides the central focus around which the other foundation areas articulate as they are applied to curriculum construction. It is a guide or filter through which theoretical knowledge can be assessed for consistency with the basic curriculum and instruction principles.

NATIONAL TEACHING STANDARDS

Teachers are dedicated to exposing students to the social, cultural, ethical, and physical worlds in which they live and use the subjects they teach as entries into those worlds.

Social and Cultural Implications

The curriculum must reflect social and cultural expectations. Particularly in a diverse society, cultural differences must be considered so that no student feels alienated by what happens in school. Culture provides the basis for social discourse and interaction and the framework for interpersonal actions and influence. Culture thus gives meaning to personal and social activities and provides a way to interpret human behavior. In other words, behavior makes sense within a social and cultural context. Without a knowledge of culture, human activities do not make sense. Herein lies the difficulty of appropriate understanding between cultures. Without an understanding of various cultures, there is less acceptance since various culturally-based behaviors may appear odd or inappropriate when examined with limited cultural perspectives.

Because life is lived within culture, cultural considerations cannot be removed from school life and expectations, nor can the dominant culture be the only acceptable view of social behavior and interactions. Various cultures need to be celebrated in the school to help children understand and value them. Diversity should be accepted as a strengthening factor in society, not as a denigrating one. Of course, common elements must be established in the school community. Otherwise, successful interactions will be difficult, if not impossible. However, while there must be some common expectations within a community, diversity provides a variety of perspectives and helps students learn how to live successfully within a world community full of contrasts. Diversity also provides alternative views of situations in which students may find themselves, as well as insights regarding problem solving that they might not otherwise have considered. Thus, diversity in the schools provides a more authentic representation of social life along with valuable perspectives for excellence in problem solving.

Learning and Development

Although learning is the purpose of schooling, curriculums may ignore that aspect when children are expected to acquire a huge quantity of information. Education is sometimes defined as a process of storing information for later retrieval. The quality of education may be seen as a reflection of how much information is recalled. Schooling is commonly criticized when students seem unable to remember the names of state capitals or the major exports of South American countries. An educated person should supposedly know these things, when in fact this information is likely to fade from memory only two months after a student supposedly learned it. The tendency to quickly forget much of what is learned in school has been known for a good long time (Cronbach, 1954). In addition, information recall is a function of personal values and utility. Few children consider state capitals and the like to be important enough to remember after being tested on them. They fail to remember, in part, because they see no valid reason for doing so.

Learning and development must be properly conceptualized and consistently integrated within the curriculum. The school curriculum should be an accurate reflection of how children actually learn and grow. Educators generally accept that children learn constructively. They personally construct meaning and are reluctant to forfeit world views they already hold. Intellectual development appears to depend not only on natural physiological growth, but also on problem-solving activities. Intellectual development depends on the development of learning capacities enhanced by problem solving that may exceed the student's ability. Intellectual growth depends on efforts to work beyond current capacities, not on teachers providing the appropriate levels of learning activities. This involves risk-taking by students as well as considerable teacher support (Piaget, 1952).

Values and Value Analysis

Learning depends substantially on the perceived value of what is learned. Some content is not valued except as a means for achieving something else: college entrance, for example. In addition, potential learning opportunities might be valued by students if they realized their worth, but they don't always have the background knowledge to determine that. Unfortunately, students are unlikely to value learning opportunities just because the teacher says they should. Students need to value what they learn from their own investigations, and draw conclusions from their own searching and contemplation. This occurs most often when students can pursue personally meaningful learning and when their teachers, at strategic times, encourage them to expand or refocus their efforts, or perhaps provide a new complimentary resource. In such cases, the teacher acts as a resource for enhancing personally significant learning, rather than directing learning and robbing students of the empowerment inherent in directing their own affairs.

Values may also be studied for their social importance, as they define them as individuals and as members of larger communities. Values provide a basis for understanding others and sharing common expectations; without these expectations, social interactions deteriorate and conflict erupts. Students need to believe in the importance of values and develop a personal value system. Value considerations are a strategic backdrop for curriculum development. All curriculum development efforts should consider values and input them as appropriate. Values of all interested parties should be considered, especially those of students.

Interpersonal Interaction and Influence

When possible, curriculum developers should consider the implications of interpersonal interaction and influence. When students are engaged in learning, they are not only influenced by input from their teachers and peers, but also by their own understandings, experiences, attitudes, and values. All of these elements are difficult to anticipate, but as far as possible teachers need to predict what will happen in the dynamics of classroom operations. For example, a teacher might believe that important events in the school, community, or world at large may occasionally intrude on lesson plans. Experienced teachers may anticipate some of these because of similar happenings in the past. Teachers also need to take note of changes in student behavior. Events like the onset of war, natural disasters, or the devastating death of a classmate can also profoundly affect students. In addition, interesting events like cloning, terrorism, or school violence could lead to interesting learning opportunities.

Astute teachers capitalize on world events and students' lives to give the curriculum greater substance and provide a reason for redirection during study, thereby promoting greater immediacy and consequent enthusiasm for the study topics. Allowing important real-life events to influence the course of study provides greater meaning and usefulness for what is learned and also increases positive teacher-student relationships. Students appreciate teachers who are flexible in responsible ways and do not cling to the curriculum as sacred and immutable.

Sometimes students deliberately disrupt instruction by bringing up irrelevant issues or by being rude. These distractions require skilled intervention to maintain classroom discipline and unimpede the flow of instruction. Wise teachers anticipate these happenings and arrange classroom conditions to prevent them where possible. A teacher may, for example, have a discussion about rules and the consequences for breaking them with the class. Most discipline problems can be prevented if the class helps determine rules and consequences.

Excellent teachers also have the resources and inclination to alter a lesson course when useful. All possible valuable teaching strategies cannot be planned in advance, but some planned flexibility is useful. Having two or more easily implementable plans and being open to change can greatly enhance teaching and learning.

The Nature and Structure of Knowledge and Meaning

Every discipline is composed of numerous concepts and principles. Properly organizing and sequencing these knowledge components for understandability and accessibility is one of the major tasks of teachers. Teachers must understand the basic conceptual structure of a discipline and organize it in a way that helps students understand and remember the information better. The knowledge structure created must be organized conceptually in order to increase its utility and meaning for students. This skill depends on the teacher's ability to examine the subject matter taken from a body of knowledge and identify its most basic ideas along with related subordinate component ideas. Unfortunately, much subject matter, as it appears in textbooks, is topically organized, with little or no indication as to how the various fundamental ideas in each topic are related, nor are there directions available regarding how to best conceptually organize a specific subject. Perhaps the most helpful way for teachers to conceptually organize their subject is to create concept maps, a topic discussed later in this chapter, which provide teachers with a systematic way to organize knowledge and sequence instruction to enhance student learning and understanding. Teachers can also teach their students to create their own concept maps. This is a particularly useful when preparing students for learning community experiences.

 ## *Decision Points*

Write the basic components of your educational philosophy and include a statement about each of the foundation areas, detailing how you anticipate using this information to formulate curricula.

Constructing Objectives

Educational goals should reflect educational philosophy as well as the other curriculum foundations. Philosophy provides a template for instruction both in terms of desired outcomes and in the means for achieving them. It also encourages consistency. Formulating curriculum requires creating general goals that set the tone for the total school program. For example, one school objective might be for students to be good citizens. From these general goals, educators write more specific secondary goals, such as getting students acquainted with the court system, since all good citizens should be well-acquainted with how the courts operate. Finally, they generate specific instructional objectives that guide the learning process. These objectives provide specific instruction and lead to achieving the more general goals. For instance, students might be expected to explain differences in the roles of courts of original jurisdiction, appeals courts, and supreme courts.

Specific Instructional Objectives

Specific instructional objectives, or performance objectives, are usually written in a behavioral objective format and contain three specific components: a clearly stated behavior, conditions, and a measurable standard (Mager, 1962; Popham & Baker, 1970). The **statement of behavior** ordinarily indicates what a learner should be able to do after instruction. The key element is a word, ordinarily a verb, that clearly communicates a specific behavior. For instance, if students are to "know" the first 10 amendments to the U.S. Constitution in order to more completely understand the court system and thereby become better citizens, they might be asked to write the first 10 amendments and explain their meaning, along with an example and explanation of how each protects individuals' rights. Notice that students are asked to give written examples, make written descriptions, and provide written explanations. Table 7.1 contains a list of helpful behavioral terms to use in constructing performance objectives.

The second element in a performance objective is the **statement of the conditions** under which learners are to perform the specified behavior. Conditions refer to such circumstances as, "with the aid of the periodic table." This informs the student that, during the specific task, he or she will be able to use the periodic table. A teacher might, for example, want students to determine the relative number of atoms in various molecules. The objective would read as follows: "With the aid of the periodic table, students will be able to determine the relative number of atoms in a list of molecules provided to them."

The following is a list of sample conditional statements for various objectives:

1. Without use of aids . . . "
2. Given a political statement . . . "
3. With the textbook and notes . . . "
4. With a tailwind of no more than 15 miles per hour . . . "
5. Given a skeletal diagram of the bones in the body . . . "
6. Given definitions of the parts of speech . . . "
7. Given a copy of the Declaration of Independence . . . "

Conditions provide learners with an understanding of what reference materials to use as they demonstrate their proficiency. Obviously the conditions must be clearly stated and realistic, since they along with any applicable aids or constraints, help learners more clearly visualize the circumstances needed to demonstrate proficiency. Formulating conditions helps the teacher properly consider what is reasonable and appropriate for students to use

TABLE 7.1   *Behavioral Terms.*

Write	Explain	List	Discuss	Recite
Identify	Differentiate	Solve	Construct	Compare
Contrast	Define	Derive	Repair	Formulate
Sing	Dance	Measure	Create	Select
Paint	Subtract	Add	Multiply	Divide
Name	Run	Swim	Adjust	Diagram
Spell	Compose	Calculate	Separate	Draw

while showing what they have learned. For example, using a periodic table to solve chemistry problems is reasonable because memorizing all the atomic weights and numbers from the periodic table generally serves no useful purpose.

The third element of a properly constructed instructional objective is a **performance standard,** a level of acceptable performance expected of all students. Students should continue working until they can achieve the specified minimum level, thereby providing students a clear view of teacher expectations. The standard ordinarily consists of a quantifiable performance: for example, students may be expected to name 80 percent of the bones depicted on a human skeleton diagram. Performance objectives are sometimes called *measurable behavioral objectives,* denoting the necessity of quantifying the performance standard. The criterion measures may be given in the following different forms:

1. Without aids, students will be able to correctly factor **80 percent of the problem set.**
2. With the use of a lathe, students will be able to turn a piece of wood **within a 1 mm tolerance.**
3. Without reference to the periodic table, from a list of element symbols, students will be able to name **at least nine out of ten elements.**
4. Given a series of 15 ground balls hit within the fielding area, students will be able to field **at least 10 balls without any errors.**

Sometimes teachers will want to establish class minimum levels. Instead of expecting all students in a class to achieve a particular minimum level, the teacher may want to raise the standard for a certain percentage of students and allow the remainder of the class to perform at a lower level. A teacher might, for example, expect 80 percent of the class to be 90 percent proficient at inserting commas in a text, while the rest of the students can be 75 percent proficient. Teachers might also specify that a particular student or group of students should achieve a specific objective or level of performance; thereby recognizing differences between students, as well as maintaining a reasonable achievement level for all class members. When minimum achievement standards are provided, some students may perform at a level far below that of which they are capable. Establishing different minimum levels for class subgroups helps avoid this problem.

Experiential Objectives

There are at least two reasons some educators are critical of behavioral objectives. First, in expressing expectations in behavioral terms, important educational outcomes may be traded for less useful ones. For example, a teacher may prefer that students be able to formulate a well-controlled experiment, but because it is hard to specify exactly what this means in behavioral terms, he or she may just have students name the steps in the scientific method. Second, insisting that performance standards be quantitatively measurable may eliminate valuable things from the curriculum in favor of measurable ones. For example, the quality of a piece of visual art must be subjectively assessed. A subjective evaluation of aesthetic quality shouldn't be replaced by a measurement like "students use nine out of the ten colors provided by the teacher."

Sometimes the only legitimate instruction is assumed to be framed from measurable behavioral objectives. The rationale is, "If you can't measure it, you can't tell if it has been achieved." However, subjective teacher assessments are appropriate, particularly if deferring to quantitative measures inappropriately modifies what ought to be expected. Restricting instruction to only those behaviors having quantitatively measurable outcomes can undermine the quality of education; thus, the scope of acceptable objectives has been enlarged to include not only objectives containing subjectively measurable standards, but also experiential objectives. *Experiential objectives* not only lack performance standards, but they do not carefully specify expected behaviors. They denote worthwhile educational experiences that have neither common behavioral expectations nor simple quantitative measures. A group of students may perform a research project where different students have different roles to perform, with no way of specifying the exact performance of any particular student. Nonetheless, this kind of activity is indisputably worthwhile, as is a field trip or an unstructured class discussion. The following are criteria which can be used to determine the value of experiential goals (Raths, 1971):

1. Does the activity engage students in higher intellectual processes?
2. Does the activity cause the student to reflect seriously on his or her values and to rationally organize that value system?
3. Does the activity require the student to make reasoned choices and accept the consequences for these choices?
4. Does the activity require the student to engage in purposeful interaction with peers and to support and defend ideas in an active interchange?
5. Does the activity encourage the student to experiment with and test personally relevant problems?

Parameters and Evaluative Adjuncts

Often, even though objectives may clearly state a behavior, the teacher's total expectation may not be clear. This is particularly true of objectives requiring complex student responses. For example, a teacher might want students to explain what a food web is in a biological community. The word *explain* is a behavioral term, but explaining a food web contains a sufficient number of complex ideas that the teacher must specify what he or she means beyond what the word *explain* communicates (Smith, 1972). Thus, a teacher might want students to show the relationships between food webs and food chains, or indicate the energy transfer in food webs and chains, along with such concepts as the law of the minimum, the law of tolerance, limiting factors, population oscillations, trophic levels, life cycles, and other related concepts and ideas. To sufficiently describe what is expected, an objective **parameter** needs to be included. The parameter specifies all of the components required to fulfill what the teacher expects. The following is an example of an objective with its parameter:

Objective:

Students will be able to create an original oil painting.

Parameter:

The painting must make appropriate use of the concepts of perspective, light, color, texture, drawing, and balance and must portray a new and interesting view of contemporary society.

Students often have only a vague idea of how their classroom performance will be evaluated. Teachers may have various biases and preferences not specified in the objective that are applied while evaluating student work. In these cases, an **evaluative adjunct** can be added to the objective to help clarify how the teacher will evaluate. An art teacher might, for instance, believe that an oil painting should first and foremost show creative elements, while less attention may be paid to the more technical aspects. In addition, perspective may be considered more important than appropriately using light, and indicating the direction and intensity of light may be more important than texture. Students should be informed of the judgment criteria weighting before beginning their paintings, not after. The following is an evaluative adjunct for the oil painting example:

1. The most important aspect of the painting is the student's ability to create an original view of contemporary society.
2. A judgment will be made in terms of how well the factors of perspective, light, color, texture, drawing, and balance contribute to the display of the theme. None of these factors, by itself, will be considered more important than any other.

Students' Role in Determining Objectives

State departments of education ordinarily create educational objectives in designing the state core curriculum in order to ensure that state school instruction meets expectations and standards. The instructional goals usually reflect national standards and articulate goals established by various professional associations and accrediting bodies. Teachers take these goals and use them to create specific classroom objectives. To ensure that the state objectives are achieved, most states administer either state competency tests or one of the available standardized tests. Considerable pressure is thus exercised to ensure that teachers teach the prescribed curriculum. The tests provide the evidence.

Many purposes exist for state core curricula, and considerable energy is expended to create them. Ordinarily, the goals are for greater commonality of educational experiences all over the state, for achievement of specified levels of accomplishment by students, for proper sequencing of various educational experiences, and for articulation of the content presented from one grade level to the next. These are valuable and justifiable reasons for establishing a common curriculum. However, other considerations, such as the role of students in the process, may be ignored under these conditions. Students ordinarily give little to no input during curriculum development, but this is a costly mistake since a lack of involvement produces a lack of interest and negligible commitment. The true value of the prescribed curriculum can be forfeited when students reject it as irrelevant.

Many students have little interest in the academic part of their schooling, and may be much more interested in the extracurricular program. This is not because the curriculum is inherently distasteful to students; rather, they would be more amenable to it if they were given an opportunity to provide input so they could feel a part of the decision-making process, thereby achieving a greater sense of self-determination. Student needs for significant involvement in their academic program, even when they do not know how to proceed, must be applied in determining educational goals. A number of things can be done to accomplish this. First, students can have an opportunity to discuss their various options. In a core curriculum often only 50 to 60 percent of the curriculum is specified. Curriculum developers recognize that teachers need to create unique experiences for a particular student population. Students should be made aware that a common curriculum core is meant to ensure that certain basic requirements are met, and these requirements constitute legitimate components of a study in the subject. However, a variety of approaches may be taken to achieve these goals, and students should have a significant voice in this determination. The remaining 40 to 50 percent of the curriculum is open to classroom deliberation and determination. State competency tests, however, may encourage teachers to devote all the class time to achieving state-determined objectives and ignore opportunities to individualizing the curriculum to meet the needs of the community or a specific group of students.

Second, students should understand that their involvement in decision making about the curriculum is only possible so far as they can make valid judgments about potential classroom learning activities. Teachers must train students in decision making so they can help assess the relative value of various possible curriculum components. Of course, any specific topic may be of greater importance to one student than to another because of how it will be put to use. A student who intends to attend college, for example, may be better served with school experiences focused on college prerequisites, while a student who plans to run the family farm or work in a local factory will have a different set of priorities. There are also some common experiences of value. Thus, students must recognize the implications of their choices on themselves and their classmates, and they should help make appropriate decisions. Some students may not have decided to attend college or know the occupation for which they wish to prepare. In these cases, students' interests should be evaluated through various career choices to determine the educational needs of each. As far as possible, students need to see that what they do in school is meaningful in achieving their educational goals and that choices made have the benefit of thoughtful decision making.

In decision making, students must be able to recognize the assumptions associated with various options, since ignoring inherent assumptions and failing to check their validity can lead to poor decisions. Students must also learn to apply properly prioritized criteria in decision making. Criteria comprise the standards for judgment and must be consistently used in decision making. Youth commonly fail to use these skills in decision making and, therefore, must be thoroughly taught before thoughtful decision making can be anticipated from them.

Decision Points

Take and defend a position on the use of behavioral objectives in teaching.

QUESTION FOR REFLECTION

1. To what degree should students be involved in decisions about curricula?

The Taxonomy of Educational Objectives

Deficiencies in educational objectives have been pointed out over the years. Historically, the first concern was that objectives were too obscure or nonexistent. Second, many educators felt that even though objectives were present, they were given in terms that did not denote particular behaviors and standards, resulting in a movement to legitimize the exclusive use of measurable behavioral objectives. Third, educators realized that even though objectives might be stated in the form of specific behaviors, they might not be justified if they contained only superficial expectations. These objectives were judged to lack substance and worth. As a consequence of this last concern, taxonomies of educational objectives were created: one for the cognitive domain (Bloom, 1956), one for the affective domain (Krathwohl, Bloom, & Masia 1964), and one for the psychomotor domain (Harrow, 1972). These taxonomies specified various levels or categories of objectives with the purpose of ensuring the development of all intellectual, affective, and psychomotor skills.

NATIONAL TEACHING STANDARDS

Knowledge of subject matter is not synonymous with knowledge of how to reveal content to students so they build their own systems of thinking. Teachers must possess what is called "pedagogical content knowledge." This involves an understanding of the most common misconceptions held by students; aspects that they will find most difficult; and the kinds of prior knowledge, experiences, and skills that students of different ages typically bring to the learning of a particular topic. This knowledge is used to structure further instruction to facilitate further learning.

Cognitive Domain

In developing the cognitive domain, educators rejected the common school practice of almost exclusively depending on memorization, thereby neglecting experiences that promoted other kinds of thinking, particularly higher-level thinking. Lower-level thinking was probably focused on due to a desire to maintain the status quo in education, but was possibly also a result of test-driven curricula. It is much easier to assess memorized information than analytical expertise, for instance. The cognitive domain, as suggested by Bloom, could be represented with a hierarchical arrangement of six general levels of thinking, with each thinking skill being a subcomponent of all goals at a higher level in the hierarchy.

Knowledge

Knowledge, the first level in the taxonomy, is characterized by the recall of specifics, universals, methods, processes, patterns, structures, and settings. At this level, the only skill required is the ability to bring appropriate information to mind. No understanding of, or ability to manipulate, the information is expected.

The following are examples of knowledge level objectives:

1. Without the use of aids, students will correctly define at least 80 percent of the words on the weekly vocabulary list.
2. Without the use of notes, students will be able to correctly quote any five of the amendments contained in the Bill of Rights.
3. Given a model of the human skeletal system, students will be able to name the bones of the body with 90 percent accuracy.

Comprehension

Comprehension refers to understanding the meaning of information. The student ordinarily demonstrates an understanding by using information in a limited way or by explaining a concept or idea. The student does this without being able to relate one component of the information to another or visualizing the implication of the information. The comprehension is composed of three subcomponents: interpretation, translation, and extrapolation. Interpretation involves sufficient understanding of a piece of information that the student can explain or summarize. The ability to make an explanation in his or her own words is evidence that a student comprehends.

Translation is a skill of accurately rendering a communication into a different form. Translating from one language to another or from a social or political event into a political cartoon would be examples of this skill. Translation has been properly performed when the result preserves the intent of the original communication.

A student extrapolates by extending trends or tendencies beyond the data given and determining the implications, consequences, and effects that are consistent with the original communication conditions. Extrapolation occurs when an individual is able to take a set of research data collected from a sample population and describe how it fits a general population.

The following are examples of comprehension objectives:

1. Without the aid of a dictionary, students will be able to translate nine out of ten paragraphs from Spanish to English without altering the intent of the paragraphs (*translation*).
2. Based upon data collected regarding economic cycles for the past 25 years, students will be able to make a written prediction of economic trends for the next 10 years, which properly reflects previous trends (*extrapolation*).
3. Without reference to the textbook or notes, students will be able to explain the Krebs cycle without errors (*interpretation*).

Application

Application requires students to make use of abstract information in particular unfamiliar situations: to use rules, methods, concepts, principles, laws, and theories under conditions unfamiliar to them. Application provides a way to make information learned in school useful. It helps not only to bridge the gap between theory and practice, but also helps students use what they have learned in a variety of settings. Students often learn information in one context and are unable to see how it applies to various other situations. Information that cannot be applied to a variety of real-life situations is of little practical use to students. In school, what is learned is commonly useful only for test purposes. Students may not see its broader applications and, therefore, fail to use what they have learned to solve everyday problems.

The following are examples of application objectives:

1. Given an experience of creating plots and gathering data to study ecological relationships in a quaking aspen forest, students will be able to use the same methods to gather valid data from other biological communities.

2. Given the principles of how to render a zone defense impotent, the basketball players will be able to show their application by consistently scoring against any zone defense employed against them.

3. After having an experience of applying the supply and demand principle to the development and sale of a particular line of products, students will be able to create a similar plan with a whole new product line that will achieve a profit of at least 20 percent. Students must defend their plan.

Analysis

Analytical skills are used to break communications down into their subcomponent parts so that the organizational structures can be understood and various related tasks undertaken. Analysis can be used for the following purposes:

1. to ascertain the nature of communications so that the intended meaning can be made clear
2. to determine the way in which a communication is organized so that the relationships of the subcomponent parts can be compared
3. to visualize how the parts of a communication are related and convey their effects and impressions

Analyzing involves separating the important from the unimportant, fact from fiction, logical from illogical, and relevant from irrelevant. Analyses can be made not only of communicated material, but also of such information as complex psychomotor movements, paintings, or the scene of an accident. Teachers should not limit analysis opportunities to a formal-logical assessment of written statements. The skill should be broadly applied so students are allowed to comprehensively develop their skills.

The following are examples of analysis objectives:

1. Given a list of 10 political statements made by individuals seeking public office, students will be able to identify at least one inconsistency in each statement.
2. Given an unfamiliar 16-line poem, students will be able to identify those similes and metaphors which adequately promote the general theme of the poem.
3. From a film clip depicting the swing of a golf club, students will be able to identify what aspect of the swing led to the individual "slicing the ball."

Synthesis

Synthesis consists of the ability to create a unique product by putting together various parts to form a new whole. The student needs to combine various elements into a pattern that was not initially evident. Synthesis involves creative effort while at the same time formulating something that can be judged to be useful or worthwhile, not just the product of undisciplined expression. Synthesis occurs when the individual carefully formulates something by fitting together disparate pieces into a coherent whole that works to accomplish something useful or that is judged to have explicit esthetic qualities.

The following are examples of synthesis skill:

1. Students will be able to formulate a research design for a physics project that is properly controlled for possible confounding variables and that properly addresses the research problem and applicable hypotheses.
2. Students will be able to design a functional municipal building to house all departments of city government for the next 30 years for a cost of less than $20 million.
3. Students will be able to compose an original poem in a style of their choosing that uses at least five metaphors to formulate a well-integrated sequence of ideas.

Evaluation

Evaluation is accomplished when students successfully judge the quality of something, such as statements, paintings, novels, project designs, essays, poems, or musical renditions. In the process of judging, criteria are used as standards. Students should not only be able to justify the evaluation standards, but also provide coherent explanations of how they made their assessment and why they reached the conclusions they did. Evaluation is not merely an intellectual process requiring good cognitive ability, but it also involves affective components. Thus, evaluation includes values, liking, and enjoying along with cognitive assessment and judgment. Evaluation requires the evaluator to carefully examine the subcomponent parts of a product to determine internal consistency while also judging the quality of construction. Two kinds of judgments can be made: The individual can either determine which is best among a number of different products or options, or a number of items can be assessed to determine which of them adequately satisfies a set of criteria.

The following are examples of evaluation objectives:

1. Given 10 pieces of pottery, the student will be able to determine which is best and provide an explanation of how criteria were used to reach this conclusion.
2. Given reports of a set of five research projects, the student will be able to determine which satisfy a given set of criteria and explain why.
3. Given 10 paintings, students will be able to arrange them from best to worst. They must be able to justify the criteria they used and explain how they used these criteria to make their assessment.

Affective Domain

In schools, affective goals tend to get ignored, as cognitive objectives receive much more attention, even though those who have a major stewardship over schools, such as state legislators, tend to emphasize affective achievements. Many affective objectives are so important that their inclusion in the school curriculum is dictated by the school code. Affective objectives receive limited treatment by teachers for various reasons. Teachers may see themselves as transmitters of information, or find difficulty defining accepted affective goals because of value differences in the communities they serve and the potential for controversial confrontations. Values often have different shades of meaning and importance, thereby posing a greater possibility of disagreement. It is much easier to confine school instruction to safe cognitive topics and much more difficult to create affective experiences that can be validly assessed. For example, if the goal of instruction is to help students achieve a greater degree of patriotism, a teacher may deliver instruction designed to make students more sensitive to national symbols, such as showing respect to the flag. Evidence of respect may include observing students as they participate in a flag raising ceremony and seeing which students show the proper respect by taking off their hats and placing their hand over their heart during the playing of the national anthem. If the teacher is present and students know they are being observed, they may show the outward signs of respect even if they do not have any respectful feelings for the flag in their hearts and minds.

Finally, teachers may fail to pursue affective instruction because they are unaware of how to effectively go about providing it. Teachers often engage in the ineffective practice of "preaching," although this rarely achieves the desired ends since students tend to reject this kind of instruction. One of taxonomy's purposes is to provide an instructional format that can more effectively engage students and achieve results.

The affective domain is arranged in a hierarchy from initial to more advanced forms of value development, ranging from the point of receiving value-based information to making particular values an integral part of one's life. Say, for example, the teacher wanted to help students acquire a viable value system including a properly organized conception of the relationship between honesty and courtesy and have this relationship become a part of the students' lifestyle. Instruction might start by helping students more completely understand both of these values. Students could be placed in instructional setting circumstances where both values could be extensively explored so that the ramifications of each, along with appropriate behaviors, would be addressed. Students would ideally achieve a level of truly appreciating both values and periodically demonstrating commitment for these values in various contrived classroom situations. Students might arrange a debate or present their views to various groups in the school or community.

In the final stages of instruction, students are confronted with situations where potential conflicts between these two values are presented. The teacher could, for example, make the following presentation to students:

TEACHER: Class, I want you to consider the following situation. I notice that Amy is wearing a blue and red checkered blouse today. What if Amy came up to you and asked whether or not you thought she looked good in the blouse, and you thought she looked horrid, but you wanted to be courteous to her and felt some reluctance telling her what you actually thought. How would you respond to her?

STUDENT 1:   I'd tell her that it looked interesting.

STUDENT 2:   But she'd know immediately that you didn't like it.

STUDENT 3:   You could tell her that it looked OK, but she should not wear it on a date with a boy she wanted to impress.

TEACHER: Would it matter whether Amy wanted to find out how the blouse might or might not impress her date, or if she was just seeking approval?

STUDENT 4:   I think it would. For a date she wants your honesty. She doesn't want to screw up the situation. But if she is seeking approval we might have to avoid being as brutal.

TEACHER: What would you say to her in this case, so that there was honesty as well as courtesy?

STUDENT 5:   I'd ask her if she wanted me to be completely honest. I don't think we should worry about protecting a person so much that they go off and get ridiculed for looking stupid in their clothes. The kind and courteous thing would be to help the person even though they appear to just want approval.

There are five major categories or levels in the affective domain: (1) receiving, (2) responding, (3) valuing, (4) organization, and (5) characterization. In preparing affective objectives, it is important to include a statement of the desired value, attitude, or appreciation, along with a behavior accepted as evidence of attaining it. For example, if the goal is to value honesty, an objective like the following may be written: *The students will indicate their commitment to the value of honesty by exhorting their classmates to exhibit honest behavior.*

Receiving

At this level, the learner is sensitized to a desired affective goal and is willing to **receive** instruction. Students might engage in a conversation about the chosen value and evidence a positive attitude about it, demonstrating how they feel by contributing to the discussion about implications for including it in their value system. The following are examples of receiving level objectives:

1. The student will demonstrate sensitivity to present social problems in the school by contributing relevant statements on the subject during class discussions.
2. Students will indicate an interest in learning about democratic society by bringing newspaper clippings to class regarding the actions of the three branches of government and current political issues.
3. Students will indicate an interest in good classroom discipline by making thoughtful comments on the subject in class discussion.

Responding

At the **responding** level, student behavior is consistent with a particular value, although commitment for the value is not present. In the beginning the particular value may not be fully accepted, even though students respond as if they have the value. Student behavior is ordinarily in deference to the teacher's request. As the students experience the value in life, they grow to accept it. Whereas they needed to be encouraged earlier, students now demonstrate a willingness to respond appropriately. Finally at this level, the students achieve a sense of satisfaction from living in accordance with the value. The following objectives are written at the responding level:

1. The students will value safety by obeying safety rules in the woodworking shop.
2. The students will demonstrate good study habits by designating a specific time and place to study and by turning in at least 95 percent of their homework assignments on time.
3. The students will demonstrate a value for classical music by voluntarily attending at least four out of the five concerts scheduled during the year.

Valuing

Valuing refers to the worth attached to an object, phenomenon, or behavior. Valuing is usually composed of both personal and social preferences, and through the interaction of these two components the value is slowly internalized and accepted by the individual as his or her personal criterion of worth. Behavior at this level is very consistent, stable, and characteristic of an individual's beliefs. Students at this level move from a preference for holding a particular value to exhibiting considerable acceptance of it. They eventually become sufficiently committed that they actively defend the value and recommend it to others. The following are valuing level objectives:

1. Students will show their commitment to service by joining a service organization on campus or the community and becoming an active member.
2. Students will evidence a high degree of commitment for the safety of others in the automotive shop by abiding by safety rules and encouraging fellow students to do the same.
3. Students will exhibit a lot of school loyalty by attending most of the school functions during the year and encouraging their fellow students to do the same.

Organization

As students experience various possible values, they may encounter situations where values need to be cognitively examined and judgments made. The fit between situations and values needs to be examined because values sometimes conflict with one another, and strategies have to be created that allow for consistent, integrated behavior that does not compromise important value considerations. Emphasizing cognitive value **organization** aids the student in making conscious choices that can be adequately defended if challenged. Carefully organized values permit consistent behavior that is less likely to be weakened when attacked. With an organized value system, students not only behave more predictably, but they also achieve more confidence in the validity of their values.

Caution must be exercised in helping children organize their values within a school setting. For example, children may equate good citizenship with obeying school rules, yet fail to adequately relate citizenship to the total community. Good citizenship is a volitional act, not an act of compliance like obedience to rules. Distinctions of this kind need to be part of the value development process. In this way, students can acquire a comprehensive set of values from which to compare social expectations with personal wants and needs, and thus live their lives in a well-understood and consistent way. The following are examples of organization level objectives:

1. Students will exhibit an organization ability of the values of honesty and courtesy by making consistent written responses to 15 situations where these two values potentially conflict.
2. Students will show the proper organization of individual needs and group expectations by incorporating both values consistently into a series of written responses to a set of contrived social episodes.
3. Students will show that materialism is moderated appropriately within their value system by writing a paper wherein materialism is logically related to paternal responsibility, family living, and social responsibility.

Characterization

Once values have been carefully organized, students should consistently live within their value systems and make it their lifestyle. The individual is no longer concerned when his or her belief system is challenged, as the student's behavior is very predictably consistent with his or her value system. The person is comfortable with his or her philosophy of life and sees no reason to change it. Various disparate life situations do not automatically stimulate questions and self-analysis; however, it is still possible for the individual to acquire altered perspectives and modify his or her values to a limited extent. The following are examples of **characterization** objectives:

1. Students will show growth in the value of honesty by consistently being honest in all their dealings with teachers and fellow students.
2. Students will demonstrate behavior consistent with a written philosophy of life.
3. Students will show a consistent objectivity by always approaching problems in an objective way.

Reflections About Self

1. Attempt to identify specific values that were deliberately taught to you when you were in the public schools. Name as many as you can remember.
2. What values would you attempt to teach in the schools? How would you go about doing this?

Psychomotor Domain

The taxonomy of psychomotor objectives represents a model for viewing, explaining, and categorizing students' movement behaviors. It is organized in a hierarchical arrangement along a continuum of increasing complexity of movement and its purpose is to help categorize relevant movement sequences within the curriculum. There are six major categories in the taxonomy, with each having several subdivisions. The first two major levels, reflex movements and basic fundamental movements, are ordinarily acquired before a child enters school. In fact, these movement skills are usually well-developed early in childhood. The final four levels include perceptual abilities, physical abilities, skilled movements, and non-discursive communication.

Perceptual Abilities

Perceptual abilities contain cognitive components; they are essentially an interaction between the psychomotor and cognitive domains. These cognitive perceptions provide appropriate motor reactions. The first of these, *kinesthetic discrimination,* consists of the individual's perceptual judgments regarding the body in relation to surrounding objects in space; in other words, the body's ability to recognize and control its parts in movement while maintaining balance.

Visual discrimination includes visual acuity, which allows the individual to distinguish form and details and differentiate between various observed objects; visual tracking, by which objects can be followed through coordinated eye movements; visual memory, which equips the individual to recall past movement experiences; figure-ground differentiation, which is the ability to select the dominant figure from the surrounding background; and consistency, which is the ability to routinely recognize shapes and forms, even though they may have been modified in some way.

Auditory discrimination is the ability to receive and differentiate between the pitch and intensity of different sounds, distinguish the direction of sound and follow its movement, and recognize and reproduce post-auditory experiences like the notes used to play a song on the piano.

Tactile discrimination refers to a learner's ability to differentiate between different textures simply by touch. The individual can differentiate between the silkiness or smoothness of an object or surface and execute psychomotor movements when the body comes in contact with surfaces.

With *coordinated abilities,* the individual is able to incorporate two or more perceptual abilities and movement patterns. At this level, a student is able to differentiate between figure and ground and coordinate a visually perceived object with a manipulative movement, such as kicking a moving soccer ball. The following objectives focus on perceptual abilities:

1. Without outside assistance, students will be able to walk the full distance across a balance beam and back without falling on each of five tries (*kinesthetic discrimination*).
2. When a soccer ball is rolled along the ground at various angles, the student will be able to intercept the ball and kick it while it is moving 90 percent of the time (*coordinated abilities*).
3. Students will be able to observe a demonstration of any of the waltz movements and then perform these movements without error (*visual memory*).

Physical Abilities

Physical abilities, including endurance, strength, flexibility, and agility, provide a basis for the successful execution of skilled psychomotor movements. *Endurance* is the body's ability to supply and utilize oxygen and dispose of increased concentrations of lactic acid in the muscles. The lack of endurance reduces the learner's ability to perform physical movements efficiently over long periods of time. The development of endurance requires sustained, strenuous activity.

Strength, the relative ability to exert tension against resistance, is ordinarily developed through gradually increasing the extent of resistance through the use of weights and springs. Exercises such as pull-ups and push-ups allow the student's own body to be used as a resistance. All physical activities require some degree of strength, and improvement can usually be acquired through muscle strengthening.

Flexibility, the ability to engage in a wide range of motion in the joints, depends on the extent muscles can be stretched during movement. Hurdlers, gymnasts, and dancers are particularly concerned about flexibility.

Agility, the learner's ability to move with dexterity and quickness, is involved with the deftness of manipulation, rapid changes of direction, and starting and stopping activities. Typing, playing the piano or other musical instruments, and playing basketball are examples of activities that require a good deal of agility. The following are examples of objectives requiring physical abilities:

1. Following the Harvard-Step Test, the student's recovery period pulse count will decrease to a point at or above the next highest classification level when compared to the norms (*endurance*).
2. Students will be able to do 50 push-ups and 15 pull-ups (*strength*).
3. While sitting on the ground in the hurdlers position, students will be able to touch their extended foot with their fingers and hold this position for 10 seconds with minimal discomfort (*flexibility*).
4. Students will be able to complete the run and dodge course in less than 20 seconds (*agility*).

Skilled Movements

Skilled movement refers to an individual's effectiveness in performing reasonably complex psychomotor behaviors. These movements are differentiated in terms of their relative difficulty. *Simple adaptive skills* refer to basic movement skills that have developed through learning. Thus, dancing is an adaptation of walking, and hurdling is an adaptation of running. These skills include skating, typing, and sawing wood.

Compound adaptive skills are also built upon basic skills, but at this level the learner must incorporate the management of an implement or tool while executing a movement. Examples of these skills include tennis, hockey, golf, badminton and ping-pong, or playing string instruments such as the violin. Not all skills involving an implement fit this skill level; for example, the paddle used in canoeing is not used in a skilled way.

Complex adaptive skills are skilled movements that require a high-level mastery of body mechanics. In these movements, the performer must judge space and estimate timing. These very complex movements involve the performer without a base of support, and necessitates a series of delicate adjustments resulting from cues received from unanticipated occurrences during the skills' execution. Examples of this type of movement include aerial gymnastic stunts, twisting dives, and complicated trampoline stunts. Examples of skilled movement objectives include the following:

1. In a five-minute timed test, students will be able to type at a rate of 40 words per minute and make no more than five errors (*simple adaptive skill*).
2. From a distance of at least 20 feet, students will be able to putt a golf ball into the cup 25 percent of the time (*compound adaptive skill*).
3. Students will be able to score at least a rating of 4.5 while executing the following dives: forward one and one-half, one-half gainer, and one and one-half twist (*complex adaptive skill*).

Non-Discursive Communication

Non-discursive communication consists of nonverbal communications used to convey a message to an observer. These movements may be facial expressions or postures, as well as complex dance choreographies, and may be either expressive or interpretive. *Expressive movements* are modifications used in everyday life, like facial expressions, posture and carriage, and gestures. These movements are adapted for use in the fine arts to convey various messages to an audience during a play or performance.

Interpretive movements can either be aesthetic in nature, with the purpose of creating an image of effortless beautiful motion, or creative, designed to communicate a visual message. These movements require the performer to have highly-developed movement skills, along with a knowledge of body mechanics and well-developed physical and perceptual abilities. The following is an objective at the interpretive movement level:

Students will be able to create an original dance sequence for a piece of music of their own choosing that contains unusual rhythmic patterns and movements in presenting a message to viewers on a contemporary social theme.

NATIONAL TEACHING STANDARDS

Subject-specific pedagogical knowledge is not a bag of tricks, but rather a repertoire of representations that combines instructional techniques with subject matter in ways that take into account the mix of students and school contexts that confront the teacher.

Decision Points

Create a series of objectives for a unit of instruction in your subject area.

Learning Strategies

As stated earlier, state departments of education commonly establish core curricula with associated objectives that teachers are required to use as the focus of instruction. Teachers are commonly asked to contribute some objectives of their own as they interpret their students' needs and assess their resources and district expectations. Students are usually not involved in this process. In learning communities, however, groups of students determine their own learning activities with the help of their teachers, whose role is to keep children on track with their curricular decisions and help them identify meaningful and attractive experiences. The teacher also helps students work toward achieving excellence by drawing attention, as appropriate, to quality educational experience considerations. In this way, the teacher can help legitimize the curriculum in the learning community. All students obviously don't have common experiences, but the experiences they do have are of the highest quality, both because students are more self-directed in their studies and because their teachers routinely counsel with them to ensure high-quality learning. Different strategies are needed to promote excellence in learning communities as compared to traditional classrooms.

Classroom Strategies

Strategies for structured classroom settings ordinarily consist of a plan for achieving specified objectives. In developing a plan, teachers must be aware of obstacles that might thwart their efforts to help students achieve the objectives. It is unwise to assume that a single approach to instruction will be effective for all students. Because students vary dramatically in terms of their abilities and interests, any instructional strategy must provide learning opportunities for students that satisfy the objectives but still cater to student differences. For many years, this has been an essential principle in education. The differences between students should not be ignored, but rather made an integral part of the teaching strategy.

The first strategy consideration is determining how to get students to enthusiastically accept and pursue the objectives, which can be difficult when students have not helped create the objectives. Grounds other than personal involvement must be used to convince them to accept classroom goals. Teachers will ordinarily want to show students how achieving the objectives can help them obtain something they desire, typically something relevant in the future. For example, youth ordinarily have little concern regarding health matters until confronted with a devastating illness. If health was a concern, little encouragement would be needed to get them involved in studying health-related concepts in their health or biology classes. If students do not have an imminent need to acquire health knowledge, teachers have to create conditions that help students realistically visualize possible future needs, such as showing a video depicting various health problems and revealing the real potential for infections among the class. Having a doctor or nurse make a class presentation regarding the nature of community health problems might be helpful to provide a "touch of reality." The teacher could also lead a discussion where health concerns are addressed.

The next consideration in planning teaching strategies is to differentiate instruction. In a regular classroom, there are realistic limitations regarding how much instruction can be differentiated to accommodate various student learning styles, needs, and inclinations. These considerations make classrooms very complex places. Determining common needs and interests along with similar student learning styles simplifies this process. In addition, teachers can gear most instruction to a constructivist learning approach by involving students in a variety of group problem-solving experiences. Children are assumed to inherently learn in constructive ways. Teachers should conduct discussions about the various options available for study and determine topics that different students will have an interest about. Students can then be grouped and allowed to focus their learning on their interests.

Because constructivism denotes the natural way children learn, fewer difficulties are expected if students have instructional experiences consistent with constructivist theory. Students should be involved in self-directed learning experiences and have the opportunity to interact with other students and their teachers during these inquiry episodes. Such episodes require hands-on activities allowing students to examine various phenomena, manipulate and study them, and assess how well any new conceptions fit already-formed concepts. Teachers can draw attention to possible new experiences or unexplored considerations that may help students gain a more credible understanding. However, teachers should avoid making excessive verbal clarifications of student understanding. Students are better off making their own discoveries and drawing their own conclusions with expert guidance from teachers.

Decision Points

Prepare an objective from your subject area for a student population of considerable diversity. Explain how you would get a group of students to pursue the objective.

NATIONAL TEACHING STANDARDS

Teachers are able to modify the social and physical organizational structure of the learning environment to cater to differences in students' learning styles and to take advantage of the fact that different settings offer different learning opportunities.

Even though all children learn constructively, they vary in terms of learning style and preferences. Gardner (1991) identified a set of learning preferences he calls multiple intelligences (see Chapter 4). According to Gardner, people possess at least eight types of intellectual abilities in varying degrees, with decided preferences for particular ones. Unfortunately, the curriculum content, and especially the tests that go with them, emphasize the linguistic and logical-mathematical abilities and neglect the others. A properly conceived strategy should consist of experiences that allow students opportunities to utilize the learning style they prefer. A better rounded curriculum, with more use of project learning methods, would allow students to develop a more complete range of abilities. It is important to pay attention to students' full range of abilities and to view these abilities not as limiting factors, but as resources that students will both personally develop and use to enhance their peers' learning during classroom activities (Good & Brophy, 2000).

With students simultaneously engaging in a variety of classroom activities, teachers cannot be expected to be intimately involved with all the learning that takes place. Student groups can work independently for long periods of time with limited teacher input, and they need to experience considerable autonomy so they can effectively assume personal responsibility for their efforts. Much of their activity can be observed intermittently, with the teacher occasionally interacting with them to raise questions or provide needed assistance.

NATIONAL TEACHING STANDARDS

Teachers need not only use the factual information associated with their subject, but also its central organizing concepts and the ways in which new knowledge is created, including the forms of creative investigation that characterize the work of scholars and artists.

Planning for Higher-Level Thinking

In school, little attention is given to higher-level thinking; more time is actually devoted to memorizing factual information. Interestingly, many consider a person uneducated unless he or she has accumulated a stockpile of information and can remember it when called upon. Unfortunately, most individuals quickly forget a good share of what they learn. However, intellectual skills are remembered and can be used for a lifetime. Students need to acquire the skills of analysis, synthesis, and evaluation and use these skills often in processing concepts and ideas that they encounter in their quest for understanding. Strategically, instead of students being given a list of facts to memorize, they should become involved in

The teaching of values is a central consideration in learning communities.

learning projects, including activities calling for them to think. Teachers should know the different kinds of thinking, so they can periodically ask questions or suggest activities that require specified kinds. However, a good variety of thinking opportunities can be experienced when students are involved in learning projects requiring them to cooperatively investigate various topics with other students and solve problems. Teachers need to be able to track the nature of and quality of students' thinking and enter into active dialogue with them to expand their thinking experiences.

Strategies for Promoting Affective Growth

Attitudes and values are essential components of every child's education. Much of the cognitive curriculum has value implications that need to be addressed. In addition, values and attitudes such as kindness, helpfulness, and honesty, as well as values like the freedom of expression associated with the Constitution and the Bill of Rights, are important for children to learn.

Value considerations identify what is learned and how, in addition to values associated with the various subjects. The degree to which student autonomy, cooperative learning, learning communities, and inquiry-based activities are valued during instruction is a critical educational consideration. Other values are also connected to topics in the various disciplines. For example, in biology values are associated with topics such as genetic engineering, cloning, population control, and in vitro fertilization. In physics, values associated with nuclear power plants, space exploration, and nuclear waste dump sites may be addressed. In social studies, values related to democracy, social responsibility, and voting rights might be studied.

There are values connected with personal growth and development like good health, and values associated with successful social living such as community responsibility. In addition, in a free society the opportunity for free speech and assembly, freedom of religion, freedom from unreasonable searches, and the right to due process are fundamental values that should be exercised in schools, and students should learn of their central role in democratic living.

All the previously listed values are justifiable and appropriate for school instruction, but how can they be effectively taught? Students often resist efforts to teach them values, choosing instead to accept the values of their peer group or of individuals whose beliefs may be inconsistent with community values. In addition, the school is also in a position to assist students in carefully examining their values to help them formulate consistent value systems that can promote more successful interpersonal interactions and social responsibility.

Because students may resist the kind of direct instruction designed to have them adopt the values presented to them, it is wise to create strategies that allow them to discuss the viability of various values with their peers. In this process, the teacher can raise questions and considerations that students, in their naivete, may fail to acknowledge or examine. Students might reject certain values if they understood all the implications associated with them, but because of their lack of knowledge they are unable to make wise choices. For example, students may value verbal cruelty and bluntness because their peers interact in an unkind, blunt way. Students may not realize the devastating effects of this behavior and engage in unkind exchanges only because they observe others doing it, thinking that somehow such actions add to their status in the group. There are a number of implications of such behavior that could be raised, including: (1) a friend could be deeply hurt by such talk, (2) you might be hurt by other's bluntness, (3) untruths are often spread, (4) such actions can lead to extreme violence, (5) patterns can be established that can have future devastating consequences, and (6) such behavior can reduce the effectiveness of learning in groups. In raising these issues, teachers should not get preachy, but rather bring up questions to be considered, thereby allowing students the chance to arrive at their own conclusions. Again, students may reject values that their teachers try to impose on them. Questions like the following might be used to introduce a discussion about the six issues raised above:

1. What might happen to a friend if you use direct cruel, blunt accusations? How might your friend react? What kinds of things might the friend say about you? What other kinds of conversations might replace those that are cruel?
2. How might you react to statements by your peers that are cruel and unkind? What impact might that behavior have on your friendships? What kind of behavior promotes good friendship?
3. Have you ever had someone say something about you that was untrue just to be mean? Did you learn why the statement was made? What did you have to do to set things right?
4. What happened in Columbine, Colorado, as a result of students saying unkind things about one another? What was determined to be the cause of the violence? What should your role be in situations where you overhear other students being unkind to one another?
5. In our class, we are organized into a learning community. What would be the impact on our ability to work together successfully if students said cruel things to one another? What is your responsibility if you hear such conversations anywhere in the school?

It is particularly useful to present issues for consideration in the form of questions. This communicates to students that the issue is open for discussion and that their input is desired and valued. The previous questions are just a few of many that might be raised in considering the issues. Discussion would continue until students reached an agreement about the means for solving these problems. Students should be encouraged to employ their new perspective in their daily activities and make future plans to assess their own attitudes and the behavior of their peers. In this way, students are able to understand that their values are important and can be modified to improve their lives.

 QUESTION FOR REFLECTION

1. What are some values that might be legitimate to teach in the public schools? Explain why you consider them to be appropriate.

Planning for Diverse Populations

Students not only differ in terms of their interests and learning styles, but also in terms of different races, classes, cultures, and religions. Students also vary in terms of learning capabilities: some have special learning or behavioral problems, as explained in detail in Chapter 5. These differences must be considered in creating a teaching-learning strategy. For example, students with learning problems might receive help from more able students as they work together in groups. Group work can be differentiated so students with different abilities and interests can assume different responsibilities. Students who lack an English language facility may work with students who have bilingual capabilities, or receive assistance from specialized staff. During group activities, students should probably be heterogeneously organized, as this helps to avoid exclusivity. All student activities should be arranged to send a clear message that diversity is valued and that it adds strength to the classroom.

The education of diverse student populations is primarily centered in cooperative learning strategies and includes such topics as cooperative learning activities, positive interdependence, lesson planning and cooperative structures, teaching cooperative skills, cooperative discipline, adaptations for students with disabilities, cooperative learning and cultural diversity, and cooperative student support teams (Ryan & Kurda, 1997). Cooperation is a key factor in efforts to promote better learning in inclusive classrooms. Cooperative learning has been recommended for instruction in regular classrooms for many years (Johnson & Johnson, 1994). Various models for cooperative learning are presented in Chapter 8. The particular model advised for use depends on classroom purposes.

Learning communities may constitute an even more potent learning strategy for diverse student populations since diversity is considered to be a strength rather than a problem. While the group as a whole must take priority over any individual, the purpose of group activity is to ensure that each individual becomes an integral part of the community and has his or her needs and learning desires addressed. The total group is able to achieve many things at a higher level because the diverse attributes of the group are accentuated in group activities. For example, if the learning community decided to study the Middle East conflict, they may acquire more insight if all group members contribute personal views toward a more comprehensive understanding.

Strategies for Learning Communities

The first step in forming a learning community is to put together a group of participants who desire this learning format. The decision to fully participate in a learning community requires individuals to have a fairly complete understanding of what it entails. The community has to be carefully contrasted with other learning schemes, particularly learning in traditional classrooms. Students should first be shown the assumptions about learning as well as human growth and development from the perspective of learning communities. They should be informed that a learning community involves group decision making about learning with the purpose of promoting personal growth with community support. Students should learn that diversity should not only be accommodated, but be highly valued for the growth potential it provides. Group agendas and shared governance should be emphasized, promoting interpersonal growth and personal responsibility. Much of the learning should develop from solving relevant problems. Students should participate in the learning community if they feel the previous conditions are desirable. However, some students might not be ready for a learning community. Because commitment is necessary for learning communities to properly function, students must want to be involved.

The next step in creating a learning community is to establish a sense of caring among group members and a sense of commitment to one another. However, it may take some time before the requisite level of acceptance and interdependence is achieved. Various interpersonal building activities can be arranged to help students become better acquainted with one another and to find "common ground." True friendship is sought in this development stage. Group members need to be willing to stand up for one another and permit other group members sufficient personal autonomy so that any group member can feel secure suggesting potential group activities. Group members should be assured that any input they give will be respected and explored with integrity. Some of this development can be routinely achieved as teams work together on projects. There doesn't have to be a defined level of interpersonal development before profitable learning projects can be successfully undertaken. Part of this growth will occur over time.

Once group members feel secure learning with one another, viable learning projects should be designated. There needs to be some agreement about what projects to pursue and who should be involved. A learning community contains room for subgroup projects, thus allowing for greater variety in the activities undertaken. Some projects may be initiated with the understanding that others will be started once the initial, more popular ones are begun. Sometimes after working on a project for a time, a small number of students may choose to move in a different direction. This needs to be assessed in terms of how it fits into the total group agenda and contributes to the well-being of individual group members. Most diversions will naturally develop from group learning and be consistent with the goals of the learning community. Only rarely should such requests fail to achieve group support. In the inquiry process one learning project might naturally spawn off equally valuable additional learning opportunities. These new directions should be supported and even encouraged, particularly when they help the learning community acquire new insights and promote the learning skills of individual members.

Students should understand that the shared leadership inherent in learning communities indicates that particular project leaders can evolve just like their interests. The person who initiates an area of study may ordinarily be the logical candidate to provide leadership, although at times someone else may emerge during the process to provide necessary guidance and stimulate group cohesiveness. Group leadership may shift. The person who originated the idea may prefer conducting research rather than managing group efforts.

How are projects identified and how do group members align themselves with a particular learning effort? Individuals with an idea they wish to investigate should first determine if others share their interest. If no one else is interested, the individual may wish to do a little further exploration to determine the degree of his or her own interest. If he or she remains interested, the group should make additional efforts to elicit support from others. Although they are not particularly consistent with the group orientation of learning communities, individual projects are acceptable. Once an individual undertakes a project of personal interest, other group members may want to get involved. These situations should play themselves out until the individual is satisfied with the results. Over time there will likely be fewer of these independent projects undertaken. Most members will prefer cooperative efforts, where individuals lobby for group support before initiating any research, and other individuals participate more willingly on projects others propose. Thus, each individual in a learning community operates within a "give and take atmosphere" between attending to personal interests and becoming involved with others.

How can such efforts be evaluated? Tests are, of course, the traditional method of assessing student achievement. In learning communities, instead of preparing for common examinations, students solve problems or create products that represent the level of skill or understanding they have achieved. These products may be music compositions, paintings, poetry, essays, research reports, and the like. A better idea of excellence and accomplishment can be achieved this way than by having students take a traditional test with questionable validity.

NATIONAL TEACHING STANDARDS

Teachers' instructional repertoires include knowledge of available curricular resources such as primary sources, models, reproductions, textbook series, teachers' guides, videotapes, computer software, and musical recordings. They keep abreast of technological developments that have implications for teaching, and they can use a computer to enhance their own teaching.

Teachers must know how to employ a variety of instructional skills and methods including such approaches as outdoor experiments, mock trials, economic simulations, discovery learning, conceptual mapping, playlets, debates, brainstorming, and working with computers. These must be employed in a way that optimizes the relationship between knowing and doing.

Planning a Traditional Course of Study

A significant part of teachers' responsibilities is creating long-range and short-range teaching plans. They organize courses of study, create units of instruction, and make lesson plans that appropriately guide instruction for the particular group of students they have. Teachers have an obligation not only to carefully analyze their students, but also to organize their classes, while taking into account available resources and text materials, national standards, and state curriculum requirements. Before the 1990s, national curriculum standards did not exist in the United States (Kim & Kellough, 1995). In order to create national standards in all core subjects, the National Council on Educational Standards and Testing recommended that national standards be created for the arts, civics/social studies, English/language arts/reading, geography, history, mathematics, and science (see Appendix A). National standards were intended to be used by the states to guide the development of courses of study, along with the creation of textbooks and other instructional materials. The standards were intended to have a positive effect upon student achievement by ensuring high-quality curricula nationwide. The national standards are reflected in many of the various state core curricula.

The first step in organizing a course of study is to create a properly sequenced list of topics to be covered in the course. This list of topics is ordinarily determined by state core curricula and adopted textbook materials, along with national standards, but the individual teacher must sequence them in terms of learning prerequisites. The following is a course outline for a course in psychology:

Unit One: The Study of Psychology and its Applications
    A. Historical Perspectives
    B. Theories in Psychology
    C. Psychological Research and Methodology
    D. Psychological Concepts and Their Applications
Unit Two: Human Growth and Development
    A. Theories of Human Growth and Development
    B. Physical Development
    C. Intellectual Development
    D. Emotional Development
    E. Social Development
Unit Three: Personality
    A. Theories of Personality
    B. The Measurement of Personality Variables
    C. Individual Differences
Unit Four: Learning
    A. Theories of Learning
    B. Thinking and Learning
    C. Performance Measures
    D. Learning Styles
    E. Self-Directed Learning
Unit Five: Motivation
    A. Motivational Theory
    B. Extrinsic Motivation
    C. Intrinsic Motivation
    D. Motivation to Learn
Unit Six: Abnormal Psychology
    A. Mental Health Indicators

B. Neuroses and Psychoses
C. Prevention of Mental Illness
D. Physiological Factors in Mental Illness
Unit Seven: Social Psychology
A. Theories of Social Psychology
B. The Nature of Culture
C. Integration and Social Theory
D. Persuasion and Group Dynamics

The next step is to visualize the kind of course the teacher wants. For example, in the psychology course previously outlined, the teacher may wish to create a format through which his or her students engage in original research regarding each of the major topics. Alternatively, they may opt to conduct searches to accumulate and sift through information about each topic, synthesize the data, and draw conclusions about the most appropriate explanations. Students would need to identify investigation sources and acquire permissions for some of these information sources.

The teacher in a biology course may wish to extensively promote inquiry. Each course outline topic would need to be examined to determine where best to employ inquiry. The teacher then determines general categories for inquiry and obtains appropriate materials for student research. The supply and equipment purchases will need to be correlated with the budget allowances, and inventories of current resources and equipment determined. Teachers will need to find additional supply sources, order materials, and differentiate specimens that students collect from those that need to be ordered from a biological supply house. Because not all possible lines of student inquiry can be anticipated in advance, money should be kept in reserve for later purchases. This kind of effort is needed to realistically prepare for potential student research during the year. Teachers should also address any unusual considerations for students with special needs.

Objectives are often created in a state core curricula, with varying levels of specificity. Additional objectives can be generated as deemed appropriate. These need to be correlated with the course topics and supply requirements.

Units of Instruction

A unit of instruction is usually created for each of the topics in a course outline. The unit is ordinarily organized conceptually to allow proper sequencing for instruction. It is useful to construct a concept map, a diagrammatic representation of unit concepts and their relationships, for each unit (see Figure 7.2). This map provides a template for helping students relate the concepts currently being studied to other concepts in the unit. Thus, students are able to visualize the context in which to learn and understand various related concepts and ideas. Learning the parts while comprehending the whole provides a more meaningful approach to learning. In addition, students are able to use the concept map to better remember what is taught.

In the concept map illustrated in Figure 7.2, four separate lines of instruction help promote a comprehensive understanding of the relationships between living things in producing an ecological balance in nature. These four lines of instruction include food webs, limiting factors, oscillations, and energy transfer. Each of these lines of instruction has four

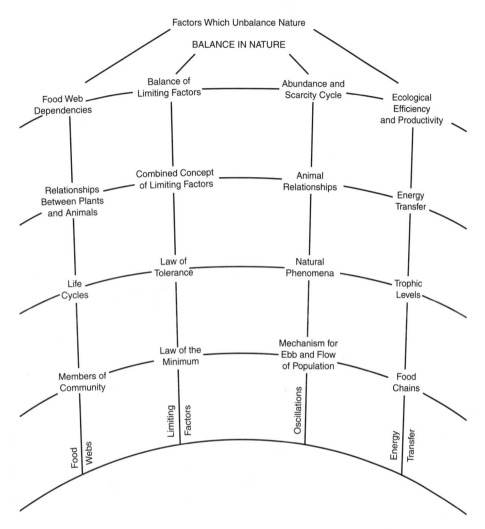

Figure 7.2   Balance in Nature Concept Map

sequentially arranged centers for conceptual organization. *Food webs*, for example, provide a line of instruction that begins with identifying membership in plant and animal communities. Next, life cycles are examined, as well as how these cycles bring plants and animals into close relationships with one another. Finally, there is a consideration of how these relationships constitute life dependencies that contribute to the balance in nature.

Limiting factors, the next line of instruction, center around specific factors that limit the growth and development of plants and animals. The law of the minimum states that the amount of essential material most closely approaching the critical minimum needed for survival will tend to be the limiting one. In close association with the law of the minimum is the law of tolerance, which states that the presence and success of an organism depends upon the completeness of a complex array of environmental conditions. Absence or failure of an organism can be controlled by the qualitative or quantitative deficiency or excess of any one of several factors that may approach an organism's limits of tolerance. Any condition that approaches or exceeds an organism's limits of tolerance is said to be a *limiting condition* or *limiting factor*. If factors in the environment are altered so that a critical minimum is approached for an organism, nature can become unbalanced.

A third line of instruction is to explore *oscillations* that exist in nature and examine the delicate balance often present in these ebbs and flows. Understanding how populations of animals increase and decrease in response to one another indicates how closely related and interdependent they are. This illustrates how artificially altering one population can have far reaching repercussions through all of nature. In some cases, the dependency is so complete that the entire populations oscillate with one another with no other factors having an apparent effect. Students first consider mechanisms for the ebb and flow of particular populations. This predator-prey relationship is tenuously balanced and dependent upon a narrow range of tolerance. For example, in one location red-tailed hawks feed on ground squirrels, who in turn feed on vegetation with a narrow tolerance for temperature change. When the plants the squirrels browse on die off due to temperature changes, the squirrels hibernate underground and become unavailable for predation. In this case, a natural phenomenon like temperature change is a mechanism for the ebb and flow of species. The reduction of ground squirrels is almost instantaneous, as is the presence of red-tailed hawks in the area.

The fourth line of instruction deals with *energy transfer*. In this case, the sequence starts with an understanding of food chains that involve plant and animal relationships. Students are taught that given plants constitute the base of all food chains. Plants capture energy from the sun and transform it into a usable form for animals. In a food chain, energy is transferred from one trophic level to another until it reaches a top predator. As energy is transferred from one trophic level to another, some of it is always lost; there is never 100 percent efficiency. Productivity in a biological community depends on the continuity of energy transfer within food chains. Breaks in the chain deprive animals higher on the chain of their source of energy, thereby leading to the unbalancing of nature.

Not only are there relationships in each line of instruction in a concept map, but there are also relationships between the lines. In the example on ecology, each of the lines is related to the others and helps make up a comprehensive, interrelated conception about plant and animal dependencies as they relate to balance in nature. This represents an effort to conceptualize many of the factors that, in an interactive way, contribute to understanding the balance of nature and how humans might have to respond to preserve that balance. Students can use a concept map to keep a general conceptualization of an area of study in front of them. Then, as they learn various aspects of the topic, they can automatically see where each fits.

Units of instruction take many forms, and are usually created for the convenience of the individual using them. In the biology example, the teacher might consider the concept map and associated concepts, while at the same time formulating achievable objectives to reach while working with the concepts. Objectives would be selected that both engage students in a variety of intellectual processes and also satisfy the aims of the state core curriculum. Key learning activities would be identified to support the achievement of the objectives. Teachers should prepare in advance for activities like labs, demos, and field trips along with their necessary supplies and equipment. All these items would be sequenced in the unit plan for easy reference.

Decision Points

Create a unit of instruction that is based on a carefully organized concept map and that incorporates not only cognitive but also affective goals.

Lesson Planning

The format of lesson plans depends on the kind of lesson being planned and the classroom configuration it will be used in. In some cases a school district may specify a particular format for writing lesson plans. The content of a lesson plan depends primarily on the degree of structure student learning is to have. The more teacher direction desired, the more detail needs to be provided regarding objectives and learning activities. With less-structured learning, fewer learning activities can be planned in advance, and consequently the lesson plans include lists of reminders to the teacher rather than sequences of activities planned for students.

Lesson Plans for Structured Learning

A structured lesson plan ordinarily has a teacher-determined objective, a list of concepts or questions that make up the content of the lesson, a series of learning activities for achieving the objective, a list of materials and/or arrangements required to teach the lesson, and a description of how student competency will be evaluated. It may also include a description of the strategy being employed by the teacher, particularly if special activities are planned for students with special needs.

In creating a lesson plan for structured learning, the teacher must first decide upon an objective and related concepts. This requires an interactive process where the concepts are considered for their strategic utility in achieving appropriate objectives, and objectives are examined to determine how well they promote the understanding and use of important concepts. Strategies are then devised that take the particular student population into account and optimize the chances of achieving the objectives. The strategy is reflected in a sequenced set of learning activities, which are arranged to create motivation, promote understanding, and move students from initial knowledge conceptualization to using what is learned to effectively engage in various kinds of research or to solve problems. The following is a lesson plan regarding energy transfer created as a component of the unit on ecological balance:

Title:
Energy Transfer in Biological Systems

Objectives:
1. Students will be able to satisfactorily explain the transfer of energy in a food chain, pointing out the influence on energy transfer of the following items:
   a.   the length of the food chain and available energy
   b.   the efficiency of energy transformation
   c.   the size-metabolism relationships and trophic structure of biological communities
2. Students will design and carry out experiments that determine how size-metabolism relationships dictate the trophic structure in biological communities.

Concepts:

1. Energy may be transformed from one type to another, but is never created nor destroyed.
2. No process involving an energy transformation will spontaneously occur unless there is a degradation of energy from a concentrated form into a dispersed form.
3. Because some energy is always dispersed into unavailable heat energy, no spontaneous transformation (light, for example) into potential energy (protoplasm, for example) is 100 percent efficient.
4. In each energy transfer in a food chain, a large portion of the potential energy is lost as heat.
5. Due to the loss of energy, the number of links in a food chain is usually limited to four or five.
6. The shorter the food chain, the greater the available energy that can be converted into biomass (biomass = living weight, including stored food).
7. The smaller the organism, the greater its metabolism per gram of biomass.
8. The smaller the organism, the smaller the biomass that can be supported at a particular trophic level in the ecosystem. *Example:* Fewer bacteria could be supported than a crop of fish in terms of grams of biomass.
9. The interaction of the food chain (energy loss at each transfer) and the size-metabolism relationship results in communities having a defined trophic structure that is often characteristic of a particular type of ecosystem (lake, forest, coral reef, etc.).

Learning Activities:

1. Have students read Chapter 3 in *Fundamentals of Ecology* (Odum, 1959).
2. Show the video clips that detail the destruction of an ecosystem by disrupting an energy transfer chain.
3. Using an overhead projector, portray the energy flow diagram and discuss it.
4. Discuss each of the concepts outlined in the content of the lesson and focus on how they are related to the concept of energy transfer.
5. Take a field trip to Strawberry Canyon to observe the blue spruce climax community in the forest ecosystem.
6. Inform students they are to design an inquiry investigation regarding the transfer of energy. They are to work in groups of about five and create a research question along with appropriate hypotheses, and design a study that can determine the validity of their hypotheses. Any possible confounding variables should be controlled. Conclusions should be reasonable and supported by the data collected.
7. Students are to prepare reports of their research and make a presentation to the class on their findings and conclusions.

Materials and Arrangements:

Overhead projector and overlays, laboratory equipment, biological materials, bus arrangements, permission slips.

Strategy:

1. To motivate students, explain that one of the most critical problems facing the world is that of acquiring sufficient fuel and food energy. Due to the increase in world population, it is becoming increasingly imperative that new and better food sources be found. To solve this problem, a good understanding of how energy transfer occurs in food chains is necessary. Sometimes humans, in their quest for new energy sources, create imbalances in nature.
2. Some of the research regarding energy transfer can be difficult to understand. Learning groups will be organized so that more able students can help their less-able peers to understand.
3. Make sure Ben and Ronald are assigned to different teams and are involved actively in research.
4. Assign Renaldo to Mary's team so he can take advantage of her bilingual skills.

Lesson Plans for Inquiry Teaching

A lesson plan created to teach inquiry skills does not contain sequences of teacher-led learning activities. Instead, it establishes an area of study: for example, the behavior of a common ant species. Students are allowed to formulate their own questions for study and to design research. The teacher's role is to ensure that the questions raised by students are substantial and that the research is well-designed. In addition to a statement regarding the area of study, the lesson plan would include a list of possible questions for research. This list would not be shared with students, but would serve only to broaden the teacher's perspective of possible research efforts. When working with students who have little experience formulating research questions, teachers may initially need to provide various clues. The list of possible research questions provides teachers with ideas from which they can create clues. Otherwise, teachers might be unprepared to provide this important assistance. The only other necessary component of an inquiry lesson is a list of materials and equipment that should be on hand to support student research. The classroom may not contain everything necessary for the research students undertake, but there should be enough supplies to accommodate much of what is needed. Additional items can be acquired if desired. Teachers may also want to include a sequence of steps to use in organizing and carrying out these activities. The following is an example of an inquiry lesson plan:

Inquiry Topic:
Research regarding plant growth and development

Possible Research Questions:
1. What is the effect of temperature on the growth of different plant species?
2. What is the effect of the amount of water on the growth of different plant species?
3. What combinations of temperature and water provide the ideal conditions for growth of different plant species?

4. How does the amount of light and shade affect the growth of different plant species?
5. How does the schedule of light exposure affect the growth of different plants?
6. What is the effect of different ratios of plant nutrients on the growth of different plant species?
7. What tolerances do different plant species have to low levels of various plant nutrients?
8. What characteristics of plant growth are evidence of various nutritional deficiencies?
9. What effects do different light wavelengths have on plant growth as compared to full spectrum light?
10. How does the pH of the soil affect the growth of different plant species?
11. What is the relative time of recovery of different plant species exposed to various periods of drought?
12. What is the effect of auxin on plant growth and the development and setting of fruit?

Materials and Equipment to Have on Hand:

Seeds of various kinds, a number of plant species, thermometers, grow tables with light control capabilities, automatic water and nutrient dispensers, light filters, plant growth containers, Ziploc bags, paper towels, plant growth hormones, fertilizers, pH indicators, acids and bases to alter soil pH, bedding material, variety of chemicals.

Decision Points

Create a course outline for your subject area along with example units and lesson plans. Prepare lessons that accommodate a particular divergent student population.

QUESTION FOR REFLECTION

1. What problems can be anticipated in teaching in a classroom that employs learning communities? How can these problems be turned into positive learning experiences?

CENTRAL IDEAS

1. Educational philosophy not only provides the basis upon which the school curriculum is constructed, but also the guidelines for instruction.
2. The school curriculum should be built around the culture in which the school exists.
3. All curriculum should be based upon an accurate conception of how children learn.
4. Values are an integral part of life and should be reflected both in curriculum construction and during classroom instruction.
5. Teachers must be able to anticipate the influence of interpersonal interactions on the instructional process and plan experiences for children that take these influences into account; during the instructional process, they should capitalize upon worthwhile inputs that emerge.
6. Some learning is best accomplished in the absence of measurable behavioral objectives. In the rush to have instruction defined exclusively by these objectives, many of the substantial experiences students should have may be omitted.

7. Many higher-level objectives require further clarification of the teacher's instructional intent through the creation of parameters.
8. Teachers can clarify their vague expectations for students through the formulation of evaluative adjuncts.
9. The purpose of the taxonomy of educational objectives is to broaden the experiences students receive in school and to ensure valuable learning experiences receive appropriate attention.
10. The strategies employed in the classroom depend on the objectives. Objectives created by teachers usually require the teacher to also supply students with acceptable reasons to pursue them.
11. Students are more likely to pursue learning objectives they have helped create and to pursue learning activities they have some control over.
12. Thinking skills are useful for a lifetime, while memorized information may have very little long-term utility.
13. The teaching of attitudes and values is an important component of the curriculum, but values must be taught through a process by which students can assess and then accept or reject them.

REFERENCES

Bloom, B. S. (Ed.). (1956). *Taxonomy of educational objectives: Cognitive domain.* New York: David McKay Company.

Cronbach, L. (1954). *Educational Psychology.* New York: Harcourt, Brace & Company.

Gardner, H. (1991). *The unschooled mind: How children think and how schools should teach.* New York: Basic Books.

Good, T. L., & Brophy, J. E. (2000). *Looking in classrooms* (8th ed.). New York: Longman.

Harrow, A. J. (1972). *Taxonomy of educational objectives: Affective domain.* New York: David McKay Company.

Johnson, D., & Johnson, R. (1994). *Learning together and learning alone* (4th ed.). Boston: Allyn & Bacon.

Kim, E. C., & Kellough, R. D. (1995). *A resource guide for secondary school teaching: Planning for competence.* Upper Saddle River, NJ: Prentice Hall.

Krathwohl, D. R., Bloom, B. S., & Masia, B. B. (1964). *Taxonomy of educational objectives: Affective domain.* New York: David McKay Company.

Mager, R. F. (1962). *Preparing instructional objectives.* Palo Alto, CA: Fearon.

Odum, E. P. (1959). *Fundamentals of ecology* (2nd ed.). Philadelphia: W. B. Saunders.

Piaget, J. (1952). *The origins of intelligence in children.* New York: International University Press.

Popham, W. J., & Baker, E. I. (1970). *Systematic instruction.* Englewood Cliffs, NJ: Prentice Hall.

Raths, J. D. (1971). Teaching without specific objectives. *Educational Leadership, 28,* 714–720.

Ryan, S., & Kurda, D. (1997). *Alaska inclusion training modules: Building inclusive classrooms and schools.* Juneau, Alaska: Alaska State Department of Education.

Smith, P. G. (1972). On the logic of behavioral objectives. *Phi Delta Kappan, 53,* 429–431.

Dynamics of Classroom Instruction

The success of educational experiences essentially depends upon the degree to which students achieve skill in thinking, learn how to solve complex problems, and successfully relate to, and work well with others. In society, those individuals who are able to understand the social structure and properly conceptualize and solve problems have a decided advantage over those who can't. These skills are more likely achieved in learning configurations like those found in their communities. This, of course, involves problem solving. Classroom learning communities provide an excellent format for helping students learn to cooperatively work on projects with identifiable value to them and that allow them to use their thinking skills to formulate and solve viable problems. The complexity of modern society makes this kind of problem solving essential. Children need to learn how to incorporate input from disparate sources while solving problems. Various cultural influences have to be considered, and a variety of strategies employed, in order to solve many of the problems students will face. In learning communities, children learn new influences, strategies, and perspectives from one another's cultural experiences and come to visualize the true complications of modern society.

Many students come to school with little inclination to engage in their teacher's learning activities. They may find little in school that peaks their interest or satisfies their needs. Many teachers labor under the false assumption that students must be motivated before they will learn. They ordinarily provide various rewards or threaten punishment in order to induce learning. However, students are never unmotivated; they just have a different agenda than their teachers. Alternative strategies exist for motivating students. Some kinds of learning can be based on intrinsic motivation while a process called *motivation to learn* can be applied to stimulate other school activities. Strategies also exist that teachers can use to motivate even those students who suffer various kinds of learning problems.

Unmotivated students commonly create classroom disruptions. In addition, some teachers ineffectively discipline their classes and stimulate excessive misbehavior. Discipline problems can also be encouraged by school conditions students find intolerable or by soured student-teacher relationships. Ineffective discipline is probably the most critical classroom problem teachers encounter. This is no doubt responsible for more teacher failure than any other factor. The deleterious effect of poor discipline on learning is incalculable. Considerable improvement can be expected when teachers ensure student needs are met and when their learning activities are more interesting and self-directed. Students must value what they learn and see it as strategically important to them in achieving their educational goals. Students who have not been allowed to provide input regarding what they learn are less likely to accept teacher learning expectations. Students' behavior can also be improved when they are involved in determining classroom rules and consequences. Learning communities are particularly effective in eliminating classroom discipline problems.

Intellectual Development and Social Growth: Methods and Technology

CHAPTER OBJECTIVES

This chapter is designed to help you

1. Explain the nature of higher-order thinking and summarize what can be concluded from the research.

2. Critique various views about thinking and indicate what school practices tend to reduce the quality of student thinking.

3. Describe how to create an environment for school that promotes thinking.

4. Explain how learning communities are a particularly good problem-solving environment.

The intellectual growth of students requires a thorough understanding of the nature of thinking.

5. Compare what can be expected from competitive versus cooperative learning.

6. Apply various models of cooperative learning depending on their instructional intentions.

7. Apply various instructional methods in the classroom.

8. Describe how computers can be used by both students and teachers.

INTRODUCTION

For many years, student thinking has been an essential goal of schooling. Even though most student activity in school is memorization, activities that require students to engage in "higher-level mental processes" have greater value. Students come to school fully equipped with an insatiable drive to explore and experiment, but schools are predominantly oriented toward controlling rather than learning, and toward rewarding students for meeting others' expectations rather than cultivating their own natural curiosity and impulse to learn (Beyer, 1997). Even though very young children can and do engage in serious reasoning and problem solving (Case, 1992), many jump to conclusions instead of suspending judgment, consider only one or two rather than all relevant alternatives in making decisions, view problematic situations exclusively from one point of view, and accept uncritically their own hasty conclusions as well as those of other people (Perkins, 1992). In addition, most youngsters do not strategically think. They do not mentally plan what to do when carrying out a thinking task before launching into it. They fail to clarify the problem they wish to resolve or the goals they wish to accomplish before they start to solve a problem. They also fail to attend to, evaluate, and modify their thinking when necessary for more careful and consistent problem solving. Consequently, their mental processes fail, making them less able to spot thinking errors in time to make adjustments and avoid problems. However, children do not need to be taught how to think from scratch. All students can and do think. They can be taught to engage in complex thinking on their own initiative when and where appropriate (Beyer, 1997). Research indicates that thinking can be improved when a thoughtful learning environment exists and when students (1) see models and descriptions of skillful thinking practices, (2) receive guidance and support in their initial thinking efforts until they can independently accomplish them in a self-directed way, and (3) are encouraged to address problems they believe are worth thinking about (Beyer, 1983).

Ms. Tucker was convinced that most of her tenth-grade English class students could not think at the levels necessary for her literature unit. The students were instructed to read many classical works because she believed they should become acquainted with examples of great writing. She believed that exposing her students to good literature would develop their higher-level thinking abilities and appropriate social values. Despite conveying this message to her students, they seemed unimpressed, preferring instead to avoid the assigned readings. Ms. Tucker also believed her students were incapable of the necessary level of thinking to truly understand and appreciate finer literature. After teaching for many years, she found a very noticeable difference between the thinking capabilities of her current students and those of former years. She thought there was a definite decline in her students' intellectual capabilities through the years.

Ms. Tucker spent an hour considering this problem at her desk when Angelica Martinez came into the room.

"I hope I'm not disturbing you," Angelica said.

"Not at all," Ms. Tucker responded, secretly wishing to avoid whatever Angelica might be requesting.

"I was wondering if I might ask for a change," Angelica continued. "I wanted to know if I could substitute something else for *The Grapes of Wrath* that you assigned us to read? I started it, but I just can't get interested. It just comes from a different age. It doesn't apply to us now."

Ms. Tucker was a little surprised. She viewed *The Grapes of Wrath* as an important piece of literature, both because it identified timeless social problems and values, and because it was historically significant. She could not imagine anyone challenging her use of it in class, particularly a student. After all, what would a student know about the value of specific pieces of literature? Students had no experience for making a judgment like that, and no way of knowing how useful these important selections were. She responded, "You don't know now how valuable *The Grapes of Wrath* will be to you in the future. You have to trust that I know what I am doing by assigning it for reading and analysis. Some works of literature I assign are timeless. They have been considered important for years. Thousands of teachers have required their students to read them. *The Grapes of Wrath* has always been high on the list of required readings."

"Well, I don't know," Angelica said, thinking of how she might refute Ms. Tucker's response. She somehow had to change her mind. "You just have to take into account that some of us don't want to read it."

"Are there others who feel the same as you?"

"Yes, of course. There are a lot of us. You should ask the class. They'll tell you."

"Yes, maybe I should do that, just to see how others feel."

Ms. Tucker was stunned by Angelica's assertion. *The Grapes of Wrath* had such significant literary value that it was hard to accept the idea that students might not accept it as important. She went home that night puzzled, but determined to think through the situation and figure out a workable approach. A single sentence she read earlier in the week seemed to continually echo through her mind. "You can't make students think about what they don't want to think about." Although she thought the problem was a matter of the students' inability, she began to wonder if her observations of students being less intellectually capable in recent years had more to do with their interests and desires than their abilities. She had always believed that even though students may not have initially had an interest in good literature, she could eventually get them involved by exposing them to it. In thinking about the situation, she realized her success rate dropped over the past few years, but only with just a few students. The possibility now existed that there might be less interest than she had assumed.

The next morning she faced her first period class, Angelica included, with considerable trepidation. Not only was her belief in the value of classic literature at risk, but her whole approach to teaching as well. She had rehearsed the question she would ask her students.

"Class, I want to ask you something, and I want you to consider it very carefully. I want you to think about what I am going to ask you in terms of its value to you as members of our society, not in terms of what is particularly comfortable. As you know I have assigned a number of pieces of classical literature. I have tried, with each piece, to provide you with a good reason for reading it. I have recently decided that it may be a good idea to get input from students on this matter. I want to ask you, therefore, what you think about the specific selections. By show of hands, how many of you would prefer not to read *The Grapes of Wrath*, believing it to be inappropriate for the times in which we live?"

Ms. Tucker stared in disbelief as three-fourths of the students raised their hands. "What is it about this book that you find irrelevant?" Ms. Tucker asked.

Johnny Sayers raised his hand. "It's better to ask what *is* relevant. It doesn't fit the world we live in."

"I agree," added Gina Rousseau. "That stuff in there is from another age. We don't talk like that any more. We face a whole lot of different problems. They don't solve problems the way we do. They don't think like us."

The last remark hit a responsive tone in Ms. Tucker. The phrase "you can't make students think about things they don't want to think about" kept coming back to her, even though she knew a multitude of important lessons and timeless insights that could come from reading *The Grapes of Wrath*. It didn't matter that she could show students how these insights exactly fit them, would help them understand themselves and others better, and consequently help them be more successful in their lives. It also didn't matter that the book was in an excellent format to promote student thinking. It was a simple fact that *The Grapes of Wrath* didn't make them think. It didn't connect with their reality and consequently failed to engage them as a source of insight about social and historical realities they needed to address.

Decision Points

Consider Ms. Tucker's conclusion that "you can't make students think about things they don't want to think about." Decide whether or not her conclusion is true. Decide whether or not it is possible to get students to use specific intellectual processes to deal with information defined by teachers.

NATIONAL TEACHING STANDARDS

Teachers need to understand their subject in a way that helps them teach their students to think analytically. Teachers appreciate the fundamental role played by disciplinary thinking in developing rich, conceptual subject matter understandings. They are dedicated to teaching their students the different modes of critical thinking.

Fostering Thinking

Even with little or no parental effort to teach them, little children learn to think quite well. They have exquisitely efficient brains they use with inconspicuous competence to learn about the world, culture, social structure, and the language of the community into which they were born—mostly without any kind of formal instruction. However, once children are exposed to school they are often accused of being poor thinkers. This raises some serious questions regarding thinking and schooling. Do school experiences diminish the quality of thinking? Should we provide students experiences more like those they encounter naturally before entering school? What kind of school experiences could be tailored to fit with natural learning as an extension of those that promoted thinking skills in infancy and childhood? What is thinking anyway? Are there different kinds of thinking that require different teaching approaches? Is there anything lacking in the way people naturally think that can be supplied in school? To what extent is thinking socially determined? If teachers give students learning experiences that hamper the development of thinking, what assurance is there that deliberate efforts to teach thinking will be successful?

These and other questions have been addressed by researchers, but conclusions that can be drawn at the present time are extremely limited. However, in recent years more interest has gone toward helping children acquire more proficient thinking skills and informed judgment. Schools want students to be able to think critically, to reason, to solve problems, to interpret, and to refine ideas and apply them in creative ways. However, there is general agreement that students do not adequately learn these higher-order abilities (Resnick, 1987). Part of the problem may lie in the inability of cognitive scientists, psychologists, and educators to clearly define the nature of the higher-order thinking skills. Another difficulty may be insufficient knowledge of how to create proper learning environments for higher-level thinking and how to organize experiences that engage students in these learning processes. The school's natural environment may also be an impediment to higher-level thinking if students are conditioned to think in ways consistent with the low-level school practices to which they have been exposed.

Though it is difficult to define higher-order thinking with precision, it is generally recognized as containing the following elements:

- The path of higher-order thinking cannot be specified in advance.
- Higher-order thinking is very complex. Its direction cannot be ascertained from any single vantage point.
- Higher-order thinking often produces multiple solutions, each with positive and negative aspects.
- Higher-order thinking usually involves subtle distinctions and various interpretations.
- Higher-order thinking requires the application of multiple criteria that are often in conflict with one another.
- Higher-order thinking ordinarily involves uncertainty. Items that are related to the subject or task are not known in advance.
- Higher-order thinking requires the individual to be independent and self-regulating. Control by others interferes with the process.
- Higher-order thinking involves creating personal meaning and formulating organization out of apparent disorder.
- Higher-order thinking requires considerable effort in order to achieve the requisite elaborations and judgments (Resnick, 1987).

Research on thinking has produced more questions than answers. However, a few conclusions can be drawn from what has been learned:

- Higher-order thinking should not be reserved for more advanced or older learners. It should be infused in the entire curriculum across all grade levels.
- Higher-order thinking should not be taught in connection with special units, but rather as an integral part of each school subject.
- Good thinking depends on specific knowledge, but many aspects of powerful thinking are shared across disciplines and situations. In order to think, students need something to think about. Concepts and information in the various disciplines provide this necessary content.
- Some aspects of thinking are teachable. Students have been successfully taught to generate multiple ideas and alternative viewpoints on a particular topic, create summaries, skim, figure out word meaning from context, solve analogies and logical puzzles, and detect logical reasoning fallacies. Other more complex aspects of higher-order thinking have not been defined and researched.
- An integrated ability to learn, think, and reason and a broad disposition to engage in higher-order thinking are apparently not achieved by acquiring particular components of the thinking process. Thus, exposure to the various subcomponents of higher-level thinking do not add up to acquiring complex higher-order thinking skills.
- Thinking programs have not been broadly successful in promoting higher-level thinking.
- Current testing practices in American education fail to validly assess efforts to teach thinking and reasoning. Testing practices may in fact interfere with efforts to cultivate higher-order thinking (Resnick, 1987).

 ## *Decision Points*

Given the research on higher-order thinking, describe how you would apply this information in your teaching field.

Despite limited success in substantially improving student thinking in specified dimensions through instruction, particularly complex higher-order thinking, it is still an education goal. As research efforts continue, higher-level thinking, it is assumed, will eventually be defined in detail and that teaching protocols will be developed that specifically promote the desired level of thinking. In these efforts, accurate definitions are assumed to be possible; for children to acquire higher-level thinking proclivities, appropriate educational experiences must be provided. However, some experts believe that children are inherently able to think and don't require special instruction. Rather, children routinely need to have opportunities in a non-coercive environment to engage in problem-solving activities, utilizing the normal school subject content in the process. This is the case made by Frank Smith (1990), who takes issue with some of the conventional ideas about thinking that theorists commonly advocate applying in the schools. As you read a description of his views, make a careful analysis and be prepared to react.

NATIONAL TEACHING STANDARDS

Teachers appreciate the multiple perspectives and interpretations in each discipline and encourage students to question prevailing canons and assumptions and to think for themselves.

Teachers must possess the knowledge of the subject in order to help their students develop higher-level thinking skills.

Frank Smith's View of Thinking

In addressing thinking questions, "thinking" must not be regarded as exclusively intellectual. Thinking and learning inevitably involve feelings, and the way a person thinks may be determined in large measure by emotional or personality considerations rather than intellectual ability.

Discussions about thinking inevitably involve a plethora of terms, including words such as *analyze, categorize, classify, conceptualize, conjecture, create, deliberate, discover, examine, explain, hypothesize, imagine, infer, invent, judge, meditate, organize, postulate, predict, reason, reflect, speculate,* and *theorize,* to name just a few. Some of these terms, like *explain* and *reason,* are anchored in the substance of actual events. Others, like *fantasize, imagine,* and *theorize,* are more concerned with possibilities. All these words about thinking commonly refer to things people do, not to specific activities of their brains. Many specialists believe that each of these terms represents a distinctive brain process, and that various kinds of instruction can be invented to initiate and improve these processes. However, though these words about thinking may describe different overt behaviors, there is no evidence to support them as extensions of differentiated brain functions.

The brain, like a computer, is an information-processing device. Thus, learning refers to acquiring information that can be manipulated, stored, and recovered. However, the brain is far more than a computer; in fact, it might be considered more an artist than a machine. It constantly creates personal realities, both actual and imaginary. It examines alternatives, creates stories, and relates experiences to all its functions. It is capable of picking up an enormous amount of information in an incidental way without the individual willing it, while it explores the world and tries to make sense of it. People constantly think about what the world is like, what it might be, and even about unknown imaginary worlds. Thus, the brain examines the present in light of the past, along with images of the future. Otherwise, the world would be uncomprehensible. In addition, feelings are a focal aspect of thinking as we try to make sense of the world, avoid bewilderment, achieve satisfaction, escape frustration, and confirm our own identity as both the author and main character in the ongoing story of our lives.

Thinking is continuously going on even if we don't realize we are thinking, as in walking down the street avoiding collisions with other people, but thinking of nothing in particular. The brain never stops thinking. Lack of thinking awareness doesn't denote its absence. This *commonplace* thinking is actually quite complex. The brain routinely takes many considerations into account, including the balancing of contrary plans, purposes, and intentions, in helping the individual move toward a smooth flow of daily life. Individuals rarely do things for a single reason. Various alternatives are considered, and multiple purposes may be acted upon.

The brain has no direct contact with the outside world. Even the visual images sensed through the eyes are not like pictures. The brain simply receives neural impulses that are interpreted and integrated into already existing images. The brain itself must decide what is producing the neural impulses, and from this create the sights, sounds, and other events it perceives in the world. Consequently, the brain can be mistaken about the perceptual decisions it makes, but is usually accurate. It decides and creates so efficiently that we are seldom aware of all the thinking going on each time we receive sensory input from the environment. Our brain categorizes, classifies, and makes various inferences without our being consciously aware. Otherwise, we would be constantly confused because of the enormous bombardment of routinely received stimuli.

The brain also makes an enormous number of decisions regarding behavior we take for granted. We engage in many tasks without careful consideration, like deciding what to wear, what to eat for breakfast, and how to get to where we are going. We scarcely call upon conscious attention as the brain plans, organizes, anticipates, categorizes, chooses, infers, solves problems, determines relationships, and makes decisions, all done without general decision-making skills simply because no general class of decisions are needed. They all depend on circumstances and a personal set of values and attitudes.

Conventional wisdom states a generalized set of problem-solving skills can be taught that are applicable to all problems. However, the behavior used to solve one problem might not solve another. Some problems are technical, requiring specialized knowledge to solve. Others are social, like discovering how to work successfully with others without alienating them or determining the emotional condition of a friend in need of help. The strategies to carry out these actions are commonly sensitive and personal, and they must stem from how we perceive ourselves and others. These different kinds of problems have nothing in common, and no particular strategy could possibly solve them all. When we have difficulty solving problems, it is rarely because we don't know how to think or could not solve the problem if we had sufficient, appropriate data to consider. It is not failure to consider the nature of the problem or to reflect on possible solutions, which we routinely do anyway, but an inability to find an appropriate way to think about the problem. We usually do not know enough about the problem we are trying to solve. Thus, we lack knowledge rather than skills.

Many students are believed to be incapable of logical thinking. Consequently, they have poor thinking quality. Both beliefs are false. Everyone, even a child, can think logically. Formal logic, however, is not a particularly good way to think. We all have a more natural way. Humans use their values and common sense to override logic; this is the way the brain works. If we reach a conclusion that we think is undesirable, we change the premises, or we manufacture a more acceptable conclusion. We don't think logically like a computer, which is precisely why computers cannot be trusted like humans. They do not have values and common sense. They do not make adjustments to accommodate value considerations, and thus they cannot be kept from drawing absurd conclusions at times. Sense interferes with logical reasoning. In thinking, conclusions may be reached that other people might dispute, not because logic was not exercised but because there are different points of view, as evidenced by the persistence of so many profound religious, political, and scientific controversies among people with impeccable intellectual qualifications and manifest goodwill.

Sometimes the term *higher-order thinking* is used to describe a kind of thinking that is presumably well above ordinary thought. A limited number of individuals are assumed to be capable of reaching elevated levels of thought, but not without great effort and painstaking instruction. On the contrary, however, people in general are capable of all levels of thinking, which they routinely engage in. Higher-order thinking is commonplace. It is said to consist of planning, predicting, monitoring, evaluating, and questioning. Yet, we engage in this kind of thinking every moment of our lives. In addition, we consistently evaluate the consequences of our own thinking as well as the thinking of other people.

A distinction is currently made between cognitive and metacognitive reasoning. Metacognitive thought involves thinking about thinking: the process of monitoring, reviewing, reflecting, and revising thinking skills. Observing and controlling one's own thought processes is thought to be a superior mode of thinking, although one not practiced by many people because they have not learned how. However, we cannot observe our own thought processes. We are not aware of them, and thus they cannot be inspected. In a fundamental sense, thinking is a neurological and chemical process that is not presently accessible for study and analysis. When our thinking appears deficient because we are unable to solve a problem to our satisfaction, reflecting on our thought processes and making improvements in our thinking skills will not suffice. The difficulty is that we do not properly understand what needs to be done, not that we lack thinking skills. In addition, we may not be paying enough attention to the details surrounding a problem, or we may lack the disposition to properly deal with the problem in the particular circumstances.

Two fundamental requirements are needed for easy thinking. First, the individual needs to know what he or she is thinking about. Applicable knowledge is indispensable. Unfortunately, in some educational situations students are considered to be inadequate thinkers when in fact they simply lack information. Second, effective thinking requires that the brain be in charge. Thinking becomes difficult when it is contrived, as it commonly is in educational settings with teacher-imposed topics or tasks. The most difficult kind of thinking is that imposed on us by someone else.

A distinction must be made between private and social thinking. Private thought is rooted in our own intentions, values, considerations, and desires, not to mention fantasies. During private thinking our thoughts can range without being affected by other people's possible reactions. Social thinking contains more constraints. Other people influence how we think. They evaluate the consequences of our thinking, distract our purposes, and may perceive faulty thinking we are unaware of. Thus, when others evaluate our thinking, value judgments are often made that are contrary to personal commonplace thinking. When thinking mistakes are made, it is usually because the individual is using inaccurate or inappropriate data. Often the individual strongly believes these inaccuracies to be correct. It is not an easy matter to persuade the individual that his or her ideas are different from the perceptions of others, or that those with a different point of view are not necessarily wrong.

Thinking is normally a concealed process. It is commonplace, but usually effective and effortless. However, thinking the way others direct is difficult. The individual is asked to provide explanations about things he or she did not reflect on in the first place or map out a route in decision making that he or she has never pursued. Thinking is not a set of skills acquired through instruction; it is natural, based on experience, and enhanced through an understanding of particular subjects. Not everyone is an equally proficient thinker, as there are differences. However, when we think badly, it is ordinarily due to our own particular experiences, values, or dispositions, rather than a lack of essential ability to think.

Remembering information is one of schooling's primary requirements. Students are ordinarily drilled or drill themselves using various mnemonic devices to aid recall. However, remembering is easy when it is not the primary activity. Remembering is greatly aided when it accompanies a meaningful activity and when the brain is allowed its full potential. Remembering is difficult when the learning experience is contrived by someone else. Similarly, we are able to understand many things, without difficulty, as part of our normal flow of events when we can make sense of our actions. In education, if students are studying things unrelatable to their existing knowledge and interests, then comprehension is inevitably difficult. When students are diagnosed with comprehension problems, it indicates the school's failure to incorporate students' experience into instruction, not any intellectual deficiency on the student's part.

Learning doesn't require teachers to motivate their students. Learning is so natural that children are uncomfortable and restless when they are unable to learn. Most of the time learning occurs without conscious knowledge or intention. It is an educational invention that learning is sporadic, difficult, and effortful, requiring special motivation, incentives, and rewards. However, such artificial motivation seems necessary when learning is meaningless for the learner.

Imagining is another process the brain continually engages in. It doesn't represent an escape from reality, nor is it a waste of time. Rather than providing an escape from reality, imagination makes reality possible. It is the brain's way of forming mental concepts, actions, and events beyond what is actually present to the senses. Imagination is the creation of possible realities that can later be assessed and framed into real intentions and actions. The brain does not react or respond to the world; it creates the world. The form and substance of whatever is perceived comes from the brain. The senses transmit basic neurological impulses, but the brain creates the images, composes the sounds, and shapes the substances that we feel. We view the present in conjunction with perspectives from the past and images of the future. Like the past and future, the present is a product of our imagination. Thus, we would not have reality without fantasy. Reality is a fantasy that works within our world. We could not function without imagination; it is at the center of all we do.

Imagination is obviously not a process on which we deliberately focus our attention: It is a natural, fundamental condition of the brain. In fact, when we relax our attention, fantasy takes over and creates the images that provide the options we consider and act upon. Imagination is the dynamo of the brain, the source of our creativeness and intellectual inventiveness. As long as the imagination is intact, we remember, understand, learn, and think smoothly and efficiently, so long as it is not restrained and coerced into focusing on meaningless tasks.

Each person's thinking takes its own track. One person may, for example, instantly detect racist or sexist bias in anything he or she sees or hears. Another person may be totally insensitive to such concerns, but may immediately react to an attack on his or her personal chauvinism or political beliefs. All of us tend to be sensitive to the intentions and expectations of others and ready to consider various alternatives. We don't have to be taught how to engage in thought. However, if we seem unable to detect bias in others or understand their fallacies or manipulative behavior, it may be because the fallacies or manipulations of others correspond to the biases, fallacies, and manipulative inclinations we already have. The development of thinking depends on the way we perceive ourselves, which in turn depends on the way other people treat us.

Our thinking depends on the company we keep. Students become thinkers when they associate with thinking people, both their teachers and people they meet through their reading. Teachers should demonstrate the power and possibilities of thought in all they do, and should never engage their students in meaningless, thoughtless activity. Two characteristics of schools and classrooms exist in which useful thinking is facilitated. The first is *interest*. Thinking cannot be effectively and efficiently applied to boring, purposeless tasks, nor can anything worthwhile be learned from such activity. The second characteristic of effective classrooms is *respect*. There must be respect between students and their teachers. This allows

TABLE 8.1 *A Summary of Smith's Conception of Thinking.*

- In thinking, we examine the present in light of the past, along with images of the future.
- The brain takes many considerations into account and makes many decisions without conscious awareness.
- The brain depends on perceptions. It cannot interact with the world on its own.
- Thinking is personal and depends on circumstances and values rather than logic.
- People routinely engage in higher-order thinking. You don't have to be taught to do it.
- Deficiencies in thinking are really situations where the individual doesn't have adequate information, rather than some inherent inability.
- Students do not do well regarding thinking tasks imposed on them by teachers.
- Instruction is not required to learn how to think.

teachers and students to become partners in learning and empowers students to become both independent and cooperative, rather than dependent, submissive, and resentful (Smith, 1990) (see Table 8.1).

QUESTIONS FOR REFLECTION

1. What do you accept or reject about Frank Smith's description of thinking? Explain why.

2. If you have a different explanation of how thinking takes place, compare it to Smith's description and defend your position.

Decision Points

With a group of peers, present your personal ideas about Frank Smith's views of thinking. As a group, determine points of agreement and disagreement. Defend your ideas.

Creating an Environment for Thinking

Smith's description of the thinking process suggests a remarkably different context for learning than that characteristic of many school experiences. His concept of brain function is consistent with the view of constructivist learning theorists. From this perspective, learners frame their own conceptions of the world, which they are reluctant to alter except through their own efforts to gain understanding. Thus, the brain does not simply absorb transmitted information. It discriminates about what it receives and retains, and is active not only in constructing knowledge, but in seeking out what it will accept as valid. The brain naturally searches and makes inquiries about questions that are personally interesting. It is unnatural to have others frame the questions and provide the information for learning.

What kind of a learning environment is consistent with how the brain functions? First, teachers should model thinking, which can be appropriately done in interactions with their students, in shared learning, and in connection with ongoing projects. Science teachers should routinely conduct research in science that involves at least some of their students. English teachers might be involved in a joint writing project. Social studies teachers might engage in studies of demographics or other appropriate topics. Conversations with students that occur as part of these experiences can provide a stimulus to student thinking.

Second, the physical arrangement of the class should be conducive to student interaction. Seating should be arranged to foster discussion rather than lectures. There should also be interesting objects in the room that stimulate questioning by students, and places should be provided for students to conduct their research. There might also be examples of student research displayed.

Third, classroom interactions should involve information processing, rather than information reception and recall. Students should be encouraged to pose questions and identify problems with personal relevance. They should be allowed to pursue their interests through researching and presenting the results of their studies to other class members. During classroom interactions, students should continuously seek to locate and verify information, identify alternative points of view, search for hidden assumptions, and determine a wide variety of possible explanations. In a thinking classroom, students are encouraged to dissect, reflect on, and modify what they read, hear, see, or feel and to give it new meaning.

Fourth, teachers should use precise language about thinking and encourage their students to do the same. Instead of asking a student to "tell" what will happen in a given set of circumstances, the student should be asked to "predict" what will happen. Instead of asking students to "explain" what a given set of data indicate, they should be asked what "conclusions" can be drawn from the data. Using terms like *hypothesis*, *theory*, *argument*, *evidence*, *inference*, and *assumption* helps to frame thinking more precisely and encourages students to make appropriate distinctions between different kinds of thinking activities.

Fifth, classrooms should be organized around thoughtful questions and inquiry. Inquiry activities should be developed around questions that students find personally meaningful and relevant. The questions investigated should also be consistent with the course of study. Skillful teachers create conditions and provide input that will help students find meaningful questions that are basic to the course of study. It is useful for students to investigate questions for which there is no single answer and for which no single process for finding answers is evident (Beyer, 1992).

Quality thinking is intentional, efficiently carried out, consistent, deep, and productive (Nickerson, 1989). Costa (1984) identifies four classroom practices that can significantly improve thinking:

- having a thoughtful learning environment
- having students clearly see and hear descriptions of the cognitive operations they are trying to improve
- providing guidance and support for student's initial efforts to carry out thinking operations until they can carry them out on their own initiative and in self-directed ways
- providing students something worth thinking about

A thoughtful learning environment is one in which teachers provide frequent occasions for deep and personal thought. Adequate time should be set aside to engage in meaningful projects. Thinking should not be hurried.

Students should monitor their own thinking, carefully checking for unsupported assumptions and various kinds of inconsistencies. Students may benefit from seeing how others deal with similar activities so they can compare their own processes and correct possible flaws.

When students engage in thinking about new or difficult ideas, they may be reluctant to proceed without support. They may also need to be cued in the beginning to focus on important aspects of a particular project or inconsistencies in their thinking. Eventually, they should be able to be self-supporting and independent.

Finally, students must consider what they are learning about to be worthwhile, meaningful, and useful. Providing students opportunities to engage in personally meaningful learning enhances their motivation and provides a favorable environment in which to improve thinking and learning.

 ## *Decision Points*

Visualize yourself as a teacher in a typical public school classroom. Describe a classroom environment you might create to foster thinking.

NATIONAL TEACHING STANDARDS

Teachers can create learning activities of the structured type as well as inductive learning. By teaching inductively, they are able to encourage students to solve problems, determine patterns, work through alternative solutions, and make comparisons between their own solutions and those obtained by others.

Problem Solving in Learning Communities

Learning communities are highly conducive to thinking, particularly because they provide many problem-solving opportunities. Solving problems in learning communities is substantially different than the problem-solving experiences students commonly have in the schools. Problems are ordinarily defined by teachers, and "right answers" are sought. The problems selected may or may not have relevance for students. In learning communities, problems as well as problem-solving strategies are determined interactively by students and their teachers. The problems chosen are characterized by their relevance and their current importance to students. Thus, it is not just relevance that determines whether or not a problem will receive the attention of the group; the problem must also have a higher priority than other considerations. Obviously, many problems exist to which students may devote their efforts. However, working on a problem in preference to one that has greater importance to the students creates the impression that problem selection is arbitrary and out of students' control. It also undermines the students' confidence in their teachers by acknowledging the teachers' lack of sensitivity and judgment.

How can teachers create a problem identification process that helps students determine significant problems for which they will have an interest without giving the impression that the teacher is being unnecessarily controlling? Students probably won't have carefully thought through possible problems for the learning community to address. Teachers usually have this role. Students will have had very little experience formulating worthwhile questions to investigate. Because these conditions exist in many classrooms, teachers may find it necessary to help students formulate their own questions and identify meaningful problems to solve. This involves a deprogramming process, particularly for students who have experienced considerable success doggedly following teacher directions. These students may feel unsure of themselves, especially when their previous success depended on careful adherence to teacher expectations.

They must acquire confidence that they can, in fact, create meaningful experiences for themselves and that the rules for this kind of effort won't change "midstream." They must be assured that their questions and problems are considered legitimate, and that their sense of well-being will not be threatened by these new procedures. In addition, these students will require some time to get used to new procedures and orientations. Some may have little confidence in themselves. They need continued reassurance and eventual acknowledgment that learning can be personally meaningful, academically significant, and socially acceptable.

The process of problem selection may need to be modified as students become more adept at defining legitimate problems and associated learning. In the beginning, teachers may need to provide a list of appropriate problems and have students discuss which has the most personal viability. Students will discover that learning communities possess flexibility and an atmosphere of love and acceptance. They may have to learn skills of courtesy and patience while trying to promote a course of action they believe is important to the group and essential to themselves. Eventually, students can be grouped and asked to initiate the process of problem selection; with experience, they can identify valid group problems with a high priority. In addition, they will gradually need to assume a variety of roles for problem solving, which can occasionally be rotated to provide all group members an opportunity to develop a full range of skills.

The Role of Inquiry

Problem solving in learning communities should be inquiry oriented. This involves creating questions and initiating research designed to obtain valid answers to questions and powerful solutions to problems. Students must recognize the possible hazards of drawing invalid conclusions. Confounding variables need to be recognized and control exercised in designing research and collecting data. In the beginning, teachers can ask strategic questions to model the way students should approach inquiry-oriented research. However, students eventually need to routinely generate their own questions. Inquiry learning is natural for children early in life, albeit a kind of inquiry with little formal control. The inquiry orientation of little children is born of curiosity and imagination. Excessive control in school can crush a child's curiosity. Teachers may find it necessary to reignite students' curiosity to support group inquiry learning. Repeatedly going through the inquiry process can do much to stimulate students' imaginations.

The Search for Meaning

The inquiry process is born of each individual's need to acquire meaning. Meaningfulness can be pursued in a number of ways. First, students may want to learn in order to accomplish something they desire. They may plan to use knowledge in a utilitarian way: for example, a student may want to learn to write poetry to impress a boyfriend or girlfriend. Many students learn in order to prepare themselves for college entrance examinations. Students may apply themselves in an auto mechanics class to better maintain their car if they eventually hope to pursue a career in auto mechanics.

The desire to acquire meaning may also come from curiosity. Sometimes children are driven without a particular end in mind. The process itself is meaningful. A sense of accomplishment is achieved through self-direction. There is a fulfillment associated with the free exercise of curiosity.

Achieving a meaningful understanding of something also drives inquiry. Humans inherently seek understanding so they can see how things work and how their own lives can be fit within the whole. Everyone looks upon the world and wonders why things are the way they are. Little children wonder why the moon seems to follow them as they travel in an automobile. They wonder why insects have six legs and spiders have eight, why the sky is blue, where the rainbow comes from, where the sun goes at night, how a plant can grow from a seed, how a worm gets into an apple, where butterflies come from, or why their pet hamster died. They want explanations about these things and many others. Children seem driven to find out answers to their questions by asking others or by conducting primitive experiments. Little children thrust objects into their mouths, bounce them, or throw them across the room. These actions may be done repeatedly until the children achieve a satisfactory degree of understanding, and then they go on to other things. In adolescence, the quest for understanding continues. Often it shifts to the social arena, where understanding personalities and interpersonal interactions helps children discern what is needed to successfully relate to others. Many times the fulfillment is just in the knowing.

Schooling is meaningful if it provides for personal needs apart from satisfying one's thirst for knowledge or allowing one to act upon personal curiosity. Students have needs for self-direction, freedom, and fun, and they need to be involved in caring relationships. They consider school experiences that provide satisfaction of these needs to be meaningful. Traditional schools often fail to provide experiences that supply this kind of meaning for students. Learning communities, however, have the potential to supply all of them and thus create a more personally meaningful learning experience for students.

Igniting Imagination

Imagination is often viewed as a threat to legitimate instruction by teachers. Daydreaming is thought to be irresponsible, an effort to avoid the appropriate learning opportunities arranged by the teacher. Some teachers consider daydreaming to be a deliberate affront. At the very least, teachers consider daydreaming as an escape tactic students use to avoid their learning responsibilities. In a more extreme sense, teachers may consider such behavior a learning impediment and label the guilty student as defective. However, imagination is legitimately unquestioned as the normal activity of a healthy brain and as the basis upon which one's concept of reality is created (Smith, 1990). Imagination creates the useful alternatives that humans can later analyze and act upon. Without imagination there would be far fewer alternatives to consider in solving problems. The brain creates these alternatives and provides the conceptions needed to form unique and useful understandings and problem solutions. Students must therefore be allowed to engage their imagination and act upon these experiences. They should be encouraged to bring up potentially divergent views in meetings with their cooperative learning group. The group should be taught to be sensitive to these initiatives and provide support so that the imaginations of all group members can be stimulated, not repressed.

Though the brain engages in imagination without being exposed to specific educational experiences, teachers can promote this process to some degree. First, teachers should help students understand the legitimacy of their imaginations. Teachers can also provide experiences designed to promote greater divergent thinking. For example, a biology teacher might ask students what might have happened if dinosaurs had not gone extinct or what would happen if no animals or plants became extinct. A social studies teacher might ask students what kind of social practices exist in a society with no families. A history teacher might ask about the likely result of having a single religion and form of government worldwide. Such questions help promote thinking without normal constraints. Students can be helped to think more divergently and creatively.

 ## QUESTION FOR REFLECTION

1. What would you do with a student who daydreams a lot in your class and routinely fails to complete assignments?

Empowerment Through Reflection

Just as teachers can improve their practice through reflection, students can achieve a greater sense of empowerment by reflecting on life in a learning community. Students need time for thoughtful consideration of their school experiences and reflection on ways they can achieve greater excellence. A number of focal points exist to help students examine essential education elements. One of these is school culture. Just as teachers need to know the cultural influences on the instructional program, students must deal with the impact of the school culture on them, and they should use this knowledge to get the most out of their school experiences. For instance, students might think of how responsibility relates to the development of personal autonomy.

Students can also be encouraged to reflect on their own learning processes and preferences. They may be asked to examine what they learn in terms of its personal long- and short-term usefulness. They could also be asked to consider personal versus group needs. Students who have carefully thought about how they learn can skillfully determine the most valuable school experiences.

Most students try to achieve greater self-understanding. If students understand their needs and are capable of ascertaining both appropriate and inappropriate need-satisfaction strategies, along with the ability to make good behavior choices, they can create a more need-satisfying, problem-free life. Many of the problems students experience in school have to do with inappropriate choices regarding how to best satisfy their needs. Students often do not understand how to modify their behavior to avoid unpleasant consequences. Being thoughtful about these matters can greatly enhance student satisfaction in school, so long as reasonable student behavior is not thwarted by unnecessary teacher control.

Students must learn to successfully interact with their teachers and other students. Interaction involves understanding others' needs as well as recognizing teachers' responsibility to initiate and carry forth a viable educational program in their classrooms. Students who reflect on the quality of their social interactions can find ways to successfully relate to other class members and create learning opportunities that may help achieve personal as well as group desires.

NATIONAL TEACHING STANDARDS

Teachers must know how to employ teaching and learning through cooperative learning groups.

Cooperative Learning

Teachers have the choice of providing their students either competitive or **cooperative learning** opportunities, or a combination of both. Some experts suggest a combination of competitive and cooperative learning, along with independent learning experiences. Competitive learning is reserved for those activities having limited consequences related to students' grades (Johnson & Johnson, 1994). Most schooling is competitive rather than cooperative. Students are expected to demonstrate what they can independently achieve. Evaluation is, therefore, a private matter, as is most instruction. Instructional privacy is commonly orchestrated by teachers to prevent students from breaking rules and disrupting procedures. Teachers' experience suggests that when students work together their social desires, which have been suppressed by rules and sanctions, suddenly emerge. If satisfaction of social needs was an integral part of the initial teaching strategy, fewer student discipline problems would be experienced.

Sometimes the "doctrine of fairness" influences how teachers feel about cooperative learning activities. In cooperative learning, students perform different tasks at different levels and yet may share the same grade. To be fair, students should have equivalent learning opportunities and assessments. However, fairness requires teachers to provide instruction and assessments consistent with student capabilities and interests.

Cooperative learning helps satisfy students' social needs as well as encouraging achievement.

A number of myths exist regarding competition that are generally accepted in society (Kohn, 1992), including the following:

- Competition is an unavoidable fact of life. It is part of human nature.
- Competition motivates us to do our best. We would cease being productive if we didn't compete.
- Contests provide the best, if not the only way to have a good time.
- Competition builds character and promotes self-confidence.

Competition is not inherent. In contrast, a cooperative inclination has been found, even among toddlers (Yarrow, Scott, & Waxler, 1973). In society, survival demands that individuals work with, rather than against, one another. Even when competition does exist, it is superficial and superimposed on an essential mutual interdependence.

The wide acceptance of competition as a motivator is startling. Schools follow this thinking when teachers administer competitive examinations and grade students based on a normal curve. Supposedly, this motivates children. However, only high-scoring students are motivated by grades. In a meta-analysis of studies comparing competition versus cooperation, cooperation was found to be a far more potent motivator (Johnson, Maruyama, Johnson, Nelson, & Skoin, 1981). Even in sports, where competition is assumed to be essential, a focus on victory reduces the level of performance. Apparently, concerns regarding winning distracts the individual's attention from achieving excellence (Johnson, 1979).

Competition also fails to achieve the assumed benefit of promoting self-confidence and character development. During competition, one's self-esteem depends on the uncertain outcome of the contest. Losing in a competition is a particularly noxious form of failure because it conveys a message of relative inferiority and typically exposes the individual to public judgment and shame (Kohn, 1992).

Winners may experience enjoyment in a contest, but losers seldom do. Consequently, the enjoyment of competition is a relative thing. Competition always produces losers; otherwise, there could not be a winner. In some contests, like tennis, winning depends on competitors forcing their opponent to make errors. Often contests have many participants but only one winner. Therefore, there may be more unhappy than happy competitors. This is paradoxical in school where we prefer that students love learning. Competition may well drive out the love of learning, at least the school kind, for many students.

Not only do cooperative learning opportunities provide students experiences that avoid competition difficulties, but they also give students a chance to develop their social skills and cooperation roles needed in employment situations. Cooperation is more useful than competition in many occupations, since individuals have to work successfully with one another to complete projects or increase production.

A number of cooperative learning strategies exist that schools use to increase cooperative skills and provide students with an option to competitive learning. The particular strategy recommended depends on instructional purposes. Jigsaw II and Original Jigsaw's emphasis is on mastering subject content. Teams-Games-Tournaments and Student Teams Achievement Divisions have a similar purpose, but with student teams competing against one another. Thus, team members cooperate *with* one another, but *against* a team of opponents. Co-op Co-op emphasizes student self-direction. Students are able to select a topic among several offered and divide the research up among team members. Finally, Student-Directed Cooperative Learning not only provides students the opportunity to select any topic within a general subject to study, but also allows students to choose who they work with on their project (see Table 8.2).

Jigsaw II

In *Jigsaw II*, students work in heterogeneous teacher-designated teams to master the content of printed materials. Team members are given "expert sheets" that list different topics on which to focus. The topics cover themes that appear throughout the material. After all students read the material, each team member is given an aspect of the topic on which to become an "expert." An "expert group" is formed for each aspect, and the "experts" (one from each group) meet to discuss their area of expertise. The expert groups then break up, the original teams get together, and the "expert" for each topic teaches group members. When teams are confident they are prepared, they receive quizzes that cover all the material. Individual scores are added together and become team scores. Individual improvement scores can also be given to encourage students to help one another improve. Students on high-scoring teams may receive certificates (Slaven, 1986).

TABLE 8.2 *Comparisons Between Cooperative Learning Models.*

Model	Purpose	Source of Information	Student Activity
Jigsaw II	Master material	Teacher	Instruction, drill, and testing
Original Jigsaw	Master material	Other students	Instruction, drill, and testing
Co-op Co-op	Acquire information on specified topics	Cooperative student research and instruction	Independent research, group synthesis, and reporting
Student Teams Achievement Divisions	Master material	Teacher	Instruction, drill, and testing
Teams-Games-Tournaments	Master material	Teacher	Instruction, drill, and public tournament
Learning Together	Develop research and production skills	Cooperative student research and instruction	Group research and reporting
Student-Directed Cooperative Learning	Promote inquiry skills in a cooperative learning format	Students	Students select group membership, engage in independent research, synthesize and report results

Original Jigsaw

Some significant differences exist between Jigsaw II and *Original Jigsaw*. In Original Jigsaw, each student reads a different section of the material, making him or her the possessor of unique information unknown to other team members. This person provides access to the desired information. Each individual has less to read in Original Jigsaw, but because students may get an insufficient background and less–than-optimum benefit in the subject, this can be a disadvantage.

In Original Jigsaw, less use is made of quizzes. In addition, team scores and improvement scores are not used. Students are instead given grades based on individual achievement. The achievements of high-scoring students are not recognized (Aronson, Blaney, Stephan, Sikes, & Snapp, 1978).

Co-op Co-op

In *Co-op Co-op*, students may locate their own materials and share them with the rest of the class. Students are first exposed to lectures, readings, and other materials designed to ignite their curiosity. Once they are interested in a topic, team building begins. Students are assigned to heterogeneous four- or five–member groups and then involved in various activities to stimulate group cohesiveness.

After teams begin working successfully together, they are allowed to select a topic of common interest. Students select a topic they believe is of interest to the whole class after carefully discussing various possiblities. The teacher interacts with each group during this process to ensure that viable topics are selected and that there are no duplicate selections among groups. Each group member then selects a mini-topic for detailed study. Each mini-topic should provide a unique contribution to the group.

Once students determine their mini-topics, they work individually on assembling information on various aspects of their mini-topics. This may involve library research, data gathering, experimentation, or the creation of tangible products like written papers, paintings, or models. As soon as individuals complete their individual work, they present their findings to their team. From these presentations, the team formulates a plan to instruct the whole class. They must fit the different mini-topics together into a coherent team presentation. As the group tries to link the various mini-topics together, a need may exist for further research and added deliberation. Once a plan has been finalized, group members are each assigned a role in the presentation. In the end, each member of the group should not simply present a mini-topic; a well-organized, carefully structured presentation should be arranged. Each group member should have a role in the presentation. Ideally, lectures should be avoided; students may instead create displays and demonstrations, act out skits, or lead class discussions to help classmates learn the topic. If the topic is controversial, group members might well engage in a class debate. Following each presentation, the class should engage in a question-and-answer session to solidify understanding and address ideas or concepts that need further consideration. This may lead to follow-up activities for long-term learning and research.

The final step is to evaluate the team presentations. Three levels exist on which evaluation may take place:

- Team presentations can be assessed by the whole class. This might be in the form of an evaluation rubric.
- Individual team member contributions can be evaluated by teammates. This is particularly useful in determining the extent to which all team members responsibly applied themselves to the project.
- Each individual's learning can be evaluated by the teacher. The data to create this kind of evaluation may be extracted by the teacher from the group reports (Kagan, 1985).

Student Teams Achievement Divisions

In *Student Teams Achievement Divisions* (STAD), students are assigned to four-member teams by the teacher. Teams are mixed in gender and ethnicity, and matched to other teams in levels of achievement as closely as possible. The class is then provided instruction, discussions, assignments, and worksheets. Students faithfully record what they are taught, study the material together, and quiz one another until they feel prepared to take a test. Each student is tested without help from team members. Team scores are posted, with awards such as special privileges, free time, or recognition in a newsletter or on the bulletin board given to the highest-scoring team.

STAD is organized so that each team member can earn up to 10 points for the team. A 30-item test is given to determine student proficiency. On each test, students are given one team point for each point they score above their previous test average. For example, a student with an average of 20 who scores 25 would get five team points.

The composition of teams may be changed periodically so that class members have an opportunity to work with other students. However, teachers should exercise caution in changing team membership. After teams have achieved cohesiveness, they may experience displeasure about being broken up. Competition between teams may leave team members unable to successfully work with students they have formerly competed against.

Teams-Games-Tournaments

Teams-Games-Tournaments (*TGT*) is similar to STAD except that weekly tournaments replace achievement tests. As with STAD, students are given regular instruction and assignments and drill one another for a period of time in preparation for the tournament. The tournament is usually in the form of a TV quiz show. Questions are written on cards and placed on the tournament table where three students compete against one another. Students take turns choosing cards and answering questions. When the tournament is concluded, all scores are added up and the winning team receives special recognition. Students compete against individuals from other teams who are at their own achievement level. Since achievement levels are subject to change from week to week, the teacher tries to match competing students in terms of the previous week's results. The winners at each tournament table win 60 points for their team regardless of the achievement level of the participants. Low-achieving students can thus have as great an impact on team scores as students at higher levels.

Teams usually stay together for about six weeks. During this time, the team that accumulates the greatest number of points receives an overall award or recognition. Because working on a team solidifies relationships, teachers should be sensitive to the problems associated with splitting teams up. Notify teams in advance that they will eventually be split up to help prepare students (DeVries, Edwards, & Slaven, 1978).

Student-Directed Cooperative Learning

Cooperative learning models are differentiated primarily on the nature of the evaluation procedures, provision for student autonomy, incorporation of intergroup competition, nature of the materials studied, and roles of group members. *Student-Directed Cooperative Learning* has some similarities to other cooperative learning models, but is significantly different from others in the degree of student autonomy offered. Because students are allowed to make learning decisions, they come to class prepared to declare a topic of interest by writing it beside their name on the chalkboard. All class members are asked to study the topics listed on the chalkboard, compare them with their own, and form groups of five members by negotiating with classmates. Some students may see a topic listed that they prefer to study more than their own. They have to weigh the merits of various suggested topics along with deciding on a work group. Negotiation for topics and group membership continues until study groups of five members have been created, with each group prepared to study one topic.

Once groups are formed, students are free to study whatever topic materials they wish. They break their topics into subareas, and each student selects an area for independent study. He or she will then pass this knowledge on to group members. Learning thoroughness is promoted since the individual responsible for study in a particular area is the only source of information on that topic. Once individual learning is done, the group needs to decide exactly how they can teach the whole class. The group creates an organized teaching episode so they can teach classmates the most important aspects of what they have learned. Teams are encouraged to use nontraditional formats for teaching the entire class, such as demonstrations, class participation experiences, and the like, rather than lectures.

Each group determines how it wants its work evaluated. The group can, for example, have their teacher and/or classmates involved in various forms of assessment. Intragroup evaluation is encouraged, particularly as it relates to how responsible participants were in carrying out their part of the project. Self-evaluation can also be employed. The actual group presentation can also be assessed by the teacher, by class members, or by both. The knowledge of all class members can be determined through examinations if this seems desirable, or each individual student may prepare a paper about what he or she learned.

 ## Decision Points

Imagine you are a teacher in the public schools. Examine the subject you teach and describe a learning situation in which each of the cooperative learning models might best be used and explain why. Take into consideration the different learning styles of students.

NATIONAL TEACHING STANDARDS

Teachers need to help students achieve a true understanding of their subject. This involves moving far beyond the rote memorization of facts. It means learning to think in a nonlinear way, approaching issues from different angles, weighing multiple criteria, and considering multiple solutions. Thus, knowledge is a combination of skills, dispositions, propositions, and integrated beliefs that are flexible, elaborate, and deep. Furthermore, understanding involves the teacher's or student's ability to apply such knowledge to problems never before encountered.

Affective Growth in Learning Communities

Affective goals are just as important in school as cognitive ones, perhaps more, because student attitudes and values shape them as learners and help establish their aspirations. Affective goals should be promoted in connection with cognitive objectives because they provide the impetus to drive the acquisition of cognitive information and skills. Students need reasons to pursue cognitive development. Affective goals provide the necessary direction and commitment for such accomplishments. Affective goals should, therefore, be attached to cognitive pursuits to provide students a potent reason for learning.

Determining Affective Purposes

A number of important values exist that should be supported in connection with student learning. Chief among these is the value for learning itself. Learning should be valued for the personal fulfillment that one acquires, as well as the goals he or she achieves. Learning can be seen as an instrument for mastering current endeavors and bringing future possibilities to fruition. Learning is an essential part of human nature, and thwarting the natural process of learning leaves individuals unfulfilled. Humans seem compelled to investigate and examine the world around them, and to acquire sufficient understanding of it to serve their idiosyncratic purposes. Understanding just for the sake of understanding also appears highly motivating.

Lifelong learning should be valued in school. School experiences should provide the desire and means to pursue meaningful learning for a lifetime. Because books are an important source of information, students should value them and become avid readers. Unfortunately, many students not only leave school unable to read successfully, but with a negative attitude toward books.

Learners should receive assistance in perfecting the natural inquiry process. Natural curiosity drives the inquiry process, and school can help students formalize inquiry so that valid information is acquired in this process. Students can learn to value the inquiry process when careful attention is given to formulating questions and hypotheses as well as creating means for collecting valid data and drawing appropriate conclusions.

Students should value their role in learning communities, both for what they can receive from others and for what they can give. The give and take of learning communities provide students a greater sense of life in a world full of communities, along with the skills to be successful in their interpersonal interactions and group endeavors. Students should value the more-enhanced understanding possible through interpersonal interactions during the learning process.

Strategies for Promoting Affective Growth in Learning Communities

An appreciation of personal affective growth can best be realized by actively pursuing the desired goals. For example, to love learning one must be involved in the kind of learning students can honestly appreciate. Students are more likely to value self-directed learning than unnatural learning sequences planned by others. Learning in unnatural ways to achieve what is unwanted is a double "turn off." However, children will not, and probably should not, be allowed to determine all their learning curriculum without input from their teachers. Strategically, this means that learning activities generated within a learning community require teachers' knowledge and experience to help students see the implications for proposed learning projects and ascertain promising research directions. In this process, teachers must avoid the kind of controlling behaviors that may turn students off. Exactly how this process should proceed cannot be specified. Principles can be applied, however, that ensure success. Teachers learn what to do, both from experience and from plying their skills with each new group of students. Thus, autonomy is extended to students in concert with their developing responsibility. Students are empowered to choose their own learning experiences as the validity of their choices and the diligence of their efforts improve. However, these conditions are not presented to students as qualifying capabilities required before they are allowed opportunities for self-determination. Rather, these attributes are assumed to gradually develop as students receive more and more opportunities for self-regulation.

It is also strategically important to involve students in conversations about the value of learning communities and the inquiry processes employed there. Comparisons can be made regarding the quality of learning in learning communities versus other learning arrangements. Cognitively processing values helps students understand values in a more comprehensive, complete sense, allowing them to achieve greater commitment for what they are doing and greater facility to explain it to others. They can begin to understand that their group learning efforts are justifiable and defensible. Consequently, students can be expected to apply themselves more conscientiously and achieve higher levels of excellence in their school work.

Students also need an opportunity to discuss the value of their knowledge. If what is learned truly serves important student purposes, it will be valued. In addition, with self-directed learning, accountability can be encouraged. Students also need to process the results of their studies in order to apply their knowledge to new projects. When students genuinely value what they have learned, they are more likely to value the learning process and be inclined to make improvements.

Decision Points

Describe specifically what you could do in your subject area to help students achieve greater affective growth.

NATIONAL TEACHING STANDARDS

Teachers know when to apply various instructional options depending on certain students and groups. Strategies involve the use of an elegant web of alternative activities in which students are engaged with content: sometimes with the teacher, sometimes with each other, and sometimes alone.

Instructional Methods in Learning Communities

A variety of methods may be used in learning communities, even though the primary approach to learning is inquiry. These other methods are primarily used in conjunction with inquiry-based learning projects. Teachers may decide to use various methods to support the inquiry experiences of student learning groups or to provide whole class learning activities as needed. A teacher may, for example, conclude that students in all learning groups need to understand how to create better relationships. A class discussion may help with this objective.

Discussions

Discussion is one of the most used instructional methods. Teachers can choose different discussion formats depending on their purposes. If a teacher wishes to exercise considerable control over the content, a *guided discussion* format may be used. Students are usually guided through a series of questions that lead them to understand a principle, formula, relationship, or other predetermined result. With this kind of discussion, student thinking can be monitored and directed toward specific thinking processes as students are led to a common understanding or conclusion. To prepare for conducting a guided discussion, teachers should create a series of questions used to direct student thinking. At the beginning of the discussion students should be informed that a particular conclusion or understanding is being sought.

At times teachers are more interested in helping students develop intellectual skills than in arriving at a conclusion or understanding. If they want students to find alternative explanations of a specific phenomenon, solve problems, or classify concepts and ideas, a *reflective discussion* would be ideal. In a reflective discussion, the teacher defines a particular problem and then initiates a discussion with open-ended questions. Students need sufficient thinking time during a reflective discussion. Incredibly, the average response time teachers give students after questions is a mere 0.9 seconds (Rowe, 1974). This is obviously too little time for students to properly consider what is asked and to formulate an answer. A pause of at least five seconds following a question is ideal. A pause of as much as 10 seconds may sometimes be appropriate. Initial questions can be preplanned, but follow-up questions will depend on student responses and, therefore, cannot be planned for in advance.

In learning communities, teachers may wish to engage their students in *inquiry discussions*. These may introduce student investigations and will help them assess their work and make improvements in their current research efforts. In inquiry discussions, students practice critical thinking by gathering and analyzing data and by drawing conclusions on the basis of evidence rather than intuition. To initiate inquiry discussions, teachers must provide students access to appropriate resources and allow them sufficient time to become familiar with the information they contain. This may consist of personal research, peer research, or research by others, including scholars, depending on what the teacher wishes to accomplish. Discussions regarding problem identification and hypothesis formulation, as well as research design, data collection, and the conclusion development are possible. In conducting inquiry discussions, teachers may wish to help students detect poor problem definition, inappropriate data-gathering strategies, the possibility of confounding variables influencing results, or the presence of unsupported conclusions.

With inquiry discussions and activities, teachers may wish to refrain from asking questions and instead promote student questioning. Commonly, discussions address teacher questions, and students became conditioned to answering questions rather than asking them. However, students' inquiry process should be one of formulating their own investigation questions. To encourage inquiry, teachers may wish to present students with situations about which they can ask questions. For example, a biology teacher may take his class on a field trip to a quaking aspen forest and ask them to look around until they observe something that sparks a question in their minds.

When teachers wish to address controversial issues in the classroom, they may want to engage students in *exploratory discussions*. These discussions need to occur in a nonjudgmental atmosphere, where students feel free from the risk of censure. At this point there are no conclusions to be arrived at, no methods of inquiry to follow and critique, and no concern about thinking processes. All points of view are equally acceptable and encouraged with no fear of criticism. This does not preclude disagreement and disparate opinions; these inputs are, in fact, encouraged. However, there should never be any form of ridicule or excessive scrutinizing of any particular student's contributions. With exploratory discussions, Dillon (1981) recommends that teachers refrain from talking or asking questions in the following situations:

- after each student talks
- when a student pauses, falters, or has apparently finished speaking
- in an attempt to encourage a nonparticipating student to become involved
- in an attempt to probe or find out a student's feelings and other personal involvement
- to make a point
- in reply to a student's question
- in an attempt to elicit what might be on the student's mind
- by asking "why" questions
- to start a discussion
- in hopes of stimulating student thought and discussion

Dillon's recommendations appear counter to what might be considered good teaching practice. Teachers should refrain from directing the discussion to encourage student exploration. The teacher's role is to participate as a discussion group member, not as the discussion director. He or she might also serve as a referee to ensure students do not become critical of one another. It may seem awkward to initiate a discussion without a question. What else would get things going? With exploratory discussions, the teacher should tell the class that they will be engaging in a discussion about a particular controversial subject. Describing an event where the subject has come up or portraying the event in the form of a video or written material is helpful. In this case, the teacher only has to invite discussion and wait for students to respond. Even if the discussion languishes, the teacher should not make a premature effort to stimulate discussion. A period of silence might actually be helpful to allow students time to think. After a period of silence, the teacher might ask if there is more anyone wishes to contribute, or he or she may contribute new information or views.

Simulations

Sometimes actual situations cannot be experienced or studied. Teachers may want to provide simulations so students can get a better feel for actual happenings and events. In many curriculum areas, practice sets as well as board games and computer simulations give students a better idea about practical life problems and ways to solve them. Simulations also exist regarding a whole range of activities between countries, law cases, geographic factors that influence settlement and commerce, the activities of corporations, strategies for dealing with pollution, and a host of others.

Simulations are particularly helpful in dealing with complex social problems. In one simulation, students play a game regarding the problems of network television at a presidential convention. The TV networks hope to attract viewers by playing up sensational events. At the same time, they must avoid making false or distorted reports. In this simulation game, the class is divided into four groups, three teams representing three TV networks and one team representing the audience. Random drawing of information cards provides the teams with on-the-spot news from network reporters and information from wire services. Each team of broadcasters judges the reports for interest, reliability, and importance and then decides what information to pass along to their viewers. The audience rates each team's presentation for interest and social responsibility.

Modified Debates

Formal debates have limited classroom usefulness since they restrict the number of students who can actively participate. However, when properly modified the debate format can provide an interesting and exciting way to help students address controversial issues. In preparation for the debate, an issue is first defined. Students can be involved in this process. Students are then divided into two groups, one to take each side of the issue. Students are provided sufficient time to research the issue and formulate arguments for their position. Each group selects a speaker to make a five-minute presentation supporting their side of the issue. They also select an individual to provide a rebuttal of the opposing side's initial presentation. Each side makes an initial presentation and then gives a rebuttal. After the presentations and rebuttals are completed, the debate is opened up to the whole class, and anyone can enter into the debate at this time. When the teacher is satisfied that students have had an adequate opportunity to contribute, the debate can be closed, or if desired the teams can be asked to switch roles and re-debate the issue taking the opposite sides. This has the added advantage of helping students more clearly comprehend both sides of the issue. An effective way to strengthen students' ability to defend a position is to have them become more familiar with the opposing point of view by trying to defend it. More insightful counter-arguments can consequently be made.

Decision Points

Create an instruction sequence in which each of the methods outlined in this chapter are effectively used.

Using Technologies for Instruction

Computers and related technologies have opened up a new world to education. Students have at their fingertips a vast array of information to investigate and learn. Teachers also have access to an enormous amount of information to help them more effectively teach. Certain cautions are appropriate in using these important resources. One area of concern is that teachers not become too presentational in their teaching. Because they can create PowerPoint presentations consisting of effectively organized information with incorporated visuals, it is easy to conclude that presenting is effective teaching. Effective teaching, however, involves the search for meaning and understanding and not just the presentation of facts and images.

Computers and Instruction

Creating PowerPoint presentations is commonly done by computers. Excellent software programs are available for producing PowerPoint materials, along with short courses that allow even novices to create impressive presentations. With PowerPoint, teachers can string together sequences of information and images that clarify understanding and bring excitement to learning. Short segments of videos can be integrated with conceptual statements and still pictures, along with graphs and other visuals that increase conceptualization and aid understanding.

There are also many computer-assisted instruction (CAI) programs available in most subject areas, which teachers can use to provide students with computer-directed learning experiences. These programs are usually designed to help students interactively learn. Some are content oriented, while others provide practice in mastering important processes. Some of these programs must be purchased from curriculum suppliers, while others can be downloaded from the Internet. Some Internet programs are free, while others require a fee. However, locating appropriate CAI programs on the Internet by "surfing the web" can be difficult, even though this is often a fruitful source for finding very useful materials. Addresses can also often be obtained from lists maintained by professional organizations.

The Internet can provide an invaluable source of information for students.

Research and the Internet

The Internet is an enormously important source for research both for teachers and their students. Teachers can obtain information to augment their teaching as well as provide data for their ongoing research. Teachers should routinely engage in research projects themselves, with other teachers, and with their students. They can be a significant role model for students when they engage in bonafide inquiry endeavors. Teachers who have a research program are more likely to promote student research.

Searching the Internet can help students acquire critical information related to a research area as well as provide student ideas to initiate research efforts. Teachers will want to help students do successful searches by showing them how to use various search engines, as well as how to limit their searches. In current society, these skills have a broad application, but they also can enhance school learning in nearly all curriculum areas.

In many cases, it is useful for teachers to create a home page for their classes. Students can post their research on the Internet, which provides an avenue for exchanging information with others doing research in the same area. Posting research on the Internet can provide greater incentives for students to engage in more sophisticated research. By making their work public, students can be encouraged to sharpen their researching and reporting skills. Learning activities of this kind also encourage students to become more aware of the work of others and to become more attuned to learning what is going on in the world.

Decision Points

Outline an instruction sequence in your subject area that could be taught to advantage in a PowerPoint presentation.

CENTRAL IDEAS

1. Higher-order thinking is natural and involves emotional and personality considerations as well as intellectual ones.
2. Without conscious direction, the brain engages in a variety of thinking operations that are central to living successfully in a complex environment.
3. The brain has no direct contact with the outside world. It must interpret neurological impulses from sensory organs and from them create a vision of the world.
4. The brain makes an enormous number of decisions regarding behavior for which we have little conscious awareness.
5. Humans use values and common sense in their thinking to override logic and thus avoid the drawing of absurd conclusions that unmodified logical thinking might encourage.
6. Metacognitive thinking, which is thinking about thinking, is difficult due to our inability to actually observe our own thinking. We cannot visualize deficiencies in our thinking by trying to examine it. Rather, problems exist because we do not understanding what needs to be done or because we lack sufficient information to think through a problem.
7. For proper thinking to take place, students require applicable knowledge and conditions where the brain is allowed to be self-directed. The brain cannot readily set aside its own agenda and become involved with teacher-imposed activities.
8. Learning doesn't require teachers to motivate students. Rather, students are uncomfortable when they are not learning.
9. Imagination is what makes reality possible. Imagination is the creation of possible realities that can later be assessed and framed into real intentions and actions.
10. The secret to good teaching is to create learning conditions that are consistent with the way the brain operates.
11. Learning communities provide an ideal way to provide students with valid problem-solving opportunities.
12. In learning communities, students should be involved in a search for meaning through inquiry. The drive to acquire meaning fuels the inquiry process.
13. Students should be empowered by reflecting on their own learning as a tool to increase self-understanding and need fulfillment.
14. The kind of cooperative learning employed in the classroom depends on the purposes teachers have.
15. Students should be helped to value learning as well as what can be accomplished through self-directed learning.
16. Computers provide students and teachers important research capabilities. They can enhance both teaching and learning.

REFERENCES

Aronson, E., Blaney, E., Stephan, S., Sikes, J., & Snapp, M. (1978). *The jigsaw classroom.* Beverly Hills, CA: Sage Publications.

Beyer, B. K. (1983). Common sense about teaching thinking skills. *Educational Leadership, 41* (3), 44–49.

Beyer, B. K. (1992). Teaching thinking: An integrated approach. In J. W. Keefe & H. J. Walberg (Eds.), *Teaching for thinking* (pp. 93–109). Reston, VA: National Association of Secondary School Principals.

Beyer, B. K. (1997). *Improving student thinking: A comprehensive approach.* Boston: Allyn & Bacon.

Case, R. (1992). *The mind's staircase.* Hillsdale, NJ: Lawrence Erlbaum Associates.

Costa, A. (1984). Mediating the metacognitive. *Educational Leadership, 42,* 57–62.

DeVries, D. L., Edwards, K. J., & Slaven, R. E. (1978). Biracial learning teams and race relations in the classroom: Four field experiments on Teams-Games-Tournament. *Journal of Educational Psychology, 70,* 356–362.

Dillon, J. T. (1981). To question or not to question during discussion. *Journal of Teacher Education, 32* (5), 51–55.

Johnson, D., & Johnson, R. (1994). *Learning together and learning alone* (4th ed.). Boston: Allyn & Bacon.

Johnson, D. W., Maruyama, G., Johnson, R., Nelson, D., & Skoin, L. (1981). Effects of cooperative and individual goal structures on achievement: A Meta-analysis. *Psychological Bulletin, 89,* 47–62.

Johnson, W. D. (1979). From here to 2000. In D. S. Eitzen (Ed.), *Sport and contemporary society: An anthology* (p. 446). New York: St. Martin's Press.

Kagan, S. (1985). *Cooperative learning resources for teachers.* Riverside, CA: University of California, Department of Psychology.

Kohn, A. (1992). *No contest: The case against competition.* Boston: Houghton Mifflin Company.

Nickerson, R. (1989). On improving thinking through instruction. *Review of Research in Education, 15,* 4–5.

Perkins, D. (1992). *Smart schools.* New York: Free Press.

Resnick, L. B. (1987). *Education and learning to think.* Washington, DC: National Academy Press.

Rowe, M. B. (1974). Reflections on wait-time: Some methodological questions. *Journal of Research in Science Teaching, 11,* 263–279.

Slaven, R. (1986). *Using student team learning* (3rd ed.). Baltimore: Johns Hopkins Team Learning Project, Center for Research on Elementary and Middle Schools.

Smith, F. (1990). *To think.* New York: Teachers College Press.

Yarrow, M. R., Scott, P. M., & Waxler, C. Z. (1973). Learning concern for others. *Developmental Psychology, 8,* 240–260.

CHAPTER 9

Motivation in Learning Communities

CHAPTER OBJECTIVES

This chapter is designed to help you

1. Explain expectancy-value theory as it pertains to motivation.
2. Explain the nature of human interest and discuss the kind of schooling that is consistent with this definition of interest.
3. Explain how students' perception of degree of difficulty and likelihood of success influences motivation.
4. Explain the appropriate use that can be made of extrinsic reinforcement in classrooms.
5. Identify conditions under which extrinsic reinforcement can undermine intrinsic reinforcement.

Students are highly motivated when engaged in projects for which they have a personal interest.

6. Apply both extrinsic and intrinsic reinforcement effectively in the classrooms as well as motivation to learn.

7. Formulate learning experiences that satisfy basic student needs.

8. Provide instruction that promotes confidence among discouraged students, aids students with learned helplessness, and helps students avoid preoccupation with self-worth.

9. Explain the nature of motivation in learning communities.

INTRODUCTION

Educators have correctly identified motivation as one of the key elements that teachers must address if learners are to have profitable school experiences. Some have summed up the problem with the old adage, "You can lead a horse to water, but you can't make him drink." Not willing to leave it at this, some might reply, "That might be true, but you can salt the oats." Unfortunately, with student learning, a single strategy (like the metaphorical salting of the oats) will not do. Learning motivation is multifaceted. One student may be profoundly motivated by the possibility that what is being learned will affect college access. Students not bound for college are unlikely to be moved by such an appeal. Students are motivated by how they use what they learn, as well as how it satisfies needs. Various learning styles and intellectual capacities, along with personal self-concept and interests, are also part of the picture.

Ms. Van Fleet conscientiously tried to motivate her health class students. She taught six periods a day with about 30 students in each class, so it was naturally very difficult to anticipate what 180 students would find motivating. Earlier in her career she believed that all students would find the study of health interesting because it concerns their own bodies and minds. She often reminded her students about the usefulness of what they learned in class, and sometimes chided them when they were less diligent than she believed they should be.

Ms. Van Fleet carefully followed the research on nutrition as well as the latest findings on the origin, prevention, and treatment of various diseases. She accumulated a wealth of historical information on diseases and made a special study of current threats of disease around the world. She was particularly interested in the AIDS epidemic because she thought her students were especially vulnerable to this and other sexually transmitted diseases. After a careful examination of the devastating consequences of AIDS, she became especially outspoken about its prevention, taking a position that abstinence is the best defense against infection.

Because of her fears and enthusiasm, Ms. Van Fleet investigated the local incidence of AIDS in the community and discovered that a shocking number of AIDS cases were being treated and there had been several AIDS-related deaths. She confronted her students with this data, hoping they would take an interest in the AIDS epidemic as well as other diseases and apply their interest to classroom studies. Unfortunately, she discovered that, despite her warnings, there were no differences in sexual promiscuity among teenagers in the community. Even worse, all her efforts to fortify students with important health information, even accompanied with "scare tactics" regarding AIDS, had little effect on student study habits. In fact, student performance on her examinations had dropped off in recent years. However, she knew she did a better job of teaching now than before. She increased her knowledge and modified her presentations over the years to make her teaching more interesting. She created dozens of motivational episodes to get students involved. Yet, in her judgment, students were not adequately interested. She concluded her students considered themselves invincible in terms of contacting diseases. She knew they believed that if they ever got sick, a trip to the doctor would take care of any problem.

After her last class left for the day, Ms. Van Fleet thought about her classroom experience. Her concern led her to desperation. She almost felt as though she had lost the knack of teaching. Half the class failed the last major examination, but she couldn't detect any concern from the students about their poor performance. Some of her students were very unruly, and seemed to punish her for their own poor performance. A few students expressed their dismay at getting low scores, but attacked Ms. Van Fleet as the cause of their poor performances rather than themselves. Some blamed their scores on bad teaching, while others blamed the test, which they considered to be grossly unfair. A few students, troubled by their failure, pleaded for ways to earn extra credit points. Many, however, expressed no interest in making improvements. One student said she had learned all she needed to know about health, and the course covered dozens of completely irrelevant topics. These episodes and dozens of others from the past few weeks clouded Ms. Van Fleet's mind. She wondered what she could do to motivate her students.

Decision Points

Put yourself in Ms. Van Fleet's position. Think about her problems. Identify anything she has done that you believe contributes to her problems. Create a student motivation strategy you believe would help Ms. Van Fleet.

NATIONAL TEACHING STANDARDS

Teachers understand ways to motivate students and monitor student engagement.

The Nature of Human Motivation

In a perfect world, students could apply themselves to learning that they found intrinsically interesting. However, the way schooling is ordinarily conceived makes this unlikely. Teachers usually have a particular agenda they wish to employ in the classroom, based on their interpretation of state-ordered objectives along with their own instructional goals. In addition, teachers have their own personal instructional approach, which is likely a reflection of their own student and teacher experiences. Left to themselves, students are inclined to act upon intrinsic motivation based upon enjoyment. The teacher is more likely to cognitively motivate by helping students find meaning and specific usefulness in what is learned. Teachers want their students to acquire knowledge and skills which they believe are essential to success in life (Good & Brophy, 2000).

Most motivation approaches are based upon **expectancy-value theory,** which indicates that the effort students are willing to expend on learning depends on the degree to which they think they will be able to successfully learn, if they provide sufficient effort and thus qualify for a reward, as well as the degree to which they value the reward. Students are unlikely to apply themselves to learning that has no valued outcome or to engage in highly valued tasks if they believe they cannot be successful no matter how hard they try (Good & Brophy, 2000).

NATIONAL TEACHING STANDARDS

Teachers build upon student interests and spark new learning passions. This way, they can build bridges between what students know and can do and what they are capable of learning.

Unique Personal Interests

Teachers ordinarily have their students go through a set of learning activities together, even though students have different interests and their involvement is a function of their interest. Several reasons exist why teachers claim this process is necessary. First, they may act on what they perceive as prescriptive expectations from the state department of education. Second, they may feel that the common student experiences are imperative for all. Third, they may fear possible discipline problems if they allow students to choose learning activities consistent with their personal interests. Fourth, there may be concern about managing a group of students engaged in various learning activities.

While a legitimate degree of concern exists for each of these claims, none justifies withholding the students' right to engage in learning attuned to personal interests and the responsibility of self-direction that is so essential to their growth and development. The compelling nature of personal interests is best exemplified by a toddler's daily activities. Toddlers can hardly be thwarted from their ordinary learning routine. Self-directed learning takes up most of each day; no adult has to motivate them to learn, nor can they prevent them from learning. Naturally, the course toddlers pursue is highly personal. Personal interest is what imbues their efforts with sufficient intensity to keep them going until they have learned what they wish. As they get older, children interrogate adults as part of their search for understanding. Often this search is futile. Parents, with their busy schedules, may not take the necessary time to answer their children's questions, or they may fail to create conditions which inspire a quest for learning. At school, teachers may find it next to impossible to respond adequately to the many questions young children put to them, partly because teachers often feel it is necessary to simply answer students' questions rather than helping them initiate research. Feeling compelled to answer questions supports the student expectation that teachers are the source of knowledge and that students' search for understanding consists of simply asking teachers to supply answers. Children may eventually abandon their inclination to question in favor of answering teacher questions. This doesn't mean that they no longer have interests. However, because they are discouraged from asking questions, and because they care little for the enforced curriculum, their interests usually center on activities outside the classroom.

How can the unique, personal interests of students be pursued as a legitimate part of school learning? To answer this question, keep in mind that a strict standard of legitimacy should not be applied to all students. A few students may have interests that do not coincide well with the prescribed curriculum. These students are better served by allowing them to pursue their divergent interests rather than being turned off to learning altogether or overtly rebelling and disrupting class. Teachers have to ask the question, "Is it better to force students to comply and get very little from them or have them productively involved with alternative experiences?"

Some student interests generally fit the course of study, but are substantially different from the concepts the teacher plans to teach. Students may also prefer a learning format different from what the teacher plans. Ordinarily these students' needs can be accommodated by having them work in small groups after establishing a clear, student-guided learning approach with accompanying responsibility imperatives. Considerable latitude can be given to these students so long as they routinely report their activities to the teacher and the teacher consistently assesses student work and provides any necessary guidance.

Many students do not have a clear interest in a certain subject. They may not know enough about what the subject has to offer to decide how they feel. At the same time they are likely to be motivated by giving input to what and how they learn. These students need to receive greater detail about the course so that they learn what the possibilities are. Teachers could, in this case, present the possible topics for study along with possible learning strategies. They might also provide students with various accompanying implications. Some topics, for example, may be considered essential for college preparation. Others may be more useful for practical living. A few may simply satisfy student curiosity. Once students have sufficient understanding of the possibilities, they can make choices and form study groups.

Some students find success in school by very carefully following the prescribed curriculum. Their success is due to skill in determining what teachers want and carefully producing it. Perhaps their interests should be cultivated by their teachers, making it less critical that they explicitly follow the teacher's directions and providing students a number of possible options.

Perceived Difficulty

One of the challenges teachers face is how to establish an appropriate level of difficulty for student learning. As previously mentioned, students must anticipate success with reasonable effort. Their perception of how difficult the learning task is will help to determine how motivated they are. Students may consider a particular activity to be so easy that it constitutes nothing but busywork, or it may be so complex and difficult that even talented, persistent students cannot anticipate success. Either way, no strategy for motivating students is likely to succeed. An appropriate level of difficulty must be determined. An appropriate degree of difficulty exists when students understand what to do and how to do it well enough to achieve high levels of success if they persistently employ appropriate strategies (Good & Brophy, 2000). Students must be able to routinely concentrate on learning without worrying about failure (Blumenfeld, Puro, & Mergendoller, 1992).

Validly determining the relative difficulty of academic work for each student is a daunting task because each student's **perception of the degree of difficulty** must be determined, not just what the teacher supposes the level of difficulty to be. One fear that must be addressed is that students may be less energetic than their true capacity would predict. Others may take on learning activities which lead to discouragement because they are not able to accomplish them. Because students can become increasingly able to handle difficult tasks, teachers may try to move them too quickly. These factors add to the complexity of assigning students learning experiences in a prescriptive way. A far more reasonable approach would be to let students determine for themselves the kind of learning tasks for which they are prepared. If personal interest helps to frame the learning tasks, students will be more likely to stretch themselves and enthusiastically learn. They are also less likely to engage in simple busywork. Because they choose the work they do, they won't refuse to attempt something they consider too difficult, but rather seek to learn at a comfortable level and be stimulated to increase their effort and capacity in order to accomplish what they are naturally interested in doing.

Likelihood of Success

The **likelihood of success** depends not only on the perceived difficulty of the task but also on a student's view of his or her personal capacity. Students who view themselves as capable are much more likely to succeed. Without a positive view of personal learning abilities, students academically languish. When students both perceive themselves as adequate learners and see success within their reach, they are motivated to learn. Research shows that effort and persistence are greater with students who set goals of moderate difficulty, seriously commit themselves to pursuing these goals, and concentrate on trying to achieve success rather than avoiding failure (Dweck & Elliott, 1983). Students show greater effort and persistence when they view themselves as competent or efficacious and capable of being successful (Bandura, 1997). Students also do better when they attribute their performance to internal, controllable causes rather than to external factors (Weiner, 1992).

Teachers need to teach their students the following items.

- There is a predictable relationship between the level of effort and the level of expected success (Skinner, 1995).
- The potential to control outcomes is within each person rather than in factors outside them (Thomas, 1980).
- They can bring about desired outcomes through their own actions (deCharms, 1976).
- They must have confidence in their ability to succeed on a task if they choose to invest the necessary effort (Bandura, 1997).
- They must realize that their success is a function of sufficient ability and reasonable effort, and that failures are due primarily to inappropriate learning strategies rather than to luck or fate (Weiner, 1992).
- They must realize that academic ability is not a fixed capacity but something that can be developed continually through learning activities (Dweck, 1991).

QUESTIONS FOR REFLECTION

1. How can teachers determine the perceived difficulty and likelihood of success for a group of students in connection with teaching them a particular subject?

2. What can teachers do when they make inaccurate assessments of students' perceived difficulty and their likelihood of success?

3. What actions should teachers take when they discover that many of their students are unsuccessful during instruction because the subject being taught is too difficult, even though the learning experiences employed are consistent with the state core curriculum?

Extrinsic Motivation

Extrinsic motivation in schoolrooms usually consists of rewards or reinforcements provided to students for desired behavior. It is the simplest, most direct, and most adaptable means of motivating students. However, extrinsic motivation strategies do not increase the value that students place on learning itself or expand what may be acquired through learning. Rather, students link learning success to the reward.

During the 1970s and 1980s, research initially showed that extrinsic reinforcement undermined intrinsic motivation. Thus, rewarding students for doing what they were already doing for personal reasons apparently decreased their inclination to continue this behavior. They were said to become conditioned to the reward and would value the reward more than the behavior for which it was given (Deci & Ryan, 1985; Heckhausen, 1991; Lepper & Greene, 1978). Focusing attention on rewards instead of learning caused a decrease in the quality of learning (Condry & Chambers, 1978). It was initially thought that these undesirable outcomes were inherent in the use of rewards. However, the undermining effect only occurred when students were offered rewards that they knew were designed to pressure them into responding as directed. This included the awareness of behavior required to avoid punishment, behavior that was being carefully monitored, behavior that was compared to that of classmates, and performance under pressure to meet a time deadline (Kohn, 1993; Lepper, 1983). What undermines intrinsic motivation is not using rewards, but rather offering them as incentives in advance and following through in ways that make students believe that the reason for engaging in the behavior was to earn the rewards, not because the learning had value in its own right. The effects of rewards clearly depend on what they are used for and how they are presented. A decrease in intrinsic motivation can be expected when rewards

- are very attractive or are presented in ways that call attention to them
- are given for just participating in the learning activity rather than provided for achieving specific goals
- are artificially connected to a particular behavior as control devices, rather than being a natural outcome of learning (Brophy, 1998)

A number of ways exist for teachers to avoid undermining intrinsic learning motivation. First, they can provide unannounced rewards following a learning activity, so that the rewards are seen as expressions of appreciation rather than as a payment of promised incentives. Second, rewards can be used as informative feedback rather than as control mechanisms. Third, teachers can give rewards not merely for participating in activities, but for accomplishing specified goals (Cameron & Pierce, 1994, 1996; Chance, 1993). Social rewards should be emphasized over material ones so students are encouraged to value the accomplishments being rewarded.

Teachers must be discriminating about the kind of activities for which they provide extrinsic reinforcers. They should know that rewards are more effective at increasing the intensity of student effort than improving the performance quality. Thus, rewards are better used for routine tasks rather than novel ones; intentional learning rather than incidental learning or discovery activities; and tasks that can be quantified rather than those that involve creativity, artistry, or craftsmanship. For example, teachers can successfully reward activities like performing routine computation, practicing musical scales, typing, spelling, shooting free throws, and naming the parts of the human skeleton. With low-level tasks, no other source of motivation may be operating, so extrinsic rewards may be required to sustain student efforts. It is unwise to provide student rewards for activities teachers prefer they do on their own, like watching educational television programs, reading good books, or participating in community activities such as attending city council meetings, visiting nursing homes, or participating in environmental clean-up efforts.

Teachers should avoid offering incentive rewards to induce desired behavior. If it is necessary to provide rewards as incentives, they should emphasize the major objectives, the key ideas, and the skills being promoted. Teachers should also avoid giving rewards like extra credit for simply participating in class or turning in assignments. When rewards are given, teachers should emphasize the importance of learning and help students take pride in their achievements, portraying rewards as verifications of significant and worthwhile achievements of high quality (Brophy, 1998). *Most of the rewards provided to students by their teachers are given as incentives* and suffer the problems already mentioned in connection with this practice. Unfortunately, it is unlikely that teachers will be sufficiently discriminating to avoid doing this in their daily teaching activities.

When teachers praise students, commendation should be given as appreciation rather than as acknowledgment of praiseworthy performances. Students should be valued for who they are, not for what they do. When designated behavior is a condition for receiving rewards, students often feel they must perform to be accepted. Conditional acceptance can not only rob students of the development of responsible independence and creative growth, but it can keep them from acquiring a sense of well-being. Effective praise expresses appreciation for students' accomplishments in ways that draw attention to what has been done, not to the student's success in pleasing the teacher.

Praise should not be indiscriminately given. However, teachers commonly lavish praise on students with little thought as to the consequences. For example, some students may find it embarrassing to be singled out and praised. They may worry that their peers think of them as "apple polishers"; thus, praise can be aversive instead of rewarding. Students may also feel that praise by teachers is used to manipulate classmates. Teachers often hope that students will seek to emulate the individual being praised. However, praise can also diminish inquiry behavior. Many teachers have habituated a particular sequence of responses when they ask classroom questions, particularly in recitation sessions. After students correctly answer questions, teachers usually mimic the answer given by the student, then follow with a short statement of praise. This sequence not only eliminates questioning and inquiry by students, but also greatly shortens the time students spend responding to questions and issues in class and reduces the thoughtfulness of their responses (Edwards & Surma, 1980).

In place of offering artificial rewards, it is sometimes possible to make students aware of naturally existing extrinsic incentives for achieving academic excellence. This can be done by calling attention to the future applications that might be made of what is learned, when applications are possible. Possible applications have implications for the way the curriculum is constructed. Curriculum developers should always have both current and future applications in mind when they organize student learning. However, students may be more motivated by current happenings than by projected future ones. Students may not perceive future goals as applying to them personally, nor understand how current learning can help them achieve these nebulous objectives. Consequently, teachers should focus on learning experiences with current relevance, limiting projections to those things that students are actively working toward. For example, some students may be pointing to college or to a particular profession.

Some teachers involve students in competitive activities to motivate them. However, most motivation theorists oppose this practice for several reasons. First, competition adds to the risk students already feel as they compete with their peers for grades and various opportunities.

Second, competition can distract students from learning. Students working on their own are able to evaluate their progress in comparison to previous performances, with considerable appreciation of how their knowledge and skills have developed. However, students working in competitive environments are so focused on winning that they pay little or no attention to what they are learning and consequently are less able to visualize how to improve their performances (Ames & Ames, 1981).

Third, competition can enhance performance on routine, simple tasks, but it is a distraction when students engage in discovery learning or creativity. In addition, competition is effective only when all competitors have an equal chance of winning (Brophy, 1998).

Finally, competition creates losers as well as winners, even though a tendency exists to think of competition as positive because it produces winners. Like chaff on the threshing floor, losers receive little attention. This is tragic. These losers are the casualties of schooling, suffering permanent losses in confidence, self-concept, and the enjoyment of school (Epstein & Harackiewicz, 1992; Moriarty, Douglas, Punch, & Hattie, 1995; Reeve & Deci, 1996).

QUESTIONS FOR REFLECTION

1. How can praise be effectively used in the classroom?
2. Praising students for teacher-approved behaviors is habituated in the speech of many teachers. How can teachers eliminate these speech patterns? What kind of communications should they have with students to replace this kind of talk?

NATIONAL TEACHING STANDARDS

Teachers hold high expectations of students and see themselves as facilitators of student learning.

Intrinsic Motivation

Intrinsic motivation is produced by the educational experience itself. The experience is valued by the learner because it carries personal meaning or because it is viewed as an instrument for accomplishing something important. Intrinsic motivation has been commonly associated with recreational activities and play rather than with academic experiences. Academics are usually expected to require an extrinsic motivator because learning is not perceived as intrinsically motivating. However, several aspects of learning are intrinsically rewarding. For example, students find it rewarding that through their learning efforts they achieve greater competence. They find it intrinsically rewarding to achieve an enhanced sense of self and become self-actualized. Intrinsic motivation is also associated with the development of personal autonomy and a corresponding decrease in teacher manipulation.

Most motivation theorists don't consider extrinsic and intrinsic motivation to be completely antagonistic. There is a degree of compatibility. However, intrinsic motivation in teaching and learning is considered preferable to extrinsic approaches. Intrinsically rewarding, self-determined learning tends to be of higher quality than extrinsically motivated learning (Deci & Ryan, 1994).

In the past, intrinsic motivation has been thought to be exclusively connected to needs; however, wants and desires are now also included (Collier, 1994). Maslow (1962) considered needs to be arranged in a hierarchy, with self-actualization needs being sought only after lower needs are achieved. These needs include creative self-expression, satisfaction of curiosity, and exploration, all of which are self-enhancing needs that appear to be intrinsically motivated. It has also been suggested that humans are motivated to achieve competence. From this perspective, a desire exists to deal effectively with the environment and to master and control various environmental factors. To achieve these ends, the individual engages in such activities as exploration, thought, and play (White, 1959).

With extrinsic motivation, the individual is very much aware of the difference between means and ends. In fact, the means are undertaken to acquire something. In contrast, intrinsically motivated activities are not experienced with a goal in mind, but rather for their own sake. The goal and the activity tend to be one and the same. Intrinsically motivated persons engage in activities out of interest and require no external prods, promises, or threats. Their actions are experienced as wholly self-determined, emanating from the individual idiosyncratically. Learning is pursued out of interest when the individual is free from external pressures (Deci & Ryan, 1994). Extrinsically motivated behavior is performed to acquire something apart from the actions necessary to achieve it. Ordinarily these actions must be promoted by incentives or other external pressures.

When teachers have a particular curriculum agenda, but wish to capitalize to some degree on the power of intrinsic motivation, they can promote limited self-determination by (1) providing students with meaningful reasons for engaging in learning activities, (2) acknowledging students' feelings when they are required to do things they prefer not to do, and (3) using a teaching style that emphasizes choice rather than control. It would obviously be better for students to engage as much as possible in activities that they personally find meaningful. Learning communities readily accomplish this by carefully discussing potential learning projects and encouraging all members to give full input regarding learning decisions. It may be acceptable for students in traditional classrooms to engage in individual learning activities that they have chosen. For instance, a student may devote most of his or her time in a science class to working on a science fair project. If the project had merit and student interest, it might occupy a student for an entire year or more. Some of the more exemplary projects, from which students have greatly benefited, have taken four or five years to reach their potential level of excellence and sophistication. Projects that have the capacity to intrinsically motivate students for long periods of time and have recognized merit should be pursued. These experiences are ordinarily far more valuable to students than going through the structured curriculum.

Many times teachers may wish for students to be intrinsically motivated, even though they are not. This is often due to prior conditioning where extrinsic rewards have been exclusively used. Teachers can help their students become more intrinsically motivated by gradually moving them along a continuum from external regulation to intrinsically motivated, self-directed activity. In the beginning students may primarily respond to rewards and threats of punishment. As more self-regulated activities are incorporated into the classroom, students can experience a greater desire for self-determination. At this stage they do not require prodding to perform, but rather experience guilt for disappointing themselves and others.

The next stage is to help students determine goals that they wish to achieve. This often involves a desire to enter college or a chosen profession. At this stage, students are motivated to accomplish self-selected goals even if what they have to do to achieve their goals is not intrinsically motivating.

By increasing the number of self-determined student activities, teachers can promote greater intrinsic motivation. When what is done is identified as an integral part of the self, students are able to sense harmony between academic experiences and their personal goals and desired activities. This ideal requires considerable self-determination, along with expert coaching from teachers. Teachers must be skilled in helping students engage in legitimate school activities that they find personally meaningful, thereby allowing them to be increasingly more self-directed in pursuing these activities.

Social settings are good places to promote intrinsic motivation because they provide a means of satisfying students' needs for autonomy, competence, and relatedness. Students are intrinsically motivated when they feel connected to others, function effectively in social settings, and acquire a sense of personal competence while working with others (Deci & Ryan, 1994). Learning communities naturally supply these conditions, and thus intrinsic motivation can be enhanced in learning communities. A contradiction may exist in efforts to simultaneously satisfy the needs for autonomy and relatedness. However, in learning communities the focus of group activities is on enhancing group interactions while supplying individual needs and desires. This allows individuals to realistically see the importance of others in their lives and recognize how these group experiences help them achieve personally meaningful goals.

Intrinsic motivation depends essentially on the degree of autonomy students have. Students will not be intrinsically motivated if their learning is excessively managed. As much as possible, students should be offered alternatives regarding what and how they learn. A variety of information sources can be used, and various strategies can be employed that articulate well with student interests. Students are often best served by being allowed to assume responsibility for regulating their own learning.

Wise teachers offer self-directed learning opportunities for all students, not just the high-achieving ones. Low achievers are commonly excessively managed (Brophy, 1998), and some of their learning problems may be associated with this management.

Greater competence can be expected when students are intrinsically motivated, and achieving increased competence can be highly motivating (Goldberg & Cornell, 1998). No student wants to be thought of as unable. When students fail to perform well, they ordinarily excuse themselves, indicating that despite their failure, they want to be competent. They want it to appear that their poor performance is due to circumstances beyond their control, or that the particular task required of them has no value and thus does not merit their conscientious efforts. They try to avoid concluding that they tried their best and yet failed (Covington & Beery, 1976).

 ## *Decision Points*

Organize an instruction sequence that capitalizes on intrinsic motivation.

NATIONAL TEACHING STANDARDS

Teachers must find ways to capture and sustain the interests of their students and to help them efficiently and effectively learn.

Teachers must motivate their students, capturing their minds and hearts and engaging them actively in learning.

Motivation to Learn

Some educators feel that intrinsic motivation is insufficient for schooling generally, and for a predesigned curriculum in particular. They conclude that students cannot be expected to maintain intrinsic motivation for the school's legitimate subject matter. If students follow their intrinsic interests, they will drift away from important aspects of the subject and toward less-substantial ones. This, of course, is one of the most critical issues in teaching: forcing students to learn "appropriate" subject matter for which they have little interest and of which they will likely retain very little, or allowing them to select their own learning experiences with the possibility they will learn what society considers useless. It is difficult to support an approach to teaching that focuses on information acquisition, given what is known about how quickly memorized information is forgotten. It makes sense to feature processes and allow considerable flexibility in what information is used to learn these processes. In addition, in a teaching approach that emphasizes student self-direction, students are not routinely left to decide everything for themselves, particularly in learning communities. Either the learning community, the teacher, or both moderate what any individual student will spend time doing. Thus, extrinsic motivation is supported by teacher coaching so that students acquire reasonable input from their teachers, but still exercise considerable autonomy over certain aspects of their learning activities.

Because students may fail to acquire "essential knowledge" if they choose their own learning activities, theorists have coined the term **motivation to learn** to describe a teaching and learning process in which students may be motivated to learn something whether or not they find it interesting and enjoyable. Motivation to learn involves information processing, sense-making, and mastery rather than demonstrating knowledge acquisition. It emphasizes the importance of thinking and understanding over supplying right answers. In motivation to learn, teachers inform students of the purpose of what they learn and connect these outcomes to goals students value, like preparing for college or an occupation.

To promote motivation to learn, teachers would do well to include the four following factors in their teaching: opportunities to learn, press, support, and evaluation (Blumenfeld, Puro, & Mergendollar, 1992). With *opportunities to learn,* teachers (1) challenge, but do not overwhelm, students; (2) make the central ideas evident in their presentations, demonstrations, discussions, and assignments; (3) present concrete illustrations of basic principles and relate unfamiliar information to students' personal knowledge; (4) make explicit connections between new information and knowledge students have previously learned, pointing out relationships among new ideas by stressing similarities and differences; (5) carefully elaborate on written materials rather than expecting students to do it themselves; (6) guide students' thinking by posing high-level questions and then probing for understanding; (7) have students summarize what they have learned and make comparisons between the various related concepts; and (8) have students make practical applications regarding what they have learned.

Press involves teachers' encouragement for their students to think through their responses in connection with teacher expectations. In this case, teachers (1) require students to explain and justify their answers; (2) prompt students, reframe questions as necessary, and probe students when they appear to have a faulty understanding; (3) monitor students for comprehension rather than for just answering questions correctly; (4) encourage all students to participate by asking them to respond to one another in discussions and debates; and (5) have students prepare written explanations of what they are learning and create alternative representations of the information in the form of diagrams and charts.

Teachers *support* their students' understanding through modeling and scaffolding. They (1) model thinking, suggest strategies, and help students solve problems when they experience difficulty; (2) reduce the procedural complexity of manipulative tasks by demonstrating procedures, highlighting problems, showing examples, and providing planning time; and (3) encourage students to collaborate in their learning by encouraging all students to make contributions.

In the *evaluation* task, teachers should (1) emphasize understanding and learning rather than work completion, performances, comparisons between students, and right answers; (2) help students use their mistakes to check their thinking rather than denoting their failure, and thus encourage them to take risks; and (3) allow students who have not performed well to continue working until they achieve the highest-possible level of excellence.

Brophy (1998) provides three general strategies for motivation to learn. The first is for teachers to *model their own motivation to learn,* sharing their interests with their students in current events and other items that relate to the subject being taught. They can call attention to current books, articles, television programs, and movies that have special significance and stress ways that various class topics apply to everyday living. Teachers can share their thinking and show how they solve everyday problems. Teachers might also be involved in their own projects and share what they are learning with their students. Teachers can show students how they have used information from a wide variety of subjects to solve real problems they confront.

Modeling curiosity can be helpful, too, particularly if a teacher expresses an interest in response to a student question. The impact of showing interest in students' questions can be expanded by inviting the student and a few interested classmates to join the teacher in investigating the project. For example, a student named Jason might say, "You know, Mr. Lombard, I read in the paper the other day that there has been a steady increase in depression among teenagers since the early 1900s. What could be the reason for that?" Mr. Lombard might respond, "I don't know, but I'd like to find out. I'm really interested in that question. Jason, why don't you and I try to find out about it? Are there three or four other class members interested in working with us? We can set aside some class time to get started on it. OK, I see four hands up. We've got a lot of interest in this subject. I'll tell you what, let's get together during the last 15 minutes of class and see if we can break up the research responsibilities. Jason, since you brought this question up, would you like to be our leader? If it's OK, I'd like to be assigned to do some part of the research."

A teacher should not address all questions brought up in class in this way. However, to demonstrate curiosity and interest and model research strategies, it would be well to occasionally be so involved. Teachers should be engaged in research or projects that relate to the subjects they teach. Depending on the subject, teachers may be involved in artistic endeavors, writing projects, scientific investigations, or building models. As appropriate, students could be invited to participate with them.

Sometimes students have low expectations of themselves. Because competence is so highly motivating, teachers need to help students gain a desire to achieve excellence. This cannot be done by merely expressing confidence in their abilities; this is more likely to compromise a teacher's credibility than promote a student's achievement. It is better for the teacher to become involved in the learning effort as a member of the learning community and model the desired behavior. As the teacher helps the student become significantly involved and provides coaching, a higher level of accomplishment can be reached. Students can easily see the difference between prior efforts and current performances. By being involved as co-learners, teachers can help students raise their own expectations rather than relying on teachers to supply encouragement. Every student needs to be able to make a valid assessment of personal abilities and strive for learning at an appropriate level. Otherwise, students are unlikely to see themselves as able, or have a clear view of the nature of excellence.

It is normal to question how teachers can become significantly involved in students' individual learning projects and still carry out their class responsibilities. In a traditional classroom setting, this might be impossible. However, in learning communities students become accustomed to greater personal autonomy and group responsibility, so little supervision is required. The teacher has the freedom to become involved with learning groups in various ways as the situation dictates. Modeling is just one of the strategies that might be undertaken.

Teacher enthusiasm is an important motivational component, particularly when students see their teacher's enthusiasm in connection with a genuine interest in the subject. It is hard to project manufactured enthusiasm without students detecting it. There is no better way to communicate enthusiasm than to be genuinely enthusiastic about what is being learned in class. Students' motivation can be enhanced when they see that their teacher's enthusiasm is based on important matters applying what they learn in the learning community to other important matters. Teachers need to explain how they are using what they learn and what it means to them. Hopefully students will be able to put what they learn to use in a similar way. If so, teacher modeling will have served its purpose.

Curiosity is a natural component of intrinsic motivation. Motivation to learn, however, may require a teacher to stimulate curiosity. A number of strategies exist that teachers can employ to stimulate curiosity. For example, a teacher might show students an owl pellet and then ask them to figure out what it is. This could be followed-up by asking what is inside the owl pellet. This naturally leads to the development of student observation skills, along with designing experience and conducting an investigation. Students might also be shown ant or bee colonies or be asked to make observations of the fish in the classroom aquaria. From this they may be encouraged to formulate a plan to study these organisms' behavior. Students might also make observations of human behavior; for example, they might be directed to sit at a bus stop or in a library, or ride an elevator up and down until they observe something they wish to study about human behavior.

Teachers can also stimulate curiosity by asking thought-provoking questions. The following are examples of questions that students might be curious about:

1. What is behind the conflict in the Middle East?
2. What is the impact of religion on war?
3. What is the danger of producing genetically altered foods?
4. What is being symbolized by Frodo in Tolkien's writings?
5. What should be done when the economic well-being of a community directly conflicts with environmental safety?

Asking students to make predictions can also stimulate curiosity. For instance, students might be asked to predict what would happen if two students of different races were placed in a room and viewed a movie depicting a controversial episode involving people of different races. The class might be asked to explain how people of different races would view what happened in the episode.

Student curiosity can also be raised by having students assess their thorough understanding of some information needed to achieve a valued objective. If they realize they are lacking some essential skill or body of information, they are more likely to be driven to acquire it. They will experience curiosity about what is needed to provide them the required understanding.

Teachers can also present phenomena and ask students to raise questions. A teacher might show students a video of police brutality, a neighborhood where extreme poverty exists, or a radioactive chemical dump located just 35 miles from a large city. After exposing students to these situations, the teacher might ask them to think about questions they'd like to raise. They should especially consider questions requiring them to design an experiment.

Student curiosity can be further stimulated by putting them into problem-solving situations. They might be asked to figure out how water can be drawn from the roots to the leaves even in tall trees, or assigned to organize a class social that allows all to participate appropriately even though there are six different ethnic groups represented.

TABLE 9.1 *Reinforcement Comparisons.*

	Extrinsic Reinforcement	**Intrinsic Reinforcement**	**Motivation to Learn**
Teacher Actions	Teachers control student learning through rewards.	Students select from options or initiate their own learning.	Teachers supply reasons students should learn uninteresting topics.
Results	Students become conditioned to the rewards and dislike what they are rewarded for doing.	Learning is self-sustained.	Students learn to acquire something they value besides the learning itself.
Strengths	These allow the teacher to control what goes on in the classroom.	These promote independent, responsible learning.	Students accomplish objectives they might not otherwise achieve.
Weaknesses	These undermine intrinsic reinforcement.	Students may devote too much time to unessential learning.	Students may fail to value learning for its own sake.

Sometimes curiosity can be induced by creating dissonance or a state of uncertainty. A teacher might point out unexpected, incongruous, or paradoxical aspects of a particular concept, call attention to unusual or exotic elements of a phenomenon, note exceptions to general rules, or challenge students to solve a mystery. Teachers might expose students to topics such as the Trail of Tears, the Japanese internment during World War II, or the involvement of the CIA in undermining foreign governments (Brophy, 1998). These episodes in American history can be compared with traditional historical accounts of events during the period. Students can receive guidance in researching history from multiple perspectives and come to appreciate why different historians may write quite different histories of the same era (see Table 9.1).

 ## QUESTIONS FOR REFLECTION

1. How would you integrate intrinsic motivation, extrinsic motivation, and motivation to learn in a sequence of learning activities?

2. Under what conditions would you shift from a motivation to learn to intrinsic motivation? Provide an example.

3. When is it appropriate to shift away from educational experiences that students find intrinsically reinforcing? Provide an example.

Student Needs and Motivation

Personal needs are some of the most potent sources of student motivation. Student needs were detailed in Chapter 3, with the hope that student behaviors could be better understood by examining the driving force behind them. A few of these needs will now be examined within the context of learning motivation. Curiosity has already been referred to as a component of the need to learn, as well as the need to achieve competence. Some theorists consider intrinsic motivation to be associated exclusively with fun activities or games. To get children to learn what they should in school, a different motivational system must, therefore, be employed. Extrinsic reinforcement or motivation to learn techniques are recommended, with a sprinkling of intrinsic motivation as opportunities present themselves.

However, little children appear to have a need to learn. Learning occupies a good deal of their time each day, and merely calling it play would be a huge oversimplification. Their explorations appear to be directed toward understanding natural phenomena and solving problems. At times they can hardly be distracted as they concentrate on the quest for understanding. Their attention seems drawn to many things as if most of what they see has to be investigated to determine its operations and usefulness. No one has to sit at his or her side to point out what should be explored, and no one has to initiate the learning. They require no extrinsic motivation; their inherent interest is sufficient. It is not until children arrive at school that motivation seems to be a problem. Up until this time, children have been essentially self-directed. Children have little need for other strategies because they have been superbly successful in directing their own learning.

In school, however, students begin to learn what others want them to learn, and doing this in cadence with all other class members produces an unnatural state of learning that creates frustration and withdrawal by some students and begrudging compliance by others. Even those who willingly comply with the new school learning format may not adequately satisfy their learning needs. They use learning that formerly was intrinsically motivating to acquire something else that they need: attention or acceptance, for example. Teachers may give their approval to students who comply with the new learning format and punish or ignore those who don't, claiming they are less-able learners. These students may later be referred to as "learning disabled." Students are thus robbed of an inherent desire to learn and have it replaced with an unnatural mode of learning they tend to resist. Therefore, the schools may fail to satisfy the needs children have to learn because teachers employ an unnatural model.

Schools also may fail to provide students the conditions for achieving a sense of competency. Usually competence, as defined by the school, is achieved by only a few students who have been able to adapt to particular expectations. Their classmates acquire a lesser standing and may simply be judged less able. In addition, because competence is defined as achieving minimum standards, a level of competence is usually reached, even by the most-able students, that is far below their capacity. Because these students have failed to achieve excellence, they too may not acquire a true sense of competency (Glasser, 1998).

Other particularly relevant student needs for motivation were defined by Glasser (1986). They include love and acceptance, control, autonomy, and fun. Glasser considered these needs to be the fundamental motives for all behavior.

Love and Acceptance

Love and acceptance are particularly potent motivators. The question is how to capitalize on their power in the classroom and avoid the depressed motivation that ordinarily accompanies lack of love and acceptance. Children often confuse love and acceptance with teachers' controlling behavior. To achieve order in the classroom, teachers may sometimes act with anger or disdain toward problem-causing students. A teacher may occasionally embarrass a student in front of the class in an effort to stop unruliness. Teachers may find it difficult to care about unruly students who make teaching difficult. Teachers may also be seen by students as obstacles to the grades they desire. A student may find difficulty feeling love and acceptance from an individual who has just given him or her a low grade. Therefore, teachers may be put in an untenable position of wanting to show their students that they care, but finding it impossible because they have to distribute grades. Research shows that academic achievement is tied to children's sense of well-being (Covington & Beery, 1976). If grading produces an adversarial relationship between students and their teachers, a reduction in academic productivity can be expected, along with depressed self-concepts. These consequences cannot be justified just for the sake of grading students. Other kinds of assessments are available, like portfolios, which can help students achieve excellence while bolstering their sense of well-being and promoting caring relationships with their teachers.

Control

Perhaps the most compelling need humans have is to control what happens to them in life. Through personal control, other needs are satisfied. It is particularly critical to achieve personal control because each individual has idiosyncratic ways to satisfy his or her needs that may or may not make sense to others (Glasser, 1984). Even if other people knew exactly how to satisfy various needs, the individual would likely be dissatisfied because of the enormous desire each person has to individually guide this process. This human need has particular importance in terms of motivation. In common practice, teachers undertake the exclusive responsibility of directing instruction in their classrooms. Their reasons for doing this are likely based on one or more of the following questionable assumptions:

- Children are unable to make valid decisions about what they learn in school.
- Children are unable to manage their own learning as well as their classroom behavior.
- Children will allow others to make decisions for them without reacting negatively.
- All students' needs can be satisfied by a common set of classroom experiences.

Because all these assumptions have questionable validity, teachers are put in a very tenuous position of conducting their classes without assurance that what they teach is satisfying needs and is useful. In fact, according to Glasser (1998), much of what teachers routinely do in the classroom is likely to frustrate the control needs of students, causing young people, in one way or another, to reject the experience.

Whether or not they appear responsible to their teachers, students still have a need for control. When students are allowed more control over school experiences, there will be much less need to supply motivation to learn and literally no necessity for extrinsic reinforcers. Intrinsic motivation will become more strategically important. More credence must be given to the need children have to become responsibly self-governed and less adherence given to the claim that students need to follow teachers' directions as part of life preparation.

Of course, most individuals are required to do things they would prefer not to do during their lives. Sometimes they are controlled by others or the circumstances in which they find themselves. Unpleasant things are often undertaken because there is a payoff of some kind. For example, a person may work at a particularly obnoxious job, but receive excellent compensation and retirement benefits, or it may be the only job available for which the person is qualified. However, just because we are faced with necessary, albeit unpleasant, things in our lives, that doesn't mean we need school training to prepare for them. Life is filled with choices. Students probably will have more choices once they leave school. They need experiences that will help them make responsible contributions in democratic communities. In our society, we prize opportunities for self-determination and decry freedom-limiting conditions like oppressive control and prejudice.

Autonomy

Most individuals desire personal autonomy and, at the same time, wish to control others. Control and autonomy work in tandem in many, if not all, human interactions. Most people go to great lengths to ensure that they have both personal freedom and sufficient control over their associates. One of the most useful tools for understanding an individual's motivation is to examine his or her behavior in terms of efforts to enhance personal freedom and acquire control.

Students' quest for freedom can be intense. It is not ordinarily relinquished unless something especially desirable is offered in exchange. Sometimes students submit themselves to their teachers because they feel they have no recourse, since punishment or sanctions from the school or parents are often penalties for noncompliance. This doesn't mean that students just quietly acquiesce and do what they are told. Rather, they engage in overt or covert rebellion. From a teacher's perspective, students who fail to comply with their directions are thought to be unmotivated. However, students are never unmotivated; they are just not motivated to do what teachers prefer. Teachers may thus feel it necessary to compete with natural motivation by using rewards such as grades. Beyond this, teachers have very little with which to motivate students. However, students may not find grades to be a compelling reason to follow the teacher's wishes. They may have their own agenda. Freedom itself is likely more motivating than anything teachers can offer.

NATIONAL TEACHING STANDARDS

Teachers realize that motivating students is not equivalent to making learning fun, for learning can be difficult work. They have to help students face temporary failure and the inevitable doubts that students meet as they push themselves to new affective, intellectual, and physical planes. This learning provides the real joy in education: the satisfaction of accomplishment.

Enjoyment or Satisfaction

Few students are likely to say that their academic experiences in school are fun. Likewise, not many teachers would claim fun as one of their instructional purposes. Teachers are more inclined to believe that school is work and that the work is unpleasant. Students are usually

Students' inherent needs can be better satisfied if what they learn is enjoyable.

told that school learning is "just something that has to be done." This is hardly motivating. If both teachers and students believe school learning is unpleasant, it's no wonder students look for diversions to somehow make the whole experience a little more fun. Given the fact that enjoyment is perpetually sought by young and old alike, it would be surprising if students did not look for more enjoyable things to do in school than dutifully working their way through an imposed, uninviting set of learning experiences for which they have no motivation.

Not only can the academic part of school be fun, but the enjoyment of learning can satisfy basic human needs. Learning provides a way for children to satisfy curiosity, enhance meaning, solve problems, and generally achieve a sense of personal satisfaction. Some would even characterize their learning experiences as fun, particularly when they are self-directed and can learn what is personally meaningful and useful. The reason teacher-directed school learning may not be fun is because it most likely appears irrelevant to many students and doesn't provide the motivating force self-directed learning can.

Learning can be enjoyable and satisfying, and consequently fun, if it has the following elements: (1) it is self-directed, (2) it is self-initiated and composed of content the individual finds meaningful, (3) it helps in solving problems students find personally relevant, (4) it allows students to be involved with their peers, (5) it provides students opportunities to use learning modalities they prefer, (6) it incorporates elements of play, (7) it allows the individual the opportunity to serve others, (8) it includes opportunities to accomplish tasks that are valued by others and for which the individual student can acquire a sense of being accepted and valued by the learning community, and (9) it provides for and promotes excellence.

Decision Points

Create a learning sequence, including a description of teacher activities and student activities, that satisfies the students' needs for love, control, autonomy, and fun.

Accommodating Social Needs in the Classroom

Most human needs are satisfied within a social context. This probably explains why youth devote so much time to social interactions. However, schools greatly limit these experiences. Ordinarily students are expected to do their own work. Lectures are to be dutifully listened to, recorded, and studied. Students are then independently tested. These activities require relative quiet, with a minimum of student-to-student interaction. Sitting for long periods of time under these conditions frustrates the need for social interaction. The result is a lot of unruliness as students seek to satisfy basic needs in an environment that prohibits unauthorized talking. It is no wonder that talking constitutes nearly three-quarters of all classroom disruptions (Edwards, 1975).

Interpersonal Interactions

Youth have a very compelling interest in one another. They are fundamentally alike, have similar interests, and need one another to satisfy their most earnest desires. A very powerful motivation exists when significant learning is combined with the need for interpersonal interaction among youth. Although youth need meaningful experiences with adults and younger children, they crave association with their age mates. Given an opportunity, many would spend most of their time with same-age individuals. They tend to have the same interests, confront the same kind of problems, and suffer the same misgivings as they move from childhood into adulthood. They are also more interesting to one another at a time when members of the opposite sex become more physically attractive. This social exchange constitutes a test to determine how acceptable they are to one another. Various rituals and routines are born of these circumstances; as a result, youth form cliques, wear specifically defined clothing, and behave according to group norms. These identifying features separate youth from other age groups and encourage exclusivity. When these conditions become extreme, some youth are left out and the chasm between youth and adults widens, making significant interaction difficult. This is particularly true when adults fail to provide youth with opportunities to relate to one another frequently enough and when youth are excessively restricted.

Knowing that youth need to have frequent, meaningful interaction with one another, teachers should create many opportunities for them to satisfy their needs in a wholesome learning environment. If these experiences are frequent enough and meaningful enough, there will be fewer problems with students engaging in social chatting rather than substantive learning.

NATIONAL TEACHING STANDARDS

Teachers are concerned with their students' self-concepts, with their motivation, with the effects of learning on peer relationships, and with the development of character, high aspirations, and civic virtues.

Community Involvement

While learning, youth need to see in one another a partner in accessing important learning, not just an opportunity for undisciplined chitchat. They need to learn they have a vested interest in one another, to satisfy not only social needs, but intellectual needs as well. This need can be accomplished through learning communities. The desire to learn and the need to socialize create a motivating environment in which to organize group learning. Mutual interests can be explored, projects completed, research reports made, and musical and artistic renditions presented. All these can be done in collaborative ways, with group members supporting and encouraging one another. Students will find these activities motivating because community learning satisfies all their needs in the most accommodating way. Social needs can be met when interactions and activities are authentically valued by the group. Students can learn to live cooperatively with others and achieve a balance of their own needs for control and personal freedom with the needs of the group. Enjoyment will be fostered as students interact with one another and engage in learning projects that help them recognize and solve their problems and find true meaning in their lives.

Learning communities have significant power to motivate so long as they are properly organized and operated. Strategically, learning communities should be allowed to develop independent of particular external expectations except in terms of basic operations. For example, the learning agenda should evolve in terms of a particular group's needs, but it is always necessary for group members to look after one another and to promote the best interests of each member in connection with group activities. Given the experiences most students have already had in school competing with one another, considerable time will be spent helping them learn to care about one another and to sincerely look after one another rather than seeing others as competitors. Some group members will have to avoid being critical of others and develop sensitivity and courteousness. A few may have to learn how to authentically express their point of view and make requests so the group addresses their concerns. Some group members may find it hard to engage in research on projects that don't represent their primary interest, and therefore have to wait for the appropriate time when their concerns can receive full attention. Most students will need to learn the nature of true excellence, to come to understand their personal capacities and limitations, and to learn to make valid assessments of the quality of their own work and that of other group members. Developing these skills will take time. Some groups will advance more rapidly than others. Consequently, group members should always view themselves and others as being in a growth process.

In groups there are always some personalities that dominate and others that are more reserved. It is worthwhile for the more assertive individuals to learn how to follow the lead of others, and for those who are more reticent to learn how to lead out. Early in the group process teachers need to explain the desirability of shared and shifting leadership. Leadership training should be given periodically by the teacher. In all likelihood the leadership practiced by some will be incongruous with group purposes. Some will have little idea about democratic leadership if in their experience they have been exposed mostly to autocratic leadership.

Teachers must learn how to shift their leadership role. Initially, teachers must take an active leadership role, particularly while the group dynamic is evolving. Teachers also might need to help students understand what is meant by excellence and how excellence can be evaluated. Students are likely to have had very little experience making an assessment of their own learning. Teachers usually perform this task exclusively. The mindset of many students is to somehow win the teacher's approval and acquire sufficient points to get higher grades. With the concept of excellence replacing grades, students may not realize that excellence requires far more quality than they have previously assumed. Grades represent minimums, not possibilities. Students will also need to understand that unlike grades, which indicate an end to a sequence of learning, learning communities continuously promote the advancement of skill levels without foreclosing on student efforts before an acceptable excellence level is realized. Some projects might require more than a single year to complete. This kind of carryover should be encouraged, not precluded.

Motivating Students with Learning Problems

For one reason or another, many students do not reach their full potential. If the minimum standard reflected high quality, few students would show themselves worthy. However, there are a significant number of students who perform far below even minimal expectations. Some are discouraged, given their level of success in comparison to their more-competitive or more-able peers. They lack confidence in themselves and often hide their true ability for fear their real skill level will be discovered and found lacking. Some are plagued with apathy or alienation. These problems effectively keep children from finding success in school.

Promoting Confidence Among Discouraged Students

Some students have low ability, and when they try to perform in a competitive system or one in which their special needs and abilities are not seriously taken into account, they appear even less qualified. Because they are a step behind their classmates, they often feel humiliated. They usually begin to manifest a failure syndrome, giving up at the first sign of frustration. They fail at tasks they might have done successfully; they are so concerned about failure that they spend more time trying to cover up their confusion than actually learning. Many times they withdraw or behave passively, and often they only do a portion of their work. Therefore, they may develop behavior problems.

Various strategies have been suggested to help these students. McIntyre (1989) provides four sets of suggestions. The first is to individualize activities and assignments and reduce the level of difficulty. Multisensory experiences are recommended, along with assignments built around student interests. Assignments should be kept short, with the initial tasks being easy or familiar enough to ensure success.

The second group of suggestions involves providing clear directions to structure activities. Directions should be repeated until the teacher is certain students understand what is expected. Tasks should be modeled along with providing verbal explanations. Levels of achievement should be carefully explained, along with time limits for completing the work. Sufficient time should be given so these students can readily complete assignments on schedule.

The third set of strategies focuses on providing task assistance or tutoring, and rephrasing questions or providing hints when students are unable to respond. Students' responses should be praised as they achieve at acceptable levels. Unsatisfactory work should be revised with help given as necessary. Struggling students should be seated among average students with whom they have good relationships, and these peers should be instructed to help the students experiencing difficulty to stay on track and provide assistance as needed. A "study buddy" system can be employed in which low achievers are encouraged to collaborate with a neighborhood friend.

The fourth set of suggestions focuses on maintaining motivation. Students should be provided encouragement and positive feedback on papers. Teachers can help students establish realistic goals and associated learning activities, and then evaluate their accomplishments. Teachers might also call attention to their students' success and send positive notes home to parents. Each day students can be encouraged to achieve a little higher than on previous days rather than competing with classmates. Performance contracting is also useful and, if grades are used, they should be based on effort and production rather than on comparisons with other students.

Directions should be kept simple and more complex tasks should be divided into parts rather than expecting students to remember long sets of instructions. Seating students near the front of the class where more frequent eye contact can be maintained is helpful (Abbott, 1978). Low achievers seem to benefit from individualized tutoring and from strategies which guarantee success, like adjusting difficulty levels (Grabe, 1985). These individuals need frequent monitoring and supplementary tutoring, not just exposure to individualized instructional materials. Care must be exercised to ensure that students are given work that is sufficiently repetitive but not truly remedial (Good & Brophy, 2000).

Helping Students with Learned Helplessness

Unlike low-achieving students, those with **learned helplessness** fail needlessly because they do not adequately apply themselves. Instead, they begin learning activities half-heartedly and give up when they encounter difficulty. Students with learned helplessness can be found at all levels of academic ability. They may manifest helplessness in one subject but work successfully in another (Galloway, Leo, Rogers, & Armstrong, 1996). These students have low initial expectancies for success, give up quickly when they encounter difficulty, attribute failures to lack of ability rather than to controllable causes such as insufficient effort, attribute their success to external and uncontrollable causes (e.g., luck, easy task) rather than their own abilities, and make predictions of low success in the future following a failure (Butkowsky & Willows, 1980; Smith & Price, 1996).

Although some evidence of learned helplessness appears in the early grades and may be a function of parental influences, it is more often centered in school failure. Most children begin school with enthusiasm, but many soon find schooling to provoke anxiety that psychologically threatens them. Students learn early on to respond to the teacher's questions, complete assignments, and take tests. Their performances are monitored, graded, and reported to parents. These pressures might be tolerable if there was more privacy or consistent success, but they become threatening in classrooms where failure carries the danger of public humiliation. Learned helplessness is especially likely to appear in classrooms where teachers use controlling strategies and where students have to develop extrinsic motivational orientations (Boggiano, et al., 1992).

It is not surprising that students with a continuing history of failure believe that they are unable to succeed. Once this belief takes root, fear of failure begins to disrupt concentration and limit the individual's coping abilities. Eventually, serious attempts to master school work are abandoned in favor of efforts to preserve self-esteem.

Various recommendations have been presented to help students with learned helplessness abandon their failure orientation to learning and replace it with hope. Cognitive retraining is composed of three components: attribution retraining, efficacy training, and strategy training. Attribution retraining has been shown to produce significant student improvement (Ziegler & Heller, 2000).

Attribution retraining involves strategies to help students attribute failure to insufficient effort or to the use of inappropriate learning strategies rather than to lack of ability. Students are exposed to a planned series of experiences in which they are (1) helped to concentrate on the learning task rather than worrying about failure, (2) shown how to cope with failure by retracing their steps to find their mistake or by analyzing the problem to find a different approach, and (3) guided to attribute failure to insufficient effort, lack of information, or use of ineffective strategies rather than lack of ability (Craske, 1985; Dweck & Elliott, 1983).

In attribution retraining, success alone is insufficient. Attempts to alter a student's view of his or her abilities have been unsuccessful, possibly due to the individual's awareness that success can be attributed in part to help from others. The key to successful attribution retraining is controlled exposure to failure. Students need to learn how to cope with failure and overcome it to achieve success. This coping process consists of seeing failure as coming from remediable causes. Students are taught to diagnose the problem first and then to correct their mistakes by approaching the problem in different ways. They are encouraged to see failure not as having finality, but rather as a result that can and should be corrected. This is best accomplished by teachers coaching students: showing them that failure is natural and that correcting problems is a routine most people experience. Students learn how failure can be overturned and success achieved by spending more time redirecting one's efforts. In this approach, rather than just having the teacher arrange for success, students are helped to acquire tolerance for frustration, persistence in the face of difficulties, and faith that continued efforts will eventually lead to success. This approach is far different from programming student success with no possibility for failure (Clifford, 1984; Rohrkemper & Corno, 1988).

In recent years a shift of emphasis has occurred in attribution retraining. Earlier, stress was given as a reason to help students view failures as a result of insufficient effort. Now more emphasis is given to helping them realize that failure is due to ineffective strategies. They are helped to realize that they may have gone about solving problems in the wrong way. This change recognizes that students may put forth their best effort and yet fail, and that a more prevalent reason for failure is poor strategies (Brophy, 1998).

The purpose of attribution retraining is to reverse the effects of a system that encourages students to develop a debilitating view of personal ability. Of course, this is not the only appropriate strategy for dealing with this problem. It seems self-evident to suggest that preventive strategies are needed, and that it is usually much easier to avoid problems than to correct them once they exist. If, as already suggested, learned helplessness is acquired from school experiences like common assignments, testing, and grading, it seems reasonable that these practices should be abandoned. Learning communities, if appropriately conceived and operated, provide an environment in which students can properly attribute success to effort in personally meaningful, well-organized learning activities.

Efficacy training is designed to help students set realistic goals and pursue them, as they realize they are achievable with a reasonable amount of effort. Schunk (1985) recommends the following practices to increase students' self-efficacy perceptions:

- Teacher modeling of the process of cognitively creating task strategies, expressing an intention of persisting despite the appearance of problems, and acquiring confidence that success can eventually be achieved.
- Explicit training in how to effectively accomplish tasks.
- Specific performance feedback that helps to correctly conceptualize a task, remedy errors, and reassure students that they are developing mastery.
- Encouragement for students to set challenging, but attainable goals that have specific performance standards and are oriented toward immediate short-term outcomes.
- Insight regarding how students' present performances surpass prior attainments rather than how they compare with the performance of other students.
- Rewards based on actual accomplishments, not just participation.
- Attributional feedback that focuses on success achieved through a combination of sufficient ability and reasonable effort.

Strategy training involves instruction on problem-solving strategies and related self-talk that students need to successfully handle tasks. This training is especially helpful for students who have not developed effective learning and problem-solving strategies. Students are taught not only how to give attention to what they are doing, but also to give attention to how, when, and why it is to be done. They are also taught to verbally express their thinking so that their thought processes can be made visible.

In one strategy training program (Devine, 1987), students are provided training in the following learning strategies to strengthen their ability to study effectively:

1. *Rehearsal*—verbally repeating information to remember it better.
2. *Elaboration*—putting information into one's own words and relating it to prior knowledge.
3. *Organization*—outlining information in a framework that aids memory.
4. *Comprehension monitoring*—keeping track of successful learning strategies and making modifications to promote improvement.
5. *Affect monitoring*—maintaining concentration and task focus, while minimizing performance anxiety and fear of failure.

Students with learned helplessness need teachers who act as resource persons rather than judges, who focus on learning processes rather than outcomes, who react to errors as natural and useful components of the learning process rather than as evidence of failure, who stress effort over ability and individual standards rather than group comparisons, and who incorporate opportunities for intrinsic motivation rather than depending on extrinsic motivational strategies (Dweck & Elliott, 1983).

Avoiding Preoccupation with Self-Worth Protection

Some students focus on performance goals instead of learning goals, often in an effort to protect an ailing self-concept. These students may be able to perform successfully but fear that if they do so their poor self-concept may be confirmed. Therefore, they invent elaborate strategies to avoid performing, or when they have to do something in class, they find some justifiable reason why they are not able to do their best. They may claim not to have studied for a test, for example. Many of these students deliberately fail so that little will be expected of them in the future. They are often calculating in the way they pretend to study. Their hope is to appear somewhat capable, but not so much that teacher expectations exceed what they feel they can routinely meet. They usually try to avoid being called on in class, as they feel unable to correctly respond (Covington & Beery, 1976). They may also try to escape by scrunching down in their seats and avoiding eye contact with the teacher. They may hesitate in answering a question, hoping the teacher will call on someone else rather than wait for them to respond. They try to make the teacher believe they are studying when in fact they are daydreaming, and try to appear thoughtful when they are actually guessing. They tend to procrastinate, do the minimum required, and in other ways perform marginally. These strategies allow students obsessed with protecting their self-worth appear to be striving for achievement while actually avoiding genuine challenges and arming themselves with excuses for potential failures (Brophy, 1998). What they hope to avoid at all cost is to do their best and be found wanting.

The following strategies are recommended by Covington (1992) for students who are preoccupied with protecting their self-worth:

1. Provide students with inherently interesting learning possibilities that are challenging, yet manageable, and appeal to their curiosity. Allow as much autonomy as possible so students can choose for themselves, and then help them to gradually increase the levels of challenge they select.
2. If there is a reward system, make it equally possible for all students to be rewarded. Reward students for being responsibly autonomous by calling attention to their skill in setting meaningful goals, posing challenging questions, organizing insightful research, and working to satisfy their curiosity.
3. Help students understand the relationship between effort and accomplishment. Help students set realistic goals that they can accomplish with reasonable effort.
4. Help students accept their accomplishments realistically in connection with their growing expertise rather than through comparisons to other students.
5. Help students adopt a multidimensional definition of their abilities and accomplishments. They should understand that their abilities will vary from one subject to another, as will their interests.
6. Improve student-teacher relationships by being involved in meaningful learning experiences with students and by assuming the role of resource person rather than of controller and assessor of student behavior.

 ## QUESTIONS FOR REFLECTION

1. How are the instructional needs of discouraged students, students with learned helplessness, and students who are preoccupied with protecting their self-worth similar and different?
2. What kind of learning activities should be arranged that will provide students with an opportunity to satisfy most of their needs most of the time?

3. What difficulties might teachers experience in providing experiences that help students satisfy their social needs? What can be done when socially oriented learning experiences create disruptiveness?

4. What can teachers do to ensure a balance of leadership opportunities for all their students?

Motivational Strategies for Learning Communities

Motivation in learning communities involves an entirely different set of strategies than conventional learning. With conventional learning, the problem is getting students to learn what they otherwise would not choose to learn. If extrinsic motivation is employed, a sufficiently powerful reinforcer must be used to alter the course the student has set for himself or herself. This will vary from student to student. With intrinsic reinforcement, the teacher must match learning opportunities to students' inherent interests. However, once learning communities are established, motivation is an integral part of the experience itself. No one has to arrange either experiences or contingencies of reinforcement. The difficulty is in helping students respond to learning in a new way, or to make a transition from being receptive to teacher presentations to becoming active learners. For one thing, students will need to acquire skill in identifying problems to solve and questions to investigate. In traditional schooling, students are not called to determine problems and formulate important study questions; the teacher has this role. The students' role is to answer questions and memorize designated subject matter. In learning communities, with few requirements being designated in advance, students may be in a quandary regarding what is expected of them, when in reality the task of expectancy has been turned over to them. No doubt earlier expectations were supplied by their teachers, and it will not be natural to create their own goals and experiences.

Another radical adjustment students will encounter is having to value learning personally rather than in terms of extrinsic rewards. Since students may have been accepting rewards for learning for quite some time, it may be difficult for them to see learning as a reward in itself. This is because most extrinsic reinforcement is administered as an inducement to learn and consequently can be expected to have undermined the intrinsic value of learning. Life in a learning community is assumed to help students value learning rather than rewards.

Another adjustment that students will have to make concerns work ethic. The time students spend "on task" in the schools is very low. Not many students exhibit sustained effort in their learning. Under these conditions, it is unlikely they will have a valid conception of what constitutes hard work. Some students will likely experience difficulty assessing their true capacity for work, and in connection with this, the level of accomplishment of which they are capable. Hopefully this transition can be accomplished by students working on projects for which they have considerable interest and for which they make sincere commitments to other group members.

Some students will have difficulty with the freedom they experience in a learning community. The task is how to help them exercise their freedom with the requisite degree of responsibility. Because prior experiences probably were much more structured with students having little or no opportunity to regulate their own learning, they will not automatically be able to responsibly regulate their own activities. For such students, teachers need to provide an opportunity to exercise autonomy as a function of associated responsibility. Greater autonomy is encouraged, while accompanying responsibility is expected. In any episode of providing students more autonomy, trust should not be discussed as an issue. Students may question whether or not they are trusted when less freedom is offered than desired. Obviously trust is needed to promote growth. However, discussions regarding trust usually denote an unworthy student seeking it as an effort to acquire freedom with insufficient responsibility. This should be discouraged.

One issue that often comes up relative to learning communities and motivation is the tendency for youth to be interested in fewer subjects than commonly offered in school. Some feel all children need to get the full spectrum of knowledge so they will be "balanced." There is certainly value in being broadly educated; however, forcing a broad base of understanding on all students may not be wise if in so doing they get "turned off" learning. As already mentioned, the desire to learn is more important than ensuring that a broad spectrum of facts gets delivered to students. Conceivably some students could pursue many subjects to satisfy their interests, while others would be involved with just a few, without definable harm. In learning communities, students will come in contact with more subjects than under a traditional system. It is just as likely that they will pursue too many subjects and spread themselves too thin, without getting an in-depth understanding as it is that they will have too narrow a focus. When the focus seems inappropriate, teachers can have one-on-one discussions with students and help them think through the scope of their learning and research.

There is wisdom in letting students become acquainted with many problems and issues so that they can give their interests a proper test. One cannot ascertain a personal interest in a subject unless a substantial acquaintance can be made with basic concepts and issues. In doing this, textbook-oriented learning should be avoided. A much better appreciation of what a subject has to offer can be obtained by examining the exciting research currently going on in a field than by spending time mastering the basics with the hope that interest can be ascertained or generated. Studying the so-called basics rarely puts students in contact with the interesting problems and issues associated with a field of study.

QUESTIONS FOR REFLECTION

1. What would be an appropriately balanced curriculum in a learning community?
2. What can teachers do to expand the number of topics in which students find an interest?
3. What would you do if you had a single student in a learning community who had a particular interest he or she wished to pursue, but there was no one else in the class interested in the subject? Describe in detail what a teacher would have to do to promote this interest.

CENTRAL IDEAS

1. To the extent possible, teachers should capitalize on opportunities to implement intrinsically motivating learning activities.
2. Teachers should avoid teaching strategies where extrinsic reinforcers undermine intrinsic motivation.

3. The effort students expend to learn will depend on the degree to which they believe they will be successful.

4. Students have unique personal interests that should be incorporated into the curriculum as much as possible.

5. Students' efforts to learn depend on how difficult they believe learning to be, as well as their likelihood of success.

6. Intrinsic motivation can be undermined by offering rewards as incentives in advance of the learning activity.

7. Teachers should avoid providing students rewards for accepted performances and creating conditions for acceptance.

8. Teachers should avoid praise that might embarrass students, manipulate classmates, or decrease inquiry behavior.

9. It is intrinsically rewarding for students to engage in learning when they recognize that their competency is related to their efforts.

10. Learning communities provide a context in which intrinsic interests can be responsibly pursued.

11. Learning communities provide a way for students to fulfill their needs for autonomy, competence, and relatedness.

12. Motivation to learn emphasizes information processing, sense making, and mastery rather than knowledge acquisition.

13. Student needs for love, control, freedom, and fun can serve as potent motivators.

14. Motivation can be enhanced by coupling significant learning with the students' need for interpersonal interaction with peers.

15. Discouraged students can receive a boost in confidence when teachers help them find genuine success.

16. Students with learned helplessness can overcome learning problems through attribution retraining, efficacy training, and strategy training.

17. Teachers can diminish students' preoccupation with protecting their self-worth by appealing to curiosity, promoting autonomy, helping students to attribute success to effort, assessing their accomplishments without making comparisons to those of other students, and helping students realize that their level of accomplishment will vary from subject to subject.

18. Motivation in learning communities is inherent in learning activities themselves; thus, teachers are not required to create motivational strategies.

REFERENCES

Abbott, J. (1978). *Classroom strategies to aid the disabled learner.* Cambridge, MA: Educators Publishing Service.

Ames, C., & Ames, R. (1981). Competitive versus individualistic goal structures: The salience of past performance information for casual attributions and affect. *Journal of Educational Psychology, 73,* 411–418.

Bandura, A. (1997). *Self-efficacy: The exercise of control.* New York: Freeman.

Blumenfeld, P., Puro, P., & Mergendoller, J. (1992). Translating motivation into thoughtfulness. In H. Marshall (Ed.), *Redefining student learning: Roots of educational change* (pp. 207–239). Norwood, NJ: Ablex.

Boggiano, A., Shields, A., Barrett, M., Kellam, T., Thompson, E., Simons, J., & Katz, P. (1992). Helplessness deficits in students: The role of motivational orientation. *Motivation and Emotion, 16,* 271–296.

Brophy, J. (1998). *Motivating students to learn.* Boston: McGraw-Hill.

Butkowsky, I. S., & Willows, D. M. (1980). Cognitive motivational characteristics of children varying in reading ability: Evidence for learned helplessness in poor readers. *Journal of Educational Psychology, 72,* 408–422.

Cameron, J., & Pierce, W. D. (1994). Reinforcement, reward, and intrinsic motivation: A meta-analysis. *Review of Educational Research, 64,* 363–423.

Cameron, J., & Pierce, W. D. (1996). The debate about rewards and intrinsic motivation: Protests and accusations do not alter the results. *Review of Educational Research, 66,* 39–51.

Chance, P. (1993). Sticking up for rewards. *Phi Delta Kappan, 74,* 787–790.

Clifford, M. (1984). Thoughts on a theory of constructive failure. *Educational Psychologist, 19,* 108–120.

Collier, G. (1994). *Social origins of mental ability.* New York: John Wiley & Sons.

Condry, J., & Chambers, J. (1978). Intrinsic motivation and the process of learning. In M. Lepper & D. Greene (Eds.), *The hidden costs of rewards: New perspectives on the psychology of human motivation* (pp. 61–84). Hillsdale, NJ: Lawrence Erlbaum Associates.

Covington, M. (1992). *Making the grade: A self-worth perspective on motivation and school reform.* Cambridge: Cambridge University Press.

Covington, M. V., & Beery, R. G. (1976). *Self-worth and school learning.* New York: Holt, Rinehart & Winston.

Craske, M. (1985). Improving persistence through observational learning and attribution retraining. *British Journal of Educational Psychology, 55,* 138–147.

deCharms, R. (1976). *Enhancing motivation: Change in the classroom.* New York: Irvington.

Deci, E., & Ryan, R. (1985). *Intrinsic motivation and self-determination in human behavior.* New York: Plenum.

Deci, E., & Ryan, R. (1994). Promoting self-determined education. *Scandinavian Journal of Educational Research, 38,* 3–14.

Devine, T. (1987). *Teaching study skills: A guide for teachers* (2nd ed.). Boston: Allyn & Bacon.

Dweck, C. (1991). Self-theories and goals: Their role in motivation, personality and development. In R. Dienstbier (Ed.), *Perspectives on motivation: Nebraska symposium on motivation, 1990* (Vol. 38. pp. 199–235). Lincoln, NE: University of Nebraska Press.

Dweck, C., & Elliott, E. (1983). Achievement motivation. In P. Mussen (Ed.), *Handbook of child psychology* (4th ed.). Vol. IV: *Socialization, personality, and social development.* New York: John Wiley & Sons.

Edwards, C. H. (1975). Variable delivery systems for peer associated token reinforcement. *Illinois School Research, 12* (1), 19–28.

Edwards, C. H., & Surma, M. (1980). The relationship between type of teacher reinforcement and student inquiry behavior in science. *Journal of Research in Science Teaching, 17* (4), 337–341.

Epstein, J., & Harackiewicz, J. (1992). Winning is not enough: The effects of competition and achievement orientation on intrinsic interest. *Personality and Social Psychology Bulletin, 18,* 128–138.

Galloway, D., Leo, E., Rogers, C., & Armstrong, D. (1996). Maladaptive motivational style: The role of domain specific task demand in English and mathematics. *British Journal of Educational Psychology, 66,* 197–207.

Glasser, W. (1984). *Control theory.* New York: Harper & Row.

Glasser, W. (1986). *Control theory in the classroom.* New York: Harper & Row.

Glasser, W. (1998). *Choice theory: A new psychology of personal freedom.* New York: Harper Collins.

Goldberg, M. D., & Cornell, D. G. (1998). The influence of intrinsic motivation and self-concept on academic achievement in second and third grade students. *Journal for the Education of the Gifted, 21* (2), 179–205.

Good, T. L., & Brophy, J. E. (2000). *Looking in classrooms* (8th ed.). New York: Longman.

Grabe, M. (1985). Attribution in a master instructional system: Is an emphasis on effort harmful? *Contemporary Educational Psychology, 10,* 123–126.

Heckhausen, H. (1991). *Motivation and action* (2nd ed.). New York: Springer-Verlag.

Kohn A. (1993). *Punished by rewards: The trouble with gold stars, incentive plans, A's, praise, and the other bribes.* Boston: Houghton Mifflin Company.

Lepper, M. (1983). Extrinsic reward and intrinsic motivation: Implications for the classroom. In J. Levine & M. Wang (Eds.), *Teacher and student perceptions: Implications for learning* (pp. 281–317). Hillsdale, NJ: Lawrence Erlbaum Associates.

Lepper, M., & Greene, D. (Eds.). (1978). *The hidden costs of reward: New perspectives on psychology of human motivation.* Hillsdale, NJ: Lawrence Erlbaum Associates.

Maslow, A. (1962). *Toward a psychology of being.* Princeton, NJ: VanNostrand.

McIntyre, T. (1989). *A resource book for remediating common behavior and learning problems.* Boston: Allyn & Bacon.

Moriarty, B., Douglas, G., Punch, K., & Hattie, J. (1995). The importance of self-efficacy as a mediating variable between learning environments and achievement. *British Journal of Educational Psychology, 65,* 73–84.

Reeve, J., & Deci, E. (1996). Elements of the competitive situation that affect intrinsic motivation. *Personality and Social Psychology Bulletin, 22,* 24–33.

Rohrkemper, M., & Corno, L. (1988). Success and failure on classroom tasks: Adaptive learning and classroom teaching. *Elementary School Journal, 88,* 299–312.

Schunk, D. (1985). Self-efficacy and classroom learning. *Psychology in the Schools, 22,* 208–223.

Skinner, E. (1995). *Perceived control, motivation, and coping.* Thousand Oaks, CA: Sage.

Smith, J. O., & Price, R. A. (1996). Attribution theory and developmental students as passive learners. *Journal of Developmental Education, 19* (3), 2–4.

Thomas, J. W. (1980). Agency and achievement: Self-management and self-reward. *Review of Educational Research, 30,* 213–240.

Weiner, B. (1992). *Human motivation: Metaphors, theories and research.* Newbury Park, CA: Sage.

White, R. (1959). Motivation reconsidered: The concept of competence. *Psychological Review, 66,* 297–333.

Ziegler, H., & Heller, K. A. (2000). Effects of an attribution retraining with female students gifted in physics. *Journal of the Education of the Gifted, 23* (2), 217–243.

Discipline in Learning Communities

CHAPTER OBJECTIVES

This chapter is designed to help you

1. Correctly apply procedures that prevent discipline problems.
2. Explain the causes of student violence and suggest strategies for preventing violence in the schools.
3. Provide classroom experiences that promote resilience.
4. Aid pupils in modifying their disruptive classroom behavior.
5. Conduct classroom problem-solving meetings where pupils are involved in determining the curriculum along with classroom rules and procedures.

Teachers often make ineffective appeals for better discipline in their classrooms.

INTRODUCTION

The most difficult aspect of teaching for many teachers is classroom discipline and management. This involves not only student disruptiveness, but also nonparticipation. No matter how well-prepared a teacher may be, if students sabotage the instructional program, the whole purpose of schooling can be compromised. Teachers must, therefore, be experts in classroom discipline and management. One way to help avoid discipline problems is to employ learning communities. Students who have a significant role in defining the curriculum and classroom procedures will less frequently disrupt the class. Through their participation in the classroom community, they achieve greater commitment to making the instructional program effectively work.

Mr. Olsen's third-period class gave him more discipline problems than he had ever experienced. Most of the trouble came from a group of six boys who continually disrupted instruction by their antics. They yelled at one another across the room, so separating them made little difference. They also threw things to one another. It didn't seem to matter where they sat; they talked loudly with anyone around them. Whenever Mr. Olsen tried to correct their behavior, they would ignore him or defiantly glare back. Another group made up of three girls also sat together and incessantly talked. They were not excessively loud, but they never paid attention. One or another of them always seemed to be primping her hair or putting on lipstick. Their conversations were well-spiced with giggling, which had come to irritate Mr. Olsen about as much as the boisterous guffaws of the boys. Two boys seated in the back corner of the room were perpetually engaged in a hushed conversation. The other students paid little attention to them except for an occasional remark filled with biting criticism and rejection. They were treated as if they were not worth anyone's time. One day Mr. Olsen thought he heard them discussing a plan to injure those who tormented them. He laughed to himself. These two misfits were delusional.

The rest of the class, until recently, seemed reasonably well-disciplined. Now it appeared as if the chronic problem students had succeeded in getting the rest of the class to join them. Formerly well-behaved students were now involved in various forms of disruption, like throwing spit balls and talking out of turn. Little work was being accomplished: Most students neglected their assignments, and test scores dropped abysmally. Mr. Olsen routinely assigned additional work to disruptive students, but they just ignored his attempts to punish them. He found it difficult to designate even one cooperative student in his class.

Sometimes Mr. Olsen resorted to yelling at students and threatening them with punishment. He occasionally sent a particularly unruly student to the office, but this never worked. The delinquent student usually came back unaffected, sometimes with a sneer or grin on his or her face. Mr. Olsen often wondered what happened to the students he referred to the assistant principal, but wasn't bold enough to find out. He didn't want his problems aired throughout the school, and asking for administration explanations was certain to lead to schoolwide discussion about the discipline issues. He had the feeling that he wasn't particularly well-respected by the principal.

Models for Handling Discipline Problems

Various discipline theories or models exist based on disparate assumptions regarding the growth and development of adolescents, the best way to interact with them, and a means to manage their behavior. These theories can be categorized as management theories, nondirective intervention theories, or leadership theories. *Management theories* generally conclude that children are incapable of self-regulation and must be managed through reinforcement and/or punishment (Martin & Pear, 1992).

Management Theories

Management theories assume that the teacher must perpetually manage student behavior. Students are assumed to be unable to manage their own behavior and require teachers to stimulate their learning and curtail their disruptiveness. Supposedly, without teacher intervention, students would not be productive learners. They would also actively sabotage the instructional program. To avoid these problems, teachers must impose punishment or employ rewards to influence student behavior.

Behavior Modification

Perhaps the best known and fully researched management theory is **behavior modification** advocated most prominently by B. F. Skinner. This approach is employed primarily by ignoring inappropriate behavior and reinforcing desired behavior. Hopefully, ignoring unacceptable behavior will extinguish it. Appropriate behavior can be strengthened and even shaped by strategically supplying students with rewards. Rewards may be in the form of edibles or tangible objects that students prize, or they may be special privileges like being a teacher's assistant or being allowed to play educational games. Rewards can be dispensed as they are earned or provided through a token economy where students receive tokens that can later be exchanged for any of a variety of backup reinforcers (Walker & Shea, 1999).

Assertive Discipline

A second management theory called **assertive discipline,** which was devised by Lee Canter, focuses more on punishment than reinforcement. This approach depends on teachers assertively communicating their wants and feelings to students and then following-up with actions that enforce their desires (Canter & Canter, 1976). Canter believes that good discipline depends on mutual trust and respect and advocates that positive student-teacher relationships be developed before his discipline approach is employed (Canter, 1996). Once the proper environment has been established, classroom rules must be unambiguously communicated to students. Teachers must then track misbehavior and inform students in an unobtrusive way when they break rules. This tracking is commonly done by putting the misbehaving student's name on the chalkboard as a warning and following this up by adding check marks behind the student's name for each subsequent disruption. Consistent punishments are then imposed based on the number of accumulated check marks. This pattern allows teachers to specifically track student misbehavior without interrupting instruction (Canter & Canter, 1981).

With assertive discipline, students may also receive rewards for appropriate activities. For example, the teacher may place an empty jar on his or her desk into which marbles are dropped when students demonstrate acceptable behavior. Marbles are removed when students misbehave. When the jar is filled, a promised class party is held.

Nondirective Intervention Theories

Nondirective intervention theories assume that individuals develop from an inner unfolding. Thus, youth have within themselves a "blueprint" for complete rational self-determination. Therefore, control tactics by the teacher are unnecessary. Children achieve the most positive growth only when they are allowed adequate self-direction. The teacher's role is to give students opportunities for self-directed growth and development (Rogers & Freiberg, 1994). Examples of nondirective intervention theories include Teacher Effectiveness Training and Transactional Analysis.

Teacher Effectiveness Training

Teacher Effectiveness Training is based on the work of Thomas Gordon (1974, 1989). Gordon rejects the practice of providing students either rewards or punishment. Instead, he focuses on teacher influences that help students become self-governing. In applying this approach to the classroom, teachers first help students identify who owns the discipline problem. Teachers commonly try to force students to change their behavior by telling them exactly what they must do even when it is a student-owned problem that creates disruptions and when the teacher's direction blocks the flow of communication needed to help students effectively solve their problems.

One way to help students solve classroom problems is through *active listening*. Teachers allow students to process disruptive events and feelings by carefully listening to them and reflecting back the teacher's understanding of what was said. Special skills are needed to initiate this kind of interaction and then to keep information flowing.

When the problem to be solved is a teacher-owned one, the teacher sends a *confronting I-message*. An I-message contains three components: a nonjudgmental description of student behavior, a tangible effect on the teacher of the behavior, and how the teacher feels about it. For example, a student who cheats on a test may receive the following I-message from the teacher: "When you look at someone else's paper during an examination (*nonjudgmental description*), I'm not certain your work is your own (*tangible effect*), and I don't feel comfortable grading your work (*feeling*)." I-messages provide a means of constructively solving problems rather than promoting resentment and anger.

Sometimes students resist even well-constructed I-messages. When this occurs, teachers can shift to a listening mode. It does little good to continue sending assertive messages to students who resist. In addition, sometimes the issue involved is one of disagreement over values. There may be no apparent resolution of a problem because the student and the teacher have different beliefs regarding the issue. Students may have different beliefs about gang membership, religion, drug use, profanity, manners, moral behavior, justice, honesty, sexual behavior, or beards and moustaches. They may refuse to bargain about these value conflicts that put their cherished beliefs at risk. When resistance is encountered due to value differences, teachers should engage in active listening as they try to help students solve problems.

Transactional Analysis

Transactional Analysis is an outgrowth of the work by Eric Berne (1966) and Thomas Harris (1967). These theorists believed that good and bad behavior is based on one of three ego-states—The Parent, the Child, and the Adult—that develop from childhood in connection with the individual's personal experiences. The Parent ego-state is the repository of all the admonitions, rules, and laws issued by parents and other adults during children's early life. Because they are recorded in early life, they are unedited. Young children are unable to critically evaluate adult behavior and consequently misinterpret motives and fail to understand extenuating circumstances. Interestingly, no amount of new experiences can erase these recordings; they will always be a part of the person's history. This personal history consists of a mental record of the complicated, well-intentioned platitudes to which they are subjected—pronouncements of which they have only a vague understanding of like: "Clean up your plate," "Eat your dessert last," "Haste makes waste," or "You can never trust a cop." Because children are unprepared to judge these statements as good or bad, they accept them as true. They are internalized and rigidly depended on as patterns for dealing with other people and constitute the source of many of the difficulties experienced in successfully interacting with others later in life. These difficulties may be the source of discipline problems in the school.

The Child ego-state is recorded simultaneously with the Parent. It consists of the emotional responses children make to what they see and hear. While the Child is being recorded, children experience numerous uncompromising demands with which they must comply regardless of how they feel or what they want to do. If there is a sufficient difference between parents' demands and children's desires, frustration occurs and an "I'm Not OK" life position develops. These feelings can surface later in life in connection with experiences similar to those in childhood. They may be manifest with such behavior as an explosive temper or a plethora of disruptive games children play in school (Berne, 1964).

When children realize they are able to do things that arise from their own awareness and original thought, the Adult ego-state begins its appearance. In the early years, the Adult ego-state is fragile and subject to injury and distortion, which may come from experiencing too many commands from the Parent or too many fears emanating from the Child. Without such interference, the Adult ego-state is able to adequately interpret life happenings and ensure that the individual's behavior is valid and useful. It tests the rules and information from the Parent to determine whether they can be wisely used. It also examines the feelings of the Child to determine if they can be appropriately expressed. If the Adult is not unduly subdued by abuse, it will help to make appropriate modifications in both the Parent and Child. For example, the Adult will help the Child express feelings safely that might otherwise have been communicated in socially unacceptable ways. Children who are able to successfully make these adjustments experience a fruitful transition from the control-bound existence of childhood to autonomous self-regulated living as adults. Otherwise, they learn a set of responses that may be disruptive. Instead of assuming an "OK" life position, they may suffer personal and interpersonal difficulties (Harris, 1967).

The challenge of teachers is to help adolescents who have not achieved a healthy life position learn to more successfully interact with others and refrain from behavior that upsets the educational process. This is done by helping young people recognize the three ego-states, learn how to operate out of the Adult ego-state, and appropriately moderate the expressions that come from the Child and Parent. Otherwise, young people may engage in the disruptive school games that have been identified as outgrowths of improper adjustment (Ernst, 1972).

Leadership Theories

Leadership theories assume that children develop from an interaction of both inner and outer influences. Growth is believed to come from the constant interplay between the two. The teacher's role is one of leadership. Children can achieve a state of responsible self-determination if teachers carefully intervene and help children gradually assume more control over their experiences. This is done by helping youth understand the results of their behavior and make adjustments to achieve more desirable consequences. Examples of leadership theories include judicious discipline, logical consequences, and reality therapy/choice theory.

Judicious Discipline

Judicious Discipline is a leadership-oriented discipline approach proposed by Forrest Gathercoal (2001) patterned after the rights and responsibilities embodied in the United States Constitution and Bill of Rights. Students are taught that they have important personal rights that they can enjoy so long as they do not interfere with compelling school interests. The First, Fourth, and Fourteenth Amendments are focused on helping students understand their rights. They learn of their rights of free speech, due process, and protection from searches and seizures. These rights are obtained so long as they do not violate the compelling interests of the school. These include the following:

- property loss or damage
- legitimate educational purpose
- health and safety
- serious disruption of an educational process

The classroom rules and consequences are patterned after these legal standards and sound educational principles. Students are guaranteed the right to appropriate application of legal procedures if they are ever accused of violating school rules. They have the right to receive adequate notice of charges, receive a fair and impartial hearing, be provided with the evidence against them, have an opportunity to mount an adequate defense, and appeal any decisions rendered by school officials.

Judicious discipline has the benefit of familiarizing students with the legal system that exists outside the school into which they will eventually migrate. It also provides a way for them to learn how to become self-governing and responsible in school. In addition, it helps school officials interpret the various actions they may reasonably take in managing student behavior so that they can proceed in a legally and morally defensible way.

Logical Consequences

Rudolph Dreikurs created a discipline approach called **logical consequences.** Essential to this approach is offering children choices rather than controlling their behavior with rewards or punishments. Misbehavior is ordinarily considered to be the result of misguided efforts to satisfy basic needs (Dreikurs, 1960). Children satisfy their needs with limited understanding of various social implications for their choices and without examining the assumptions regarding life conditions. They may not realize, for example, that satisfying their need for acceptance depends on contributing to the welfare of others. Dreikurs (1968) believed that all behavior is motivated by the following four needs:

- gaining attention
- exercising power
- exacting revenge
- displaying inadequacy

The most predominating need is that of gaining attention and acceptance. When this need goes unfulfilled, young people may become a class nuisance as they seek to get attention. They commonly select a way to behave that is disruptive and thus encourage their teachers to control them. If they fail to acquire all the attention they wish, they often initiate a power struggle with their teachers that could have been avoided had the individual received the desired attention. Teachers should avoid entering into a power contest with students.

If students fail to satisfy their need for power, they may feel compelled to take revenge against the teacher who they believe treats them unfairly. It is very difficult to avoid problems with these children. They can become very destructive, and teachers commonly provoke more vengeful behavior when they try to correct them. Children who fail to achieve a sense of self-worth through attention, power, or revenge often become so discouraged that they give up, wrap themselves in a cloak of inadequacy, and withdraw. Ironically, this is a last-ditch effort by the individual to gain acceptance.

To help students change their disruptive behavior, teachers try to help them understand their misguided behavior and to realize that they can satisfy their needs in more acceptable ways. Teachers first attempt to ascertain the students' motives, after which they communicate them. Students are then encouraged to exchange their mistaken goals for useful ones and become committed to these new goals. Finally, students are taught how to apply logical consequences in their lives. Logical consequences do not naturally occur, but are contrived, realistic happenings (Dinkmeyer & Dinkmeyer, 1976). For example, the logical consequence for breaking a window is having to pay for it (Dreikurs & Grey, 1970). If a student pushed someone on the stairway, the teacher may let him or her decide whether to avoid pushing in the future or go back to the class and wait until everyone else has cleared the stairway before going down (Dreikurs, Grunwald, & Pepper, 1982).

Dreikurs suggests that many discipline problems can be prevented by having discipline-oriented class discussions. In these discussions, students talk about how to avoid problems and improve the class. They focus on the responsibilities of class members and formulate plans that give the class a sense of direction through the establishment of instructional goals (Dreikurs, Grunwald, & Pepper, 1982).

Student disruptions can be reduced by helping them identify and make value judgements about their inappropriate behavior and its consequences.

Reality Therapy/Choice Theory

Reality therapy/choice theory is a leadership-based approach to discipline created by William Glasser. Glasser rejects behavior management theories and provides a rationale for using a discipline approach that teaches students to assume more responsibility for their misbehavior and change it (Glasser, 1984). He believes that most discipline problems can be avoided by helping students to understand and routinely satisfy their basic needs in legitimate ways (Glasser, 1998). These needs include:

- love
- control
- freedom
- fun

Glasser indicates that many school discipline problems are a function of commonly used boss-management techniques. Students are given no recourse regarding what happens to them in school. However, students need to be given greater control over the curriculum and the instructional program (Glasser, 1992). In his research he discovered that students are able to achieve at much higher levels academically than they actually do. He concluded that greater student involvement in school decision making is required to help them realize their academic potential (Glasser, 1998). The lack of quality in young people's school experiences, along with excessive teacher and administrative control, lead to discipline problems. Classroom meetings that promote student decision making can substantially reduce discipline problems (Glasser, 1969). In those cases where discipline problems occur despite efforts to prevent them, one-on-one interactions with the disruptive student can be conducted (Glasser, 1965), including conversations in which the misbehaving student (1) identifies the inappropriate behavior, (2) indicates the consequences associated with the behavior, (3) makes value judgments about the behavior and its consequences, and (4) creates a plan to eliminate the inappropriate behavior.

Decision Points

Make a series of school observations. Determine the kind of discipline approach used by the observed teachers. Make an assessment as to the effectiveness of these approaches.

Preventing Discipline Problems

Mr. Olsen, in the vignette outlined earlier, experienced a particularly acute discipline problem. Over time, the situation deteriorated badly, as can be expected when problems are not corrected. In addition, he contributed to the problem by trying to punish students, not realizing that some students found his tactics to reinforce rather than inhibit bad behavior. Furthermore, the whole class, tiring of his responses, had apparently colluded to inflict more misery on him. The difficulties Mr. Olsen encountered are not unusual. Many teachers experience problems keeping well-ordered, productive classes. There are a number of reasons for this, including an irrelevant curriculum, boredom, insufficient need satisfaction, and coercive, punitive rule enforcement.

Teachers usually deal with misbehavior by punishing the offender. Unless punishments are sufficiently aversive, however, they are as likely to promote more misbehavior as they are to eliminate problems (Jones & Jones, 1995). However, even when punishment helps terminate the misbehavior, it commonly leads to unpredictable consequences. For example, students may refuse to work or react later in negative ways like destroying school property. In addition, punitive treatment can lead to more aggressive behavior and violence (Holms & Robins, 1988).

Punishment usually provokes resistance and resentment, which children may take out on others, including peers. Punished children commonly feel worse about themselves and resent those who punish them (Kohn, 1993). Obviously, learning conditions deteriorate as a consequence of punishment. In addition, punishment is ineffectual in eliminating inappropriate behavior in the long run. Punished children ordinarily revolt or try to calculate a way to circumvent requirements (Kammi, 1991).

Rather than punishing students for misbehavior, teachers should establish classroom procedures to prevent these problems. Obviously, if discipline problems can be prevented they should be. The reason for this is simple: once problems occur and are reacted to, difficulties are multiplied. It is much more difficult to quell a student outburst than to prevent it. After misbehavior has occurred and reactions are made, emotions flair up and add to the problem. This is particularly true after administering punishment. Students tend to react emotionally to punishment, and their reactions often interfere with solving problems. In addition, punishment routinely fails to teach correct behavior because there is an exclusive focus on misbehavior. Punishment has no place in learning communities.

NATIONAL TEACHING STANDARDS

Teachers know how to manage groups of students. They need to know how to establish social norms for student-teacher interactions and help students learn to adopt appropriate roles and responsibilities for their own learning and that of their peers. This includes teaching students to work independently without constant direct supervision by a teacher.

Teachers should examine various instructional strategies and organize structures that will best enhance learning. They should continually search for new forms of organization that may expand their repertoire and provide effective instruction.

Classroom Problem-Solving Meetings

In learning communities, teachers try to prevent discipline problems rather than reacting to misbehavior. Learning communities provide a good environment for prevention because students routinely make decisions about the curricula as well as classroom procedures. When students decide on classroom rules and reach agreements with one another regarding what they will and won't accept in terms of classroom behavior, there is greater commitment for following the rules and a greater inclination to monitor and correct inappropriate behavior. One effective strategy for preventing discipline problems is the classroom problem-solving meeting. In these meetings, the teacher initially assumes a leadership role and later transfers substantial leadership responsibility to students. Students gradually assume a more active role in guiding meetings as they become more accustomed and able. Classroom problem-solving meetings follow a five-step process:

1. determining curriculum
2. setting guidelines for formulating classroom procedures or rules
3. determining consequences for violating expectations
4. formulating guidelines for improving instruction
5. reaching agreement and making commitments

Step 1: Determining Curriculum

The purpose of determining curriculum is to help students acquire a sense of commitment for classroom learning activities, which is achievable when students are given a bonafide role in helping to determine the curriculum and accept the course of study as personally relevant and important. In addition, curriculum decisions must be valid. Student-selected curricula are more valid when choices are made that reflect the implications of various learning activities for the present and for the future. Students must be taught decision-making skills so they can properly consider alternatives and apply a rational approach to making choices. These skills prepare students to carefully examine the usefulness of what they learn. For example, some school experiences may be more important for college-bound students, while others are especially suitable for students planning to attend technical schools or enter the workforce right out of high school. Potential homemakers may require different experiences than individuals who plan to enter the job market. Of course, some experiences may be appropriate for all students. Students must consider all these implications and, with teacher guidance and input, help determine the most valuable learning experiences. Teachers should be constantly vigilant in identifying those students who change their minds about college or anticipated occupations. Students should understand that it is acceptable to make modifications in their plans at any time. However, students still need to see their schooling as contributing to their future plans even if changes become necessary.

To make valid judgments, students must know legitimate potential curriculum components. In most subjects, far more topics exist to learn about than could be included in a single course. In addition, various concepts exist that some groups or individuals consider more important than others. For example, some aspects of the curriculum are prescribed by state departments and school curriculum committees. Professional organizations often provide curriculum guidelines for the various subjects. Students should be taught to examine all the possibilities and make selections that are in harmony with state core curricula and yet reflect personal desires and interests, as well as taking into account the implications to which reference has already been made.

The first thing teachers should do is acquaint students with appropriate options for topics associated with the subject. Students should also be invited to supply some of their own suggestions. To prepare students to give input, teachers should present various references and books and allow time for students to explore these materials. They might, for example, provide various journals that report the work being done in a subject area. Sufficient time and direction should be given so that students know many of the topics that could possibly be included in the course. The teacher should draw attention to the core curriculum and to various available references, such as textbooks and so on. The teacher might also provide students with suggestions regarding approaches to the subject. In English, students might take a writing, critiquing approach to the course. In history, students might write the history of their community as a focal point, so they understand what goes into creating a world or country history. In a sociology class, students might perform a community study and compare what they find to data reported for other communities in their textbooks and field journals. Biology students may focus their study on health, inquiry, or ecology. In a chemistry class, students may take either a theoretical or a practical approach.

Along with learning the various ways a subject can be studied, students need to be taught decision-making skills. In this process, decisions they render should be consistent with what they interpret as the greatest good for the entire class, not just personal interests. The greatest good for the greatest number, with appropriate consideration for the needs of all individuals, should guide their deliberations. Individual needs should not be ignored, but they cannot take precedence over the larger group needs. This usually involves including a few units of instruction that address the needs of small groups or individuals, while focusing the bulk of instruction to larger groups of students. The teacher needs to explain this kind of differentiation early in the decision process. In considering a large number of topics, students must learn how to prioritize their selections. They must realize that they should not include too much, and that it is possible to create a curriculum that is too broad and superficial. They will need guidance to include fewer topics to study in depth so that greater scholarship and excellence can be anticipated.

Finally, students should be asked to express their commitment for the curriculum they have created. If any student has reservations, these should be addressed so that the entire class supports the final decision. Acceptance of and commitment for the proposed classroom learning activities are essential before beginning the next step.

Step 2: Setting Guidelines for Formulating Classroom Procedures or Rules

Once there is commitment for the proposed curriculum, classroom procedures can be successfully determined. To initiate a classroom procedure discussion, the teacher should indicate that procedures are being created so that the desired curriculum can be successfully implemented. In reality, "classroom procedures" consist of a list of rules. However, "classroom procedures" is a better term because of the negative connotation commonly given to the word *rules*. Usually, teachers are the exclusive authors and enforcers of classroom rules. Students, therefore, do not experience a sense of ownership. In fact, imposed rules are often actively opposed by students, sometimes causing them to misbehave. A teacher may engage the class in a discussion, something like Mr. Lott does:

MR. LOTT: Class, you have prepared a curriculum for which you have expressed your commitment. You have indicated that you're interested and excited about what you might learn. You have made your decisions about the curriculum after preparing yourselves to make valid choices. I am also excited about the part I will play in your learning. I feel the same sense of commitment that you do. However, sometimes individuals may do things in class that limit the learning of others even though they have expressed a commitment to other class members not to. What are some of the things that you believe may disrupt the learning of the class?

RAUL: The worst thing is when people talk when they should be quiet.

SABRINA: Yea, and also when they yell out answers to questions without raising their hands.

MR. LOTT: So the first problem is too much noise, and the other is not appropriately taking turns to be heard in class.

RONALD: Yes, but I don't like to have to raise my hand every time I want to ask a question or say something in class. That sucks!

SABRINA: You might not like to, but that's tough. It'd be good for you to do something someone else wants for a change. Can you imagine what it would be like to have everyone talking at the same time? I've been in classes like that. It just becomes a yelling match. I think we need to vote on this.

MR. LOTT: Yes, we do need to decide as a group how we feel about this issue, and whether or not we wish to support what the class decides. Is there further discussion?

CHARLOTTE: I have something to say about this. Ronald, you don't even have a clue. It's the pits to let anyone shout out answers. In some of my classes where that happens, teachers have become so frustrated they just give us questions to answer out of the textbook and then sit at their desks glaring at us. Mr. Lott, how do you feel about that?

MR. LOTT: I suspect most teachers want students to talk one at a time so everyone can hear what is being said. Also, it is much more difficult to manage a discussion when everyone is shouting out answers to questions. It is hard to maintain continuity and to call on students in an orderly way. Sometimes a teacher may want to call on a particular student for some reason, but other students sabotage their intentions. So, from a teaching perspective, hand-raising makes sense. I must confess I have sometimes just stopped discussion and had students work quietly at their desks rather than have a discussion full of disruptions.

CHARLOTTE: That's good enough for me. I don't want to be in a disorderly class. I don't mind if someone else answers questions I know the answer to, but I don't want people interrupting me and I certainly don't want to waste my time doing seat work just because a bunch of loudmouths make the class too noisy.

MR. LOTT: Ronald, you said you preferred being able to express yourself without coordinating with other class members. You have heard how some of them have reacted to your suggestion. Do you have a response?

RONALD: I hate formal discussions. A lot of stuff never gets said. I know I don't participate much when I have to wait to be called on. I just thought we could have a discussion without that. You know, we could just watch each other and take turns without interrupting.

VANESSA: I've been in other classes where they have tried that. It is always a miserable failure. It is hard to know when to speak and when not to. That's when I don't want to participate. I just mentally drop out. I think most of us feel that way. Ronald, I can't believe you have ever been in a class where they're doing what you suggest. What are you telling us this for? You know darn well we can't do what you suggest! The teacher has to regulate discussion! We'll never talk about what we're supposed to talk about if people just yell out stuff! And remember what Mr. Lott said about asking questions for a particular student. We have to remember that, too.

RONALD: OK, I can go along with that. Don't get so riled up. I was just suggesting a new way to do this. You don't have to get hostile.

MR. LOTT: Ronald, you say you can go along with what others are proposing. Does that mean you feel good about it, and feel it is necessary?

RONALD: Yes, I do. I just wasn't considering the whole situation. I was only thinking of some dry discussions I've participated in. But I can see that things could get a little out of hand.

MR. LOTT: Are there any other things you think will interfere with learning?

WALNETTA: If we're going to be working together, everyone has to do their part. We can't be slackers. We need to do our work on time and finish assignments when we're supposed to. I've worked in groups where I had to do it all. I won't do that anymore. I hate to work with a bunch of freeloaders.

LING: I think we need to do our own work and not bother others. That ought to take care of a lot of problems. I need it quiet to work. Some people can be so inconsiderate. And I don't want people looking at my work. I hate people who cheat.

MARLA: That depends on whether or not you're working with other students on a project. Sometimes we need to help one another and sometimes we need to do our own work. You know, Ling, you need to learn to cooperate more. You might learn something if you did.

LING: You're one to talk. I don't see you helping anyone. You certainly haven't helped me. But let's get this straight. I really mean that we should help one another but not bother people by poking them or criticizing them.

MR. LOTT: Ling has brought up an important idea. Criticizing and bullying one another can cause a lot of disruptions in class. Let's hear some more discussion about this.

ROGER: I'm one of those people who has been bullied. It's not just in class but in the hallways, too. Teachers don't see all this. Students have to help one another. I often wished there was someone who would stick up for me when bullies attack me. How come none of you guys have helped me?

MELISSA: Well, Roger, I've never seen you get attacked, but I agree with you. I've watched some other classmates being bullied. It made me sick, but I didn't know what to do about it. I guess I was afraid I would be attacked too if I interfered. But if we all stood together against bullies, that may help. And I have been publicly criticized a few times. I know how it feels. Don't you think we can fight against these things? Can't we all agree to do that?

MR. LOTT: Well, what about it, class? How many feel they want to support these classroom procedures and help one another avoid the unpleasantness of being criticized and bullied?

Other rules would be determined in a similar way with the teacher helping to create as few rules as necessary. If students fail to bring up rules that in the judgment of the teacher should be considered, cues can be given to suggest that these additional rules also be discussed.

Step 3: Determining Consequences for Violating Expectations

Classroom procedures or rules should have consequences attached. Ordinarily, students are punished for disobeying rules. Punishment is usually arbitrary and administered as retribution for misbehavior or as an aversive deterrent to future rule breaking. Sometimes it satisfies a teacher's desire to avenge indignities suffered at the hands of misbehaving students. Because punishment is ordinarily intended to be a painful deterrent, it rarely is seen by students as a logical consequence for their misbehavior. Logical consequences are better deterrents to misbehavior, particularly if students are involved in deciding what the consequences should be. If consequences seem appropriate to students for disruptive behavior, and if students have actually helped choose them, students will more likely accept them as necessary. Such consequences are better deterrents than punishment.

Consequences must be a logical result of rule breaking. If something is broken it should be paid for or replaced. If someone's feelings are hurt, an apology is needed. If some students don't do their part in a research project, they should not benefit equally with those who do the work. If students talk and interfere with the learning of other students, they should be excluded from the learning activities they disrupt until they formulate a plan for readmittance.

Teachers need to help students understand the difference between punishment and logical consequences. In identifying consequences, students are likely to list punishments instead, due to their extensive experience with them. Most will not have had experience with responsibility-based discipline. Teachers will need to help students make clear distinctions between punishment and consequences. For example, a student might suggest that anyone who destroys books or other school property should be sent to the principal's office for punishment. The teacher might respond to the student with a cue: "If someone breaks school equipment or tears books, who should have to pay for it?" Cues like this can help students learn that there are essential differences between consequences and punishment.

Students accept ownership of consequences they help determine, reaching an agreement with other class members so there can be unanimity as consequences are applied.

TABLE 10.1   *Punishment Versus Consequences.*

Behavior	Punishment	Consequences
Tearing a book	Being sent to the principal's office	Having to pay for it
Disrupting class by talking	Being sent to detention for the day	Being excluded from class until a plan is created for re-entry
Cursing the teacher in class	Being suspended	Having to appear before a student committee to give an accounting and a plan to avoid future profanity
Cheating on a test	Having test torn up and no credit given	Giving student an alternative test
Killing fish in the aquaria	Being sent to the principal's office	Replacing the fish
Throwing paper airplanes and flipping rubber bands at other students	Being sent to detention for two days	Cleaning up the airplanes and rubber bands, apologizing to the class, and creating a plan to change

When a student disrupts class, this behavior should be discussed in connection to rules and consequences he or she has helped create. Thus, students can see their inappropriate behavior as a departure from their own intentions and commitments. They should be able to simply conclude that they are violating commitments they have made to all their classmates (see Table 10.1). The following is an example of how Mr. Lott interacted with his class regarding consequences:

MR. LOTT: As a class, we have outlined our curriculum as well as classroom procedures that you believe will help you achieve your learning goals. Although we should not expect anyone to violate his or her commitment to the class by being disruptive, we must determine what the consequences should be if the expectations and commitments you have agreed on are broken. What do you think should be the consequences of not following the procedures you have outlined?

SHARON: That's easy. We should just take some points away from their grade.

CHRISTIAN: We could do that, but we could also send them to see Mr. Castro, the assistant principal. I've heard what he does to students. That would put a stop to problems.

MR. LOTT: It sounds like you want to hurt a person for misbehaving.

RICHARD: Well, they deserve it if they violate our rules, especially when they have helped make them up. They ought to know better.

MR. LOTT: Has anyone had punishment that you felt was undeserved or too severe?

OWEN: I have. One time when I was in the fifth grade I brought some marbles to school. My teacher saw me playing with them. They were still in my pocket. She took them away from me, and I never got them back. She also cussed me out in front of the whole class, telling them she was making an example of me, and they better not do what I did or worse might happen to them. I hated her. I really slacked off in that class after that.

MR. LOTT: So what do you think your teacher should have done?

OWEN: I didn't think I was disturbing the class, but even if I had been, she should have just taken my marbles away until school was out and then given them back. I had my favorite "taw" in my pocket. I still feel angry about that.

MR. LOTT: Let's look at another situation. Say that a student talks loudly during quiet study time even though he has agreed to be quiet. What should we as a class do?

TIFFANY: We should make him sit out in the hall for the next week. I don't think I'd send him to see Mr. Castro, but he should get some kind of punishment. We can't keep noisy people in class. I can't work when the class is too loud.

MR. LOTT: Remember, we don't want to punish; we just want consequences that help people recognize unacceptable behavior and honor the commitments they have made. How long should people have to sit in the hall after they have decided to change the way they behave in class?

BEXI: You probably want us to say that once they've decided to change, and tell you how they plan to act in class, they should be able to come back to class immediately. But that's not enough. That won't keep a lot of people I know from being bad. And if they act up again, it shouldn't be so easy to get back into class. Maybe they should have to make an apology to the whole class and say they won't be noisy anymore. Yea, they should tell us how they have gone against what the whole class agreed to. That will show them what liars they are.

GARN: That's too embarrassing.

JOHANNA: That's the whole point of it. If they disturb the rest of us they should have to apologize. And they should have to admit they have broken a promise to the rest of us.

MR. LOTT: Obviously, there is a difference of opinion about having to apologize and the form it should take. Perhaps we should see how the rest of the class feels. How many think disruptive students should have to apologize? (All but Garn raise their hands.) It looks like only one student opposes this. Garn, do you want to say more about this?

GARN: I would be embarrassed, but I will go along with it. I don't think that will happen to me anyway. You guys go too far to make people feel bad. You should never call a person a liar. But I can support it if everyone else wants to do it.

MR. LOTT: It is important that consequences clearly communicate what should happen to someone who ignores classroom procedures, and the point about having people acknowledge they have not kept their commitment may be appropriate. Labeling someone a liar in this case may be carrying this too far. Remember that the purpose of punishment is to make someone suffer pain and embarrassment. Garn has said he would be embarrassed to make an apology. He finds an apology punishing. Perhaps we need to think this through again. Is there any more input?

REESE: When I voted to include apologies, I was thinking of it mostly as punishment. I have always felt that people who goof off in class and ruin it for the rest of us should suffer for what they do. Now I think I oppose this policy. We shouldn't embarrass anyone. We need to think up some other consequence. I'd like to suggest that anyone who continues to be disruptive should have to make a written plan of how to avoid bad behavior in the future. It should be a very detailed plan. They could just give it to Mr. Lott. It doesn't have to be a public thing.

MR. LOTT: Reese has given another way to handle these problems. What do you think about his suggestion? Are there any more comments?

RICO: Let's vote on it. I'm ready.

MR. LOTT: Is there general agreement with Reese's suggestion? (All students raise their hands.) It looks like we agree on this policy. I think you have made an important distinction between consequences and punishment. Keep in mind that in a couple of weeks we will have another classroom meeting and at that time we can evaluate the plan you have made, changing it as needed. That is true of any classroom procedure we have made.

Additional consequences would be identified in a similar way, with the teacher providing cues for possible consequences students fail to bring up. The teacher should be careful to avoid imposing consequences or taking too dominant a role in identifying them.

Step 4: Formulating Guidelines for Improving Instruction

Formulating guidelines allows students to give input regarding approaches to learning that they personally have found successful. For example, some students do better with "hands-on" experiences, while others prefer reading or writing. Some students like to build models or create artistic representations of a topic. Some like to interact with their peers, while others choose to explore things on their own. A few students may want to engage in long-term projects they consider relevant. Some classmates may feel they benefit more from teacher-led learning activities.

When a teacher has her class discuss learning approaches, it is wise not to initiate discussion by asking students what kinds of activities are fun for them, although having fun may be a critical aspect of useful learning. Rather, teachers should ask students to suggest the kinds of learning activities they find most beneficial. Learning should be central to discussions about all of the previous steps as well, thus setting the stage for more serious student input. Otherwise, students may give suggestions that have not been seriously examined. Discussion should focus on learning excellence and on classroom activities that support the development of excellence.

Mr. Lott provides an example of how this step might take place:

MR. LOTT: Class, so far we have chosen our curriculum, created classroom procedures to help us learn effectively, and identified consequences for disrupting. Let's now consider the kind of learning activities we will include. What kind of learning activities help you learn better? Remember, we want everyone to achieve a high level of excellence. We might try some kinds of activities that we decide to discard later. Also, we may later come up with some new ones.

SHARON: I don't like lectures. I get so bored my mind wanders.

MOANA: I like to work in groups. It's a lot more fun than just sitting around being bored.

AMMON: I don't like groups. I've never been in one where I didn't have to do all the work. Other people just let you do it, too. Some people are just too lazy or dumb to do their part.

JARED: You're the stupid one. Why'd you do it all? You didn't have to. You could have told the teacher. I like to work in groups. Maybe some of us could work in groups while the rest do something else. Is it possible to do that, Mr. Lott?

MR. LOTT: Yes. It is quite all right to do some activities together as a class and others in groups or as individuals. We can provide for choices when groups or individuals are interested in different topics or when they prefer different learning methods.

JAMIE: I think it would be fun to have a party every Friday. It would make the rest of the week easier to bear. We all get so bored. We need a break.

CHRISTIAN: Yes! Let's do it! Parties would be great! Yea, party time!

MR. LOTT: It sounds like you want to have parties because you assume the learning activities you have chosen may not be enjoyable and meaningful. Do we need to examine what we have decided so far and pick more relevant activities?

CHARLOTTE: No, we don't need to pick other activities. I'm excited about what we're going to do. We don't need parties to spice things up. That's stupid. It's no solution to boredom. Jamie, you just need to get involved. That's the best way not to get bored.

RONALD: I agree, particularly when we will have a chance to change things later on. What do we need parties for? Most of the time I hate school. It really stresses me out. Everything is set in stone even when it is the biggest drag possible. We can make learning fun. Anyway, maybe we can bring in some treats occasionally when we are having group activities. Can we do that, Mr. Lott?

MR. LOTT: There is no school rule against having refreshments, occasionally, assuming we clean up after ourselves. I suppose it would depend on what refreshments you bring. Toupo, how often would you suggest having refreshments?

TOUPO: You'd better not leave that up to me. I'm a party animal, but I'd hate to be the one to arrange all this. Maybe we could do it once a month.

MR. LOTT: (Mr. Lott looks around the class for additional comments.) Unless there are more comments, let's assume we'll have some kind of simple refreshments for a month or two. Later we can reconsider how we feel about it. Are there any more comments about preferred kinds of learning activities?

CAROLYN: I like to do art, but there is nowhere I can do it except in art classes. People who like to write get to do it in most of their classes. Is there any way to use my art interests in this class?

ANGELA: I'd like to do a research project. But I know no one would let me. It would take several months. They're not going to let me do that, are they? I did a project in my biology class last year. Me and Jennifer worked on it most of the year and then entered it in the science fair. We didn't do much of what the rest of the class did. Mr. Oliverson told us what we did was more valuable than what the other students did. I felt it was, too. I think we got to do it because it was preparation for the science fair. But this is a social studies class.

MR. LOTT: You have explained some important ways you differ from one another in how you learn. It would be unwise for us as a class to ignore these differences. We should certainly arrange to accommodate different learning preferences and skills. What can be done will depend on how carefully we plan each of these variations. I hope each of you will try to achieve excellence in terms of your learning preferences. You should also be willing to experiment with new things rather than staying exclusively with the "tried and true." I think it would be wise for each of you to make a written statement about your personal learning preferences and turn them in to me so I can be aware of them. I'll report back to the class. I'm afraid some things might be overlooked otherwise.

Mr. Lott tries to keep channels of communication open by not telling students which learning approaches are appropriate and which are not. He also tries to raise issues when it appears students are not including important information in their decisions. In addition, he tries to clarify the issues so students have a better understanding of what is involved before prematurely drawing conclusions. Also notice that Mr. Lott does not comment on a request to avoid lecturing. Knowing the ineffectiveness of lecturing, Mr. Lott doesn't intend to use this method much anyway. If a number of students had asked that he lecture, he might want to point out its limitations and his own preference for not using it. It is important to realize that teacher input is also important in this process. Teachers don't simply supply what students request. Rather, they assess student input along with their own views and capabilities. For example, a teacher may consider unannounced quizzes as central to his or her teaching strategy, even though students request that quizzes not be given. It may be wise for the teacher to reconsider his position after listening to student input. If the teacher still considers quizzes to be critical, students should be appraised of the reasons and allowed to offer rebuttals. If the teacher explains that unannounced quizzes are important in getting students to prepare for class, students may indicate that they will always be prepared for classroom activities, thus negating the need for quizzes. If students were in fact conscientious in their preparations, the teacher may have little reason to give unannounced quizzes.

Step 5: Reaching Agreement and Making Commitments

The final step is to have students reach agreement on the curriculum as well as classroom procedures, consequences, and desired learning approaches, and to make commitments to one another about these matters. It is important for all class members to feel comfortable with the proposals and to accept them as binding. Otherwise, they will not enthusiastically participate. They will be unlikely to strive for excellence and instead will mark time or frustrate their classmates' learning efforts. The following is how Mr. Lott helped students to make commitments to one another:

MR. LOTT: So far you as a class have decided what the curriculum will be for the year. You have identified behaviors that may interfere with learning, and you have created classroom procedures for preventing these problems. You have also made a list of consequences for violating commitments and have given me some suggestions for the kind of learning activities that help you to learn better. It is now time to consider the degree of commitment you have for what you have planned. By show of hands, how many of you feel committed to the plan? Is there any one who doesn't feel commitment or who would like to make a comment or raise a question about the class decisions?

MARLENE: I want to object. I can't go along with all those group projects like it was decided. I hate those. I always have to do all the work.

MR. LOTT: Keep in mind, Marlene, that you are free to find alternative activities to do on your own rather than having to do group work. Also remember that, in this class, group projects will be different than what many of you have experienced. Everyone will have a responsibility that he or she can't shift to someone else.

MARLENE: Well, I don't like group work. And I don't like some of the topics that we're going to study. Some of them won't prepare us for college. I thought this course was to be college preparation.

MR. LOTT: I have tried to make sure that the class considered college preparation and other student needs as they decided on topics for study. I believe the class has created a good balance. But you feel that this curriculum does not meet your needs. Would you like to discuss some modifications in what the class has decided?

MARLENE: No. I guess not. I was just checking things out.

MR. LOTT: Does this mean that you are willing to give your full commitment and participation? Otherwise, it will not be fair to you and the other students. You'll have a better experience if you fully participate with class members and follow the classroom procedures the class has agreed upon.

MARLENE: No, I'm alright. I want to stay in the class. I think I can learn what I need to learn.

(Note: Sometimes students object in order to test the limits rather than to seek alternatives. This appears to be the case with Marlene.)

MR. LOTT: I'm glad you wish to stay, Marlene. Your decision to do so is a statement of your commitment to the class. Sometimes class members may have concerns about some aspect of the program. There may be something that isn't working well. We will meet together again in a week to evaluate what has been decided. Changes will be made as needed.

Helping Students Reaffirm Commitments

Sometimes discipline problems occur even though students have entered into agreements with their classmates as members of a learning community to participate in class responsibly and not be disruptive. In this case no imperative exists to teach students about rules and consequences, but rather to help them remember what they have agreed to and to reaffirm their commitments. Disruptive students should not be given a lecture by the teacher regarding their behavior. Instead, they should be directed to compare their behavior to community expectations, which they have been involved in making, and invited to present a proposal to the class for any changes they feel are necessary. The interaction between student and teacher may be like the following:

MR. LOTT: Rosella, how does your behavior during science lab today compare with the agreement you and the class made at the beginning of the year?

ROSELLA: How should I know? I don't know what you mean.

MR. LOTT: What kind of possible tragedy did you and the class want to prevent in the lab?

ROSELLA: We didn't want anyone to get hurt, but I wasn't doing anything that would hurt anyone. Don't tell me that a little water would hurt someone.

MR. LOTT: What did you and other class members agree was necessary behavior in the lab? (Mr. Lott sidesteps Rosella's suggestion that her violation of laboratory safety rules was a special case and should be permitted.)

ROSELLA: Well, you know. We were to observe all the safety rules.

MR. LOTT: And what were you doing that violated your commitment to class members? (Notice that commitment to class members is retained as the focus.)

ROSELLA: I was just spraying a little water at Linae through a micro-pipette. We were just having fun. That wouldn't do any harm. She didn't care. Besides, other people were doing it, too.

MR. LOTT: What did you and the class decide was wrong with doing that? (Rosella's excuse is ignored.)

ROSELLA: Sometimes there could be something harmful in the pipette, and we decided never to take a chance even though we knew exactly what was in the pipette. But I knew it was just water.

MR. LOTT: What did you and your classmates decide would be the consequences of spraying someone? (The excuse is bypassed again.)

ROSELLA: We wouldn't be allowed to participate in labs until we made a written plan the other class members considered adequate to avoid such problems in the future. But, Mr. Lott, I have to get my project done. I have to finish it today. We have to turn it in tomorrow to be graded. If I don't, I won't get any credit for it.

MR. LOTT: I realize that, but how serious did the class feel it was to obey lab rules? (The reality of the excuse was acknowledged, but given no credence because of the seriousness of what was done.)

ROSELLA: Pretty serious. But Mr. Lott, I have to get an A in this class. My dad will kill me.

MR. LOTT: And what excuses were to be allowed and what circumstances were to be considered in changing the consequences of breaking lab rules? (Mr. Lott helps Rosella to see that there are no justifiable excuses for ignoring laboratory safety rules.)

ROSELLA: We decided there were no excuses and there were no special circumstances because, if rules were violated, someone could be seriously injured. But maybe there could be an exception made in this case. I didn't do any harm.

MR. LOTT: What did we agree to do if anyone wanted to reconsider classroom procedures and consequences?

ROSELLA: We could bring it up at a class meeting. But that will be too late.

MR. LOTT: I think that we also discussed that topic. What was agreed to about that?

ROSELLA: We decided no exceptions to rules and consequences were to be made before the class met and considered proposals for modifications.

MR. LOTT: If I made an exception, whose trust would I be violating?

ROSELLA: The whole class. How I wish I'd never squirted that water. Now I'll miss out on getting credit for my project. You know if this had happened at the beginning of the term I could have finished my project. Having it happen now makes it impossible. It just doesn't seem fair.

MR. LOTT: How does the danger of disobeying a safety rule in the lab now compare with doing the same earlier in the year? (Mr. Lott wisely chooses not to discuss the idea of fairness and instead helps Rosella see that safety concerns don't depend on the time when unsafe acts are committed.)

ROSELLA: There is no difference. I should have known better. The rule is OK. I just used poor judgment. I'll start writing my plan now.

Notice that Mr. Lott is interested in teaching Rosella about the potentially devastating consequences to others for violating lab rules, not just the consequences to her. He also helps her realize she has helped formulate the rules and consequences and has a commitment to other students to abide by what was decided. Finally, Mr. Lott reaffirms his commitment to the class plan as well. He doesn't take it upon himself to make exceptions without the consent of class members. There could, of course, be times when a teacher may have to make exceptions, but these should be rare, and the justification for any exceptions should be given to the class to seek their approval at the earliest convenience. If teachers routinely override class decisions, the preventive discipline approach can be seriously undermined. Students will be less inclined to consider it binding on them. Ownership can be eroded away unless students are involved in the decisions made.

Decision Points

With a group of peers, role-play a series of discipline problems using the techniques for correcting misbehavior where students have made prior commitments regarding classroom behavior.

Student ownership of classroom rules is essential in maintaining their commitment for them.

Changing Classroom Procedures and Agreements

The instructional program and discipline procedures should be systematically assessed from time to time to determine if they are still appropriate and acceptable to the class. Past experience may show that adjustments are needed. This provides an avenue for revisions as well as for giving students an opportunity to renew their commitments to one another. These meetings will need to be more frequent in the beginning. As problems get resolved and students become accustomed to relating to one another in a different way, fewer meetings will be needed. Ordinarily, reaffirming commitments is essential in the early weeks. This is particularly true for students who have been conditioned to punishment or reward systems of discipline. It is easy to slip back into prior ways of thinking and acting.

The format for problem solving in classroom meetings is to allow students considerable autonomy. Students or the teacher may raise issues and problems for consideration. Teachers need to be careful not to take over and dominate these meetings. The teacher should be an active group member without always being the one to provide direct leadership. The teachers will need to coach students during the first few meetings and perhaps model how these meetings should proceed, but eventually students should have the opportunity to lead out.

In addressing problems, particularly regarding the discipline or failure of group members to responsibly follow-through on commitments, the group must maintain an atmosphere of caring and concern. The way in which any problem-solving session is conducted should be carefully defined in advance and followed. Differences of opinion about matters concerning the group should actually be prized as part of the group's strength. Consensus doesn't necessarily have to be sought, but there does have to be agreement that divergent views are accepted within the confines of group norms. The norms that are established must be accommodating enough to allow sufficient divergence for a variety of inputs, but not so loose that the group cannot function.

Students may not be used to having the power to change things. Often part of the accountability scheme is to follow-through on commitments regardless, as if making modifications somehow nullifies agreements and diminishes the quality of the undertaking. However, modifications can and should be made when they are desirable for improvement, particularly when modification procedures are established in advance. When quality and excellence are of primary importance, changes are inevitable.

Decision Points

With a group of peers, role-play a problem-solving meeting involved in (1) making adjustments to the curriculum and (2) solving a discipline problem.

Reflections About Self

1. Which of your teachers punished you and/or your classmates while you were in the public schools? How did you feel either about being punished or watching others being punished? Was punishment a deterrent for all students in your classes?

2. Compare the discipline tactics of teachers you considered to be effective with those who were not. What were the differences? How did you feel about each of these teachers?
3. How do you think you and your classmates in the public schools would have responded to a preventive discipline approach? Would you have acted more responsibly?

NATIONAL TEACHING STANDARDS

Teachers are able to develop systems for overseeing their classrooms so that students and teachers alike can focus on learning, not on controlling disruptive behavior.

Solving Discipline Problems Involving No Prior Commitments

In some cases, teachers may have to deal with students who have made no commitments to their classmates regarding classroom behavior. Quite different strategies need to be employed than when preventive discipline procedures are employed. In this case, one-on-one teaching is required to help the individual identify his misbehavior and its consequences and then formulate a viable plan for preventing any future problems.

Solving discipline problems is more a matter of teaching than of trying to regulate student behavior. Discipline approaches that regulate students either punish unwanted behavior or attempt to reinforce acceptable behavior. The teacher's role is to carefully monitor students and police their class actions. Assertive discipline and behavior modification are examples of approaches that use these techniques. These discipline approaches have limited power to promote student responsibility and self-discipline. They also have the inherent problems associated with punishment and rewards. Punishment can stimulate more rebellion or withdrawal, and rewards may inappropriately condition students to the reward and rob them of self-sufficiency.

Teaching students to face up to their misbehavior and make appropriate modifications involves the following steps:

1. help the student identify his or her inappropriate behavior
2. help the student identify consequences
3. help students compare intentions with behavior
4. have students make a value judgment about consequences, intentions, and behavior
5. have students make a plan for modifying behavior and express a commitment to follow the plan

Step 1: Help the Student Identify His or Her Inappropriate Behavior

Although reasons always exist behind a student's misbehavior, teachers should not investigate these motives. This usually leads to excuses and interferes with helping students identify inappropriate behavior. It is imperative that students identify their own misbehavior in order to accept ownership of the problem. Most individuals do not like to accept their own wrongdoing, so lying, shifting the blame, and giving excuses will ordinarily occur, but these reactions should be avoided as much as possible. A conversation between a teacher and a misbehaving student may go something like the following. In this case, a student has been flipping rubber bands at other students:

MR. LOTT: Jamie, I've asked you to meet with me to discuss a problem in class. What was it that you hit Eric with this morning just as we were putting away textbooks? (Notice that the misbehavior is not identified specifically, but cues have been given regarding when it occurred and with whom, so the student is less able to pretend he doesn't know what the teacher is talking about.)

JAMIE: I hit him with a rubber band, but he hit me with one first. He is always bugging me.

MR. LOTT: So you hit him with a rubber band. How many times have you flipped rubber bands at students in this class? (The teacher bypasses the student's ploy to shift the blame to Eric. He also tries to help Jamie identify the extent of the problem. Flipping rubber bands is probably not a problem unless it has happened often.)

JAMIE: Now wait a minute! I said he hit me first! He started it! You should be talking to him, not me!

MR. LOTT: OK. But how many times have you flipped rubber bands at other students in class? (Mr. Lott acknowledges Jamie's protest but continues to focus on the problem rather than being distracted and led away from directly dealing with the problem.)

JAMIE: Well, I don't know. Maybe once.

MR. LOTT: Who are the three people you hit with rubber bands during quiet study time yesterday? (Jamie is being evasive and not owning up to the problem. Mr. Lott bypasses Jamie's downplay of the problem's seriousness by providing a clue that lets Jamie know Mr. Lott is aware of his flipping activities.)

JAMIE: I hit Mark and Lisa, but I don't remember who else. But they were flipping rubber bands, too. Why don't you talk to them? (Jamie is still trying desperately to minimize his misbehavior and shift the blame.)

MR. LOTT: Yes, and how many people did you flip rubber bands at on Friday? What are their names? (Mr. Lott continues maintaining his focus on the problem by ignoring Jamie's blame shifting.)

JAMIE: I don't remember exactly, but I probably flipped about six rubber bands. (Jamie has finally indicated the extent of the problem and his role in it.)

Step 2: Help the Student Identify Consequences

If students were fully aware of the consequences of misbehavior, and if they realized their potential personal detriment, there would be far fewer discipline problems. Students seem to be unaware of certain consequences, or if they know of them, they fail to acknowledge their seriousness. No doubt some students believe that the consequences of their behavior can be avoided or that someone will keep them from suffering the full impact of these consequences. Maybe they feel they can avoid being detected when they misbehave. The purpose of Step 2 is to have them identify the unpleasant consequences of their disruptiveness. This interaction would look something like the following. This will be an extension of the case initiated in Step 1:

MR. LOTT: Jamie, you have admitted that you flipped rubber bands at class members on a number of occasions. If this continues, what are the likely consequences?

JAMIE: Mr. Lott, I didn't mean to cause any trouble. But Mark knocked my books on the floor and hit me on the head.

MR. LOTT: But what happens when you disturb others in class by flipping them with rubber bands? (Jamie hasn't given up on blaming others. However, it still has to be ignored in order to maintain focus on the problem and solve it.)

JAMIE: I don't know. I guess I'll get into trouble. (Jamie either has a vague idea of the consequences or he is pretending not to know.)

MR. LOTT: What kind of trouble are you referring to?

JAMIE: Do we really have to go through all this? I hate this garbage!

MR. LOTT: You said you could get into trouble. What do you mean by that?

JAMIE: Good grief. I suppose you'd send me to the principal. That's what teachers do and then the principal tries to figure out some terrible punishment. They just blow everything out of proportion. They kick you out of school for doing nothing.

MR. LOTT: I didn't have anything like that in mind, although that is often one of the consequences for breaking rules. What negative impact does flipping rubber bands at classmates have? (Notice that Mr. Lott doesn't want Jamie to think of punishment as the result of misbehavior. He wants him to think of more logical consequences. Also notice that there is a cue embedded in the question.)

JAMIE: I guess it might disturb them. (When Jamie senses he might avoid being punished, he becomes more cooperative.)

MR. LOTT: What would it disturb?

JAMIE: It would keep them from learning.

MR. LOTT: What about you and your learning?

JAMIE: It keeps me from learning, too.

MR. LOTT: What might happen to your right to remain in class if you disturb your classmates' learning?

JAMIE: You might kick me out, just like Mr. Kosta likes to do.

MR. LOTT: Who is responsible when you have to leave class because you disturb others' learning? (Mr. Lott helps Jamie see that he, not the teacher, is in control of the consequences.)

JAMIE: I guess it's me.

Step 3: Help Students Compare Intentions with Behavior

Students often do not have a clear picture of how their misbehavior and its consequences compare with their intentions. Usually students don't intend to disrupt class. If asked, they deny intentionally causing trouble. They try to excuse themselves by claiming that others were involved, the class was boring and they couldn't help themselves, and so on. It is particularly useful for students to see how their behavior may be inconsistent with their intentions and for the teacher to guide their behavior modifications to reflect what they really intend. Let's continue with the episode of Mr. Lott and Jamie:

MR. LOTT: Jamie, sometimes it is helpful to look at our intentions to see if our behavior is accomplishing what we want. How would you compare what you intend to have happen in class and what did happen when you flipped rubber bands?

JAMIE: I didn't mean to disturb class, but I just get tired of school and always being told what to do. Sometimes I can't stand all the boring lessons.

MR. LOTT: Are you saying that because you are unhappy with your experiences in school, it is alright to interfere with others' learning? (Notice that Mr. Lott doesn't become defensive and lecture Jamie about his school responsibilities.)

JAMIE: No, I don't mean that. It's just something I do when school isn't interesting or when things are not going well.

MR. LOTT: If you don't mean to disturb others, what do you need to do about flipping rubber bands at your classmates?

JAMIE: I should stop.

Step 4: Have Students Make a Value Judgment About Consequences, Intentions, and Behavior

Students need to eventually indicate that there are unwanted consequences associated with their classroom behavior and that they want to make modifications. They need to clarify their intentions and recognize the need for their behavior to be an accurate reflection of their intentions. For example, Jamie finally has to admit that his behavior is in fact incongruous with his intentions; thus, he may not wish to continue misbehaving. Students also need to state that they do not want the identified consequences to occur. In the episode involving Mr. Lott and Jamie, the conversation may be something like the following:

MR. LOTT: Jamie, you have said that when you flip rubber bands you could exclude yourself from class. You have said this might be necessary because your behavior interferes with the learning of classmates as well as yourself. Do you want these things to happen?

JAMIE: No.

MR. LOTT: So what do you think about flipping rubber bands?

JAMIE: I should stop doing it.

MR. LOTT: How would doing this compare with your intentions?

JAMIE: I want to learn in this class. That's what I intend to do.

Step 5: Have Students Make a Plan for Modifying Behavior and Express a Commitment to Follow the Plan

Once students have stated their intentions and expressed a desire to change their behavior, they are ready to start working on a plan to eliminate undesirable classroom behavior. Students are used to being told what to do in class. Not many will have had experience actually making their own plan to regulate their class behavior. Students also need an opportunity to commit to following their plan and assessing how well it works. They can also be told that there will be a follow-up session and that they are in charge of determining whether or not the problem has been satisfactorily solved. The dialogue between Mr. Lott and Jamie would be something like the following:

MR. LOTT: You have said you want to change. What do you think you could do to avoid the problem of flipping rubber bands?

JAMIE: I could just stop.

MR. LOTT: Is there something you could avoid doing that would help you? (Jamie's proposed solution is not a proactive plan.)

JAMIE: I could stop bringing rubber bands to class.

MR. LOTT: Are there any other possible solutions?

JAMIE: You could change my seat so I am not sitting by Alfonzo.

MR. LOTT: Which of these plans is most likely to succeed? (Mr. Lott does not reject the suggestion that changing Jamie's seat may help solve the problem, even though he believes it will not. Nor does he lecture Jamie on his poor choice or claim he is playing games and not being serious about solving the problem. He also does not focus on the inferred blaming of Alfonzo for the problem. Instead, he asks Jamie to indicate which of these plans is most likely to succeed.)

JAMIE: If I leave my rubber bands home, I won't have anything to flip. That should work well.

MR. LOTT: I suspect your plan will work. Is this what you want to do to solve this problem?

JAMIE: Yes.

MR. LOTT: OK. Why don't you do this for a week and then we can visit again about how well it is working? Your responsibility is to determine how well your plan is working and decide if any adjustments need to be made.

Many discipline problems are much more complex and difficult to deal with than those presented in the foregoing dialogues. These examples are only intended to be illustrative and provide a flavor for the kind of interactions that help students to assume more responsibility for their own behavior in a noncoercive environment. In addition, various ethnic groups have significantly different ways of interacting and responding to efforts to deal with disruptiveness. For example, some may find it hard to comfortably deal with face-to-face confrontations regarding discipline problems. Others may engage in emotional denials rather than face up to problems and help solve them. The process of helping students solve discipline problems is a complex interactive one where predicting the nature of responses is difficult. However, these nonpunitive techniques are more likely to promote student ownership and responsible student reactions.

Violence in the Schools

In addition to routine discipline problems, teachers sometimes have to deal with student violence. The level of extreme violence among youth in society, as well as in the schools, is increasing. Every year since 1950, the number of children killed by guns has doubled. In 1995, homicide was the third-leading cause of death in all children ages 5 to 14 and the second-leading cause of death for children ages 10 to 24. Youth arrests for murder have increased from a low of 1,578 in 1975 to a peak of 2,829 in 1992. The total crime statistics show a decrease, but extreme violence has nearly doubled in less than two decades. All of the mass murders of school peers occurred between 1958 and 1999 (Meloy, Hempel, Mohandie, Shiva, & Gray, 2001). Eleven percent of all crimes occur in schools, with 160,000 children staying home each day for fear of being hurt or killed (Sautter, 1995). Ironically, though in 1997 there were 370,000 children in grades 8, 10, and 12 who carried guns to school, only 6,091 of them were expelled for this reason during the 1996 to 1997 school year (National Institute of Justice, 2000).

Suggested causes for school violence include TV violence, dysfunctional families, grinding poverty, inequitable educational opportunity, latchkey homes, child abuse, domestic violence, family breakups, poor emotional and cognitive development, drugs, and gangs (Arllen, Gable, & Hendrickson, 1994; Ascher, 1994; Gaustad, 1991; Stratton, 1995). Some violence may also be a function of bullying and rejection in school. Bullying is the unacknowledged crime of violence in schools, with adults being generally unaware of its prevalence (Vail, 1999). One in six children is bullied each week in school, with bullied children manifesting an increase in suicidal thoughts, self-esteem problems, and poor mental health (Rigby, 1998; Rigby, 2000; Rigby & Slee, 1999). In a study by O'Connell, Pepler, and Craig (1999), 54 percent of the children who observe bullying on the playground gave tacit approval by watching without doing anything to oppose this abuse. Twenty-one percent modeled the bullying, while only 25 percent attempted to intervene. Most interventions were by girls, while boys predominate as bullies (Mills, 2001). Though bullying is widespread and generally not acknowledged by adults, when it is detected it is usually handled poorly (Hazler, 1999). Some schools have a zero tolerance for bullying and include instruction regarding bullying and its effects as regular units of instruction. Juyonen (2001) believes the most promising bullying prevention strategy involves (1) creating an explicit anti-harassment school policy, (2) providing instruction for all students regarding policies and procedures along with developing conflict resolution skills, and (3) dealing with incidents of bullying on a case-by-case basis, involving staff mediation that reinforces both school policies and the bullying instruction students have received.

Bullies who are caught in the act can be very difficult to handle. They ordinarily turn their aggression against those who try to intervene. The following guidelines may be helpful:

- Remove the victim from the situation as quickly as possible rather than confronting the bully.
- Inform the bully that he or she will be consulted later. Avoid telling the bully what actions might be taken.
- Avoid being aggressive with the bully.
- Avoid physical intervention unless necessary and then only when sufficient help has been acquired (Pearce, 2002).

Learning communities can be particularly effective in limiting bullying activity. Group members become protective of one another and consistently watch out for one another. Group commitment against bullying is an effective tool for eliminating its presence in school.

The most significant predictor of children's violent behaviors is a history of previous violence, including having been a victim of abuse (Huston et al., 1992). Several aspects of school organization and operations also contribute to violence, such as confining too many students in too small a space and imposing basic routines and academic conformity. School size is also a factor, as is teacher isolation (Klousky, 2002; Sautter, 1995). Violent student behavior has been observed when rules are unfair, arbitrary, or unclear; when they are perceived as unfairly or inconsistently enforced; when students do not believe in the rules; when educators disagree about the nature of the rules and the consequences for student misconduct; when teachers are too punitive; when students feel alienated; when schools are too impersonal; when misconduct is ignored; when grades are overemphasized; when curriculum is thought by students to be irrelevant; and when schools lack essential resources for teaching (Evans & Evans, 1985; Gaustad, 1992).

Students who shoot their classmates have some common characteristics. Many have experienced a recent drop in grades, hang out with delinquent friends and have a history of delinquency themselves, have been bullied, have suicidal thoughts, display an inappropriate sense of humor, and have various mental problems. Interestingly, the mental problems of these youth are not usually identified until after the shootings occur. Most adults who are in contact with these violent youth are unaware that they have dangerous inclinations. However, in most cases the shooters provide some indication to peers of their intentions a short time before the killings, sometimes in the form of a warning to stay away from a certain area or by some other cryptic remark. Many times the youth who were told of these plans understood the threat but did not believe it would take place (National Institute of Justice, 2000; National Research Council, et al., 2003).

Difficulties in Preventing School Violence

Unfortunately it is not clear how to identify shooters. For every killer youth there are many others with the same behaviors and attitudes who never come close to killing classmates. Potential violence is difficult to predict because (1) mass school killings are rare events, (2) violent events are embedded in a social and transactional sequence of events that are difficult to unravel either before or after the shootings, and (3) youth don't as yet have fully formed characters (Laub & Lauritsen, 1998). Thus, preventing school violence appears not to lie in the early identification of shooters, but rather in developing a positive and supportive organizational climate in schools (Mulvey & Cauffman, 2001).

Many violence prevention programs are ineffective, primarily because they are not designed to prevent, but rather to react to, violence problems (Hawkins, Farrington, & Catalano, 1998). Some of these efforts focus on defusing anger or identifying weapons brought into the school, but not on helping students avoid angry feelings or resist the inclination to bring weapons to school to act upon their anger (Stephens, 1998). Stringent gun laws, surveillance cameras, armed police, and metal detectors will not protect schools from students bent on revenge. Students who are intent on bringing weapons to school are inevitably a step ahead of the security (Ascher, 1994), and those who want guns seem able to acquire them despite various legislative efforts (National Research Council, et al., 2003). Not only do these efforts fail to prevent violence, but they are likely to undermine the trust needed to create conditions that prevent violent behavior. Violence prevention is more likely when schools sponsor programs that promote a disposition of nonviolence and an attitude of caring about others in the school community rather than offering courses in anger management or conflict resolution. Conflict resolution programs have common characteristics: They emphasize helping children deal with hostility through anger and stress management, impulse control, diversity awareness, active listening, creative problem solving, and peer mediation. One significant weakness of conflict resolution programs is the responsibility they place on student-to-student dialogue, thereby overestimating the impact such dialogues can have on solving problems. In addition, teachers have very little power to modify violence-promoting conditions in the home or neighborhood (Devine, 1996).

Additional strategies have been suggested for preventing school violence, like regulating television content, reducing poverty, aiding employment, providing family services, promoting early identification of children at risk for violent behavior, and reducing the size of schools (Arllen et al., 1994; Conroy & Fox, 1994; Devine, 1996; Evans & Evans, 1985; Gaustad, 1991; Smith, 1993). Some of these approaches suffer from some of the same defects as anger and stress management strategies. Others, like reduction in school size, may help reduce violence to some degree but do not focus directly on the problem.

QUESTION FOR REFLECTION

1. What steps need to be taken in the schools to limit the degree of violence often found there?

Prevention Through Resilience Training and Learning Communities

One attribute that schools can foster to prevent violence in children is resilience. Between one-half and two-thirds of children who grow up in families with mentally ill, alcoholic, abusive, or criminally involved parents or in poverty-stricken or war-torn communities seem able to cope with these potentially devastating conditions, partly due to an inborn capacity for resilience that helps them to develop social competence, problem-solving abilities, critical consciousness, autonomy, and an innate sense of purpose (Werner & Smith, 1992). It is also due to the presence of protective factors in the environment, including caring relationships, high expectations, and opportunities for participation within communities (Benard, 1993). To develop resiliency, children need a caring relationship with at least one individual. This relationship must include trust along with a desire to succeed. The most common positive role model in the lives of resilient children, outside the family, is a favorite teacher (Werner & Smith, 1989).

Students who have opportunities to participate in school in meaningful ways are empowered rather than alienated. Their need for self-regulation is satisfied, and they are more able to assume personal responsibility; they acquire a greater sense of purpose and personal commitment, and they develop resilience (Sarason, 1990).

Children have an innate capacity for resilience unless this capability is diminished by abusive conditions in the home, school, or community. Maltreated children behave provocatively and aggressively, and they have difficulty regulating affection and emotions, engaging in meaningful relationships, and performing basic cognitive functions. They have the potential for extreme violence in the schools (Lowenthal, 1999).

Schools can be ideal places to promote resilience if they focus more on cooperative learning, group problem solving, and decision making. In addition, students need opportunities to participate in classroom goal setting and to be involved in activities that provide personal and social development. Benard (1993) suggests that schools prepare a caring environment for students with high expectations. Students should be involved both in curriculum planning and achievement evaluation. In schools where these conditions are not found, children feel alienated and aggressive, and they live in quiet desperation and loneliness (Phelan, Davidson, & Cao, 1992).

Genuine community relationships are essential to developing resilience and reducing violence in the schools. However, schools are inherently deficient as moral communities. In moral communities, the interests of individuals as well as those of the society are preserved simultaneously as they are grounded in fundamental moral principles. When students are fully vested members of moral communities, their autonomy and social responsibility become focal aspects of social interplay (Sirotnik, 1990). Moral learning communities are essential to the prevalence of caring relationships. No member has to feel alone. All members stand up for one another and render assistance as needed. Love is unconditional, a significant aspect of the ongoing business of the community.

Most school communities have divergent values, since children grow up with a cultural emphasis on independence rather than on the value of community life. Thus, children may develop a sense of moral and intellectual arbitrariness (Freiberg, 1990). To combat this potential source of social alienation and rejection, schools need to create cohesive learning communities to moderate the development of shared values built upon the basic democratic principles. When learning communities have shared values, they are less-alienating places and thus have less potential for violence (Strike, 1999). In learning communities with the group offering support and devoting time to investigating problems that are personally critical, group identification and acceptance can be enhanced, and even troubled students can be helped to solve their problems in constructive ways without resorting to violence.

CENTRAL IDEAS

1. When students have a significant role in determining the curriculum, along with classroom rules, consequences, and procedures, many discipline problems can be prevented.
2. Students will behave more responsibly in class when they make a public commitment to do so.
3. In making curriculum decisions, teachers should help students to be sufficiently informed about viable alternatives and their implications so that valid selections can be made.
4. Rules in the classroom should be constructed with the help of students, and should emphasize their connection to accomplishing learning goals.

5. Consequences for breaking rules should be logical and should help to build student responsibility.

6. In correcting student misbehavior, teachers should call attention to the agreements and commitments students have made to one another regarding discipline.

7. Many discipline problems can be prevented if students' needs are sufficiently satisfied in the classroom.

8. Violence is best prevented within the context of learning communities where students help establish caring relationships and commitments to one another.

9. Teachers can help students acquire resilience by helping them participate in school in meaningful ways with groups of their peers.

10. Classroom meetings are an ideal place to solve classroom problems because they provide a way for students to give input and become actively involved and committed to solutions.

REFERENCES

Arllen, N. L., Gable, R. A., & Hendrickson, J. M. (1994). Toward an understanding of origins of aggression. *Preventing School Failure, 38* (3), 18–23.

Ascher, C. (1994). Gaining control of violence in the schools: A view from the field. ERIC Digest No. 100. New York: ERIC Clearinghouse on Urban Education. (ERIC Document Reproduction Service No. ED 377 256).

Benard, B. (1993). Fostering resiliency in kids. *Educational Leadership, 51,* 44–48.

Berne, E. (1964). *Games people play.* New York: Ballantine Books.

Berne, E. (1966). *Principles of Group Treatment.* New York: Oxford University Press.

Canter, L. (1996). First the rapport—then the rules. *Learning, 24* (5), 12–14.

Canter, L., & Canter, M. (1976). *Assertive discipline: A take charge approach for today's educator.* Seal Beach, CA: Canter & Associates.

Canter, L., & Canter, M. (1981). *Assertive discipline follow-up guidebook.* Los Angeles: Canter & Associates.

Conroy, M. A., & Fox, J. J. (1994). Setting events and challenging behaviors in the classroom: Incorporating contextual factors into effective intervention plans. *Preventing School Failure, 38,* 29–34.

Devine, J. (1996). *Maximum security.* Chicago: The University of Chicago Press.

Dinkmeyer, D., & Dinkmeyer, D., Jr. (1976). Logical consequences: A key to the reduction of disciplinary problems. *Phi Delta Kappan, 57,* 664–666.

Dreikurs, R. (1960). *Fundamentals of Adlerian psychology.* Chicago: Alfred Adler Institute.

Dreikurs, R. (1968). *Psychology in the classroom: A manual for teachers* (2nd ed.). New York: Harper & Row.

Dreikurs, R., & Grey, L. (1970). *A parent's guide to child discipline.* New York: Hawthorne Dutton.

Dreikurs, R., Grunwald, B. B., & Pepper, F. C. (1982). *Maintaining sanity in the classroom: Classroom management techniques* (2nd ed.). New York: Harper & Row.

Ernst, K. (1972). *Games students play.* Millbrae, CA: Celestial Arts.

Evans, W. H., & Evans, S. S. (1985). The assessment of school violence. *The Pointer, 29,* 18–21.

Freiberg, W. (1990). The moral responsibility of the public schools. In J. I. Goodlad, R. Soder, & K. A. Sirotnik (Eds.), *The moral dimensions of teaching* (pp. 155–187). San Francisco: Jossey-Bass.

Gathercoal, F. (2001). *Judicious discipline* (5th ed.). San Francisco: Caddo Gap Press.

Gaustad, J. (1991). Schools attack the roots of violence. ERIC Digest No. 63, Eugene, OR: Clearinghouse on Educational Management. (ERIC Document Reproduction Service No. ED 350 806).

Gaustad, J. (1992). School discipline. ERIC Digest No. 78. Eugene, OR: Clearinghouse on Educational Management. (ERIC Document Reproduction Service No. ED 350 727).

Glasser, W. (1965). *Reality therapy: A new approach to psychiatry.* New York: Harper and Row.

Glasser, W. (1969). *Schools without failure.* New York: Harper & Row.

Glasser, W. (1984). *Control theory: A new explanation of how we control our lives.* New York: Harper & Row.

Glasser, W. (1992). *The quality school.* New York: Harper & Row.

Glasser, W. (1998). *Choice theory: A new psychology of personal freedom.* New York: Harper Collins.

Gordon, T. (1974). *T.E.T.: Teacher effectiveness training.* New York: Peter H. Wyden.

Gordon, T. (1989). *Discipline that works: Promoting self-discipline in children.* New York: Penguin.

Harris, T. A. (1967). *I'm OK—you're OK.* New York: Avon Books.

Hawkins, J. D., Farrington, D. P., & Catalano, R. F. (1998). Reducing violence through the schools. In D. S. Elliott, B. A. Hamburg, & K. R. Williams (Eds.), *Violence in American Schools* (pp. 188–216). Cambridge: Cambridge University Press.

Hazler, R. J. (1999). Student perceptions of victimization by bullies in school. *Journal of Humanistic Education and Development, 29* (4), 143–150.

Holms, L. S. J., & Robins, L. N. (1988). The toll of parental disciplinary practices in the development of depression and alcoholism. *Psychiatry, 51,* 24–35.

Huston, A. C., Donnerstein, E., Fairchild, H., Fashbach, N. D., Katz, P. A., Murray, J. P., Rubinstein, E. A., Wilcox, B. L., & Zuckerman, D. (1992). *Big world small screen: The role of television in American society.* Lincoln, NE: University of Nebraska.

Jones, V. F., & Jones, L. S. (1995). *Comprehensive classroom management: Creating positive learning environments for all students.* Boston: Allyn & Bacon.

Juyonen, J. (2001). School violence prevention testimony. Presented to the California State Assembly Select Committee on School Safety, RAND Health, Santa Monica, CA.

Kammi, A. (1991). Toward autonomy: The importance of critical thinking and choice making. *School Psychology Review, 20,* 382–388.

Klousky, M. (2002). How smaller schools prevent school violence. *Educational Leadership, 59* (5), 65–69.

Kohn, A. (1993). *Punished by rewards.* Boston: Houghton Mifflin Company.

Laub, J., & Lauritsen, J. L. (1998). The interdependence of school violence with neighborhood and family conditions. In D. S. Elliott, B. A. Hamburg, & K. R. Williams (Eds.), *Violence in American Schools* (pp. 127–155). Cambridge: Cambridge University Press.

Lowenthal, B. (1999). Effects of maltreatment and ways to promote children's resiliency. *Childhood Education, 75* (4), 204–209.

Martin, G., & Pear, J. (1992). *Behavior modification: What it is and how to do it* (4th ed.). Upper Saddle River, NJ: Prentice Hall.

Meloy, J. R., Hempel, A. G., Mohandie, K., Shiva, A. A., & Gray, B. T. (2001). Offender and offensive characteristics of nonrandom sample of adolescent mass murders. *Journal of the American Academy of Child Adolescent Psychiatry, 40* (6), 719–728.

Mills, M. (2001). *Challenging violence in schools.* Philadelphia, PA: Open University Press.

Mulvey, E. P., & Cauffman, E. (2001). The inherent limits of predicting school violence. *American Psychologist, 56* (10), 779–802.

National Institute of Justice. (2000). *Safe school initiative: An interim report on the prevention of targeted violence in schools.* Washington, DC: Department of the Treasury; Department of Education; Department of Justice.

National Research Council of the Institute of Medicine and the National Academies. (2003). *Deadly lessons: Understanding lethal school violence.* Washington, DC: The National Academies Press.

O'Connell, P., Pepler, D., & Craig, W. (1999). Peer involvement in bullying: Insights and challenges for intervention. *Journal of Adolescence 22* (4), 437–452.

Pearce, J. (2002). What can be done about bullying? In M. Elliott (Ed.), *Bullying: A practical guide to coping for schools* (3rd ed., pp. 74–91). London: Pearson Education.

Phelan, P., Davidson, A., & Cao, H. (1992). Speaking up: Student's perspectives on school. *Phi Delta Kappan, 73,* (7), 695–704.

Rigby, K. (1998). *Bullying in schools: And what to do about it.* Markham, Ontario, Canada: Pembroke.

Rigby, K. (2000). Effects of peer victimization in schools and perceived social support on adolescent well-being. *Journal of Adolescence, 23* (1), 57–68.

Rigby, K., & Slee, P. (1999). Suicidal ideation among adolescent children involved in bully-victim problems and perceived social support. *Suicide and Life Threatening Behavior, 29* (2), 119–130.

Rogers, C. R., & Freiberg, H. J. (1994). *Freedom to learn* (3rd ed.). Upper Saddle River, NJ: Merrill/Prentice Hall.

Sarason, S. (1990). *The predictable failure of educational reform.* San Francisco: Jossey-Bass.

Sautter, R. C. (1995). Standing up to violence. *Phi Delta Kappan, 76,* K1–K12.

Sirotnik, K. A. (1990). Society, schooling, teaching, and preparing to teach. In J. I. Goodlad, R. Soder, & K. A. Sirotnik (Eds.), *The moral dimensions of teaching* (pp. 296–327). San Francisco: Jossey-Bass.

Smith, M. E. (1993). Television violence and behavior: A research summary. ERIC Digest. Syracuse: ERIC Clearinghouse on Information and Technology. (ERIC Document Reproduction Service No. ED 366 329).

Stephens, R. D. (1998). Safe school planning. In D. S. Elliott, B. A. Hamburg, & K. R. Williams (Eds.), *Violence in American schools* (pp. 253–289). Cambridge: Cambridge University Press.

Stratton, J. (1995). *How students have changed: A call to action for our children's future.* Arlington, VA: American Association of School Administrators.

Strike, K. A. (1999). Can schools be communities? The tension between shared values and inclusion. *Educational Administration Quarterly, 35,* 46–70.

Vail, K. (1999). Words that wound. *American School Board Journal, 186* (9), 37–40.

Walker, J. E., & Shea, T. M. (1999). *Behavior management: A practical approach for educators* (7th ed.). Upper Saddle River, NJ: Merrill/Prentice Hall.

Werner, E., & Smith, R. (1989). *Overcoming the odds: High-risk children from birth to adulthood.* New York: Cornell University Press.

Werner, E., & Smith, R. (1992). *Vulnerable but invincible: A longitudinal study of resilient children and youth.* New York: Adams, Bannister, and Cox.

Improving Teaching and Learning

To make improvements in teaching and learning, valid assessments must be conducted and the acquired data used to appropriately modify these processes. However, evaluations of learning are commonly shortsighted and misapplied. Thus, tests are commonly used to determine how students compare with one another, as well as the more critical concern of determining if what children are learning is necessary for success in life, or if it should be ignored. Too often various standardized tests are assumed to provide this more important kind of information when in fact they do not. Very little attention is given to determining whether or not what is learned should be learned. Educational evaluation should not only determine if objectives are being met, but also if the objectives achieve the desired ends. For instance, educators need to find out if graduates can really solve complex social problems or occupy an effective leadership role in civic and social associations.

Learning evaluation tends to be confined to students' memorization of knowledge. Knowing a body of information is assumed to be sufficient preparation for a variety of rather disparate purposes, including the degree that the information (1) prepares the individual for a successful career, (2) prepares the individual for college, (3) provides for parenting excellence, (4) helps the individual enjoy good health, (5) encourages lifelong learning, (6) leads to an active civic role, (7) prepares the individual to solve complex problems, (8) prepares the individual to appreciate and protect the environment, and (9) inclines individuals toward an appreciation of the arts. Objectives like these commonly contain various national commission goals, but rarely get explicitly assessed.

Neither the careful assessment of teaching nor teacher development receive much attention in the public schools. However, teacher improvement can be greatly enhanced through self-assessment, collegial interactions, and action research. Instructional leadership along with adequate funding are necessary to make these improvements a reality. National certification efforts and the creation of national standards can provide a much-needed impetus toward the improvement of teaching.

Students do better academically when they have parental support and when both teachers and parents support student learning. Seeking parental help and offering them a decision-making role in school affairs generally leads to better parent support. Parents need to stay informed about their children's learning efforts and remain appraised about course requirements, their children's academic progress, and the schedule of various school events and activities.

CHAPTER 11

Measuring and Evaluating Learning and Schooling

CHAPTER OBJECTIVES

This chapter is designed to help you

1. Explain the original purposes of grading, along with modifications that have been made over the years.
2. Explain the three related assessment tasks.
3. Explain the purposes for which different forms of measurement are constructed.
4. Create appropriately written objective and essay examination questions.
5. Formulate a rubric for evaluating students' papers and projects.
6. Create multiple-choice test items that measure higher levels of thinking.
7. Explain the issues involved in assessing affective goals.

Most student evaluation is based on traditional testing even though alternative assessments may be more valid.

8. Perform norm-based grading.

9. Explain the effects of grades on self-concept.

10. Explain the nature and effects of grade inflation.

11. Appropriately define excellence for student achievement.

12. Create authentic assessments.

13. Help pupils create academic portfolios.

14. Implement assessment procedures for learning communities.

INTRODUCTION

Assessment is generally seen as a necessary component of effective education. Teachers must continuously determine whether or not their students are learning the intended knowledge and skills. Differences of opinion exist, however, regarding what should be evaluated and how to accomplish it. Some believe using standardized, high-stakes tests provides teachers a means to determine how students in various geographic areas compare against one another, as well as the degree that students meet national standards. These tests will hopefully provide administrators with the necessary information to modify and improve the curriculum. Others believe that making geographical comparisons takes away the local school districts' autonomy to more validly determine their curriculum and standards. Teacher-made tests, in addition to various forms of alternative assessments like portfolios, can be used to authentically measure student accomplishments in terms of local expectations.

Mr. Dimetri spent an hour sitting at his desk, staring at his roll book, debating what he should do regarding grades. His students performed so poorly in his algebra class that he could hardly justify passing most of them. He carefully analyzed his exams and felt they were no more difficult than those he had given in previous years. He felt certain that he taught the material in ways comparable to earlier years; in fact, his students performed so poorly on his first exam that he took special pains to ensure they would do better on subsequent ones. However, it didn't seem to matter what he did. Student performance on his exams was abominable. More than half the class had an average less than 50 percent, and 25 out of 158 students scored below 25 percent. As his tests were multiple choice, these students could have scored that well by chance, without even looking at the test questions. Five students performed well enough to get As, while 10 were worthy of Bs. If he curved his grades, as in the past, 37 students would get Cs, 30 would receive Ds, and 76 students would receive Fs. Mr. Dimetri prided himself on being able to create valid tests that distributed student scores to form a nearly perfect bell-shaped curve. In addition, the center of his curve was always very near 75 percent, allowing him to distribute grades in a reasonable way from year to year.

As Mr. Dimetri considered the various issues involved, he finally concluded that his students hadn't really tried to learn; they hadn't taken their responsibility in his class seriously. He felt he had done everything in his power to prepare them for each of the examinations, from going over all the concepts in class to providing many examples. In addition, students were given a study sheet and participated in a review prior to each exam. Mr. Dimetri went so far as to organize game activities to make the reviews more interesting and enjoyable. Now he was faced with a very difficult decision. He knew that if he graded students in terms of their actual performance many would fail, and a good number would get grades below what they anticipated. "How can they expect to get acceptable grades when they don't prepare?" he wondered. He considered holding to the standards, thereby sending a message to students and parents alike that good grades require an excellent performance based on considerable effort. Inflating students' grades would send a distorted message, not only to students but also to prospective employers and the universities to which some students intended to apply. However, he also knew parents wanted their children to get high grades. Some gave their children substantial amounts of money for getting As. A few parents even offered their children new cars if they brought home straight As. He knew that grading on actual performance meant sitting in the principal's office the day after grades came out, and the superintendent's office not more than a week later. The only argument in his favor was the value of supporting the issue's moral side. But he also knew that many people allow practical considerations to outweigh moral imperatives. "I guess I'm just from the old school," he said to himself out loud.

Mr. Dimetri's mind continued to wander. What would be wrong with giving good grades to these students? They want them, and their parents want them. The principal and the superintendent want them to have them, rather than receive flack from parents. Don't rock the boat, he thought. "Well, I'll give them just what they want," he said to himself. "Why should I be the only one enforcing standards? If it's ever going to happen, the school and the whole community will have to support it. But that's not likely to occur. Maybe they will fire me if I support standards. It is just not worth it." He picked up his pen and added enough points to each student's average so that no one failed, while a good portion of the class got As and Bs.

Mr. Dimetri's problem is faced by many teachers. Others encounter problems because they are held accountable for student scores on standardized achievement tests. The pressure to give higher grades than performances justify or the responsibility for poor performances on standardized achievement tests creates intense interest in student achievement evaluation, as well as differences of opinion about what should be given priority. Teachers have a significant influence on how students respond on tests, and are believed to have the power to guarantee student success. However, students' prior experiences and home environment, as well as limitations placed on teachers regarding learning conditions, class size, and available materials, impact teacher effectiveness. Placing accountability on teachers shifts the burden from other factors that influence student achievement, making them less amenable for study and adjustment.

Decision Points

Assume you are Mr. Dimetri. What would you do to solve the problem? Why?

Traditional Purposes and Means of Measurement, Evaluation, and Grading

The original purpose of testing and grading was to sort students for college entrance. According to testing theory, test scores for groups of students should form a bell-shaped curve if the groups tested are representative of the population and the test is valid. The assumption of normality dictates that students receive grades based on where their scores fit on the normal curve. Tests that fail to produce easy-to-curve results do not satisfy the assumption of normality and thus require modification. Evaluating competence takes a back seat to determining how well the tests create score distributions approximating the normal curve.

Grading practices have changed over the years, as have their purposes. Grades have come to have different meanings. Some applications have abandoned strict application of the bell curve to grading. Perhaps the most significant adjustment is grade inflation. As grades artificially inflate, they lose their historical meaning (Bracy, 1994), as seen at the university level over the past three decades and even longer in secondary schools (Gose, 1997). Formerly, only 5 percent of students in a given class could anticipate receiving A grades, whereas now many more students receive high marks.

Grades still carry some of their historical purposes, but they are also used to chart students' progress and motivate them. Earlier definitions required modifications as they were too narrow or threatened to injure students in one way or another. Some teachers, for example, believed grades could damage students' self-concepts. Others saw grades as a source of unhealthy competition and cheating. A few educators took issue with the "normality assumption," preferring to believe that most students could achieve mastery if given sufficient time to learn (Kindsvatter, Wilen & Ishler, 1992). Criterion-referenced grading has gradually begun to make inroads in the assessment of student achievement. With criterion-referenced grading, instead of working for a set time and then being tested, students are allowed to study for varying periods and continually be tested until they achieve the designated competency level.

In addition, criterion-referenced grading has led to greater recognition that students have different learning skills and preferences. Norm-referenced tests narrowly focus on a limited number of skills and areas of knowledge. Guilford's model of the intellect (Guilford, 1962), along with Gardner's (1985), work on multiple intelligences and other efforts, broaden educators' views of acceptable and appropriate school experiences, and complicate the means for assessing school learning. Educators have been required to rethink the purposes and means of student evaluation, and various alternative assessment procedures have come from these efforts. In place of traditional tests, some educators use authentic assessment and portfolios. These assessment formats increase the validity of student evaluation while lessening the detrimental impacts of traditional testing.

 QUESTION FOR REFLECTION

1. To what extent are the changes made in grading practices appropriate, given the fact that grades still are supposed to represent relative student achievement?

The Relationship Between Measurement and Grading

Three related tasks make up student assessment: measurement, evaluation, and grading. **Measurement** is the process of obtaining assessment data. These data are often quantifiable, but they can also be based on a quality assessment. Quantifiable data are ordinarily sought to simplify the evaluation process. Supposedly, greater precision and objectivity occur when student performance data can be quantified. Questions of objectivity regarding evaluation devices such as multiple-choice, matching, and true-false tests also need to be addressed. Commonly referred to as "objective tests," these differ from essay tests and other "subjective" forms of evaluation. Objective tests offer greater objectivity in scoring. However, objectivity does not extend to the tests' construction, a differentiation that is often ignored when it should not be. A multiple-choice test is not necessarily an objective assessment, since subjective judgments are made in the test's construction.

Two basic issues regarding measurement are validity and reliability. **Validity** refers to the degree a test measures what it purports to measure. A test with *content validity,* the type of validity sought in teacher-made tests, will appropriately sample the course of study and determine the extent that course objectives have been accomplished. Students commonly complain that tests are not accurate course measurements. They may have emphasized the wrong areas while studying based on instructor's input. If the instructor prepared a criterion-based test, such a criticism may be valid. If the test is norm based, it is designed to spread scores out. Therefore, the test's validity not only depends on properly representing the course content, but also articulating with test assumptions and purposes.

Reliability refers to the consistency of tests results. A test is **reliable** if, on repeated administrations, the same results are obtained. Reliability can be acquired by administering the same test to students on two successive occasions. If they score about the same both times, the test is considered reliable. An estimate of reliability can also be made by comparing the results of two different but equivalent tests.

Teachers want to use valid and reliable tests so they can make accurate, justifiable measurements. Inaccurate measurement leads to ineffective evaluations and erroneous grading. Too often, validity considerations are not seriously addressed. The language in a test may lead students to draw inappropriate conclusions regarding what is expected. If less-important content receives more emphasis than more-critical information, or only a few of the course objectives receive coverage, the test is invalid. These issues cannot be ignored if tests are to be validly constructed.

Once valid and reliable measurement has been achieved, teachers must use this data to **evaluate** student performance. Evaluation is the process of using information obtained from several sources, such as tests, questionnaires, direct observation, written and oral performances, and/or interviews, to determine the quality of student achievements. Once all the information is assembled, teachers must sift through it and render a value judgment. Unfortunately, not all data can simply be appropriately quantified and added up to determine a grade; in fact, a student's performance usually cannot be simply quantified. Student academic efforts such as research projects, constructed models, paintings, sculptures, musical renditions, and classroom presentations should be considered as part of the overall evaluation.

Once an evaluation is made, teachers ordinarily provide **grades,** an expected condition of their employment. In recent years some modifications have been made in this grading process. Some school districts are now providing alternative assessment programs. In a few cases, students create portfolios of their best work. Self-evaluation is often involved as students include what they consider their best work in their portfolios. Teachers and others can then make an assessment of the work. Sometimes portfolios are evaluated and graded by teachers. Although these are contradictory evaluation processes, schools may acquiesce to the demands of colleges or parents who want a simple, quantitative way of comparing student achievement.

The Vital Role of Evaluation in Curriculum and Instruction

Although various ways exist to assess learning, some kind of evaluation is needed so that the effectiveness of instruction can be determined and improvements can be made. It is also important to understand student performance so there can be proper articulation of learning events and application of the necessary remediation. Evaluation provides the necessary feedback to chart student progress and appropriately sequence instruction.

Though the assessment of student achievement is an essential component of an evaluation program, it is only one component. All aspects of the school need to be evaluated, for they all have a bearing on the success of the instructional program. Sometimes these more-comprehensive evaluation tasks are turned over to central office personnel, leaving teachers responsible only for classroom learning. Even classroom learning is increasingly framed and assessed through standardized tests administered by central office personnel. However, the teacher's role extends beyond collecting important assessment data: he or she is well-qualified to evaluate and make important decisions about many aspects of school life that articulate with learning.

NATIONAL TEACHING STANDARDS

Teachers can judge the relative success of the activities they design.

Teachers can make judgments about themselves as teachers in relation to students and classes.

Evaluation and Instructional Decisions

Classroom tests can both assess student performance and modify instruction. Teachers should examine test results to ascertain where students are experiencing difficulty. The tests may reveal misunderstood concepts or inadequate skills requiring additional instruction, or there may be evidence suggesting that a teacher reframe the instruction the next time a particular lesson is taught. In addition, teachers must determine the reasons students do not satisfactorily learn. A teacher might find that students have received insufficient practice or misleading examples. They may have been unmotivated, or unable to comprehend the material. These types of questions may not necessarily be answered by examining test results, but the results may prompt teachers to consider additional avenues for investigating instructional problems.

What kinds of information should teachers focus on in examining test results? Perhaps the first is whether students have conceptual understanding. Teachers need to consider whether students simply failed to understand, whether the test questions were misleading, or whether insufficient time was allotted for mastering the concepts. The presentation pace of instruction may have a bearing on student performance. In addition, there may have been little or no student interest in the subject or desire to achieve at the expected level of competency.

In checking essay test questions, teachers may determine the fundamental importance of the presented information and the degree to which students are given directions that can easily be followed in organizing and presenting ideas. In examining the quality of student responses, teachers should focus on the extent to which students provide appropriate transitions between sentences and between paragraphs in their writing. They should also demonstrate higher-level thinking if that is expected. If these skills are lacking, instruction should specifically focus on enhancing them.

Some students learn slower than others, but they eventually satisfy expectations. They do not lack understanding or skill; they just move at a slower pace. Unless tasks specifically require speed, these students should not be penalized for being slow. If teachers determine that their tests and other evaluation devices unnecessarily require speed, then slower students should be allowed to demonstrate their competency within more reasonable time limits.

Unfortunately, teachers tend to ignore the fact that students require varying amounts of time to achieve mastery, and pace instruction to accommodate the mythical "average student." As a result, quicker students get bored and slower students struggle. Teachers need to determine how much time is required for their students to learn, even though it should not be a deciding factor in assessing student performance. Students should be given adequate time to learn, even though doing so will necessitate changes in organizing instruction.

NATIONAL TEACHING STANDARDS

Teachers frequently do not assign grades, as evaluation may have other purposes; rather, it allows students and teachers to assess where they stand. Teacher assessments help teachers determine what follow-up activities are needed to enhance learning.

Curriculum and School Assessment

The school curriculum is the product of many considerations, most notably the process of learning itself. Values to acquire, subjects to be learned, objectives to be achieved, and skills to be developed must be considered. In making an analysis of the school and curriculum, all entities involved in constructing and delivering the curriculum need to be considered. Therefore, in addition to school achievement, teaching, administration, and a host of other elements need to be examined. Libraries and other learning facilities need to be inspected, along with their rules and procedures. Even the lunch room and busing operations are related to learning. The activity program should receive special attention, and its contribution to the overall instructional goals of the school should be determined.

The goals of instruction are a central aspect of schooling. In evaluation, less attention is often given to identifying goals rather than achieving them. This is a critical error. It is far more important to achieve the *right goals* than to simply measure the extent to which objectives have been met. Instructional goals need to reflect what *ought* to be taught in the schools, which is a complex issue full of value considerations. Sometimes teachers allow the state core curriculum to circumscribe the entire content they teach. However, even though a core curriculum may specify many instructional objectives, a great deal is ordinarily left up to teachers in terms of both what and how to teach. Teachers are at liberty to create learning experiences that help promote higher-level skills, encourage value development, and greatly expand individual opportunities. State core requirements only specify minimums and should be built upon and expanded. Teachers are in a particularly critical position to do this and to organize classroom experiences that articulate well with student interests and learning proclivities.

 ## Decision Points

Determine what you feel should be taught in your subject and compare this with what you have experienced in the public schools.

NATIONAL TEACHING STANDARDS

Teachers can carefully track what their students are learning as well as what they, as teachers, are learning.

Teachers make judgments about average student performance but realize that very few students are average, and they must interpret data in that light. Teachers are able to accommodate what they know about individual students to the whole class.

Forms of Measurement

The form measurement takes should depend on the nature of information sought. For example, to test students' abilities in constructing coherent paragraphs, using a test on diagramming sentences would be inappropriate. Likewise, if you wanted students to demonstrate their ability to perform a science inquiry investigation, giving them a paper-and-pencil test about the steps in the inquiry process would not do. Unfortunately, sometimes the form of a measurement instrument depends on the ease of preparing and scoring test items rather than on the ability of the test to validly measure an understanding or capability. For example, it is much easier to measure the recall of memorized facts than more complex skills and understandings.

Objective Tests

Although objective tests *can* measure higher-level mental processes, these devices are primarily used to measure the students' ability to recall information. Considerable effort is ordinarily required to frame objective questions that validly engage students in higher-level thinking. In addition, evidence of an adequate education is often considered simply an accumulation of information. Schools are frequently criticized for failing to teach all the facts someone considers essential.

Multiple-Choice Tests

The most commonly used objective test form is *multiple choice.* A number of advantages exist for using multiple-choice items: (1) They are easy to prepare in a variety of subjects, (2) they are easy to score, and (3) they can be created to measure higher-level thinking more readily than other objective test forms. Multiple-choice tests are composed of two parts: (1) a stem, and (2) a list of suggested answers. From the list, students select the correct or best answer. The incorrect responses are called *distractors.* A difficulty in constructing effective multiple-choice test items is supplying distractors that are plausible answers so students lacking a sufficient understanding of the materials don't simply guess rather than making fine discriminations between right and wrong answers. Carelessly written distractors tend to give away the correct answer, even to students who do not know the content well (Armstrong & Savage, 1998).

In preparing multiple-choice test items, the stem should be clearly written and all distractors should be written grammatically consistent with the stem. Consider the following example:

Alluvial fans

A. consisting of clay.
B. are land deltas.
C. accumulating in a dry basin near the tops of mountains.
D. emerges from the gentle slopes of an upland onto a steeply sloping plain.

A student totally unfamiliar with this subject could identify *b* as the correct answer because it is the only choice that is grammatically correct. Furthermore, a student might easily conclude answer *c* is wrong because a basin would be unlikely to appear near the tops of mountains. A similar deduction could be made for answer *d.* Since plains are gently sloped, it is highly unlikely that there would be a gentle slope upland onto a steeply sloping plain.

Sometimes a stem contains insufficient information regarding what students should be looking for in the list of alternatives. Examine the following example:

Charles Darwin

A. discovered the fossilized remains of the extinct dodo bird.
B. made interesting discoveries supporting the theory of evolution on the Galapagos Islands, off the eastern coast of Africa.

C. sailed on a ship called the *Titanic.*
D. proposed the concept of natural selection as the explanation for evolution.

Because the stem gives such limited information, students need to ponder four true-false statements. In addition, there are some misleading aspects of the alternative choices as well as "giveaways." In distractor *a,* the student may realize that the dodo bird became extinct so recently that there would not have been time to develop fossilized remains. Distractor *b* locates the Galapagos Islands off the eastern coast of Africa. Darwin did explore the Galapagos Islands and made interesting discoveries supporting the theory of evolution. However, these islands are located off the western coast of South America adjacent to Equador in the Pacific Ocean. The problem with distractor *c* is that most students are likely to know the *Titanic* sank in the Atlantic Ocean after striking an iceberg on its maiden voyage. There is no chance that Darwin sailed on this ship, and there probably was not a second *Titanic.* The following example shows a much better way to format this question:

The individual who proposed a theory of natural selection after visiting the Galapagos Islands off the western coast of South America was
A. Alfred Russell Wallace.
B. Charles Darwin.
C. Gregor Mendel.
D. T. H. Huxley.

In this question, the data for consideration are all located in the stem. In addition, all of the distractors are reasonable. Alfred Russell Wallace is often considered a co-discoverer of the theory of organic evolution with Darwin. He is credited with such concepts as survival of the fittest, the topic of a paper he sent to Darwin. They were contemporaries and working on the same biological problems in their research. Huxley, another contemporary of Darwin, interacted with him as he formalized his theory and published it. Gregor Mendel is credited with discovering the mechanism that makes evolution possible through his work with garden peas. However, Darwin is the only one whose voyage to the Galapagos Islands was monumental in helping him understand natural selection as an evolutionary principle.

Sentence-Completion Tests

Another kind of objective test item is *sentence completion.* Although these items are less useful in assessing student thinking than multiple-choice items, they are easier to construct and can be used to sample a broad range of content. One difficulty often encountered in sentence-completion tests is creating items with only one right answer. Look at the following test item, for example:

The person who ran against George W. Bush in the 2000 presidential election was_____.

The answer the teacher probably had in mind was Al Gore. However, other plausible alternatives exist. A student may include answers such as "a democrat," "a liberal," or "nearly victorious." To avoid this problem, the teacher should clearly identify the type of response wanted. A revision of the previous question may look something like the following:

The name of the person who ran against George W. Bush in the 2000 presidential election was _____.

Each completion item should have only one blank, which should appear near the end of the sentence. This allows students to pick up relevant cues regarding the nature of the expected response as they read the item. Items with multiple blanks tend to be confusing.

Matching Tests

Matching test items are also relatively easy to construct and easy to correct. In making matching test items, the focus should stay on a single topic or theme listed at the beginning of the matching item. For example, a test that includes the names of U.S. Presidents on one side and their party affiliation on the other might be labeled "U.S. Presidents and Party Affiliations."

Ordinarily the list on the right-hand side (the one providing alternative descriptions or definitions from which students are to select answers) should contain about 25 percent more items than the list on the left-hand side. This makes it possible for students to miss one question without being forced to miss another. When there are equal components to matching questions, students receive a double penalty for missing a question. It is also important for the entire matching test to be printed on one page. Students may fail to realize that part of the test is on another page and therefore make unnecessary errors.

Directions for matching tests need to be carefully written. Students should be told that the letter representing an answer on the right-hand side of the test should be placed in the blank in the left-hand margin opposite the item for which the answer is appropriate. Otherwise, students may draw lines connecting the items and answers, making the test extremely difficult to score. In addition, the directions should clearly state that there is only one correct response for each item.

True-False Tests

True-false test items are easy to create and score. However, they have the disadvantage of encouraging guesses. Furthermore, the nature of true-false testing may encourage teachers to steer away from the main focus of their instruction in order to find the odd examples in the subject that are absolutely true or absolutely false rather than assessing students' ability to make fine discriminations. In addition, true-false items often suffer from ambiguity and misinterpretation.

In developing true-false tests, teachers should prepare items that are clearly true or false. In addition, leaving a blank in front of each question and giving instructions regarding when and how to record answers is helpful. Students should be instructed to make "+" for true and "−" for false or write the words *true* or *false* out completely. Otherwise, students may use the letters *t* or *f*. Because of the idiosyncracies in students' handwriting, these letters can sometimes be hard to differentiate. An alternative is to precede each item with the words *true* and *false* and instruct students to circle the right answer.

Essay Examinations

Essay questions provide a powerful means of assessing students' ability in all cognitive levels. However, they also have a number of problems. Due to the time required to respond to questions, they may create a problem in covering the important components of a course. The result can be a narrow sampling of content.

Another problem teachers face with essay examinations is inconsistent scoring. Grading essay exams usually takes a long time, and it is difficult to maintain the same standards while reading a lot of tests over lengthy periods of time. The standards tend to drift. It is also difficult to avoid bias if teachers know the students' names. This information needs to be concealed. One way to achieve greater reliability is to read each student's response to a single question before going to the next one. This helps avoid the problem of drift. In addition, teachers should avoid reading student tests in the same order for each question. There may be an unfair advantage to students whose tests are read either first or last (see Table 11.1).

In writing essay exams, teachers need to be certain the test items are as precise and clear as possible. Otherwise, students often have to guess what teachers want. Compare the following two sets of instructions:

1. Write an essay in which you discuss continental drift and plate tectonics.
2. Write an essay, of about six pages, in which you explain the theory of continental drift and discuss how this theory eventually led to the theory of plate tectonics. In your response, provide specific reference to (1) the land masses that at one time were associated with one another, (2) the biological and geological evidence for believing particular land masses were once connected, and (3) the process included in the theory of plate tectonics and the explanation it provides for continental drift.

With the first question, students may very well ramble and cover items the teacher considers unimportant. In addition, because the expected length of the response is not given, students could very well write anywhere from one to ten pages or more. The second question provides clearer and more detailed instructions, and gives the specific kind of response expected. This makes it much easier for students to write an acceptable answer and for teachers to fairly evaluate responses.

TABLE 11.1   *Examination Strengths and Weaknesses.*

Type of Test	Strengths	Weaknesses
Multiple choice	Easy to score; can measure higher-level thinking	Difficult to create plausible distractors
Matching	Easy to create and score	Sometimes confusing to students
True-false	Easy to create and score	Encourages guessing; may cause teachers to create test items that are off the main focus of the lesson
Essay	Powerful means of assessing cognitive levels; easy to create	Can create a narrow sample of content; may result in inconsistent scoring

Decision Points

For the subject you teach, construct a test including multiple-choice, sentence-completion, true-false, matching, and essay items.

Evaluating Papers and Projects with Rubrics

Although tests are often considered the fairest and simplest way to evaluate student achievement, papers and projects can also provide an assessment format for more complex, comprehensive student learning, as well as a more valid means of determining the quality of students' thinking and organizing abilities. A **rubric** is often used to communicate expectations. For example, a rubric for a research report may specify that the document must include a question derived from a careful analysis of some phenomena that appears to be a useful next step in research efforts. The rubric can specify that the question should be substantial, not one for which the answer is already known. A different number of points would be given for different levels of quality. The following example shows a rubric for formulating a research project study question in sociology about the impact of control on human relationships:

1. The question relates to the impact of control on human relationships. The question is clearly important for investigation. The question appears to be a logical next step in research efforts, and it can be anticipated that answering the question will provide important insights in human relationships. (30 points)
2. The question relates to the impact of control on human relationships. The question involves something that may be useful to know but is not necessarily a strategic next step in a research effort. (20 points)
3. The question relates to the impact of control on human relationships. The question deals with an interesting but peripheral aspect of the issue. (10 points)

For a research project, rubrics might also be created for other aspects of the report, such as research design; measurement instruments and their reliability, validity, and potential bias; control of possible confounding variables; data analysis; and strategies for drawing conclusions. All of these would receive point values in terms of how closely the student project followed the expectations detailed in the rubric.

Carefully delineated expectations should also be provided for student-written papers. If teachers hold students accountable for specific content or for particular formats in writing papers, these specifications should be supplied to students in advance, along with the rubrics used for grading. It is inappropriate for teachers to pose loosely structured requirements and then hold students accountable for stringent expectations. If teachers wish students to exercise more creativity, less structure should be provided and fewer specific expectations given. In grading, sufficient latitude is needed for students to be truly creative.

Decision Points

Create a rubric for a research project report you might assign in your subject area.

Evaluation and Educational Purposes

Various forms of evaluation are more or less useful in assessing specific kinds of student achievements. Objective tests, for example, are less effective in measuring higher-level thinking processes. They are primarily designed for recall and other less-advanced skills. In addition, common testing practices usually ignore affective goals. However, many times these goals are considered as important as cognitive ones. An effective testing program includes not only various levels of cognitive functioning, but also the development of attitudes and values.

Evaluating Higher-Level Cognitive Processes

As already mentioned, the tests teachers construct often exclusively measure recall. However, most agency-created lists of objectives, such as those from state departments of education and national societies interested in the quality of education, include emphasis on higher cognitive functioning. Analysis, synthesis, and evaluation skills are emphasized in these groups' goals, but they are not often achieved in classrooms, nor routinely sought and achieved through tests. Test items that validly measure higher thinking processes are difficult to effectively use in making assessments, not to mention tricky to create. In making assessments, subjective judgments are necessary and various biases and inequities are inevitable. Creating test items is difficult and tedious, and there are many possible ways for students to misinterpret them or become confused. The following is an example of an *analysis* level test item:

Items 1, 2, and 3 refer to the following situation:

A college housing committee held an open meeting regarding a proposal to have male and female students living in adjacent dormitory rooms. One student made the following remarks:

A. This whole meeting is ridiculous.
B. Males and females should not be restricted in their living arrangements.
C. Students will do what they want to in spite of the rules and arrangements regarding room occupancy in the dorms.
D. Separate dormitories are supposed to guarantee that everything will be respectable.
E. This is absolute hypocrisy.
F. Anyway, students will never develop maturity unless they are able to exercise their own freedom with regard to this issue.

1. One of the above statements in the student's argument offers reasons, but doesn't function as a reason for any other statement. This statement also has a main conclusion. Identify this statement.
   1. A   2. B   3. C   4. D   5. E   6. F
2. The student offered A as a reason for
   1. B   2. C   3. D   4. E   5. F
3. The student offered *B* as a reason for
   1. A   2. C   3. D   4. E   5. F

Item 1 asks respondents to analyze the elements of the statement, while items 2 and 3 ask them to analyze the relationships between parts of the statement. Notice that these questions require students to analyze specific components of statements, not respond to some nebulous conceptualization. Questions that refer to poorly described information fail to provide a basis for developing analysis skills.

Synthesis questions provide more latitude for responses, but they can also be confusing and inappropriate, especially when teachers don't make their expectations clear. Look at the following two test items. The first allows considerable latitude, while the second lays out more specific expectations:

1. Complete a 12-line poem from this first line: "The night was cold with eerie still." The poem should have a rhyme scheme of the student's own choosing, but there should be consistency from beginning to end.
2. Given the following data, formulate a plan to determine the nature of chemical pollution in the Bear River that may be attributed to agricultural run-off, including recommended procedures to terminate the pollution problem. Prepare a defense for your plan.
   A. The plan must be comprehensive and deal with all the potential pollutants likely to occur from farming operations.
   B. The plan must contain processes that can isolate not only pollutants, but also the levels of concentration of these pollutants.
   C. The plan must include potential courses of action recommended to rectify the suspected pollution problems that help to deal with the problem without making excessive demands on local farmers.

The first question is designed to have students produce a unique poem. Considerable latitude is given so that true creativity is possible. Consistency is sought in order to delineate quality as writing that is creative yet well-organized and integrated. With synthesis, it is important to remember that the final product should be creative and yet internally consistent.

The second question asks students to produce a plan with particular guidelines regarding assessment of a potential pollution problem and potential actions that may be undertaken to deal with the problems. Considerable latitude is again given, but the proposed plan must consist of more than a loose set of ideas. The various parts of the plan must form an organized, well-articulated, appropriately sequenced set of procedures, as well as be defended as plausible.

Evaluation level thinking requires students to either judge the quality of a set of items against a set of criteria or judge which of a number of items is best. Students must use a set of self-created criteria or criteria that have been given to them. They must also provide an explanation of their evaluation process, along with a rationale, so the teacher can be satisfied that the student rendered careful analyses and judgments. The following are examples of evaluation questions:

1. Rank order the five pieces of poetry displayed in class from best to worst. Provide a rationale for your evaluation, explaining why you selected the criteria you did and how you applied them in making your judgments.

2. If the 1973 Middle East War crisis could have been equitably settled, some subsequent problems might have been prevented. Using a set of criteria that you create and prioritize, select which of the following solutions would have been the best and explain why.

   A. Israel should simply have moved back to their pre-1967 war borders.
   B. Israel should have been allowed to keep all occupied territory at the close of the 1967 war provided they guaranteed that Arabs within its borders would be treated as equals.
   C. Because the Arab world started the 1973 war, Israel should have been allowed to keep territory gained prior to the onset of negotiations.
   D. All territory presently held by Israel through both the 1967 and 1973 war efforts should have been equitably divided among all concerned.

When students are required to provide a rationale for their evaluation level responses, greater assurance exists that they are not just stating preferences without benefit of careful analysis and judgment. Teachers should give careful attention to student responses concerning the criteria they generate, while students should preferably prioritize criteria so any weightings given in their assessments are evident. Students need to give detailed explanations of their thinking so that teachers can make appropriate assessments of their skill.

Decision Points

From your teaching subject, write test items to appropriately evaluate each of the following intellectual levels: analysis, synthesis, and evaluation.

Evaluating Affective Goals

Affective goals are rarely sought directly. Teachers do not ordinarily create strategies to develop values, nor create the means to assess them. No doubt some teachers believe students will learn to appreciate aspects of a subject, but most values are acquired inadvertently if at all. In an English class, for example, teachers hope students will appreciate good literature. In biology, the goal may be for students to act favorably upon environmental considerations. Teachers of U.S. history likely wish students to come away with positive attitudes regarding the Constitution and democratic government. Some teachers likely hold such values as very important, but make little effort to address them in the curriculum and take even less time to determine if these values have been acquired by students.

One difficulty in assessing affective goals is that students may be able to ascertain what teachers are evaluating and pretend they have a value when in fact they do not. For example, if students are expected to show reverence for the flag, they may act as if they do because they know the teacher is looking on, not because they sincerely respect the flag. In addition, students' responses usually have to be observed rather than obtained via a paper-and-pencil test or an essay. Thus, appropriate data may be infrequent and difficult to collect and interpret. This kind of information cannot ordinarily be acquired through self-report. Students may try to provide the information they believe the teacher values rather than reporting their own thoughts and feelings.

Most affective data must be collected by teachers through observations at times when students are unaware assessments are being made, which can be particularly difficult when students have been instructed in a particular value prior to assessment. The instruction obviously raises student awareness. Performing multiple observations over an extended time period can help capture the desired information and satisfy teachers that goals have been met.

Purposes and Forms of Evaluation

Evaluation serves three distinct purposes. The first, **diagnostic evaluation,** includes efforts to determine individual levels of competency prior to instruction. With diagnostic information in hand, teachers can more efficiently organize instruction. If students already have certain understandings and skills, they can be excused from learning experiences that are unnecessary duplications of previous learning. Diagnostic information also provides a way to arrange students into appropriate groupings for instruction.

The second kind of evaluation, **formative evaluation,** is used to guide and monitor learning progress during instruction and to provide appropriate feedback to students and parents. Individual students can learn of their deficiencies, and teachers can procure data for modifying what and how they teach.

Summative evaluation, the third type of assessment, is usually administered at the end of a unit or grading period as a final assessment of student achievement. Summative evaluation typically determines the student's broad ability as compared to the more-detailed examinations found in formative evaluation (Bloom, Madaus, & Hastings, 1981).

Standardized Achievement Tests

Standardized achievement tests are ordinarily used to chart students' progress relative to acceptable norms. The norming of these tests involves groups of students who are considered typical. In addition, these tests are assumed to provide a valid assessment of school achievement. In addition, high test scores are an indication of teaching effectiveness and low scores a measure of ineffectiveness.

These assumptions have been questioned by educators for a number of reasons. First, standardized achievement tests frequently consist of a mere 40 or 50 items and thus provide a very narrow sample of knowledge and skills from the content domain. Second, standardized tests are credited with an unwarranted precision in measuring student performance. Decisions are sometimes made regarding students' progress when the differences in scores from year to year are simply due to the standard error of the test itself.

The procedures involved in creating these tests do not contribute to accuracy or precision. Companies that create and sell standardized achievement tests, like all for-profit businesses, primarily exist to produce revenue for their shareholders. Pressure exists to sell to the largest market possible, which creates a dilemma due to the considerable diversity in the United States. Different states choose different educational objectives. In some states, counties or individual school districts are empowered to make decisions concerning localized curriculum. Despite these curricular differences, test makers are obliged to create one-size-fits-all assessments. Thus, any particular test may be a poor fit for instruction emphasized in any specific area. This mismatch between what is taught locally and what is tested through standardized achievement tests is illustrated in the research of Freeman and colleagues (1983). This group analyzed five nationally standardized achievement tests in mathematics and studied their content for grades 4 to 6. Then, assuming that the textbooks used would reasonably define classroom instruction, they examined four widely used textbooks designed for grades 4 to 6. In their analysis, they identified the standardized achievement test items that did not receive meaningful attention in the textbooks, concluding that 50 to 80 percent of what was measured on the tests was not adequately addressed in the textbooks.

Another reason to question the use of standardized achievement tests concerns the process used to formulate test items. These tests require items that only about half of the students answer correctly in order to spread students' scores out. If a test item is answered correctly by around 80 percent or more of the test takers, it is usually discarded. As a result, the vast majority of items on standardized achievement tests are of "middle difficulty." Items students perform well on are eliminated, even though these items usually represent content that teachers stress because they consider it important. Consequently, the important knowledge and/or skills that teachers teach well are not likely to be measured on standardized achievement tests. Therefore, it is fundamentally foolish to use these tests as a measure of student achievement and teacher effectiveness (Popham, 1999).

Additionally, scores are heavily influenced by the students' native intellectual ability, as well as knowledge learned outside of school. Students are not equal in intellectual abilities. Gardner (1994) suggests there are at least eight distinctive abilities. Thus, a child who has less aptitude on quantitative or verbal tasks might possess greater interpersonal or intrapersonal intelligence. Children with varying innate abilities respond differently to the items commonly found on standardized achievement tests. Furthermore, these tests are designed to measure only a few of the intellectual abilities defined by Gardner.

Standardized achievement tests routinely assess what students have learned outside of school. This, of course, favors students from advantaged families who have been provided stimulus-rich environments, since they ordinarily have a background similar to the test makers.

A final reason to be wary while using standardized achievement tests is that, because of the pressure usually exerted on schools to achieve high student test scores, schools may teach to the test and ignore the defined curriculum. These efforts take time away from more valuable academic pursuits.

 ## QUESTIONS FOR REFLECTION

1. What evaluation processes do you think could be used to replace standardized achievement tests that would provide a more valid assessment of teaching and learning?

2. To what extent is it desirable to establish common standards for all students in the United States?

3. From a particular topic in your area of teaching, what kind of assessment would be most appropriate? Why?

Grading Practices

In order to grade students' achievement, quantifiable data are ordinarily secured. This information can then be manipulated in various ways to determine grades. One of the most common ways to structure student response information is to compute **means** and **standard deviations.** The mean, which refers to the average, is determined by adding all the scores together and dividing by the total number of scores. In contrast, the standard deviation is the degree of variability between the scores. A large standard deviation denotes a good deal of variability between student scores while a small standard deviation indicates little variability. Sufficiently accurate estimates of the standard deviation can be computed by dividing the range of scores by five. For example, look at the following list of scores:

76, 78, 68, 78, 78, 89, 85, 78, 79, 76, 65, 82, 82, 87, 80

92, 82, 80, 78, 79, 88, 82, 75, 79, 76, 79, 91, 72, 95, 78

The range of scores from 65 to 95 is 30. If we divide the range of 30 by 5, the standard deviation is 6. Now observe what this means in terms of assigning grades. When the standard deviation (SD) of 6 is added to 65, the lowest score, we obtain the range of scores in the *F* category. Thus, the scores of 65 to 71 are in the *F* range. Adding the SD to 72 gives the upper level of the *D* range. The following is the range for each grade, along with the number of scores that fall within this category:

Scores	Grade	Number of Scores
65 to 71	F	2
72 to 77	D	5
78 to 83	C	16
84 to 89	B	4
90 to 95	A	3

Notice that grades are not determined by the numerical value of student scores, but rather by range and standard deviation. Grades are given in terms of how scores compare with one another and how they fit within the normal bell-shaped curve. Sometimes teachers wish to grade students on how well their performances fit **criterion-referenced standards.** On a 100-item test, for example, the grade breakdown may be as follows: 90 to 100 = *A*, 80 to 89 = *B*, 70 to 79 = *C*, 60 to 69 = *D*, and 0 to 59 = *F*. With criterion-referenced grading, teachers may decide that students must reach a particular standard to receive a passing grade. They may say, for example, that the minimum acceptable level of performance is a score of 80. Students scoring below this level are given more time to study and practice and are then retested. This process can be repeated as often as necessary until students reach the designated level.

One criticism of criterion-referenced grading is that the minimum level of competency defined becomes the maximum achieved. Thus, students may only learn until they can demonstrate minimum competency when they could, in fact, have done better. However, there is no reason to exceed the minimum. Consequently, some students who could have achieved higher levels of excellence may be encouraged not to do so. With norm-referenced grading, a different kind of problem is created. Low-scoring students may see no hope of achieving higher levels of performance, and thus they may quit trying. Also, when the conditions of norm-based grading are strictly maintained, an entire class may perform far below their capabilities. For example, on a 100-item test the mean may be something like 35, with a high score of 60. Assume the range is from 10 to 60. In this case, the SD is 10. Grades would be given out as follows: 10 to 20 = *F*, 21 to 30 = *D*, 31 to 40 = *C*, 41 to 50 = *B*, and 51 to 60 = *A*. Over a period of time, students may realize that there are no particular standards; whatever the class scores is considered normal. If little or nothing is required to acquire an acceptable grade, low achievement can be expected. Teachers may question whether this is due to hard tests or low student effort and performance. As is generally the case with norm-referenced testing, only a one-time measure is taken for an area of study. Students do not have an opportunity to improve their performances. If the norm-based procedure for calculating grades is strictly employed, students may achieve far below acceptable levels and still receive high grades.

Rather than a norm-referenced or criterion-referenced system, teachers may wish to use a contract where individual students contract for a particular grade. This is usually done by having students select from a list of competencies or projects and contracting to complete a certain number of them for a particular grade. When this approach is used, teachers have to determine when projects have reached an acceptable level of quality.

Some teachers wish to have improvement or effort reflected in students' grades. It seems reasonable for students with low ability who work very hard, or who make substantial improvements, to have that reflected in their grades. There may be some objection to this, however, because it distorts the competency level that a grade is supposed to represent. Other problems exist as well. When teachers try to include effort in a grade, they have the almost-impossible task of classifying the relative efforts of students. Students who are rewarded for their efforts may pretend to be hard-working when, in fact, they are not. The real efforts of students may be so distorted as to be impossible to assess. If improvement is factored into grades, teachers are faced with the dilemma of how to credit improvement relative to actual achievement. For example, one student may improve the scores on tests from 30 to 50 while another student may improve scores from 87 to 93. The first student has an improvement score of 20, while the second only has an improvement of 6. The second student obviously has less room for improvement; therefore, the teacher is faced with the dilemma of giving appropriate credit for improvement without penalizing anyone. Assuming the improvement score of 6 is the lowest in the class, the second student may not merit much. Through lack of improvement, this student's final grade should be in the *B* range rather than *A*, while the first student, who might have made the most improvement in the class, merits a much higher grade than his achievement would indicate.

Effects of Grading

Grading is not benign in its potential negative impact on students, even though that is the general assumption. Educators and parents would naturally not intentionally inflict harm on children by supporting grading if it were recognized as potentially harmful. Teachers as well as parents need to be aware of the potential dangers imposed on children through grades so that appropriate modifications can be made in the evaluation process. Generally speaking, the justification given for grading is that grades make it easier for university admissions officers or prospective employers to sort students and find the most qualified candidates. High school grade point average (GPA) is, in fact, a good predictor of success in college (Pettijohn, 1995; Tan, 1991). However, neither college nor high school GPA is a cogent predictor of success after school (Cohen, 1984). Some grading proponents claim that employers use grades for hiring decisions. However, most employers are far more interested in creative, responsible employees with balanced personalities, relevant experiences, good work habits, and the ability to work cooperatively with others (Glasser, 1998).

What do parents want to know about their children's achievement? Many parents want to know their children's relative standing, but they are much more concerned that their children are happy, balanced, independent, fulfilled, productive, self-reliant, responsible, functioning, kind, thoughtful, loving, inquisitive, and confident (Kohn, 1998). Since most of these attributes may be compromised by grades, parents have good reason to reject traditional evaluation practices. For example, grades and other extrinsic rewards tend to damage creativity (Amabile, Hennessey, & Grossman, 1986), reduce intrinsic motivation (Harackiewicz & Manderlink, 1984), diminish responsibility, produce less helpfulness and generosity (Fabes, Fultz, Eisenberg, May-Plimles, & Christopher, 1989), decrease concern for others (Balsam & Bondy, 1983), and curtail cooperation (Kanter, 1987). Thus, imposing grades on students to sort them for college may come with too high a price.

Self-Concept Development

School grades take their toll early in life. They foreclose on the hopes and aspirations of many students and consign them to lower academic ranks, lesser social status, and reduced employment opportunities. Even as early as kindergarten, children can identify the brightest and dullest among their peers and, given an opportunity, often point out these differences with relish. Moreover, kindergartners seem convinced that ability, not effort, is the main ingredient of success, and that failure comes from lack of ability, which many of them fear (Covington & Beery, 1976). This attitude, which is promoted through grading, has fateful consequences for both successful and unsuccessful students. Successful students are subject to elitism and arrogance (Kohn, 1998), while less-able students are convinced that their efforts have little effect on their achievements (Weiner & Kukla, 1970).

In lower-achieving students, grading establishes a failure-expectation pattern that some students then tend to perpetuate themselves. Failure-prone students may actually sabotage their own efforts (Aronson & Carlsmith, 1962). They may create standards for themselves that exceed what they believe they can achieve and then deliberately do low-quality work, which helps them avoid setting a precedent they feel unable to repeat on demand. Ironically, teachers often mistakenly accept the elevated standards as evidence of the student's willingness to try. In this way, irrational goal setting is unwittingly reinforced (Covington & Beery, 1976).

Children who receive extrinsic rewards for academic work choose easier tasks rather than challenging ones, make more errors, do lower-quality work, and use illogical problem-solving strategies (Condray, 1977). While children receiving no extrinsic rewards pursue optimal challenges, are more innovative, take responsible intellectual risks, and perform better under challenging conditions, children who receive extrinsic rewards have a tendency to be dependent, conform, do low-quality work, and have a low self-improvement orientation (Butler, 1992).

Rewards not only depress some forms of intellectual development and responsible independence, but they also have crippling effects on ethical and social development. Grades promote intolerance and interfere with communication between students who achieve at different levels (Kohn, 1998). They also encourage cheating. Grades reduce students' sense of control over their fate, and cheating is an attractive way to acquire more control and reduce the risk of failure (Milton, Pollio, & Eison, 1986). Rewards may encourage corner cutting and duplicity to reach desired achievements (Bok, 1979). They also produce anxiety, hostility, resentment, disapproval, envy, distrust, contempt, and aggression (Horney, 1973).

QUESTIONS FOR REFLECTION

1. What are your experiences and opinions about the effects of testing on students and students' self-concepts? Explain what kind of measurement instruments you might use that can make valid assessment of student achievement without having negative effects on students' self-concepts. Defend your selections.

2. From your field of teaching, describe specific content areas where different forms of assessment would be appropriate. What specific kinds of testing would you use?

Grade Inflation

In an effort to soften the blow to the self-concepts of students, educators have inflated grades. This practice began at least 40 years ago in the secondary schools and almost as long ago at the university level (Gose, 1997). A study by Levine (1994) determined that the number of As given to college students quadrupled between 1969 and 1993, while the number of Cs given dropped 66 percent. Between 1960 and 1979 there has been a .432 rise in GPA (Juola, 1980). Grade inflation generally promotes lower academic standards (Basinger, 1997) and gives students a distorted view of their academic achievements and abilities (Baummeister, 1996). Inflated grades encourage students to believe they are better prepared for the work than they actually are. Though grades have never properly represented working skills, inflated grades create an impression of student preparation that is even more distorted. Employers are less able to identify qualified candidates, and many must provide unanticipated training for new employees (Gose, 1997; Nagle, 1998). Ironically, students report that they could have achieved a much higher level of excellence than they actually did in the public schools. They routinely perform below their capability, and they know it. They persist in low performance because a low level is all that is expected of them. The incentives that students are conditioned to acquire are not compelling (Glasser, 1998). Thus, inflated grades fail to promote excellence because they establish low standards and do not encourage students to attain their potential.

One of the reasons often given for grade inflation is the increase in the quality of students over the years. However, the decline in Scholastic Aptitude Test (SAT) scores and American College Training (ACT) scores seem to indicate that current high school students are less qualified than their predecessors. Ironically, these scores have dropped while the preparation for these tests has been emphasized (Goldman, 1985). It is unlikely that student aptitudes have decreased; rather, grade inflation has probably led students to believe they are more prepared than they actually are. Budgetary pressures on universities related to enrollment declines and concern for credit-hour production may also be responsible for grade inflation at the college level. The struggle to increase enrollments to justify continued existence of various academic programs is also thought to create some pressure. Finally, grade inflation is connected to the student evaluation of faculty (Eiszler, 2002). College faculty realize that giving poor grades is not in their economic best interest. They believe that low grades lead to low student ratings and a corresponding reduction in class sizes, putting their jobs at risk (Beaver, 1997).

Grades are supposedly inflated to create a more pleasant atmosphere in the classroom so that achievement levels can be raised (Sykes, 1995). Unfortunately, self-esteem is known to play only a minor role in academic performance, possibly because these efforts to raise self-worth are contrived and children know it. A preference is for what researchers call *earned self-esteem*, the result of students working hard to attain goals rather than simply being given credit for poor work out of fear that expecting excellence may interfere with self-esteem (Baummeister, 1996).

Excessive focus on self-esteem has significantly affected a dramatic increase of pessimism and depression. These negative states occur when individuals do not have to meet challenges, overcome frustration, or demonstrate persistence in order to be successful (Seligman, 1995). Inflated grades undermine these important experiences: when students do not need to engage in learning that takes effort and persistence, they are protected from experiences that would have bolstered their sense of accomplishment and improved the quality of their performances. The increase in depression since the early 1900s has been well-documented, and Seligman believes its cause is an excessive focus on developing self-concept. He states that educators predict dire consequences unless students' feelings of anger, sadness, and anxiety are cushioned. These feelings, however, serve important purposes. They motivate the individual to change when necessary to achieve his or her goals, and by doing so help eliminate negative emotions. Depression occurs when individuals fail to achieve their goals or when they reach their goals but realize it has not been through personal effort. When children encounter obstacles, if teachers jump in to bolster self-esteem, soften the difficulties, and distract them by distorting what real success requires, children find it hard to eventually achieve excellence. If they are thus deprived of mastery, their self-esteem is weakened rather than strengthened, just as certainly as if they had been belittled, humiliated, and physically thwarted at every turn (Seligman, 1995).

Seligman (1995) is among those who believe that academic excellence can best be promoted by maintaining standards and support a return to strict grading patterns. However, excellence cannot be guaranteed through strict traditional norm-based grading practices. Norms are established in terms of how groups of representative individuals perform. Thus, typical performance sets the standards. When students commonly perform well below their capabilities, as indicated by Glasser's (1998) research, their level of achievement should not be taken as an appropriate standard of performance. Seligman's sense of well-being is accomplished by student efforts that represent their best work and are consistent with high standards of excellence.

QUESTIONS FOR REFLECTION

1. Reflect on your own experiences as a student. What kinds of actions did teachers take in an effort to grade fairly? What specific grading practices did you observe that you believe may have been harmful to students? What kinds of alternative evaluations do you think might have been appropriate?

2. Assume that, as the research shows, the grades in the school you attended were inflated. What was your attitude about the grades you got? Did you have to do your best to achieve the grades you were given? What do you think would be a helpful approach to student evaluation that could avoid some of the problems often associated with grading?

Evaluation and Excellence

One of the problems in defining excellence is that it differs for everyone. There are, of course, world standards achieved by Nobel prize winners, world class athletes, master painters and composers, and the like. These are not the levels of excellence sought after in school. If a student is capable of such attainments, his or her efforts should be encouraged. However, most students will define their potential at lesser levels. The degree of mastery possible for any student should not be undermined. The level of excellence sought should be defined by the student. Teachers can help in this process by teaching students how to realistically assess their own capabilities. Students should set their own expectations. The teacher's role is to help students honestly assess themselves and accept levels of excellence within their capability range.

Sometimes educators believe that their students should work at a level that stretches them a little but does not create frustration and discouragement. Although too much frustration may thwart learning, teachers need to remember that students may avoid trying simply to protect themselves from failure. This tendency is acquired when students are unduly protected from frustration. Rather than making a student withdraw, an appropriate level of frustration should provide a challenge and the drive necessary to achieve less-accessible levels of success. In doing this, students must evaluate their own performances and not be compared with peers. Attribution for failures should be correctly addressed. Students should always see their failures as a work in progress, not a final state. A student's reaction to failure must primarily be linked to discovering new learning strategies. An analysis of effort may be made to determine if more effort would have led to better accomplishments. Some students, however, may be putting forth a lot of effort and will not be encouraged by an admonition to work harder (Brophy, 1998).

Teachers should resist the common practice of encouraging students to improve by continually raising standards. This may seem harmless and even beneficial, particularly when children demonstrate that they can improve, but indiscriminate raising of standards by someone other than the student himself or herself can cause considerable harm. Some students who have been subject to such raising of standards suffer from a condition called *over-striving*. For these students, higher expectations define their worthiness, and they may feel that their acceptability depends on their achievements. When they start to reach the upper limit of their capability, they fear they won't be able to continue to produce, and this puts their self-concept in jeopardy. Instead of seeking success, these children work hard out of a fear of failure. Sometimes suicide seems to be the only alternative when children conclude they are no longer able to satisfy others' expectations (Covington & Beery, 1976).

Another type of problem occurs when students underestimate their abilities. Achieving excellence at an appropriate level gives students a sense of well-being. However, due to grade inflation, many students have accepted levels of achievement far below their capacity. Some underperforming students avoid true tests of their ability because they fear being inadequate. Many of these students do not even accurately know their intellectual strengths. Ironically, students may even feel unable to reach the lowered expectations, and therefore keep their abilities secret. Trying to provide these students with successful experiences is counter-productive, because they don't see such experiences as authentic representations of their ability.

QUESTIONS FOR REFLECTION

1. In your experience, what is the likelihood of students achieving true excellence in the schools? What are some unique ways you believe teachers could increase the level of classroom excellence?

2. What do you think the effect on academic excellence would be if students were allowed to evaluate themselves? Explain your thinking.

NATIONAL TEACHING STANDARDS

Teachers must be able to properly assess not only the achievements of groups of students, but of individual students as well. Teachers realize that classes don't learn; individual students do. However, they learn different things in different ways and at different paces.

Teachers understand that the purposes, timing, and focus of an evaluation affect its form. They are astute observers of students. Teachers use a variety of evaluation methods. They are able to create their own evaluation tools including portfolios, videotapes, demonstrations, and exhibits. They can also use traditional exams and quizzes to assess student work. Teachers are able to make assessment of students' work in a variety of ongoing instructional contexts.

Alternative Assessment

Because of the potential hazards of grading, as well as the need to make evaluation more authentic and valid, educators have created alternative assessments. Many times grades do not adequately represent student achievements. Although grades provide a sense of how students compare, if the tests do not accurately represent useful knowledge and skills, they fail to provide essential information about student performances. Critics of traditional tests and grades point out that tests often do not validly measure school content. Critics also indicate that testing encourages teachers to "teach to the test." Standardized tests in particular have received this criticism. Documented instances show teachers eliminating much of the intended curriculum in order to devote adequate time to preparing students for standardized achievement tests. In some instances, teachers have been required to abandon their curriculum and prepare students for standardized tests in areas outside their expertise (Clinchy, 2001; McNeil, 2000; Merrow, 2001). Interestingly, some of the standardized tests contain items that have no right answer, items that have multiple right answers, and items where the official answer is wrong (Bracey, 2001).

Sometimes there is little congruency between school purposes and assessment, which causes two potential problems. First, the anticipated form of testing may be allowed to frame the curriculum. Curriculum created around a test may not be an authentic preparation for life. The second potential problem is failure of the test to measure what ought to be taught. In some classrooms, high-level intellectual skills may be emphasized, but the tests used may not really determine how well students perform. Consequently, testing and grading may reduce the quality of educational experiences as well as provide poor evidence for what students can accomplish.

Authentic Assessment

Because tests may inappropriately frame the curriculum as well as fail to validly measure what is taught, some educators have proposed that authentic evaluation be used to determine the quality of student work. One of the problems of traditional testing is that it fails to assess students on complex performances that reflect sophisticated levels of understanding and achievement. **Authentic assessment** encourages students to perform in ways consistent with expert performances in the subject area. Thus, authentic assessments replicate the challenges and standards of performance that typically face writers, businesspeople, scientists, community leaders, designers, or historians; examples include writing essays and reports, conducting individual and group research, designing proposals and mock-ups, and so on (Wiggins, 1989).

Critics may believe such standards of performance are too high and there is no way to assess them. Some fear that insufficient standards exist to adequately judge quality.

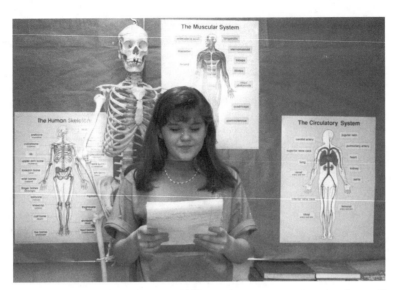

Alternative assessments, like student research reports, can increase the quality of student learning and accomplishment.

However, this problem is less significant than continuing to administer tests that do not measure acceptable life expectations. Other criticisms have also been given, such as the following list created by the Educational Testing Service (*Performance assessment: Different needs, difficult answers,* 1995):

- Authentic assessment tasks can be difficult to develop.
- Teachers may need additional training in how to create authentic assessment experiences.
- Teachers may experience difficulty scoring authentic assessment experiences.
- Authentic assessment procedures may require a lot of class time.
- There will have to be commitment to different kinds of instructional techniques.
- There may be difficulty establishing high levels of reliability in authentic assessment.

     None of these criticisms attacks the credibility of authentic assessment. Rather, they indicate potential problems and suggest that these problems need to be dealt with by creating an authentic assessment program of strength.

     To develop authentic assessment, instructional goals must authentically represent the kind of knowledge and skills required in the various forms of work performed in society. Teaching and learning should be designed to provide the necessary training to perform these complex tasks. Assessments need to be developed that provide valid measurement. Some believe this requires tests to be created in the usual testing format. However, many of the skills used in various occupations require independent construction of something that cannot be represented in a test. For example, an individual may be required to prepare a research proposal, write an essay, perform skilled personal interactions, build models, conduct research and prepare reports, create architectural plans, construct houses, keep accounting records, and the like. Many of these skills are impossible to simulate in a testing format.

No doubt teachers will require specialized training not only in creating authentic tests, but in formulating and arranging authentic learning experiences. They will also need to develop skills to judge the quality of student work and help them make self-assessments. Teachers need to examine how they use their classroom time. Many may feel that the additional time required for these authentic activities is wasted. Complex student learning activities do require more time, but this time is more wisely spent than preparing for traditional tests. Teachers need to offer substantially different learning activities for students, experiences that obviously will need to be more self-directed. Students cannot acquire many of the required skills without considerable independence, thus giving the process of learning greater authenticity.

Finally, teachers need to decide whether the validity of learning experiences and assessment processes or the reliability of measures carries more weight. Reliability is an important concern, but it should not outweigh the more important validity considerations. Validity needs to be addressed first, followed by whatever degree of reliability is achievable.

 ## QUESTION FOR REFLECTION

1. Compare criticisms of authentic assessment with traditional testing. Explain which you believe to be more appropriate and discuss why.

Portfolios

Using **portfolios** for assessment is becoming more widespread (Calfee & Perfumo, 1993). The portfolio should consist of the best work a student has done, such as art work, models, furniture, a house, or equipment constructed to perform research. If possible, the portfolio should be maintained in a file. Sometimes photos are used if the items are bulky. Computer filing of portfolio materials is becoming more common and is a very useful way to collect and modify it as needed. The quality of a portfolio, as well as the need for modifications, should be judged by the student with teacher assistance (Herbert, 1998).

Sometimes educators fall into the trap of trying to grade student portfolios, even though a portfolio system should replace grades. Grades are meant to compare students' achievements. If students are encouraged to do their best work and allowed sufficient autonomy to achieve it, items in their portfolios won't provide a basis for making comparisons. What one student chooses to include may be substantially different from the work chosen by another. Therefore, grades should not be imposed on this process. It defeats the desired strengths of the portfolio method. When portfolios are graded teachers may urge, if not require, students to do exactly the same kind of projects so their work can be more readily compared.

Portfolio work should primarily be evaluated by the student. The student's assessment should determine whether new items should be developed, or whether the work in the portfolio represents the student's desired level of achievement. The teacher may assist students in comparing their work with similar work by others. For example, an art teacher may help a student ascertain whether or not her illustrations can be expected to qualify her for a good job or allow her to access advanced training. The level the student seeks should depend on her aspirations. This requires an honest evaluation. Students should eventually become expert in assessing their own work, as the ability to assess one's own work is enormously empowering, since students can accurately visualize their current level and discover what they may need to advance to a higher level. These assessments display their abilities better than potentially irrelevant or inaccurate testing.

Different standards exist that students might use to judge the quality of their work: (1) They might judge their current work compared to previous work. (2) They might attempt to compare their work to similar work by other individuals at the same age and experience level. (3) They might compare their work against that of people with advanced training and experience. (4) They might evaluate the work history accomplished by others and compare it to their own rate of progress. Both the work and relative progress provide students with a valid means to determine the quality of their efforts.

In making assessments, students should be taught to generate and apply appropriate criteria and incorporate them in terms of relative importance. Some criteria are more important and should be more heavily weighted in the evaluation process. The following criteria are examples that may be generated by students to make assessments of their work. Keep in mind that these are examples and do not constitute an exact, appropriate list of criteria:

For oil paintings: (1) The project should display an unusual view of some life phenomenon. (2) The project should display the appropriate use of perspective, light, color, and texture. (3) The project should demonstrate excellence in drawing skill.

For a science research project: (1) The research must address a question that the student has personally determined and be formated for scientific investigation. (2) The project must apply appropriate controls so that there are not confounding variables influencing the experiment results. (3) Data collection must be appropriate, accurate, and devoid of any biasing factors. (4) Conclusions must be supported by the data collected. (5) The results must be significant.

For a sociology survey project: (1) The research must be based on a meaningful, personally determined question. (2) The sampling must adequately represent the population it is drawn from. (3) The questions must not be leading and must be properly sequenced. (4) Appropriate statistical routines must be used. (5) Conclusions must be supported by the data. (6) Extrapolations to the general population must be justifiable.

Teachers need to help students use criteria to make work assessments and formulate plans for improvement. Greater assistance is needed in the beginning. Evaluation is a very complex intellectual skill; students should learn how to make valid judgments and understand the difference between evaluation and personal preferences.

How can you tell if the work in a portfolio is really a student's own? There is probably no foolproof way to guarantee this. However, as teachers work closely with students, they can monitor the authenticity of the students' work as they consult with students and observe them perform. Portfolios may be less subject to fraud than tests. There is a substantial amount of cheating on tests, despite teacher efforts to curtail it.

What kind of work can be included in a portfolio? The following list provides some examples:

1. Writings, including essays, poetry, and plays
2. Research proposals, reports of science, and social research

3. Paintings, drawings, sculptures, and illustrations
4. Compositions and performances of music
5. Records of participation in plays and operettas
6. Competitions in athletics, speech, debates, commercial contests, foreign language fairs, and science fairs
7. Completed accounting practice sets
8. Examples of letters typed
9. Computer programs created
10. Research papers written
11. Jewelry, furniture, and home construction
12. Architectural designs
13. Results of judging competitions
14. Physical fitness tests and intermural competitions
15. Simulations
16. Auto repairs
17. Agricultural projects
18. Terms in student government
19. Activities as a teacher assistant
20. Summaries of learning in various subjects
21. Documentaries produced

Teachers can guide students through portfolio development by helping them (1) identify the characteristics of good academic work, (2) apply criteria in assessing their own work, (3) promote the use of peer assessment to help them refine and revise their work, and (4) select the work included in the portfolio so that it accurately creates a portrait of the learner. Teachers who have implemented a portfolio system report that (1) students have a richer, more positive, and expanded sense of their progress, (2) assessment becomes collaborative rather than competitive, (3) teachers obtain a richer, clearer view of their students, (4) records of what students can actually do are made available to teachers, and (5) student organization skills and academic performance is improved (Shultz, 1998; Tierney, Carter, & Desai, 1991). Portfolios are a more equitable and culturally fair way to assess students, particularly culturally and linguistically diverse children (Hadaway & Marek-Schroer, 1994).

Decision Points

Take a position regarding the usefulness of portfolios for student assessment. After comparing the pros and cons of portfolios and of norm-based evaluation, explain which position is most supportable and why.

NATIONAL TEACHING STANDARDS

Teachers should help their students engage in self-assessment, instilling in them a sense of responsibility for monitoring their own learning.

Assessment in Learning Communities

In learning communities, evaluation is broad based. Student achievements, as well as learning and instructional processes, receive attention. Traditional schooling exclusively spotlights comparative student achievements, with the general focus on students' memorized information. In learning communities, student achievement is assessed, as is the teaching-learning processes employed in the instructional program. In addition, they consider different kinds of achievements and use different formats for evaluation. Student self-evaluation is considered an essential element in assessing learning communities.

Nature and Purpose of Assessment

While comparing student performances on tests is the prevalent assessment in most schools, comparative assessments are avoided in learning communities since they are viewed as hostile to the evaluation purposes, not to mention the general learning community purposes. Learning communities depend on sincere affection and cooperative associations among members; traditional testing and grading can undermine group commitment. In learning communities, evaluation focuses on consistency with group purposes and methods for improved and more effective group processes.

Determining how well students perform is important in learning communities. Rather than making comparisons, however, evaluation focuses on a degree of excellence. Excellence is variously defined, depending on purposes. If students want to assess performances relative to the world of work, one set of standards may be applied. If college entrance is the goal, another set of standards may be appropriate. Many students wish to acquire living skills, and excellence in this domain may depend on the specific aspirations of each student. Considerable flexibility is needed: students' interests and purposes can help to shape criteria and levels of achievement. For example, one student may look upon art as a potential occupation, another as a field to teach, a third as a possible hobby, and a fourth as simply something to appreciate. In each case, the kinds of experiences needed and levels of competence required are greatly varied.

The following possible assessment concerns in learning communities are suggested as essential:

1. Are community members achieving the defined level of excellence?
2. Are student needs being met within the learning community?
3. Are levels of excellence flexible in terms of how they are defined among group members?
4. Are levels of excellence adaptable for change as individuals see a need for altering them?
5. Are leadership and cooperation validly assessed?
6. Does the evaluation determine the expertise of group members to conduct inquiry-based research and prepare appropriately written reports?
7. Do members of the learning community coherently and openly express themselves?
8. Do members of the learning community acquire a high level of skill in social interactions?

9. Are appropriate materials accessible to group members to support their study and investigations?
10. Do members acquire a cohesive set of values to skillfully articulate and carefully follow?
11. Do members achieve a high level of intellectual development?
12. Do members acquire the ability to validly assess their own growth and achievement?
13. Does the curriculum created by the learning community provide valid experiences for all students that lead to accomplishing appropriate goals and objectives for the kind of background students will need to live a full life?
14. Are the student portfolios an accurate representation of the students' accomplishments and capabilities?
15. Does the role of the teacher contribute appropriately to individual achievement and group development?
16. Does the school administration provide appropriate avenues for the learning community to be purposeful and fruitful?

Assessment Procedures

Learning communities need to assess their members' accomplishments. Such assessment requires careful analysis of the various definitions of excellence generated for each student's purposes. Teachers and students can then carefully examine each student's work and compare it to his or her aspirations. This process involves determining the degree of student progress. They need to see that their efforts produce desirable increases in their accomplishments and realize that they can continue to progress toward the levels of excellence they have set for themselves.

Teachers need to ensure that they honor each student's level of excellence rather than impose a single set of standards on all students. Varying abilities and interests, along with the goals students have set for themselves, should be the focus for this evaluation. Students working on a single project may aspire to different outcomes and work side by side with other students to achieve them. Teachers will need to assess the extent to which students allow sufficient differentiation between their own goals and those of their peers. Students may initially have a tendency to project their own expectations on classmates. However, all participants in learning communities should allow associates to carve out expectations for themselves and pursue their own expectations without inappropriate interference. Teachers need to systematically assess expressions of students' intentions and determine if these are carried out with group support.

Teachers must also ascertain whether or not students feel free to modify their learning goals, opportunities, and associated excellence levels. Learning communities should provide an atmosphere where students are free to modify their learning goals within group expectations. The teacher should help ensure that changes are not made thoughtlessly and without thorough dialogue with group members. The group should give approval for proposed changes so these alterations do not substantially interfere with group projects and processes. This kind of data can be acquired through observations, but also via student opinion surveys.

Leadership skills and cooperative learning abilities need to be evaluated. Each participant in a learning community should have the opportunity to serve as a team leader and assume all the attendant responsibilities. These activities ensure that students are optimumly benefiting from these experiences and being provided improvement directions. Direct observation is the appropriate format for this kind of evaluation. Teachers can create checklists that identify skills they consider essential elements of leadership and cooperation. For example, leaders should not be coercive, should delegate, should assume appropriate work responsibilities, should provide encouragement, should deal successfully with disputes, should create useful agendas for meetings, and so on. Cooperative learning abilities include the inclination to share, to help others, to shoulder an appropriate share of work responsibilities, to make sincere commitments and follow-through, to be punctual, to refrain from annoying others and making their work difficult, and the like.

Inquiry research is the predominant methodology for learning communities. This process must be well-understood and expertly executed. In evaluating it, students should carefully research questions they have formulated and properly employ the processes of the scientific method. Teachers should examine the way students generate hypotheses to ensure they are educated guesses, not "shots in the dark." Teachers should also examine research designs to determine the extent they can provide relevant information regarding the research question and ensure that potential confounding variables are addressed. Teachers need to decide if their students can determine when variables might interfere with a correct data interpretation. Finally, teachers need to examine students' research conclusions to ensure that these conclusions are properly supported by the data. This process can only be accomplished by a careful analysis of the students' research reports and by scheduled observations of student research activity.

By participating in learning communities, students can obtain skills in communicating coherently and expressively. These skills can be formally evaluated with observation checklists. Students' abilities to appropriately sequence a set of ideas and draw conclusions could be assessed, along with their ability to communicate with a suitable level of emotion.

Students in learning communities need to have social skills; their success in the group depends on it. Here again, observations are necessary. Students' observations are needed during the group learning process so any problems can be detected and interventions applied. No doubt students will need instruction on how to engage in successful social interactions. Such attributes as sensitivity, thoughtfulness, sincerity, helpfulness, and conscientiousness can be examined and encouraged.

Whether or not students have sufficient materials for the projects they do can be assessed in part from teacher observations, but learning teams should be periodically surveyed to determine what is lacking. In addition, the teacher should determine if necessary learning materials have been made available in a timely way and if they are in good condition. Some equipment or supplies are difficult to acquire, or they may be too costly. Students may occasionally find access to what they need at a university or research lab. Often appropriate materials can be obtained from federal agencies or local businesses. Teachers need to find as many sources as they can, not only for equipment and materials, but also for funding. School budgets are commonly insufficient to support the kind of research efforts that would be most beneficial for students. Students must, of course, have access to computers and related resources.

The development of a value system is an important outcome of schooling. State departments of education, state legislatures, and other bodies are commonly interested in helping students accumulate a set of values that properly reflect social norms and responsibilities. Though schools may be responsible for transmitting these values to students, little actual teaching concerning values occurs in the schools. Learning communities, however, have values as a central focus. For instance, the "democratic values," a reflection of the United States Constitution, are incorporated into the basic operation of learning communities. Additional values like courtesy, honesty, and integrity are directly sought in conjunction with students' group interactions. Values should be regularly assessed both by observation and from students' writing. Groups of students may periodically engage in conversations about value issues with one another. Student position papers also provide an excellent resource for assessment.

Although the most acclaimed goal of schooling is the intellectual development of students, most tests are inadequate in determining intellectual skills. However, students take initiative for learning in various projects that reveal what skills students have. Much of what students do in learning communities may serve as a basis for this assessment, including all of their writing, such as reports of their work, explanations of a point-of-view, or artful presentations of ideas and feelings. Various kinds of projects are also excellent sources to assess students' intellectual development. A proper assessment examines a broad range of intellectual functions, including the routine assessment of analysis, synthesis, and evaluation skills.

In learning communities, students should become experts in valid self-assessment. Teachers should give instruction on how to validly self-evaluate and then ask students to provide them with their own assessments of their work, along with the criteria they used and a rationale for the judgments. Teachers should frequently provide students feedback on their self-assessment skills by helping students make careful analyses of their work in comparison to other pieces of similar work. Remember, students are not being taught to grade their work. Comparing their work with that of their peers is not done to determine which is best, but rather to evaluate it against similar work that appropriately represents their aspirations.

The concern exists that the work students undertake on their own initiative will somehow be inferior to that prescribed by others. Thus, teachers rarely use student input in curriculum construction. However, students' commitment for learning is essentially a function of their interests. In this regard, the extent to which students maintain interest and commitment for their learning plans, and also the extent to which the topics they select can be judged as viable school experiences, need to be evaluated. Teachers need to carefully examine student projects to determine if they are substantial and if certain topics are avoided that should logically be included in the curriculum. The purpose of this evaluation is not to ensure that student learning projects exactly represent the curricular expectations outlined by state departments of education and others, but rather to ensure that viable curricula have been identified and included. Perhaps the best way to do this is to create a set of criteria against which to make judgments. The following are some examples of possible criteria:

Experiences selected should

1. provide a means to develop students' intellectual capacity.
2. help students develop a valid value system.

3. provide for the development of excellence.
4. familiarize students with information valued by the culture.
5. involve students in active inquiry through which they can learn firsthand about the usefulness of the scientific methods in learning.
6. help students value the democratic process.

Portfolios are an especially useful way for learning community participants to assess their own work and demonstrate the level of their knowledge and skill. With the help of their teachers, students should routinely examine their portfolios and assess their progress. Students should also determine if the examples of their work represent the level of excellence they wish to achieve and make plans to enhance their portfolio.

Decision Points

Create an assessment program for a learning community in your subject area.

CENTRAL IDEAS

1. The original purpose of testing and grading was to sort students for college entrance. Current grading practices have a variety of other purposes.
2. Student assessment has three distinct components: measurement, evaluation, and grading.
3. Valid tests measure what they claim to measure.
4. A test is reliable when it is consistent in measuring achievement.
5. Tests should not only be used to assess curricula, but also to help teachers modify it.
6. Objective tests should be written in an appropriate format with understandable language.
7. Specific procedures need to be followed in scoring essay exams to ensure sufficient reliability.
8. Papers and projects should be graded with an appropriate rubric.
9. In evaluating affective goals, teachers should make sure the conditions under which data are collected do not contain biasing factors.
10. There are three forms of evaluation: diagnostic, formative, and summative. Diagnostic evaluation precedes and guides instruction. Formative evaluation helps to monitor and direct instruction. Summative evaluation is administered at the end of instruction for grading purposes.
11. Norm-based grading depends on means and standard deviations being computed from a set of test scores.
12. Both norm-based grades and minimum levels of competency in criterion-referenced grades may depress the excellence levels of which students are capable.
13. Grades and grade inflation are related to low performance and self-concept problems.
14. Excellence in school can be enhanced by helping students acquire a valid understanding of their capabilities.
15. Students can suffer a debilitating condition called over-striving when teachers and parents continually raise standards without allowing students to assess their own work.

16. Authentic assessments are designed to determine how students perform complex, sophisticated skills; they authentically represent the kind of knowledge and skills required in various kinds of work performed in society.
17. Portfolios are collections of what students consider to be their best work; they can be used to give an authentic view of student accomplishments.
18. Assessment in learning communities goes far beyond student achievement to include evaluation of the learning community operations, students' development of interpersonal skills, leadership, attitudes, and school support.

REFERENCES

Amabile, T. M., Hennessey, B. A., & Grossman, B. S. (1986). Social influences on creativity: The effects of contracted-for reward. *Journal of Personality and Codical Psychology, 50,* 14–23.

Armstrong, D. G., & Savage, T. V. (1998). *Teaching in the secondary school: An introduction* (4th ed.). Upper Saddle River, NJ: Prentice Hall.

Aronson, E., & Carlsmith, J. M. (1962). Performance expectancy as a determinant of actual performance. *Journal of Abnormal and Social Psychology, 65,* 178–182.

Balsam, P. D., & Bondy, A. S. (1983). The negative side effects of reward. *Journal of Applied Behavior Analysis, 16,* 283–296.

Basinger, D. (1997). Fighting grade inflation; A misguided effort? *College Teaching, 45,* 88–91.

Baummeister, R. F. (1996, Summer). Should schools try to boost self-esteem? *American Educator, 22,* 14–19.

Beaver, W. (1997, July). Declining college standards: It's not the course, it's the grades. *The College Board Review, 181,* 2–7+.

Bloom, B. S., Madaus, G. F., & Hastings, J. T. (1981). *Evaluation to improve learning.* New York: McGraw-Hill.

Bok, S. (1979). *Lying: Moral choice in public and private life.* New York: Vintage.

Bracey, G. W. (1994). Grade inflation? *Phi Delta Kappan, 76* (4), 328–329.

Bracey, G. W. (2001). The 11th Bracey report on the condition of public education. *Phi Delta Kappan, 83* (2), 157–169.

Brophy, J. (1998). *Motivating students to learn.* Boston: McGraw-Hill.

Butler, R. (1992). What young people want to know when: Effects of mastery and ability goals on interest in different kinds of social comparisons. *Journal of Personality and Social Psychology, 62,* 934–943.

Calfee, R. C., & Perfumo, P. (1993). Student portfolios: Opportunities for a revolution in assessment. *Journal of Reading, 36* (7), 532–537.

Clinchy, E. (2001). Needed: A new educational civil rights movement. *Phi Delta Kappan, 83* (7), 493–498.

Cohen, P. A. (1984). College grades and adult achievement: A research synthesis. *Researcher in Higher Education, 20* (3), 281–293.

Condray, J. (1977). Enemies of exploration: Self-initiated versus other-initiated learning. *Journal of Personality and Social Psychology, 35,* 459–477.

Covington, M. V., & Beery, R. G. (1976). *Self-worth and school learning.* New York: Holt, Rinehart & Winston.

Educational Testing Service. *Performance assessment: Different needs, difficult answers.* (1995). Princeton, NJ: Educational Testing Service.

Eiszler, C. F. (2002). College student evaluation of teaching and grade inflation. *Research in Higher Education, 43* (4), 483–501.

Fabes, R. A., Fultz, J., Eisenberg, N., May-Plimles, T., & Christopher, F. S. (1989). Effects of rewards on children's prosocial motivation: A socialization study. *Developmental Psychology, 25,* 509–515.

Freeman, D. J., Kuhn, T. M., Porter, A. C., Floden, R. E., Schmidt, W. H., & Schwille, J. R. (1983). Do textbooks and tests define a natural curriculum in elementary school mathematics? *Elementary School Journal, 83* (5), 501–513.

Gardner, H. (1985). *Frames of the mind: The theory of multiple intelligences.* New York: Basic Books.

Gardner, H. (1994). Multiple intelligences: A theory in practice. *Teacher's College Record, 95* (4), 576–583.

Glasser, W. (1998). *Choice theory: A new psychology of personal freedom.* New York: Harper Collins.

Goldman, L. (1985). The betrayal of the gatekeepers: Grade inflation. *The Journal of General Education, 37* (2), 97–121.

Gose, B. (1997). Efforts to curb grade inflation get an F from many critics. *The Chronicle of Higher Education, 43,* A41–A42.

Guilford, J. P. (1962). Factors that aid and hinder creativity. *Teacher's College Record, 63,* 384–392.

Hadaway, N. L., & Marek-Schroer, M. (1994). Student portfolios: Toward equitable assessments for gifted students. *Equity and Excellence in Education, 27* (1), 70–74.

Harackiewicz, J. M., & Manderlink, G. (1984). Process analysis of the effects of performance-contingent rewards on intrinsic motivation. *Journal of Experimental Social Psychology, 20,* 531–551.

Herbert, E. A. (1998). Lessons learned about student portfolios. *Phi Delta Kappan, 79* (8), 583–585.

Horney, K. (1973). Culture and neurosis. In T. Milton (Ed.), *Theories of psychopathology and personality* (2nd ed. pp. 161–162). Philadelphia: W. B. Saunders.

Juola, A. (1980). Grade inflation in higher education—1979: Is it over? (ED 189 1299).

Kanter, R. M. (1987). *Men and women of the corporation.* New York: Basic Books.

Kindsvatter, R., Wilen, W., & Ishler, M. (1992). *Dynamics of effective teaching* (2nd ed.). White Plains, NY: Longman.

Kohn, A. (1998). Only for my kid: How privileged parents undermine school reform. *Phi Delta Kappan, 79,* 569–577.

Levine, A. (1994, Jan. 19). To deflate grade inflation: Simplify system. *The Chronicle of Higher Education, 40,* B3.

McNeil, L. M. (2000). Creating new inequalities: Contradiction of reform. *Phi Delta Kappan, 81* (10), 729–734.

Merrow, J. (2001). Undermining standards. *Phi Delta Kappan, 83* (9), 653–659.

Milton, O., Pollio, H. R., & Eison, J. A. (1986). *Making sense of college grades.* San Francisco: Jossey-Bass.

Nagle, B. (1998). A proposal for dealing with grade inflation: The relative performance index. *Journal of Education in Business, 74* (1), 40–43.

Pettijohn, T. F. (1995). Correlations among students' grade point averages and American College Test scores. *Psychological Reports, 76* (February), 336–338.

Popham, W. J. (1999). Why standardized tests don't measure educational quality. *Educational Leadership, 56* (6), 8–15.

Seligman, M. E. P. (1995). *The optimistic child.* New York: Harper Collins.

Shultz, D. (1998). Improving student organization through the use of portfolios (ED 412 275). Action Research Project. Saint Xavier University and Skylight Training and Publishing Field-Based Master Program.

Sykes, C. (1995). *Dumbing down our kids.* New York: St. Martin's Press.

Tan, D. L. (1991). Grades as predictors of college and career success. *Journal of College Admissions, 132,* 12–15.

Tierney, R. J., Carter, M. A., & Desai, L. E. (1991). *Portfolio assessment in the reading-writing classroom.* Norwood, MA: Christopher-Gordon.

Weiner, B., & Kukla, A. (1970). An attributional analysis of achievement motivation. *Journal of Abnormal and Social Psychology, 15,* 1–20.

Wiggins, G. (1989). A true test; Toward more authentic and equitable measurement. *Phi Delta Kappan, 70* (8), 703–713.

Teacher Improvement

CHAPTER OBJECTIVES

This chapter is designed to help you

1. Explain some obstacles to improving teaching and the factors that help teachers make better assessments of their teaching.
2. Explain how to make a self-analysis of your teaching.
3. Employ the use of researchable questions in your quest for improving your teaching.
4. Engage in peer collaboration to improve your teaching assessments.
5. Point out ways to improve teaching by improving the school environment.
6. Explain ways to improve teaching in learning communities.

Teaching can be markedly improved through teacher collaboration and action research.

INTRODUCTION

The quest for teaching excellence is elusive: There is no proven best way to teach, and there are diverse learning purposes for which different kinds of teaching are appropriate (Good, 1996). According to tradition, Socrates once took a prospective student into deep water, pushed his head under, and held it there until the aspiring pupil nearly drowned. When Socrates finally lifted the student to the surface, he told the young man to come back when his desire to learn was as strong as his recent desire for air. This anecdote provides a metaphor for good teaching: Teachers should somehow get students to the point where they are desperate to learn. This would be ideal, of course, but it rarely happens. Instead, teachers typically impose a curriculum that students do not really want and struggle to get many of them involved in learning. Good teachers may be adept at providing students with discrepant events that catch students off guard or create dissonance in some way. Students may be motivated to resolve incongruity, which might sustain learning over an extended period of time.

Student surveys are sometimes used to define good teaching, and teachers are urged to make changes producing greater student satisfaction. Unfortunately, this procedure may not lead to better teaching. The teacher's charisma may influence students' evaluation scores more than the quality of teaching (Coats & Swierenga, 1972). Students will more likely evaluate the quality of teaching on personally defined criteria than on comprehensive, valid standards. Student biases may also make data acquired from student surveys unacceptable.

Supervisors and principals have traditionally assessed the quality of teaching both to improve it and to evaluate teacher performance for retention decisions. These efforts have not improved teaching, partly because teachers feel uncertainly about administration expectations and how to satisfy them (Good & Brophy, 2000).

Teaching quality can be more appropriately assessed when it is compared to teacher intentions and the goals of instruction. Because the various educational outcomes require different kinds of teaching, "quality" is hard to define. What might a teacher do who wishes to help students become more intense, independent learners? Even a very excellent lecture is unlikely to help these students become more capable of inquiry, nor will charisma alone provide what students need to become responsible, independent learners. Students need someone to help them confront curious life phenomena, creating interesting questions for conducting research. A teacher who is actively involved in personal research efforts lets students know about his or her work and involves students in research as their interests develop.

Ms. Chadwick collapsed in exhaustion as the final period of the day came to a close. She felt like she was in the middle of a war zone and losing the battle. As a first-year teacher near the middle of the school year, her lessons focused on the civil war, specifically the economic and racial aspects of the conflict. She included true stories of families with children fighting on the opposing sides, slaves who escaped and secretly moved to the North, and battle experiences recorded in the journals of both Confederate and Union soldiers. She tried to present all the conflict issues, in an interesting way, to help students understand, from the views of both sides, why this conflict took place. She also presented information on the government's reconstruction policy after the war, explaining how Southerners were exploited by "carpetbaggers" and others seeking to benefit from their misfortunes. Putting all these factors together gave Ms. Chadwick a sense of understanding and competence, along with a greater sense of the need for government unity and freedom in citizen's affairs. She thought her students would also appreciate the lessons and wish to diligently learn. However, many of her students seemed disinterested and disrupted her class. She tried to follow the recommendations of her mentor teacher; in fact, she tried to apply the advice exactly after being assured the tactics always "worked." However, while contemplating her frustrating day, she concluded that these tactics didn't work for her and that maybe she didn't have what it took to be a good teacher. "Maybe," she thought, "I should give up teaching and find something more placid that doesn't involve complex interaction and management difficulties." Never before had she seriously thought about giving up teaching. She always viewed herself motivated and ready to teach, and no other profession seemed to suit her better. However, she began to realize that her simplistic views about teaching were causing her to fail at things she thought she understood. She also suspected there were aspects of teaching she didn't even know about that might help her be more successful. Other teachers occasionally talked about them in the teachers' lounge. Alice Cardner, for example, mentioned attribution retraining, while Jim Peters gave a lengthy rationale for peer tutoring. Roland Mecham tried to explain the benefits of using the Co-op Co-op cooperative learning system over the Jigsaw Method. Ms. Chadwick never learned the details of different cooperative learning models, receiving instead only a very sketchy outline of the general concept with an admonition to seriously consider it in her classroom. However, during her student teaching, she had asked her cooperating teacher, Mr. James, about cooperative learning and was told to forget about it. Group learning was too hard to manage, she was told, and most of the group work was done by only one student. Mr. James explained that cooperative learning just alienates better students while teaching less-able students to be lazy and take advantage of their brighter counterparts. Now Ms. Chadwick started to wonder who was right, Mr. James or Mr. Mecham. Was cooperative learning something she could learn to do, and would it help her teach more effectively? Or would it be like Mr. James predicted? She couldn't afford to lose any more classroom control. However, Mr. Mecham said that his students seemed to learn more with cooperative learning. What about that? He said he didn't have problems managing the class either. Maybe he just had a knack for teaching that way.

 ## QUESTIONS FOR REFLECTION

1. If you were in Ms. Chadwick's place, what would you do and why?
2. What do you consider the most effective kind of learning for different kinds of learners? What techniques have you been exposed to and what do you think you would be comfortable with as a teacher? How can these forms of teaching be assessed without attributing quality exclusively to one form?

Obstacles to Teacher Improvement

Teacher improvement is often discussed among educators, as well as individuals and agencies outside the schools. At various times the government becomes particularly active in trying to promote education improvements. These efforts have a long tradition, but seem to have been unsuccessful: Direction and funding have repeatedly been given for the same kind of reform efforts, year after year. These endeavors rarely have an impact on teaching, even though improvement in teaching quality is the most necessary change. What factors are responsible for limiting the improvement of teaching despite numerous efforts to increase it?

Insufficient Time and Inadequate Finances

For teachers to improve, time must be set aside for a number of activities. Even after teachers have identified a desired teaching style, they need to experiment with new methods, make observations, engage in discussions, and analyze theoretical work as well as apply theory to their teaching. They need to constantly reflect on their teaching and stay abreast of new research and developments. However, given the demands of class preparation and its related work, finding time for professional reading and interacting with peers is usually difficult. Nonetheless, these things are essential to becoming a talented professional and a knowledgeable teacher (Darling-Hammond, Bullmaster, & Cobb, 1995; Goodson, 1997).

School officials who are serious about improving teaching need to provide sufficient time for teachers to engage in consistent, long-term improvement. In many schools, efforts to improve teaching consist of one or two annual workshops. Teachers may do little serious thinking before these training sessions, and there is usually no follow-up. Consequently, no articulated development program and little or no support for teacher improvement exists (Good & Brophy, 2000).

School funding is often in short supply. The availability of funding ordinarily depends on state and local revenues, which may be subject to the ups and downs of tax collections and state legislature allocations. Teachers tend to focus on increases in their paychecks more than funding for inservice training. The money provided to teachers to run their classes is often inadequate, and teachers end up using their own resources to finance some learning activities. Under these conditions, having sufficient money available to finance a comprehensive teacher improvement program is unlikely.

Status Quo

Even if improvements are needed and the resources are available, changes are often difficult to make. Many teachers have established comfortable and reasonably successful routines and are unlikely to depart from them without good reason. Changing routines requires considerable effort. Teachers already overburdened with responsibilities are unlikely to make changes requiring a lot of time and energy. In addition, making changes implies that past activities were inadequate, something most people do not like to admit. Administrative edicts that are simply imposed on teachers ordinarily fail to inspire cooperation. Teachers need to help determine what changes are needed as well as their implementation. Teachers need to believe that the changes not only will be in their own best interest, but will also benefit the children. A change, like implementing a team approach to teaching, that consumes a lot more teacher time will not be readily accepted even if it appears to be advantageous to children.

Teacher improvement is also limited by the way teachers have been socialized. Most teachers seldom take part in evaluation processes designed to both discover and eliminate weaknesses. Even in early school experiences, people are not expected to correct their mistakes and incorporate new ideas in their work. Indeed, time is rarely given to think about what has been accomplished with the idea of trying to improve it. Instead, students are simply expected to go on to the next assignment and turn everything in on schedule. Students do not have to do original, practical thinking because most teachers only require analytical thinking, at best. Most teachers have limited practice identifying problems and little experience either solving them or generating alternatives. In addition, schools do not ordinarily provide students an opportunity to evaluate themselves. With current grading practices, teachers perform evaluations providing students information regarding their current status, but make few suggestions about how students might improve. These practices usually make students fearful about evaluation and improvement, as they run the risk of exposing their weaknesses and being labelled. Finally, teaching candidates are not given training experiences to help them develop a sense of collegiality and understand the virtue of self-learning through peer feedback. To develop professionally, teachers need to study collegial relationship models and practice giving and receiving feedback (Good & Brophy, 2000). Not only do teachers have little inclination to work together to make improvements in their practice, but it is unlikely an organizational structure exists in the school that supports teacher interaction for improvement purposes during the instructional day (Smylie, 1992).

NATIONAL TEACHING STANDARDS

In seeking excellence, teachers should have a reverence for the craft, recognize its complexities, and have a commitment to lifelong professional development.

Complexity of Teaching

Teaching is one of the most complex of human activities. Teachers are not only confronted with the personal idiosyncrasies and learning styles of many students, but also with the dynamics of human relationships in various classroom configurations. They also have to consider the social structure of the school, as well as more general levels of social functioning. Each student comes to school with an individual history and personal ways of satisfying specific needs and goals. Teachers also bring their own history and culture to the classroom, along with expectations and strategies for helping students learn. Teachers also have personal philosophies to help simplify classroom situations. They are usually more or less successful depending on how well-defined and predictable their theories are. In addition, the professional culture in the school includes various opinions about what a quality education is and the best means to achieve it. Working within this structure and determining the best teaching method using colleagues' insights and assessments in addition to one's own is perplexing indeed.

A teacher must carefully study expert knowledge and research about teaching, examine his or her own views about numerous issues, consult with colleagues, conduct cultural and social analyses, and consider dozens of other possible inputs that influence curriculum development and instruction. Most especially, teachers must carefully study the nature of learning and assess their teaching practices accordingly. Teaching improvement requires extensive, thoughtful analysis of all relevant inputs.

Nowhere is the complexity of teaching more apparent than in the classroom during instructional sessions. Many teachers struggle to practice their craft despite this perplexity.

Some are marginally successful, but many others flounder. Sometimes they employ tactics designed for simple interpersonal interactions. Successful teachers employ theories that simplify complex classroom situations and makes them more manageable. Teaching improvement depends extensively on the degree to which teachers carefully study and apply appropriate theoretical knowledge about teaching and learning (Johnson, 1998). When teachers have insufficient time or inclination to conscientiously focus on this task, extensive improvement is unlikely at best.

In the quest to improve teaching, teachers must acquire a well-organized, comprehensive philosophy of education. Although constituents of an educational philosophy vary, some elements are likely to be the same for most teachers. Some may change from time to time or be periodically refined and redefined; however, some components, like students' needs and ways they learn, are likely to be more permanent. Having a well-organized, defensible educational philosophy provides teachers with a way to simplify their teaching, making it easier to be successful in the complex classroom environment. Teachers must be theoreticians rather than technicians; in this way, theory not only simplifies their work, but also allows them to apply their teaching skills and knowledge to their practice (Giroux, 1994).

 ## QUESTION FOR REFLECTION

1. What can you do as a teacher to reduce classroom complexity to a manageable level?

NATIONAL TEACHING STANDARDS

Aware that experience is not always a good teacher, proficient teachers search out other opportunities to cultivate their own learning. They involve others in observing and offering critiques of their teaching. They also write about their work and solicit parent and student reactions. Thus, masterful teachers develop specialized ways to listen to their students, colleagues, and administrators and to reflect on their teaching as a way to improve their practice.

Student Evaluation

Student evaluations provide one of the more controversial sources of teaching data. This information is best used only when it can foster improvement. For example, students can tell what they like or dislike about a class but may not truthfully specify why. The course may be difficult, or the student may be getting a low grade. The teacher's charisma, or lack of it, may skew the evaluation so that it does not make helpful suggestions for improvement. In addition, students may not understand the full implications of their responses. For instance, course objectives may be judged nebulous when, in fact, these objectives have been clearly stated by the teacher. The student, however, may rate objectives unclear because she was not present when they were presented. A poor test performance may produce a similar reaction.

Charisma may bias student evaluations. In one study a charismatic actor presented nonsubstantial information to students who evaluated him. These results were then compared to those of regular teachers teaching important conceptual information. The charismatic actor was not only judged to be a better teacher, but students stated that the information he taught was much more substantial than that taught by the regular teachers (Coats & Swierenga, 1972). Other factors influencing student evaluation include the age and sex of the teacher, the subject being taught (Bledsoe, Brown, & Strickland, 1971), and the grade students expect (Weaver, 1960). In one study, the same group of students evaluated six teachers. The results indicated that any particular student may have a significant tendency to evaluate all the teachers the same, as there were high-rating students and low-rating students. Also, any one student may use the same rating category for all items on the evaluation instrument. Thus, students were not discriminating when evaluating the various aspects of teaching (Edwards & Fisher, 1985). Their evaluations were influenced by a single trait rather than reflecting the multifaceted reality of teaching (Shelvin, Banyard, Davies, & Griffiths, 2000). The validity of using student evaluations to modify instruction is questionable. Student evaluations have been shown to produce course changes that have reduced the quality of instruction (Tuckman & Oliver, 1968). However, rather than suggest that student assessment of teaching be avoided altogether, these data imply that student input should be scrutinized and used in discriminating ways. Teachers should not be pressured to modify how and what they teach simply on the basis of student evaluations. Finally, research indicates that student ratings don't reflect actual teacher effectiveness (Shelvin, Banyard, Davies, & Griffiths, 2000), as instructor performance is essentially underdetermined by student evaluation data (Sproule, 2002).

Decision Points

Create an evaluation instrument that would allow students to provide valid information about your teaching, but would avoid as many biasing factors as possible.

Administrative and Supervisory Analysis

The average teacher is only visited by a supervisor once a year, and typically receives only general and vague feedback. Principals who are good supervisors frequently visit classrooms and provide teachers help by giving timely, insightful feedback. Strong principals encourage teachers to frequently consult with them, and offer help without demeaning them. They also encourage teachers to assume responsibility for self-evaluation and improvement (Good & Brophy, 2000). Unfortunately, evaluation experts agree that supervision is generally poor (Peterson, 1995; Stronge, 1997). Many supervisors lack the necessary skills to assist teachers in a variety of subjects and/or the sensitivity required to give assistance without bruising egos. Many principals are so inundated with other responsibilities that they allow non-instructional matters to take precedence over instruction improvement.

Teachers often confuse supervision with evaluation. When a principal or other supervisor comes into a classroom, the teacher may wonder if he or she is there to foster improvement or to make decisions about tenure or accountability. Even if the supervisor indicates that the purpose is to improve teaching only, the teacher is unlikely to separate the two supervision functions. Thus, the teacher often plays a role to ensure positive evaluations rather than seeking help for needed improvement. Formal evaluation systems can seriously erode teachers' professional development programs (Good & Brophy, 2000).

An effective teacher evaluation program should not be a threat to teacher development. However, because different individuals support different conceptions of good teaching and also have various opinions regarding appropriate schooling outcomes, this threat is difficult to prevent. These differences may undermine cooperative efforts to improve teaching. Currently there is considerable support for constructivist learning in classrooms, which is a significant departure from traditional teaching. Some teachers have spent their careers operating on a different set of assumptions about how children learn. What should be expected of them? Should they be required to change their teaching approach just to adapt to constructivist principles, or should they be allowed to continue trying to improve their practice along traditional dimensions? Trying to make everyone fit new conceptions, and doing so by edict, will only alienate teachers, making them defensive and uncooperative. When teachers are forced to follow a particular theoretical teaching conception, assessment is often based only on the preferences and beliefs of a few individuals without considering processes that work for a particular teacher with a particular group of students (Wheeler & Scriven, 1997). Constructive changes are more likely when teachers practice self-assessment and reflect on their own practice. Teachers should be encouraged to examine theory and research and use this information as the basis of improvement. Teachers can acquire important insights by reading the literature and consulting with colleagues. However, when changes or modifications suggested through the evaluation process are mandated, teachers may be prevented from applying their own professional judgment and thus limited in their commitment to the process.

Accrediting and Certifying Agencies

Teachers are sometimes assumed to improve through meeting accreditation or certification requirements. While these processes can promote improvement, they focus primarily on programs rather than teaching and learning. Accrediting agencies ordinarily examine curricula, evaluation procedures, and instructional support. They do not make systematic observations of teaching nor determine the quality of teaching in the school. The same applies when state departments of education examine school operations. Their concerns center on teacher preparation, the curriculum, and support functions such as library holdings and the like.

One exception is the establishment of the National Board for Professional Teaching Standards (NBPTS). The NBPTS was estasblished by the Carnegie Task Force on Teaching as a Profession in 1987 as a voluntary, advanced certification procedure. Veteran teachers were encouraged to seek this certification in an effort to upgrade their skills. Teachers are certified by presenting portfolios and videotaped evidence of the quality of their teaching, which is then assessed by the organization (Cascio, 1995). The categories of teacher expertise include the following:

- Teachers are committed to students and learning.
- Teachers know the subjects they teach and how to teach them.
- Teachers are responsible for managing and monitoring student learning.

- Teachers think systematically about their practice and learn from experience.
- Teachers are members of learning communities (Helms, 2001).

NBPTS is claimed to validate good teaching, create excellent mentors and professional development opportunities, help retain good teachers, and have a positive impact on student learning. Forty-seven states and nearly 400 school districts have currently approved incentives encouraging teachers to seek this advanced certification (Castor, 2002). By the year 2001, over 16,000 U.S. teachers were certified (Mylord & Engelhard, 2001). There have been various improvement in NBPTS standards since its inception (Darling-Hammond, 1999). Currently the incorporation of standards that adequately address the need for helping teachers truly understand culture as it relates to school learning and deal with all aspects of children's lives in connection with school learning has been emphasized. At present these are seen by some as deficient (Ladson-Billings & Darling-Hammond, 2000). The National Board for Professional Teaching Standards are listed in strategic text locations to draw attention to associated content that addresses these important concerns.

Self-Directed Improvement of Teaching

Self-directed efforts to improve teaching generally meet with more success than administratively guided endeavors because of differences between teachers as well as the teachers' inclination toward independence and consequent commitment. Teachers work less enthusiastically when they cannot take control of their own improvement. Empowering teachers by providing necessary improvement resources, but also offering freedom for self-determination, enables greater commitment. Without commitment, improvement efforts are likely to be ineffective (Crandall, 1983). As indicated by the research of Linda McNeil in Chapter 3, teacher autonomy is central to the improvement of teaching.

McNeil (1988a) discovered that when bureaucratic controls shape the schools, the curricula are often trivialized, undermining valid educational considerations. Teachers tend to react to administrative mandates by reducing educational quality, thereby controlling their students just as administrators control them. When students judge their school experiences as trivial and not credible, they comply minimally and fail to achieve the excellence of which they are capable. When principals see boring, uninspired teaching resulting in apathetic students (brought about, ironically, by their controlling administration), they react by imposing more restraints, thereby trying to solve the problem by increasing its cause. McNeil also explains that when schools exercise bureaucratic controls, tension develops due to the contradictory goals of educating students and controlling them. When controlling and processing are overemphasized, teachers may feel their suggestions that students pursue viable educational purposes are not taken seriously. In addition, administrators commonly emphasize minimum standards rather than excellence. Teachers respond by expecting less of students and accepting minimal compliance from them. Rather than encouraging students to gather and interpret important conceptual information, teachers instead tend to require students to memorize lists of unrelated facts.

McNeil's (1988a) analysis revealed that when teachers are confronted with excessive administrative control and fail to find support for their own authority as school professionals, they create their own domain of authority. They tightly control course content by creating strict classroom routines along with carefully packaged lectures and objective tests. Students then react with calculated resistance. Under these conditions, teachers and students report feeling "herded." Interesting behavioral problems develop in schools with these coercive environments. McNeil's study found that attempts to control student misbehavior were so blatantly disproportionate to the offenses students committed that the management strategies seemed like acts of desperation; as a result, students rebelled in such petty ways as littering the halls and cafeteria. Finally, McNeil (1988b) discovered that teachers were less controlling when they were in a less-controlled environment themselves. When experiencing greater autonomy, teachers tended to stimulate more and better student learning and to continue learning themselves. The school environment, particularly the relative autonomy teachers and students have, must receive careful analysis in a teacher's efforts to improve instruction.

Useful procedures exist for helping teachers in their quest for improvement, including structuring a useful educational philosophy, making a detailed self-examination, examining the literature, conducting experiments, and engaging in collaborative efforts with peers.

QUESTION FOR REFLECTION

1. What level of administrative control would be appropriate in order to avoid the problems McNeil identifies? Make specific suggestions. What effect do you believe this can have on students and their learning?

Educational Philosophy

Because an educational philosophy provides a consistent set of beliefs that act as a road map for educational practice, it should be carefully assessed along with the related practices in order to help determine teaching effectiveness. Philosophical consistency is essential because it enables a predictable and defensible course of action, thereby avoiding confusion. A philosophy contains teachers' critical beliefs—principles they are willing to defend. Teachers equipped with a well-articulated philosophy feel committed to a way of teaching, possess a strong sense of ownership, and apply consistent guidance for their practice.

Analyzing one's educational philosophy involves looking at personal beliefs and values. It also entails a careful study of educational research and philosophy. Various conceptions of education have been put forth to guide educational practice, each based on different assumptions and goals for education. There is also a body of teaching research that needs to be consulted in the process of formulating a justifiable education philosophy. The broader the base of information, the more comprehensive and useful an educational philosophy is likely to be.

The primary considerations in an educational philosophy include learning, teaching, curriculum, and desired outcomes. Learning should reflect current research and be spelled out in specific terms. For example, constructivist theory indicates that children construct personal meaning that is personally relevant and resistant to change. Efforts to modify children's conceptual understanding must focus on helping students discover new inputs for themselves before changes can be effectively made.

In defining the nature of teaching used in a teaching philosophy, a teacher must thoughtfully articulate teaching practice with learning. For example, teaching that employs constructivist learning should provide student experiences that allow them to discover new conceptions rather that engage in processes intended to directly alter misconceptions. Inquiry based on students' personal questions would be an appropriate strategy for much of what is learned.

Involving students in curriculum determination is useful since constructivist theory states students should be self-directed. For consistency, the curriculum should exemplify the accepted theory of learning and teaching.

To some extent, learning theory dictates the outcomes sought for schooling. If students learn in a natural way, then the outcomes sought should incorporate these natural learning proclivities. Constructivism is currently the preferred interpretation of how children naturally learn. Consequently, educators seek for students to become active learners who initiate personally relevant learning activities and try to make sense of the world from personal experiences. Such a student is not considered a receptacle for the stock of knowledge acquired by researchers over the years, but rather as an individual who can analyze knowledge in light of personal research and experience and make sense of it. This student will actively pursue understanding in order to make personally relevant adjustments to an ongoing, perpetually changing world environment.

Decision Points

Identify the principles included in your educational philosophy and decide what your classroom will be like if you apply them to your teaching. How might you go about assessing how well your philosophy is being employed in day-to-day classroom activities?

Self-Examination

Self-examination can be one of the more fruitful strategies to improve teaching because of the multiple sources of information a teacher can apply to assessment and improvement. Individual teachers can take student input and assessments from supervisors and other teachers, as well as their own observations, and draw conclusions about their teaching. Even though video recordings do not capture all that happens in the classroom, teachers can use them to gather a wealth of information for careful analysis later.

Self-analysis provides several advantages over other types of assessment. First, self-analysis provides for more frequent evaluation episodes. Teachers can choose to evaluate their work any time they desire. Getting feedback from supervisors can be very sparse indeed. On one survey only 34 percent of secondary teachers reported being observed for more than five minutes even once during their first year of teaching (Good & Brophy, 1994). Such lack of feedback may dissatisfy teachers who wish to receive help dealing with classroom complexities (Wise, Darling-Hammond, McLaughlin, & Bernstein, 1985).

Second, teachers are more likely to change their behavior when they are personally involved in identifying problems and determining solutions. Self-analysis allows teachers a degree of personal control over what they deem necessary for self-improvement. They are able to assess their own needs and find ways to accommodate them (Rodriguez & Johnstone, 1986). Interestingly, the success of new school practices are mainly due to teacher efforts, primarily the commitment they acquire when they are significantly involved in the decision-making process (Crandall, 1983).

Third, self-evaluation is a non-intrusive way to gather a lot of information about teaching, providing a format for making judgments about teacher behavior in nonthreatening ways. In addition, it requires little or no disruption of ongoing classroom procedures and often leads to a more accurate, comprehensive source of data than that available through supervisory evaluations. It is also more likely to reveal how teachers behave under typical classroom conditions. Self-assessment provides teachers a way to engage in introspection and consistent self-analysis, leading to greater confidence in making needed changes and stronger commitment for following-through on the changes initiated (Armstrong & Savage, 1998).

In making self-assessments, teachers need to avoid being haphazard and unsystematic. Data needs to be systematically and carefully gathered; otherwise, assessments will not be valid (Brown, 1983). It is not easy to make accurate and complete teaching records, especially given the complexity of classrooms. Much goes on in fast-paced classrooms that cannot be reconstructed from memory; even audio recordings and video recordings may miss many things. However, researchers have found that teachers' instructional skills improve more from recording and assessing their own teaching than from feedback received from outside observers (Good & Brophy, 1994) (see Table 12.1).

Teachers may find it useful to focus on questions like the following when assessing teaching:

1. What aspects of teaching do I most enjoy, and what does this imply about my beliefs concerning what good teaching is?
2. How many different students were involved in discussions?
3. How do my instructional goals compare to those of my peers?
4. Do my lessons follow a good pedagogical sequence?
5. Are both low and high achievers involved in the lessons?
6. How effectively do I use praise?
7. How effectively do I use wait-time?
8. Do discussions involve a depth of understanding or just superficial knowledge?
9. How frequently do I use control statements?
10. How effectively do I use student questions as a focus of instruction?

TABLE 12.1 *Supervisory Versus Personal Teaching Assessment.*

	Advantages	**Disadvantages**
Self-analysis	Doesn't disrupt class; more likely to change teaching behavior; teachers more likely to be committed	May be haphazard and unsystematic; hard to capture the fast-paced happenings in the classroom
Supervisory assessment	Emphasizes school expectations	Too infrequent; may not be considered credible by teachers

11. Are appropriate discipline prevention procedures effectively employed?
12. Are my reactions to discipline problems consistent with my discipline program?
13. How effectively do I manage small-group activities?
14. How skillful am I in dealing with students' feelings and emotions?
15. Are transitions between different kinds of activities smooth and efficient?
16. Are teacher-directed lessons effectively summarized so students acquire a sense of closure?
17. Are there any students who are isolated and uninvolved who need help in becoming more effective learners?
18. Do students come to class prepared for the lessons?
19. Are learning activities based on student interests?
20. Do I effectively deal with students' cultural differences and keep my teaching free of gender problems?
21. Does my instruction cater to individual differences?
22. Does my teaching properly fit all aspects of my philosophy, particularly my view of learning?

Decision Points

Examine the list of questions teachers might use to assess their teaching. From this list, create a list of questions you believe are appropriate to assess your own teaching.

NATIONAL TEACHING STANDARDS

Teachers have a responsibility to be lifelong students of their craft, seek to expand their repertoire, deepen their knowledge and skill, and become wiser in rendering judgments.

Teachers are inventive in their teaching and, recognizing the need to admit new findings and continue learning, stand ready to incorporate ideas and methods developed by others that fit their aims and their students.

Able teachers are students of education scholarship and are cognizant of the settled and unsettled territory in their field. They stay abreast of current research and, when appropriate, incorporate new findings into their practice.

Examining the Literature

A wealth of literary information exists on teaching. Each teacher should be a student of teaching and make it a lifetime quest to familiarize himself or herself with all teaching aspects so improvements can routinely be made. Teachers may be unaware of new teaching developments. Sometimes research suggests that changes be made in methods that have a long history of use in education but may go unnoticed if teachers fail to regularly consult current research. For example:

Teachers can acquire a wealth of important information about teaching from the literature.

- Extrinsic reinforcers are ordinarily dispensed after notifying students they can receive rewards for specific behavior. This has been shown to undermine intrinsic reinforcement (Brophy, 1998).
- Verbal praise is ordinarily delivered in conjunction with a statement that mimics the response students make to a question. Thus, a teacher may ask a student, "What is seven times seven?" The student would answer "49." The teacher then responds, "49, very good." This routine greatly reduces the number of inquiry responses by students and the length and quality of their classroom contributions (Edwards & Surma, 1980; Rowe, 1974).
- Teachers ordinarily wait an average of 0.9 seconds after asking a question before making additional comments or asking other questions, leaving students with less time than needed to think up an answer to the question. Teachers need to wait much longer for student responses (Rowe, 1986).
- Teachers may be unaware of the specific differential responses to male and female students that creates gender bias, or they may not understand that their differential behavior toward high and low achievers (percentage of time that they "stayed with" or "gave up on" students) affects student performance (Good & Brophy, 1974).

These and other research findings provide useful data to teachers. When teachers are presented with information on how to improve teaching, they ordinarily succeed in doing so (Good & Brophy, 2000). However, teachers cannot depend on supervisors to provide all the necessary information. Face-to-face interactions between teachers and supervisors are generally insufficient; teachers need to search for additional insights themselves.

NATIONAL TEACHING STANDARDS

Good teachers attend teacher centers, special conferences, and workshops. They also may conduct and publish their own research.

Teachers draw upon diverse sources to enrich their teaching. They have a commitment to continued professional development. In their learning they become a role model for their own students through their critical and analytical thought. They also provide a model for commitment to creativity and a disposition to take risks in exploring new intellectual, emotional, and physical or artistic territories.

Action Research

Teachers can produce knowledge about teaching for themselves and others through **action research,** which allows teachers to pursue personally relevant insights that are applicable to their work. The result can be professionally beneficial and personally invigorating for teachers. They are able to pursue personal goals, increase reflection on their practice, become involved in collegial relationships with their peers, raise their own status and efficacy, reduce the gap between doing research and making applications, and create legitimacy for action research in the classroom (Lieberman, 1986). When teachers are personally involved in research efforts, they are able to more readily apply what they learn to improving their own classrooms. Action research often yields information with specific applicability, enabling teachers to move from the theoretical to the practical. Teachers are thus able to improve their performance by the direct study of their work (McKernan, 1987).

For action research to be successful, teachers must be given sufficient time and resources. Not only do they need time to collect and organize data and draw conclusions, but they also require opportunities to discuss their findings with colleagues. Action research provides a format for teachers to reflect on their teaching, interact with their peers, and eventually extend their knowledge of alternative teaching practices. When teaching is properly researched, the perceptions of teachers and others change regarding the scientific basis for teaching improvement (Good, 1996; Weinert & Helmke, 1995). Until teaching can be studied and improved though research efforts, there is less chance that teaching will be considered anything more than an art (Billups & Rauth, 1987). The results of action research can provide teachers with information on improving their own practice, prepare them to become active participants in conferences and workshops, and publish what they have learned from their research for consideration by larger audiences. This often can initiate collegial associations beyond the school that help teachers advance their professional competence.

Action research has the potential to improve education more than any other kind of educational innovation of the past century. Action research is a process for improvement directed by individual teachers. It is geared to teachers' particular situations and thus can appropriately represent their concerns in a research format. Teachers who routinely engage in action research can repeatedly ask themselves, "Is there a better way to teach?" Action research empowers teachers because they are not just consumers of others' research. They are able to determine for themselves what works best in their particular classroom and their view of learning and teaching (McLean, 1995). Action research places more emphasis on "how to" and has less of a "philosophical bent." It assumes that teachers are autonomous and interested in making teaching improvement. It also assumes that teachers have the necessary skills to conduct controlled studies of their work by properly framing important questions, designing ways to answer these questions, and making careful non-biased conclusions regarding their findings (Mills, 2000).

Action research accomplishes very little unless the potential improvements identified can be put into practice and tested further without fear of administrative veto. There needs to be a school atmosphere that not only encourages action research, but also the application of new classroom methods and strategies. There can't always be an "ironclad" guarantee regarding the effectiveness of particular teaching procedures before they are allowed to be employed.

NATIONAL TEACHING STANDARDS

Teachers need to know how to improve their teaching by involving their colleagues in terms of their skills, knowledge, and expertise to provide their students learning experiences that are as rewarding as possible. They must know the strengths and weaknesses of providing these options and their suitability or incompatibility for certain students and groups.

Teachers enlist the knowledge and expertise of their fellow faculty members in a variety of ways as they seek to provide their students with rewarding learning experiences.

Improving Teaching Through Peer Collaboration

Useful teaching insights can be obtained from colleagues, either through study groups or between a teacher and one close associate. Study groups can broaden the inputs but may foment distractions if there are too many agendas to create a proper focus. To avoid multiple agendas, study groups should ordinarily be formed on the basis of interest. The group needs a narrow enough topic that consistent progress can be achieved toward a desired objective.

Participation in study groups should probably be voluntary if an effective team atmosphere is to materialize. Sometimes groups are formed in an effort to "fix" teachers' deficiencies identified by administrators or persons representing outside teacher assessment and development programs. Outside assessment groups generally focus teacher development without regard to the specific problems and needs of particular teachers. Too often teachers view these inservice activities as unrelated to their teaching needs (Smylie, 1995; Spencer, 1984). Some study groups are created to encourage teachers to teach in a particular way. However, it is more helpful if teachers are encouraged to develop their own teaching style (Gordon L., 1992).

Good and Brophy (2000) suggest three rules for the successful operation of inservice groups. First, group operations should provide teachers with information that augments their self-development and provides an opportunity to see unique perspectives from other members. Individuals should be encouraged to make their own decisions and establish their own goals. The group members should provide insights and give group perceptions, even though the group's purpose is not to achieve consensus about the best teaching model.

Second, group members should not overwhelm one another with information. An agenda should be set restricting interaction to a few key areas. Group members may be asked to limit their input on any one presentation to simply bringing up two or three strengths and two or three weaknesses. Suggestions might be made regarding how to make improvements.

A third rule is to be honest. Teachers must be willing to say what they feel about another teacher's teaching. They must be frank but kind. The purpose of getting together is not to bolster or protect egos, but to improve teaching. Teachers need honest, objective feedback to accomplish this. Troubling teacher behavior needs to be examined openly, and changes should be suggested as needed. Strengths also need to be identified and encouraged, and suggestions about possible new strategies should be brought up and considered. Providing teachers with information along with suggestions helps improve instruction more than giving information alone or giving information along with a supervisor's directives (Pajak & Glickman, 1989).

A particularly helpful teaching improvement format is for two teachers to collaborate. With only two teachers working together, there are fewer divergent inputs to consider, and yet teachers are able to broaden their insights beyond their own perceptions. Sometimes another person can see faults and difficulties that are only vaguely evident to the person doing the teaching.

Selecting a partner who has philosophical views similar to one's own is important. Though such similarity may seem to limit the kinds of available information, working with a person who has shared perspectives has a number of advantages that ordinarily outweigh those of divergence. Teachers can gain the multiple perspectives from working in groups on other occasions.

When two persons work together, they should continually discuss philosophical positions regarding education, reaffirm the principles that make up each person's philosophy, and reinforce appropriate teaching applications. Thus, both individuals can acknowledge their common philosophical orientation as they engage in dialogue and research and consider avenues for making improvements.

One of the obvious advantages of a two-person team is that feedback can be consistent with what each individual is trying to accomplish in the classroom. It is not very useful to give recommendations that apply to a different set of purposes and hopes. Teacher supervision, evaluation recommendations, and even administrative directives may be in opposition to what the teacher is trying to accomplish. For example, a supervisor may recommend that a science teacher stop providing hands-on experiences for students because having students move around the room interferes with the orderly classroom environment preferred by the supervisor. However, student movement is an essential ingredient to the teacher's inquiry-based instructional program.

In the two-member team approach, participants need to have lengthy discussions involving their research efforts and current beliefs about teaching, followed-up with an indi-

TABLE 12.2 *Organizational Strategies for Teacher Improvement.*

Group Configuration	Advantage	Disadvantage
Two-member teams	Analysis and change more consistent with a single teaching philosophy; limits the number of inputs to a manageable level; can identify faults the teacher may not see	Time-consuming
Small study groups	Provides a broad base of input	Groups may be formed to "fix" a particular teacher's deficiencies
School-wide improvement	Is more likely to lead to school-wide improvements	Managing the change process may be unwieldy
Individual teachers	Analyses can be more frequently made	Teacher might not see personal faults without others' input

vidual lesson. The nature and purpose of each individual's lesson is discussed before it is presented. Ideally, team members are able to observe one another teach, although video recordings can also be analyzed. This should be followed by a candid discussion regarding observations. Each team member should take the assessments, reconstruct the lesson, and if possible reteach it. Afterward there can be additional discussion concerning new assessments. At this point, these two teachers may wish to study the topic further by examining research in the area or conducting some action research themselves. This process may go on until both are satisfied with the obtained results. A different topic can then be addressed (see Table 12.2).

 QUESTION FOR REFLECTION

1. What do you believe your weakness is as a teacher? What kind of improvement program might you establish in a two-person group?

Focus of Teacher Analysis

What should be the focus of teaching analysis? The teaching process cannot be exclusively limited to the teacher's classroom actions. Student achievements must also be considered in terms of both accomplishments and outcomes as they relate to intentions. Ongoing discussion is needed about what is happening in the school versus what *should* be happening, lest the former takes precedence. This instructional intention issue is most likely to become distorted during student achievement. It is easy to talk about improving the efficiency and effectiveness of learning, but unless a discussion of the nature and purpose of what should be learned follows, little good is served. For example, in some schools student achievement assessment is limited almost exclusively to the recall of information when higher-level cognitive capabilities and the development of appropriate attitudes and values are considered more essential.

Teaching cannot be improved without simultaneously studying the curriculum and appropriately modifying it. Teaching is not just a set of skills that apply methods of instruction; it also involves knowledge regarding curriculum construction. The formulation of curricula involves a complex of considerations including the nature of knowledge, the nature of learning and development, values and value analysis, and interpersonal interaction and influence, as well as educational philosophy and the community's nature. An interaction exists among these elements both in the construction of the curriculum and in actual teaching. Good teaching involves both curriculum and instruction, and consequently its improvement must deal with both of these interrelated considerations.

Curriculum assessment requires that all the elements be taken into account in formulating curricula. Thus, a careful study is needed of how children learn and develop. This is related to the instruction goals and the means for achieving them, including the nature of student-teacher interactions and the influence teachers have on students in the instructional process. Student needs and interests are also taken into account, assessing the extent to which these needs are satisfied during instruction. Teaching assessment includes an analysis of how well teachers employ learning experiences for students that satisfy their needs and interests and achieve goals that are defensible ends of instruction.

How well does the school fit within its community, and to what extent are school experiences authentic representations of community life? Do children take an active part in the community in conjunction with school experiences, and are children prepared for effective service as community members? These questions should be addressed during teacher assessment. School experiences must be genuine in terms of community life. Students should be prepared for their world. Therefore, the study of teaching must include assessments of how well graduates are integrated into the community, as well as how they contribute to community life. The school should not exist as a social system apart from the community. When there is an integration of school and community, students are able to visualize the relationship of their school experiences to real life. They can see the meaning in what they do in school and find justifiable reasons for being there. Students frequently cannot successfully make connections between their school experiences and their lives outside school, as well as their post-education lives. Teaching assessment should focus on this problem and help provide the means for identifying dysfunctions between desires and experiences. Excellent teaching provides a close articulation between the real world and classroom experiences.

Improving Teaching by Improving the Workplace

Opportunities for improving teaching are plentiful, but may go unrecognized due to time constraints and inadequate budgets, as well as traditional roles commonly given to teachers. Leadership, for example, is not usually a role defined for teachers. School administrators often exclusively occupy leadership roles even though sharing leadership responsibilities with teachers would be wiser. However, teacher leadership can be encouraged by providing them opportunities to deal with many of the school problems ordinarily reserved for administrators. For example, teachers could provide leadership in such areas as parent-teacher relationships, curriculum development, community-school relationships, custodial affairs, the school lunch program, busing operations, school office procedures, and the like. Although these opportunities may have nothing to do with teaching, each one is a strategic aspect of the school that often requires teachers' special knowledge. Nothing in the school is exclusively administrative. Even the acquisition of supplies and equipment and the upkeep of the school grounds have implications for teaching. Certainly the school activity program has important teaching opportunities, although it may seem to exist apart from school purposes. The athletic program sometimes doesn't articulate well with the academic program. Another problem area is the extent to which interschool athletics that involve only a few students supersede the intermural program, which involves many more students. Increased teacher leadership may create better perspectives on how these different programs should be operated in conjunction with the school's central mission.

Many teachers may benefit from attending conventions sponsored by various professional societies. At these gatherings, teachers can meet other professionals who share common concerns and have similar interests, find new teaching approaches or access to helpful materials, and attend sessions on a variety of interesting topics. They can also discover teaching support resources, as publishing companies usually send representatives to provide the latest updates in books and materials. Teachers are thus able to keep abreast of new developments and find ways to improve instruction.

Conventions help prepare teachers for leadership and decision-making responsibilities. When teachers' status is raised through increased competence and critical decision-making roles, they can exhibit enhanced commitment and better teaching. Strategically involved teachers have more responsible roles, higher morale, deepened intellectual background, and increased confidence in their usefulness (Maeroff, 1988). Teachers rarely see themselves as key players in school change; more often, they are dedicated to simply carrying out the wishes of others. However, essential change in schools and teaching requires teachers to willingly carry out school reforms. Unless teachers provide leadership and initiate necessary changes, very few useful modifications will be made in teaching or in other school operations (Smylie, 1992). Substantial literature has appeared in recent years concerning teachers as school leaders. Teachers should examine this literature for suggestions on how to more effectively prepare themselves for leadership opportunities (Smylie, 1997).

Teachers can profoundly affect schools and teaching by collaborating with colleagues. Teachers need to be colleagues with educators at various levels, including administrative personnel and university faculties. Collaboration areas include research with professors regarding classroom operations (Lieberman, 1986) and collegial interactions with professional educators regarding teacher education (Rosenholtz, 1989). In this role, teachers can participate in discussions regarding teaching issues, including items related to the subject matter being taught, motivation, ability grouping, student autonomy, learning communities, leadership, multicultural issues, and so on.

Discussion can be conducted in three stages. The first stage emphasizes acquiring external knowledge, or what can be found in the literature, regarding a particular problem. At this stage, participants should explore available knowledge and understand rather than dispute it. Teachers should seek to understand disagreements among experts and carefully document their views.

In the second stage, discussion should center on personal knowledge or participant experience. Those involved can compare their views to identify differences. This phase involves active listening, sharing, and reflection, plus an effort to integrate personal knowledge and information gleaned from the literature.

In the third stage, participants explore future actions. From the literature and from personal experiences, teachers should be able to visualize directions for improvement. Implications for both individual teachers and the entire school can be explored as directions for change are considered and action plans created.

In discussions regarding change, teachers will need to explore various teaching models in light of personal values. One topic, personal commitment to teaching, involves participants exploring the reasons he or she decided to become a teacher. In this case, participants may want to examine their own feelings in depth before making literature reviews (Brookhart & Freeman, 1992) or before considering examples of how other teachers' decisions have evolved throughout their careers (Bullough, 1992).

Teacher Improvement in Learning Communities

Teacher improvement assessment in learning communities includes some of the same elements as teacher evaluation in traditional classrooms. However, these assessments must contain components dealing with the unique concerns of learning communities. Different role expectations exist for both teachers and their students, along with different conceptions of learning. Specific aspects of teacher-student interactions are much different from those of traditional classrooms. In addition, the nature of a learning community must be critically examined as it authentically represents the community at large. The student empowerment process and the degree to which students are truly autonomous in the learning community must also be examined, particularly the degree that student roles help to encourage personal responsibility.

Role Expectations

Teachers in learning communities devote their time to strengthening community relationships and promoting leadership responsibility. They consistently focus on the task of ensuring that all participants have their personal as well as academic needs met as part of the group agenda. They have to successfully communicate to group members that the group takes precedence, even though the major group responsibility is to ensure individual fulfillment. They must also help all group members secure a sense of empowerment and engage in intrinsically interesting and meaningful learning activities. Skillful teachers provide a means for group members to work through difficulties and move toward meaningful learning and cooperative growth. In learning communities, teachers also need to be especially adept at acquiring resources and arranging for various kinds of instructional inputs. Although teachers in learning communities are unlikely to consider presenting information as their primary role, they still need to be well-qualified in making necessary student presentations.

Student roles are also substantially different in learning communities. As the learning format is essentially inquiry, students need to become skilled in relating to other class members, completing group projects, and working independently as needed. They are required to periodically assume leadership roles, as well as function as supportive, involved learning group members.

Those who assess learning communities must understand the purposes and operations of community learning and all its implications for teachers and learners. Teachers as participants must have the ability to evaluate themselves as well as their students. Teachers are required to make assessments of long-term, interactive associations as well as astute judgments regarding complex interpersonal interactions and task performances occurring over extended periods, which necessitates ongoing evaluation. Other than teacher self-assessment, two-person teams may be the most helpful teaching improvement configuration. In either case, constructing a checklist of items on which to make assessments is essential. The items on the checklist reflect the instructional intentions of the teacher being evaluated, along with some aspect of role expectations for both students and teachers. The following areas might be examined: community relationships, leadership promotion, student need satisfaction, group process skills, student empowerment, articulation of study topics with student interests, cooperative skills, resource management, and teacher presentation skills.

Teacher and Student Interactions

In traditional teaching, the relationship between teachers and students may be adversarial due to coercive classroom environments that may fail to satisfy student needs. Student grading practices may lead many to become disillusioned with teachers as well as education in general. In learning communities, student-teacher and student-student relationships must be positive and productive. Assessments consequently must ascertain to what degree relationships provide the necessary atmosphere for caring associations and productive learning to take place. These evaluations can involve teacher observations as well as surveys of student opinion. Insights to improve relationships can then be applied so that improvements can be made.

Many students spend much of their schooling in competitive environments where some students acquire a higher academic and social status than others. Designations like "smart" or "dull," given by teachers as early as kindergarten, tend to continue with students as they move through the school system. This categorizing process is often based on the children's appearances. Children become very much aware of the assigned categories and tend to interact with one another according to this school caste system (Covington & Beery, 1976). In learning communities, this categorization must be eliminated before successful student relationships can be established. Once negative personal identities are established, they are not easily changed. Old patterns may be reinforced in homes and communities. Those placed in higher categories likely prefer to retain their privileged positions, and those in lower categories may feel insecure if given greater status and responsibility. Yet these changes in learning communities must be made. Presently there are no carefully researched strategies for helping students make this transition aside from assigning them a variety of learning community roles and helping them successfully occupy these roles. Teachers may occasionally provide instruction regarding student attitudes and attribution. Students who suffer self-worth problems probably need extensive experiences in leadership roles, along with support in making accurate attributions for failure and success.

Student-teacher relationships also need to be improved in learning communities. Students must be able to act in good faith with their teachers, with assurance that their well-being will not be jeopardized. Some students will have had many positive experiences with their teachers, while others may have had alienating encounters. Students differentially receive praise and correction from teachers, and in the process may develop negative patterns of behavior and attitudes. Teachers cannot expect immediate changes from students with a history of negative teacher interactions. However, successful learning communities require that negative attitudes be changed so teachers and students can work together in an atmosphere of trust and love. Teachers should be particularly astute in assessing students' attitudes and at creating opportunities for positive student-teacher interactions. Improvements can be made if teachers consistently show affection and caring and if they empower students to be self-governing learners. Even then, considerable time may be required before students are willing to relinquish suspicions and fears.

Authenticity of Community Life

Learning communities must be authentic places where students can acquire a sense of trust, put forth effort toward community integration, and remain committed to personal and group excellence. Learning communities need to be authentically democratic. Teachers must not reserve veto power to themselves and routinely override student decisions and aspirations. Teachers will only need to draw the attention of community members to possible consequences of questionable activities for students to reexamine their intentions and make changes. Teachers may help supply data that students have not considered, or raise relevant questions that have not been addressed. For example, students may have decided on activities that keep them at school long after school hours. Such issues as parents' wishes, custodial clean-up, school insurance requirements, adequate teacher supervision, and transportation may not have been considered in students' quest for a particularly zestful learning activity. Teachers simply need to raise such issues and allow students to deal with them. Once the potential conflict is dealt with, students can decide whether to change or carry out the decision.

Sometimes teachers may need to have students reassess the kind of learning events they propose. They may select activities unlikely to require excellence or pick study topics without relevance to their aspirations. Some students might propose a curriculum inconsistent with the course of study or excessively different from state guidelines. When these issues are raised, students should be given time to deliberate their proposals in light of the additional information. The purpose of having students reassess their plans is not to force them to change, but rather to have them examine additional information so their decisions can reflect a more complex set of conditions. Students could, for example, continue to pursue learning that is inconsistent with state guidelines agreeing to limit time on such projects, as they feel justified by their interests but recognize the prominence of state guidelines. They may decide to follow state mandates, but give less time to these endeavors and more to topics of group interest. Students can expect little harm and anticipate considerable worth from engaging in this kind of decision making. Teachers need to be experts in managing these group affairs; accurate assessments are needed to increase their effectiveness.

Student and Teacher Empowerment

Learning communities cannot function properly if curriculum requirements are too rigid. Ordinarily state curricula allow latitude to accommodate substantial decision making by students and their teachers. State-mandated curricula usually consist of a set of objectives for each subject, objectives that evolved out of standards proposed by learned societies with inputs from state officials and classroom teachers. These educational goals are generally reasonable and acceptable both to teachers and to students as the subject is examined for learning possibilities. A viable classroom curriculum can be constructed that is sufficiently harmonious with both state expectations and student aspirations.

Both teacher and student empowerment is essential to successful learning communities. If no decisions are invited, there can be no genuine democratic learning experience. When democratic processes are subverted, there can be little commitment and less hope for excellence. The potential for learning when teachers and students are empowered far outweighs any benefit of prescribed curricula.

Teacher empowerment comes not only from allowing students to make more decisions in their individual classrooms, but also from providing them opportunities to make decisions on important matters throughout the school. Teachers can often provide insights due to their knowledge and experience. In addition, their participation in making decisions raises the level of their commitment. Many school decisions require teachers' perspectives for validity. Administrative expedience should not prevail when teaching and learning considerations predominate. In recent years, teachers have been given a more extensive role in school decisions. This trend toward teacher empowerment needs to be supported at all levels. Teaching improvement depends on teachers being empowered to make decisions regarding all aspects of school. There is no valid way to judge the success of schooling unless the teachers who are responsible are given authority to make decisions regarding instructional matters. Learning communities are particularly supported by teacher decision making and adversely affected by interference with this process.

Successful teachers in learning communities know how to empower their students. Perhaps the most critical skill these teachers possess is the ability to teach students about making helpful learning opportunity decisions and to responsibly pursue these activities. Teacher improvement, consequently, should focus on this important skill. How well can teachers decondition students who have experienced excessive teacher control so they accept roles that call upon them to make valid decisions about curricula and follow-through responsibly? How successfully do teachers help students satisfy all their needs? How conscientiously do teachers try to determine students' interests and create strategies for them to pursue their interests? How successful are teachers in helping students acquire skills for productive interaction with their peers? These are some of the questions that need to be addressed in order to increase teacher competence in learning communities.

Personal Autonomy and Community Responsibility

Successful learning communities provide all participants with sufficient autonomy to satisfy their personal interests and needs. Interests are not static; they cannot be initially determined and then perpetually pursued without modification. Teachers can anticipate that student interests will change, and students' ways of satisfying their needs will adjust from time to time. However, teachers cannot expect to always know what their students' interests are and to track these interests when modified. Students are in a better position to identify interests and track changes; however, teachers must provide the necessary conditions. Doing so requires giving students sufficient autonomy so they can direct their own learning in connection with group projects and modify the nature of their participation as desired.

Responsibility should always accompany efforts to enhance student autonomy. Students are obligated to follow-through on commitments and make sure that any desired modifications have group approval before they are implemented. Democratic purposes cannot be achieved unless students act upon their privilege of moral agency and learn how to explicitly articulate their independence with the community's social values and expectations. These privileges are critical in attaining a real sense of belonging and acquiring a desire to assume a responsible community role (Edwards, 2000).

Responsibility also includes student actions in support of the community in an effort to enhance community life and interpersonal relationships. It consists of actions taken by one caring person for another. Thus, student actions in the learning community are characterized by courtesy, service, support, collegiality, cooperation, and fairness. In a learning community, members look after the interests of one another in order that the whole community can be strengthened and the desires of each individual fulfilled. Thus, individuals in effective learning communities seek not only to preserve their own integrity, but to promote the welfare of others. Social justice requires that all members' interests are protected and supported, for in safeguarding the individual, the community fortifies itself (Sirotnik, 1990).

Fostering student autonomy and responsibility are central to a teacher's role in a learning community. These skills are not prescriptive. A well-defined sequence of teacher behaviors does not exist that will dependably promote autonomy. Teachers must apply principles that support student autonomy and responsibility, and they must invent productive ways to interact with individual students. Ordinarily questions rather than admonitions are used to help students focus on the limits of personal autonomy in relation to community responsibility. A teacher may, for example, ask a student how the group will likely be affected if she abandons her committed area of study. If a student is having difficulty getting along with another community member, the teacher may ask, "What can you do to improve your relationship with Angela?" Teachers must apply the principle of agency to these interactions. They must also communicate genuine feelings of acceptance and love. However, appropriately applying the agency principle is not particularly easy. Teachers usually use control to interact with students. If teachers sincerely wish to promote learning communities, they need to avoid their inclination to control and instead focus on kindling a desire in students to be autonomously responsible.

Moral communities depend extensively on the rational inquiry process for community survival. An inquiry orientation helps them deal with the unexpected and devise more effective strategies as needed. This can only be accomplished in an atmosphere of trust and interpersonal commitment. All members of the community must feel that associates have their best interest at heart and that everyone is interested in having all community members do well. To increase effectiveness, teachers need to determine the extent of students' high level of commitment and routinely engage in inquiry-based learning. A critical aspect of any effort learning community assessment is to find ways to improve. The various aspect of learning communities must be carefully analyzed by teachers in their quest for improvement. These considerations must be systematically researched in terms of desired effects and adjustments made accordingly.

 ## QUESTION FOR REFLECTION

1. What are the essential differences between a teacher's role in a traditional classroom and in a learning community? How can you be certain that conflicts between these different role expectations do not get confused in personal analysis of your teaching and in assessments made by others?

CENTRAL IDEAS

1. More time and money, as well as more emphasis on improvement, are required if teachers are to adequately develop their teaching skills.
2. Teachers need to take the initiative for self-improvement and admit that there are appropriate changes that can be made in their teaching.
3. Teaching is extremely complex, requiring the development of an educational philosophy that can be expertly applied in order to simplify teaching to a manageable level.
4. Teachers cannot expect student evaluations to provide valid data for teaching improvement.
5. Evaluation by supervisors can be a threat to teachers and thus fail to foster improvement in teaching.
6. Coercive administrative practices stimulate a coercive classroom environment in which teachers fiercely control students and students excessively rebel.
7. The most critical aspect of an educational philosophy is to properly conceptualize learning and teaching so that teaching practices properly articulate with the way children learn.
8. Teaching practice can be greatly improved through teachers' self-analysis. This involves teachers considering relevant literature and conducting action research.
9. Improvements in teaching can be made by consistent collaboration with colleagues, most effectively through two-person teams.

10. The improvement of teaching depends on making the workplace more conducive to teachers' professional development. Leadership opportunities, as well as increased association with other teachers on a broader scale, can help in this development.

11. Teacher development in learning communities is substantially different than in traditional classrooms. The teacher's role involves promoting positive group interactions, fostering relationships, and helping students occupy leadership positions in the instructional process. These skills are far more complex than traditional teaching and more difficult to validly assess.

12. Teachers and students are better able to function in learning communities when empowered with sufficient autonomy to develop a true sense of responsibility and commitment.

REFERENCES

Armstrong, D. G., & Savage, T. V. (1998). *Teaching in the secondary school: An introduction* (4th ed.). Upper Saddle River, NJ: Prentice Hall.

Billups, L., & Rauth, M. (1987). Teachers and research. In V. Richardson-Koehler (Ed.), *Educators' handbook: A research perspective* (pp. 167–187). White Plains, NY: Longman.

Bledsoe, J. C., Brown, I. D., & Strickland, A. D. (1971). Factors related to pupil observation reports of teachers and attitudes toward their teacher. *The Journal of Educational Research, 65* (3), 119–126.

Brookhart, S., & Freeman, D. (1992). Characteristics of entering teacher candidates. *Review of Educational Research, 62,* 37–60.

Brophy, J. (1998). *Motivating students to learn.* Boston: McGraw-Hill.

Brown, R. (1983). Helpful and human teacher evaluations. In W. Duckett (Ed.), *Teacher evaluation: Gathering and using data* (pp. 9–26). Bloomington, IN: Phi Delta Kappa.

Bullough, R., Jr. (1992). Beginning teacher curriculum decision making, personal teaching metaphors, and teacher education. *Teaching and Teacher Education, 8,* 239–252.

Cascio, C. (1995). National Board for Professional Teaching Standards: Changing teaching through teachers. *Clearing House, 68* (4), 212–213.

Castor, B. (2002). A measure of quality. *American School Board Journal, 189* (2), 52–53.

Coats, W. D., & Swierenga, L. (1972). Student perceptions of teachers: A four analysis study. *The Journal of Educational Research, 65* (8), 357–360.

Covington, M. V., & Beery, R. G. (1976). *Self-worth and school learning.* New York: Holt, Rinehart & Winston.

Crandall, D. P. (1983). The teacher's role in school improvement. *Educational Leadership, 41,* (3), 6–9.

Darling-Hammond, L. (1999). *Reshaping teaching policy, preparation, and practice: Influences of the National Board for Professional Teaching Standards.* American Association of Colleges for Teacher Education, Washington, DC; National Partnership for Excellence and Accountability in Teaching, Washington, DC.

Darling-Hammond, L., Bullmaster, M., & Cobb, V. (1995). Rethinking teacher leadership through professional development schools. *Elementary School Journal, 96,* 87–106.

Edwards, C. H. (2000). Moral classroom communities and the development of resiliency. *Contemporary Education, 71* (4), 38–41.

Edwards, C. H., & Fisher, R. L. (1985). The use by student evaluators of general constructs vs. specific teaching skills in the evaluation of instructors. *Illinois School Research and Development, 21* (3), 25–30.

Edwards, C. H., & Surma, M. (1980). The relationship between type of teacher reinforcement and student inquiry behavior in science. *Journal of Research in Science Teaching, 17* (4), 337–341.

Giroux, H. A. (1994). Teachers public life and curriculum reform. *Peabody Journal of Education, 69,* (3), 35–47.

Good, T. (1996). Teaching effects and teacher evaluation. In J. Sikula, T. Buttery, & E. Guyton (Eds.), *Handbook of research on teacher education* (2nd ed.). New York: Macmillan.

Good, T., & Brophy, J. (1974). Changing teacher and student behavior: An empirical investigation. *Journal of Educational Psychology, 66,* 390–405.

Good, T. L., & Brophy, J. E. (1994). *Looking in classrooms* (6th ed.). New York: Longman.

Good, T. L., & Brophy, J. E. (2000). *Looking in classrooms* (7th ed.). New York: Longman.

Goodson, I. (1997). The life and work of teachers. In B. Biddle, T. Good, & I. Goodson (Eds.), *International handbook of teachers and teaching* (Vol. 1, pp. 135–152). Dordrecht, The Netherlands: Kluwer.

Gordon, L. (1992). Educational reform in New Zealand: Contesting the role of teacher. *International Studies in Sociology of Education, 2* (1), 23–42.

Helms, R. G. (2001). The right form of certification. *Kappa Delta Pi Record, 38* (1), 20–23.

Johnson, E. C. (1998). The importance of theory. *Teacher Education Quarterly, 25* (4), 37–38.

Ladson–Billings, G., & Darling-Hammond, L. (2000). The validity of National Board for Professional Teaching Standards (NBPTS), Interstate New Teaching Assessment and Support Consortium (INTASC) assessments for effective urban teachings: Findings and implications for assessment. National Partnership for Excellence and Accountability in Teaching. Washington, DC.

Lieberman, A. (1986). Collaborative research: Working with, not working on. . . . *Educational Leadership, 43,* 28–33.

Maeroff, G. (1988). *The empowerment of teachers.* New York: Teachers College Press.

McKernan, J. (1987). Action research and curriculum development. *Peabody Journal of Education, 64,* 6–19.

McLean, J. E. (1995). *Improving education through action research: A guide for administrators and teachers.* Thousand Oaks, CA: Corwin Press.

McNeil, L. M. (1988a). Contradictions of control, part 1: Administrators and teachers. *Phi Delta Kappan, 45,* 333–339.

McNeil, L. M. (1988b). Contradictions of control, part 2: Contradictions of reform. *Phi Delta Kappan, 45,* 478–485.

Mills, G. E. (2000). *Action research: A guide for the teacher researcher.* Upper Saddle River, NJ: Prentice Hall.

Mylord, C. M., & Engelhard, G., Jr. (2001). Examining the psychometric quality of the National Board for Professional Teaching Standards: Early childhood/generalist assessment system. *Journal of Personnel Evaluation in Education, 15* (4), 253–285.

Pajak, E., & Glickman, C. (1989). Informational and controlling language in simulated supervising conferences. *American Educational Research Journal, 26,* 93–106.

Peterson, K. (1995). *Teacher evaluation: A comprehensive guide to new directions and practices.* Thousand Oaks, CA: Corwin Press.

Rodriguez, S., & Johnstone, K. (1986). Staff development through a collegial support group. In K. Zumwant (Ed.), *Improving teaching; 1986 ASCD yearbook* (pp. 87–99). Alexandria, VA: Association for Supervision and Curriculum Development.

Rosenholtz, S. (1989). *Teachers' workplace: The social organization of schools.* New York: Longman.

Rowe, M. B. (1974). Relation of wait-time and rewards to the development of language, logic and fate control: Part II-rewards. *Journal of Research in Science Teaching, 12,* 291–308.

Rowe, M. B. (1986). Wait-time: Slowing down may be a way of speeding up. *Journal of Teacher Education, 37* (1), 43–50.

Shelvin, M., Banyard, P., Davies, M., & Griffiths, M. (2000). The validity of student evaluation of teaching in higher education: Love me, love my lectures? *Assessment and Evaluation in Higher Education, 25* (4), 397–405.

Sirotnik, K. A. (1990). Society, schooling, teaching, and preparing to teach. In J. I. Goodlad, R. Soder, & A. Sirotnik (Eds.), *The moral dimensions of teaching* (pp. 296–327). San Francisco: Jossey-Bass.

Smylie, M. (1992). Teachers' reports of their interactions with teacher leaders concerning classroom instruction. *Elementary School Journal, 93,* 85–98.

Smylie, M. (1995). New perspectives on teacher leadership. *Elementary School Journal, 96,* 3–8.

Smylie, M. (1997). Research on teacher leadership: Assessing the state of the art. In B. Biddle & T. Goodson (Eds.), *International handbook of teachers and teaching* (Vol. 1, pp. 521–592). Dordrecht, The Netherlands: Kluwer.

Spencer, D. (1984). The home and school lives of women teachers: Implications for staff development. *Elementary School Journal, 84,* 299–314.

Sproule, R. (2002). The underdetermination of instructor performance by data from the student evaluations of teaching. *Economics of Education Review, 21* (3), 287–294.

Stronge, J. (1997). Improving schools through teacher evaluation. In J. Stronge (Ed.), *Evaluating teaching: A guide to current thinking and best practice* (pp. 1–17). Thousand Oaks, CA: Corwin Press.

Tuckman, B. W., & Oliver, W. F. (1968). Effectiveness of feedback to teachers as a function of source. *Journal of Educational Psychology, 59,* 297–301.

Weaver, C. H. (1960). Instructor rating by college students. *Journal of Educational Psychology, 51* (1), 21–25.

Weinert, F., & Helmke, A. (1995). Learning from wise Mother Nature or Big Brother Instructor: The wrong choice as seen from an educational perspective. *Educational Psychologist, 30,* 135–142.

Wheeler, P., & Scriven, M. (1997). Building a foundation: Teacher roles and responsibilities. In J. Stronge (Ed.), *Evaluating teaching: A guide to current thinking and best practice* (pp. 27–54). Thousand Oaks, CA: Corwin Press.

Wise, A. E., Darling-Hammond, L., McLaughlin, M. W., & Bernstein, H. T. (1985). Teacher evaluation: A study of effective practices. *Elementary School Journal, 86* (1), 61–121.

Working with Parents and the Community

CHAPTER OBJECTIVES

This chapter is designed to help you

1. Explain what teachers must understand about parents in order to have successful communications with them.

2. Explain how the school can support parents in preparing their children for successful school experiences.

3. Engage in various forms of parental communication as a means to develop good relationships and get them actively involved in helping their son or daughter succeed in school.

4. Engage in well-organized parent-teacher conferences by building rapport, obtaining information from parents, providing parents with critical information about their child, and arranging for useful follow-up strategies.

Better classroom adjustment and academic achievement can be promoted through regular parent involvement in the schools.

5. Formulate strategies to get parents and older adults involved in meaningful activities to help children learn in school.

6. Explain ways parents can participate in school governance and decision making.

7. Explain the different ways parents can participate in traditional schooling and in learning communities.

8. Discuss the purpose of having parents and their children involved in solving community problems.

9. Explain the usefulness of service-learning in learning communities.

INTRODUCTION

Students benefit from close communications between parents and the school. When parents are involved with their children's schooling, better attendance can be expected, along with more positive student attitudes and behavior, greater willingness to complete homework assignments, and higher academic achievement (Becher, 1984; Epstein, 1984; Haynes, Comer, & Hamilton-Lee, 1989; Henderson & Berla, 1995).

When teachers make positive contacts with parents and open friendly two-way communications with them, teachers and parents begin to see one another as allies instead of adversaries. When contact is made early in the school year, teachers can establish a working relationship with parents that they can continuously build on. This close coordination helps deal with problems that may surface in a timely way, and avoid many difficulties regarding expectations, student behaviors, and achievements.

Early contact also provides teachers with critical data about their students' home conditions. This kind of information can help teachers understand why students respond as they do in the classroom. Sometimes teachers can discover such factors as marital problems and divorce, a limited ability to communicate in English, excessive pressure to excel academically, or various kinds of abuse in time to help students get along in school better than they might otherwise.

In order to help their children, parents need to know school expectations as well as the schedule of school events like Back-to-School Night. They also need to know how their son or daughter is doing. This information should be timely and include students' academic performances, general behavior, and involvement in school activities. Parents need to know teacher policies regarding homework, late papers, and grading guidelines. They also need to be acquainted with the course content and with due dates for tests and papers so that they can help their children meet expectations.

Becoming acquainted with parents puts teachers in a position to solicit assistance in the academic program. Some parents have had interesting experiences or occupations that are relevant to study topics. Some parents may be willing to act as aides during classroom instruction or serve as chaperones for special events. Occasionally parents may have access to materials that teachers find useful for instruction.

Parents need to know the disciplinary policies of the school. Parents should ideally agree with the actions taken to discipline their child, or at least not be surprised by such actions. Significantly involving them in school disciplinary actions may be even better.

Mr. Brenchley blankly stared out his window and considered what the next two or three hours might bring. He was facing his first series of parent-teacher conferences as a new teacher and was unsure of himself. Several teachers in the faculty lounge offered advice suggesting he should not take criticism from parents. "Let them know that you are the boss," Mr. Dunbar said. "Tell them if their child is disruptive," Mr. Shipley added. "Make sure you have your roll book handy so you can justify the grades you gave out," warned Ms. Catanni.

Mr. Brenchley mulled over these recommendations and found himself unable to imagine showing some of the parents who was boss. He knew most of them would be much older than he was, and some were professionals not used to having others talk down to them. He tried to get himself prepared by creating a folder for each of his students that contained some of their work. He intended to start each conference by having parents examine their child's work, followed by a look at the good things the student was doing in class. He thought this should precede any discussion of student problems.

As he considered what he might say about some of the more disruptive students, his first appointment came through the door. It was Ms. Cordasco, Francesco's mother. Before he was part way through his introductory remarks, he noticed a cross-cultural miscommunication. The Cordascos recently immigrated from Mexico, and Ms. Cordasco reflected the collectivist orientation that each member should help the family as a whole. She was not interested in talking about Francesco's achievement nor hearing what Mr. Brenchley predicted about his potential success in college and future profession. She appeared almost frightened at the prospect of her son giving up his family for academic achievements. Several weeks later, Mr. Brenchley would discover that his glowing report of Francesco's achievements seemed like a threat to the Cordasco family's Latino culture.

Immediately after Ms. Cordasco left, Mr. Bosco strolled into the room, wearing a sharp business suit and displaying an air of confidence that immediately intimidated Mr. Brenchley. Mr. Bosco's daughter, Brittany, was one of the top students in the class. However, Mr. Brenchley thought she always seemed to be under pressure. He tried not to pressure his students to perform, but Brittany seemed pressured by some imaginary force. As Mr. Brenchley looked at Mr. Bosco, he wondered if Brittany was not feeling excessive pressure at home to perform. He wondered how he would bring the issue up, and was relieved when Mr. Bosco brought it up himself. "I'm concerned about Brittany," he started. "She seems to have decided that she needs to be the school valedictorian by the time she graduates. She works well into the night on homework even when we offer to take her out for breaks. She refuses to go on family outings, locking herself in her room to pour over her school books. We're concerned and wondering if there is something happening here at school that might be driving her. She doesn't get pressured at home to perform well in school. We have never cared that she get good grades. We are more interested that she become a well-adjusted human being. Now it seems she may be going off the deep end."

"I really appreciate your insight," Mr. Brenchley responded. "I had hoped to bring up the issue with you but wondered how you would respond to my suggestion that Brittany seems to be a compulsive academic. I notice that she does not participate in school activities much. She seems almost devastated when she fails to get a hundred percent on all her tests, even though she almost always gets the highest score in class."

"We've been considering having Brittany see a counselor. After talking to you, I believe that would be a good step. In the meantime, maybe you could help by speaking to her. It can help her get a better perspective on things."

Mr. Brenchley indicated that he would be willing to try to help Brittany, but realized that he was ill-equipped to undo what had likely taken several years to develop. He decided, however, that he could try to help all his students realize that learning is more important than grades.

Ms. Wolters was the next parent to arrive. Her son, Jacob, was struggling in the class, although Mr. Brenchley suspected that he was much more capable than his academic record indicated. As Ms. Wolters approached the desk, Mr. Brenchley automatically reached for his roll book, anticipating that Jacob's mother had come to question the *C* grade Jacob received in the class. His fears were confirmed. Mr. Brenchley tried to create a warm, friendly atmosphere, but Ms. Wolters cut him off mid-sentence.

"Let's cut to the chase, Mr. Brenchley," she said with a sharp edge to her voice. "You gave Jacob a *C*. He needs an *A* in your class if he hopes to get into college. He is a bright boy and has always had good grades. The school is failing to properly motivate him to work up to his potential. It is your responsibility in this history class to make sure he achieves at the level that fits his ability. His bad grade is a measure of your failure, and it is your responsibility to do something about it."

Mr. Brenchley drew in a long breath, calculating what he might say. He knew that Jacob ran with a rather rough crowd at school, and he suspected that he might be into drugs, although he had never been caught with drugs in school. Jacob's grades steadily declined for about a year, and he didn't even seem to care about doing poorly.

Decision Points

1. With a peer, role-play actions you might make in response to Ms. Wolters' attack on Mr. Brenchley and the school for Jacob's poor academic performance.

2. Role-play the following additional situations you might encounter in the school during parent-teacher conferences:
   a. Ms. Hemingway requests that you force her daughter, April, to wear the clothes she has on when she leaves home. Apparently April changes her clothes once she arrives at school to wear something more consistent with the lifestyle she follows with her friends.
   b. Mr. Robben complains that his son, Aaron, is picked on by bullies at school and wants something done about it.
   c. Ms. Gonzales is concerned that her son, Manuel, is doing poorly in school. He works hard on his homework, but seems to be making little progress. He has made good progress learning the language of normal discourse in English but apparently lacks the more technical language of the school.

NATIONAL TEACHING STANDARDS

Accomplished teachers have the skills and understandings to avoid conflicts between parents and the school and successfully foster collaborative relationships between school and families.

Understanding Parents

Understanding parents is essential to successfully working with them. Most parents are interested in seeing their children succeed academically and believe teachers also have their children's best interests at heart. Misunderstandings are often a matter of miscommunication, although mistrust or alienation occasionally results from school happenings that the parents resent; these can be prevented with proper communication. Not only do different parents have different expectations of the schools their children attend, but their reactions to problems can also markedly differ (Walker & Shae, 1995).

Sometimes parents are uncooperative when their children have academic difficulties. Some are apathetic, expecting the school to solve the problems, while others may be defensive or aggressive. Some parents may have had unhappy experiences themselves as students, and since they felt there was no hope for them in the schools, they harbor similar feelings about their children (Menacker, Hurwitz, & Weldon, 1988). They often have disparaging views about the school's ability to help their children through difficulties. Some have adopted ways to avoid dealing with any school personnel (Walker & Shae, 1995). Others view school personnel as the experts and excuse themselves from interfering with any school operation (Greenwood & Hickman, 1991; Turnbull & Turnbull, 1997).

Some parents are overwhelmed by the size of schools and the bureaucratic way schools operate. They are uncomfortable with the busy pace and absence of private areas where parents can come in and discuss problems (Lightfoot, 1978). When the school serves a diverse population, some parents have difficulty when they sense cultural differences between their family and school personnel (Swap, 1993). For example, Asian-American immigrant parents who are asked by a teacher for a conference may think the purpose of the interview is to be "checked up on," an expression of disrespect (Yao, 1988).

Parents may also be uninvolved for practical reasons. They may have limited English-speaking ability, have limited access to transportation or babysitters, or have work hours that make them unable to meet face-to-face with teachers. Some may not understand what is expected of them or what they can contribute to their child's education. These parents may take issue when school personnel attempt to arrange meetings to discuss their child's academic problems. Sometimes parents may feel that a simple request to meet with a teacher implies poor parenting and may therefore react with resentment or anger.

In order to successfully relate to parents and create a positive atmosphere during parent-teacher conferences, teachers must be knowledgeable regarding their students' cultures. Otherwise, teachers may fail to get important information about students or acquire critical support from parents. Teachers need to obtain valid information about cultures so they can increase the level of cordiality needed and the special insights required to enlist parental cooperation both for school activities and home support. Care must be exercised in this process to avoid stereotyping parents. Many times general descriptions of cultural phenomena may be inaccurate and contribute to poor understanding of the differences between members of the school constituency.

 QUESTION FOR REFLECTION

1. Explain how you, as a teacher, might approach parents in a collaborative manner. Design an approach to a parent-teacher conference.

Parent Involvement

Because of the enormous impact parents can have on their children's academic performance, the various obstacles to good parent-school relationships should be overcome, and positive associations need to be promoted. All children do better with a solid home and school support system. Many problems can be overcome through a comprehensive program of parent-school involvement like that suggested by Epstein (1984, 1987). She recommends the following categories of parent involvement:

1. Parents have an obligation to address the health and safety concerns of their children; however, some parents lack the basic child-rearing and parenting skills necessary to successfully prepare children for school. They may need instruction in how to properly supervise, discipline, and guide their children through the various phases of their school experiences. Parents need to learn how to support learning and appropriate school behavior in their children.
2. Sufficient communication is needed between home and school so parents are adequately appraised of school programs and of their children's progress. Communications should be accurate and positive, providing not only a means for parents to receive information, but also ways to express their concerns.
3. As far as possible, parents should be involved as school volunteers. They may be asked to help with a wide variety of school-related activities in addition to spending time in classrooms.
4. Parents need to learn how to work cooperatively with teachers to help their children with learning activities at home. They need to understand how the work children do at home correlates with school learning.
5. Although school governance is commonly left to school personnel, there are appropriate roles for parents in school governance. They can take an active part in decision making through participating in advisory councils or other committees at the school, district, or state level. They have a critical role in helping to monitor schools and in making recommendations for improvements.

Home Support

Parents need to learn that many of their school experiences were substantially different than the experiences their children will receive. Teachers can help parents overcome these negative prejudices through home support. When teachers provide help in coordinating a child's school work at home, parents can become more convinced that teachers are committed to their children's success. Some parents are still in school themselves and are unlikely to have the necessary skills to help their children be successful students. When the parents of young children are involved in school or are struggling economically, a potential exists for neglect. Such parents may also lack good parenting skills, which could result in various kinds of abuse that will eventually limit their children's ability to successfully work in school and effectively learn. Some states have taken Epstein's suggestions seriously and initiated training programs for parents (Epstein, 1991). Illinois (Chapman, 1991) and California (Solomon, 1991), for example, have implemented programs providing parents with training in child-rearing, including how to promote better self-concept and prepare students for school.

NATIONAL TEACHING STANDARDS

Teachers communicate regularly with parents and guardians, listening to their concerns and respecting their perspectives, enlisting their support in fostering learning and good habits, informing them of their child's accomplishments and successes, and educating them about school programs.

Teachers have to be alert to instances where school interests and parents' interests diverge and where there may be insufficient support from the home. In these difficulties, teachers must hold the interest of the student and purposes of the school paramount.

Home-School Communications

Communication between the home and school should be positive and informative, allowing parents to feel that someone is hearing and considering their concerns. Initial contact should be made with parents at the beginning of the school year to inform them of academic programs, grading guidelines, homework policies, rules and procedures, and school activity programs. After this, ongoing contact should be made with parents regarding various classroom activities and the academic success of their children. Student progress should frequently be communicated to parents, particularly if their child is experiencing difficulties that require immediate attention. It is wise not only to contact parents when problems arise, but to keep them informed regarding the positive accomplishments of their children. Many parents are used to receiving school contact only when problems develop, leaving them with negative impressions of the school.

Parent-teacher conferences have been the most common mode of communication between parents and the school. These are usually twice-a-year sessions conducted in a semi-formal situation. The formality of these sessions sometimes promote parent discomfort. Parents indicate that teachers tend to be too businesslike, too patronizing, and too inclined to talk down to them (Lindle, 1989). Parents prefer school contact in which teachers listen to and value their opinions and request their involvement in solving problems.

Many parents prefer that teachers and administrators keep them informed of situations involving their children. They wish to learn about potential problems as soon as they become evident, rather than being told about them later. Early parent involvement may help avert more serious problems that could eventually develop. Various ways exist for teachers to communicate with parents, keep them informed, help create positive attitudes, and elicit parental support for school programs.

Introductory Letters

An introductory letter can be an effective way for teachers to make an initial contact with parents. Such a letter might include an invitation to attend a Back-to-School Night at the beginning of the school year, along with some basic information about the class like schedules, homework expectations, curriculum, school policies regarding absences and tardies, discipline rules, and school regulations. Consequences for misbehavior might also be listed. Parents should be informed of these matters so they can offer their support. A teacher might want to identify those items to modify and then seek parental input, perhaps presenting those changes at the Back-to-School Night. If teachers do not wish to have lengthy discussions regarding such matters, they may ask parents for written suggestions. An introductory letter might also include a description of the teacher's academic background and experience, along with a short statement of the teacher's philosophy so that parents have some idea of what to expect. Parents might be invited to discuss the school's rules and policies with their children, particularly after parents have had an opportunity to express their concerns to the teacher and clear up any possible misunderstandings. Thus, parents could lend their support to the school program and let their children know that they are well-informed and in agreement with the school's program and regulations. In some schools, parents are expected to indicate their support of school discipline rules and consequences without first having an opportunity to give input. Some acquiesce and sign the form, indicating they are aware of the rules and consequences, but withhold giving full support. This may be an alienating experience for some parents and should be avoided if possible.

Decision Points

Write an introductory letter designed to inform parents about yourself as a teacher and explain your philosophy, telling parents what they and their children may expect in your class. In addition, state the nature of communications parents can expect to keep them informed and involved in their child's education.

Back-to-School Night

Back-to-School Night is ordinarily designed to supply parents with comprehensive information about school programs and policies. The school issues a letter stating that programs and policies will be distributed at the Back-to-School Night, with an invitation to come, learn, and raise appropriate questions. Back-to-School Night should come early in the school year. Parents usually receive a copy of their child's schedule and follow this schedule like a student, only with shortened sessions. Because the sessions in each class are fairly short, perhaps only 15 minutes, parents who have concerns requiring more time should be invited to schedule a follow-up conference with teachers. In these conferences, teachers need to be open-minded and receptive. They may, however, receive suggestions from some parents that cannot be implemented. For example, a parent might suggest that students be punished when most parents prefer their children experience reasonable consequences of misbehavior rather than punishment. The teacher should explain the most preferred treatment for misbehavior and attempt to obtain support from the parent. Impasses do occur, yet teachers should make an effort to maintain respect for parents' opinions and consider the parents' point of view.

In preparing for Back-to-School Night, the teacher should make the classroom as attractive as possible. It is a good idea to have displays of former students' work if there has not been time for the current class members to prepare something. Copies of textbooks, equipment, and other instructional materials may also be displayed.

Teachers might also prepare a list of needed instructional supplies that parents may be able to supply. Sometimes parents can acquire useful materials free or at low cost. Parents might also be given an opportunity to sign up to volunteer as guest speakers or as teacher's aides. If field trips are planned, parents' permission and possible participation may be solicited at this time.

Back-to-School Night should be carefully organized so that various activities are efficiently accomplished. It is a good idea for the teacher to greet each parent at the door, then make a short presentation about the class so parents can become better acquainted. Much of the information given should be in printed form in order to economize the time, as well as provide parents with material they can refer to later. Parents should receive an explicit invitation to sign up for a follow-up conference so they understand that conferences are not just for expressing trouble with some aspect of what is presented, but are an opportunity to become more involved with the school and their child's education.

Not all parents are likely to attend Back-to-School Night. Consequently, teachers may send a packet of materials to non-attendees, providing them the same essential information covered during the meeting. This material should include an invitation to conference with the teacher. If the teacher wishes to make follow-up telephone calls, parents might be informed that they can expect a call in the next two or three weeks.

Decision Points

Explain how you would organize and conduct a successful Back-to-School Night.

Open House

During the year, schools may periodically wish to sponsor an open house featuring students' work, possibly around a science fair or foreign language fair. Teachers in other subject areas may also wish to have a fair where their students' work can be displayed. These activities can encourage students to actively pursue substantial projects they can present to their parents. Art and photography contests and displays provide a good opportunity to get parents into the school to view their children's work. Concerts featuring the school band and orchestra can be held in conjunction with these activities or as separate events.

Decision Points

Identify an appropriate activity for an open house in your subject area. Outline how you would involve parents and conduct the activity.

Newsletters, Notes, and Letters

Schools can periodically provide parents with information about special events, new programs, student activities, and so on. Student accomplishments can be presented in a newsletter, along with special projects like zero tolerance for drugs and alcohol. Student groups can prepare newsletters, thereby bringing up their desires and concerns. Teachers may also want to send notes or letters to individual parents presenting a particular issue concerning their child. Letters can arrange conferences with parents, invite parents to various school and class functions, inform parents about a student's work, or provide parents with lists of suggestions to enhance their children's work in school. Although teachers can inform parents of child difficulties through letters, they should also routinely send home notification of positive happenings.

Telephone Calls

For many situations, sending a letter is inadequate. Many issues require direct interaction and responses from parents. In such instances, teachers may wish to contact parents by telephone. For example, one teacher, in an attempt to get students more involved, would call a difficult student's parent and say, "Mrs. Holmes, I am Carolyn's science teacher. I have called to tell you that Carolyn did something quite wonderful and remarkable in class today." The teacher would then hang up without telling the parent what the student had done or allowing the parent to ask about it. When the student came home, the curious parent would ask what he or she did in science class that was so wonderful. The student, of course, had no idea, but as a result these students became more involved in their science class. This teacher obtained good results by focusing on positive things about students, even when these positive behaviors were somewhat insignificant. Emphasizing positive behavior rather than pointing out negative, inappropriate behavior ordinarily has better consequences.

Some teachers routinely call parents when their children excessively misbehave. This is not always a good idea, particularly if a specific parent receives only negative calls. Telephone calls are more appropriate for short, positive messages. Sometimes a face-to-face meeting is better. Teachers can miss a good deal without nonverbal cues.

Home Visits

For some families, home visits may be appropriate. Parents who do not attend Back-to-School Night may respond to a personal visit by becoming more supportive of their child's academic work both at school and at home. A teacher might convey the information ordinarily given at Back-to-School Night and discuss ways the parent can help his or her son or daughter be more successful in school. Parents can also benefit from having more detail about class content and ways the teacher hopes students will become involved. If students need to complete home projects, teachers can explain the role parents may play in helping their child be more successful. In addition, home visits may give teachers an opportunity to observe the home conditions under which students live that may affect classroom performance or behavior. A teacher might find, for instance, that a child's home may not have a quiet study area or that a child's home responsibilities leave little time for study. Teachers may justifiably suggest some modifications to help the involved students acquire a more conducive study environment. For some students, teachers may need to augment learning at school if conditions in the home are inadequate for sustained study.

Teachers who wish to make home visits must become familiar with the area of the community in which students live. In some neighborhoods, safety issues may make it necessary for a teacher to be accompanied by another teacher, counselor, or school nurse when visiting students' homes.

The Use of Technology

In some school districts, communications between parents and school have been greatly enhanced by technology, since parents have Internet access to much of what is going on in the school. A schedule of events can be posted on the school's web page, along with various categories of helpful information. Teachers can give parents access to all class assignments, activities, and test results. Parents can monitor missing assignments, grades, and even attendance. Though the Internet resources may keep some parents effectively informed, teachers can find it time-consuming to enter all the data onto the system. In addition, students may feel oversupervised, and parents without Internet capabilities may feel disenfranchised since they will miss information about important school happenings.

NATIONAL TEACHING STANDARDS

Teachers work successfully with various other professionals like school counselors, school psychologists, curriculum coordinators, and the like.

Working with School Professionals

Teachers need to consult school counselors and school psychologists as they work with parents to help students in their classes. Teachers need to be alert to possible child abuse and refer it as necessary to the school psychologist. Teachers may also notice problems like depression and potential suicide that should be brought to the attention of school counselors or the school psychologist. School counselors can identify learning problems and help teachers plan study programs that may provide students with expanded benefits. Teachers can also obtain vocational information for their students, along with information regarding college scholarship opportunities. Teachers can help solidify their relationships with parents by providing them this information.

Teachers should also work with curriculum coordinators to ensure that their programs are consistent with state learning goals and objectives. This information needs to be communicated to parents so they can compare state expectations to the program of studies outlined by teachers. When parents become knowledgeable about curricular issues, they prepare themselves to provide input in modifying state core curricula. This knowledge also gives parents a better idea of how they might be involved in the teaching-learning process. Too often parents have only a vague idea of school curricula and related issues. Parents need to understand teachers' views of learning so they can see more clearly why teachers teach the way they do. Thus, parents can render more valuable service to the schools when they know both the curriculum and the learning processes employed by teachers.

Parent-Teacher Conferences

Parent-teacher conferences present opportunities to report a variety of information to parents and obtain their cooperation regarding children's school activities. These conferences should not focus exclusively on academic performance and behavior problems; various social and psychological adjustments should also be explored. Parents should expect to learn how their child relates to other children, how much he or she participates enthusiastically in classroom activities, and how the child has grown in a variety of intellectual capacities. Teachers can prepare for conferences by keeping accurate anecdotal records of students' activities, along with examples of each student's work. Students might help assemble a portfolio of their best work that teachers can use to initiate parental conversations. In conducting parent-teacher conferences, the following steps are recommended:

1. *Build rapport.*   Parent-teacher conferences will ordinarily be more successful when teachers make parents feel comfortable. Because parents may be apprehensive and fearful, considerable effort may be required to make them feel at ease. Teachers should create an informal atmosphere and display friendliness and acceptance, regardless of the parents' appearance.
2. *Obtain information.*   Teachers need to be good listeners so that they do not miss critical student information. Parents should not feel they are being interrogated; thus, negative or emotionally laden questions should be avoided. One way to get things started is to ask parents to express how they believe their child feels about the class. Teachers should not feel threatened by negative comments, but rather respond by asking how to make the class more acceptable to the student. When teachers get parents to open up and express themselves, they get better insight into parents' expectations and are thus better able to give them a valid report of their child's school success.
3. *Provide information.*   Teachers might begin by trying to make an accurate assessment of their students' school successes and problems, followed by some suggestions about specific plans they might have to enhance student learning. They should also ask for suggestions from the parents to help their son or daughter make a better social, psychological, and academic adjustment to school.

Teachers should then assure parents that they will act upon the parents' concerns. Together, the teacher and parents should make plans to coordinate school work students might do at home.

4. *Follow-up strategies.* At the close of the conference, teachers should review the major points covered in the meeting and identify any unresolved issues that may need additional discussion or follow-up actions. Specific commitments made by both parents and teachers can be brought up and affirmed; if additional conferences are needed, they can be scheduled at this time. Teachers should do everything they can to ensure a cordial atmosphere exists during conferences and a positive attitude prevails as conference agendas are concluded (Wolf & Stephens, 1989).

Teachers should ensure that parents' concerns are addressed in parent-teacher conferences. Patience and skill may be necessary to get parents to open up and express themselves about troubling matters regarding their children's schooling. Often they see school as a source of child difficulties they experience at home, or they might believe that the school is responsible for their children's academic needs as well as their personal and social problems, regardless of their source. If parents feel a sense of failure in raising their children, they may claim that the school caused the problem. Sometimes their accusations may be accurate. In these cases, schools may need to make adjustments to ensure a more invigorating and emotionally safe learning environment. Teachers must be careful not to defend the school as if it is impossible for children to have harmful experiences there. Some children do have devastating school experiences. The duty of both parents and teachers is to minimize negative school experiences and help students optimally benefit during the time they spend there.

Decision Points

With peers, role-play the following situations in a parent-teacher conference:

1. A parent brings a child to the parent-teacher conference in an effort to publicly force the child to be more involved in school work.
2. A parent comes into a parent-teacher conference very angry that her child has received a failing grade in your class. She blames you for the student's failure and tells you so.
3. A parent claims that his child has so much homework in your class that the family can no longer enjoy family activities.
4. A parent says her daughter boasts that she gets all *A* grades without studying. The parent wants her daughter to do excellent work if she is to get As.

NATIONAL TEACHING STANDARDS

Teachers need to know how to mobilize the efforts of community members to augment the learning opportunities for students. They need to be able to include tutors, aides, and volunteers as teaching assistants.

Volunteer parents can be a valuable resource for teachers in the classroom.

Parents as Volunteers

While some parents are inclined to turn all matters of their children's learning over to the school, others readily accept opportunities to become intimately associated with their children's learning as volunteers. However, parents have an important role to play in their children's education. Teachers need to find out how parents might make important contributions to the school. Teachers can survey parents to determine their skills, talents, and interests, and then create nontraditional opportunities for parental involvement (Christenson & Sheridan, 2001). At least three categories of volunteer participation exists whereby parents can make significant contributions to their children's education:

- skills in hobbies and crafts
- direct knowledge and experience in occupations
- knowledge about various aspects of different cultures

Parents who have interesting hobbies and knowledge of crafts can be asked to provide displays, do demonstrations, or teach students about a hobby or craft. In teaching about various occupations, parent volunteers can provide examples of a typical day at work, explain the training and skills needed for a particular occupation, explain the pros and cons of going into a particular field, and indicate the employment possibilities. In some instances they might provide on-the-job training or student internship opportunities. Students might also benefit from spending time with parent volunteers on the job in an effort to learn more fully the kind of work people do in various occupations. Children may have difficulty gaining an appreciation of what the work world is actually like; these firsthand experiences may also help students realize the knowledge and skills they need if they plan to enter a particular occupation. If parents have spent time in foreign countries, they may be particularly helpful in explaining the history, geography, customs, art, music, and political environment in these countries (Hunter, 1989).

Parents can also act as teachers' aides. Under the supervision of teachers, parents can perform such tasks as tutoring children who are experiencing difficulty, acting as chaperones, or working with small groups when they need to go to alternative instructional sites like the computer room or the library. Parent volunteers can provide an enormous service to teachers by helping with duties without which some valuable learning activities might be too difficult to provide.

One commonly untapped source of school helpers that can augment the shrinking pool of parent volunteers is senior citizens, who bring a wealth of experience and knowledge (Armengol, 1992). For example, the Salt Lake City School District is noted for recruiting and training a cadre of older adults to participate in school activities like story reading, field trips, tutoring, arts and crafts, and sports (Salt Lake City School District, 1992). Older adults can provide unique perspectives, including historical understanding, on a variety of topics. They can also serve as surrogate grandparents, filling a significant gap in the lives of many young people caused by the decline in extended family relationships. Their involvement can help dispel negative stereotypes that youth and older adults may have about one another (Matters, 1990).

NATIONAL TEACHING STANDARDS

Teachers should work collaboratively with parents and other teachers in an effort to improve the school's effectiveness. This involves the analysis and construction of curriculum, coordination of instruction, professional development of staff, and other school-site policy decisions fundamental to the creation of highly productive learning communities.

School Governance and Parental Decision Making

There is no better way to acquire parental support for schools than giving parents an opportunity to participate in governance matters. Schools should routinely involve parents in governance, decision making, and advocacy, including responsible participation in parent-teacher organizations and in various decision-making and advisory roles (Epstein, 1991). Parents will not become enthusiastically involved in their children's schooling without significant decision-making potential; some recommend a say in policy formulation as well. In reality, schools belong to the parents. School boards are elected and school employees hired to carry out parents' wishes. Too often these efforts get insulated behind closed doors that parents are reluctant or unable to penetrate.

When parents get involved, not only is there increased commitment for school purposes, but there is greater potential for schools to gain new insights. These associations also provide a way of energizing the community in promoting school programs and funding. With the increase in diversity that most schools are currently experiencing, they need the creativity, resourcefulness, and ingenuity of all stakeholders, whether they are school personnel, parents, students, or members of the outside community. Involvement in critical matters like education energizes and affirms people and challenges them to contribute their energy, time, and ideas for the common good. Parental involvement is particularly helpful because parents have the greatest stake in ensuring that their children have a good education. Parents often provide the input necessary to examine practices that have become entrenched in the schools and help spearhead needed changes (Christenson & Sheridan, 2001; Jennings, 1989).

NATIONAL TEACHING STANDARDS

Teachers need to know how to work with parents in a changing society. An increasing number of youth live with single parents, working parents, and low-income parents. Teachers need to work successfully with youth who have emotional needs that are not being met at home so they can enhance students' learning.

Parental Involvement in Learning Communities

While recommended parental involvement in instruction, decision making, and policy formulation is extensive, parents' roles in learning communities can be substantially different. Parents can be involved in all the ways defined for parents in traditional classrooms, but more instructionally integrated roles are also suggested. In traditional teaching, the parents' role is often to help teachers with ancillary functions such as putting up bulletin boards, chaperoning, tutoring individual students, presenting hobbies and crafts, and providing instruction on various occupations and cultures. The teacher has the responsibility for teaching the bulk of what students are to learn. The teacher is ordinarily the one who selects and organizes all of the instruction, with parents given a helping role as needed. In learning communities, parents may participate as active members of a learning group just as the teacher commonly does. Parents can assume the role of learner, and periodically of group leader, while studying a particular topic of interest. Parents' participation should not be limited to supervising students, but rather participating as a co-learner. All group members must share an interest in the topic and find some aspect that they can energetically investigate and eventually share with the group. Parents, as fullfledged participants, learn right along with students.

Though parents are co-learners in learning communities, their role should have a little different aspect than that of the students. Adults are able to bring a wealth of experience and knowledge to learning communities. Students may have naive ideas about the level of sophistication and understanding appropriate and possible in studying an area of knowledge. Some parents may be able to set an example of greater excellence than students are accustomed to by bringing their maturity to the tasks of researching and reporting their findings. Students can therefore observe excellence firsthand and begin to learn how to become more sophisticated learners themselves. Some parents will have a wealth of practical knowledge and can help students apply what they learn to the real world. There will be a wide range of parents' backgrounds and training levels. Some are involved in highly technical fields, while others work at jobs requiring little training. All these potential inputs should be included without highlighting one as being more valuable than another. Students will eventually fill a wide range of occupations, just as their parents have. All kinds of abilities and interests make up the communities the school serves and should be represented as much as possible in the work of learning communities.

Including parents in learning communities to the optimum extent may not be possible. Parents usually have heavy responsibilities with jobs and commitments that likely overlap the school schedule. Still there may be some parents, in particular older adults, who can become intimately associated with learning communities and provide the benefits that their participation offers. By making some modifications, learning communities may be able to find creative ways to include parents whose schedules don't map onto those of the school.

 QUESTION FOR REFLECTION

1. What problems do you foresee in having parents involved in learning communities? How can these problems be avoided?

The Role of Families and the School in Communities

When children participate in learning communities in school, they become better qualified to participate in the larger community outside the school. Unfortunately, various levels of government ordinarily function without input from either the schools or families in the community. However, many of the issues that groups deal with have important implications for students and their families; had student and parent input been received and taken seriously, some problems might have been solved. For example, youth crime and drug abuse are problems where youth and their families may have significant input.

Community Service Learning Programs

Community service learning should be an integral part of school learning communities. Schools can use service learning opportunities to get students out into the community and participating in learning opportunities that enhance their understanding of community issues as well as extend their sense of community beyond the school. Research on the impact of service learning suggests positive effects on students' intellectual and social/psychological development. Students develop a heightened sense of personal and social responsibility, acquire positive attitudes toward adults and others, become more active in exploring careers, develop greater self-esteem, grow in terms of moral and ego development, engage in more complex patterns of thought, and achieve greater mastery of skills and content that are directly related to their experiences (Conrad & Hedin, 1991).

Successful service learning programs have the following features:

- Significant, necessary, and measurable service is accomplished.
- Youths are directly involved in planning and implementing activities.
- A clear institutional commitment to the service program exists as reflected in goals and mission statements.
- Strong community support exists for students to be involved in the program.
- Learner outcomes for the program are clearly expressed and publicized.
- A well-designed and articulated curriculum for service exists that includes preparation, supervision, and active reflection on experience.

- Regular and significant recognition exists of the youths and adults who participate in the program (Cairn & Kielsmeier, 1991).

The fundamental task of schools is sometimes asserted to be preparing students for the work world. In a democratic society, an equally important objective is to prepare students for active, informed citizenship. One aspect of being an informed citizen is knowing how to get and keep a job; another is to know how to build a better world. For example, everyone will likely experience events in their communities that are discriminatory or potentially dangerous, like pollution. Schools must help youth acquire experiences that prepare them to work for justice and equity, not just pass examinations and exhibit specific job-related skills. Service learning can help youth develop helpful attitudes and make commitments to the communities in which they live, thereby participating in solving problems that significantly affect them and their neighbors.

NATIONAL TEACHING STANDARDS

Teachers need to know where and how to draw upon the community for valuable resources to enhance student learning. These resources include other students and teachers, senior citizens, parents, businesspeople, and local organizations.

Professional teachers cultivate knowledge of their school's community as a powerful resource for learning.

Good teachers cultivate knowledge about the character of the community and its effects on the school and students. They develop an appreciation of ethnic and linguistic differences of cultural influences on students' aspirations and expectations and of the effects of poverty and affluence.

The Role of Community Government Agencies

When youth authentically participate in neighborhood decision making, they are more likely to think of themselves as contributing community members, particularly if they are significantly involved and their input is valued. By participating, youth can become better at making decisions that directly involve them, and they can learn to value their role in the community. If youth are not taken seriously, they will not take the actions of community leaders seriously and may become oppositional. No better way exists to obtain the cooperation of youth in matters that concern them than through soliciting their authentic participation, and there is no more certain way to predispose them to resist decisions made by governing authorities than to ignore their concerns and pay no heed to their views.

Great benefit can come from involving youth with older community leaders. Authentic communities need to have dissimilar membership. Without a varied membership configuration, the insights needed may not be obtained, and the concerns of all members of the community may not be adequately addressed. Unfortunately, while in school, youth work almost exclusively with age-mates. This commonly produces an *us and them* mentality. Youth may then suffer a detachment from the broader community in which they live. When this occurs, despite the fact that community issues still impact them, these students are likely to take less interest in community problems and issues and feel less receptive regarding decisions that are made without their input.

When students have an opportunity to give valued input, they feel essential and develop a sense of caring and responsibility. They also learn to respect others' contributions as they learn to feel connected with community members. Youth can and should be taught that they have a crucial role in community matters and that they are wanted and needed. They will come to believe that they can make a difference.

When youth are empowered through significant community roles, they develop resilience and experience a reduction in the inclination toward violence (Edwards, 2000). Youth desire meaningful participation. They want to be counted as significant and needed. When this happens, they have little reason to rebel. Their lives become more meaningful, and their contribution to the community seems more significant.

The parents of youth need to assume roles with their children in community and neighborhood governance. Community issues impact them personally as well as being important to their families. These critical considerations impact younger children as well. If young children are able to experience a community environment that promotes social and emotional growth, they will be less inclined to become involved with gangs or to engage in various criminal activities as youth. This is particularly true when family members have participated in decisions regarding important community issues. In some communities, decisions are often made behind closed doors with limited public input, even during open meetings. When local governments isolate themselves from the public regarding issues that impact the community's youth, thwarting the input that might have been given in a more open forum, less cooperation is expected from their constituency. Even in representative type governments, participation should be sought in order to empower individual citizens and to enlist their cooperation in dealing with community problems. Citizens often provide important insights that, if ignored, can lead to less-effective government and a less-involved citizenry.

 ## QUESTION FOR REFLECTION

1. How reasonable is it to expect that parents and youth can be involved in community and neighborhood governance? How might more of their participation be expedited?

The Role of Business and Other Community Entities

Various community entities can make a positive impact on schools, particularly when learning communities are the basic learning configuration. Learning communities inherently reach out into the larger community to elicit cooperation in a number of important educational matters. Business could, for example, provide additional funding to ensure that school programs are sustained. Educators might enlist the help of businesses to help finance science fairs or support the research efforts by school youth. These efforts can be sold to businesses as being in their best interest, because students can become better educated when they have proper backing. Youth may also get involved with nursing homes, youth organizations, hospitals, agencies that house individuals with special needs, and hospices in service learning situations. They can also get involved in various businesses and other community organizations to learn about the work world and provide assistance in various aspects of these organizations. This kind of an outreach program can have a positive impact on the whole community: better relationships can be established, and better articulation of school and various occupations can be achieved. In addition, students can develop lifetime involvement with community matters and take on a responsible citizenship role. These arrangements can also contribute to reducing community problems like drug trafficking and alcohol consumption. When children are meaningfully involved in community affairs, they are less likely to initiate problems (Conrad & Hedin, 1991; Van Hoose & Legrand, 2000).

Many times students in learning communities require data from community agencies in order to learn about a particular topic. There may also be agencies, housed in the community as branches of federal or state government, through which important research information may be obtained on topics such as pollution, soil erosion, deforestation, social problems, race relations, and the like. In the process of doing research, students can benefit from making contact with community individuals who oversee these agencies as well as learning about the purposes and programs they promote.

Decision Points

Make a list of commonly available community agencies that might become involved either in sponsoring student activities or in providing information and opportunities for student research.

CENTRAL IDEAS

1. The more parents are involved in the school, the more likely they are to support the school and its programs.
2. Parents coming from different cultural and socio-economic backgrounds have different views of the school and consequently are more or less able to have successful interactions with school personnel.
3. Parents should play an active role in addressing children's health and safety concerns.
4. Communications with parents should be comprehensive and varied so that parents are well-informed of school programs, school expectations, and their children's progress.
5. Parents should be enlisted as school volunteers. They can be involved in a wide variety of activities that can make significant contributions to student learning.
6. Parents should be involved in school governance and in making important school decisions.
7. Teachers need to learn how to build rapport with parents; obtain critical information about their child; provide useful, insightful information about their child; and skillfully arrange for follow-up meetings to help parents become meaningfully involved in helping their child effectively learn.

8. Parents can greatly benefit their children by significant involvement in learning communities. In learning communities, parents take on a role like that of their son or daughter in group learning and leadership.
9. Community problems, like drug dealing and gangs, can be better solved through the involvement of parents and youth in neighborhood government.
10. Service learning is an excellent way to extend learning communities out into neighborhoods.
11. Teachers should solicit the help of agencies outside the school to provide support and access to important student research opportunities.

REFERENCES

Armengol, R. (1992). Getting older and getting better. *Phi Delta Kappan, 73* (6), 467–470.

Becher, R. M. (1984). *Parent involvement: A review of research and principles of successful practice.* Washington, DC: National Institute of Education.

Cairn, R. W., & Kielsmeier, J. C. (1991). *Growing hope: A source book on integrating youth service into the school curriculum.* Roseville, MN: National Youth Leadership Council.

Chapman, W. (1991). The Illinois experience: State grants to improve schools through parent involvement. *Phi Delta Kappan, 72* (5), 355–358.

Christenson, S. L., & Sheridan, S. M. (2001). *Schools and families: Creating essential connections for learning.* New York: Guilford Publications.

Conrad, D., & Hedin, D. (1991). School-based community service: What we know from research and theory. *Phi Delta Kappan, 72,* 743–749.

Edwards, C. H. (2000). Moral classroom communities and the development of resiliency. *Contemporary Education, 71* (4), 38–41.

Epstein, J. L. (1984). *Effects on parents of teacher practices in parent involvement.* Baltimore, MD: Johns Hopkins University, Center for Social Organization of Schools.

Epstein, J. L. (1987). What principals should know about parent involvement. *Principal, 66* (3), 6–9.

Epstein, J. L. (1991). Paths to partnerships: What we can learn from federal, state, district, and school initiatives. *Phi Delta Kappan, 72* (5), 345–349.

Greenwood, G. E., & Hickman, C. W. (1991). Research and practice in parent involvement: Implications for teacher education. *The Elementary School Journal, 91* (3), 279–288.

Haynes, N. M., Comer, J. P., & Hamilton-Lee, M. (1989). School climate enhancement through parent involvement. *Journal of School Psychology, 27,* 87–90.

Henderson, A. T., & Berla, N. (1995). *A new generation of evidence: The family is critical to student achievement.* Washington, DC: Center for Law and Education.

Hunter, M. (1989). Join the "par-aide" in education. *Educational Leadership, 47* (2), 36–41.

Jennings, W. B. (1989). How to organize successful parent advisory committees. *Educational Leadership, 47* (2), 42–45.

Lightfoot, S. L. (1978). *Worlds apart: Relationships between families and schools.* New York: Basic Books.

Lindle, J. C. (1989). What do parents want from principals and teachers? *Educational Leadership, 47* (2), 12–14.

Matters, L. (1990). *Intergenerational relations: Older adults and youth.* Columbia, MO: Center on Rural Elderly.

Menacker, J., Hurwitz, E., & Weldon, W. (1988). Parent-teacher cooperation in schools serving the urban poor. *Clearing House, 62,* 108–112.

Salt Lake City School District. (1992). SMILES (Senior Motivators in Learning and Educational Services). Unpublished manuscript. (ERIC Document Reproduction Service No. #D 346 983).

Solomon, Z. P. (1991). California's policy on parent involvement: State leadership for local initiatives. *Phi Delta Kappan, 72* (5), 359–362.

Swap, S. M. (1993). *Developing home-school partnerships: From concepts to practice.* New York: Teachers College Press.

Turnbull, A. P., & Turnbull, H. R. (1997). *Families, professionals, and exceptionalities: A special partnership* (3rd ed.). Upper Saddle River: NJ: Merrill/Prentice Hall.

Van Hoose, J., & Legrand, P. (2000). It takes parents, the whole village, and school to raise children. *Middle School Journal, 31* (3), 32–37.

Walker, J. E., & Shae, T. M. (1995). *Behavior management: A practical approach for educators* (6th ed.). Upper Saddle River: NJ: Merrill/Prentice Hall.

Wolf, J. S., & Stephens, T. M. (1989). Parent/teacher conferences: Finding a common ground. *Educational Leadership, 47* (2), 28–31.

Yao, E. (1988). Working effectively with Asian immigrant parents. *Phi Delta Kappan, 70* (3), 223–225.

Appendix A

National Curriculum Standards

1. *Arts*—The standards were developed jointly by the American Alliance for Theater and Education, the National Art Education Association, the National Dance Association, and the Music Educators National Conference. For information, contact the Music Educators National Conference (MENC), 1902 Association Drive, Reston, VA 22091.
2. *Civic/social studies*—The Center for Civic Education and the National Council for the Social Studies developed these standards. For current information, contact the National Council for the Social Studies (NCSS), 3501 Newark St., NW, Washington, DC 20016.
3. *English/reading/language arts*—Standards were developed jointly by the International Reading Association, The National Council of Teachers of English, and the University of Illinois Center for the Study of Reading. For information, contact the Center for the Study of Reading, 174 Children's Research Center, 51 Gerty Drive, Champaign, IL 61820.
4. *Foreign languages*—The American Council on the Teaching of Foreign Languages developed outlines for three levels of language proficiency based on the number of years a language is taken. For information, contact ACTFL, Six Executive Plaza, Yonkers, NY 10701.
5. *Geography*—The Association of American Geographers, the National Council for Geographic Education, and the National Geographic Society developed standards for geography education. For information, contact the Geography Standards Project, 1600 M St., NW, Washington, DC 20036.
6. *History*—The National Center for History in the Schools developed standards for history education. For information, contact the National Center for History in the Schools, UCLA, 231 Moore Hall, 405 Hilgard Ave., Los Angeles, CA 90024.
7. *Mathematics*—Mathematics standards can be ordered from the National Council of Teachers of Mathematics, Order Processing, 1906 Association Drive, Reston, VA 22091.
8. *Physical education*—Standards are found in *Outcomes of Quality Physical Education Programs* published by the National Association of Sports and Physical Education (NASPE). For information, contact NASPE, 1900 Association Drive, Reston, VA 22091.
9. *Science*—Standards were prepared by the National Research Council's National Committee on Science Education Standards and Assessment, the American Association for the Advancement of Science, and the National Science Teachers Association. For information, contact the National Science Education Standards, 2101 Constitution Ave., NW, HA 486, Washington, DC 20418 (Kim & Kellough, 1995).

Reference

Kim, E. C., & Kellough, R.D. (1995). A resource guide for secondary school teaching: Planning for Competence (6th ed). Upper Saddle River, NJ: Prentice Hall.

Index